BEST PRACTICES
IN LITERACY INSTRUCTION

Also from
Lesley Mandel Morrow and Linda B. Gambrell

Breaking Through the Language Arts Block:
Organizing and Managing the Exemplary Literacy Day
Lesley Mandel Morrow, Kenneth Kunz, and Maureen Hall

Handbook of Research on Literacy and Diversity
Edited by Lesley Mandel Morrow, Robert Rueda, and Diane Lapp

Lenses on Reading, Third Edition:
An Introduction to Theories and Models
Diane H. Tracey and Lesley Mandel Morrow

Maximizing Motivation for Literacy Learning: Grades K–6
Barbara A. Marinak, Linda B. Gambrell, and Susan Anders Mazzoni

Oral Language and Comprehension in Preschool:
Teaching the Essentials
Lesley Mandel Morrow, Kathleen A. Roskos, and Linda B. Gambrell

BEST PRACTICES
IN LITERACY
INSTRUCTION

SIXTH EDITION

edited by
Lesley Mandel Morrow
Linda B. Gambrell

THE GUILFORD PRESS
NEW YORK   LONDON

To Bob, who has spent a lifetime as an avid reader;
how lucky we are to spend hours filled with rich conversation
discussing our readings both for pleasure and for information
—L. M. M.

To my beautiful 3-year-old granddaughter,
Brielle Renee Gambrell, who is already an avid reader
—L. B. G.

Copyright © 2019 The Guilford Press
A Division of Guilford Publications, Inc.
370 Seventh Avenue, Suite 1200, New York, NY 10001
www.guilford.com

Printed in the United States of America

This book is printed on acid-free paper.

Last digit is print number: 9   8   7   6   5   4   3   2

Library of Congress Cataloging-in-Publication Data

Names: Morrow, Lesley Mandel, editor. | Gambrell, Linda B., editor.
Title: Best practices in literacy instruction / edited by Lesley Mandel
    Morrow, Linda B. Gambrell.
Description: Sixth Edition. | New York : The Guilford Press, [2019] |
    Previous edition: 2015. | Includes bibliographical references and index.
Identifiers: LCCN 2018037281| ISBN 9781462536771 (paperback : acid-free
    paper) | ISBN 9781462536788 (hardcover : acid-free paper)
Subjects: LCSH: Language arts—United States. | Reading comprehension—
United
    States. | Literacy—United States.
Classification: LCC LB1576 .B486 2019 | DDC 372.6—dc23
LC record available at *https://lccn.loc.gov/2018037281*

About the Editors

Lesley Mandel Morrow, PhD, is Distinguished Professor of Literacy and Director of the Center for Literacy Development at the Graduate School of Education at Rutgers, The State University of New Jersey. Her research deals with early literacy development and the organization and management of language arts programs and literacy-rich environments. Dr. Morrow has published more than 300 journal articles, chapters, and books. Her work has been recognized with awards including the Outstanding Teacher Educator in Reading Award and the William S. Gray Citation of Merit, both from the International Literacy Association (ILA), and the Oscar S. Causey Award for outstanding contributions to reading research from the Literacy Research Association (LRA). Dr. Morrow is past president of the ILA and is a member and past president of the Reading Hall of Fame.

Linda B. Gambrell, PhD, is Professor Emerita in the Eugene T. Moore School of Education at Clemson University. Her major research interests are in the areas of reading comprehension, literacy motivation, and the role of discussion in teaching and learning. Dr. Gambrell has published numerous books and articles on reading instruction, comprehension strategy instruction, and literacy motivation. She is a recipient of the Outstanding Teacher Educator in Reading Award from the ILA, the Laureate Award from the Association of Literacy Educators and Researchers (ALER), and both the Albert J. Kingston Award and the Oscar S. Causey Award from the LRA. Dr. Gambrell is past president of the ILA, LRA, and ALER, and is a member of the Reading Hall of Fame.

Contributors

 Peter Afflerbach, PhD, is Professor of Education at the University of Maryland. His research interests include reading assessment, reading comprehension, and the verbal reporting methodology. Dr. Afflerbach is a standing member of the Reading Committee of the National Assessment of Educational Progress, and he serves as chair of the Literacy Assessment Committee of the International Literacy Association (ILA). He served on the Common Core State Standards Review and Feedback panels. Dr. Afflerbach is an author or editor of numerous books, including the *Handbook of Individual Differences in Reading: Reader, Text, and Context*. He has served as coeditor of the journal *Metacognition and Learning* and on the editorial advisory boards of several other journals. He is a former elementary school Title I reading teacher, middle school remedial reading and writing teacher, and high school English teacher.

 Janice F. Almasi, PhD, is the Carol Lee Robertson Endowed Professor of Literacy Education at the University of Kentucky. Her research focuses on comprehension; in particular, her work examines the strategic processing that occurs while children read, and as they discuss text with peers. Dr. Almasi is currently a co-principal investigator on a federally funded grant in which she is examining the efficacy of interventions to assist struggling readers' narrative comprehension. Her research has been acknowledged with several awards and has been published in leading journals in the field of literacy. She has served as president of the Literacy Research Association (LRA) and on the Board of Directors of the ILA.

 Donald R. Bear, PhD, is Professor Emeritus in Literacy Studies at Iowa State University and the University of Nevada, Reno, where he directed reading centers and taught at all levels. He is a former classroom teacher, and is an author on several instructional programs and assessments. Dr. Bear researches orthographic development in different and second languages, and the sequence students follow across the synchrony of literacy learning. He recently served as a board member of the ILA.

Heather Kenyon Casey, PhD, is Professor of Literacy Education at Rider University, where she teaches undergraduate and graduate courses in literacy, coordinates the graduate-level literacy concentration, and is Site Director of the National Writing Project. Her research focuses on adolescent literacy and the use of collaborative learning structures and new literacies to motivate and support adolescent literacy development and engagement. A former middle school language arts teacher and a certified reading specialist, Dr. Casey is past cochair of the Adolescent Literacy Task Force and the Literacy Reform Task Force of the ILA. She has published numerous articles and book chapters and is author of the book *Literacy Learning Clubs.* Dr. Casey has led several grants in partnership with the National Writing Project focusing on building teacher leadership.

Byeong-Young Cho, PhD, is Assistant Professor in the Department of Instruction and Learning and Research Scientist in the Learning Research and Development Center at the University of Pittsburgh. His major research interests include reading comprehension, digital literacies, higher-order thinking, reading assessment, and verbal data analysis. He is currently conducting research projects on middle and high school students' history learning in multisource digital-text environments, the impact of metacognitive intervention on digital literacy performance, and the assessment of digital literacy competence. Dr. Cho has published his work in peer-reviewed journals such as *American Educational Research Journal, Reading Research Quarterly, Cognition and Instruction, Journal of Adolescent and Adult Literacy,* and *The Reading Teacher.*

Sarah K. Clark, PhD, is Associate Professor of Literacy Education and Leadership in the Department of Teacher Education at Brigham Young University. She spent over 25 years in the field of education as a classroom teacher, a teacher trainer/coach, and an author of educational books and curriculum resources. Dr. Clark is an expert in the areas of providing effective literacy education, integrating literacy and STEM topics to provide authentic learning experiences, supporting and mentoring novice teachers, teacher development, and supporting struggling readers. She is a recipient of multiple awards, including the Promising Researcher Award from the Association of Literacy Educators and Researchers (ALER), the School of Teacher Education and Leadership Teacher of the Year Award, and the Emma Eccles Jones College of Education and Human Services Teacher of the Year Award.

Maria Elliker Crassas, PhD, is a former elementary classroom teacher and a certified reading specialist. Dr. Crassas is currently doing personal study on the language and literacy skills of children who have Down syndrome and autism and the relation of these skills to health and wellness, as her eldest son has this dual diagnosis. She is host of the podcast *The Quest for Healing,* which explores this and other related topics.

Michael Domínguez, PhD, is Assistant Professor in the Department of Chicana and Chicano Studies at San Diego State University. His research interests focus on the schooling experiences of Chicana/o youth, particularly issues of identity construction, sociopolitical development and activism, racialization, affect, and community and family ingenuity. Dr. Domínguez's current work employs social-design and critical-ethnographic research methodologies to explore the ways in which Latina/o youth are constructing new identities and navigating difficult affective experiences across the diaspora, and the implications of this for youth, communities, and schools nationwide. Previously a middle school teacher in Nevada, he is also passionate about liberatory teacher education, ethnic studies curriculum, and the emerging field of culturally sustaining pedagogy.

Susan M. Dougherty, EdD, is Associate Professor of Literacy Education in the College of Education and Human Services at Rider University. Her areas of research interest include parent–preschooler talk, family literacy, and early literacy and science learning. She teaches undergraduate and graduate courses in literacy and has a particular interest in preparing preservice and future literacy specialists to support children who find literacy learning difficult. Dr. Dougherty began her career in education as an elementary teacher in New Jersey and is currently on the board of the New Jersey Literacy Association. She has published many articles and book chapters in her areas of concern and coedited the book *Pivotal Research in Early Literacy: Foundational Studies and Current Practices.*

Nell K. Duke, EdD, is Professor in Literacy, Language, and Culture and in the combined program in Education and Psychology at the University of Michigan. Her work focuses on early literacy development, particularly among children living in poverty. Her specific areas of expertise include development of informational reading and writing in young children, comprehension development and instruction in early schooling, and issues of equity in literacy education. She has received a number of awards for her work, including the P. David Pearson Scholarly Influence Award from the LRA. Among her most recent books are *Inside Information: Developing Powerful Readers and Writers of Informational Text through Project-Based Instruction* and *Beyond Bedtime Stories: A Parent's Guide to Promoting Reading, Writing, and Other Literacy Skills from Birth to 5, Second Edition.*

Patricia A. Edwards, PhD, is Distinguished Professor of Language and Literacy in the Department of Teacher Education at Michigan State University. A member of the Reading Hall of Fame, she is an internationally recognized expert in parent involvement; home, school, and community partnerships; multicultural literacy; early literacy; and family/intergenerational literacy, especially among poor and minority children. Dr. Edwards served on the Board of Directors and as president of the ILA. She was also the first African American president (2006–2007) of the LRA, and will serve as president of the Family, School and Community Partnerships Special Interest Group (2018–2020) of the American Educational Research Association (AERA). Dr. Edwards has published seven books, including *Change Is Gonna Come: Transforming Literacy Education for African American Students,* which won the LRA's Edward B. Fry Book Award in 2011. In 2012, she received the Albert J. Kingston Service Award from the LRA. More recently,

Dr. Edwards was named as the 2017–2018 Jeanne S. Chall Visiting Researcher at Harvard University's Graduate School of Education.

Douglas Fisher, PhD, is Professor of Educational Leadership at San Diego State University and a teacher leader at Health Sciences High and Middle College. He is the recipient of the William S. Gray Citation of Merit from the ILA, the Farmer Award for Excellence in writing from the National Council of Teachers of English (NCTE), as well as a Christa McAuliffe Award for Excellence in Teacher Education from the American Association of State Colleges and Universities. Dr. Fisher served as president of the ILA for 2017–2018. He has published numerous articles on reading and literacy, differentiated instruction, and curriculum design, as well as books, such as *Text Complexity: Raising Rigor in Reading*, *Visible Learning for Literacy*, *Rigorous Reading*, and *Building Equity: Policies and Practices to Empower All Learners*.

Elena Forzani, PhD, is Assistant Professor in Literacy Education at Boston University. Her work focuses on digital literacies learning, with a particular emphasis on understanding how students comprehend and evaluate the credibility of online text. Dr. Forzani seeks to understand how to design learning and assessment that targets the needs of different kinds of learners within these contexts. Previously, she was a fellow at the New Literacies Research Lab at the University of Connecticut and taught high school English and Reading as well as first grade.

Nancy Frey, PhD, is Professor in the Department of Educational Leadership at San Diego State University. Her research interests lie in school-wide practices, literacy interventions, and the leadership of teachers and administrators who create these positive changes in the lives of young people. She is a recipient of the Early Career Achievement Award from the LRA and a corecipient of the Christa McAuliffe Award for Excellence in Teacher Education from the American Association of State Colleges and Universities. She is the author of *Engagement by Design: Creating Learning Environments Where Students Thrive; Developing Assessment-Capable Visible Learners: Maximizing Skill, Will, and Thrill;* and *Text-Dependent Questions: Pathways to Close and Critical Reading.* Dr. Frey is a credentialed special educator, reading specialist, and administrator in California, and a teacher leader at Health Sciences High and Middle College, where she learns from her colleagues and students every day.

Linda B. Gambrell (*see* About the Editors).

Kathy Ganske, PhD, is Research Professor in the Department of Teaching and Learning at Vanderbilt University's Peabody College. Her current research interests include the development of vocabulary knowledge and increased cognitive engagement during word study instruction, especially with language-minority students and students from low-income backgrounds; and literacy reform in challenging schools, including those in international settings. Dr. Ganske's work is grounded in extensive teaching experience in elementary classrooms. She is the author, coauthor, or editor of several books, including *Word Journeys, Second Edition; Word Sorts and More, Second Edition; Mindful of Words;* and *Comprehension Across the*

Curriculum, as well as numerous articles and book chapters. She also serves on the board for Ride for Reading, a national nonprofit that helps children in low-income areas become healthy and literate.

Vicki B. Griffo, PhD, is Literacy Instructor in the Department of Special Education at San Francisco State University, as well as an independent literacy consultant. Her research interests are in reading development and disabilities, refining instructional methods, and developing teacher education. These interests first took root while she served as a first- and second-grade teacher working with bilingual students in a rural, high-poverty district in central California. Dr. Griffo has conducted educational research on a variety of topics, such as improving reading comprehension and reading assessment and remediation of at-risk students.

John T. Guthrie, PhD, is the Jean Mullan Professor Emeritus in the Department of Human Development at the University of Maryland. He is a member of the Reading Hall of Fame and received the Oscar S. Causey Award for Outstanding Research from the LRA. Dr. Guthrie is a Fellow of the AERA and the American Psychological Association. He received the University of Maryland Regents Faculty Award for research/scholarship/creative activity in 2004. In 2011, he was elected to the National Academy of Education, an honorary society of scholars that connects education research to policy. The ILA awarded him the William S. Gray Citation of Merit for lifetime contributions to literacy in 2017. Dr. Guthrie was principal investigator for a federally funded grant to examine adolescents' motivation, engagement, and learning in a districtwide study of concept-oriented reading instruction. He has published several articles and books about motivation and engagement.

Kris D. Gutiérrez, PhD, is the Carol Liu Chair in Educational Policy and a Professor of Language, Literacy, and Culture at the University of California, Berkeley. Her research examines learning in designed learning environments, with attention to students from nondominant communities and English learners. Dr. Gutiérrez is a member of the National Academy of Education and a past president of both the AERA and the National Conference on Research in Language and Literacy. She was appointed by President Obama as a member of the National Board for the Institute of Education Sciences, where she served as vice chair. She also served on the U.S. Department of Education Reading First Advisory Committee and as a member of President Obama's Education Policy Transition Team. Dr. Gutiérrez has received numerous awards, including the Distinguished Contributions to Social Contexts in Education Research—Lifetime Achievement Award from the AERA and the Oscar S. Causey Award from the LRA. She has published widely in academic journals and is coauthor of *Learning and Expanding with Activity Theory*.

Susan J. Hart, EdD, is Assistant Principal at Cassidy Elementary School in Lexington, Kentucky. She began her career as an elementary school teacher in the District of Columbia Public School System and also worked as a research assistant for Dr. Janice F. Almasi at the University of Kentucky, where she assisted with various research endeavors, including collecting and analyzing data related to the Kentucky Reading Project and implementation of response to intervention across the state of Kentucky. Her doctoral dissertation examined an online interactive community of practice that sought to better support teachers, specifically as it related to literacy and strategy instruction.

Troy Hicks, PhD, is Professor of English and Education at Central Michigan University (CMU). He directs both the Chippewa River Writing Project and the Master of Arts in Educational Technology degree program. A former middle school teacher, he collaborates with K–12 colleagues and explores how they implement newer literacies in their classrooms. In 2011, he was honored with CMU's Provost's Award for junior faculty who demonstrate outstanding achievement in research and creative activity; in 2014, he received the Conference on English Education's Richard A. Meade Award for scholarship in English education; and in 2018, he received the Michigan Reading Association's Teacher Educator Award. Dr. Hicks has authored numerous books, articles, chapters, blog posts, and other resources broadly related to the teaching of literacy in our digital age.

Jong-Yun Kim, PhD, received his doctoral degree from the Department of Teaching and Learning, Policy and Leadership at the University of Maryland, College Park. His major research interests are reading comprehension of multiple texts; the relationship between reader beliefs, biases, and reading strategies; and classroom assessment of reading. He was a high school teacher of Korean language and literature in South Korea.

Melanie Kuhn, PhD, is Professor and Jean Adamson Stanley Faculty Chair in Literacy at the Purdue University College of Education. In addition to reading fluency, her research interests include literacy instruction for struggling readers, comprehension development, and vocabulary instruction. Her instructional experience includes teaching at Rutgers Graduate School of Education, in the Boston Public Schools, and at Centre Academy in London. She was co-principal investigator on an Interagency Education Research Initiative grant that explored the development of reading fluency with second graders and served as a member of the Literacy Research Panel for the ILA. Dr. Kuhn has authored or coauthored three books—*Developing Fluent Readers: Teaching Fluency as a Foundational Skill*, *Fluency in the Classroom*, and *The Hows and Whys of Fluency Instruction*—and numerous journal articles and chapters.

Donald J. Leu, PhD, is Professor of Education and the Neag Endowed Chair in Literacy and Technology at the University of Connecticut. Dr. Leu's research focuses on the new skills and strategies required to read, write, and learn with Internet technologies and the best instructional practices that prepare students for these new literacies. He directs the New Literacies Research Lab and is a member of the Reading Hall of Fame. He is a past president of the LRA and former member of the Board of Directors of the ILA. He has received the A. B. Herr Award from the ALER, the Maryann Manning Medal from the University of Alabama, Birmingham, and the Friday Medal for Innovation and Leadership in Education from North Carolina State University.

Christina L. Madda, PhD, is Associate Professor of Literacy Education at Northeastern Illinois University, where she teaches courses in literacy instruction for elementary and secondary grades, assessment and diagnosis, and technology integration. Her current research interests include the use of iPads for intervention with struggling readers, and developing the language of literacy coaching within clinical settings. Dr. Madda is also involved with the Illinois Grow Your Own Teachers initiative, which aims to improve urban education by creating a pipeline of community-based teachers of color. Her recent publication in the *New Educator* journal addresses the potential of university–community partnerships like Grow Your Own Teachers to strengthen teacher preparation.

Jacquelynn A. Malloy, PhD, is Associate Professor of Elementary Education in the Department of Teaching and Learning, College of Education, Clemson University. She teaches undergraduate courses in English language arts methods and social justice for 21st-century learners, as well as master's- and doctoral-level courses in theory, research, and literacy. Her research focuses on motivation and engagement, integrated instruction, and teacher visioning, with publications in *The Reading Teacher, Elementary School Journal,* and *Teaching and Teacher Education.* Dr. Malloy collaborates with numerous colleagues to create and field-test instruments for assessing motivation to read. She is a design-based research enthusiast.

Barbara A. Marinak, PhD, is Professor and Dean of the Division of Education at Mount St. Mary's University, where she teaches literacy and research courses. Dr. Marinak's research interests include reading motivation, intervention practices, and the use of informational text. Her dissertation was awarded the 2005 J. Estill Alexander Future Leaders in Literacy Dissertation Award from the ALER. She is also the 2016 recipient of the ALER's A. B. Herr Award, which recognizes a professional educator who has made outstanding contributions to the field of reading. Before joining the faculty at Mount St. Mary's, Dr. Marinak spent more than two decades in public education, where she held a variety of leadership positions. She has published numerous journal articles and book chapters, and is coauthor of the books *No More Reading Junk* and *Maximizing Motivation for Literacy Learning: Grades K–6* and coeditor of *Essential Readings on Motivation.*

Nicole M. Martin, PhD, is Assistant Professor in the Department of Elementary Education at Ball State University. Her research focuses on K–8 disciplinary literacy, informational reading and writing, and literacy instruction in urban schools. She has received several awards, including Outstanding Dissertation Award Finalist from the ILA and Teacher of the Year. Dr. Martin has authored and coauthored many journal articles, book chapters, and the book *Reading and Writing Genre with Purpose in K–8 Classrooms.*

Lesley Mandel Morrow (*see* About the Editors).

Lisa M. O'Brien, EdD, is Assistant Professor of Reading/Language Arts in the School of Education and Social Policy at Merrimack College. Her research focuses on ways to provide all children access to opportunities that ameliorate early and later opportunity and knowledge gaps and support families and teachers (i.e., preservice and inservice) in understanding and implementing these practices. These efforts include investigation of family literacy program effects, transformative technology integration practices, and relations between text type, knowledge, and comprehension. Prior to earning her doctorate, Dr. O'Brien worked as a head preschool teacher serving children from low- to middle-income families. She has also worked as an elementary grade classroom teacher, supported special education students in middle and high school, and served as a reading specialist/literacy leader in a K–4 school.

Jeanne R. Paratore, EdD, is Professor Emerita in Language and Literacy Education at Boston University Wheelock College of Education and Human Development. She is research advisor to the Intergenerational Literacy Program, a family literacy program she founded in 1989 to support the English literacy learning of immigrant parents and their children. Dr. Paratore has conducted research and written widely on issues related to family literacy, classroom grouping practices, and interventions for struggling readers. She is a recipient of the New England Reading Association's Lifetime Achievement Award and a member of the Reading Hall of Fame.

P. David Pearson, PhD, is an emeritus faculty member and Professor in the Graduate School of Education at the University of California, Berkeley, where he served as Dean from 2001 to 2010. He also serves as the Evelyn Lois Corey Emeritus Chair in Instructional Science. Long interested in comprehension and balanced literacy, his current research focuses on literacy history and policy. Dr. Pearson has received numerous honors, including the William S. Gray Citation of Merit and the Albert J. Harris Award from the ILA, the Oscar S. Causey Award from the LRA, the Alan Purves Award from the NCTE, and the Distinguished Contributions to Research in Education Award from the AERA. In 2012, the LRA established the P. David Pearson Scholarly Influence Award to honor research that exerts a long-term influence on literacy practices and/or policies. He has written scores of articles and chapters and written or edited several books, most notably the *Handbook of Reading Research*, now in its fourth volume.

Taffy E. Raphael, PhD, is Professor Emeritus at the University of Illinois at Chicago and Senior Advisor in SchoolRise LLC. Her research interests include comprehension and writing instruction, frameworks for literacy curriculum and instruction, and whole-school reform. Dr. Raphael designed and researched pedagogical frameworks such as Question Answer Relationships and Book Club. She has been honored by awards such as the ILA's Outstanding Teacher Educator in Reading Award, the University of Illinois at Urbana–Champaign's Distinguished Alumni Award, and the LRA's Oscar S. Causey Award for lifetime contributions to literacy research. Dr. Raphael is a fellow of the National Conference on Research in Language and Literacy and a member of the Reading Hall of Fame. She served on the board of the LRA, where she also served as treasurer and president. Dr. Raphael has published several books and over 100 chapters and articles in leading journals.

Timothy Rasinski, PhD, is Professor of Literacy Education at Kent State University. He began his career as an elementary and middle school teacher. His scholarly interests include reading fluency and word study, reading in the elementary and middle grades, and readers who struggle. Dr. Rasinski's research on reading has been cited by the National Reading Panel and has been published in journals such as *Reading Research Quarterly, The Reading Teacher, Reading Psychology,* and the *Journal of Educational Research.* He has served on the Board of Directors of the ILA, as the president of the College Reading Association, and as coeditor of *The Reading Teacher* and the *Journal of Literacy Research.* In 2010, he was elected to the Reading Hall of Fame. Dr. Rasinski has written over 200 articles and has authored, coauthored, or edited over 50 books or curriculum programs on reading education, including *Fluency Instruction, Second Edition: Research-Based Best Practices.*

D. Ray Reutzel, PhD, is Dean of the College of Education at the University of Wyoming. Dr. Reutzel is a past editor of *Literacy Research and Instruction* and *The Reading Teacher* and the current Executive Editor of the *Journal of Educational Research.* He has received more than 17 million dollars in research/professional development grant funding. A recipient of the 1999 A. B. Herr Award and the 2013 Laureate Award from the ALER, Dr. Reutzel served as president of that organization from 2006 until 2007. He was presented the John C. Manning Public School Service Award from the ILA in 2007 and has served as a member of the Board of Directors of both the ILA and the LRA. Dr. Reutzel was elected a member of the Reading Hall of Fame in 2011 and is serving as its president from 2017 to 2019. He is the author of more than 225 published research articles, book chapters, monographs, and books.

Cary B. Riches, EdD, is Director of Curriculum and Instruction, PreK–12, in the Brandywine School District, Delaware. A former high school English and reading teacher, instructional coach, and high school assistant principal, she recently earned her doctorate in Education from the University of Delaware. Dr. Riches is interested in building and sustaining systems to effectively deliver multi-tiered systems of support focused on reading and writing. She has successfully built an elementary and secondary system to support response to intervention. The system includes comprehensive professional learning for teachers and administrators.

Victoria J. Risko, EdD, is Professor Emerita in the Department of Teaching and Learning at Vanderbilt University. Her research focuses on teacher education and professional development, teacher reflection, reading comprehension and meaningful learning, and uses of cases and multimedia environments to enhance learning, especially with English learners and readers who are experiencing difficulties. Dr. Risko was the 2011–2012 president of the ILA and is a former president of the ALER. She has received the New York Chancellor's Award for Outstanding Teaching, a Distinguished Research in Education Award from the Association of Teacher Educators, the A. B. Herr Award and Laureate Award from the ALER, the Literary Award for distinguished leadership and contributions to global literacy from the ILA, and, with coresearchers, the Alan C. Purves Award from the NCTE for recognition of research supporting

English learners. She is a member of the Reading Hall of Fame. She is coauthor of several books, has published in numerous journals, and is past coeditor of the "Research in the Classroom" column in *The Reading Teacher.*

John Z. Strong, MEd, is a doctoral student in Education with a specialization in literacy development and learning problems at the University of Delaware. Previously, he taught high school English language arts. His research interests include integrated reading and writing interventions in grades 4–12. Mr. Strong is a recipient of the University of Delaware's Richard L. Venezky Award for Creative Research in Literacy. He has coauthored articles published in *The Elementary School Journal,* the *Journal of Adolescent and Adult Literacy,* and *The Reading Teacher,* and he is a coauthor of the forthcoming book *Differentiated Reading Instruction in Grades 4 and 5, Second Edition.*

Ana Taboada Barber, PhD, is Associate Professor in the Department of Counseling, Higher Education, and Special Education at the University of Maryland, where she is also Codirector of the Language and Literacy Research Center. Dr. Taboada Barber studies reading comprehension from a cognitive and motivational perspective. Her work centers on studying the influence of specific motivational variables (e.g., autonomy support, self-efficacy) and cognitive variables (e.g., executive functioning skills, inference making) on the literacy and language development of upper elementary and middle school students. She is interested in studying reading comprehension within classroom instructional contexts and as an individual-difference variable. As a former English as a second language teacher, her work in reading comprehension development is principally concentrated within the population of English learners or emergent bilinguals within the United States.

Nicole Timbrell, MEd, is Head of Digital Learning and Australian Curriculum Coordinator at the Australian International School, Singapore. Her research interests are in the new literacies of online research and comprehension, and the use of technology in teaching reading and writing skills to adolescents.

Diane H. Tracey, EdD, is Professor of Education at Kean University and author (with Lesley Mandel Morrow) of *Lenses on Reading, Third Edition: An Introduction to Theories and Models.* She has written widely on topics related to literacy achievement and is an active presenter at local, state, and national conferences. Dr. Tracey has served as secretary of the LRA and on the editorial review boards of the *Journal of Literacy Research, The Reading Teacher,* the *National Reading Conference Yearbook,* and *Education and Urban Society.* She is a recipient of Kean University's Presidential Scholars Challenge Award. Prior to her work at the university level, she was an early childhood educator and a research assistant on a large, federally funded grant project studying children's reading disabilities. Dr. Tracey is also a graduate student at the Center for Modern Psychoanalytic Studies, training to become a modern psychoanalyst.

Doris Walker-Dalhouse, PhD, is Professor of Literacy in the College of Education at Marquette University and Professor Emerita at Minnesota State University, Moorhead. Her research, conducted in after-school reading programs with preservice teachers and struggling readers, refugee children, and families, addresses the impact of sociocultural factors on the literacy development of ethnically and culturally diverse learners. Dr. Walker-Dalhouse cochaired the ILA Response to Intervention Task Force, was lead writer for Standard 4: Diversity and Equity for the 2017 ILA Standards for the Preparation of Literacy Professionals, and is presently chair of the LRA Student Outstanding Research Award Committee. She is a member of the Board of Directors of the ALER, past member of the Board of Directors of the ILA and the LRA, past coeditor of the "Research in the Classroom" column in *The Reading Teacher,* and recipient of the 2013 Albert J. Mazurkiewicz Special Services Award from the ALER. She has published in several professional journals and research association yearbooks.

Sharon Walpole, PhD, is Director of the Professional Development Center for Educators and Professor in the School of Education at the University of Delaware. She has extensive school-based experience designing and implementing tiered instructional programs. Dr. Walpole has also been involved in federally funded and other schoolwide reform projects. She is a recipient of the Early Career Award for Significant Contributions to Literacy Research and Education from the LRA and the Excellence in Teaching Award from the University of Delaware. Her current work involves the design and effects of the open educational resource *Bookworms Reading and Writing.* She has coauthored or coedited several books, including *How to Plan Differentiated Reading Instruction, Second Edition: Resources for Grades K–3; The Literacy Coach's Handbook, Second Edition;* and *Organizing the Early Literacy Classroom.*

Chase Young, PhD, is Associate Professor in the Department of Language, Literacy, and Special Populations at Sam Houston State University. His research aims to develop reading fluency and support struggling readers. In 2014, the ALER selected him as their Jerry Johns Promising Researcher. His research articles have appeared in the *Journal of Educational Research,* the *Journal of Research in Reading, The Reading Teacher,* the *Journal of Adolescent and Adult Literacy,* and *Literacy Research and Instruction.* Along with Timothy Rasinski, he recently coauthored *Tiered Fluency Instruction: Supporting Diverse Learners in Grades 2–5.* Previously, he taught elementary school and served as a reading specialist.

Lisa Zawilinski, PhD, is Associate Professor at the University of Hartford. Her research examines methods for helping young children develop literacy skills and strategies across various learning contexts. She focuses on the skills and strategies necessary for elementary grade students to communicate and gather information on the Internet. Dr. Zawilinski also examines how best to support preservice teachers' use of technology to meet the varying needs of all students. She has published in *The Reading Teacher, Reading Today,* and a variety of other journals and books.

Introduction

HEATHER KENYON CASEY

In 1999, Linda B. Gambrell, Lesley Mandel Morrow, Susan B. Neuman, and Michael Pressley came together to develop the book *Best Practices in Literacy Instruction*. In that first edition, the editors offered a platform for bringing together leading literacy scholars in the field to give voice to preferred practices for literacy instruction in grades PreK–8. Among the areas investigated in the first edition were classroom context, motivation to read, teaching methods, and the social nature of learning. Each edition since has offered expert guidance in the preferred practices of literacy education closely linked to relevant research, pedagogy, and policy. In this, its sixth edition, almost 20 years later, Lesley Mandel Morrow and Linda B. Gambrell continue to provide a place where experts in the field of literacy education can give voice to current research trends and pedagogy in ways that will continue to positively influence children and adolescents and the educators who work alongside them.

The sixth edition addresses evidence-based practices from PreK through 12th grade with an increased emphasis on understanding how to best support the linguistic needs of the diverse learners that make up our classrooms. This edition also contributes to the conversation about the thoughtful and purposeful use of technology in today's classrooms. It provides evidence-based strategies for supporting students' literacy needs across grade levels in ways that prepare our current children and adolescents for success in their futures. Important, too, are the places in this volume where issues of assessment and standards are addressed in ways that offer educators an understanding of accountability that empowers best practices.

Preservice and practicing teachers, reading/literacy specialists and coaches, and administrators and teacher educators will find this new edition helpful to their work. *Best Practices in Literacy Instruction* provides evidence of teaching practices that work across grade levels and sound research that is an important resource for those who develop and implement curriculum and policy. As these editors get ready to mark the 20-year anniversary of this important work, the sixth edition promises to continue to inspire educators.

The 19 chapters in this edition are organized into four parts. In Part I: Perspectives on Best Practices, the contributing authors provide a theoretical framework for understanding current perspectives of best practices. The contributions include an investigation of the social nature of literacy learning, a discussion of current issues influencing the field, and an examination of the theories and research concerned with motivating readers. In Part II: Best Practices for All Students, the contributing authors offer frameworks for supporting the diverse learners in our PreK–12 schools. These contributions include a discussion of preferred practices for literacy learning from the early years through adolescence. In addition, this section also offers contributions that center on supporting struggling readers as well as dual language learners across this continuum. In Part III: Evidence-Based Strategies for Literacy Learning and Teaching, the contributing authors examine the evidence for strategic literacy instruction. They contribute information and ideas about word study and vocabulary, fluency, comprehension, writing, and assessment. Part IV: Perspectives on Special Issues, explores current trends and topics that are influencing all areas of literacy instruction and learning. These contributions examine the influence of new literacies and digital tools, strategies for organizing for effective literacy teaching and learning, and understanding the emotional component of literacy learning. These topics are discussed alongside the importance of creating strong home–community partnerships outside of the school as well as building strong professional learning communities within the school.

As we continue this important dialogue at the local, state, national, and international levels around literacy policy and pedagogy that the current editors began nearly 20 years ago with the original publication of this seminal text, the sixth edition of *Best Practices in Literacy Instruction* is poised to continue to make important contributions to the field of literacy instruction and learning.

PART I: PERSPECTIVES ON BEST PRACTICES

In Chapter 1, Jacquelynn A. Malloy, Barbara A. Marinak, and Linda B. Gambrell explore the importance of creating a literacy community within the classroom. The authors contend that when meaningful relationships are constructed in classrooms, then learning can best occur. Drawing on decades of research, they describe how the classroom community contributes to literacy learning and examine strategies classroom teachers and related personnel can incorporate to foster a shared sense of responsibility for students' literacy development and learning. At the center of this development is the *teacher* implementing evidence-based instructional and assessment practices that honor the cultural and linguistic needs of each child and create opportunities for social collaboration and engagement around texts in their multiple mediums.

In Chapter 2, Christina L. Madda, Vicki B. Griffo, P. David Pearson, and Taffy E. Raphael provide a broad vision of current practices that create a sense of balance in the literacy curriculum. They trace the history of the sometimes politicized term "balance" and demonstrate how research supports the need for literacy programs that incorporate a variety of instructional and assessment strategies alongside multiple resources and pedagogical choices. Essentially, they argue for the need for teachers to be equipped with a strong understanding of how to understand and support individual literacy learners and how to match that knowledge of the learner with appropriate strategies and resources that will support continued learning across disciplines. The authors contend that this framework is often challenged by policy debates that shape curriculum in ways that do not always reflect best practices. At the heart of the need for a balanced literacy curriculum, they argue, is the evidence that demonstrates how this approach best supports students' literacy development and learning across grade levels.

In Chapter 3, John T. Guthrie and Ana Taboada Barber discuss the value of considering theories of motivation and engagement when designing classroom instruction. The authors describe the strong evidence base for strategies to motivate and engage students. In this chapter, these theories and frameworks are updated to reflect current trends in education around supporting students' capacity to develop a growth mindset. The capacity to motivate and engage children and adolescent literacy learners is dependent on a classroom that offers choice, collaboration, and relevant materials and resources. The authors provide evidence and strategies that demonstrate that key to universal success is an awareness of the linguistic differences among the growing diversity in our classrooms.

PART II: BEST PRACTICES FOR ALL STUDENTS

In Chapter 4, Lesley Mandel Morrow, Susan M. Dougherty, and Diane H. Tracey offer a robust theoretical framework for best practices in literacy education. These are offered alongside an overview of historical trends in government initiatives as well as recent policy shifts around standards initiatives and the influence on early literacy education in the United States. The authors offer an overview of how policy trends and the rise of social media and young children's access to digital tools in early literacy have shaped pedagogy and children's literacy development in recent years. They provide specific strategies for success in word study, concepts about print, comprehension, and writing development alongside the importance of building positive relationships with children and a strong classroom community. Indeed, they contend, one cannot happen without the other. The authors take the reader through a possible day in an early literacy classroom that is inclusive of all of these components in a way that is responsive to current trends in digital literacy and an awareness of the linguistically diverse classrooms that early literacy educators support.

In Chapter 5, Victoria J. Risko and Doris Walker-Dalhouse offer best practices for shifting the pathway of struggling readers. The authors recall a tradition of a narrow instructional focus for those students identified as "struggling readers" that can create misconceptions for children about their identity as literacy learners and the classroom expectations for their success. They offer evidence for the need for students who struggle at all levels to experience instruction in balanced literacy programs with rich contexts for learning that are inclusive of a variety of authentic texts that can be paired to meet students' needs. According to Risko and Walker-Dalhouse, this goal requires assessment practices that target students' abilities along with their challenges, and that understands reading as inclusive of decoding, fluency, and comprehension across a variety of genres and disciplines. This focus on comprehensive strategies instead of discrete skills results in sustained literacy growth and development. The authors resist a "one-size-fits-all" approach for supporting struggling readers and instead call for these authentic and contextualized practices to be situated according to the diverse cultural and economic contexts in which literacy instruction and learning occur.

In Chapter 6, Michael Domínguez and Kris D. Gutiérrez offer a comprehensive description of the diverse linguistic communities across the United States alongside specific evidence-based practices for supporting dual language learners. The authors remind readers that as this population grows, it becomes critically important to understand best practices in relation to the specific communities in which educators are working as well as the sociopolitical demands of supporting these children and their families in the current political climate. Vital to this is an understanding of the importance of debunking a deficit model of dual language learning. The authors call on educators to implement practices that encourage continual literacy development within all of the languages that students speak.

In Chapter 7, Douglas Fisher and Nancy Frey remind the reader of the robust literacy practices both in school and out of school with which today's adolescents engage. They cite a strong evidence base that learning is based in language. This translates to discipline-specific literacy practices that motivate learning across content areas. Specific strategies and examples are offered to support adolescent literacy learners through purposeful classroom discourse patterns and collaborative grouping practices. Close reading and writing practices are defined and described through classroom examples that demonstrate the capacity to motivate adolescent learning and learners.

PART III: EVIDENCE-BASED STRATEGIES FOR LITERACY LEARNING AND TEACHING

Practices for the developmental approach to word study are offered by Donald R. Bear in Chapter 8. Bear describes the developmental framework and stages around the development of word knowledge. This leads to specific strategies designed to motivate learners across this continuum in the continual development of word study as a key element in comprehensive literacy development. Bear offers a lens for understanding word study with diverse linguistic communities. A collection of strategies such as picture and word sorts, the study of word families, and the larger connection to reading and writing practices are explored. Bear contends that central to the success of meeting students at the appropriate word-study level are the formative assessments teachers use to understand where on the developmental continuum to focus instruction with students.

In Chapter 9, Kathy Ganske expands the discussion of word study in her deep dive into best practices for vocabulary instruction. In this chapter, Ganske provides important evidence for explicit attention to the morphological features of language as an avenue for vocabulary development alongside rich, varied, and authentic reading, writing, and speaking experiences in classrooms. She offers specific strategies such as small-group study of vocabulary, attention to academic vocabulary, and understanding how to use context to understand new words and phrases, among others.

In Chapter 10, Janice F. Almasi and Susan J. Hart describe instructional practices that support the comprehension of narrative text. The authors argue for the use of narrative text to develop strategic readers who can then turn these developing strategies to multiple text types, including digital platforms, to arrive at independent conclusions and meanings. Specific recommendations for classroom instruction include creating a sense of community where diverse and divergent views of text and the capacity to feel comfortable to voice confusion are respected and in fact celebrated. Critical to this development is the opportunity for rich discourse and peer collaboration around the shared reading and writing of text. Almasi and Hart argue that paying particular attention to how context influences learning is central to this robust view of comprehension instruction.

Nell K. Duke and Nicole M. Martin focus on best practices in the instruction of comprehension of informational text in Chapter 11. Central to this instruction, Duke and Martin suggest, is viewing the classroom as a community of learners and unpacking the contexts in which many pieces of informational text (e.g., news media, medical resources) are authored. The authors recommend that teachers welcome students' curiosities and model how texts can provide evidence and ideas, while offering opportunities to collaborate with others during and after reading experiences to deepen understanding. Explicit instruction in text structures and their associated visuals (e.g., graphs, charts, images) as well as opportunities to engage in these different text types are important. The use of whole-class read-alouds and small-group and/or independent reading activities are identified as critical to the continual development of the comprehension of informational text.

In Chapter 12, Melanie Kuhn, Timothy Rasinski, and Chase Young examine fluency instruction. This chapter highlights the importance of fluency in students' reading achievement and cites a robust tradition of research to document this need. The authors suggest this is accomplished when students are given the opportunity to read texts multiple times, when they are supported during read-aloud sessions, and when ample time is provided for reading in its many forms in the classroom. The authors detail the fluency-oriented reading instruction method as a pathway for supporting fluency in the effort to boost deeper comprehension and higher reading achievement. They call for continued research in this developing area as texts and text types evolve. Kuhn, Rasinski, and Young also call for educators to consider the importance of attending to fluency beyond the primary grades.

Troy Hicks examines writing instruction in Chapter 13. Hicks offers the same call for community as a vehicle for writing development that the earlier chapter authors suggest is necessary for reading instruction. He draws on the historical tradition around writing communities that documents the value of developing a community for supporting writing development. Newer to this discussion, however, is the rise of digital literacies and their influence on developing writers and writing. Hicks recommends that in order to create a writing community, teachers need to be specific and transparent about how particular strategies and processes can influence writing, to offer their students the opportunity to engage with multiple genres, and to encourage them to collaborate with peer writers in meaningful ways. Central to writing development is developing an identity as a writer, which is often best accomplished through this community approach, the opportunity to write for real audiences, and the chance to celebrate the culmination of writing pieces with the classroom community. Hicks suggests that digital literacies invite teachers and students to do this together in transformative and powerful ways.

In Chapter 14, Peter Afflerbach, Byeong-Young Cho, Maria Elliker Crassas, and Jong-Yun Kim bring Part III to a close with their discussion of reading assessment practices. In this chapter, the authors examine classroom-based assessments that have the potential to inform daily instruction and learning. They offer strategies for supporting readers through these formative assessments in light of standards-based initiatives and the trend toward high-stakes and digital assessments that sometimes minimize teacher input. To do this effectively, the authors call for assessing process and product and skills and strategies in relation to the wide range of print and digital texts students are expected to work with frequently. To do this well, they call for assessments that truly measure all areas of reading development. The authors advocate for appropriate professional development to ensure that those who will administer and analyze the assessments understand how to do so effectively. Important, too, is learning how to use the data to inform instructional decisions in ways that will purposefully and positively support developing readers.

PART IV: PERSPECTIVES ON SPECIAL ISSUES

In Chapter 15, Lisa Zawilinski, Elena Forzani, Nicole Timbrell, and Donald J. Leu explore the integration of new literacies into PreK–12 instruction. In this chapter, the authors suggest that current practices require an expanded conception of literacy that extends beyond traditional print-based reading and writing. In doing so, they argue for understanding best practices for online reading comprehension and research as inclusive of what we know to be effective literacy instruction across text types as well as new strategies for navigating these blended worlds. The authors offer examples of online tools that can be paired with traditional text and text-based instruction to support literacy learning and development. They offer a series of strategies such as understanding the hashtag as a literacy skill, using explanatory thinking as a think-aloud alongside screencasts, and understanding how to navigate online searches. The authors suggest that consistent across all literacy texts is the need to develop independent, critical thinking skills and strategies to support comprehension.

In Chapter 16, D. Ray Reutzel and Sarah K. Clark describe practices for organizing literacy instruction to best meet students' needs. According to the authors, at the center of this discussion is differentiation. They argue for the need to differentiate according to the global and national context in which literacy teaching and learning is positioned along with the specific needs of each classroom and student in those unique and diverse settings. Reutzel and Clark take the readers inside classrooms and describe evidence-based strategies for supporting literacy development, multiple methods for grouping, and a variety of scheduling options to support the literacy development of children. They explicate the need to understand these decisions within the broader policy landscape that includes the influence that the Common Core State Standards and response to intervention have had on the expectations for many students and teachers and the larger goal of closing the literacy achievement gap.

In Chapter 17, Diane H. Tracey asks us to consider the importance of understanding the physiological, emotional, and behavioral foundations of literacy learning. Tracey argues that literacy development can only be understood in relation to the social, emotional, physiological, cultural, and linguistic development of children. She, like her colleagues in previous chapters, values the classroom as a community. Tracey looks at the classroom community through the lens of the holistic development of children. In this chapter, she offers evidence that there is a direct correlation between food insecurity, emotional distress, and delayed literacy development. To respond to this growing phenomenon, Tracey offers guidelines for educators to consider things such as sleep, nutrition, exercise, and building relationships, among others, as gateways for learning. She demonstrates that when children feel safe and secure and are in good physical health, their literacy development is optimized. One cannot occur without the other.

In Chapter 18, Jeanne R. Paratore, Patricia A. Edwards, and Lisa M. O'Brien explore the importance of home, school, and community partnerships. The authors examine this important bridge through the lens of culturally relevant teaching. A strong evidence base is presented that demonstrates the long understood value of these partnerships. Newer to this discussion is the understanding of the need to build these partnerships through the lens of culturally relevant pedagogy. According to the authors, in order for productive relationships that foster learning to develop, teacher awareness of the specific dispositions and backgrounds of all involved is essential. The authors share a variety of strategies educators can use to build these meaningful partnerships.

In Chapter 19, Sharon Walpole, John Z. Strong, and Cary B. Riches suggest that effective literacy instruction is closely aligned with effective professional learning. The authors present a robust view of professional learning that is inclusive of focused workshop and training sessions, curriculum development, professional collaborations, and focused coaching, among others. Understanding the necessity to differentiate professional learning based on need and topic is described. In addition, the authors argue that in order to create a culture of sustained professional learning, there is a need for literacy specialists to coordinate these efforts and create plans that are inclusive of a range of evidence-based professional learning structures (e.g., coaching, professional learning communities, classroom visits). The accessibility of digital tools widens the scope of these collaborations as increasingly professional learning can be connected to online communities.

The sixth edition of *Best Practices in Literacy Instruction* is a robust exploration of essential issues and scholarship in literacy education. The different editions of this book are all part of a rich literacy tradition, and the new edition continues to align with current trends and initiatives that are influencing literacy learning today. It is an important resource for all educators.

Contents

PART IV. PERSPECTIVES ON SPECIAL ISSUES

PART I

PERSPECTIVES ON
BEST PRACTICES

CHAPTER 1

Evidence-Based Best Practices for Developing Literate Communities

JACQUELYNN A. MALLOY
BARBARA A. MARINAK
LINDA B. GAMBRELL

This chapter will:

- Explore the importance of developing a well-supported learning community.
- Present 10 evidence-based best practices for comprehensive literacy instruction.
- Discuss how these practices can be expressed in ways that support and sustain a community of learners.
- Emphasize the central role of teachers as visionary decision makers who thoughtfully design litearcy instruction to support learning within the classroom community.

CLASSROOMS AS COMMUNITIES OF LEARNERS

When students are excited to learn, teaching is a joy. Creating a classroom community that sparks enthusiasm for learning, and where each and every student is a valued contributor to this learning, can make that ideal a reality. Research on the relationships among classroom climate, student engagement, and achievement has increased of late (see Baker,

3

2006; Kaplan Toren & Seginer, 2015), and this research suggests that the culture of the classroom is shaped by many factors, including the attitudes and beliefs of the students and the teacher, the quality of classroom interactions, and the instructional practices employed by the teacher.

A *culture of learning* can develop in a classroom when teachers and students embrace the idea that we learn best together. A *community of learners* can be described as a group of people who share values and beliefs about learning and who actively engage in learning from one another. This engenders an atmosphere wherein students and teachers construct knowledge together in connected, collaborative, and supportive ways. Creating a positive classroom learning community provides a risk-free context in which students can engage in learning at their own level of expertise and comfort. In this environment, students are willing to take on learning challenges and make mistakes—all necessary to continued learning and development.

Community-centered pedagogies that facilitate student learning have been highlighted in educational literature and recent research. This research suggests that the classroom environment plays a critical role in supporting students' motivation, engagement, and achievement (Patrick, Kaplan, & Ryan, 2011). As far back as 1939, Lewin, Lippitt, and White recognized that classrooms have very distinct psychological environments. A common thread in the literature on community-centered pedagogy is that positive social interactions need to occur in a regular and timely manner in order to foster a sense of community.

The basic tenets of community-centered pedagogy are grounded in the work of Dewey (1963) and Vygotsky (1978) who posited that learning is facilitated through individual participation in social interactions. This approach is framed within the social-constructivist view and supports activities that promote and nurture student-to-student interactions in co-constructing knowledge. Community-centered pedagogy focuses on learning activities that involve group work and purposeful collaboration.

According to Kent and Simpson (2012), a classroom community is comprised of the collective cultures, values, and rules enacted by the group. They contend that "participating as a contributing member of a community is essential for the well-being and academic success of all students" (p. 28). This builds on work by Schaps and Lewis (1997) who suggest that a strong sense of classroom community contributes to positive student outcomes. A growing body of literature highlights "the importance of positive classroom social processes—children's positive interactions with teachers and peers—for improving children's social and academic performance" (p. 130) (Brock, Nishida, Chiong, Grimm, & Rimm-Kaurman, 2008; Flook, Repetti, & Ullman, 2005; Hamre & Pianta, 2005).

It is the classroom teacher who is responsible for creating and cultivating this positive classroom community as the instructional leader and facilitator of knowledge. The theoretical perspective of Connell and Welborn (1991) advances the idea that children have three basic psychological needs: *competence, autonomy,* and *relatedness.* According to Brock et al. (2008), these three needs can be met in the classroom through children's interactions with teachers and the learning environment—with some intentionality on the part of the teacher, that is.

Connell and Wellborn (1991) define *competence* as the need to see oneself as capable. Teachers can promote feelings of competency by providing specific feedback that values the learning process (e.g., "You read that passage with such good expression—I really believed you!"), rather than using vague praise (e.g., "Nice job"). *Autonomy* describes the experience of choice in initiating, maintaining, and regulating learning activities. Teachers support autonomy when they encourage students to make informed choices about what they read and how they show what they know. *Relatedness* is defined as the need to feel connected to the social environment and to the learning that occurs there. Teachers support relatedness by knowing their students' interests, strengths, and challenges and by modeling, and then supporting, the prosocial interactions that will help students get to know and value each other.

The fulfillment of these three key psychological needs—competence, autonomy, and relatedness—sparks student engagement in learning and mediates classroom performance (Brock, et al., 2008; Kent & Simpson, 2012). Teachers, through their use of quality interactions and their choice of comprehensive and community-supporting classroom practices, can create learning communities that support students' social and academic development. In classrooms that operate as communities of learning, students are actively engaged in directing their own learning—again, a classroom where teaching is a joy.

EVIDENCE-BASED BEST PRACTICES: A RESEARCH SYNTHESIS

While no single instructional program, approach, or method has been found to be effective in teaching all students to read, *evidence-based best practices* that promote high rates of achievement have been documented. An "evidence-based best practice" refers to an instructional practice that has a record of success in improving reading achievement and is both trustworthy and valid. There is evidence that when this practice is used with a particular group of students, they can be expected to make gains in reading achievement (International Reading Association, 2002a, 2002b). Providing comprehensive literacy instruction in the increasingly diverse classrooms of today requires teachers to assess skillfully in order to design appropriate instruction to meet the individual needs of all students. In addition, the classroom teacher must be adept at identifying student needs through ongoing formative assessments and providing appropriate whole-group, small-group, and individual instruction.

What counts as evidence of reliable and trustworthy practice? Evidence-based best practices are established in two ways: by data collected according to rigorously designed studies and by expert consensus among practitioners who monitor student outcomes as part of their practice (U.S. Department of Education, 2012). A position paper published by the International Reading Association (2002b) asserts that such evidence provides:

- *Objective* data that any evaluator would identify and interpret similarly.
- *Valid* data that adequately represent the tasks that children need to become successful readers.
- *Reliable* data that will remain essentially unchanged if collected on a different day or by a different person.
- *Systematic* data that were collected according to a rigorous design of either experimentation or observation.
- *Refereed* data that have been approved for publication by a panel of independent reviewers.

According to a U.S. Department of Education report (2012), research has produced the following findings that form the basis of evidence-based literacy practices:

- Instruction that focuses on students' strengths and needs in the five core elements of reading: phonemic awareness, phonics, fluency, vocabulary, and comprehension;
- Instruction that is systematic and sequenced;
- Instruction that uses materials that are engaging and relevant to the students' needs;
- Instruction that is continuously monitored to gauge effectiveness.

In our view, evidence-based instruction involves teachers making decisions using "professional wisdom integrated with the best available empirical evidence" (Allington, 2005, p. 16). This definition of evidence-based instruction honors the wisdom and verification derived from professional experience while at the same time recognizes the important role of empirical research. Furthermore, no single investigation or research study ever establishes a practice as effective. When evaluating claims of evidence for best practices, we must determine whether the research was data-based, rigorous, and systematic (Bogdan & Biklen, 1992; International Reading Association, 2002b). It is important to note that it is the *convergence of evidence* from an array of research studies, using a variety of research designs and methodologies, that allows us to determine best practices.

In order to provide instruction using best practices, as well as to make appropriate instructional and assessment decisions, teachers need a strong knowledge of good evidence, drawn from both professional wisdom and the research. One of the most important questions a teacher can ask is "What evidence is available that suggests that using this practice in my classroom will support comprehensive literacy instruction and increase litearcy achievement for my students?"

We must acknowledge that some students are at risk of academic failure because of their life conditions. Furthermore, we need to acknowledge that school cultures require specialized academic abilities. Life conditions and experiences that do not support and encourage the development of those specialized academic abilities "tend to produce children who are deficient in the ability to handle academic work" (Gordon, 2009, p. ix). We think Gordon has it right when he states, "We know in the 21st century that the absence of a certain developed ability because of the absence of opportunity to learn should not be interpreted as absence of ability to learn, and the recognition of the fact of diverse human characteristics demands accommodation and differentiation in pedagogical treatment" (p. x).

COMPREHENSIVE LITERACY INSTRUCTION

For literacy instruction to be *comprehensive,* an all-encompassing definition of literacy needs to be considered. Literacy is, after all, the means by which we communicate, whether by comprehending the thoughts, ideas, and intentions *of* others, or in communicating our thoughts, ideas, and intentions *to* others. While the traditional view of literacy addresses primarily reading and writing, a *comprehensive view* of literacy encompasses three reciprocal modes of communicating: *speaking/listening, reading/writing,* and *viewing/representing.* Just as oral skills precede and continue to support reading and writing activities, the signs, symbols, and images that are present and exchanged in the environment are valued literacies in terms of understanding the "unwritten" messages that exist around us. In our increasingly global society, these nonlinguistic arts of viewing and representing hold increasing power to communicate across languages. We are remiss as educators if we do no support our students in devloping both the linguistic and nonlinguistic modes of communicating because they are all essential literacies.

Comprehensive literacy instruction, then, addresses these reciprocal modes of communication, building both receptive skills (listening, reading, viewing) as well as expressive skills (speaking, writing, visually representing). It is formed around high expectations for continued student growth based on future-looking standards of what students know and are able to do involving these modes. In order for students to become independent communicators, instruction should be provided to each student in their zone of proximal development (Vygotsky, 1978) such that they are supported in moving from what they can do with support to what they can do on their own. Further, as communication occurs for social reasons and in a social context, developing literate learners can support the growth of a purposefully functioning literate community. The best practices that are described in this chapter, and throughout this volume, are designed to prepare educators toward reaching that worthy end.

THE ROLE OF DIFFERENTIATED INSTRUCTION IN COMPREHENSIVE LITERACY INSTRUCTION

There is no doubt that as contemporary student populations become increasingly more diverse, teachers and administrators are focused on honing literacy practices that prove to be effective for all students (McCoy & Ketterlin-Geller, 2004; Tomlinson, 2001). For more than three decades, literacy professionals have recognized the need to study our students in order to determine their strengths and needs. However, this careful examination is now taking place in classrooms welcoming students with disabilities, students who are culturally and linguistically diverse, and students with a wide variety of print experiences, interests, and motivation (Stronge, 2007). In addition, in order to deliver comprehensive literacy instruction for all students, it is important to use pedagogically sound assessment techniques to support differentiated literacy instruction.

The Role of Assessment in Differentiated Instruction

The goal of assessment is to obtain useful and timely information about desired goals as literacy learning evolves. To capture the dynamic nature of students becoming more proficient, teachers need to use tools and practices that reflect the complexities of reading and writing (Lipson, Chomsky-Higgins, & Kanfer, 2011). In other words, obtaining authentic information about literacy performance should not be sacrificed for the efficiency of contrived texts and tasks created specifically for assessment purposes. Such contrived assessments may misrepresent a student's profile, resulting in instruction that is narrowly focused and limiting. Teachers can obtain an accurate profile of students' needs and growth with less frequent, but more authentic, diagnostic tools and/or practices. Performance-based measures such as running records and writing samples are assessment practices so closely aligned to daily practice that they are virtually indistinguishable from instruction.

The first step in arriving at a shared understanding of differentiated instruction is to accept that learners are all essentially different and that instruction matters (Brighton, 2002; Tomlinson, 2001). Differentiation seeks to accommodate the differences in students' learning needs in light of theory, research, and common sense. It is an approach to teaching that includes active planning for student differences. In other words, when teachers differentiate, they are meeting the individual needs of their students without diminishing expectations or sacrificing curricular rigor.

TEN EVIDENCE-BASED BEST PRACTICES FOR COMPREHENSIVE LITERACY INSTRUCTION

In keeping with our understanding of comprehensive literacy instruction, we present the following 10 evidence-based best practices that are generally supported by experts in the field (Table 1.1). These practices are based on a broad view of the reading and writing processes, one that incorporates the full range of experiences that students need in order to reach their literacy potential. Further, these literacy practices support students in developing relationships as colearners in a literate classroom community. We believe that best practices are characterized by meaningful literacy instruction that encourage students to become proficient, persistent, passionate, and prepared to meet the literacy challenges of the 21st century.

BEST PRACTICES IN ACTION

1. *Implement practices that invite students to be active, contributing members of a literacy community.* The profession of teaching literacy requires as much art as skill. Knowledge of the reading and writing processes, sound instructional methods, and ways to assess and differentiate learning are essential components of effective literacy instruction. But just as important is the give-and-take; the back-and-forth that occurs (or not) as readers engage with print, digital, and visual texts; their teacher; and each other. We refer to these interactions as "the dance" (Malloy, Marinak, & Gambrell, 2010). *The dance* occurs in the space between what is taught and

TABLE 1.1. Ten Evidence-Based Best Practices for Comprehensive Literacy Instruction

1. Implement practices that invite students to be active, contributing members of a literacy community.
2. Understand that maintaining an engaged community requires the ongoing monitoring and adjustment of literacy practices.
3. Promote engagement in your community of learners by planning and delivering literacy instruction through the ARC (access, relevance, and choice).
4. Provide students with small-group differentiated instruction that reflects the complex nature of literacy: reading, writing, listening, speaking, viewing, and representing.
5. Utilize a wide variety of text (fiction, nonfiction, poetry, digital, periodicals, etc.) within and across all content areas.
6. Promote close reading and critical thinking by engaging students in annotation, text-based discussions, and writing with evidence.
7. Use formative and summative assessments that reflect the complex and dynamic nature of literacy.
8. Replace less relevant guided practice (worksheets, repetitive center-based drills) with more authentic, inquiry-based opportunities to experiment and apply evolving literacy strategies.
9. Ensure that all voices are heard and honored by reducing teacher talk and prompting more student-led discussions.
10. Provide instruction in and practice with technologies that expand concepts and modes of communication.

what is learned—the carefully choreographed back-and-forth construction/negotiation of knowledge that occurs in literacy spaces. Whether the dance is unfolding beautifully or not can be felt when you enter the classroom. It can be heard in the way students and teachers relate to each other, and seen in work that is created. If all are enjoying the dance, they are seeking and sharing knowledge; they are occupied and involved, inclusive and responsive. You feel, as you enter, that you're witnessing a community of literate souls.

Specifically, research suggests that four practices can invite students to be active, contributing members of a literacy community (Turner & Kim, 2005). These include building relationships among community members, fostering a sense of collective responsibility, promoting ownership of literacy for all community members, and reflecting on the community's learning.

Let's briefly consider each of these practices. *Building relationships among community members* suggests that every child feels that he or she belongs and that each has something important to contribute. One way to welcome readers into a literacy community is for teachers to honor students' interests. Students' reading interests are highly individual. Factors such as age, gender, home environment, classroom environment, and academic ability are a few of the factors that influence students' reading preferences. Moss and Young (2010) suggest several ways to help determine an individual student's interests. First, observe, note, and record students' interests as they participate in various classroom reading tasks and activities. Second, engage in informal discussions with students, parents, peers, and others to help identify particular areas of interest both in and out of school (Marinak & Gambrell, 2016).

When teachers foster a sense of collective responsibility, they recognize that meaning is constructed through the readers' social interactions (Bruffee, 1989). Hence, knowledge is not fixed. If all members of the literacy community share roles and celebrate the social contexts that shape their views, knowledge is not simply imparted from teacher to student; rather, it is mutually constructed and verified through exciting, dynamic interactions (Applebee, Langer, Nystrand, & Gamoran, 2003). Therefore, *promoting ownership of literacy for all community members* means that all readers have various responsibilities related to text.

Reflecting on the community's learning means that students are encouraged to collaborate, consider, reconsider, and rearrange their ideas. It also involves recognizing the cultural practices that students bring to their engagement with text, including influences from home, school, and neighborhood as well as the digital and cyberspaces where students are interacting. Street (2003) suggests that reflecting on a literacy community's learning must include attempts to bridge the divide between school literacies and out-of-school literacies.

2. *Understand that maintaining an engaged community requires the ongoing monitoring and adjustment of literacy practices.* Literacy communities are complex sociocultural spaces where independent literacy learning is facilitated and high expectations are established (Morrow, Wamsley, Duhammel, & Fittipaldi, 2002; Taylor, 2002). Ideally, they are dynamic environments where cooperation (vs. competition) is valued, specific feedback is individualized, and multiple opportunities for application are provided (Wharton-McDonald, 2005). Given the dynamic nature of literacy communities, student engagement requires ongoing monitoring and adjustment as students assume more responsibility for their own learning. Practices that result in high levels of student engagement one week might need to be adjusted in the next. Adjustments are effective when teachers redefine their role in a literacy community to one of facilitator versus "holder of all knowledge" and when engagement is monitored within and across the disciplines.

Research indicates that literacy communities remain effective and engaging when teachers embrace a facilitative role and students are seen as active, capable decision makers. (Moje, Collazo, Carrillo, & Marx, 2001; Swafford, Chapman, Rhodes, & Kallus, 1996). If teachers learn alongside their students, literacy experiences become egalitarian and the entire community becomes the source of feedback for necessary revisions/readjustments. This occurs when differences are not viewed as deficits, but as perspectives that can enrich all members. By adopting this stance, teachers and students can celebrate the diversity in all classrooms, valuing everyone's stories and experiences as a resource to achieve shared goals (Nieto, 2015).

3. *Promote engagement in your community of learners by planning and delivering literacy instruction through the ARC (access, relevance and choice).* There is congruence across theoretical perspectives, research findings, and literacy experts (Guthrie, McRae, & Klauda, 2007; Malloy & Gambrell, 2011; Marinak & Gambrell, 2016) that a number of classroom characteristics promote and enhance literacy motivation. Three classroom characteristics have emerged as powerful and influential factors in fostering literacy motivation. Marinak and Gambrell (2016) refer to these as the ARC of motivation: access, relevance, and choice.

a. *Access.* Having access to rich and abundant materials to read is critical to the development of literacy motivation. Access to reading materials supports and encourages students to engage in reading and writing in a voluntary and sustained manner (Neuman & Roskos, 1993; Edmunds & Bauserman, 2006). Access to reading materials provides the foundation for students to choose what they want to read (Turner, 1995; Edmunds & Bauserman, 2006, Guthrie et al., 2007). If we want students to be motivated readers, we must create a classroom context that is text-rich and celebrates the joy and value of reading. In literacy communities that nurture instrinsic reading motivation, teachers display books to pique students' interests, select interesting and informative text to read aloud, and introduce new books as they are added to the classroom library (Marinak & Gambrell, 2016).

b. *Relevance.* Relevant literacy activities are reading and writing events such as those that occur in people's everyday lives, as opposed to reading and writing that has a school-based value alone (Purcell-Gates, 2002; Purcell-Gates, Duke, & Martineau, 2007). We know that as young children learn and use their developing oral language, they do so for real reasons and purposes (Halliday, 1975). Therefore, in order for literacy learning to be meaningful to students, teachers need to be mindful of the reasons and purposes they establish for reading and writing tasks.

Relevant and authentic literacy activities are often designed to focus on communicating ideas for shared understanding rather than simply to complete assignments or answer teacher-posed questions (Gambrell, Hughes, Calvert, Malloy, & Igo, 2011; Teale & Gambrell, 2007; Guthrie et al., 2007).

Assor, Kaplan, and Roth (2002) found that when teachers emphasized the relevance of reading tasks and activities, the students rated classroom tasks as important and worthy of their best cognitive effort. Relevant literacy tasks enable students to see the connection between school literacy tasks and "real-life" literacy tasks.

c. *Choice.* Numerous studies report that students' intrinsic motivation increases when teachers support student choice of literacy tasks (Guthrie et al., 2007; McCombs, 2003; Turner, 1995). When students are supported in choosing what they read, there are indications that they engage in reading more often (Reynolds & Symons, 2001), understand more of what they read (Guthrie & Humenick, 2004), and are more likely to continue reading (Gabriel, Allington, & Billen, 2012). Research supports the notion that the texts that students find most interesting are those they have selected for their own reasons and purposes (Pressley, 2007).

Middleton and Perks's (2010) 4WH framework may be useful in providing students with choices and fostering collaborative literacy relationships. The framework includes four questions. *Who will students work with?* Students can be afforded choices when slelecting literacy partners. *What strategies/skills will students work with?* Readers can provided with a choice of skills to enage in and/or response options for showing what they know. *When will students engage in specific reading tasks and activities?* Many reading tasks can be completed in various ways and in different orders. For example, if students are reading text sets of a fiction book and a nonfiction book on the same topic, let the students select the order for reading the texts. *Where will students read?* As adults, we can often select where we want to read. Encourage students to do the same, supporting them in finding their own "most comfortable" spot (Marinak & Gambrell, 2016).

4. *Provide students with small-group differentiated instruction that reflects the complex nature of literacy: listening/speaking, reading/writing, viewing/representing.* Current literacy research, theories, and policies place a strong emphasis on deep comprehension as the ultimate goal of reading instruction. Students are expected to engage in critical thinking about text and to be able to analyze multiple accounts of an event, note similarities and differences in points of view represented in the text, assess the warrant behind people's ideas, integrate information across several texts, and

explain the relationships between ideas and the author's craft (Calkins, Ehrenworth, & Lehman, 2012).

Though students often need concentrated instructional support in foundational skills and strategies, it is important that they be provided with differentiated instruction that reflects the complex nature of literacy at all grade levels. In other words, literacy instruction in K–12th grade should include explicit instruction in, practice with and application of reading, writing, listening, speaking, viewing, and representing. The gradual-release-of-responsibility model provides a framework for differentiated instruction.

In general, the gradual-release model describes a process in which students increasingly assume responsibility and independence toward a targeted learning outcome. We view the gradual-release-of-responsibility model as consistent with the notion of explicit instruction. During each phase of the gradual-release model, teachers can—and should—be explicit in their instruction and feedback. For example, during the first phase, teachers should provide clear explanations and modeling for a specific skill or strategy. As responsibility is gradually released, feedback to students should be specific and understandable. Small-group and one-on-one configurations can be particularly effective in differentiating the support for students with variable learning needs. The gradual-release-of-responsibility model and scaffolded instruction are in keeping with constructivist principles when they are used to plan opportunities that result in students listening, reading, viewing and discussing, writing, and representing knowledge in authentic ways (Graham & Perin, 2007; Tracy, Menickelli, & Scales, 2016).

5. *Utilize a wide variety of text (fiction, nonfiction, poetry, digital, periodicals, etc.) within and across all content areas.* It has long been our contention that the literacy modes are *tools* for learning. *Listening, reading,* and *viewing* are modes of accessing new knowledge, and *speaking, writing,* and *representing* are modes of showing what has been learned. Taking literacy out of the silo of the English language arts block affords the classroom teacher multiple ways of bringing his or her students to the content in each of the other disciplines in meaningful and purposeful ways (Neuman & Roskos, 2012; Sailors, Kumar, Blady, & Willson, 2013). Integrating content instruction with literacy learning encourages students to learn and practice literacy in ways that promote the advancement of both content and literacy. As Greenwald and Schelino (2017) observe, "when academic content is integrated, students explore a concept or skill repeatedly through the day in different ways and through various lenses, allowing for broader application of the individual skills and a greater conceptual understanding of the world" (paragraph 3).

One of the most inspiring recent expressions of using multiple texts to teach is offered by Tracy et al. (2016), wherein a sixth-grade teacher explores the topic of "courageous voices" in literacy instruction that incorporates multiple historical contexts. Using an evolving text set to survey the myriad ways that people use their voices to enact change in society, students were encouraged to find a cause that they could promote and to develop a plan for enacting that change. Going beyond simply providing poems, song lyrics, trade books, and videos, this teacher explicitly taught students to garner meaning and to layer these meanings through multiple perspectives and societal issues to come to a personal understanding of courage and voice. In so doing, the teacher selected texts that were attentive to her students' interests and needs and incorporated her instructional goals and required content.

Across a 3-week unit of study, the teacher offered explicit instruction in how to read, view, and interact with texts with a critical lens. Not only were students learning to listen, to read, and to view, but they were also being exposed to multiple historical contexts and societal issues. In the second week, students moved from whole-class engagement to small-group interactions where they were charged with refining their personal interpretations and determining their own passions regarding issues that were important to them. By the third week, students were writing and presenting their plans for change to an audience of parents and other school members. This report of content integration by Tracy and colleagues (2016) is particularly rich in description of the numerous and varied instructional activities that were used to immerse students in these texts, in exploring and expanding their interpretations as they looked across texts and perspectives, and in empowering students to use their developing literacy skills to create solutions to problems that were meaningful to them.

6. *Promote close reading and critical thinking by engaging students in annotation, text-based discussions, and writing with evidence.* By selecting rich texts for students to read, teachers have opportunities to guide their students in reading and rereading, viewing and re-viewing, and listening again and again to harvest ever-deeper meanings. Providing students first with a purpose for engaging with the text, an initial exploration brings first impressions and personal connections. Repeated interactions with the text can then be more purposeful and critical, as students make notes of excerpts that are particularly compelling, or delve into the language, rhetoric, or context of the text to understand more deeply what the author intended, as well as what he or she did not include.

Close examinations of text do not come naturally; rather, the teacher leads students to discover the discipline of deep observation by first modeling his or her interaction with the text and thinking aloud about what "brings the meaning" in his or her view. In this way, students come to realize that listening, reading, and viewing are *acts of thinking*—whether about the ideas being expressed or the way those ideas are expressed—and that our existing schemas and interpretations should be challenged and reshaped as we move through and across texts (Fisher & Frey, 2012).

These deep interactions with texts should, ideally, be combined with multiple modes of "encoding" the meanings that are being developed. Initially, students may highlight or annotate their discoveries, but it is important that these initial forays are extended to promote questioning, synthesis, and new interpretations. Repeated interactions with the text provide avenues for discussing, writing, and graphically representing the multiple meanings that are brought to the fore as a community of learners.

7. *Use formative and summative assessments that reflect the complex and dynamic nature of literacy.* When selecting assessment tools and/or practices, we should keep in mind the old adage, "What gets tested gets taught." And more importantly, according to Johnston and Costello (2005), what gets assessed and how it gets assessed has implications for literacy learning. Literacy is complex. It involves competencies, strategies, and beliefs, as well as dispositions about print, symbols, images, and the spoken word that transcend the classroom. Literacy prepares students for life. Hence, it is critical that literacy assessments reflect the dynamic and reciprocal nature of listening/speaking, reading/writing, and viewing/representing. In other words, as Carr and Claxton (2002) assert, there must be "a willingness to engage in joint learning tasks, to express uncertainties and ask questions, to take a variety of roles in joint learning enterprises and to take others' purposes and perspectives into account" (p. 16). Subscribing to the belief that literacy assessment should be as complex as literacy instruction means utilizing a wide variety of ongoing and summative assessments. The International Reading Association (2017) suggests that "literacy assessment needs to reflect the multiple dimensions of reading and writing and the various purposes for assessment as well as the diversity of the students being assessed" (p. 1).

The goal of *ongoing assessment* is to engage in tasks that allow teachers to monitor student learning and provide ongoing feedback to students. Ongoing assessments that are closely aligned to instruction yield valuable data that can be used to differentiate text and practices. They also help students identify their strengths and weaknesses and allow teachers to adjust instruction in real time. Formative assessments are referred to as *low stakes* because the evaluative consequences of adequate yearly progress are not attached to such data. Running records, writing samples, and constructed responses are examples of formative assessments.

On the other hand, *summative assessments* are used to evaluate student learning at the end of an instructional unit by comparing student performance to a standard or benchmark.

Summative assessments include more traditional evaluative tasks such midterms, finals, research papers, and so forth. Running records, writing samples, and constructed responses could also be used as summative assessments if grade level, building and/or district standardization has occurred. This might include standardizing scoring rubrics, text passages, or administration schedules. Many districts also use data from informal reading inventories in a summative fashion to benchmark student progress.

Some summative assessments, often termed *terminal assessments,* are synonymous with the phrase *high stakes*. These literacy assessments are given at the end of the school year under very strict testing conditions that do not often reflect day-to-day literacy learning. In addition, data from these high-stakes terminal assessments are usually not available to teachers and reading specialists until the following school year. The International Literacy Association (2017) states:

> Finally, all assessments—regardless of purpose—should provide useful and timely information about desired literacy goals. They should be composed of authentic literacy activities as opposed to contrived texts or tasks generated specifically for assessment purposes. The quality of assessment information should not be sacrificed for the efficiency of an assessment procedure. It is incumbent upon all users and consumers of literacy assessments to interpret results within the context of the purpose for which an assessment is best suited (p. 4).

Without a doubt, ongoing and summative literacy assessments should always reflect the complex and dynamic nature of literacy and yield information that improves teaching and learning.

8. *Replace less relevant guided practice (worksheets, repetitive center-based drills) with more authentic, inquiry-based opportunities to experiment and apply evolving literacy strategies.* One way to encourage and support students' literacy development is to view every subject or content-area lesson as an opportunity to expose students to authentic uses of literacy. According to Hattie (2009), when teachers use effective vocabulary and comprehension strategies in the content areas, student learning of subject-matter information increases. Other studies have reported that having students engage in writing activities on a regular basis during content-area lessons increases their learning of content information (Bangert-Drown, Hurley, & Wilkinson, 2004; Graham & Perin, 2007).

One important consideration when integrating literacy across the content areas is the notion of having students engage in literacy tasks and activities for authentic purposes. The dreaded "hoop-jump" of completing a worksheet that will be graded by the teacher and then tossed in a wastebasket is rarely as engaging as creating a product that demonstrates knowledge in a creative and real-world way. Students who study the requirements for plants to live can express their understandings just as clearly by creating a "how to" video of green-thumb skills for taking care of plants in the home. Moving up the rungs of Bloom's Taxonomy of Learning Domains (Krathwohl, 2002), units that result in students *creating* products (as opposed to completing them) encourage higher-order thinking skills and provide opportunities to demonstrate a deep understanding of a topic.

Moreover, elucidating the ways that historians conduct their research and that scientists prepare reports of their experiments makes learning relevant for students. Historians learn to master the language and context of primary documents, and this brings them closer to the moment in time that is being explored (Morgan & Rasinski, 2012). Creating a mini-museum of primary documents when investigating a particular period in history or a historical event allows students to enter into a slice of time and to understand why people acted and reacted in the way that they did. For example a mini-museum of primary documents gathered around the topic of the Japenese internment camps could be used to first understand issues of trust and otherness, leading to a class debate about current issues regarding immigration and refugees. Thinking like a historian supports students in developing new ideas about how we might learn from the past to develop policy in the present.

9. *Ensure that all voices are heard and honored by reducing teacher talk and prompting more student-led discussions.* The type of discussion that occurs in classrooms speaks volumes about the roles of the teacher and students in the classroom context as well as the opportunities provided for promoting deep understanding of content and the development of language skills. In classrooms where teachers view themselves as the "keepers of knowledge," discussions typically follow an *initiation/response/evaluation* model (IRE). The teacher asks a question, the student responds, and the teacher evaluates the response (Cazden, 2001). While this approach is a traditional one, it often impedes engagement and learning (Alexander, 2008; Galton, 2007) by privileging only the students who know the answer and diminishing opportunities for students to explore or think through what they are learning.

As an alternative to this *monologic* approach to classroom discussion, a body of research is growing to support *dialogic* discussions where teachers serve as facilitators of knowledge who guide students in developing understandings of text and content (Mercer & Littleton, 2007; Reznitskaya, 2012). In dialogic classrooms, teachers do not focus on questions that have a single answer, but guide students in thinking through the content they are learning with open-ended questions. Teachers who facilitate knowledge model how to *include others* in a discussion and *follow up* on each other's responses; *look for evidence* from text to *support claims*; and *make connections* to other texts and personal experiences. In this system, more students can be involved and engaged because the onus of understanding is a collaborative venture where knowing a correct answer is no longer a required point of entry; rather, *thinking* and supporting one's thoughts become the driving force toward comprehension and consensus (Malloy & Gambrell, 2011).

10. *Provide instruction in and practice with technologies that expand concepts and modes of communication.* While the integration of Internet use and other computer-mediated instruction in the K–12 classroom is becoming well established, new technologies and applications continue to emerge. Similarly, the empirical evidence to support instructional strategies for using these technologies continues to be developed (Cviko, McKenney, & Voogt, 2012; Zawilinski, 2016). What we have come to understand is that digital literacy requires different skills than those required to access traditional text and that it is important that we understand these differences in order to provide appropriate instruction for our students (Leu et al., 2015). It is incumbent on teachers, therefore, to become acquainted with new research as it emerges and to incorporate this new knowledge into their classrooms to suit their particular instructional needs. Our students are growing to adulthood in an age when knowledge of technology is a necessity and not a luxury. As educators, we are obligated to prepare them for that reality.

Perhaps the most powerful aspect of new technologies is the seemingly infinite possibilities for communicating and creating. Students can interact with their teachers, classmates, schoolmates, and indeed the world using a fascinating array of tools and platforms. Twitter, Facebook, Edmoto and blogs can be used for discussion. Wiki, Nings, and Google Docs are user-friendly venues for digital collaboration. A host of programs such as iMovie, Playpod, and Soundcloud are participatory media that encourage students to create digital products. New technologies and media have the potential to remove barriers to reading, writing, learning, communicating, and creating. Assistive and adaptive technologies from the past are replaced with iPad apps. All students, regardless of ability, disability, or language proficiency can participate fully in literacy conversations. And when children are valued, heard, encouraged, and understood, they will be successful.

TEACHERS AS VISIONARY DECISION MAKERS

Literacy researchers have converged on a word to describe the driving force that guides teachers in coordinating and integrating practices effectively: *vision*. Although this is not a word you might expect to see in a discussion of evidence-based practices, the teacher's vision of literacy achievement has long been heralded as the crucial factor in ensuring that the goal of improving literacy instruction for all students is met. According to Calfee (2005), ensuring that "children have the opportunity to acquire the level of literacy that allows them full participation in our democratic society depends on a corps of teachers who possess extraordinary minds and hearts" (p. 67).

Calfee asserts that teachers not only must possess a domain of skills and knowledge to lead students to acquire this level of literacy success but also must acquire a sensitivity to student needs and be passionate in their willingness to make their vision work. Duffy (2005) describes the teachers' ultimate goal as that of *inspiring students to be literate*—to engage students in "genuinely literate activities" where they are doing something purposeful with literacy. This engagement should reflect the teachers' instructional vision—the reason they are passionate about teaching literacy.

Teachers who are visionary decision makers are empowered to identify and select evidence-based literacy practices to create an integrated instructional approach that adapts to the differentiated needs of students. A teacher's vision should clearly be knowledge-based and should encompass what he or she wishes to achieve for each student. How detailed one's vision becomes is certainly an individual matter and subject to personal experiences and situations, but without a vision the teacher is left to sway and sputter as a candle facing the winds of curricular change and federal-, district-, and school-level impositions. It is the teacher with vision who is able to stand firm in the belief that with knowledge and heart, evidence-based best practices can be selected and adapted to meet the needs of each student within a community of learners where it is a joy to teach.

ENGAGEMENT ACTIVITIES

1. Articulate your vision for literacy teaching and learning. Commit to writing what you wish to accomplish as a literacy teacher as well as what you wish for each of your students to achieve. Refer to this vision statement often as you teach or as you learn more about teaching. Be certain to adjust and enhance your vision statement as new knowledge and expertise dictate.

2. As an extension of your vision for teaching and learning, consider the ways that you can build a community of learners in your classroom. In those first important weeks of school, do two important things: make it your mission to learn the interests and strengths of your students. Are they leaders, artists, atheletes, or have strong skills in weaving stories? Are they interested in sports, extreme weather, animals, or politics? Then help your students to get to know each other through discussion and collaboration. Coming to value your students' strengths and interests, and creating opportunities for them to value each others' interests and abilities, will take you far in developing a community where learning is a shared endeavor.

3. In each content area that you teach, give some thought to the professions and real-world applications of knowledge that the content implicates. Scientists conduct experiments, write reports, and make recommendations based on what they find. Mathemeticians solve problems in economics, engineering, and architecture. Authors write novels, speeches, and letteres to the editor. How can you promote literacy as a means of showing knowledge that is commensurate with the skills required in the adult world of professions and experience?

4. Embrace technology and multimodal texts. Create content-relevant text sets that support learners with differing abilities and interests to engage students in learning across the various visual, print, and digital texts. Challenge yourself to incorporate new applications and interfaces to enrich learning and support students in learning to meaningfully and reliably negotiate new literacies.

REFERENCES

Alexander, R. J. (2008). *Essays on pedagogy*. New York: Routledge.

Allington, R. L. (2005). What counts as evidence in evidence-based education? *Reading Today, 23*(3), 16.

Applebee, A. N., Langer, J. A., Nystrand, M., & Gamoran, A. (2003). Discussion-based approaches to developing understanding: Classroom instruction and student performance in middle and high school English. *American Educational Research Journal, 40*(3), 685–730.

Assor, A., Kaplan, H., & Roth, G. (2002). Choice is good, but relevance is excellent: Autonomy-enhancing and suppressing teacher behaviours predicting students' engagement in schoolwork. *British Journal of Educational Psychology, 72*, 261–278.

Baker, J. A. (2006). Contributions of the teacher–child relationships to positive school adjustment during elementary school. *Journal of School Psychology, 44,* 211–229.

Bangert-Drown, R. L., Hurley, M. M., & Wilkinson, B. (2004). The effects of school-based writing to learn interventions on academic achievement. *Review of Educational Research, 74,* 29–58.

Bogdan, R. C., & Biklen, S. K. (1992). *Qualitative research for education: An introduction to theory and methods* (2nd ed.). Boston: Allyn & Bacon.

Brighton, C. M. (2002). Straddling the fence: Implementing best practices in an age of accountability. *Gifted Child Today, 25*(3), 30–33.

Brock, L. L., Nishida, T. K., Chiong, C., Grimm, K. J., & Rimm-Kaurman, S. E. (2008). Children's perceptions of the classroom environment and social and academic performance: A longitudinal analysis of the contribution of the *Responsive Classroom* approach. *Journal of School Psychology, 46,* 129–149.

Bruffee, K. A. (1989). Thinking and writing as social acts. In E. P. Maimon, B. F. Nodine, & F. W. O'Connor (Eds.), *Thinking, reasoning, and writing* (pp. 213–222). New York: Longman.

Calfee, R. (2005). The mind (and heart) of the reading teacher. In B. Maloch, J. V. Hoffman, D. L. Schallert, C. M. Fairbanks, & J. Worthy (Eds.), *54th yearbook of the National Reading Conference* (pp. 63–79). Oak Creek, WI: National Reading Conference.

Calkins, L., Ehrenworth, M., & Lehman, C. (2012). *Pathways to the Common Core: Accelerating achievement.* Portsmouth, NH: Heinemann.

Carr, M., & Claxton, G. (2002). Tracking the development of learning dispositions. *Assessment in Education: Principles, Policy and Practice, 9*(1), 9–37.

Cazden, C. B. (2001). *Classroom discourse: The language of teaching and learning.* Portsmouth, NH: Heinemann.

Connell, J. P., & Wellborn, J. G. (1991). Competence, autonomy, and relatedness: A motivational analysis of self-system processes. In M. Gunnar & A. Sroufe (Eds.), *Minnesota Symposium on Child Psychology* (Vol. 22, pp. 43–77). Hillsdale, NJ: Erlbaum.

Cviko, A., McKenney, S., & Voogt, J. (2012). Teachers enacting a technology-rich curriculum for emergent literacy. *Educational Technology Research and Development, 60*(1), 31–54.

Dewey, J. (1963). *Experience and education.* New York: Collier. (Original published 1937)

Duffy, G. G. (2005). Developing metacognitive teachers: Visioning and the expert's changing role in teacher education and professional development. In S. E. Isreal, C. C. Block, K. L. Bauserman, & K. Kinnucan-Welsch (Eds.), *Metacognition in literacy learning: Theory, assessment, instruction and professional development* (pp. 299–314). Mahwah, NJ: Erlbaum.

Edmunds, K. M., & Bauserman, K. L. (2006). What teachers can learn about reading motivation through conversations with children. *The Reading Teacher, 59*(5), 414–424.

Fisher, D., & Frey, N. (2012). Close reading in elementary schools. *The Reading Teacher, 66*(3), 179–188.

Flook, L., Repetti, R. L., & Ullman, J. B. (2005). Classroom social experiences as predictors of academic performance. *Developmental Psychology, 41,* 319–327.

Gabriel, R., Allington, R., & Billen, M. (2012). Middle schoolers and magazines: What teachers can learn from students' leisure reading habits. *The Clearing House, 85*(5), 186–191.

Galton, M. (2007). *Learning and teaching in the primary classroom.* London: SAGE.

Gambrell, L. B., Hughes, E., Calvert, W., Malloy, J., & Igo, B. (2011). Authentic reading, writing, and discussion: An exploratory study of a pen pal project. *Elementary School Journal, 112*(2), 234–258.

Gordon, E. W. (2009). Foreword. In L. M. Morrow, R. Rueda, & D. Lapp (Eds.), *Handbook of research on literacy and diversity* (pp. ix–xi). New York: Guilford Press.

Graham, S., & Perin, S. (2007). A meta-analysis of writing instruction for adolescent students. *Journal of Educational Psychology, 99,* 445–476.

Greenwald, B., & Schelino, A. (2017). Seamlessly weaving concept, content, and skills. *Literacy Daily.* Retrieved July 7, 2017, from *www.literacyworldwide.org/blog/literacy-daily/2017/07/07/seamlessly-weaving-concept-content-and-skills.*

Guthrie, J. T., & Humenick, N. M. (2004). Motivating students to read: Evidence for classroom practices that increase reading motivation and achievement. In P. McCardle & V. Chabra (Eds.), *The voice of evidence in reading research* (pp. 329–354). Baltimore: Brookes.

Guthrie, J. T., McRae, A., & Klauda, S. L. (2007). Contributions of concept-oriented reading instruction to knowledge about interventions for motivations in reading. *Educational Psychologist, 42*(4), 237–250.

Halliday, M. A. K. (1975). *Learning how to mean.* London: Arnold.

Hamre, B. K., & Pianta, R. C. (2005). Can instructional and emotional support in the first grade classroom make a difference for children at risk for school failure? *Child Development, 76,* 949–967.

Hattie, J. (2009). *Visible learning: A synthesis of over 8000 meta-analyses relating to achievement.* New York: Routledge.

International Literacy Association. (2017). *Literacy assessment: What everyone needs to know.* Retrieved from *www.literacyworldwide.org/get-resources/position-statements.*

International Reading Association. (2002a). *Evidence-based reading instruction: Putting the National Reading Panel Report into practice.* Newark, DE: Author.

International Reading Association. (2002b). *What is evidence-based reading instruction?* Newark, DE: Author.

Johnston, P., & Costello, P. (2005). Theory and research into practice: Principles for literacy assessment. *Reading Research Quarterly, 40*(2), 256–267. (Position statement)

Kaplan Toren, N., & Seginer, R. (2015). Classroom climate, parental educational involvement, and student functioning in early adolescence: A longitudinal study. *Social Psychology of Education, 18*(4), 811–827.

Kent, A. M., & Simpson, J. L. (2012). The power of literature: Establishing and enhancing the young adolescent classroom community. *Reading Improvement, 49*(1), 28–32.

Krathwohl, D. R. (2002). A revision of Bloom's taxonomy: An overview. *Theory into Practice, 41*(4), 212–218.

Leu, D. J., Forzani, E., Rhoads, C., Maykel, C., Kennedy, C., & Timbrell, N. (2015). The new literacies of online research and comprehension: Rethinking the reading achievement gap. *Reading Research Quarterly, 50*(1), 1–23.

Lewin, K., Lippitt, R., & White, R. K. (1939). Patterns of aggressive behavior in experimentally created "social climates." *Journal of Social Psychology, 10,* 271–299.

Lipson, M. Y., Chomsky-Higgins, P., & Kanfer, J. (2011). Diagnosis: The missing ingredient in RTI assessment. *The Reading Teacher, 65*(3), 204–208.

Malloy, J. A., & Gambrell, L. B. (2011). The contribution of discussion to reading comprehension and critical thinking. In R. Allington & A. McGill-Franzen (Eds.), *Handbook of reading disabilities research* (pp. 253–262). Mahwah, NJ: Erlbaum.

Malloy, J. A., Marinak, B. A., & Gambrell, L. B. (2010). We hope you dance: Creating a community of literate souls. In J. A. Malloy, B. A. Marinak, and L. B. Gambrell (Eds.), *Essential readings on motivation:* Newark, DE: International Reading Association.

Marinak, B., & Gambrell, L. (2016). *No more reading for junk: Best practices for motivating readers.* Portsmouth, NH: Heinemann.

McCombs, B. L. (2003). A framework for the redesign of K–12 education in the context of current educational reform. *Theory into Practice, 42*(2), 93–101.

McCoy, J. D., & Ketterlin-Geller, L. R. (2004). Rethinking instructional delivery for diverse student populations: Serving all learners with concept-based instruction. *Intervention in School and Clinic, 40*(2), 88–95.

Mercer, N., & Littleton, K. (2007). *Dialogue and the development of children's thinking: A sociocultural approach.* London: Routledge.

Middleton, M., & Perks, K. (2014). *Motivation to learn: Transforming classroom culture to support student achievement.* Thousand Oaks, CA: Corwin Press.

Moje, E. B., Collazo, T., Carrillo, R., & Marx, R. W. (2001). "Maestro, what is 'quality'?": Language, literacy, and discourse in project-based science. *Journal of Research in Science Teaching, 38*(4), 469–498.

Morgan, D. N., & Rasinski, T. V. (2012). The power and potential of primary sources. *The Reading Teacher, 65*(8), 584–594.

Morrow, L. M., Wamsley, G., Duhammel, K., & Fittipaldi, N. (2002). A case study of exemplary practice in fourth grade. In B. M. Taylor & P. D. Pearson (Eds.), *Teaching reading: Effective schools, accomplished teachers* (pp. 289–307). New York: Routledge.

Moss, B., & Young, T. A. (2010). *Creating lifelong readers through independent reading.* Newark, DE: International Reading Association.

Neuman, S. B., & Roskos, K. (1993). Access to print for children of poverty: Differential effects of adult mediation and literacy-enriched play settings on environmental and functional print tasks. *American Educational Research Journal, 30*(3), 95–122.

Nieto, S. (2015). *The light in their eyes: Creating multicultural learning communities.* New York: Teachers College Press.

Patrick, H., Kaplan, A., & Ryan, A. M. (2011). Positive classroom motivational environments: Convergence between mastery goal structure and classroom social climate. *Journal of Educational Psychology, 103*(2), 367–382.

Pressley, M. (2007). Achieving best practices. In L. B. Gambrell, L. M. Morrow, & M. Pressley (Eds.), *Best practices in literacy instruction* (pp. 397–404). New York: Guilford Press.

Purcell-Gates, V. (2002). Authentic literacy in class yields increase in literacy practices. *Literacy Update, 11*(1), 1–9.

Purcell-Gates, V., Duke, N., & Martineau, J. (2007). Learning to read and write genre-specific text: Roles of authentic experience and explicit teaching. *Reading Research Quarterly, 42*, 8–46.

Reynolds, P. L., & Symons, S. (2001). Motivational variables and children's text search. *Journal of Educational Psychology, 93*(1), 14–22.

Reznitskaya, A. (2012). Dialogic teaching: Rethinking language use during literature discussions. *The Reading Teacher, 65*(7), 446–456.

Sailors, M., Kumar, T., Blady, S., & Willson, A. (2013). Literacy tools created and used within print-rich classroom environments for literacy teaching and literacy learning. In B. M. Taylor & N. K. Duke (Eds.), *Handbook on effective literacy instruction* (pp. 46–71). New York: Guilford Press.

Schaps, E., & Lewis, C. (1997). Building classroom communities. *Thrust for Educational Leadership, 27*(1), 14–21.

Street, B. (2003). What's "new" in new literacy studies?: Critical approaches to literacy in theory and practice. *Current Issues in Comparative Education, 5*(2), 77–91.

Stronge, J. H. (2007). *Qualities of effective teachers* (2nd ed.). Alexandria, VA: Association for Supervision and Curriculum Development.

Swafford, J., Chapman, V., Rhodes, R., & Kallus, M. (1996). A literature analysis of trends in literacy education. In D. J. Leu, C. K. Kinzer, & K. A. Hinchman (Eds.), *Literacies for the 21st century: Research and practice* (pp. 437–446). Chicago: National Reading Conference.

Taylor, B. M. (2002). Highly accomplished primary grade teachers in effective schools. In B. M. Taylor & P. D. Pearson (Eds.), *Teaching reading: Effective schools, accomplished teachers* (pp. 279–289). New York: Routledge.

Teale, W. H., & Gambrell, L. B. (2007). Raising urban students' literacy achievement by engaging in authentic, challenging work. *The Reading Teacher, 60*, 728–739.

Tomlinson, C. A. (2001). *How to differentiate instruction in mixed-ability classrooms*. Alexandria, VA: Association for Supervision and Curriculum Development.

Tracy, K. N., Menickelli, K., & Scales, R. Q. (2016). Courageous voices: Using text sets to inspire change. *Journal of Adolescent and Adult Literacy, 60*(5), 527–536.

Turner, J. C. (1995). The influence of classroom contexts on young children's motivation for literacy. *Reading Research Quarterly, 30*, 410–441.

Turner, J. D., & Kim, Y. (2005). Learning about building literacy communities in multicultural and multilingual classrooms from effective elementary teachers. *Literacy, Teaching and Learning, 10*(1), 21–41.

U.S. Department of Education, Office of Vocational and Adult Education. (2012). *Adult Education Great Cities Summit: What is evidence-based reading instruction and how do you know it when you see it?* Washington, DC: Author.

Vygotsky, L. S. (1978). *Mind in society: The development of higher psychological processes.* (M. Cole, V. John-Steiner, S. Scribner, & E. Souberman, Trans.). Cambridge, MA: Harvard University Press.

Wharton-McDonald, R. (2005, May). *Linking best practice to literacy in diverse populations.* Presentation at the 50th annual convention of the International Reading Association, San Antonio, TX.

Zawilinski, L. M. (2016). Primary grade students create science eBooks on iPads: Authentic audiences, purposes and technologies for writing. *New England Reading Association Journal, 51*(2), 81–90.

CHAPTER 2

Current Issues and Best Practices in Literacy Instruction

CHRISTINA L. MADDA
VICKI B. GRIFFO
P. DAVID PEARSON
TAFFY E. RAPHAEL

This chapter will:

- Revisit the notion of balance within today's literacy curriculum.
- Examine current issues in education including the importance of cultivating classroom learning communities that foster student agency and engagement.
- Synthesize the research base on best practices in literacy instruction.
- Discuss seven dimensions of literacy teaching and learning that illustrate competing demands and priorities at work.

Some of education's most enduring and polarizing debates have revolved around questions of what constitutes best practice within the literacy curriculum. When we speak of "literacy," we refer to the requisite skills, strategies, and experiences that readers and writers bring to bear when interacting with text in the world. It's no surprise, then, that such an essential set of skills and practices have attracted so much attention in the education field given their fundamental role in shaping future citizenry, building a foundation for college and career readiness, and enhancing one's overall quality of life. As we set out to identify and define a range of best practices for literacy instruction, we begin by revisiting what we believe continues to be a fundamental construct within the literacy curriculum today: the construct of balance.

As described in earlier editions of this book (Griffo, Madda, Pearson, & Raphael, 2015; Madda, Griffo, Pearson, & Raphael, 2011; Pearson & Raphael, 1999, 2003; Pearson, Raphael, Benson, & Madda, 2007), the notion of a "balanced curriculum" was born out of the 1990s' antagonistic "Reading Wars" debate (Pearson, 2004). This debate pitted those in favor of teaching reading using a whole-language approach against proponents of a more phonics-based approach (see Lyon, 1997; McIntyre & Pressley, 1996; Pressley, 2006). Naturally, each side claimed to advocate for the more effective instructional methodology (see Chall 1967, 1997, for a historical treatment of this debate).

One legacy of the Reading Wars is that educators and researchers now see the shortcomings of unidimensional, dichotomous, "either/or" approaches to literacy instruction (Pearson, 2004). For example, modern debates no longer focus on the issue of phonics versus whole language. In fact, few in the field today contest the necessity of teaching foundational skills, including phonemic awareness and phonics, in key balance with reading comprehension. Instead, issues now center on which model of close reading will prevail, how we will support students in meeting the comprehension and vocabulary demands of more complex texts, or how to best help students develop specialized ways of thinking, reading, and writing in the various disciplines.

As we have argued in past editions, regardless of the policy context in which we construct our vision, balance must be recognized as a complex and multidimensional construct to be artfully orchestrated across many facets of literacy teaching and learning (Griffo et al., 2015). Thus in this chapter, we continue the conversation of what it means to enact a balanced literacy curriculum that reflects the demands of 21st-century citizenry, enhances the schooling experience of students, and ensures high levels of literacy for all. We begin by outlining current issues that frame today's educational context including policy influences, persistent disparities in reading achievement among U.S. students, the complexity of digital age learning, and the need to cultivate classroom communities that foster student agency and engagement. Next, we revisit what we've learned from research about core elements that form the foundation for a balanced literacy program. We then extend the discussion by addressing balance within a series of dimensions relevant to issues of content and context within literacy teaching and learning.

CURRENT ISSUES IN BEST PRACTICES

While the National Reading Panel (NRP; 2000) report was central to shaping policy and informing earlier editions of this chapter, today the

Common Core State Standards (CCSS) Initiative dominates the policy context and frames current thinking (National Governors Association Center for Best Practices & Council of Chief State School Officers [NGA & CCSSO], 2010). This nationwide effort to create a set of rigorous standardized learning goals for students across the United States maps English language arts and mathematics skills from kindergarten through high school, emphasizing college and career readiness. Prior to this effort, states were individually responsible for defining their educational goals, resulting in incongruence across state lines and prompting textbook publishers, for all practical purposes, to focus their curricula on standards in states with the largest populations (e.g., California, Texas). For the most part, the CCSS Initiative has gained wide acceptance, with almost 40 of the 50 U.S. states participating, and many of the opted-out states revising their standards to closely align with the CCSS.

The national CCSS offer a vision of balance for the English language arts that reflects much of the research conducted in recent decades. In the CCSS document, foundational skills of early literacy instruction make up one piece of the standards puzzle for K–5th grade, with strong supporting roles played by word-level processes, vocabulary, oral discourse, and the conventions of written language. At center stage, comprehension and composition play a critical role across the grades, with a fresh focus on a range of higher-order processes: close reading of challenging texts to ferret out both essence and nuance, literacy in the disciplines, writing from text-based sources, and understanding, constructing, and critiquing argument. The CCSS's increased focus on deeper learning as well as higher-order reading and writing processes represents a much-needed shift away from an overemphasis on basic skills (Raphael, Au, & Popp, 2013). While still in its nascency, the field has yet to determine the impact of the CCSS in promoting equity in literacy achievement and preparing today's students to meet the college and workplace demands of tomorrow.

With education's current emphasis on college and career readiness, we are compelled to contemporaneously survey present-day achievement within U.S. schools. Results from large-scale assessments of U.S. students' literacy achievement remain a cause for concern. The National Assessment of Educational Progress (NAEP) serves as one gauge of literacy achievement based on a national representative sample of students. NAEP's most recent administrations (reading in 2015 and writing in 2011) illustrate that while students are making gains in literacy, less than 40% of students score at a level considered proficient in reading, and a mere 25% do so in writing (National Center for Educational Statistics, 2012, 2017). These results suggest that our educational system has a long way to go in adequately preparing students for college and the workplace. Furthermore, NAEP scores reveal ongoing disparities in performance between students of diverse backgrounds (i.e., from racial and ethnic minority groups, non-native English speakers, and with low socioeconomic status) and their "mainstream" peers (i.e., white, middle-class, native English speaking). These results are particularly troubling because more than half of U.S. children are expected to be part of a minority race or ethnic group by the year 2020 (U.S. Census Bureau, 2015).

As the demographics of U.S. classrooms continue to diversify, educators must look closely at factors affecting student performance in order to ensure that all students are achieving high levels of literacy. There are many ways to explain the achievement gap reflected in tests such as the NAEP. These explanations include many factors outside of schools' control such as economic disparity, access to health services, family involvement, and school funding, to name just a few (National Education Association, 2017). Yet, studies indicate that there are important factors that we can control within schools and classrooms that influence student achievement levels—in particular those of curriculum that frame instruction (i.e., *what* to teach) and the quality of teaching in implementing the curriculum (i.e., *how* it is taught). For example, research has demonstrated the centrality of concept knowledge or vocabulary learning in general and particularly for students who do not speak English as their native language (Carlo et al., 2004). Taylor, Pearson, Peterson, and Rodriguez (2003, 2005) identified a set of classroom practices, dubbed "teaching for cognitive engagement," that support higher levels of achievement; the set includes teacher coaching rather than telling, high levels of questioning, students' active participation in activities that nurture high levels of thinking (e.g., book club discussions, inquiry groups), and time for students' sustained engagement in reading and writing. However, research indicates that students from diverse backgrounds often have limited exposure to high-quality instruction, even within what teachers believe to be a balanced curriculum. When compared to "mainstream" peers, low-income or minority students tend to receive a great deal of instruction in lower-level skills and little instruction in reading comprehension and higher-level thinking about text (see Amendum & Fitzgerald, 2010; Amendum et al., 2009; Darling-Hammond, 1995, 2004; Kong & Fitch, 2002). It may be a conspiracy of good intentions—one that might be labeled "first things first," where the logic is something like "Let's get the words right and the facts straight before we get to the 'what ifs' and 'I wonders' of classroom instruction." And, of course, the conspiracy is that many lower-performing students spend their entire school careers getting the words right and the facts straight, but never being pushed toward that higher-level thinking. One reason for this disparity and conspiracy—limited instructional focuses rooted in lowered expectations for students from diverse backgrounds—is something we can and should change.

Ensuring academic success for all students requires that we attend to evolving social, cultural, and technological landscapes that shape our notion of what it means to be literate today. While literacy continues to represent a set of shared communicative practices among social and cultural groups, the nature of those practices and the texts consumed has changed immensely (National Council of Teachers of English, 2013). Within today's age of digital learning, multimodal text forms and their media-driven environments accompany, augment, and even supplant print-based literacy practices. For example, when researching a topic, students may access online digital texts in addition to print materials; may supplement print materials with websites, online images, and videos; and even solely source content online. As students consume information in these new ways, the cognitive tools they need at their disposal extend well beyond deciphering the printed word or simply comprehending words on the page. Twenty-first century literacy demands that students learn to evaluate and think critically about information and its source(s), to curate and manage information for myriad purposes, and to communicate and collaborate with others utilizing a variety of digital tools (International Society for Technology in Education, 2016; Howland, Jonassen, & Marra, 2011; Partnership for 21st Century Skills, 2016). These literate competencies not only enable success in the classroom, but are essential to actualize the broader objectives of literacy education to support lifelong learning, live a more fulfilling life, accomplish personal and professional goals, and contribute to the social and civic fabric of a global world.

The nature of the classroom environment bears strong implications for learners' development of 21st-century literacy proficiencies. Meaningful student engagement and favorable learning outcomes are often linked to school environments where students exhibit personal agency, exercise choice, and collaborate with peers (Watkins, 2005). In classrooms that nurture learning communities, students are more likely to be reflective, engaged, willing to take risks, and thereby tackle increasingly more challenging tasks and texts (Watkins, 2005), all important portrayals of a "growth mindset." The work of psychologist Carol Dweck (2006) suggests that students with a "growth mindset" do not shirk challenge, but believe that through effort and persistence they can develop their abilities. In other words, operating from a "growth mindset" (believing we can or will be able to succeed if we put forth effort and seek new strategies and support when we are stuck) as opposed to a "fixed mindset" (believing we inherently possess or lack what it takes to succeed) can enhance one's self-efficacy, academic tenacity, and overall academic performance (Dweck, Walton, & Cohen, 2014). The classroom environment, including the nature of classroom tasks, social relations in place, and language used by teachers, can help cultivate a growth mindset. For example, Dweck's

(2006) research points to the importance of praising student effort and persistence over ability. Research shows that teachers can also nurture dispositions of persistence, resilience, and endurance through supportive classroom learning communities (Dweck et al., 2014; Watkins, 2005). In these environments, a higher premium is placed on knowledge *construction* rather than knowledge *consumption* through collaborative student dialogue and problem solving. Many of the best practices showing up in modern-day literature emphasize the sociocultural role in knowledge building and remind us that the essentials of best practice are not only rooted in knowledge of literacy skills tantamount today, but also in awareness of how we as educators optimally grow literate citizens of the future.

EVIDENCE-BASED BEST PRACTICES: A RESEARCH SYNTHESIS

In reflecting on the notion of balanced literacy within today's policy context, the demands of 21st-century citizenry, and the challenge of ensuring a high level of literacy achievement for all students, it's important to take stock of lessons learned as a foundation for moving forward. As we have suggested, the Reading Wars debate pitting phonics against comprehension abated in favor of balance between the two. We are armed with strong evidence now to ensure this sort of balance. The work of the NRP (2000), and the long tradition of research in curriculum and pedagogy stemming back to the 1980s (e.g., Anderson, Hiebert, Scott, & Wilkinson, 1984), 1960s (e.g., Chall, 1967), and even earlier (e.g., Gray, 1948) confirms the importance of uniting methodologies. This unification requires the use of lower-level processes (e.g., phonemic awareness, phonics) in service to the pursuit of higher-order goals (e.g., comprehension, composition, critique). In what follows, we synthesize the research base that not only has served to establish the foundation for the literacy curriculum, but has also paved the way for more nuanced and sophisticated discussions about balanced literacy today.

Phonemic Awareness and Phonics

The research (NRP, 2000) suggests that explicit instruction in the auditory processes of phonological awareness, such as rhyming, phonemic segmentation (breaking a word into its phonemic units—*bat* → /buh/aa/ tuh/), and phonemic blending (putting the parts together— /buh/ /aa/ /tuh/→ *bat*) pays dividends in the long run in terms of its transference to word-decoding ability and beginning reading achievement. While many dense skill-oriented phonemic awareness programs exist, studies suggest that there is no need to privilege such programs over more authentic and engaging activities such as oral language games (see Snow, Burns, & Griffin, 1998), working with rhyming or alliterative texts, and practicing with invented spelling (see Adams, 1990; Clarke, 1988).

With regards to phonics, we know that the NRP report, notwithstanding its narrow sample, concluded that an early emphasis on code matters. We know from other work (e.g., Ehri, Nunes, Stahl, & Willows, 2001; Gaskins, Ehri, Cress, O'Hara, & Donnelly, 1997) that word recognition approaches should be complementary and that students need a full repertoire of tools to meet the challenges of pronouncing unknown words they encounter in text. Ehri (1995) describes four approaches to helping young students learn to read words: sequential decoding, analogy, contextual analysis, and sight-word recognition. Sequential decoding is letter-by-letter sounding out, whereas decoding by analogy focuses on word families or phonograms—words that are spelled and pronounced similarly, such as *cat, fat, sat,* and *bat.* Gaskins (2005) found analogy instruction to be much more effective following instruction in sequential decoding. Contextual analysis is a form of word solving that involves the use of clues within the word (morphological analysis) as well as around the word (the surrounding context). Finally, there is immediate sight-word recognition, which plays two roles in word reading. First, some words, such as *have, the,* and *break,* must be learned as sight words because their pronunciations cannot be predicted from their orthographic patterns. Second, sight-word recognition helps move students' repertoire of word reading from "arduously analyzable" (I can figure these out if I work at it) to "immediately recognizable" (I know that word; it's *irrefutable*), an important step toward fluency. In short, the goal of phonics and context instruction is to get to the point where readers need them minimally, thus freeing up their thinking skills for higher-level processes. Balanced phonics instruction—or, more accurately, balanced word reading instruction—is essential to fluent and skilled reading.

Comprehension and Vocabulary

We know from the NRP (2000) that comprehension can be improved by explicit strategy instruction and by a variety of approaches to vocabulary instruction. We also know from previous work (see Murphy, Wilkinson, Soter, Hennessey, & Alexander, 2009; Pearson & Fielding, 1991) that rich conversations about text can improve comprehension of both the texts within which the instruction is embedded and new texts that students subsequently read on their own. Hence, we are prepared to conclude that all three of these approaches—strategy instruction, rich talk about text, and semantically rich conversations about word meanings (see Beck,

McKeown, & Kucan, 2002; Blachowicz & Fisher, 2009) should be included in a balanced literacy curriculum. At this point in the history of literacy research, we have no evidence for privileging any one of the three over the other two. Moreover, they seem to comprise a complementary set.

Writing

While the role of writing was not within the scope of the NRP report, we know that writing is a core component of any literacy program and that reading and writing are mutually supportive and interactive processes. Just as with reading, the area of writing has also seen its share of polarizing debates. Mutually exclusive dichotomies—those between *product* versus *process* approaches—have lingered for years. While the *product* contingency employs attention to form and grammar of the text produced, the *process* side focuses on meaning making by emphasizing the stages of writing such as brainstorming, drafting, revising, and editing with little attention to convention. Where the product side can be too heavily focused on form, the process side too often relies on familiar registers, such as personal narratives, rather than more complex registers that better prepare students for future academic demands (Schleppegrell, 2004). Similar to the processes in reading, these methodologies are complementary; both are needed. Focus on product alone can lead to formulaic writing, while process orientations may not sufficiently equip students with the necessary conventions to adequately communicate their ideas, nor sufficient knowledge or ideas to fuel the composition process.

Since the publication of the NRP (2000) report, literacy researchers and educators have come to recognize that literacy is far too complex a process to frame effective instruction—as simply coordinating a balance between lower-level and higher-order processing of text. As students traverse myriad texts, language, and comprehension demands vary accordingly—and tools deemed effective within one particular content or context may differ greatly in another. Thus, students need to develop a set of skills and strategies that can be flexibly deployed across complex settings characteristic of today's literacy environment. For the remainder of this chapter, we build a profile of balanced literacy instruction that relies on a rich teacher knowledge base to adapt and orchestrate a wide range of classroom experiences that challenge and grow student literacy toolkits. Specifically, we describe several dimensions of the literacy curriculum that illustrate the competing demands and priorities at work within any comprehensive literacy program. In so doing, we demonstrate just how far the field has moved beyond the code versus meaning debate (i.e., balance in the past) to argue that there are many aspects of literacy that must be simultaneously and artfully balanced (i.e., balance today) to equip

students with the depth and breadth of proficiencies necessary to meet a
wide array of 21st-century literacy demands.

BEST PRACTICES IN ACTION

In what follows, we elaborate on seven dimensions of the literacy
curriculum that teachers must balance to build, challenge, and refine
students' skills across a wide range of texts and disciplines. We characterize
these dimensions as "content dimensions"—those that concern textual or
curricular considerations of *what to teach*—and "contextual dimensions"—
those that concern instructional considerations of *how to facilitate* student
learning. These dimensions, we argue, rest upon the foundation of
evidence-based best practices informed by research and previous debates.
In other words, we believe teachers are best prepared to navigate issues
of balance within these dimensions when equipped with a rich knowledge
base of the pillars of the literacy curriculum. These dimensions,
therefore, illustrate added layers of complexity, and are reflective of the
more nuanced and sophisticated discussions of what it means to enact a
balanced curriculum today.

Content Dimensions

We are quite privileged in our modern education to have much greater
access to texts that vary according to level of difficulty, genre, and subject
matter. These content dimensions underscore the fact that not all texts
are created equal; with changes in structure, format, and purpose come
associated shifts in linguistic, comprehension, and cultural demands.
Thus, students need the chance to learn and grow their core literacy skills
and strategies across a diverse platform of texts. Below we address the
need for balance when attending to (1) text difficulty, (2) genre, and (3)
disciplinary literacy (see Table 2.1).

Text Difficulty

One issue that has gained currency in education since the last iteration
of this chapter is that of balancing text difficulty with text complexity.
Where texts were once categorized as age- or grade-appropriate, classrooms are now using texts leveled in difficulty by characteristics affecting
the ease of reading: word repetition, word length, and sentence length
(and sometimes syntax complexity and text cohesion). The ubiquitous use
of assigning leveled texts for independent reading practice is grounded
in the underlying logic that access to books within individual zones of

TABLE 2.1. Balancing Content Dimensions

Dimension	Competing forces	
Text difficulty	Matched to individual	Stretching limits
Genre	Explicit instruction	Inductive learning
Disciplinary emphasis	Literacy as a skill	Literacy as a tool

Note. Content dimensions consist of three areas: (1) text difficulty, (2) genre, and (3) disciplinary emphasis. Each dimension has two competing forces: text difficulty—(a) matched to individual and (b) stretching limits; genre—(a) explicit instruction and (b) inductive learning; disciplinary emphasis—(a) literacy as a skill and (b) literacy as a tool.

comfort and ability will drive students to read more often, and thus improve reading skills and overall reading ability (Pearson, 2013).

Recent focus on the importance of text complexity brings balance to a heavy reliance on text difficulty. For example, national standards assert the need for students to read a high proportion of complex, challenging text at their grade level and beyond in order to adequately prepare for texts they will encounter in college and the workplace. The rationale is that if students who are reading below grade level are assigned a strict diet of texts solely at their reading level, it provides little occasion to exercise and stretch their repertoire of literacy skills and strategies needed to access more challenging, complex texts. Thus, the risk is that if challenging texts are withheld until students are deemed "ready" to receive them, they are robbed of invaluable exposure to the rich language and content of more complex texts (Raphael, Florio-Ruane, George, Hasty, & Highfield, 2004).

This emphasis on text complexity in the CCSS is based upon the sobering observation that when students finish secondary school (in grade 12 in the United States) the average level of challenge in texts they are reading is about a whole grade level below texts assigned at the freshmen level in college. The authors of the standards point to, and we think rightly so, the tremendous amount of resources devoted to remedial education in the first year of college. This is not only true of community colleges (where one might expect a larger proportion of students who find themselves less well prepared) but also in regional and even research-intensive universities. But teachers can mitigate the growing discrepancy between student reading achievement and grade-level content demands by providing a healthy diet of appropriately leveled texts in addition to frequent access and exposure to more complex texts that are chosen based on students' interests and goals. The CCSS solution to closing this text complexity/text difficulty gap is to gradually increase the expectations (and instructional support) at every grade level from the primary years onward so that by 12th grade, the gap stands a chance of being closed altogether. While more research is needed in this area, it is our contention that making more difficult texts accessible to students requires a good deal of teacher support and scaffolding to assist comprehension through use of reading strategies and text discussion.

Genre

A second notable dimension of balance concerns the incorporation of a wide range of genre pedagogies into the literacy curriculum (e.g., Duke & Purcell-Gates, 2003; Hicks, 1998; Nodelman, 1992; Pappas & Pettegrew, 1998). "Genre" refers to an evolving classification of texts that form the basis of school-based curriculum—most notably literary texts (e.g., stories, personal narratives, and poetry), and informational texts that employ a range of structures (e.g., descriptive, explanatory, cause–effect, problem–solution). Readers encounter a wide range of genres that span printed and digital texts as they read across topics and for various purposes. Moreover, as readers take up a single field of study, they encounter variation in genre structure as they access information across a variety of formats such as textbooks, scientific reports, historical documents, personal narratives, or the myriad of multimedia web-based texts.

The consideration of genre variation is an important instructional factor because of textual properties that range across a host of features such as structure, word choice, style, and purpose (Graesser, McNamara, & Kulikowich, 2011). The more familiar readers are with the conventions of genre types, the better off they are in comprehending and even composing their own texts. For example, by the time students leave elementary school, they are keenly aware that narrative text structures are organized around characters, setting, and plot; similarly, they are likely familiar with common expository structures, such as sequence, comparison, description, cause–effect, and problem–solution.

Explicit instruction in deconstructing the conventions of various genres has proven productive in supporting comprehension, such as alerting readers to linguistic and other discourse markers commonly used to communicate important ideas and signal text interconnectivity. For example, to demonstrate a comparison of ideas texts may utilize key words such as *however, nevertheless,* and *similarly,* whereas a text showing sequence will contain words like *first, then,* and *previously* (see Almasi, 2003, for more information). However, even within a single text, it is common to encounter multiple text structures. Today's information age often requires students to navigate multiple, overlapping, and blended genres characteristic of web-based multimedia text formats. Thus, attending to a range of genres within the literacy curriculum often means transcending traditional notions that contrast narrative with informational texts. The complex, varied, and sophisticated literate actions one must employ with print and digital-based texts emphasizes the imperative need to expose students to a full scope of genres in order to develop their proficiency and versatility in using appropriate genre conventions to build and access texts for a variety of purposes and contexts.

Disciplinary Literacy

The third content dimension concerns disciplinary literacy. Toolkits of literacy skills and strategies not only vary across text and genre, but across disciplinary or subject-matter emphasis. Literacy today is envisioned as a versatile tool central to learning that has application and utility across disciplines, but not necessarily as meaningful in and of itself as a subject area. As previously mentioned, the CCSS strive to bring balance to the curriculum by integrating English language arts with other disciplines. This integration offers students myriad contexts in which to genuinely apply their literacy strategies, as well as assures them a steady source of knowledge to fuel comprehension and composition processes. However, there are also distinctions among literacy practices in various disciplines including the specific types of high-level thinking that accompany subject-matter learning. By illustrating how different standards for comprehension and composition get realized in literature, science, and social studies, the CCSS demonstrate both commonalities and differences across disciplines. It is important, therefore, to strike a balance in helping students develop both the generalizable and content-specific literacy competencies that can facilitate disciplinary learning.

The expanding knowledge base of *disciplinary literacy* has contributed much to current thinking and research around what it means to meet the requirements of the CCSS and support literacy learning in content areas, particularly within secondary settings (see Goldman et al., 2016; Shanahan et al., 2016; Shanahan & Shanahan, 2015). Shanahan and Shanahan (2008; 2012) distinguish between content-area reading (or content-area literacy) and disciplinary literacy approaches to instruction. One of the primary distinctions they make is relevant to how literacy is thought about and developed. Through a content-area reading lens, reading tasks are viewed as similar across content areas, and as such, a set of generic or generalizable skills (e.g., previewing, questioning, summarizing, note taking) or activities (e.g., Know, Want to Know, Learned [KWL]; word maps; Directed Reading Thinking Activity [DRTA]) can be taught or utilized to support students' comprehension and retention of text. A disciplinary literacy perspective, on the other hand, emphasizes the unique language, purposes, and ways for using text among the disciplines, and therefore calls for the teaching of discipline-specific strategies. While we know that more generalizable content-area reading strategies are an important staple, especially for younger students as well as for those who struggle with reading comprehension (NRP, 2000), studies suggest the need to also equip students with additional, more specialized literacy tools required for meeting the textual and conceptual demands of more advanced disciplinary coursework (Shanahan & Shanahan, 2012). For example, as students actively engage with disciplinary texts, they must navigate various registers that include technical vocabulary and syntactic forms; draw upon knowledge of text structure and genre to predict and connect main and subordinate ideas; pose relevant questions; compare claims and propositions across texts; and use appropriate norms for reasoning to evaluate evidence or claims (Lee & Spratley, 2010). While we still have much to learn about characterizing and addressing the unique literacy demands of differing disciplines (Moje, Stockdill, Kim, & Kim, 2011; Shanahan & Shanahan, 2008), students benefit when teachers recognize the complementarity but also distinct purposes between content-area reading and disciplinary literacy approaches to instruction. Successful literacy integration within the disciplines means acknowledging both the demands of the content and the needs of the learner.

Contextual Dimensions

Content dimensions remind us that students must be given a variety of experiences and opportunities to become skilled in meeting the literacy demands present within a diverse range of texts across genre and discipline. Achieving a balanced literacy curriculum, however, is also dependent on managing contextual dimensions related to the instructional surround. Over the past 30 years, the definition of effective literacy instruction has broadened beyond what needs to get taught (i.e., developing an ability to decode and comprehend many types of texts) to also consider how it gets taught. An important part of balance today, therefore, includes considerations of student interest and motivation, the nature of student–text interactions, and how to best facilitate or support such interactions. Below we address balance within the contextual dimensions of (1) authenticity, (2) talk about text, (3) teacher control, and (4) professional prerogative (see Table 2.2).

Authenticity

Authenticity has been identified as important to students' literacy learning and motivation (Florio-Ruane & Raphael, 2004; Guthrie et al., 2004;

TABLE 2.2. Balancing Context Dimensions

Dimension	Competing forces	
Authenticity	Skill decontextualization	Real-world relevance
Text discussion	Culturally sanctioned	Personal interpretation
Teacher control	Minimal	Maximal
Professional prerogative	Distant	Local

Note. Context dimensions consist of four areas: (1) authenticity, (2) text discussion, (3) teacher control, and (4) professional prerogative. Each dimension has two competing forces: authenticity—(a) skill decontextualization and (b) real-world relevance; text discussion—(a) culturally sanctioned and (b) personal interpretation; teacher control—(a) minimal and (b) maximal; professional prerogative—(a) distant and (b) local.

Purcell-Gates, Duke, & Martineau, 2007). Balance in authenticity lies between the idea that students need to develop and practice a set of conventional skills that enables them to access texts, and the reality that too often school tasks are inauthentic, decontextualized, and, by implication, do not mirror real-world literacy activities. The content students read, write, and talk about, and the activity settings in which students work, should whenever possible be grounded in authentic tasks and goals. These tasks and goals should map to the purposes for which we, as a society, use literacy: to communicate, to learn, and to enjoy.

Authenticity, as talked about here, is relative to a person, meaning that what counts as interesting, entertaining, or relevant to read and write about is individually determined and variable. As such, authentic texts are those that individuals would typically seek out and engage with outside of a learning-to-read-and-write context (Purcell-Gates et al., 2007). Many literacy educators proclaim the numerous benefits of reading and responding to authentic literature—books, for example, that are written for the purpose of entertaining, informing, persuading, or inspiring—which reflects purposeful language use, complex natural language, and compelling story lines (e.g., Dyson, 2003). Even our youngest students must be given opportunities to read (even if it's "pretend-read") and respond to high-quality literary texts that demonstrate the many rewards and pleasures of reading. Studies have also demonstrated the benefits of more authentic informational texts as the basis for instruction in facilitating students' engagement with, comprehension of, and composition of informational and procedural texts across content areas (Purcell-Gates et al., 2007; Guthrie, Anderson, Alao & Rinehart, 1999; Guthrie et al., 2004). Other authentic practices include writing for real audiences and purposes (e.g., Cappello, 2006), writing to make sense of one's life (Dyson, 2003;

Genishi & Dyson, 2009; Schultz, 2006, 2009), and reading to engage in book club or other discussions with teachers and peers (e.g., Raphael et al., 2004).

The digital world also bears strong implications for literacy and authenticity in a 21st-century context. Today's authentic texts are increasingly more multimodal—those in which print is inextricably linked with visual, audio, and/or spatial patterns of meaning—and linked to multicultural and multinational sources and audiences (Coiro, Knobel, Lankshear, & Leu, 2014). Authentic tasks and purposes in this context have become increasingly more about one's ability to think critically about "text" (i.e., not solely "print"), analyze and evaluate sources, organize information, communicate information, and collaborate utilizing a variety of tools (Howland et al., 2011). These "information literacy" skills, necessary for participation in 21st-century citizenry, should be at the heart of school-based literacy activities. Authentic learning in classrooms today should not narrowly focus on students acquiring information via traditional text types, but rather on students finding, using, creating, and sharing multiple forms of media around the world (Frey & Fisher, 2012).

On the face of it, it might seem hard to disagree with an emphasis on authenticity. But, if pursued in too single-minded a fashion, there might be little occasion for treating formal features of language (e.g., its structure, sound–symbol system, punctuation) as objects of study, meaning where useful skills get practiced and acquired. One way of labeling what might be lost under a regime of "hyperauthenticity" is knowledge *about* language and how it works in different contexts.

Talk about Text

The second contextual dimension of balanced literacy is nurturing a classroom environment rich in talk about text. Conversations about text offer invaluable student opportunity to build on prior knowledge, ideas, and experiences, as well as to voice and refine understandings (Nystrand, 2006). Ideally, text discussions should be predominately student-led in topic selection, turn taking, and interpretation, with the teacher playing a supporting role. While the goal of these practices is for students to take ownership of the conversation, discussion left too open-ended can leave students floundering in the absence of set purpose, organizational structure, and support.

While conversing may seem on the surface to be an intuitive skill, students often need explicit guidance on how to engage in sustained and collaborative discussion. Many text-talk routines incorporate explicit student instruction on the discourse conventions for engaging in conversation such as (1) restating an idea, (2) agreeing or disagreeing, (3) asking for clarification, and/or (4) elaborating on an idea. In addition to teaching students how to talk, several well known text-talk routines also provide important frameworks for questioning the meaning and purpose of texts such as reciprocal teaching (Palinscar & Brown, 1984), questioning the author (Beck, McKeown, Sandora, & Worthy, 1996; Sandora, Beck, & McKeown, 1999), and literature circles (Daniels, 2002), to name a few. Many of these routines were endorsed in the NRP (2000) report and continue to serve the goals of literacy education due to their power to help students contextualize text in their own experience and understanding.

While it is often appropriate and oftentimes more efficient for teachers to simply tell students things they ought to know, we also recognize that learning is enriched when students are driven to ask authentic questions and derive answers from a rich set of experiences including talking with peers. In a range of studies, however, researchers have demonstrated that teacher–student discussions predominately follow a teacher-driven pattern of teacher initiation of a question (I), student response (R), and teacher evaluation (E) of the response (Cazden, 2001; Mehan, 1979). This I-R-E pattern is grounded in the transmission model of learning (one that assumes the teacher holds all the knowledge that must then be transmitted to students) that places a premium on recitation and correct answers. Yet, discussion has also been shown to be a powerful device for developing cognition such as in building persuasive ability. During peer discussions, students are prompted to state their position on a topic, motivated to supply evidence in support, challenged through counterarguments, and compelled to develop sound reasoning. Therefore, text discussions have been demonstrated to enhance student engagement, understanding, and internalization of the knowledge and skills necessary to engage in challenging literacy tasks (Applebee, Langer, Nystrand, & Gamoran, 2003).

Consistent and frequent opportunities to talk about text allow learners to work collaboratively to build shared understanding and strategies to reach consensus as well as accept difference. The teacher plays a key role in cultivating positive and respectful interactions through establishing discussion routines and structures to help foster student expression.

Teacher Control

A third contextual dimension of balance that must be sought in a balanced literacy program is the degree of teacher control. By "teacher control" we refer to the level of support or involvement on behalf of the teacher within a given activity or pedagogical context. While it is mistake to assume that literacy learning is limited only to situations in which a teacher provides explicit instruction, it is also erroneous to assume that learning is only meaningful when the teacher is out of the picture. Depending on the goal of the literacy event, activity, or lesson, different levels of teacher and student input are appropriate and necessary. Rodgers's (2004) observations of teaching and learning over time illustrated that effective teachers varied the amount of support and the related degree of teacher control and levels of student activity according to their perceptions of student need. Au and Raphael (1998) characterize variations in teachers' roles in terms of the amount of teacher control and student activity. They define five teacher roles: (1) explicit instructing, (2) modeling, (3) scaffolding, (4) facilitating, and (5) participating. These roles reflect a gradual release of responsibility (Pearson & Gallagher, 1983) where there is decreased control by the teacher and increased activity on the part of the student (see Figure 2.1). That is, teachers don't just start out with greater control and steadily move to lesser control, but rather teachers cycle back and forth between these roles in response to student performance and understanding.

Professional Prerogative

The fourth and final contextual dimension concerns professional prerogative, or who, or what, "calls the shots" with respect to how teachers and students spend their time in classrooms. At the one extreme, teachers may rely on a predetermined curriculum of skill instruction, often tied to a curricular scope and sequence that operates within and across grade levels. At the other extreme, the texts and the tasks that arise in the course of instruction, or, even more common, the needs that a given student or set of students demonstrate, are the determining force behind what is taught. In the latter view, the curriculum is unveiled as teachable

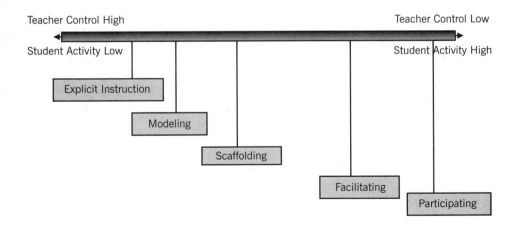

FIGURE 2.1. Teachers' roles.

moments occur, with the text, the tasks, and the students functioning as springboards to skill or strategy instruction. Teachers will find many moments when it's necessary to deviate from materials to adhere to their basic professional responsibility to adapt to individual differences.

We suggest the need for teachers to operate flexibly between these two poles. Curricular standards, which have been a "fact of life" in American education since the early 1990s, have attracted both praise and concern. On one hand, they can provide educators with a standardized baseline from which to teach by making goals explicit and creating an expectation of what content will be covered prior to students entering and exiting the classroom. On the other hand, there is no predetermined formula that will support the variation that comes our way when we meet the constellation of students and environments in each and every classroom. Effective literacy instruction is not simply about teachers enacting curriculum or possessing a good bag of tricks that, if designed well enough, can be applied successfully by any novice. Rather, literacy instruction is the art of knowing how to assemble the tools in concert with each other to make worthwhile instruction that is particular to the students and purposes in a given classroom.

REFLECTIONS AND FUTURE DIRECTIONS

In reflecting on balance in past iterations of this chapter, and considering balance in today's educational environment, we remain convinced that the scholarly evidence and the world in which today's students will live and work requires attention toward multiple facets of literacy. The research suggests appropriating the metaphor of "ecological balance" as it has unfolded in our understanding of ecosystems from environmental science. Most appealing about this metaphor is the idea that various elements do their part to support both their own survival and the survival of all of the other elements in the system. So it is in a comprehensive literacy curriculum. The seven content and contextual dimensions previously described are to be held in harmony. In doing so, they help to prepare students for a future that we may not even be able to imagine today, of continually evolving forms for accessing information as well as evolving forms for literate practice for personal growth and satisfaction.

What we aim for is that teachers are able to do a thorough job of teaching literacy—one that nurtures and grows a rich set of literacy skills and strategies across a wide variety of texts, for myriad purposes that map to real-world challenges. The inherent complexity is that teachers need a broad knowledge base in order to respond to and act adaptively to students and situations that are always in flux. Thus, a balanced literacy curriculum can only be realized through artful orchestration by teachers who achieve balance by weighing their professional knowledge with their intimate knowledge of their students and environment.

ENGAGEMENT ACTIVITIES

1. *Redefining our goals for literacy teaching in a 21st-century context.* We promote the definition of teaching literacy in a 21st-century context as supporting students' abilities to access information; think critically about a wide array of texts that vary in content, format, and platform; analyze and evaluate sources; organize information; communicate information; and collaborate using a variety of tools. How does this definition align with your current thinking, practice, and curricular goals? Reflect on how you and your colleagues utilize technology in your classroom or school. How are you helping your students develop 21st-century competencies including the information literacy skills cited above? What challenges do you face? Create a plan for technology integration that emphasizes information literacy and authentic tasks in support of your curricular goals.

2. *A close look at current practices.* Reflect on how your teaching is achieving balance across the seven content and context dimensions discussed. What dimensions are you balancing well? Where do you need to seek more balance? How might you go about achieving greater balance in the classroom?

3. *Cultivating a "growth mindset."* Find an article related to growth mindset or visit Dweck's website (listed below under Resources for Further Learning). What benefits do you see of a growth mindset for your students or for yourself as a learner? What practices or actions can you put into place to cultivate a growth mindset? What are the challenges within curriculum or policy that might undermine developing a growth mindset?

RESOURCES FOR FURTHER LEARNING

Brock, C. H., Goatley, V. J., Raphael, T. E., Trost-Shahata, E., & Weber, C. M. (2014). *Engaging elementary students in disciplinary learning and literacy.* New York: Teachers College Press.

Connelly, F. M., He, M. F., & Phillion, J. (Eds.). (2008). *The SAGE handbook of curriculum and instruction.* Thousand Oaks, CA: SAGE.

Hoffman, J. V., & Goodman, Y. M. (2009). *Changing literacies for changing times: An historical perspective on the future of reading research, public policy, and classroom practices.* New York: Routledge.

Li, G., & Edwards, P. A. (Eds.). (2010). *Best practices in ELL instruction.* New York: Guilford Press.

Morrow, L., Rueda, R., & Lapp, D. (Eds.). (2009). *Handbook of research on literacy and diversity.* New York: Guilford Press.

www.ciera.org—Center for the Improvement of Early Reading Achievement.

www.corestandards.org—Common Core State Standards Initiative.

www.iste.org—International Society for Technology in Education.

www.mindsetworks.com—Carol Dweck's website on mindset training for educators and students.

www.projectreadi.org—Reading, Evidence, and Argumentation in Disciplinary Instruction.

www.SchoolRiseUSA.com—School Rise: Enlightened Teaching.

REFERENCES

Adams, M. J. (1990). *Beginning to read: Thinking and learning about print.* Cambridge, MA: MIT Press.

Almasi, J. (2003). *Teaching strategic processes in reading.* New York: Guilford Press.

Amendum, S., & Fitzgerald, J. (2010). Reading instruction research for English-language learners in kindergarten through sixth grade: The last 15 years. In R. Allington & A. McGill-Franzen (Eds.), *Handbook of reading disabilities research* (pp. 373–391). Mahwah, NJ: Erlbaum.

Amendum, S., Li, Y., Hall, L., Fitzgerald, J., Creamer, K., Head-Reeves, D. M., & Hollingsworth, H. L. (2009). Which reading lesson instruction characteristics matter for early reading achievement? *Reading Psychology, 30*(2), 119–147.

Anderson, R. C., Hiebert, E. H., Scott, J. A., & Wilkinson, I. A. G. (1984). *Becoming a nation of readers: The report of the Commission on Reading.* Washington, DC: U.S. Department of Education.

Applebee, A. N., Langer, J. A., Nystrand, M., & Gamoran, A. (2003). Discussion-based approaches to developing understanding: Classroom instruction and student performance in middle and high school English. *American Educational Research Journal, 40*(3), 685–730.

Au, K. H., & Raphael, T. E. (1998). Curriculum and teaching in literature-based programs. In T. E. Raphael & K. H. Au (Eds.), *Literature-based instruction: Reshaping the curriculum* (pp. 123–148). Norwood, MA: Christopher–Gordon.

Beck, I. L., McKeown, M. G., & Kucan, L. (2002). *Bringing words to life: Robust vocabulary instruction.* New York: Guilford Press.

Beck, I. L., McKeown, M. G., Sandora, C., Kucan, L., & Worthy, J. (1996). Questioning the author: A yearlong classroom implementation to engage students with text. *Elementary School Journal, 96*(4), 385–414.

Blachowicz, C., & Fisher, P. (2009). *Teaching vocabulary in all classrooms* (4th ed.). Columbus, OH: Prentice-Hall.

Cappello, M. (2006). Under construction: Voice and identity development in writing workshop. *Language Arts, 83*(6), 482–491.

Carlo, M. S., August, D., McLaughlin, B., Snow, C. E., Dressler, C., Lippman, D. N., . . . White, C. E. (2004). Closing the gap: Addressing the vocabulary needs of English-language learners in bilingual and mainstream classrooms. *Reading Research Quarterly, 39*(2), 188–215.

Cazden, C. B. (2001). *Classroom discourse: The language of teaching and learning.* Portsmouth, NH: Heinemann.

Chall, J. S. (1967). *Learning to read: The great debate.* New York: McGraw-Hill.

Chall, J. S. (1997). *Learning to read: The great debate* (3rd ed.). New York: McGraw-Hill.

Clarke, L. K. (1988). Invented versus traditional spelling in first graders' writings: Effects on learning to spell and read. *Research in the Teaching of English, 22*(3), 281–309.

Coiro, J., Knobel, M., Lankshear, C., & Leu, D. J., Jr. (Eds.). (2014). *Handbook of research on new literacies.* Mahwah, NJ: Erlbaum.

Daniels, H. (2002). *Literature circles: Voice and choice in book clubs and reading groups.* Portland, ME: Stenhouse.

Darling-Hammond, L. (1995). Inequality and access to knowledge. In J. A. Banks & C. A. M. Banks (Eds.), *Handbook for research on multicultural education* (pp. 465–483). New York: Macmillan.

Darling-Hammond, L. (2004). What happens to a dream deferred?: The continuing quest for equal educational opportunity. In J. A. Banks & C. A. M. Banks (Eds.), *Handbook of research on multicultural education* (pp. 607–630). San Francisco: Jossey-Bass.

Duke, N., & Purcell-Gates, V. (2003). Genres at home and at school: Bridging the known to the new. *The Reading Teacher, 57*(1), 30–37.

Dweck, C. S. (2006). *Mindset.* New York: Ballantine.

Dweck, C. S., Walton, G. M., & Cohen, G. L. (2014). Academic tenacity: Mindsets and skills that promote long-term learning (Report prepared for the Bill and Melinda Gates Foundation). Retrieved October 15, 2017, from *https://ed.stanford.edu/sites/default/files/manual/dweck-walton-cohen-2014.pdf.*

Dyson, A. H. (2003). *The brothers and sisters learn to write: Popular literacies in childhood and school culture.* New York: Teachers College Press.

Ehri, L. C. (1995). Phases of development in reading words. *Journal of Research in Reading, 18,* 116–125.

Ehri, L. C., Nunes, S., Stahl, S., & Willows, D. (2001). Systematic phonics instruction helps students learn to read: Evidence from the National Reading Panel's meta-analysis. *Review of Educational Research, 71*(3), 393–447.

Florio-Ruane, S., & Raphael, T. E. (2004). Reconsidering our research: Collaboration, complexity, design, and the problem of "scaling up what works." *National Reading Conference Yearbook, 54,* 170–188.

Frey, N., & Fisher, D. (2012, April). Literacy 2.0: Finding, using, creating, and sharing information. *Principal Leadership,* pp. 58–60.

Gaskins, I. W. (2005). *Success with struggling readers: The Benchmark School approach.* New York: Guilford Press.

Gaskins, I. W., Ehri, L. C., Cress, C., O'Hara, C., & Donnelly, K. (1997). Procedures for word learning: Making discoveries about words. *The Reading Teacher, 50*(4), 312–327.

Genishi, C., & Dyson, A. (2009). *Children, language, and literacy: Diverse learners in diverse times.* New York: Teachers College Press.

Goldman, S. R., Britt, M. A., Brown, W., Cribb, G., George, M., Greenleaf, C., . . . Project READI. (2016). Disciplinary literacies and learning to read for understanding: A conceptual framework for disciplinary literacy. *Educational Psychologist, 51*(2), 219–246.

Graesser, A. C., McNamara, D. S., & Kulikowich, J. M. (2011). Coh-Metrix providing multilevel analyses of text characteristics. *Educational Researcher, 40*(5), 223–234.

Gray, W. (1948). *On their own in reading: How to give children independence in attacking new words.* Chicago: Scott Foresman.

Griffo, V. B., Madda, C. L., Pearson, P. D., & Raphael, T. E. (2015). Balance in comprehensive literacy instruction: Evolving conceptions. In L. B. Gambrell & L. M. Morrow (Eds.), *Best practices in literacy instruction* (5th ed., pp. 37–60). New York: Guilford Press.

Guthrie, J. T., Anderson, E., Alao, S., & Rinehart, J. (1999). Influences of concept-oriented reading instruction on strategy use and conceptual learning from text. *Elementary School Journal, 99*(4), 343–366.

Guthrie, J. T., Wigfield, A., Barbosa, P., Perencevich, K. C., Taboada, A., Davis, M. H., . . . Tonks, S. (2004). Increasing reading comprehension and engagement through concept-oriented reading instruction. *Journal of Educational Psychology, 96*, 403–423.

Hicks, D. (1998). Narrative discourses as inner and outer word. *Language Arts, 75*(1), 28–34.

Howland, J. L., Jonassen, D., & Marra, R. M. (2011). *Meaningful learning with technology* (4th ed.). Boston: Pearson.

International Society for Technology in Education. (2016). ISTE standards for students. Retrieved September 1, 2017, from *www.iste.org/standards/for-students?sfvrsn=2.*

Kong, A., & Fitch, E. (2002). Using book club to engage culturally and linguistically diverse learners in reading, writing, and talking about books. *The Reading Teacher, 56*(4), 352–362.

Lee, C. D., & Spratley, A. (2010). *Reading in the disciplines: The challenges of adolescent literacy.* New York: Carnegie Corporation of New York.

Lyon, G. R. (1997). *Report on learning disabilities research* (Adapted from testimony by Dr. Reid Lyon before the Committee on Education and the Workforce in the U.S. House of Representatives on July 10, 1997). Retrieved January 2, 2002, from *www.ldonline.org/ld_indepth/reading/nih_report.html.*

Madda, C. L., Griffo, V. B., Pearson, P. D., & Raphael, T. E. (2011). Balance in comprehensive literacy instruction: Evolving conceptions. In L. M. Morrow & L. B. Gambrell (Eds.), *Best practices in literacy instruction* (4th ed., pp. 37–66). New York: Guilford Press.

McIntyre, E., & Pressley, M. (1996). *Balanced instruction: Strategies and skills in whole language.* Boston: Christopher–Gordon.

Mehan, H. (1979). "What time is it, Denise?": Asking known information questions in classroom discourse. *Theory into Practice, 18*(4), 285–294.

Moje, E. B., Stockdill, D., Kim, K., & Kim, H. (2011). The role of text in disciplinary learning. In M. Kamil, P. D. Pearson, P. Mosenthal, P. Afflerbach, & E. B. Moje (Eds.), *Handbook of reading research* (Vol. 4, pp. 453–486). Mahwah, NJ: Erlbaum/Taylor & Francis.

Murphy, P. K., Wilkinson, I. A. G., Soter, A. O., Hennessey, M. N., & Alexander, J. F. (2009). Examining the effects of classroom discussion on students' comprehension of text: A meta-analysis. *Journal of Educational Psychology, 101*(3), 740–764.

National Center for Educational Statistics. (2012). *The nation's report card: Writing 2011* (Publication No. NCES 2012470). Retrieved September 12, 2017, from *https://nces.ed.gov/pubsearch/pubsinfo.asp?pubid=2012470.*

National Center for Educational Statistics. (2015). *The nation's report card: Mathematics and reading assessments 2015* (Publication No. NCES 2015136). Retrieved September 12, 2017, from *https://nces.ed.gov/pubsearch/pubsinfo.asp?pubid=2015136.*

National Council of Teachers of English. (2013). The NCTE definition of 21st century literacies. Retrieved August 15, 2017, from *www.ncte.org/positions/statements/21stcentdefinition.*

National Education Association. (2017). Identifying factors that contribute to achievement gaps. Retrieved September 28, 2017, from *www.nea.org/home/17413.htm.*

National Governors Association Center for Best Practices & Council of Chief State School Officers. (2010). *The Common Core Standards for English language arts and literacy in history/social studies, science, and technical subjects.* Washington, DC: Authors. Retrieved August 17, 2013, from *www.corestandards.org/ELA-Literacy.*

National Reading Panel. (2000). *Teaching children to read: An evidence-based assessment of the scientific research literature on reading and its implications for reading instruction* (National Institute of Health Pub. No. 00-4769). Washington, DC: National Institute of Child Health and Human Development.

Nodelman, P. (1992). *The pleasures of children's literature.* New York: Longman.

Nystrand, M. (2006). Research on the role of classroom discourse as it affects reading comprehension. *Research in the Teaching of English, 40*(4), 392–412.

Palinscar, A. S., & Brown, A. L. (1984). Reciprocal teaching of comprehension-fostering and comprehension-monitoring activities. *Cognition and Instruction, 1*(2), 117–175.

Pappas, C., & Pettegrew, B. S. (1998). The role of genre in the psycholinguistic guessing game of reading. *Language Arts, 75*(1), 36–44.

Partnership for 21st Century Skills. (2016). Framework for 21st century learning. Retrieved September 1, 2017, from *www.p21.org/storage/documents/docs/P21_framework_0816.pdf.*

Pearson, P. D. (2004). The reading wars: The politics of reading research and policy—1988 through 2003. *Educational Policy, 18*(1), 216–252.

Pearson, P. D. (2013). Research foundations for the Common Core State

Standards in English language arts. In S. Neuman & L. Gambrell (Eds.), *Reading instruction in the age of Common Core State Standards* (pp. 237–262). Newark, DE: International Reading Association.

Pearson, P. D., & Fielding, L. (1991). Comprehension instruction. In R. Barr, M. L. Kamil, P. Mosenthal, & P. D. Pearson (Eds.), *Handbook of reading research* (Vol. 2, pp. 819–860). New York: Longman.

Pearson, P. D., & Gallagher, M. C. (1983). The instruction of reading comprehension. *Contemporary Educational Psychology, 8*(3), 317–344.

Pearson, P. D., & Raphael, T. E. (1999). Toward an ecologically balanced literacy curriculum. In L. B. Gambrell, L. M. Morrow, S. B. Newman, & M. Pressley (Eds.), *Best practices in literacy instruction* (pp. 22–33). New York: Guilford Press.

Pearson, P. D., & Raphael, T. E. (2003). Toward a more complex view of balance in the literacy curriculum. In L. M. Morrow, L. B. Gambrell, & M. Pressley (Eds.), *Best practices in literacy instruction* (2nd ed., pp. 23–39). New York: Guilford Press.

Pearson, P. D., Raphael, T. E., Benson, V. L., & Madda, C. L. (2007). Balance in comprehensive literacy instruction: Then and now. In L. M. Morrow, L. B. Gambrell, & M. Pressley (Eds.), *Best practices in literacy instruction* (3rd ed., pp. 30–54). New York: Guilford Press.

Pressley, M. (2006). *Reading instruction that works: The case for balanced teaching* (3rd ed.). New York: Guilford Press.

Purcell-Gates, V., Duke, N., & Martineau, J. (2007). Learning to read and write genre-specific text: Roles of authentic experience and explicit teaching. *Reading Research Quarterly, 42*(1), 8–45.

Raphael, T. E., Au, K. A., & Popp, J. (2013). Transformative practices for literacy teaching and learning: A complicated agenda for literacy researchers. *Annual Yearbook of the Association of Literacy Educators and Researchers, 35,* 9–32.

Raphael, T. E., Florio-Ruane, S., George, M., Hasty, N. L., & Highfield, K. (2004). *Book Club Plus: A literacy framework for primary grades*. Littleton, MA: Small Planet Communications.

Rodgers, E. M. (2004). Interactions that scaffold reading performance. *Journal of Literacy Research, 36*(4), 501–532.

Sandora, C., Beck, I., & McKeown, M. (1999). A comparison of two discussion strategies on students' comprehension and interpretation of complex literature. *Reading Psychology, 20*(3), 177–212.

Schleppegrell, M. J. (2004). *The language of schooling: A functional linguistics perspective*. New York: Routledge.

Schultz, K. (2006). Qualitative research on writing. In C. A. MacArthur, S. Graham, & J. Fitzgerald (Eds.), *Handbook of writing research* (pp. 357–373). New York: Guilford Press.

Schultz, K. (2009). *Rethinking participation: Listening to silent voices*. New York: Teachers College Press.

Shanahan, C., Heppler, J., Manderino, M., Bolz, M., Cribb, G., & Goldman, S. R. (2016). Deepening what it means to read (and write) like a historian:

Progressions of instruction across a school year in an eleventh grade U.S. history class. *The History Teacher, 49,* 241–270.

Shanahan, C., & Shanahan, T. (2015). The what and why of disciplinary literacy. In M. Hougan (Ed.), *Fundamentals of literacy instruction and assessment, 6–12* (pp. 127–140). Baltimore: Brookes.

Shanahan, T., & Shanahan, C. (2008). Teaching disciplinary literacy to adolescents: Rethinking content-area literacy. *Harvard Educational Review, 78*(1), 40–59.

Shanahan, T., & Shanahan, C. (2012). What is disciplinary literacy and why does it matter? *Topics in Language Disorders, 32*(1), 7–18.

Snow, C. E., Burns, M. S., & Griffin, P. (Eds.). (1998). *Preventing reading difficulties in young children.* Washington, DC: National Academy Press.

Taylor, B. M., Pearson, P. D., Peterson, D. P., & Rodriguez, M. C. (2003). Reading growth in high-poverty classrooms: The influence of teacher practices that encourage cognitive engagement in literacy learning. *Elementary School Journal, 104*(2), 3–28.

Taylor, B. M., Pearson, P. D., Peterson, D. P., & Rodriguez, M. C. (2005). The CIERA School Change Framework: An evidenced-based approach to professional development and school reading improvement. *Reading Research Quarterly, 40*(1), 40–69.

U.S. Census Bureau. (2015). New Census Bureau report analyzes U.S. population projections (Release Number: CB15-TPS.16). Retrieved September 5, 2017, from *www.census.gov/newsroom/press-releases/2015/cb15-tps16.html.*

Watkins, C. (2005). Classrooms as learning communities: A review of research. *London Review of Education, 3*(1), 47–64.

CHAPTER 3

Best Practices for Motivating Students to Read

JOHN T. GUTHRIE
ANA TABOADA BARBER

This chapter will:

- Convey the research evidence for the importance of motivation and classroom practices to foster motivation and engagement in reading.
- Present the prevailing motivations that impact students' reading including interest, confidence, and dedication.
- Portray classroom practices such as assuring relevance, providing choices, generating success, arranging collaborations, setting up thematic units, and emphasizing importance to build valuing.
- Illustrate how to connect to the power of growth mindset for literacy advancement.
- Reflect on Spanish-speaking readers and digital literacy motivations.

WHAT DO WE MEAN BY MOTIVATION?

Many teachers think of a motivated reader as a student who is having fun while reading. While this is often true, motivation is diverse. What we mean by motivation are the values, beliefs, and behaviors surrounding reading. Some productive values and beliefs may lead to excitement, yet other values may lead to determined hard work. We talk about three powerful motivations that drive students' reading. They operate in school and out of school, and they touch nearly every child. Some students may have all of these motivations and some may have only one. For some students, these motivations appear in the positive form of driving students toward reading. Other motivations are negative and push students away from books. When we talk about reading motivations we refer to (1) interest, (2) dedication, and (3) confidence. An interested student reads because he or she enjoys it, a dedicated student reads because he or she believes it is important, and a confident student reads because he or she can do it. All these students possess the positive mindset that they are growing in literacy.

Key Motivations to Read: Interest, Confidence, Dedication

Interest

When we think of motivation, our mind first turns to interest. Motivation is enjoying a book, being excited about an author, or being delighted by new information. Researchers refer to interest as intrinsic motivation, meaning something we do for its own sake. On a rainy day, we might rather read our favorite book than do anything else. We are not trying to get a reward when falling into a novel.

Motivation also brings to mind the reward for success. Who doesn't like to win a trinket for hitting the target with a dart at the state fair? Who doesn't want to earn serious money for working hard in a career? These are extrinsic rewards because someone gives them to us. We do not give them to ourselves, and these rewards do propel us to put out effort, focus energy, and get up in the morning. Yet extrinsic rewards do not motivate reading achievement in the long term. Students who read only for the reward of money, a grade, or a future job are not the best readers. The reason is that if you read for the reward of a good quiz score, what happens after the quiz is that you stop reading. If the test score is the only thing that matters, it is okay to take shortcuts, not really understand, or cheat. It encourages students to become more interested in the reward than the learning. None of these generate long-term achievement. Sometimes a reward, such as candy or early recess, will jump-start a group of students to read in this moment for this purpose. But if the motivation is not intrinsic, it will not increase achievement in the long term (Wigfield & Guthrie, 1997).

Confidence

Believing in yourself is more closely linked to achievement than any other motivation throughout school. The reason is that confidence, which is belief in your capacity, is tied intimately to success. This link occurs for simple, daily reading tasks. A student who reads one page fluently thinks he can read the next page in the same book proficiently. The link is also forged for reading in general. A student who reads fluently and understands well is also sure of him- or herself as a reader. In and out of school, people like the things they do well.

Conversely, students who struggle begin to doubt their abilities. They expect to do poorly in reading, writing, and talking about text. The real dilemma is that lower-achieving students often exaggerate their limitations. Believing they are worse than they really are, they stop trying completely. Retreating from all text interactions, they reduce their own opportunity to do what they want to do more than anything—to be a good reader. Their low confidence undermines them even further in a cycle of doubt and failure. By middle school, breaking this cycle is a formidable challenge for teachers.

Dedication

Although intrinsic motivation is desirable, this type of motivation is not always possible in school. There are assignments that are not desirable to a student, yet are part of the curriculum. There are books that do not appeal to some individuals, yet at a given moment in a given school, it is necessary to read them. What motivation enables students to read in this situation? The reason to read in this case is the students' belief that reading is important, and the students' persistence in reading, whatever the assignment. We call this dedication and researchers call it behavioral engagement (Skinner, Kindermann, & Furrer, 2009).

Every student has the potential to be dedicated. Skills are hard for some students to develop, but dedication is related to will. It is up to a student to decide whether to be dedicated or not. Students are either avoidant, dedicated, or somewhere in between the two. Students who value reading are dedicated in the sense that they devote effort, time, and persistence to their reading. These are the three key signs of dedication in students.

One of the most important distinctions between dedicated and avoidant students is that avoidant students do not make the connection between their efforts and the outcomes. A fourth-grade teacher, Taysha Gateau-Barrera, told us that "dedicated students know that they don't improve by mistake. They make continued efforts to try hard and be well organized because they want to be successful in school." Avoidance is a particularly powerful sign because it stops all learning abruptly. If a student wants to read and tries to read well, he or she may learn. If another student refuses to interact with text, all hope for gaining skill, knowledge, or experience from text is dashed.

Dedicated students read to attain information that expands their knowledge of their perceived world. Reading is a vehicle to take them to the knowledge they want. Unlike the kids who are reading for practice, these students are reading to know. In our interview study (Guthrie, Klauda, & Morrison, 2012), one middle school student said reading was important because "it informs us because we read about the *Titanic,* and it happened on April 12. It's not boring, it's more like fun because they give you information and stuff about the past." Another student remarked, "Reading actually teaches you things and makes you really think about life that's going on on this Earth." Still another said, "In science [we read about] this bacteria that I didn't know about and it's called hiking disease. When you're hiking and you get some water from the pond, and it's this little bug that if it hits you too long it can make you very sick."

Growth Mindset

Motivated students have a growth mindset. They believe they can improve in literacy. To these students, literacy is attainable with effort and persistence. Carol Dweck, the author who coined the term "growth mindset" showed that students who believe they can grow in literacy made rapid progress (Xiaodong, Dweck & Cohen, 2016). Unfortunately, some students doubt that effort helps them. They think that literacy is a skill that you either possess or do not possess. Working hard cannot help you achieve or protect you from failing. But we know this is not true. For teachers, it is crucial to realize that we can teach growth mindset and promote its development. Growth mindset is connected to interest, confidence, and dedication. A teacher who promotes these motivations is fostering growth mindset.

EVIDENCE-BASED PRACTICES
IN CLASSROOM MOTIVATION

Evidence for the Power of Motivation and Engagement Is Expanding Rapidly

Evidence that motivation is vital to achievement is now expressed not in a few studies, but in many reviews and handbooks. The *Handbook of Research on Student Engagement* contains more than 800 pages of literature reviews by more than 55 authors (Christensen, Reschly, & Wiley, 2012). In the *Reading Research Quarterly,* reading motivation and its roles in building proficient and dedicated readers was comprehensively documented (Schiefele, Schaffner, Moller, & Wigfield, 2012). Classroom practices that energize motivated students have been systematically reviewed (Guthrie,

Wigfield, & You, 2012). Reading motivation has come of age as in indispensable ingredient of teacher preparation. The International Reading Association's Literacy Research Panel was charged to identify the central issues in reading education. In 2012, the original ILA Literacy Research Panel stated that the highest priority for literacy education is to transform all classrooms into places where students are extensively immersed in meaningful learning through literacy by placing an emphasis on motivation and engagement.

Most teachers and the International Literacy Association aim to nurture lifelong readers. Motivation is a goal. At the same time motivation is a means. It stands as a vital link to attainment of the proficiency. As the research shows, and the Literacy Research Panel has articulated, motivation is imperative in progressing toward 21st-century literacy.

Intervention Research in Reading Motivation

Following a meta-analysis of motivation studies involving text interaction, Guthrie and Humenick (2004) concluded that a variety of positive motivations were increased by experimental conditions related to relevance, content goals, choices, and collaborations. Contributions of these practices to middle school students' reading engagement and proficiency with information text in concept-oriented reading instruction (CORI) has been demonstrated (Guthrie, Klauda, & Ho, 2013).

Although interventions are rare in motivation research, a few studies can be identified. Vansteenkiste, Lens, and Deci (2006) compared experimental groups who received either intrinsically motivating goals for reading or extrinsically motivating goals for reading the same text. In the intrinsic condition, students who were obese were asked to read a text on nutrition for their own purposes. In the extrinsic condition, similar students were asked to read the same text for the extrinsic goal of memorizing facts to score well on a test. The students with intrinsic goals recalled the text more fully and reported more involvement in the reading than students with the extrinsic goals (Vansteenkiste et al., 2006). Furthermore, when a brief computer-based instructional unit was embellished with personalized features and inconsequential choices, students showed more intrinsic motivation for the activity than if the program did not have the embellishments (Cordova & Lepper, 1996).

In summary, a variety of correlational, experimental, and qualitative research confirms the positive impacts of motivational practices on students' interest, confidence, and dedication in reading. This body of research affirms the effectiveness of specific practices that will be described next, including making reading relevant, affording choices, assuring success, arranging for collaborations, emphasizing the importance of reading, organizing thematic units, and integrating multiple motivation supports during instruction.

From kindergarten to 12th grade, teachers can and do use motivational practices in their classrooms. Each practice described here has been afforded to students across the age range. For example, kindergartners can be given the choice of which story they want the teacher to read aloud; and secondary students can choose which two or three subtopics to pursue in a long-term multigenre inquiry. In this chapter, we often provide examples for middle elementary-age students. You can generate how to apply the practice for students of the age, ethnicity, background, ability, and currently existing motivation in your classroom.

BEST PRACTICES IN ACTION

Collaboration

Collaboration is a central process in CORI. Teachers implementing collaboration are initiating the following activities: (1) reading as partners or in small groups, (2) exchanging ideas and sharing expertise, (3) student-led discussion groups, (4) book talks, (5) team projects such as a poster-making activity, and (6) peer feedback. As with the other motivation supports, these activities are contextualized within the conceptual theme and books on the theme. For example, partners may be given 5 minutes to discuss the inferences they generated from reading three pages of text on the conceptual question of the day. In each 90-minute lesson, teachers arrange for students to work in whole-group, partnerships, small-team interactions, and individually. The structure for small-team interaction is collaborative reasoning, based on research from Chinn, Anderson, and Waggoner (2001). In this interactive structure, students make claims about the text, add to each other's interpretations, raise clarifying questions, and attempt to synthesize their own brainstorming. Shown to impact higher-order thinking about text, collaborative reasoning is not merely a social break from learning or an open discussion, but a scaffolded process of cumulative contributions based on reading about a topic. The outcome is a collective understanding about text.

Collaboration can occur in every lesson. It may be a broad plan or a brief event. As collaboration between partners, within a team, and across all students, the classroom becomes a community. To assure that the community spirit is expanding, teachers can be sure each lesson includes one or more of the following:

1. Partners reading aloud together.
2. Partners exchanging questions to answer over text.

3. Teams summarizing a chapter.
4. Literature circles debating story themes.
5. Peers collaborating in reasoning.
6. Students interacting in a jigsaw.
7. Classmates editing each other's writing.

Relevance

Appealing to students' interest is a popular motivational approach. In a book-length treatment on building reading motivation for boys, Brozo (2002) found that boys respond when teachers become aware of their students' personal interests and needs. Some boys may want to read about heroes, adventurers, magicians, or tricksters. If their curiosities can be identified through interest inventories, they may become engrossed in a book or a topic and learn to find satisfaction through literacy. Although this suggestion is useful for book clubs or free-reading activities, it is not easily used for instruction with information books and is not easy to relate to curriculum-connected, academic accountabilities that are widespread in middle schools.

Real-World Materials

When it is possible to bring media based in the real world into classroom instruction, the text becomes relevant. For example, in a social studies class studying civil rights, the teacher found a poignant newspaper article. It described an elderly female protester who was on a picket line objecting to racist policies. Although she was a civil rights activist she behaved hypocritically by owning a segregated grocery store. The article captivated students' attention and through their critical analysis of the text and the historical situation, they developed keen insights about the economic and moral pressures surrounding racism (Johnson & Cowles, 2009).

Relevant texts are commonplace in vocational schools or courses. One vocational school's students worked in shops that were run like real job sites. Students were presented many opportunities to participate in work-related scenarios. As well as providing services to the community such as changing the oil or repairing people's car brakes, they read texts on auto mechanics, construction, electricity, plumbing, graphic design, and computer technology. The school did not have to stretch to provide students with authentic tasks or reading materials. Because of their relevance, the students valued these reading tasks. The vast majority of students dedicated themselves to mastering these texts despite their complexity (Darvin, 2006). Whether they are newspapers, job-related texts, or part of the popular culture, texts from the real world are relevant in themselves.

For elementary school students in urban settings, a team of teachers built relevance by forming linkages between students in the upper elementary grades and adult pen pals in local businesses, nonprofit organizations, and government agencies in the area. Adult pen pals read the same books as the students and wrote questions and commentaries guided by a website. Teachers selected grade-level books from five domains: fiction, social studies, biography, folk tales, and science. In communicating with their pen pals students eagerly read, wrote, and explored exciting worlds beyond the classroom. In this case, it was not the real-world materials, but the real-world members of their community and authentic questions that inspired reading dedication (Teale, Zolt, Yokota, Glasswell, & Gambrell, 2007).

Poignant Topics

A powerful source of relevant texts for young adolescents is novels or biographies on the theme of freedom. As Bean and Harper (2006) showed, young adolescents are captivated by *The Breadwinner,* a novel about Parvana, a 12-year-old girl living in Afghanistan under Taliban rule. In an act of survival, Parvana poses as a boy selling goods to earn money for her family. She achieves some freedom by making her femininity invisible, but she loses some of her ethnic identity. Reading this book, students became immersed in her loss of religious identity as she gained economic freedom. Many of them discovered they had paid a price for freedom as well. The relevance of this text to their lives generated dedicated reading.

In a study at the elementary school level, students volunteered that their personal interests were the main factor that made them want to read a narrative text. In asking why they chose certain books students replied:

- "I like dolphins. I think they are cool because they live in the ocean and I like oceans."
- "It was important because I like different cultures."
- "Because it was about an Indian and I am interested in Indians."

Identifying students' topical interests through a conversation or a questionnaire can enable teachers to heighten the relevance of books and entice students into dedicated reading.

Teachers Create Relevance

It is often impossible to locate real-world materials. On many occasions, the teacher needs to create relevance by designing events that enable students to see connections of text to themselves. For example, a middle school class was reading *Night* by Elie Wiesel, an account of the author's experiences during the Holocaust. Students did not take much interest in the scene in which Jewish individuals were herded like cattle into a railroad car because it was taking place on another continent in an earlier generation. To render the scene more personal, the teacher made a large rectangle of red tape on the classroom floor. He asked the class to crowd into this limited space. After students' giggling and complaining subsided, the teacher explained that this is how Jews stood for days at a time on a moving train. Following this weak simulation, students began to ask about the people and their circumstances, and their reading desire was reignited.

A teacher-guided event that is relevance-generating consists of enabling students to create their own questions about text. In one social studies class, students wrote their questions about the freedoms of religion, speech, assembly, petition, and the press. Students were expected to learn about the five basic freedoms embodied in the Constitution. They read for definitions, historical origins, and limits of all these freedoms and prepared a 6–8 minute oral report. Their report centered on a single person, event, battle, or place during the Civil War that was connected to one of these freedoms. By enabling students to be guided by their own questions, as well as the curriculum framework, they bring their own knowledge, interests, and idiosyncrasies into their reading activities. As a consequence, their willingness to spend time and effort grows and their products display the benefits of dedicated reading.

For students at many ages, the teacher may set up situations involving a discrepant event, a reality that conflicts with what the students might expect to see. For example, as Duke, Purcell-Gates, Hall, and Tower (2006) reported in a study on light, one teacher set up a prism on the overhead projector while her class was out of the room. This caused rainbows to appear on the ceiling. When the students returned there were many oohs and aahs and a rush of questions about how the rainbow effects occurred. The teacher led the students to find and read information text on light to help them answer their own questions. Such discrepant events may be created for literature and fiction as well. If students are asked to predict the outcome of a chapter or what a character will do in a scene, the teacher can create a discrepancy between the students' expectations and the events in the book. Exploring and explaining the discrepancies between students' predictions and the actual events can lead to teachable moments that deepen students' comprehension and enhance their reading dedication.

Relevance is an instructional practice central to CORI activities (Guthrie, McRae, & Klauda, 2007). In this context, relevance refers to linking books and reading activities to the students' personal experiences. These connections to "me" as a person are especially poignant for adolescents who are centered on thinking about who they are. Such links to self can be tied to long-term history, such as students' cultural experiences in their ethnic group, to a personal interest such as skateboarding, or to a recent personal experience. In CORI for middle school students, we give context through videos related to the conceptual theme. For example, in Week 1, we present a video on predation where a cheetah is capturing a gazelle on the Serengeti Plain. After watching the 3-minute video, students make observations about it, draw inferences, and make connections between the events. The students then read a paragraph of text to learn more about predation in cheetahs and other animals. They draw inferences from the text and share their observations with peers.

In this 20-minute activity, reading information text is made relevant by connecting it to a vivid personal encounter with the phenomenon through video. Needless to say, the color, audio effects, and drama of the video rivet the students' attention and arouse their interest. Asking students to perform the processes with the video that we later ask them to perform with the text brings a linkage not only in content, but in the process of learning across the media. Thus, relevance is formed through the immediacy of experience with video and text. It is relevance situated in a disciplinary domain and information texts on the subject matter. We believe that this level of relevancy is effective as a starting point for learning the relevance of other texts on other topics in the future.

When students view a video on predation in the Serengeti the experience is effortless, eye opening, and interesting. It activates what they already know and arouses natural curiosities. Watching the video is intrinsically motivating, which means that students will do it for their own enjoyment. Students often ask to see the video many times. Linking a readable trade book to this interesting event projects the qualities of the video enjoyment into the text interaction. For this moment, in this situation, reading becomes interesting. Thus, the students' interest in reading is scaffolded by creating situated interest in an extremely concrete situation. Then we extrapolate outward from it. Students are weaned from the relevance-generating event and learn to find interest in other texts and other topics.

Choices

The most widespread recommendation for motivation is providing choices. In the classroom, students are often thrilled to have a choice in their reading. They rise to it with enthusiasm, at least temporarily. A theoretical framework for choice in the classroom is self-determination theory (Ryan & Deci, 2000), which argues that students' development of autonomy, or being in charge of their own lives, is central to their academic achievement and emotional adjustment. After reviewing self-determination theory, Reed, Schallert, Beth, and Woodruff (2004) stated, "When it comes to addressing specifically the motivational processes of adolescents in literacy-focused classrooms, the single, most powerful suggestion we can make is to encourage teachers to develop learning environments that are autonomy-supportive" (p.274).

Autonomy support in this context refers to enabling students to become self-directing and self-controlling of their literacy and academic work. Reeve (1996) explained autonomy support in the classroom in a book-length treatment entitled *Motivating Others: Nurturing Inner Motivational Resources.* As Reeve noted,

> Autonomy support refers to the amount of freedom a teacher gives a student so the student can connect his or her behavior to personal goals, interests, and values. The opposite of autonomy support is coercion or being controlled. Teacher autonomy support expresses itself when teachers allow students choices, respect their agendas, and provide learning activities that are relevant to personal goals and interests. (p. 206)

Among the proposals for instructional practices described in this section, autonomy support may enjoy the largest amount of empirical verification, which has been reviewed in Guthrie and Humenick (2004).

Providing choice is a motivational support system in CORI for middle school that enables students to develop self-direction in the classroom. Teachers provide the following kinds of choices within the 6-week CORI program: self-selection of books or sections of books, student input into topics or sequence of topics, student suggestions for strategy use for comprehension, options for demonstrating learning from text, and selecting partners for teams. As these examples show, we are not affording students open opportunity to take complete charge of everything they do for a week in reading/language arts. These are mini-choices during literacy lessons. Yet as small as these choices may appear to be, they enable students to feel a stronger sense of investment and to commit larger amounts of effort to their reading work.

On a daily basis effective teachers can give mini-choices. They empower students to increase their investment in learning. When appropriate, in every lesson have students do at least one of the following:

1. Select a story.
2. Select a page to read.
3. Select sentences to explain.

4. Identify a goal for the day.
5. Choose three of five questions to answer.
6. Write questions for a partner exchange.

Success

Support for students' self-efficacy in reading and other subjects is crucial. Without belief in themselves, students in the upper elementary and middle school grades often retreat from books. As portrayed by Schunk and Zimmerman (2007), several explicit teaching practices increase students' self-efficacy. The self-efficacy-fostering framework consists of providing students with process goals. These are steps for performing reading tasks successfully. Teachers provide feedback for success in the process goals rather than feedback for the students' products or outcomes. That is, teachers give specific direction to students about the effectiveness of their strategy for performing work. They help students set realistic goals for reading. Also beneficial to students' self-efficacy is their perception of coherence in the texts and tasks of instruction. When students can identify the links across contents of reading and perceive themes in the substance of their reading materials, they gain a belief that they can succeed in reading and writing about text.

To afford your students practices that boost success, assure that at least one of the following is very prominent in every lesson:

1. Text matched to students' reading levels
2. Frequent feedback for reading
3. Authentic reading merged with skills
4. Multiple opportunities for reading
5. Sharing competency with peers
6. Student goal setting
7. Rewarding effort

Emphasizing Importance

Too many students avoid reading because they believe it is not important to them now or in the future. They do not value reading and do not think it will benefit them. To address this dilemma, we believe in providing students with a concrete experience rather than an abstract principle. Rather than attempting a global strategy of persuading students that reading will enable them to go to college or enter a career of their choice, we attempt to situate the benefit of literacy in a concrete situation. For example, have students view a video of plant and animal relationships. Then have them read a related text and share their new learning with a partner. After the lesson, ask the question, "What were your sources of new learning today?" Students will respond by saying, "the video" or "my partner" or "my writing." Soon they will discover that it was the text that enabled them to gain knowledge most effectively on this particular topic on this particular day. This recognition is an awareness of the value of reading. It often comes as a surprise to the students. The teacher may also ask how a choice made during the lesson benefitted them. Students' awareness of how well they enjoyed the choice, and how it helped them focus cognitively, raises their estimate of the value of reading.

For each lesson you can ask students to show the importance of reading. Have them:

1. Identify the portion of text they used to answer a question.
2. Point to a text that was most informative about a character in literature.
3. Identify a text that enabled them to explain a concept in information text.
4. Compare what they learned from a text versus what they learned from a video on the topic.
5. Contrast the content they learned from reading, writing, or discussing in a lesson.
6. Explain how the content of a text could help them in an out-of-school situation.

Thematic Unit

Thematic units can be taught on many topics. First, you begin with a main theme, or big idea. Next, identify supporting concepts to explain the big idea. Then, identify texts that contain the concepts. Texts should also afford you the opportunities to teach reading strategies, such as concept mapping. In one unit of CORI for grade 7, the theme is the diversity of plants and animals in community interactions. The superordinate idea of the unit is *symbiosis,* including such forms as mutualism and parasitism. To accentuate the conceptual theme, teachers give students a big question for each week, as well as daily questions related to the week's big question. This does not preclude student questioning, but sets a frame for the topic. In Week 1, the following four questions were presented on the first 4 days of instruction:

1. What are the characteristics of an ecosystem?
2. How does predation contribute to balance in an ecosystem?
3. How do different species of animals rely on their environment for feeding?
4. In what ways do animals adapt to their environment for survival?

To provide resources for literacy on this theme all books are unified around it for the 6 weeks. Texts for whole-class instruction, individual guided reading, and individual books for group projects are selected to be theme-relevant. Strategies that are taught for comprehension, including summarizing and concept mapping, are placed within the context of the conceptual theme. For example, student summaries represent their reading related to a particular question on a given day. Motivation supports, such as choice, are provided in the context of thematic learning. For example, the teacher may provide a choice for which chapter in a selected book to read on a given day. Students make their selection based on their view of what will enable them to learn about the question of the day and to discuss it effectively with a peer. Thus, motivational support of choice is not global, but is framed by the content question of the day and undergirded by the content learning of yesterday.

Build in the following qualities to your thematic units:

1. Instructional units have conceptual complexity and duration.
2. Students learn big ideas of survival, war and peace, discovery, and oppression.
3. Topics persist over days and weeks.
4. Students write concept maps of pages, chapters, books, and unit.
5. Connect diverse genre (stories, nonfiction, poems) to each other.
6. Have overarching guiding questions that link texts.

REFLECTIONS AND FUTURE DIRECTIONS

Since this chapter was originally written, two motivational issues have come to prominence. We briefly sketch them as a starting point for new research and classroom action.

Spanish-Speaking Readers

I know I can read most of the words; I can also read long words. But I still forget what the sentence means when I finish the paragraph. If I have to answer questions from my teacher I forget even more! I really liked it when I got to answer my own and my buddy's questions and when the questions made me think not just remembering
—MIGUEL, grade 4.

Miguel is an English learner (EL). He speaks Spanish at home and English with his friends at school. While the languages spoken by EL students are diverse, Spanish is spoken by 71% of the EL population in the United States (Ruiz Soto, Hooker, & Batalova, 2015). However, ELs are an underserved group, one that is vulnerable and struggling significantly with academics, especially with reading comprehension (Taboada Barber, 2016).

ELs' struggles with reading comprehension are not limited to the cognitive system alone. In fact, ELs' cognitive challenges with comprehension are closely intertwined with their motivations for reading. Although many of the motivations described in this chapter apply to ELs, two of them have been identified as particularly salient in these students: self-efficacy for reading and student interest (Taboada Barber et al., 2015). Why these two? Research studies in upper elementary and middle school classrooms tell us that the challenges ELs face with reading content area (mostly expository texts, but also narratives) is compounded by the academic language they found in these texts. That is, the language encountered in school texts presents a steep learning curve for Spanish-speaking ELs, who, in their majority, acquire conversational English relatively quickly, but consistently struggle with the language structures of academic English in texts.

It is a disservice to these students to make them wait until they are fluent English speakers to teach them subject matter or the comprehension skills that can lead to deep text understanding—and the pacing of school curricula cannot afford that either! Yet their limited content background knowledge and sparse academic language preclude their development of self-confidence. That is, their competence beliefs as readers are low, or weak at best. Taking the case of Miguel, he perceives the reading task as word decoding mostly; he is aware that he can decode words, but he is also quite aware that he does not have the skills to make meaning out of text: How can he remember what the paragraph is about if he struggles with sentence-level comprehension?

How can ELs like Miguel feel competent about his reading when his text understanding fails when faced with teacher questions? Miguel's perception of his strengths as a reader is fractured, his beliefs in his reading are broken. He needs help with understanding reading as a process, and specifically with establishing process goals that will allow him to break down the process of comprehension into manageable parts—such as the student text questioning that he appears to enjoy so much. Being taught how to formulate student-led text-based questions can help children like Miguel with the syntax of question forms as well as with the enthusiasm and ensuing competence that comes from searching out answers to those questions. If students like Miguel are to be nurtured in their self-efficacy for reading, they must understand the steps needed to perform comprehension tasks successfully. They need to see comprehension as a goal that they can manage and achieve. In working toward their comprehension goals, students benefit from becoming aware of their successes and learning to set realistic next steps for themselves, as described previously in the section "Success."

Experiencing relevance is particularly valuable for Spanish-speaking

ELs. The practice of fostering relevance is in direct relation to nurturing students' interests, or intrinsic motivation for reading. The use of real-world materials and the use of poignant topics, as discussed earlier, are key ways to facilitate students' interests, irrespective of their language or cultural backgrounds. But fostering relevance as a motivational practice requires nuance for EL students. Precisely because ELs are used to very direct, explicit instruction (e.g., language-explicit instruction to meet English proficiency goals), they tend to be less exposed than their monolingual peers to the affordances of autonomy-supportive instruction. Establishing relevance, such as providing explanations on how a topic relates to students' lives, or seeking to meet students' interests through a variety of texts, is an autonomy-supportive practice (Assor, Kaplan, & Roth, 2002). Yet, autonomous supportive experiences are not common-place practices in the school experiences of many ELs (Taboada, Kidd, & Tonks, 2010; Taboada Barber & Buehl, 2013). When asked about why answering his own questions was enjoyable for Miguel, he blurted out with a smile: "Because I got to ask what I wanted to ask! And read what I wanted to read to find an answer. I liked that!" In sum, similar relevance-affording practices used for English monolingual students can be used for ELs—the difference may lie in the fact that ELs may respond to these practices with unusual motivations and enthusiasm for reading because practices such as nurturing reading self-efficacy and student interests are foreign to many of them. Often these are not seen as a priority in academic-language-packed curricula. Absent motivation practices such as fostering relevance and competence, ELs could meet content and language standards but they would do so barely, and most likely deprived of opportunities to engage with reading that ought to be afforded to every student, especially to those who struggle with reading the most.

Digital Literacy Motivation

Most teachers and students carry a super computer in their pockets. Reading and writing on a smart phone is the new literacy. What are the motivations for this rising tide of digital literacy? Here we are referring to digital literacy as reading and writing online, although others have given fuller descriptions. (Leu, Kinzer, Coiro, Castek, & Henry, 2013). Briefly, we mention the known similarities, differences, and mysteries of print and digital literacy motivations.

Most of what you read in this chapter applies to digital literacy. Motivation counts. Two key motivations of self-efficacy and interest have been shown in research to drive digital reading achievement. More highly motivated students not only attain higher digital literacy proficiency but they grow faster. There is an upward spiral because not only does motivation ignite achievement, but accomplishment spurs motivation gains. Motivation has another effect. It also creates digital engagement—the doing, persisting, and sustaining of digital interaction. As teachers are aware, doing leads to success. Avid readers are the achievers in digital as well as print literacy.

A surprise for some is that social media—Facebook, Instagram, and more—are a drag on literacy achievement. A negative correlation between using social media and proficiency in the full range of complex digital skills is the reality. Not all digital literacy produces achievement, and some literacy practices are detrimental (Naumann, 2015). However, this is not unique because the old-world practice of reading comic books is negatively correlated with achievement. High amounts of low-level text interaction goes together with lower achievement, whether they are print or digital.

Not many motivations have been systematically investigated in digital literacy. Only the fundamentals of self-efficacy (self-confidence as a reader) and intrinsic motivation (enjoying reading for its own sake) have been shown to be important for digital comprehension (Shang, 2016) and engagement (Lee & Wu, 2012). A wealth of other motivations such as belonging, mastery goals, identity, valuing, prosocial tendencies, effort beliefs, and frames of mind are waiting to be explored by digital literacy researchers. In addition, online dispositions such as reflection, critical stance, persistence, and collaboration have been identified, but their contributions to achievement have not been established (O'Byrne & McVerry, 2009). It is nearly certain that deep ethnographic inquiries and sensitive qualitative research will yield insights into powerful dispositions for interacting with digital sources.

A unique aspect of digital literacy is that the computer can follow your processes during the act of reading. A person's clicks, time spent on pages, sequences of selections, evaluations of text, and frequency of getting lost can easily be captured by the computer. When these are melded into indicators of engagement, a person's digital engagement can be collected and connected to success or failure. It's already known that computer measures of engagement during reading, consisting mostly of counting the number of relevant pages selected and read in an Internet literacy task, can forecast success in deep digital comprehension (Lee & Wu, 2012; Naumann, 2015).

What we see online is more complex than print. Beyond paragraphs and pictures, animated diagrams, video, audio, emogies, and nonlinguistic games are part of our daily digital panorama. Because they elicit novel ways of seeing, understanding, and connecting ideas, these diverse modes will likely involve diverse motivations. Yet research has not discovered or documented what they are.

We can expect that digital motivations will be strong. Our basic needs for being capable (competency), feeling free (autonomous), and staying connected (relatedness) will be more fulfilled in a digital world than in a print environment. Such need support derives from the fact that during online literacy activities we can select texts at our level, choose from a wide variety of materials, and share reactions socially more readily than in print. This empowerment likely works to expand the best and the worst parts of ourselves. For some individuals, heightened digital literacy motivations will generate more knowledge of biology, history, and community. For other individuals, the digital motivations will increase time spent playing games, boasting, bullying, or exercising other primitive tendencies.

Digital literacy will amplify who we are. In this light, it is vital for teachers to emphatically encourage students to interact digitally with authentic literature, breakthroughs in science, innovations in technology, and stories from multiple cultures. It is equally crucial for teachers to dramatically discourage the digital literacy actions that demean people, destroy worthy beliefs, or misinform others. Time on social media is enjoyable, but should not subtract significantly from substantive learning and creating. To foster growth of healthy digital literacy practices, teachers will want to promote students' constructive rather than destructive uses of this powerful tool.

Every teacher is a motivator. Teachers empower students to become active with print. Otherwise reading never happens. At the same time, motivating students to their fullest is rare. When students become interested, confident, and dedicated, almost every teacher is rewarded.

ENGAGEMENT ACTIVITIES

1. **Reflection.** To grapple with the ideas in this chapter, first make an appraisal of where you are. Many teachers support motivation—some more than others. Where are you? For each motivational practice, such as providing relevance, ask the following questions. You might do it alone or in a grade-level school team. Take a few notes on each question and share your perceptions. You can almost certainly take steps forward, especially if you do so with your colleagues.

   a. Do I do this practice already?
   b. How often do I do this?
   c. When do I do this?
   d. How well does it work?
   e. How can I do this more?
   f. How can I do this better?
   g. How can I connect this practice to my teaching more deeply?

REFERENCES

Assor, A., Kaplan, H., & Roth, G. (2002). Choice is good, but relevance is excellent: Autonomy-enhancing and suppressing teacher behaviors predicting students' engagement in schoolwork. *British Journal of Educational Psychology, 72,* 261–278.

Bean, T. W., & Harper, H. J. (2006). Exploring notions of freedom in and through young adult literature. *Journal of Adolescent and Adult Literacy, 50,* 96–104.

Brozo, W. G. (2002). *To be a boy, to be a reader: Engaging teen and preteen boys in active literacy.* Newark, DE: International Reading Association.

Chinn, C. A., Anderson, R. C., & Waggoner, M. A. (2001). Patterns of discourse in two kinds of literature discussion. *Reading Research Quarterly, 36,* 378–411.

Christensen, S., Reschly, A., & Wylie, C. (Eds.). (2012). *Handbook of research on student engagement* (pp. 601–634). New York: Springer Science.

Cordova, D. I., & Lepper, M. R. (1996). Intrinsic motivation and the process of learning: Beneficial effects of contextualization, personalization, and choice. *Journal of Educational Psychology, 88,* 715–730.

Darvin, J. (2006). "Real-world cognition doesn't end when the bell rings": Literacy instruction derived from situated cognition research. *Journal of Adolescent and Adult Literacy, 49,* 10–18.

Duke, N. K., Purcell-Gates, V., Hall, L. A., & Tower, C. (2006). Authentic literacy activities for developing comprehension and writing. *The Reading Teacher, 60,* 344–355.

Guthrie, J. T., & Humenick, N. M. (2004) Motivating students to read: Evidence for classroom practices that increase reading motivation and achievement. In P. McCardle & V. Chhabra (Eds.), *The voice of evidence in reading research* (pp. 329–354). Baltimore: Brookes.

Guthrie, J. T., Klauda, S. L., & Morrison, D. A. (2012). Motivation, achievement, and classroom contexts for information book reading. In J. T. Guthrie, A. Wigfield, & S. L. Klauda, *Adolescents' engagement in academic literacy* (pp. 1–51). Retrieved from *http://cori.umd.edu.*

Guthrie, J. T., Klauda, S. L., & Ho, A. (2013). Modeling the relationships among reading instruction, motivation, engagement, and achievement for adolescents. *Reading Research Quarterly, 48,* 9–26.

Guthrie, J. T., McRae, A., & Klauda, S. L. (2007). Contributions of concept-oriented reading instruction to knowledge about interventions for motivations in reading. *Educational Psychologist, 42,* 237–250.

Guthrie, J. T., Wigfield, A., & You, W. (2012). Instructional contexts for engagement and achievement in reading. In S. Christensen, A. Reschly, & C. Wylie (Eds.), *Handbook of research on student engagement* (pp. 601–634). New York: Springer Science.

Johnson, A. S., & Cowles, L. (2009). Orlonia's "literacy-in-persons": Expanding notions of literacy through biography and history, *Journal of Adolescent and Adult Literacy, 52,* 410–420.

Lee, Y., & Wu, J. (2012). The effect of individual differences in the inner and outer states of ICT on engagement in online reading activities and PISA

2009 reading literacy: Exploring the relationship between the one and new reading literacy. *Learning and Individual Differences, 22,* 336–342.

Leu, D. J., Kinzer, C. K., Coiro, J., Castek, J., & Henry, L. A. (2013). New literacies: A dual-level theory of the changing nature of literacy, instruction, and assessment. In D. E. Alvermann, N. J. Unrau, & R. B. Ruddell (Eds.), *Theoretical models and processes of reading* (6th ed., pp. 1150–1181). Newark, DE: International Reading Association.

Naumann, J. (2015). A model of online reading engagement: Linking engagement, navigation, and performance in digital reading. *Learning and Individual Differences, 53,* 263–277.

O'Byrne, W., & McVerry, J. (2009). Measuring the dispositions of online reading comprehension: A preliminary validation study. *National Reading Conference Yearbook, 58,* 362–375.

Reed, J. H., Schallert, D. L., Beth, A. D., & Woodruff, A. L. (2004). Motivated reader, engaged writer: The role of motivation in the literate acts of adolescents. In T. L. Jetton & J. A. Dole (Eds.), *Adolescent literacy research and practice* (pp. 251–282). New York: Guilford Press.

Reeve, J. (1996). *Motivating others: Nurturing inner motivational resources.* Boston: Allyn & Bacon.

Ruiz Soto, A. G., Hooker, S., & Batalova, J. (2015*). States and districts with the highest number and share of English language learners.* Washington, DC: Migration Policy Institute.

Ryan, R. M., & Deci, E. L. (2000). Self-determination theory and the facilitation of intrinsic motivation, social development, and well-being. *American Psychologist, 55,* 68–78.

Schiefele, U., Schaffner, E., Moller, J., & Wigfield, A. (2012). Dimensions of reading motivation and their relation to reading behavior and competence. *Reading Research Quarterly, 47,* 427–463.

Schunk, D. H., & Zimmerman, B. J. (2007). Influencing children's self-efficacy and self-regulation of reading and writing through modeling. *Reading and Writing Quarterly: Overcoming Learning Difficulties, 23,* 7–25.

Shang, H. F. (2016). Online metacognitive strategies, hypermedia annotations, and motivation on hypertext comprehension. *Educational Technology and Society, 19*(3), 321–334.

Skinner, E. A., Kindermann, T. A., & Furrer, C. J. (2009). A motivational perspective on engagement and disaffection: Conceptualization and assessment of children's behavioral and emotional participation in academic activities in the classroom. *Educational and Psychological Measurement, 69,* 493–525.

Taboada, A., Kidd, J. K., & Tonks, S. M. (2010). A qualitative look at English language learners' perceptions of autonomy support in a literacy classroom. *Research in the Schools, 17,* 39–53.

Taboada Barber, A. (2016). *Reading to learn for ELs: Motivation practices and comprehension strategies for informational texts.* Portsmouth, NH: Heinemann.

Taboada Barber, A., & Buehl, M. M. (2013). Relations among grade 4 students' perceptions of autonomy, engagement in science, and reading motivation. *Journal of Experimental Education, 81*(1), 22–43.

Taboada Barber, A., Buehl, M. M., Kidd, J., Sturtevant, E., Richey, L. N., & Beck, J. (2015). Reading engagement in social studies: Exploring the role of a social studies literacy intervention on reading comprehension, reading self-efficacy, and engagement in middle school students with different language backgrounds. *Reading Psychology.* *36*(1), 31–85.

Teale, W. H., Zolt, N., Yokota, J., Glasswell, K., & Gambrell, L. (2007). Getting children in2books: Engagement in authentic reading, writing and thinking. *Phi Delta Kappan, 88*, 498–502.

Vansteenkiste, M., Lens, W., & Deci, E. L. (2006). Intrinsic versus extrinsic goal contents in self-determination theory: Another look at the quality of academic motivation. *Educational Psychologist, 41,* 19–31.

Wiesel, E. (1960). *Night.* New York: Bantam Books.

Wigfield, A., & Guthrie, J. T. (1997). Relations of children's motivation for reading to the amount and breadth or their reading. *Journal of Educational Psychology, 89,* 420–432.

Xiaodong, L., Dweck, C., & Cohen, G. (2016). Instructional interventions that motivate classroom learning. *Journal of Educational Psychology, 108,* 295–299.

PART II

BEST PRACTICES
FOR ALL STUDENTS

CHAPTER 4

Best Practices in Early Literacy

Preschool, Kindergarten, and First Grade

LESLEY MANDEL MORROW
SUSAN M. DOUGHERTY
DIANE H. TRACEY

This chapter will:

- Provide an overview of the primary theories underlying best practices in early literacy education.

- Present a brief summary of the major governmental initiatives, including the English Language Arts Common Core Standards, that have significantly affected early literacy education in the United States.

- Offer a research synthesis and research-based instructional strategies related to early literacy best practices.

- Examine special issues related to early literacy instruction including digital literacies, dual language learners, and response to intervention.

- Suggest an approach to developing a classroom community that supports motivation for literacy learning and prompts the development of an "I can do this" mindset.

- Illustrate best practices in early literacy through the presentation of a case study.

EVIDENCE-BASED BEST PRACTICES:
A RESEARCH SYNTHESIS

There has been much controversy regarding best practices for early literacy instruction. At times, the idea that young children's education should be child-centered has been a dominant theme. At other times, ensuring that young children's education addresses specific skills and content has been emphasized. Teachers wonder if their methods should be formal and explicit, or play- and discovery-oriented. They wonder how to make optimal use of technology in early childhood classrooms. They want to know how to best help children who are learning English as an additional language and others for whom literacy learning seems unusually challenging. More recently, early childhood educators have renewed their focus on the best ways to help children develop a positive mindset toward learning and school. They think about ways to build children's recognition that they can overcome learning challenges. To support our readers' thinking about these issues, we share theory, policy, and research that have helped to shape best practices in early literacy education. Then, we conclude with a case study of an exemplary early childhood classroom and ideas for engagement activities.

Best Practices: Theoretical Influences

Historically, many theorists have addressed early childhood learning from child-centered theoretical perspectives. Child-centered approaches suggest that it is best to provide children with motivating opportunities that stimulate exploration in playful environments. Rousseau (1712–1778) believed that children's learning evolved naturally as a result of their innate curiosity. Pestalozzi (1746–1827) also believed in natural learning, but felt that children needed adult facilitation to enhance their development.

Froebel (1782–1852) emphasized the importance of play as a vehicle for learning, and coined the term "kindergarten," which literally means "children's garden." Piaget emphasized the idea that children acquire knowledge by interacting with objects and experiences and, subsequently, change and reorganize their knowledge in response (Piaget & Inhelder, 1969). Dewey's (1916) philosophy of early childhood education led to the concept of a child-centered curriculum built around the interests of children and a problem-based learning approach.

In contrast to child-centered theoretical approaches, Vygotsky (1978, 1986) put forth the theory of social constructivism. Vygotsky recognized that children learn as a result of their social interactions with others. He particularly emphasized the idea that children learn from interacting with others who are more developed than they are—linguistically, cognitively, socially, and emotionally.

Skills-based instructional models involve the systematic explicit teaching of literacy. Skills-based instruction has its roots in *behaviorism*, which suggests that complex cognitive activities, such as reading and writing, can be broken down into their composite skills that are taught one at a time (Tracey & Morrow, 2012). Direct reading instruction is a skills-based approach. In direct instruction, teachers explicitly focus students' attention on specific reading skills and provide information to students about those topics.

The term "emergent literacy" refers to the period in a child's life between birth and when the child can read and write conventionally, usually at about the third-grade level. In emergent literacy theory, literacy is viewed as beginning at birth and growing through authentic learning experiences at home and in school. Emergent literacy theory is based on the beliefs that children's development in the areas of listening, speaking, reading, and writing are all interrelated, and that the strengthening of any one of these four areas will have positive effects on the others.

Best Practices: Policy Influences

In addition to theoretical influences, governmental policies have shaped early literacy instructional practices. In 1965, President Johnson authorized the first federal policy directed at preschool education by creating Head Start. The goal of the initiative was to prepare low-income children for kindergarten. The program is still in operation today and grants are made directly to public and private nonprofit Head Start organizations.

Consistent with a child-centered model of early literacy education, Head Start services address children's cognitive, physical, emotional, and social needs. Initially, Head Start was mostly focused on the emotional and social needs of the child. But research has demonstrated that even very young children can be and should be engaged in learning appropriate literacy skills in Pre-K. Therefore, Head Start and other Pre-K programs have embedded literacy learning in Pre-K.

In 1997, Congress requested that the National Institute of Child Health and Human Development (NICHD) establish the National Reading Panel (NRP) to determine the most effective practices for teaching reading. Made up of a group of distinguished scholars, the panel reviewed scientifically based reading research and then published *The National Reading Panel Report: Teaching Children to Read* (NICHD, 2000). From the research, five key areas were identified as essential for effective reading instruction: phonemic awareness, phonics, vocabulary, comprehension, and fluency.

The five key areas identified by the NRP then became central to the Reading First and Early Reading First initiatives. These programs provided competitively based, large grants to at-risk school districts that revised their language arts curricula to address the five key areas identified by the NRP.

Another influential policy group has been the National Early Literacy Panel (NELP). The NELP was charged with conducting a synthesis of the scientific research specifically related to early literacy development from birth through kindergarten. The variables identified as essential to early literacy success include (1) expressive and receptive oral language development, (2) knowledge of the alphabetic code, (3) phonological and phonemic awareness, (4) use of invented spelling, (5) print knowledge including environmental print, and (6) other skills such as rapid naming of letters and numbers, visual memory, and visual perceptual abilities (NELP, 2010).

Since the 1990s, teaching at all levels has been influenced by the creation of standards, that outline what children at various grade levels are expected to know and to be able to do. Initially, these efforts were conducted within states, resulting in somewhat different expectations for students across the United States. In 2009, educators were introduced to the Common Core State Standards (CCSS), which were developed by several national groups, including the National Governor's Association. These new standards and the standardized tests created alongside them affected how the English language arts were taught. Today, following criticism and controversy, many states have returned to state-level standards; however, the influence of the CCSS remains evident. Kindergarten and first- and second-grade learning expectations are included in these standards; preschool standards are often also developed by states.

Best Practices: Research Influences

Theoretical frameworks and research suggest that there is no single method or approach to teaching language arts that is universally effective with all young children. In contrast, teachers need to possess a broad repertoire of theories and instructional strategies, and draw from this repertoire to address students' varied learning needs.

Literacy must be emphasized throughout the school day. Children who do not become fluent grade-level readers by the end of the third-grade level face great challenges as they attempt to meet academic expectations throughout the rest of their school years.

Building a Supportive and Positive Mindset in the Classroom

Before thinking about *what* to teach, it is important to consider the environment within which learning will take place. Classroom environments that encourage children to take risks and overcome challenges are vital to development. The goal should be to develop a context in which the teacher and children collaborate, help each other, and share a warm and supportive relationship. The way in which teachers interact with students affects what they will learn—about themselves, about others, and about literacy.

The language teachers use with children and the manner in which it is delivered will set the tone of the classroom. First, we encourage educators to be aware that tone of voice is very important. The same statement can feel like positive reinforcement or sarcasm. For example, "Wow, you chose a great book there!" can make a child feel good or bad about the book chosen, depending on how it is said. Sarcasm and criticism are hurtful, especially for young children, and therefore should always be avoided. It is also important that teachers focus on what children are saying and doing, despite the many demands for their attention. Positive reinforcement of desired behaviors and redirection of off-task or undesired behaviors is much more effective and creates a much more pleasant environment than negative reinforcement. Although currently very popular, techniques that make children's behavior public (e.g., red-, yellow-, and green-light behavior charts) often do more harm than good.

Language that positively reinforces desired behaviors is best when focused on the class as a group, rather than calling out specific children. For example, rather than saying, "I love how Tiffany and Damon have cleaned up," say, "Many of you are remembering the rules about cleaning up the literacy stations." Similarly, use language that specifically points out the desired behaviors. For example, instead of saying, "Good job," name the task: "You did a really good job of cleaning up the stations today." Asking questions that prompt children to think about the effects of particular behaviors provides them with a feeling of ownership and pride. For example, you might say, "The library corner looks great. I see that you remembered to put books back neatly where they belong. Why is this important?"

As you interact with children for instructional purposes use techniques that give all children a voice and an opportunity to participate. When you ask a question be sure to employ sufficient wait time (approximately 5 seconds) before selecting a student to answer. Doing so allows for greater participation and provides children with an opportunity to think before answering. Also, avoid asking questions that reward only children who have knowledge of something that you haven't yet taught.

For example, don't begin a study of the rain forest by asking, "What do we call a forest that is very warm and wet?" This question may be appropriate on day 3 or 4 of learning about rain forests, but not on day 1. When you ask a question that has a specific answer, be sure to provide verbal reinforcement that explains why the response is correct; don't simply repeat the correct answer. Use words that extend the child's answer when appropriate.

Remember that we want to balance our use of teacher-directed discussions with opportunities for children to talk and explain their thinking without trying to supply a specific "correct" answer. For example, after watching a video clip of a species of monkey that lives in the rain forest, you might ask the children to think about how the animal uses different body parts to help it move around from tree to tree. Give the children a chance to talk to one another about the parts of a monkey's body that help it move well in the trees (e.g., "Turn to a friend and tell her what you notice . . . ").

Afterward, you might return to a whole-class discussion, during which you would ask children to share their discussions. For example, you might say, "As you were talking, I heard several groups talking about the monkey's tail. José, can you tell everyone what you and Michael were saying about how the monkey was using its tail?"

Children in early childhood classrooms should often be engaged in small-group or individual activities, which means that the teacher will need techniques for getting attention in a busy, noisy classroom. It will likely be useful to develop a repertoire of attention-getting techniques. Having several techniques will allow you to switch to a new method if one used previously is no longer effective. A few of the attention-getting techniques that we've observed teachers use include:

- Ringing a bell
- Using a clapping rhythm
- Using a catchy phrase such as "Hocus, Pocus, it's time to focus" or "1, 2, 3, eyes on me" (to which children respond "1, 2, eyes on you.')
- Holding up a hand with fingers extended and putting one finger down at a time during a count down from 5.

Recently, the work of psychologist Carol Dweck (2006), who wrote the influential book *Mindset,* has influenced thinking about the qualities of learning environments that most benefit young learners. The teaching of skills and the modeling of learning strategies, while essential, should be accompanied by messages that help children develop a mindset of "I can succeed." We want young children to view learning through a lens of growth through effort (e.g., working hard to overcome challenges), rather than what is called a "fixed mindset" (e.g., believing that people are either naturally good or bad at something). As teachers, we can use language that helps children adopt a *growth mindset*. We can explicitly talk about responses to tasks that are hard and encourage children to "keep trying" and to notice their improvements over time (Pawlina & Stanford, 2011).

Examples of language that will promote a "growth mindset" include:

- "I was watching you gather all of the materials for your report on the yellow-eyed tree frog. You worked hard to find books and to find pictures online. What do you think will be the hardest part about writing the report? What will be the easiest part?"
- "Last week you remembered how to make the first letter in your name. Today you remembered how to make the first three letters! Pretty soon you are going to be able to write all five letters."
- "I knew you could beat yesterday's time for sitting and looking at your book. You are within reach of your goal."
- "I noticed that you haven't finished your project yet and see that you are pretty frustrated. Can you tell me what is hard? Can we come up with some things you could do to help you get going again?"

During literacy instruction, teachers can simultaneously work toward building growth mindset and developing students' strategies—for decoding new words, for comprehending, for learning new vocabulary, and for writing. This can be accomplished by talking directly about the challenges students face during literacy-related tasks and by encouraging students to talk about how they approached various challenges and then overcame them. For example, the popular CAFE system focuses on the development of strategies for four domains of literacy: comprehension, accuracy, fluency, and expanding vocabulary (Boushey & Moser. 2009). Within accuracy, students are taught a range of strategies for decoding words they don't automatically recognize. As teachers share each of the strategies with young readers and provide them with opportunities to practice using them, they can also talk directly about the challenges posed by new "big" words in texts and invite students to decide which strategies work best for them and how they used these strategies with success. At the end of a guided reading lesson, a teacher might say, "Emily, I noticed that you figured out the word *careful* after a few tries. I was so glad you kept at it and didn't give up. A few months ago, I think you would have stopped after one try. Do you agree? Can you tell us what strategy you used to figure out the word *careful*?" By both focusing on the strategies used for decoding and on the students' increasing confidence and willingness to employ strategies, the teacher encourages a growth mindset among her young readers.

When classroom environments are supportive and encourage risk taking and when teachers help children acquire a growth mindset, opportunities to learn literacy skills and strategies are maximized.

Comprehension of Fictional Text

A primary goal of an early literacy education is to help young children comprehend and enjoy stories. Comprehension and enjoyment are facilitated when teachers engage their students in prereading, during reading, and postreading activities. Prior to reading a story to children, prereading activities build youngsters' background knowledge and strengthen understanding of new vocabulary; as a result, text comprehension is improved (van Kleek, 2008). A "picture walk" is an example of an effective prereading activity. During picture walks, children and teachers talk about the pictures in the book prior to reading it. This activity helps prepare the students' minds for the upcoming text, thus enhancing story comprehension. The picture walk, or other prereading activities, should be very short and not give too much of the story away; otherwise children often will be tired before they start to read.

During a read-aloud of a fictional story with young children, the teacher can model the thinking of a skilled reader by commenting at pivotal points (Dickinson & Smith, 1994; McGee & Schickedanz, 2007). Teacher comments demonstrate for young children the kind of thinking readers do about characters' motivations and connecting them to events; the comments also support comprehension of the plot as it unfolds. For example, when reading *Strega Nona* (dePaola, 1975) aloud to a group of kindergarteners, the teacher might pause when reaching the point in the text at which Strega Nona leaves Big Anthony on his own for a few days with the admonition not to touch the pasta pot.

The teacher might say, "I know Big Anthony really wants to prove to everyone that Strega Nona has a magic pasta pot and I see in this illustration that he is thinking about the pasta pot right now. I am thinking that he might not keep his promise not to touch the pot." A few strategically placed comments during a read-aloud support young children as they begin to acquire the ability to comprehend. It is important to remember that the comments should focus on pivotal moments within the story. The reader should not interrupt the story too frequently; it is important to keep the story flowing so that children pay attention to and connect the events of the story.

After reading, students benefit from experiences that help them to deepen and extend their comprehension of the text. For fictional texts, story retelling, with or without storytelling props, helps children to connect the main events of the narrative (Curenton, 2011; Morrow, 2009). Discussions that focus on open-ended questions also serve to consolidate children's understanding of a fictional text (McGee & Schickedanz, 2007).

Comprehension of Informational Text

In addition to the ability to comprehend and enjoy narrative text, young students' ability to comprehend and enjoy informational text is an important component of their early literacy development. Books about science, social studies, music, art and procedural (how-to) texts are included in the category of informational text.

Research has demonstrated that PreK and kindergarten children are able to learn content from informational texts, learn about different types of informational texts, and learn about how informational texts are organized (Duke, Bennett-Armistead, & Roberts, 2003). Duke, Halladay, and Roberts (2013) recommend that informational texts be used throughout the day in early childhood classrooms. They note that these texts are ideal for whole-class read-alouds, small-group guided reading lessons, independent reading, and as supplements to content-area lessons. Duke, Halladay, and Roberts suggest that classroom teachers provide students with topic choices of the informational texts, and pay close attention to the difficulty level of the texts used in lessons. These researchers also remind classroom teachers to carefully craft the questions they ask young students during discussions of informational texts. Because informational texts for young children often contain photographs or illustrations that work alongside the words to explain concepts, teachers can demonstrate how a reader uses all these sources of information during reading by making comments and asking questions. Questions teachers might ask include (1) "What can we learn from this picture that the words did not tell us?"; (2) "Why did the author/illustrator choose to put this picture here?"; (3) "How does this picture help us understand the words better?"; and (4) "What pictures could be added to help explain the words I just read?" (Duke, Halladay, & Roberts, 2013, pp. 55–56).

Guthrie (2004) has spent a great deal of his professional life researching how to engage and motivate students, especially in the use of informational text. He has developed a framework called concept-oriented reading instruction (CORI). CORI has five central features: (1) theme-based instruction, (2) an emphasis on student choice for both what is read and how to respond to it, (3) the use of hands-on activities for responding to readings, (4) the availability of a wide variety of text genres at different reading levels chosen to interest students, and (5) the integration of social collaboration into reading response activities. Research on the effects of

CORI showed increased motivation for reading, increased use of meta-cognitive skills, and increased gains in conceptual knowledge among elementary grade students (Tracey & Morrow, 2012). Given the features of CORI, we believe it can effectively be applied in early childhood class-rooms.

In fact, Patrick, Mantzicopoulos, and Samarapungavan (2009) describe the outcomes of using Scientific Literacy Projects (SLP), which incorporate many of the elements also seen in CORI, with children in kin-dergarten. They found that using thematic, inquiry-based units that also incorporate literacy activities such as writing and recording in science notebooks and interactive read-alouds of science tradebooks resulted in greater motivation for science learning. Particularly notable was the increased enthusiasm for science learning among kindergarten girls when compared to children not engaged in the SLP units.

Word Study

During the early childhood years, young children learn an array of skills that lead to success in reading the vast majority of printed words by the elementary grade years. In this section we address print concepts, phono-logical/phonemic awareness, phonics, high frequency words, and fluency.

"Print concepts" is a term used to capture the ways in which print works in a particular language. Print concepts include (1) the relationship between spoken and written language; (2) concepts of words, letters, and sounds; and (3) the directionality of print (in English, left to right and top to bottom). Children learn print concepts through being exposed to books and writing and through explicit instruction (Gehsmann & Tem-pleton, 2013).

Phonological awareness refers to the ability to recognize various-sized units of sound within spoken language. These units of sound include whole words, syllables, and individual sounds (phonemes). The ability to recognize individual sounds is so important to early literacy learning that it has been given a special name. "Phonemic awareness" refers to the abil-ity to hear and manipulate phonemes—the smallest units of sounds in the English language. Both phonological and phonemic awareness are solely auditory processes; young children can become aware of units of sound without knowledge of what symbols (letters) might be used to rep-resent them in print. Research has demonstrated that phonemic aware-ness is linked to success in early reading (Cardoso-Martins & Pennington, 2004). Presenting young children with rhyming texts and oral activities that require them to substitute sounds, blend sounds to form words, and segment words help children to learn phonemic awareness (Yopp & Yopp, 2000).

Phonics, the ability to correctly associate letters with their corresponding sounds, is an essential word recognition skill for young children (Shaywitz et al., 2004). Of course, the ability to correctly associate letters with their corresponding sounds (phonics) is dependent on the subskills of (1) letter recognition and (2) knowing the sounds that letters can represent. In other words, a young child learns to recognize the letter *B* (and differentiate its form from other, similar looking letters) and learns that the letter *B* is often used to represent the /b/ sound. Later, children will learn common letter combinations for representing common larger sound segments (e.g. the letters *–ight* are sometimes used to represent the /īt/ heard in words such as *light* and *right*). An early phonics activity might involve having children sort pictures or small items based on their initial, medial, or final *letter* (e.g. "Put all the objects that begin with the letter *B* in the blue basket and all the objects that begin with the letter *P* in the purple basket). If young students are having difficulty mastering phonics, it is important to determine if their weakness is a consequence of a visual (letter recognition) deficit, an auditory (phonological-processing) deficit, or both, and to intervene accordingly.

Another essential word recognition skill is the ability to recognize the most frequently seen words by "sight" (Gehsmann & Templeton, 2013). These words are often referred to as "sight words" and the goal is for children to automatically identify them without having to engage in "sounding out." Words that occur with great frequency in the English language (e.g., *the, is. was*) are the focus of attention in classroom materials such as the morning message or big books. *The Reading Teacher's Book of Lists* (Kress & Fry, 2015) is an excellent resource for lists of high-frequency words and sight-word activities. It is useful to also point out that any word a reader recognizes instantly can be called a sight word and that words such as child's first name, words related to thematic study, and other words that are personally meaningful to a child might become sight words.

Children learn the relationships between letters and their corresponding sounds and between printed and spoken words through a process of creating neural connections in their brains between these items (Adams, 1990; Kuhn, Schwanenflugel, Meisinger, Levy, & Rasinski, 2010). These connections become stronger and faster with practice, eventually contributing to automatic and fluent word recognition. Since young readers build their bank of words recognized automatically by developing neural connections that connect written words to their pronunciations and because these connections become stronger and faster with practice, one of the most effective approaches to teaching word identification is through the use of word families (e.g., the *"at"* family, the *"in"* family, the *"et"* family). The use of word families strengthens the brain's ability to perceive these groups of letter as single chunks, eliminating the need for letter-by-letter reading, and strengthening automaticity and fluent reading. Again, *The Reading Teacher's Book of Lists* (Kress & Fry, 2015) is a great resource for creating word family activities.

Automatic word recognition is one component of fluency, which is the third foundational skill for young readers. "Fluency" is the term used to describe reading that sounds *natural*; it is smooth and appropriately paced and the reader reads individual words correctly and with ease. Fluency develops as a function of practice, often in the form of repeated readings. Activities ideal for promoting fluency are shared reading (teacher-led instruction typically with a big book), paired reading (students in homogeneous or heterogeneous pairs), choral reading (the teacher and students all read aloud at the same time), rereading (reading a text multiple times in order to develop fluency), and Readers' Theater (children are assigned parts in a play and reread to develop proficiency to present the play).

Writing

Since the 1970s, educators have included writing as an integral part of best practices in early literacy (Morrow, 2009). Writing ability begins in a child's first year of life and is developed through authentic learning activities. Young children begin writing when they make their first scribbles on a page. Later, scribbles become random letters, and next children engage in invented spelling—writing that reflects the relationships between sounds and letters but without concern for correct spelling or punctuation. Eventually, children's writing and spelling become conventional.

As with reading, writing development is best supported through authentic experiences. Examples of authentic activities include: writing notes and letters that are actually mailed (electronically or through the postal service), writing recipes that will be shared, writing in journals or creating blog posts that will be read and responded to, and writing stories and poetry that will be listened to by others. Writing instruction in the classroom includes the use of a writing center, and whole-class and small-group writing lessons in which teachers explicitly teach skills and mechanics.

Speaking and Listening

Children's oral language, both expressive (speaking) and receptive (listening) provides the foundation upon which their reading and writing skills are built (Gillam & Reutzel, 2013). Therefore, helping young children to develop their listening and speaking skills is one of the most important jobs of early childhood educators.

Children's speaking and listening skills are enhanced through experiences that provide language opportunities (Isbell, Sobol, Lindauer, & Lowrance, 2004). Gillam and Reutzel (2013) emphasize that teachers do not need to create isolated lessons to address children's listening and speaking skills in classrooms. Rather, Gillam and Reutzel advocate that teachers embed interactions that support language growth into storybook reading and content-based lessons by (1) encouraging children to always speak (and answer questions) in full sentences; (2) helping children learn conversational rules such as listening to each other, taking turns when speaking, staying on topic, and responding to others' comments; and (3) supporting students as they learn to fully describe their experiences, perceptions, and opinions on a wide variety of topics.

Vocabulary Development

Vocabulary development is a special area of importance for young children. We now recognize that children come to school with a wide range of vocabulary knowledge. In the early years, vocabulary is developed through exposure to oral language; in general, children who are exposed to lots of language input learn more words than children who hear less spoken language or a smaller range of words (Hart & Risley, 1995, 1999; Weizman & Snow, 2001). When adults use tactics to help children understand the meanings of new words (e.g., gestures, explanations), vocabulary learning is enhanced (Weizman & Snow, 2001).

Jalongo and Sobolak (2011) determined that in order to become proficient readers, children should know approximately 10,000 words by age six. According to Byrnes and Wasik (2009), this can be accomplished during the early childhood years if children learn approximately five to six new words per day, which equates to about 38 new words per week and approximately 2,000 new words per year.

Teachers help students learn vocabulary when they explain new words as they are encountered during storybook reading and content-area instruction (e.g., science, social studies, health.) There is a positive correlation between how often children listen to storybook read-alouds and the size of their vocabulary (Walsh & Blewitt, 2006). Often it takes more than simply hearing a word in a book to learn its meaning, however. When teachers read with expression, explain word meanings, ask open-ended questions, and model language expansion, vocabulary knowledge will grow (Beck & McKeown, 2001).

It is important to remember that repetition and deep explanation are essential to learning word meanings (Harris, Golinkof, & Hirsh-Pasek, 2009; Neuman & Wright, 2014). Children rarely learn the meaning of a new word through just one exposure to the word's meaning. Therefore, simply mentioning the meaning of a word while reading a story is not going to be enough for many of your students to learn and remember it.

Instead, you will want to find additional times to use the word and discuss its meaning. You might (1) explain the word's meaning in greater detail after reading aloud, (2) provide a synonym, (3) use the word as you talk about the story in a postreading discussion, (4) use the word again in a piece of classroom writing (e.g., the morning message), (5) present an illustration or a video that shows the word's meaning visually, (6) find ways to have the children use the word verbally (e.g., turn to a partner and talk about something you would be *cautious* around).

It's also true that children seem to be able to learn more word meanings when the words are linked by a theme or category (Pollard-Durodola, et al., 2011). Especially when you are targeting children's content vocabulary, you will want to select words that are connected by theme or topic (e.g., nature, transportation, animal body parts).

SPECIAL ISSUES IN EARLY LITERACY INSTRUCTION

In this section, we discuss best practices that relate to recent societal changes and newly acknowledged challenges. First, we respond to the increasing availability and influence of technological tools both in schools and in everyday life. Next, we explore emerging understandings about the education of young dual language learners. Finally, we describe how schools use the response to intervention (RTI) framework to structure interventions right from the start for students performing below expectations.

Digital Literacies in the Early Childhood Classroom

To be successful in the 21st century, young learners must become proficient in both traditional (print) and digital literacies (McKenna, Conradi, Young, & Jang, 2013). There are similarities between traditional and digital literacies. For example, both types of texts may have page numbers, a table of contents, headings, and an index. However, the differences between the two types of text may be greater than their similarities. While traditional text is almost always read from the top of the page to the bottom, and from the left to the right, digital texts are often navigated in a nonlinear manner as the reader clicks on links to move through a variety of pages and websites. Additionally, digital texts often contain hyperlinked resources such as on-demand pronunciations, dictionaries, audio texts, and video clips (McKenna et al., 2013). These additional resources, which can be considered scaffolds for learning, may be the reason that digital texts have been found to be at least as effective as traditional texts in supporting literacy achievement, and sometimes more so (Korat & Shamir, 2012; Moody, Justice, & Cabell, 2010; Tracey & Young, 2007).

McKenna et al. (2013) suggest three ways in which the interactions between young children and the use of technology in the classroom can be conceptualized and implemented. First, young children must learn to comprehend digital texts. Using an LCD projector, teachers can model how to read e-books, navigate websites, and engage in software activities. Virtual field trips can also be taken (McKenna et al., 2011). Second, young children can be taught to generate digital creations (drawn, spoken, and written). Third, young children must learn to use and navigate the unique scaffolds offered in digital environments such as hyperlinks. A digital morning message can be used as the means for introducing young children to these features (Labbo, 2011). Again, teacher modeling followed by students' paired and independent practice is the route to learning success.

Dual Language Learners in Early Childhood Classrooms

In early childhood classrooms it is critical to acknowledge the strengths and to address the needs of children whose primary language is a language other than English. Often these students have been referred to as "English language learners," but terminology is changing as we recognize that supporting the maintenance and continued development of language and literacy skills in the primary language has great benefits (Roberts, 2017). For this reason, the terms "emergent bilingual," which suggests the child is on a path to becoming fully bilingual, and "dual language learner," which suggests that the child is learning to use two languages at the same time, are replacing earlier terms.

We will use the term dual language learner (DLL), which has been adopted by Head Start and the National Association for the Education of Young Children. It is estimated that 40% of the United States' elementary and secondary school population by 2030 will be acquiring English alongside another language (Thomas & Collier, 2002), making it essential that teachers engage in best practices for supporting these students. The majority of young children from this group will be born in the United States, making it especially appropriate to use the term DLLs; they will be raised in home environments within which they are highly likely to have exposure to their family's primary language and English. Each child's level of exposure to the primary language and English will vary from a great deal to just a little, depending on a whole range of factors (e.g., length of time in the United States, language use in the surrounding community, sibling language use, exposure to English-language television).

While DLLs must master phonological awareness and word identification strategies just like their peers who are acquiring English only, *The
Report of the National Literacy Panel on Language and Minority Children and
Youth* (August & Shanahan, 2006) demonstrated that the greatest ongoing areas of instructional need for DLLs are "English vocabulary, English
proficiency, and other higher-level text processing skills" (Carlo & Bengochea, 2011, p. 118). Of particular importance to this group of students
is the mastery of academic vocabulary, those words that are needed to
complete school tasks such as "circle, underline, sentence, page, syllable,
paragraph, capitalize, and indent" (Carlo et al., 2004).

Early childhood educators working with DLLs might (1) include print
in the classroom in children's first languages, such as labels on objects;
(2) strategically pair students with stronger oral English communication
skills with students who need support in English communication; (3) provide daily, extensive, and explicit vocabulary instruction; (4) have children collect 'Very Own Word' (VOW) cards for new English vocabulary;
(5) use visuals and manipulatives to support instruction; and (6) engage
with family members and encourage them to teach primary language
vocabulary that connects to the topics/themes being taught in English in
school and to read storybooks and other texts in their primary language.

At-Risk Early Childhood Students and Response to Intervention

Despite the best efforts of educators, some students still struggle to master literacy skills. To respond, many school districts are implementing
RTI programs. RTI was created with the goal of reducing the need to clas-
sify students through early diagnosis and treatment of young children's
learning difficulties. Instead, the model of RTI is based on the idea that
some children require more focused, intensive instruction in order to
succeed. Therefore, RTI suggests that educational initiatives in schools
should be organized in three tiers. The first tier of instruction is offered
to all students in general education classrooms. This instruction is usually based on grade-level curriculum using grade-level texts; it involves all
types of grouping, with whole-class, small-group, and individual instruction occurring. For students who have difficulty mastering grade-level
concepts and texts within the grade-level curriculum, small-group, more
intensive instruction that addresses their needs is implemented. This
small-group instruction is the second tier of RTI and may occur within
the classroom or in a separate setting. Students who do not respond to
the intensified instruction offered in Tier 2 after an established period
of time will be offered Tier 3 support. The third tier is meant to be even
more intensive and focused on specific learning goals and is often conducted in a one-on-one situation. If Tier 3 instruction does not support

the student in reaching instructional goals, an evaluation to determine eligibility for special education services is conducted.

BEST PRACTICES IN ACTION

The Physical Environment

A classroom's physical environment sets the foundation for literacy learning. The classroom should be inviting, with well-defined centers around the room. Ideally, displays on the walls reflect a theme being studied and demonstrate evidence of the children's growing literacy development. In the whole-group area (a large carpeted space), there should be an interactive whiteboard for the morning message and other computer-based activities, a calendar, weather chart, helper chart, daily schedule, classroom rules, and a pocket chart for assembling cut-up words into sentences.

The literacy center should contain a rug for independent reading and multiple bookshelves for storing books. There should be baskets of books grouped by level of difficulty. Other shelves can hold baskets organized by topics and authors. Colored stickers on the books and baskets assist students in returning them to the correct spot. Books about the current theme can be placed on a special open-faced shelf, and rotated monthly as the class theme changes. Ideally, the literacy center has a flannel board and flannel board characters, puppets, and props for storytelling. There is a rocking chair for the teacher and other adults to read to the class. The listening area in the center can have a CD player for listening to stories and multiple headsets. There are manipulatives for learning about print. These include magnetic letters, puzzles, rhyme cards, and letter groups (e.g., word families) on small tiles for making words.

The writing center is an extension of the literacy center. There is a round table for children to meet with the teacher for guided writing instruction and individual conferencing. At least one computer should be a part of the writing center. The center offerings should include many types of paper, a stapler, markers, crayons, colored pencils, dictionaries, alphabet stamps, and ink stamp pads. The writing area should include a word wall that is divided into sections for each letter of the alphabet. When the children learn a new word, it is taped under its initial letter where it can be located for help in later spelling or to practice reading. Other classroom centers include science, math, dramatic play, and art.

Classroom Management and Affective Climate

Best practices in literacy instruction take place in classrooms that are well managed and in which children feel accepted and are motivated to take risks. Research consistently finds that student–teacher relationships play an important role in learning (Griggs, Gagnon, Huelsman, Kidder-Ashley, & Ballard, 2009; Jennings & DiPrete, 2010). Teachers who are warm, well organized, and set realistic expectations for student behavior are more likely to develop relationships with students that set the stage for learning.

Case Study

Kim Jackson has been teaching kindergarten for the past 7 years. She recently completed a master's degree with a reading specialist certification. She teaches in a working-class community and has 22 students of diverse backgrounds in her all-day kindergarten class. Ms. Jackson's philosophy of teaching includes integration of the curriculum so that students can build connections between content areas. She implements whole-class, small-group, and center-based instruction in her classroom. She focuses on explicit skills instruction embedded within meaningful, authentic contexts.

Center Management

Ms. Jackson uses daily center-based instruction. To ensure that students visit two specific centers a day, Ms. Jackson has designed a contract for her students. The contract has the name of each center and an icon representing the center.

These same labels and icons are visible at the actual centers. When children complete their center work, they check it off on their contracts. The completed work is placed in the basket labeled "Finished Work." After children complete their two assigned centers, they can work at any center they choose. At the end of each day, Ms. Jackson reviews the children's completed work. Any incomplete work, or work that indicates a child needs additional help with a concept, is placed in the "Unfinished" folder. There is a time during the next day for addressing these tasks. This system is consistent with Ms. Jackson's commitment to differentiate instruction based on her students' needs.

Assessing Students to Determine Instructional Needs

In order to provide instruction that meets the varied levels of her students, Ms. Jackson devotes time to assessment, using both formal and informal measures. In September, January, March, and June, Ms. Jackson assesses students' knowledge about print and book concepts, phonological and phonemic awareness, letter recognition, phonics, sight words, vocabulary, listening comprehension, and writing ability. As children begin to read conventionally, she takes monthly running records of each child's reading. Running records are used to record reading behaviors including the types of reading errors made, the word identification strategies used, and the students' reading comprehension ability. Ms. Jackson also takes anecdotal notes about her students' behaviors that indicate both progress and points of difficulty. She collects samples of children's writing, analyzes them, and places them in student portfolios. Ms. Jackson also monitors the students' social, emotional, and physical development.

Small-Group Reading Instruction

As stated above, in addition to whole-class lessons, Ms. Jackson works with small groups of children for reading instruction. With the assessment information she collects, she places students with similar levels of ability and need together. As she works with her students, she takes careful notes regarding literacy progress, and adjusts the group members as needed. Ms. Jackson presently has four small groups and meets with each group three times a week. If time permits, she will meet with students who need additional support to reach grade-level expectations for additional guided reading sessions.

A Typical Day in Kim Jackson's Classroom

Children Arrive at School (8:45 AM)

It is a Monday morning, and chatter begins to fill the classroom as Ms. Jackson's students arrive. Quiet music plays in the background as children complete their morning routines. Children move their nametags on the attendance board from the side labeled "Not Here" to "Here," and they place their name sticks into cans labeled with different lunchtime options (e.g., buying lunch, lunch from home).

DO NOW

So that children are engaged from the very beginning of the day Ms. Jackson has a daily *Do Now*. Students know they should move right into writing in their journals. Ms. Jackson circulates among the writers, reminding some children to use spaces between words and suggesting others use classroom tools such as the word wall for their spelling needs. As she listens to completed entries, she has the opportunity to chat with the children about their weekend activities. She also uses this time to engage in strategic conversations with her DLLs, asking them at times to tell her a vocabulary word in their primary language that relates to their journal entry. She might say, "You wrote that your aunt baked a cake for your mom's birthday. I don't think I know the word for cake in Spanish. Can you tell me?" When the 2-minute warning bell rings, the children begin to put away their writing journals and transition to the morning meeting on the carpet.

The Morning Meeting and Reading Comprehension Workshop (9:00 AM)

The weather and calendar are discussed very quickly. Using an interactive whiteboard, Ms. Jackson draws the students' attention to the text on the screen. Since it is the month of May, the students echo-read a poem called "May" from *Chicken Soup with Rice* (Sendak, 1962), and then individual students are invited to the board to locate target letters, sight words, and punctuation marks within the text. Ms. Jackson then distributes copies of the text to all of the children, and leads them in an activity in which they circle letters, sight words, and punctuation marks previously learned.

Continuing to use the whiteboard, Ms. Jackson draws her students' attention to a book related to the class monthly theme of animals, titled *Animals Should Definitely Not Wear Clothing* (Barrett, 1988). There is a copy for each child. The purpose of her lesson is for children to learn about making inferences while reading. Before beginning, Ms. Jackson gives some examples of making inferences in everyday life, saying "People are always thinking and sometimes you can figure out what is happening without someone telling you." She continues, "Once, when I got home from work, I saw that the muffins I'd left on the counter were gone. The container was on the floor and the dog, who usually runs to greet me seemed to be hiding behind a chair. Without anyone telling me, I knew that the dog had pulled down the muffins and had eaten them." She explains that this kind of thinking is called "making inferences." After giving a few examples of making inferences in everyday life, she explains that authors of books don't tell us everything and that readers always have to be making inferences too. She tells the class that she is going to read them a funny book and that as she reads it, they will notice that the author does not tell them why the things that happen in the book are funny. She explains that as they listen to the book, they will have to look at the pictures and think about the words to make inferences about why each is funny. Next, Ms. Jackson reads *Animals Should Definitely Not Wear Clothing* to the class. After the first reading, Ms. Jackson has the children echo-read each page with her and they laugh together at the silly pictures. After this second reading, Ms. Jackson points out that the author's words don't explain exactly what is funny and they have to "think about" why each animal wearing clothing is funny. She turns to the pages featuring a snake and the words "because a snake would lose it" and explains that as she reads those words, she also looks at the picture of the snake slithering out of a pair of pants. She explains that she "makes an inference" that it is funny that a snake would wear clothes because if a snake wore pants, they'd fall right off. Ms. Jackson asks the group if they remember any other funny things that happened when different animals tried to wear clothing. She turns to some of the pages the students suggest and encourages them to explain their inferences.

Next, Ms. Jackson asks students to work with their discussion partners to look through their copy of the book and make more inferences about why it is funny for each animal to wear clothing. Ms. Jackson walks around and listens to the conversations. The class then comes together as a whole and talks about the inferences they made. In future lessons, Ms. Jackson will focus on making inferences in additional texts, each time emphasizing that readers have to think about the words and illustrations to understand.

Because Ms. Jackson knows that the DLLs in her class will benefit from engaging with these concepts in their primary language, she sends home a Spanish-language version of *Animals Should Definitely Not Wear Clothing* (*Los animales no se visten;* Barrett, 2004) with the children in her class whose families are Spanish speakers. In her weekly newsletter for all families, she communicates about the thematic focus and shares the Bronx Zoo web address, encouraging all parents to engage in conversations with their children about the animals they encounter online.

Center Time (9:30–10:30 AM)

Ms. Jackson spends a few minutes reviewing the center activities. A description of what has been added to each center relating to the animal theme is below.

- *Writing Center*: Books about farm, rain forest and forest animals. Animal stickers, an animal dictionary, and paper to make animal books. Two computers are embedded that can be used either for composing or for revisiting the Bronx Zoo website.
- *Literacy Center*: Fiction and nonfiction animal books, animal books with accompanying CDs, an animal puzzle with word labels, an animal concentration memory game, and an animal lotto game.
- *Computer Center*: There is software for printing animal stationery, postcards, and animal masks, a website bookmarked for visiting the Museum of Natural History's animal exhibits and another linking to the PBS Kids *WildKratts* Creature Photoshoot game.
- *Science*: Pictures and small figures of desert, forest, and rain forest animals are available to promote discussion of the characteristics of these animals and why they live where they do. There are also animal cards to sort into desert, rain forest, and forest categories, and recording sheets for all activities.

- *Math*: Little plastic animals in an estimation jar are placed in the math center, with a sheet on which students can record their estimation. There is also a basket containing 50 little animals numbered from 1 to 50, the task being to put the animals into sequential order.
- *Blocks*: In addition to the regular blocks, there is an area called *the desert,* one called *the rain forest,* and one called *the forest.* Each has been decorated with plastic foliage and other items to represent its habitat. Toy animals of the appropriate type are placed in the desert, rain forest, or forest.
- *Art Center*: Animal stencils and animal stamps are added to the art center. There are pictures of desert, forest, and rain forest animals, and Play-Doh for children to make models of an animal of their choice.
- *Dramatic Play*: The dramatic play area is transformed into a veterinarian's office. There is a phone and calendar for taking appointments, paper and folders for the doctor's records, a stethoscope, and a prescription pad.

Small-Group Guided Reading Instruction (9:30–10:30 AM)

Small-group reading instruction and center time occur simultaneously, with Ms Jackson alternating between meeting with small groups and then spending a few minutes checking in with children at the centers. The first group with which Ms. Jackson meets is reviewing a book they have read before, *We Went to the Zoo* (Sloan & Sloan, 1994). Ms. Jackson provides a picture walk as the children look through each page and discuss what they see. During this book introduction, the students are asked to find the words *saw* and *many,* since these words caused some difficulty during the first reading. They also discuss the names of the animals in the book. As the group reads, Ms. Jackson notices that one student makes no errors in reading and finishes quickly. Ms. Jackson makes a note to possibly move this student to a more advanced guided-reading group. During guided reading, Ms. Jackson was able to complete a running record on one child. She noted that this student reads *seals* instead of *otters* and said "pander bears" instead of "bears." Ms. Jackson decides that she will help this child to pay more attention to the print as he reads. Ms. Jackson also calls two more small reading groups in the remaining time.

Snack and Play (10:30–10:45 AM)

By midmorning everyone needs a break. The children relax during snack and socialize with each other.

Writing Workshop (10:45–11:45 AM)

The children gather for writing in the whole-class meeting area. Using the whiteboard again, Ms. Jackson introduces the writing activity for the week. The children will be writing informational texts about an animal of their choice. Students have the option of working with a partner, which is particularly beneficial for the DLLs in the class. Ms. Jackson is supportive of students with the same primary language working together because she knows that opportunities to discuss ideas in their primary language actually supports their ability to write more sophisticated ideas in their English language products. The students are told to select an animal they like and brainstorm about their animals, including what the animal looks like, what it eats, and where it lives. The students produce writing reflective of different developmental levels; their pieces include pictures, scribble writing, letter strings, invented spelling, and conventional writing. Ms. Jackson moves about the classroom, holding brief conferences with individuals or pairs of students. In each of these meetings, she offers support for one targeted skill. She helps one child record the sounds in a word to label his picture; she helps another pair of students decide where end-of-sentence punctuation should be placed, and she helps another child write a sentence by stretching out the sounds in each word. Once complete, the animal writings will be compiled into a class informational text.

Play and Lunch (11:45 am–12:45 PM)

Children play either inside or outside depending on the weather. Play time is followed by lunch time.

Science or Social Studies (12:45–1:30 PM)

The next portion of the day is reserved for content-area teaching, most often related to science or social studies themes. Ms. Jackson's science teaching is guided by the Next Generation Science Standards (NGSS Lead States, 2013). Keeping with her animal theme, she is currently focused on helping students meet the life science standard "Use observations to describe patterns of what plants and animals (including humans) need to survive." Since they have been learning about animals living in three different habitats (deciduous forests, rain forests, and deserts), Ms. Jackson is helping the students to discover how animals in each of these ecosystems find food and water. Today, they watch video clips about ant species living in each of these environments and they record the types of food they see ants eating in each of the video clips on a chart divided into sections by habitat. They talk about the feeding behaviors that the ants seem to have in common and the differences that they see.

Next, Ms. Jackson introduces the students to an "ant farm" kit that she has ordered from a science education supply company. The students help her to assemble the kit and place the ants (also ordered and sent through the mail) inside the kit. She introduces the students to an "ant observation journal" and explains that they will have time each day to watch the ants and to record what they see. The students get right to work on their first entries, recording what they notice about the ants' behavior when they are first placed in the kit. She explains that they will attempt to understand more about how ants live and survive by carefully observing them over the next few weeks.

Math (1:30–2:15 PM)

There is a specific math curriculum followed in Ms. Jackson's kindergarten. Since the class is working on counting and categorizing, math time begins with a theme-related activity. The students work together to brainstorm as many desert, rain forest, and forest animals as they can. The animal names are written on three different color Post-it notes (one color for each habitat) and then arranged in a bar graph. The children can then count the number of animals they knew from each habitat and use the words *fewer* and *more* to compare groups.

Art, Music, Physical Education, or Library (2:15–3:00 PM)

The class goes to special teachers for art, music, physical education, and library. Ms. Jackson has coordinated with these teachers about the theme being studied, so the art teacher is working on paper mache animal sculptures, the music teacher has found some great animal songs, and the physical education teacher has thought of animal movements to help the students run like chickens on the farm, swing like monkeys in the jungle, and lumber like bears in the forest. The librarian features informational books and storybooks related to animals in her read-alouds.

Closing Circle with Read-Aloud (3:00–3:15 PM)

At end of the day Ms. Jackson uses the whiteboard to take her students on a virtual field trip to the Bronx Zoo, via the zoo's website (*www.bronx-zoo.com*). Ms. Jackson asks the students questions, encouraging them to answer in full sentences, and responds to her students' inquiries about the zoo and its animals. Ms. Jackson encourages each child to choose an animal that he or she would like to learn more about the next day in school.

Finally, she and the children review the activities of the day that they particularly liked and she writes them on a chart so children will remember to tell to their parents when they go home.

Family Involvement

Before the animal unit began, Ms. Jackson sent home a short note about the activities that would be done in school, the skills being taught, and suggestions for activities for parents to do at home. During the unit she asked for volunteers to come into the classroom to read animal books, and she asked for artifacts about animals that parents might share with the class. Ms. Jackson also asked for parent volunteers to help her students during writing workshop and for help during center time to assist children with activities while she worked with small groups of children for guided reading instruction. Ms.Jackson offered multiple options and time slots for parent participation. At the end of the unit, parents were invited to school to see all the work done about animals. In her weekly newsletter (distributed electronically to parents) she also includes photographs that show the students engaged in projects and lessons related to animals.

REFLECTIONS AND FUTURE DIRECTIONS

In this chapter, we have (1) provided an overview of the primary theories that underlie best practices in early literacy education, (2) presented a brief summary of the major governmental initiatives, including the English Language Arts Standards, (3) offered a research synthesis and research-based instructional strategies related to early literacy best practices, (4) examined special issues related to early literacy instruction including digital literacies, DLLs, and RTI, and (5) illustrated best practices in early literacy through the presentation of a case study.

ENGAGEMENT ACTIVITIES

1. After reading the case study in Ms. Jackson's room, compare it to your own early childhood classroom or one that you observe. In what ways are your classrooms similar? In what ways are they different? Are there aspects of Ms. Jackson's classroom that you would like to incorporate into your own (or the one you are observing)? If so, what are they? Are there additions or changes that Ms. Jackson should make in her room?

2. Record the lessons and activities that you implement for your students (or students that you observe) for a full day. At the end

of the day, review what you have recorded and determine how they connect to objectives for learning in early childhood discussed early in the chapter. Which objectives did you address most, which the least? How can your instruction be strengthened based on your findings?

3. Meeting the needs of DLLs and continuing to optimize the potential of digital technologies to support students' literacy growth are two pressing educational issues. Choose one of these two topics, and locate and review 10 related websites. Describe each website and report its strengths and weaknesses. Then, share what you have found with at least two other educators.

REFERENCES

Adams, M. J. (1990). *Beginning to read.* Cambridge, MA: MIT Press.

August, D., & Shanahan, T. (2006). *Developing literacy in second-language learners: Report of the National Panel on Language Minority Children and Youth.* Mahwah, NJ: Erlbaum.

Beck, I. L., & McKeown, M. G. (2001). Text talk: Capturing the benefits of read-aloud experiences for young children. *The Reading Teacher, 55,* 10–20.

Boushey, G., & Moser, J. (2009). *The CAFE book: Engaging all students in daily literacy assessment and instruction.* Portland, ME: Stenhouse

Byrnes, J. P., & Wasik, B. A. (2009). *Language and literacy development: What educators need to know.* New York: Guilford Press.

Cardoso-Martins, C., & Pennington, B. F. (2004). The relationship between phoneme awareness and rapid naming skills and literacy acquisition: The role of developmental period and reading ability. *Scientific Studies of Reading, 8*(1), 27–52.

Carlo, M. S., Aigust, D., Mclaughlin, B., Snow, C. E., Lippman, D., Lively, T. J., & White, C. (2004). Closing the gap: Addressing the vocabulary needs of English-language learners in bilingual and mainstream classrooms. *Reading Research Quarterly, 39*(2), 188–215.

Carlo, M. S., & Bengochea, A. (2011). Best practices for literacy instruction for English-language learners. In L. M. Morrow & L. B. Gambrell (Eds.), *Best practices in literacy instruction* (4th ed., pp. 117–137). New York: Guilford Press.

Curenton, S. M. (2011). Understanding the landscapes of stories: The association between preschoolers' narrative comprehension and production of skills and cognitive abilities. *Early Child Development and Care, 181*(6), 791–808.

Dewey, J. (1916). *Democracy and education.* New York: Macmillan.

Duke, N. K., Bennett-Armistead, V. S., & Roberts, E. M. (2003). Filling the great void: Why we should bring nonfiction into the early-grade classroom. *American Educator, 27*(1), 30–35.

Duke, N. K., Halladay, J. L., & Roberts, K. L. (2013). Reading standards for informational text. In L. M. Morrow, T. Shanahan, & K. Wixson (Eds.), *Teaching with the Common Core Standards for English Language Arts, Pre-K–2*. New York: Guilford Press.

Dweck, C. (2006). *Mindset*. New York: Ballantine.

Gehsmann, K. M., & Templeton, S. (2013). Reading standards: Foundational skills. In L. M. Morrow, T. Shanahan, & K. K. Wixson (Eds.), *Teaching with the Common Core Standards for English language arts* (pp. 67–84). New York: Guilford Press.

Gillam, S. L., & Reutzel, D. R. (2013). Speaking and listening standards. In L. M. Morrow, T. Shanahan, & K. K. Wixson (Eds.), *Teaching with the Common Core Standards for English language arts* (pp. 107–127). New York: Guilford Press.

Guthrie, J. (2004). Teaching for literacy engagement. *Journal of Literacy Research, 36*(1), 1–29.

Harris, J., Golinkoff, R. M., & Hirsh-Pasek, K. (2009). Lessons from the crib for the classroom: How children really learn vocabulary. In S. B. Neuman & D. K. Dickinson (Eds.), *Handbook of early literacy research* (pp. 49–65). New York: Guilford Press.

Hart, B., & Risley, T. R. (1995). *Meaningful differences in the everyday experience of young American children*. Baltimore: Brookes.

Hart, B., & Risley, T. R. (1999). *The social world of children: Learning to talk*. Baltimore: Brookes.

Jalongo, M. R., & Solobak, M. J. (2011). Supporting young children's vocabulary growth: The challenges, the benefits, the evidence-based strategies. *Early Childhood Education Journal, 38*, 421–429.

Jennings, J. L., & DiPrete, T. A. (2010). Teacher effects of social and behavioral skills in early elementary school. *Sociology of Education, 83*(2), 135–159.

Korat, O., & Shmir, A. (2012). Direct and indirect teaching: Using e-books for supporting vocabulary, word reading, and story comprehension for young children. *Journal of Educational Computing Research, 46*(1), 135–152.

Kress, J. E., & Fry, E. B. (2015). *The reading teacher's book of lists* (6th ed.). San Francisco: Jossey-Bass.

Kuhn, M. R., Schwanenflugel, P. J., Meisinger, E. B., Levy, B. A., & Rasinski, T. V. (2010). Aligning theory and assessment of reading fluency: Automaticity, prosody, and definitions of fluency. *Reading Research Quarterly, 45*(2), 230–251.

Labbo, L. D. (2011). From morning message to digital morning message: Moving from the tried and true to the new. *The Reading Teacher, 58*(8), 782–785.

McGee, L. M., & Schickedanz, J. A. (2007). Repeated interactive read-alouds in preschool and kindergarten. *The Reading Teacher, 60*(8), 742–751.

McKenna, M. C., Conradi, K., Young, C. A., & Jang, B. G. (2013). Technology and the Common Core Standards. In L. M. Morrow, T. Shanahan, & K. K. Wixson (Eds.), *Teaching with the Common Core Standards for English language arts* (pp. 152–169). New York: Guilford Press.

McKenna, M. C., Labbo, L. D., Conradi, K., & Baxter, J. (2011). Effective use of technology in literacy education. In L. M. Morrow & L. B. Gambrell (Eds.), *Best practices in literacy education* (4th ed., pp. 361–394). New York: Guilford Press.

Moody, A. K., Justice, L. M., & Cabell, S. Q. (2010). Electronic versus traditional storybooks: Relative influence on preschool children's engagement and communication. *Journal of Early Childhood Literacy, 10,* 294–313.

Morrow, L. M. (2009). *Literacy development in the early years: Helping children read and write* (7th ed.). Needham, MA: Allyn & Bacon/Pearson.

National Institute of Child Health and Human Development. (2000). *Teaching children to read: An evidence-based assessment of the scientific research literature on reading and its implications for reading instruction* (NIH Publication No. 00-4769). Washington, DC: U.S. Government Printing Office.

Neuman, S. B., & Wright, T. S. (2014). The magic of words: Teaching vocabulary in the early childhood classroom. *American Educator, 38*(2), 4–13.

NGSS Lead States. (2013). *Next generation science standards: For states, by states.* Washington, DC: National Academies Press.

Patrick, H., Mantzicopoulos, P., & Samarapungavan, A. (2009). Motivation for learning science in kindergarten: Is there a gender gap and does integrated inquiry and literacy instruction make a difference? *Journal of Research in Science Teaching, 46*(2), 166–191.

Pawlina, S., & Stanford, C. (2011). Preschoolers grow their minds: Shifting mindsets for greater resiliency and better problems solving. *Young Children, 66*(5), 30–35.

Piaget, J., & Inhelder, B. (1969). *The psychology of the child* (H. Weaver, Trans.). New York: Basic Books.

Pollard-Durodola, S. D., Gonzalez, J. E., Simmons, D. C., Davis, M. J., Simmons, L., & Nava-Walichowski, M. (2011). Using knowledge networks to develop preschooler's content vocabulary. *The Reading Teacher, 65*(4), 265–274.

Roberts, T. (2017). *Literacy success for emerging bilinguals: Getting it right in the preK–2 classroom.* New York: Teachers College Press.

Shaywitz, B. A., Shaywitz, S. E., Blachman, B. A., Pugh, K. R., Fulbright, R. K., Skudlarski, P., . . . Gore, J. C. (2004). Development of left occipitotemporal systems for skilled reading in children after a phonologically-based intervention. *Biological Psychiatry, 55*(9), 926–933.

Thomas, W., & Collier, V. (2002). *A national study of school effectiveness for language minority students' long-term academic achievement.* Santa Cruz, CA: Center for Research on Education, Diversity, and Excellence.

Tracey, D. H., & Morrow, L. M. (2012). *Lenses on reading: An introduction to theories and models* (2nd ed.). New York: Guilford Press.

Tracey, D. H., & Young, J. W. (2007). Technology and early literacy: The impact of an integrated learning system on high-risk kindergartners' achievement. *Reading Psychology, 28,* 443–467.

van Kleek, A. (2008). Providing preschool foundations for later reading comprehension: The importance of, and ideas for, targeting inferencing in storybook-sharing interventions. *Psychology in the Schools, 45*(7), 627–643.

Vygotsky, L. S. (1978). *Mind in society: The development of higher psychological processes.* Cambridge, MA: MIT Press.

Vygotsky, L. S. (1986). *Thought and language.* Cambridge, MA: MIT Press. (Original work published 1962)

Walsh, B., & Blewitt, P. (2006). The effect of questioning style during storybook reading on novel vocabulary acquisition of preschoolers. *Early Childhood Education Journal, 33*(4), 273–278.

Weizman, Z. O., & Snow, C. E. (2001). Lexical input as related to children's vocabulary acquisition: Effects of sophisticated exposure and support for meaning. *Developmental Psychology, 37*(2), 265–279.

Yopp, H. K., & Yopp, R. H. (2000). Supporting phonemic awareness development in the classroom. *The Reading Teacher, 54*(2), 130–143.

CHILDREN'S LITERATURE

Barrett, J. (1988). *Animals should definitely not wear clothing.* New York: Simon & Schuster.

Barrett, J. (2004). *Los animals no se visten.* Buenos Aires, Argentina: De La Flor.

dePaola, T. (1975). *Strega nona: An old tale.* Englewood Cliffs, NJ: Prentice-Hall.

Sendak, M. (1962). *Chicken soup with rice.* New York: Harper & Row.

Sloan, P., & Sloan, S. (1994). *We went to the zoo.* Boston: Sundance.

WEBSITES

Common Core State Standards: *http://www.corestandards.org.*

ESL Kid Stuff: *www.eslkidstuff.com.*

Everything ESL: *www.everythingesl.net.*

Teach Children ESL: *www.teachchildrenesl.com.*

TeacherTube: *www.teachertube.com.*

CHAPTER 5

Best Practices to Change
the Trajectory of Struggling Readers

VICTORIA J. RISKO
DORIS WALKER-DALHOUSE

This chapter will:

- Describe characteristics of dialogic learning communities that hold potential for changing the trajectory of struggling readers.
- Discuss current issues related to assessment and instruction of struggling readers.
- Present evidence-based practices for K–12 instruction.
- Describe how these practices are implemented within authentic instruction.
- Recommend future directions for assessment and instruction of struggling readers.

This chapter focuses on evidence-based assessment and instructional best practices for students identified as struggling readers. The best practices we identify (1) are supported by a convergence of evidence, often outcomes of divergent research methodologies; (2) provide a comprehensive and balanced view of students and literacy learning; (3) have a history of demonstrated effectiveness in classrooms and authentic settings; and (4) hold the potential, as demonstrated in instructional settings, to be sustainable and to support optimal learning, going beyond short-term testing of impact.

A comprehensive and balanced view of students' literacy processes is particularly needed to change the trajectory of students who experience reading difficulties (Risko & Walker-Dalhouse, 2012). Students identified as struggling readers have multiple literacy capabilities that go unrecognized in some school settings, and thus "mistaken identities" are frequently aligned with deficit views of students' capabilities (Gholson & Wilkes, 2017). Too often these identities are consequences of assessment and instructional practices that are narrow in conception rather than wider methods for leveraging students' strengths, including their linguistic, cultural, and experiential knowledge (Duran, 2017). Additionally, students may develop misconceptions about what is expected of them as literacy learners (e.g., such as expectations for classroom discourse) and/or require explicit instruction that addresses areas of need situated within environments that acknowledge students' capabilities (Suoto-Manning, Dernikos, & Yu, 2016). And even within a broader conception of students and instruction, there is a tremendous gap between what is intended to be and what actually is implemented in classrooms (Schmidt & McKnight, 2012).

Rich contexts for learning benefit all students, but are particularly effective for struggling readers across the grades (Camburn & Wong, 2011; Alvarez & Risko, 2010; Guthrie, 2004), including beginning and young readers (Sharp et al., 1995). Students who benefit the most from support with contextual and conceptual learning are those who receive it the least. Rich contexts and accelerated learning opportunities are typically situated in high-socioeconomic status (SES) and higher-achieving schools, while students in low-SES schools receive more of a focus on basic and isolated skill instruction that is less effective for low-achieving students (Camburn & Wong, 2011).

The goal to "play catch up" by teaching a wide array of skills out of authentic reading and writing contexts might provide short-term gains but not lasting ones; students can become skilled but not strategic or thoughtful about their reading. The rush to teach basic skills minimizes comprehension of complicated texts and deep learning of academic content. Teaching that minimizes comprehension instruction, especially for students in the upper grades, has small-to-moderate effects as compared to much larger effects for comprehension interventions (Lipson & Wixson, 2012).

Redirecting instruction requires recognizing the multiple layers of knowledge, languages and language interactions, interests, and experiences that all students need to draw on as they engage in new learning. Required is a focus on both skills-based and knowledge-based development within dynamic classroom learning communities in which literacy assessment and instruction build on students' knowledge, previous skill development, experiences, and diversity (Varelas & Pappas, 2013).

The practices we identify are optimal when situated within dialogic learning communities that hold expectation for students to "grow into the intellectual life around them" (Vygotsky, 1978, p. 88). Students' cultural and ethnic identities, experiences, and linguistic histories are honored and validated as they interact with and collaborate with their peers during text discussions (Stevenson & Beck, 2017). The teacher's focus is on student learning instead of classroom management (Watkins, 2005), facilitating connections to students' capabilities and histories with scaffolds that support connectivity and engagement (Moll, 2015). Such learning communities have several characteristics that hold the potential for accelerating the knowledge and cognitive development of students, especially students who may be experiencing reading difficulties. These include engaging (1) students and teachers in shared learning opportunities where knowledge is co-constructed; (2) students in book talks where they explain, elaborate, and take ownership of their own ideas and accept and build upon the ideas of others; (3) students in collaborative problem solving that spurs learning and active knowledge building; and (4) students in drawing on their prior knowledge, experiences, and interests to generate questions that are respected as integral and important to the learning community. Each student is seen as a knowledgeable contributor to the learning community (Johnston, 2012), and the learning of each is influenced by the learning and thinking of others, as students learn about others' perspectives, share in revealing "intensity" of text ideas, and resolve confusions (Ivey & Johnston, 2017; Maine, 2013).

EVIDENCE-BASED BEST PRACTICES

High-quality best practices for struggling readers require the expertise of classroom teachers and reading/literacy specialists. These practices all share the following characteristics.

Are Informed by Continuous and Multiple Assessments

There is widespread agreement that appropriate and differentiated instruction is informed by continuous and multiple assessments. Both summative and formative assessments are needed to capture the patterns of students' abilities and difficulties (Spear-Swerling, 2015) that develop over time, in different trajectories, and across contexts of school and life experiences. Assessments that are grounded in simple views of literacy (e.g., cognitive processes as the sole indicators of students' literacy performance) fail to capture the range of abilities, social interactions, linguistic background, and cultural histories that influence literacy development (McIntyre, 2011). Allington and McGill-Franzen (2010), for example, found that an overemphasis on the word-reading skills of young readers skews representation of students' literacy development, not attending to areas (e.g., concept and vocabulary knowledge) that will affect comprehension. In contrast, assessments that hold power for a positive influence on instruction assess a wide array of factors (e.g., word-learning skills, motivation, text comprehension, linguistic history) that affect reading development (Afflerbach, 2016). Assessments that capture performance *during* learning activities, especially those that are more challenging, are associated with large and meaningful student gains (Merchand & Furrer, 2014). Representation of knowledge should be captured in multiple formats, including multimodal assessments (Risko & Walker-Dalhouse, 2010). These could include drawings, graphic organizers, and computer software to create digital texts and illustrations (Stover, Yearta, & Harris, 2016; Kervin & Mantel, 2017).

Provide Rich Contexts for Learning

Classrooms with rich learning contexts support active learning and engagement, use of strategies for making sense of words and text ideas, and comprehension of academic content. These classrooms have the following elements.

Use of Knowledge as Analytical Tools

Rich contexts for learning provide a content focus for identifying and resolving real-world problems. Broad, central concepts (e.g., challenges faced by explorers, resettlement efforts of immigrants and refugees) taught for knowledge building are examined from different disciplinary perspectives, and in depth. Students, often in collaboration with peers, are invited to think analytically (e.g., pose problems, hypothesize and generate questions, challenge conventional understandings) as they participate in disciplinary inquiry (Windschitl & Thompson, 2006). Students need to gather evidence and build arguments to address their inquiry and content-relevant questions, and students are accountable for accurate, comprehensive, and disciplinary-specific representation of information (e.g., graphing survey data, creating pictorial displays for interview information; see Resnick & Hall, 2001). When students' interests direct their goals for learning and problem solving, there is a likelihood of increased motivation, finding relevance and connections to content goals, choosing to read more widely, and increased confidence (Guthrie & Humenick, 2004). Students' understandings and appreciation of disparate disciplinary perspectives (Bransford & Vye, 2015) develop along with critical thinking and use of information for problem solving and explaining text meanings (Pianta, Belsky, Houts, Morrison, & the NICHD Early Child Care Research Network, 2007).

Anchor Texts Ground Disciplinary Learning

Rich learning contexts are typically organized around anchor texts, which are sufficiently dense to "seed" interest, and enable prolonged examination of complex content. Anchor texts represent students' lived experiences in and out of school. They might include the text shared during a teacher read-aloud, a science experiment, or the study of a film viewed by the class. A basic requirement, though, is that the anchor is accessible to all students; thus, a reading level is not required to access its content.

Anchor texts set up the major concepts to be investigated and rein-forced through additional texts that will deepen knowledge and provide reasons to revisit concepts, reread texts and access resources online, for verifying literal and inferential understandings, and to advance analytical and critical thinking (Cognition and Technology Group at Vanderbilt, 2003). Videos are particularly strong anchors for setting up the examination of complex concepts. They, like other texts, require guided instruction for alerting students to organizational features and important information. Videos are dynamic and embedded with several levels of information with much to notice and examine with each re-viewing, and to explore for accuracy of disciplinary knowledge (Bransford & Vye, 2015).

Sufficient Time and Resources Support Intensity

Resources include a wide array of texts and interactive technologies, and students' firsthand experiences. These resources are impactful when used coherently and with sufficient time for developing knowledge in depth (Windschitl & Thompson, 2006). Needed are multiple occasions to revisit content, expand on understandings through guided instruction and dialogic conversations, and engage in multiple reading and writing activities. Additionally, this could include engaging students in digital think-alouds to enhance their comprehension of informational texts that they locate online (White, 2016). Coherence and focus on content provides prolonged engagement and instructional intensity.

Multiple Organizational Formats Support All Learners, Especially Struggling Readers

Rich learning classrooms have multiple organizational formats to support differentiated instruction. There may be whole-class instruction to initiate the study of concepts embedded in the anchor, small-group instruction that is teacher-led, small and large groups where students collaborate in shared learning activities, and one-to-one instruction. This flexible formatting for learning opportunities allows for additional time for teachers to organize small groups or individual instruction to support struggling readers.

Provide Explicit Instruction

Struggling readers benefit from additional explicit instruction to help them acquire and apply tools to gain success in reading (Cantrell & Wheeler, 2011; Barth & Elleman, 2017). These tools include providing students with strategies and skills, and facilitating understanding and use of the academic discourse necessary to respond to and understand text (Wharton-McDonald, 2011). Skills and strategies address all areas of literacy development (e.g., word learning, comprehension monitoring, composing texts, supporting arguments with evidence). Additionally, flexible use of strategies and choosing those that are most appropriate for the genre and content comes with teacher guidance (Shanahan, 2009). Thus, teachers, guided by their assessment data, are responsible for articulating and demonstrating the metacognitive work of choosing and applying strategies to aid comprehension. This is especially the case when students are reading texts across disciplines that require increased use of inferential and abstract thinking, and use of academic language.

Additionally, guided reading instruction supports students' learning with increasingly difficult concepts and texts (Sandoval & Morrison, 2003). And while there are different formats for guiding reading instruction, it typically engages students in previewing, careful reading, use of strategies, and interpretive and critical analysis before, during, and after reading a text (including digital and video texts). And it includes dialogic discussions and students' generative productions (e.g., written, digital, artistic, or dramatic projects).

Previewing and guided text discussions engage students' curiosity and interest in the texts' central concepts while building new knowledge. Previews are designed to invite curiosity and questions and, if needed, to activate and expand knowledge on central, complex concepts that may otherwise remain distant from the students. Central text concepts provide the conceptual glue for related details and facts (Alvarez & Risko, 2010). Text content is more comprehensible when students are reading with knowledge that is relevant to central concepts and related high-level text content; knowledge development "levels the playing field" for struggling readers (Snow & O'Connor, 2013, p. 4).

Revisiting texts to confirm accurate recall, to search for evidence supporting claims, to confirm and expand interpretations, and more, are characteristics associated with strategic reading, and they are associated with close reading. These actions occur in tandem with activation and extension of prior knowledge. Guided instruction that neglects to engage students' prior knowledge is attempting to build comprehension in a vacuum, in the absence of a foundation that is needed to anchor new learning.

Teach to Students' Capabilities and Cultural and Linguistic Histories While Targeting Specific Areas of Difficulties

Instruction that is well matched to both optimize students' capabilities and target areas of need can change the trajectory of reading disabilities (Wharton-McDonald, 2011). For example, students may know how to search for details and facts during close reading but require guidance and strategies for mapping these details and facts around central concepts and main ideas. Reteaching skills and strategies already mastered by students holds them in place rather than advancing their literacy development.

Additionally, culturally responsive teaching closes achievement gaps (McIntyre, Hulan, & Layne, 2011). There are multiple demonstrations of effective culturally responsive instruction (Souto-Manning, 2016; Souto-Manning, Dernikos, & Yu, 2016). For example, there are benefits to developing social justice themes to study world and community problems (Morrison, Robbins, & Rose, 2008), such as the *Social Justice Education Project*, in which Mexican American high school students investigate the impact of local living and school policies on families and students in the community (Moll, 2015), or teachers share their own histories to reify the importance of one's experience for building positive identities in classroom communities (Milner, 2011).

May (2011) demonstrated that animated text talk (e.g., interpreting, paraphrasing, and or modeling expressions and meaning of text ideas) around informational multicultural texts engaged students in comprehending complex life experiences and drawing on their "insider" knowledge and comprehension skills to make connections and draw inferences to address culturally relevant issues and events. Irvine and Armento (2001) and Siddle Walker (2001) describe culturally specific teaching styles that promote the academic success of African American and other racially diverse groups of children. Intentional and focused interactions between teachers and students and positive teacher feedback are important for student achievement and academic engagement (Dolezal, Welsh, Pressley, & Vincent, 2003). Building effective learning opportunities for students across ethnic and racial groups can be initiated by holding respectful and dialogic conversations with families and students to engage and address issues related to race and racial literacy (Milner, 2017).

Carol Lee and colleagues implemented a form of cultural modeling as one example of a robust learning opportunity to bridge students' cognitive development, lived experiences, and text content (Lee, 2017). Cultural modeling involves analyzing the content to be addressed, requiring generative tasks (e.g., interpretation of symbolism), and making connections to students' routine literacy practices (listening to music, digital composing) and students' conversational patterns. Implementations of this instruction with African American middle and high school students impacted increased comprehension, student-generated questions, comprehension monitoring, writing performance, and engagement (Lee, Rosenfeld, Mendenhall, Rivers, & Tynes, 2004). Students' use of their African American vernacular and rhetorical patterns and prior knowledge and experiences, defined as dynamic and not fixed in time, were key elements for scaffolding connections between cultural and linguistic resources and instructional goals.

Translanguaging instruction is well documented for its support of English learners and is best implemented within classrooms with differentiated instruction. Working in small groups or with a partner, English learners are encouraged to process text ideas in their home languages and with peers that share their home languages, interrogating their translations and interpretations before presenting their understanding of texts in English with the class. Students are generating cross-language comparisons that enable them to analyze similarities and differences with English used in texts for word choice, complex sentence and text composition, and language that is content-specific. Additionally, these cross-language comparisons support acquisition of foundational skills in English, as students compare likenesses and differences of phonemes across languages or apply print concepts, such as those required to support reading right to left or left to right. This instruction makes explicit to students that their linguistic knowledge is useful for learning a new language and for text comprehension (Garcia & Godina, 2017; Jiménez et al., 2017).

Provide Multiple Opportunities to Build Students' Identities as Readers and Writers, Problem Solvers, and Producers of Knowledge

Students thrive in classrooms that involve students in multiple opportunities to read and write engaging texts (Spear-Swerling, 2011), and where multiple dimensions of students' identities are made visible. Building students' confidence with positive student–teacher and student–student relationships enables engagement and feelings of self-worth (Triplett, 2007), and persistence in tasks where they feel they can succeed. For example, Stevenson and Beck (2017) report high engagement in reading and positive identity development of migrant preadolescent farm-working students, enrolled in a summer literacy program, that provided access to multiple texts focusing on the lives of migrants, deepening knowledge of the challenges migrants face and encouraging advocacy methods for seeking educational support when coming to new schools and balancing work demands of families. Drawing on the texts they read as mentor texts, these students collaborated with each other writing texts representing their own migrant histories, and in the process came to view themselves as capable readers and writers. Embedded in this example is explicit inclusion of students' knowledge and culture and development of genre-specific information and processes that enhance writing (Kganetso, 2016).

Time during the day (i.e., at school and home) to engage in multiple literacy activities during and across the year, including summers, is fundamental to the depth and breadth of reading growth and development. Achievement gaps are persistent in the development of literacy skills between young children in low-income neighborhoods compared to those in more affluent neighborhoods during the elementary grades (Dyson, 2010). Research documenting summer reading loss for low-income children (Allington & McGill-Franzen, 2017) and children whose parents speak languages other than English supports the need for student reading engagement that extends across the calendar versus the academic year and involves classroom and home interventions (Kim & Quinn, 2013).

Embed Skills and Strategies

There are compelling arguments for teaching struggling readers skills within larger contexts. For example, phonemic awareness can be taught as a separate skill or in combination with other skills, such as associating sounds with printed letters simultaneously (see Morris, 2011). The advantage for the latter is that students can learn several skills simultaneously, such as the knowledge of sounds *and* the alphabetic principle of reading English (Perfetti, 1992). Similarly, interactive phonemic awareness (Morris, 2011) provides students with the opportunity to use the context of reading to help them complete parts of words that may be unfamiliar to them (e.g., students may know beginning sounds and then fill in the rest of the word). Use of multiple cues allows students to cross-check their hypotheses about word choice, drawing on language, meaning, and sound cues to confirm their hypotheses, thereby fostering adaptability and independence (Clay, 1993; Morris, Tyner, & Penney, 2000).

Instruction that addresses multiple components, not only in word learning, but also in comprehension strategies, appears to be more effective than instruction of single strategies (Gelzheiser, Scanlon, Vellutino,

& Hallgren-Flynn, 2010: Mahdavi & Tensfeldt, 2013), especially for older students whose reading difficulties are influenced by several factors (Wanzek, Wexler, Vaughn, & Ciullo, 2010). Vocabulary learning also benefits from instruction of multiple strategies (e.g., identifying vocabulary critical to text meanings, attending to word parts, using context to confirm hypotheses about word meanings, self-monitoring for understanding) (Graves & Silverman, 2011), and, in turn, text comprehension benefits from instruction on word meanings (Wright & Cervetti, 2017).

Draw on Multiple Forms and Complexity Levels of Texts to Afford Access to New Knowledge and Academic Learning

Struggling readers have a long history of being held in place with limited trajectories in achievement gains, due partly to instruction with texts that are too easy, the use of difficult texts without appropriate instructional supports, and too few opportunities to read texts with success (Allington, 2012). Limited access to a wide range of genre and more challenging texts can restrict struggling readers' trajectory in attaining academic content and accelerating their learning (Chall & Jacobs, 2003; Rasinski, Rupley, Paige, & Nichols, 2016).

Struggling readers need volumes of practice with both challenging, grade-appropriate texts, texts that provide opportunities to address instructional needs, and easy texts that have varying organizations and genre (e.g., narratives, informational, digital, pictorial texts) and instruction with texts matched to students' instructional reading levels. Allington (2013), for example, recommends multiple opportunities to read texts at a 98% accuracy level. Ehri, Dreyer, Flugman, and Gross (2007) reported reading gains for primary students, when tutored, with reading texts at 98 to 100 % accuracy. O'Connor and colleagues (2002) found that for upper grades, instructional-level (not grade-level) texts were optimal for advancing the development of struggling readers (O'Connor et al., 2002).

A common goal to increase students' access to complex texts is embedded in many of the current revisions of state standards focusing on the English language arts. Typically, complex texts are identified by an examination of quantitative and qualitative features of texts (e.g., explicit vs. implicit text structures, knowledge demands on readers) and reader and task characteristics (e.g., students' prior knowledge and reading strategy development, students' interest, students' experiences with similar tasks). One strategy that seems to hold promise to support struggling readers' access to complex texts is the interactive read-aloud (Santora, Baker, Fien, Smith, & Chard, 2016). Needed, however, is a careful assessment of and accommodation for potential difficulties of selected texts and tasks based on students' histories. One form of support is the use of a graphic organizer, such as a "complex text analysis chart" (Witte, 2016, p. 32) used with narratives, that makes explicit author's central messages, key events, character development, and plot development. Witte (2016) reports gains in text comprehension, vocabulary development, writing, and text discussions for first-grade students.

The central aim for struggling readers and text choice is to provide instruction with texts that are moderately challenging and provide high success rates (Wharton-McDonald, 2011), gradually moving students to more difficult texts with deliberate instructional support. One powerful instructional support is "just in time scaffolding" (Frankel, Pearson, & Nair, 2011, p. 227), in which teachers provide timely cues and demonstrations to advance students' strategic work and text understandings followed by repeated practice with the goal of students' independence. Another is dialogic conversations occurring around texts, with advantages for lower-achieving students. Dialogic conversations are most effective when discourse expectations (e.g., norms for supporting claims) are taught and accessible to all students (Michaels, O'Connor, & Resnick, 2007), and when they occur in small groups in which students feel comfortable exchanging ideas (Applebee, Langer, Nystrand, & Gamoran, 2003). Further, Lightner and Wilkinson (2016) report the benefits of alignment of goals, student needs, and discussion frameworks (e.g., questioning the author) for optimal dialogue among teachers and their students.

Texts provide scaffolds for other texts. Less challenging texts (e.g., videos, wordless picture books or highly illustrated texts, graphic novels that introduce concepts with pictorial or graphic support) can scaffold more complex texts while building concepts and extending students' prior knowledge. Similarly, text sets that have overlapping concepts and vocabulary can couple easier texts with more challenging ones, or video texts matched with print text, can advance learning of content and academic knowledge and ease transition to more complex texts.

Differentiate Instruction to Support Identities as Readers and Writers and Literacy Success

Changing the trajectory of struggling readers requires differentiated instruction, provided by highly knowledgeable teachers, and coordinated efforts and guidance from the specialized knowledge that reading/literacy specialists can provide (Allington, 2013). Differentiated instruction gives readers access to the same curriculum as their classmates, multiple opportunities to participate in mixed-ability grouping learning, learning outcomes commensurate with the students' skill and ability, and learning assignments designed to meet students' needs (Hall, Strangman, & Meyer, 2003). Additional instruction provided for small groups and individuals is significantly more effective than instruction for large groups; and when compared, individual instruction is associated with greater acceleration than instruction for small groups (Wanzek & Vaughn, 2007).

Effective teachers consider their instructional practices, materials, assessments, and grouping arrangements, especially in efforts to meet the mandates of the response to intervention (RTI) legislation (Watts-Taffe et al., 2012). Consistent with planning for all students, RTI places the first level of intervention for struggling readers in the classroom. Classroom teachers have control over the *process* (e.g., how we plan for and instruct students, how we establish the learning environment) and the *products* (i.e., assessments of learning). Specific instruction for struggling readers should implement instruction and planning carefully with the reading/literacy specialists. This coordinated effort insures that expert teachers are providing the instruction for struggling readers instead of less qualified support staff (Allington, 2013).

BEST PRACTICES IN ACTION

Ms. George, a fifth-grade classroom teacher of a heterogeneous group of middle school students, 18 native English speakers (10 white and eight African American) and six English language learners (four Bosnian and two Sudanese), is beginning her school year with challenges that face her and other teachers each year. She realizes that she has little knowledge of her students' home literacies and cultural backgrounds, so she plans to communicate with each of her students' families. To do this, Ms. George contacts each child's parent with support where needed by school liaisons familiar with the language and cultural norms of the families, and invites them to share family stories about their lives and experiences, and their child's development as a reader and writer during home visits (Compton-Lilly, Papoi, Venegas, Hamman, & Schwabenbauer, 2017) and/or through family dialogue journals (Allen et al., 2015). Ms. George also listens to the parents as they describe their expectations for their child and their beliefs about his or her progress in reading, and for ways to collaborate with them during the school year. Her actions indicate that she understands that parent–teacher collaboration is essential for student learning, and that home literacy environments in which parents and children are engaged in literacy activities and where children have access to literacy materials are associated with positive outcomes in reading performance (Skibbe, Justice, Zucker, & McGinty, 2008; Tichnor-Wagner, Garwood, Bratsch-Hines, & Vernon-Feagans, 2016).

Ms. George has devoted weeks to planning for alignment of her instructional goals, preliminary assessment information, and district and state standards. As in the past, she will continue to teach conceptually and thematically, integrating the English language arts across the curriculum while ensuring that each student is achieving progress and feels successful. She is confident that her goals complement directives of her state standards (e.g., interdisciplinary teaching, accessing multiple text levels and genre to support knowledge development, engaging students in hands-on experiences and productions representing their knowledge development).

Ms. George realizes that she must differentiate instruction to accommodate the needs of all students, and in particular, her struggling readers and English language learners. As a classroom teacher, she is responsible for providing the first level of intervention and progress monitoring of her struggling readers based upon the requirements for Tier 1, high-quality classroom-based instruction, of the RTI model used in her school district. Ms. George will engage in collaborative planning with the reading/literacy specialist in her school who will both work with struggling readers within Ms. George's classroom and provide intensive instruction outside of the classroom for students identified as needing Tier 2, supplementary reading instruction.

Ms. George begins by reviewing the data about her students' performance on standardized measures of achievement administered the previous spring. She uses the scores to make preliminary plans for adapting her instruction and to identify additional assessments to identify specific students' capabilities and needs, and to plan appropriate differentiations.

Dynamic Assessment

During the first week of school, Ms. George meets with students in small groups and during individual conferences to implement the first of multiple formative assessments that will occur throughout the year. Students are asked to choose their favorite texts to read and topics for writings that will be shared with peers. Ms. George is an eager and active participant, recording data on her electronic tablet organized within folders for each student. She is listening to oral readings, text retellings, discussion of purpose and style of writings, and expressions of interests and aspirations. She is analyzing miscues and distinguishing those that affect meaning from those that don't; she is recording word and comprehension monitoring strategies; she is noticing English usage of English learners and records students' use of home languages that may provide hints of language cues she can incorporate into her own language repertoire; she records students' questions and accounts of experiences. She is beginning to gather a wealth of data, including information about the students' cultural and linguistic histories that can be leveraged for instruction. She has information of strategies that struggling readers in her class use to identify unknown multisyllabic words and monitor their reading comprehension. *Using the Motivation to Read Profile–Revised* (Malloy, Marinak, Gambrell, & Mazzoni, 2013–2014), Ms. George has begun to identify her students' evaluation of the value they place on reading, their self-concept as readers, and their literacy instruction. And she identifies difficulties that include limited understandings of novel vocabulary, overattention to memorizing details and facts, low comprehension of main ideas, and limited attention to use and critique evidence for forming arguments.

Because block scheduling is used in Ms. George's middle school, she is confident that the 90-minute block for language arts instruction will provide her with the time for explicit instruction, independent reading and writing in response to reading by students, and monitoring of students' progress and engagement using formative assessment (i.e., conferences, projects, teacher-constructed tests, and observation).

Rich, Anchored Instruction with Explicit Teaching

Ms. George's vision of thematic teaching is not the thematic teaching of past decades; it is not the form of thematic instruction that she experienced during student teaching where themes were shallow and content connections were vague. Instead, her themes are grounded in informational-loaded concepts that invite multiple real-world connections and opportunities to examine and respond to problematic situations.

Ms. George has assembled a set of materials that relate to a social studies topic of immigration that is part of the fifth-grade curriculum. She chooses texts based upon the Lexile scale that uses quantitative measures (i.e., sentence length and word frequency) to match readers to text. In addition to easier texts, she includes instructional-level and complex texts that will be introduced to her struggling readers with guided instruction to increase their conceptual understanding of the content. Among her texts are *Somos como las nubes/We Are Like the Clouds* (Argueta, 2016); *Their Great Gift: Courage, Sacrifice, and Hope in a New Land* (Coy, 2016); *Faraway Home* (Kurtz, 2000); the graphic novel *The Arrival* (Tan, 2007); *Journal of Otto Peltonen–A Finish Immigrant* (Durbin, 2002); biographies of refugees; and primary sources (e.g., oral histories recorded at Ellis Island). Additional texts will come from the students and families who will generate brief stories about their families' immigration history. Ms. George plans evening meetings during potluck suppers, hosted by the school principal, to assist the students and their parents in sharing their experiences and beliefs about immigration.

Ms. George attends to both content- and standards-based goals. Her content goals focus on building understandings of immigrants and refugees and conditions favoring and challenging immigration, laws that regulate immigration, and the history of immigration cycles and demographics. The central concept for her unit of instruction is "leaving home for a new life—the reasons, the challenges, the laws, and potential contributions." This central concept will ground the choice of texts, discussions, and learning activities.

Ms. George starts the school year with the study of this content because related concepts were currently discussed in the school neighborhoods, and by state and national legislators. Most recently, community leaders and legislators have argued for and against a new refugee settlement project that is proposed for their city.

While several standards-based goals from Ms. George's state standards for English language arts, grade 5, are addressed in her unit, she includes three that are specifically targeted for those struggling readers who are experiencing difficulty in identifying main ideas (both stated explicitly and inferred), determining meanings of academic words, and identifying and comparing different points of view with supporting evidence.

Her anchor text is a set of school-approved digital videos that appeared on the local public education channel and that display interviews with refugees who have settled in this city and in other national communities and interviews with church leaders and legislators who state their arguments for and against resettlement programs. This anchor seeds connections to historical information on immigration and refugee status and laws, statistics of refugee relocation programs, decisions that affect allocation of public and private funds supporting resettlement programs and affect city budgets, and challenges refugees face in their new home communities and country.

Differentiated Instruction

The anchor will be viewed by the entire class followed by small group discussions and guided instruction, using graphic organizers, to identify main ideas, different points of view and supporting evidence, and to generate arguments that are substantiated with text details. Both Ms. George and the reading/literacy specialist will join the small groups and engage students through interactive read-alouds of the related texts paired with the anchor text. They will conference with individuals to provide guided instruction to meet the goals for understanding the anchor content and the related texts. The reading/literacy specialist, with the chosen texts, provides intensive tutoring for those students requiring additional support. Instruction will acknowledge strategies that students are using appropriately and provide intense practice in use of strategies that aid students' ability to identify main ideas, make connections to details to support evidence for building arguments about different perspectives, define new vocabulary and nuanced text meanings, and draw conclusions. Teacher guided reading lessons will assist students' transition to and comprehension of increasingly more complex texts. Ms. George plans to guide students through the development of a digital text with hypertext commentaries (Dalton, 2013) as one way to demonstrate their close reading and knowledge acquisition. Students will have multiple opportunities (often guided by the classroom teacher or reading specialist) to read, write, dramatize, and develop digital products (e.g., a graphic novel with selected illustrations and captions) that enhance their literacy identities and their developing expertise regarding content (Bransford & Vye, 2015).

REFLECTIONS AND FURTHER DIRECTIONS

In this chapter we identify current issues related to the assessment and instruction of struggling readers. We also sought to contextualize these practices in research and authentic classrooms. However, it is clear to us that the number and depth of documented accounts of teacher practices in urban and rural settings, across multiple grade levels, and in national and international school settings, along with research on the assessment and instruction of struggling readers, must become an even greater educational priority.

ENGAGEMENT ACTIVITIES

1. Examine the ELA standards for your state as they relate to the students you teach. Develop a separate chart for each standard on which you record the *frequency* and *type* of instruction that you have provided for students on a weekly or biweekly basis. Include a column for recording the type of assessment used to denote student progress.

2. Think about your current knowledge of the ethnic, cultural, and linguistic background of *one* specific student in your class who struggles with reading and/or writing. Identify five ways that you can use this information to differentiate reading materials, methods, and instruction for this particular student. Later complete the activity with other students who struggle in these areas.

3. Discuss with others in your professional learning community the extent to which staff and students in your school and classroom

reinforce a negative identity as "struggling readers" for students with reading difficulties. To what extent are they isolated socially and in learning experiences from more successful students? How might you foster positive changes in student identity development in your classroom?

4. Examine your school and/or district's literacy plan to determine the provisions made for supporting students who experience literacy difficulties. Assess your individual and school progress in implementing the plan. Identify obstacles. Identify strengths.

5. Interview a member of the local school board about the literacy program in your district. How does it meet the needs of linguistic, ethnic, and culturally diverse students in the district? How does it meet the needs of students who struggle in reading and writing? Are literacy support personnel (i.e., literacy coaches or reading/literacy specialist) available and utilized effectively to support classroom teachers? Are there community groups supporting children and their parents?

REFERENCES

Afflerbach, P. (2016). Reading assessment: Looking ahead. *The Reading Teacher, 69*(4), 413–419.

Allen, J., Beaty, J., Dean, A., Jones, J., Smith Mathews, S., McCreight, J., . . . Simmons, A. M. (2015). *Family dialogue journals: Three-way partnerships that support student learning.* New York: Teachers College Press.

Allington, R. L. (2012). *What really matters for struggling readers: Designing research-based programs* (3rd ed.). Boston, MA: Allyn & Bacon.

Allington, R. L. (2013). What really matters when working with struggling readers. *The Reading Teacher, 66*(7), 520–530.

Allington, R. L., & McGill-Franzen, A. (2010). Why so much oral reading? In E. H. Hiebert & D. R. Reutzel (Eds.), *Revisiting silent reading: New directions for teachers and researchers* (pp. 45–56). Newark, DE: International Reading Association.

Allington, R. L., & McGill-Franzen, A. (2017). Summer reading loss is the basis of almost all the rich/poor reading gap. In R. Horowitz & J. Samuels, (Eds.), *The achievement gap in reading: Complex causes, persistent issues, possible solutions* (pp. 171–183). New York: Routledge.

Alvarez, M. C., & Risko, V. J., (2010). What comes before matters in the end: Directions for reading comprehension instruction. In S. Szabo, T. Morrison, L. Martin, M. Boggs, & L. Raine (Eds.), *Yearbook of the Association of Literacy Educators and Researchers: Vol. 32. Building literacy communities* (pp. 32–46). Commerce, TX: University of Texas A&M.

Applebee, A. N., Langer, J. A., Nystrand, M., & Gamoran, A. (2003). Discussion-based approaches to developing understanding: Classroom instruction and student performance in middle and high school English. *American Educational Research Journal, 40*(3), 685–730.

Barth, A. E., & Elleman, A. (2017). Evaluating the impact of a multistrategy intervention for middle-grade struggling readers. *Language, Speech and Hearing Services in Schools, 48*(1), 31–41.

Bransford, J. D., & Vye, N. J. (2015). Anchored instruction: Then and now. In J. M. Spector (Ed.), *Encyclopedia of education technology* (pp. 27–29). Thousand Oaks, CA: SAGE.

Camburn, E., & Wong, S., (2011). Two decades of generalizable evidence on U.S. instruction from national surveys. *Teachers College Record, 113*(3), 561–610.

Cantrell, S.C, & Wheeler, T. (2011). Pedagogy/instruction: Beyond "best practices." In R. Powell & E. C. Rightmyer (Eds.), *Literacy for all students: An instructional framework for closing the gap* (pp. 152–189). New York: Routledge.

Chall, J. S., & Jacobs, V. A. (2003). Poor children's fourth-grade slump. *American Educator, 27*(1), 14–15, 44.

Clay, M. M. (1993). *Reading recovery: A guidebook for teachers in training.* Portsmouth, NH: Heinemann.

Cognition and Technology Group at Vanderbilt. (2003). Connecting learning theory and instructional practice: Leveraging some powerful affordances of technology. In H. F. O'Neil Jr., & R. S. Perez (Eds.), *Technology applications in education* (pp. 173–209). Mahwah, NJ: Erlbaum.

Compton-Lilly, C., Papoi, K., Venegas, P., Hamman, L., & Schwabenbauer, B. (2017). Intersectional identity negotiation: The case of young immigrant children. *Journal of Literacy Research, 49*(1), 115–140.

Dalton, B. (2013). Engaging children in close reading: Multimodal commentaries and illustration remix. *The Reading Teacher, 66*(8), 642–649.

Dolezal, S. E., Welsh, L. M., Pressley, M., & Vincent, M. M. (2003). How nine third-grade teachers motivate student academic engagement. *Elementary School Journal, 103*, 239–269.

Duran, L. (2017). Audience and young bilingual writers: Building on strengths. *Journal of Literacy Research, 49*(1), 92–114.

Dyson, L. (2010). The trend of literacy development during the early years of children living in low-income neighborhoods: A cross-sectional study. *International Journal of Learning, 16*(12), 53–65.

Ehri, L. C., Dreyer, L. G., Flugman, B., & Gross, A. (2007). Reading rescue: An effective tutoring intervention model for language minority students who are struggling readers in first grade. *American Educational Research Journal, 44*(2), 414–448.

Frankel, K. K., Pearson, P. D., & Nair, M. (2011). Reading comprehension and reading disability. In A. McGill-Franzen & R. L. Allington (Eds.), *Handbook of reading disability research* (pp. 219–231). New York: Routledge.

Garcia, G. E., & Godina, H. (2017). A window into bilingual reading practices of fourth-grade, Mexican American children who are emergent bilinguals. *Journal of Literacy Research, 49*(2), 273–301.

Gelzheiser, L., Scanlon, D., Vellutino, F., & Hallgren-Flynn, L. (2010). Interactive strategies approach—extended: A responsive and comprehensive intervention for intermediate-grade struggling readers. *Elementary School Journal, 112*(2), 280–306.

Gholson, M. L., & Wilkes, C. E. (2017). (Mis)taken identities: Reclaiming identities of the "collective black" in mathematics education research through an exercise in black specificity. *Review of Research in Education, 41*, 228–252.

Graves, M. F., & Silverman, R. (2011). Interventions to enhance vocabulary development. In A. McGill-Franzen & R. L. Allington (Eds.), *Handbook of reading disability research* (pp. 315–328). New York: Routledge.

Guthrie, J. T. (2004). Teaching for literacy engagement. *Journal of Literacy Research, 36*(1), 1–30.

Guthrie, J. T., & Humenick, N. M. (2004). Motivating students to read: Evidence for classroom practices that increase reading motivation and achievement. In P. McCardle & V. Chhabra (Eds.), *The voice of evidence in reading research* (pp. 329–354). Baltimore: Brookes.

Hall, T., Strangman, N., & Meyer, A. (2003). *Differentiated instruction and implications for UDL implementation.* Washington, DC: National Center on Accessing the General Curriculum. Retrieved May 8, 2018, from *http://aem.cast.org/about/publications/2003/ncac-differentiated-instruction-udl.html.*

Irvine, J., & Armento, B. (2001). *Culturally responsive teaching: Lesson planning for elementary and middle grades.* New York: McGraw-Hill.

Ivey, G., & Johnston, P. (2017). Emerging adolescence in engaged reading communities. *Language Arts, 94*(3), 159–169.

Jiménez, R. T., David, S., Pacheco, M., Risko, V. J., Pray, L., Fagan, K., & Gonzales, M. (2017). Creating responsive teachers of students learning English. In R. Horowitz & J. Samuels (Eds.), *The achievement gap in reading: Complex causes, persistent issues, possible solutions* (pp. 38–56). New York: Routledge/Taylor & Francis.

Johnston, P. (2012). *Opening minds: How classroom talk shapes children's minds and their lives.* Portland, ME: Stenhouse.

Kervin, L., & Mantel, J. (2017). Children creating multimodal stories about a familiar environment. *The Reading Teacher, 70*(6), 721–728.

Kganetso, L. M. W. (2016). Creating and using culturally sustaining informational texts. *The Reading Teacher, 70*(4), 445–456.

Kim, J. S., & Quinn, D. M. (2013). The effects of summer reading on low-income children's literacy achievement from kindergarten to grade 8: A meta-analysis of classroom and home interventions. *Review of Educational Research, 83*(3), 386–431.

Lee, C. D. (2017). Integrating research on how people learn and learning across settings as a window of opportunity to address inequality in educational processes and outcomes. *Review of Research in Education, 41*, 88–111.

Lee, C. D., Rosenfeld, E., Mendenhall, R., Rivers, A., & Tynes, B. (2004). Cultural modeling as a frame for narrative analysis. In C. Dauite & C. Lightfoot (Eds.), *Narrative analysis: Studying the development of individuals in society* (pp. 39–62). Thousand Oaks, CA: SAGE.

Lightner, S. C., & Wilkinson, I. A. G. (2016). Instructional frameworks for quality talk about text: Choosing the best approach. *The Reading Teacher, 70*(4), 435–444.

Lipson, M. Y., & Wixson, K. K. (2012). RTI: To what interventions are students responding? *The Reading Teacher, 66* (2), 111–115.

Mahdavi, J. N., & Tensfeldt, L. (2013). Untangling reading comprehension strategy instruction: Assisting struggling readers in the primary grades. *Preventing School Failure, 57*(2), 77–92.

Maine, F. (2013). How children talk together to make meaning from texts: A dialogic perspective on reading comprehension strategies. *Literacy, 47*(3), 150–156.

Malloy, J. A., Marinak, B. A., Gambrell, L. B., & Mazzoni, S. A. (2013, December–2014, January). Assessing motivation to read: The Motivation to Read Profile—Revised. *The Reading Teacher, 67*(4), 273–282.

May, L. (2011). Animating talk and texts: Culturally relevant teacher read-alouds of informational texts. *Journal of Literacy Research, 48*(1), 3–38.

McIntyre, E. (2011). Sociocultural perspectives on children with reading difficulties. In A. McGill-Franzen & R. L. Allington (Eds.), *Handbook of reading disability research* (pp. 45–56). New York: Routledge.

McIntyre, E., Hulan, N., & Layne, V. (2011). *Reading instruction for diverse classrooms: Research-based, culturally responsive practice.* New York: Guilford Press.

Merchand, G. C., & Furrer, C. J. (2014). Formative, informative, and summative assessment among curriculum-based measurement of reading, classroom engagement, and reading performance. *Psychology in the Schools, 51*(7), 659–676.

Michaels, S., O'Connor, C., & Resnick, L. (2007). Deliberate discourse idealized and realized: Accountable talk in the classroom and in civic life. *Studies in Philosophy and Education, 27*(4), 283–297.

Milner, H. R., IV. (2011). Culturally relevant pedagogy in a diverse urban classroom. *Urban Review, 43,* 66–89.

Milner, H. R., IV. (2017). Race, talk, opportunity gaps, and curriculum shifts in (teacher) education. *Literacy Research: Theory, Method, Practice, 66*(1), 73–94.

Moll, L. C. (2015). Tapping into the "hidden" home and community resources of students. *Kappa Delta Pi Record, 51,* 114–117.

Morris, D. (2011). Interventions to develop phonological and orthographic systems. In A. McGill-Franzen & R. L. Allington (Eds.), *Handbook of reading disability research* (pp. 279–288). New York: Routledge.

Morris, D., Tyner, B., & Penney, J. (2000). Early steps: Replicating the effects of a first-grade reading intervention program. *Journal of Educational Psychology, 92,* 681–693.

Morrison, K. A., Robbins, H. H., & Rose, D. G. (2008). Operationalizing culturally relevant pedagogy: A synthesis of classroom-based research. *Equity and Excellence in Education, 41*(4), 433–452.

O'Connor, R. E., Bell, K. M., Harty, K. R., Larkin, L. K., Sackor, S. M., & Zigmond, N. (2002). Teaching reading to poor readers in the intermediate grades: A comparison of text difficulty. *Journal of Educational Psychology, 94*(3), 474–485.

Perfetti, C. (1992). The representation problem in reading acquisition. In P.

Gough, L. Ehri, & R. Treiman (Eds.), *Reading acquisition* (pp. 145–174). Hillsdale, NJ: Erlbaum.

Pianta, R. C., Belsky, J., Houts, R., Morrison, F., & the NICHD Early Child Care Research Network. (2007). Opportunities to learn in America's elementary classrooms. *Science, 315*(5820), 1795–1796.

Rasinski, T. V., Rupley, W. H., Paige, D. D., & Nichols, W. D. (2016). Alternative text types to improve reading fluency for competent to struggling readers. *International Journal of Instruction, 9*(1), 163–178.

Resnick, L. B., & Hall, M. W. (2001). *The principles of learning: Study tools for educators* (Version 2.0) [CD ROM]. Pittsburgh, PA: Institute for Learning, University of Pittsburgh.

Risko, V. J., & Walker-Dalhouse, D. (2010). Making the most of assessments to inform instruction. *The Reading Teacher, 63*(5), 420–422.

Risko, V. J., & Walker-Dalhouse, D. (2012). *Be that teacher!: Breaking the cycle for struggling readers.* New York: Teachers College Press.

Sandoval, W., & Morrison, K. (2003). High school students' ideas about theories and theory change after a biological inquiry unit. *Journal of Research in Science Teaching, 40,* 369–393.

Santora, L. E., Baker, S. K., Fien, H., Smith, J. L. M., & Chard, D. J. (2016). Using read-alouds to help struggling readers access and comprehend complex, informational text. *Teaching Exceptional Children, 48*(6), 282–292.

Schmidt, W. H., & McKnight, C. C. (2012). *Inequality for all: The challenge of unequal opportunity in American schools.* New York: Teachers College Press.

Shanahan, C. (2009). Disciplinary comprehension. In S. E. Israel & G. G. Duffy (Eds.), *Handbook of research on reading comprehension* (pp. 240–260). New York: Routledge.

Sharp, D. L. M., Bransford, J. D., Goldman, S. R., Risko, V. J., Kinzer, C. K., & Vye, N. J. (1995). Dynamic visual support for story comprehension and mental model building by young, at risk children. *Educational Technology Research and Development, 43*(4), 25–41.

Siddle Walker, V. (2001). African American teaching in the South: 1940–1960. *American Educational Research Journal, 38*(4), 751–779.

Skibbe, L. E., Justice, L. M., Zucker, T. A., & McGinty, A. S. (2008). Relations among maternal literacy beliefs, home literacy practices, and the emergent skills of preschoolers with specific language impairment. *Early Education and Development, 19*(1), 68–88.

Snow, C., & O'Connor, C. (2013). Close reading and far-reaching classroom discussion: Fostering a vital connection: A policy brief from the Literacy Research Panel of the International Reading Association. Retrieved September 13, 2013, from *www.reading.org.*

Souto-Manning, M. (2016). Honoring and building on the rich literacy practices of young bilingual and multilingual learners. *The Reading Teacher, 70*(3), 263–271.

Souto-Manning, M., Dernikos, B., & Yu, H. M. (2016). Rethinking normative literacy practices, behaviors, and interactions: Learning from young immigrant boys. *Journal of Early Childhood Research, 14*(2), 163–180.

Spear-Swerling, L. (2011). Patterns of reading disabilities across development.

In A. McGill-Franzen & R. L. Allington (Eds.), *Handbook of reading disability research* (pp. 149–161). New York: Routledge.

Spear-Swerling, L. (2015). Common types of reading problems and how to help children who have them. *The Reading Teacher, 69*(5), 513–522.

Stevenson, A., & Beck, S. (2017). Migrant students' emergent conscientization through critical, socioculturally responsive literacy pedagogy. *Journal of Literacy Research, 49*(2), 240–272.

Stover, K., Yearta, L., & Harris, C. (2016). Formative assessment in the digital age: Blogging with third graders. *The Reading Teacher, 69*(4), 377–381.

Tichnor-Wagner, A., Garwood, J. D., Bratsch-Hines, M., & Vernon-Feagans, L. (2016). Home literacy environments and foundational literacy skills for struggling and nonstruggling readers in rural early elementary schools. *Learning Disabilities Research and Practice, 31*(1), 6–21.

Triplett, C. F. (2007). The social construction of "struggle": Influences of school literacy contexts, curriculum, and relationships. *Journal of Literacy Research, 39*(1), 95–126.

Veralas, M., & Pappas, C. C. (2013). *Children's ways with science and literacy: Integrated multimodal enactments in urban elementary classrooms.* New York: Routledge.

Vygotsky, L. S. (1978). *Mind in society: The development of higher psychological processes.* Cambridge, MA: Harvard University Press.

Wanzek, J., & Vaughn, S. (2007). Research-based implications from extensive early reading interventions. *School Psychology Review, 36,* 541–561.

Wanzek, J., Wexler, J., Vaughn, S., & Ciullo, S. (2010). Reading interventions for struggling readers in the upper elementary grades: A synthesis of 20 years of research. *Reading and Writing: An Interdisciplinary Journal, 23*(8), 889–912.

Watkins, C. (2005). *Classrooms as learning communities: What's in it for schools?* New York: Routledge.

Watts-Taffe, S., Laster, B. P., Broach, L., Marinak, B., Connor, C. M., & Walker-Dalhouse, D. (2012). Differentiated instruction: Making informed teacher decisions. *The Reading Teacher, 66*(4), 303–313.

Wharton-McDonald, R. (2011). Expert classroom instruction for students with reading disabilities. In A. McGill-Franzen & R. L. Allington (Eds.), *Handbook of reading disability research* (pp. 265–272). New York: Routledge.

White, A. (2016). Online reading comprehension: Using digital think-alouds to build comprehension of online informational texts. *The Reading Teacher, 69*(4), 421–425.

Windschitl, M., & Thompson, J. (2006). Transcending simple forms of school science investigation: The impact of preservice instruction on teachers' understandings of model-based inquiry. *American Educational Research Journal, 43*(4), 783–835.

Witte, P. G. (2016). Teaching first graders to comprehend complex texts through read-alouds. *The Reading Teacher, 70*(1), 29–38.

Wright, T. S., & Cervetti, G. N. (2017). A systematic review of the research on vocabulary instruction that impacts text comprehension. *Reading Research Quarterly, 52*(2), 203–226.

CHILDREN'S AND ADOLESCENT LITERATURE

Argueta, J. (2016). *Somos como las nubes/We are like the clouds* (A. Ruano, Illus.). Toronto, ON, Canada: Groundwood.

Coy, J. (2016). *Their great gift: Courage, sacrifice, and hope in a new land.* Minneapolis, MN: Carolrhoda.

Durbin, W. (2002). *The journal of Otto Peltonen–A Finnish immigrant.* New York: Scholastic.

Kurtz, J. (2000). *Faraway home.* Orlando, FL: Harcourt Brace.

Tan, S. (2007). *The arrival.* New York: Levine Books.

CHAPTER 6

Best Practices for Teaching Dual Language Learners

Leveraging Everyday Literacies

MICHAEL DOMÍNGUEZ
KRIS D. GUTIÉRREZ

This chapter will:

- Provide background information relevant to understanding the demographic, social, cultural, and policy context surrounding instruction for English language learners (ELLs).
- Challenge typical discourses and assumptions related to ELL students.
- Draw attention to the special considerations at work for ELL students in literacy instruction.
- Highlight the important role of thoughtfully constructed, situated literacy practices that draw on students' everyday repertoires of practice to enhance their learning.

THE CLASSROOM AS A COMMUNITY OF LEARNING FOR ENGLISH LEARNERS

We want to begin this chapter by helping readers understand English learners and their contexts for learning. As Rumbaut and Massey (2013) elaborated in their report, "Immigration and Language Diversity in the

United States," the United States has always been a multilingual nation. Yet, policies and practices, as well as the tense recent political climate, continue to ignore this history, and the linguistic variability and promise of this nation's population, particularly in its youth. Youth who are learning English are a diverse group: they differ along a number of dimensions, including race, ethnicity, their country of origin, immigration status and length in the United States, home language(s), and access to teachers with experience and preparation in the areas of bilingualism, biliteracy, and second language acquisition. Despite this heterogeneity, English learners are too often misunderstood and taught as if they were a demographically homogenous population, found only in self-contained classroom settings and programs. The reality is that this is simply not the case. Rather, English learners—in their rich heterogeneity—are found in many types of classrooms, in many contexts, and with many different linguistic skillsets. They are, rather than outliers in our classrooms, vital parts of the communities of learning that we as educators must be striving to encourage and develop in the 21st century.

Toward that end, this chapter is for *every* literacy educator—veteran and novice alike—not just those teaching in contexts specific to ELL students. Our schools are changing, and as diverse youth with a wide array of multilingual practices and skills enter our classrooms, crafting effective communities for, and communities of, learners is dependent on our ability to employ best practices that recognize the powerful mediating role students' linguistic and sociocultural repertoires—those assets they bring with them from home and their life beyond the curriculum—have in developing language and literacy skills. We hope to emphasize the importance for all literacy educators of leveraging these skills in culturally sustaining ways to construct inclusive, multilingual communities of learning that support English learners' development.

EVIDENCE-BASED BEST PRACTICES: A RESEARCH SYNTHESIS

The Demographic Imperative: Contextualizing the Conversation

Simply put, the demographic and educational landscape of the United States is changing, making this conversation, and pedagogical skillset, of the utmost importance to the communities of learning teachers will be creating in the future. As of 2014 (Strauss, 2014), youth of color had become the majority in U.S. public schools, and by 2036, greater than 65% of U.S. public school students are projected to be from racially and ethnically diverse backgrounds (Taylor, 2014). To dispel the notion that racial and ethnic demographic change—and the presence of bicultural youth in our classrooms—is explained wholly by immigration, it is worth noting that the vast majority of EL students are United States–born (85% of elementary age, and 62% of secondary age, respectively; Zong & Batalova, 2015). Home language and home language practices, then, indicate little about an English learner student's nationality, citizenship, or country of origin (Capps et al., 2005), and indeed, 21% of the U.S. population spoke a language other than English at home (U.S. Census Bureau, 2015).

Unpacking these demographics further, shifting demographics means increasing diversity in a true sense; not simply a more prevalent Spanish-speaking Latinx population. While Spanish is the first language of the majority of English learner students in the United States (they make up 62% of EL populations), there are significant numbers of youth speaking other languages, including Chinese, Vietnamese, Haitian Creole, Hindi, Korean, Tagalog, Russian, Arabic, and First Nations/Indigenous American languages, with many of these other languages growing in prominence at significant rates (U.S. Census Bureau, 2015). Several states have EL populations in which Spanish is not the first language of the majority of the EL student population: North and South Dakota, Alaska, and Montana (First Nation/Indigenous languages), Vermont (Bosnian), and Maine (Somali), for example (Batlova & McHugh, 2010a, 2010b).

The most recent estimates from the National Clearinghouse for English Language Acquisition (NCELA) and the National Center for Education Statistics (NCES) report that the total English learners preschool–grade 12 student enrollment represents 9.6% of the total preK–12 student population (NCELA, 2018; NCES, 2017). While these most recent data show a stabilization of the English learner population as a percentage of the total U.S. population, it is important to note that states in the Midwest, in the South, and on the East Coast are undergoing drastic growth in their EL student populations, with Virginia, Kentucky, Indiana, Alabama, and North and South Carolina experiencing greater than a 200% growth rate in the last decade (Carnock, 2017; NCELA, 2011). While major metropolitan areas in these states may be hotbeds of cultural and linguistic diversity, the biggest shift in these "New Latinx Diaspora" states' demographics has been in rural communities, where many previously homogenous rural districts now find 10–12% of their student body speaking a language other than English (Batlova & McHugh, 2010a, 2010b; NCES, 2017). In short, English learners are, and will continue to be, increasingly commonplace rather than the exception. Thus, the need to develop robust literacy practices for English learners is no longer an issue limited to certain areas, but a need in *all* of our learning communities.

So where does this leave us? To summarize, by 2025, one in four public school students will be designated as an EL student, and at least three out of four of those students will be native-born U.S. citizens (National

Education Association, 2008; Zong & Batalova, 2015). Yet at a time when there is an increased need for more robust bilingual and biliterate peda-gogical models, there remains institutionalized and informal resistance to such approaches, despite overwhelming evidence of their effectiveness (August & Shanahan, 2006). Increasing inequity and lack of access to meaningful instruction in the nation's poorest schools have translated into a woeful gap between the instructional models available to serve English learners, and those that are needed. With all this in mind, the language ideologies, assumptions, and discourse we as educators bring to our classrooms—and that are brought to our classrooms from the socio-political context beyond—merit a close, and thoughtful, reexamination.

Rethinking Our Discourse: Situating Best Practices in the Present Contexts

In the casual discourse of schools nationwide, the term English learner—despite this demographic group's linguistic and demographic diversity—has come to be synonymous and used interchangeably with the immigrant student, particularly the Latinx immigrant, or to imply an equivalency between language use/ability, and race, ethnicity, or national origin. Such discourse inaccurately conflates deficit assumptions about minori-tized students with English proficiency, and as a consequence, youth who are English learners are too often characterized in ways that frame their emergent bi/multilingualism itself as a deficit. This monolithic, and prob-lematic, view of EL students fails to capture the strength of their linguistic repertoires. As Wong-Fillmore and Snow (2005) have noted, understand-ing the trajectory of second language acquisition can support teachers in developing more effective and asset-based communicative and pedagogi-cal practices (p. 6). Considering this, we believe strongly that educators and policymakers need to understand the difference between (1) sequen-tial and simultaneous bilingualism, and (2) additive and subtractive bilin-gualism, as well as the idea of (3) translanguaging.

"Sequential bilingualism" refers to youth who are monolingual in a first home/community language, and who begin school with little to no knowledge of English (Peña & Kester, 2004). "Simultaneous bilinguals," on the other hand, have had access to both their first languages and Eng-lish (their second language) in their home/community contexts from an early age and have some proficiency with both languages as they begin school. Recent research suggests that as more English learner students are born in the United States, more of these youth will fall into this lat-ter, simultaneous bilingual, category (Almanza de Schoenwise & Kling-ner, 2012). This underscores the point that nearly all English learner students, regardless of their exposure to English, arrive in schools with some literacy knowledge and linguistic skills, and the acquisition of English should be framed by educators as a process of *additive* bilingualism—adding an additional, complementary linguistic and literacy system to their existing language. This framing is in contrast to a *subtractive* one, in which English supplants the home language, resulting in a monolingual, or monoliterate, English-speaking student, who has—to the detriment of their development and learning—lost access to the linguistic repertoires they arrived in school with from their home/community (García & Kleifgen, 2010, pp. 41–43). To be clear, an additive (or ideally, dynamic) framing of bilingualism has been consistently shown to be more beneficial to a student's development in all languages and across academic disciplines (Escamilla et al., 2014; García & Kleifgen, 2010).

This distinction, then, is important to understand, for school policies and practices often assess and label entering students solely based on their proficiency in English, rather than their broader language and literacy abilities. In doing so, whether intentionally or not, schools exercise what Quijano (2000) calls a "coloniality of power," implicitly or explicitly overvalidating English literacy skills, ignoring the other linguistic repertoires upon which consequential learning might be built, and perpetuating a subtractive language ideology, or negative orientation to English learner's bilingualism. This ideology is alive in current labels such as limited English proficient students (LEP), non-English proficient (NEP), and even English learners (ELs), for example, all of which are problematically English-centric, and not very useful in terms of developing robust teaching strategies, as they discursively erase students' fuller capacities, linguistic repertoires, and experiences. And while classifications can be useful for particular purposes, the danger here is that focusing on perceived regularities in the group—defining students solely by their lack of English—makes it easier to rely on ill-conceived, one-size-fits all approaches to language and literacy learning that ignore the significant variance across members of categories. Further, such labels make it difficult to develop teaching practices that account for students' extant literacy strengths, abilities, and skills. This concern is exacerbated (if not created) by federal, state, and local policies related to the teaching and funding of English learners. Consider, for example, the lack of consistency across districts and states about who counts as an English learner, as the assessment and classification systems are highly variable and of differing quality. In some cases, students can receive years of services even as they approach fluency, while in others, students with basic English skills may be quickly reclassified as English-proficient, entering a system that no longer attends to their ongoing needs as English learners working to develop more expansive forms of academic literacy. Such policies belie the fact that recent research shows that the development of robust, academic biliteracy takes seven to 10 years; 3–5 years longer than traditional estimates recognized (Wong-Fillmore & Snow, 2005).

While the growth of the WIDA Consortium (Gottleib, Cranley, & Cammilleri, 2007) across many states has helped to mitigate these variances in classification, these findings still have vital implications for practice, especially as practitioners can be easily mislead or confused about how to best address the needs of the English learner. English learners need a range of ongoing forms of assistance regardless of their classification, to negotiate the ongoing and varying language and literacy demands across their academic trajectories. As researchers have pointed out, students who may be at the same level of proficiency with their English-speaking peers at one point in their learning trajectories may fall behind at another time because of the increasingly complex language demands of disciplinary content, and the natural ebb and flow of linguistic development (Carlo & Bengochea, 2011; Nakamoto, Lindsey, & Manis, 2007).

Thus, to ratchet up students' learning, robust forms of language and literacy support need to continue beyond students' "official" reclassification, and should be oriented toward leveraging students' complete linguistic and literacy toolkit in additive fashion. That is to say, we need to find ways to leverage their home, everyday, and school language practices without focusing solely on their deficits in relation to a cultural standard of English monolingualism. Such an approach invites the possibility for *translanguaging* pedagogies (Garcia, 2011); or pedagogies and approaches to language learning that invite hybridity among and across linguistic repertoires and languages beyond code switching, encouraging students to, for instance, take notes in their home language, while reading in English, and discussing in a fusion of the two. At its core, translanguaging encourages us to see literacy and linguistic practices in the way a bilingual speaker/learner might: as a single coherent, flexible, communicative system, and not discrete abilities fixed to particular languages (Otheguy, García, & Reid, 2015).

Finally, as we examine the complicated terrain in which English learners are being served, it is not just important, but essential, to place these factors and realities into their present sociopolitical context. Language ideologies about languages other than English remain a legal and public deterrent to developing a rich menu of approaches for English Learners (Razfar, 2005), and recent political rhetoric around racially diverse and immigrant Americans has exacerbated such tensions. Though acute in the given moment, these tensions are hardly new. Indeed, the place of English learners in U.S. schools is wrapped in a long social, political, and legal history of exclusion, from the erasure of indigenous languages in Bureau of Indian Affairs boarding schools, to the *Lau v Nichols* (1974) case meant to guarantee equal-access rights of English learner students, to more recent efforts like California's Proposition 227 that attack bi/multilingualism in schools, serving English learners has always been contested (Santa Ana, 2004). Moreover, English language teaching has itself far too often been guided by colonial ideologies that operate in subtractive terms, using the acquisition of English to undermine cultural heterogeneity, identity, and affinity (Garcia, 2017; Motha 2014). As Schmidt (2000) notes, "The dispute [over the use of non-English languages] in society and schools is essentially a disagreement over the meanings and uses of group identity in the public life of the nation state, and not language, as such" (p. 47).

With this in mind, we want to emphasize the important role that teachers and practitioners have in disrupting such problematic language ideologies, sociopolitical ills, and exclusionary constructions of citizenship through their pedagogies, and the communities of learners they build. By actively embracing best practices that leverage students' full linguistic repertoires, and encouraging multilingual communities of learners who learn with and from one another, educators are in a unique position— regardless of whatever policies and curricula they may be saddled with—to support linguistic pluralism in additive, culturally sustaining ways.

Thus, we argue that fuller and more accurate discourses and descriptions of young students help to challenge deficit explanations for their schooling performance, and are more accurate in understanding their academic potential, and future place in society. In short, discourse—the words we choose to use—matters to our practice, and labels and narrow descriptors can shape how we see our students' learning potential. With this in mind, we believe the term dual language learners (DLLs)[1] more accurately captures the complex and developmental character of English language learning; it is an asset-based conception of these students, the multiple languages and literacies they are acquiring, and their potential. We use the term in this spirit.

Dual Language Learners and Language Socialization

We know from research on the cultural dimensions of learning that there is both regularity and variance within and across groups of people, including those who share a common language or country of origin (Gutiérrez & Rogoff, 2003; Rogoff, 2003). From a teaching and learning perspective,

---

[1]We choose to use DLLs noting that recently, other scholars and educators with similar, humanizing intentions have selected emergent bilinguals (EBs), or multi-language learners (MLLs) as their terms of choice. Though each term is chosen for specific reasons, and no term can capture the full range of experiences English learner students may have, each of these are productive, asset-based alternatives to English-centric labels like ELL or LEP.

these differences among students learning a language are best attributed to youths' participation in the practices that constitute everyday family and community life, and the way they are socialized both through their participation in the valued practices of the home and in the community (Ochs, 1993; Ochs & Schiefflin, 2011, 2017). Recognizing this reality helps us to challenge simplistic and overly general conceptions of youth linguistic practices, as there is no monolithic way in which DLL youth acquire language, nor is there a particular learning style that they embody. The language practices of DLL youth are as diverse and dynamic as the other cultural practices of which they are a part, even if they are too often characterized in ways that do not capture their linguistic repertoires or the important differences that distinguish learners of English from other student learners (Gutiérrez, Zepeda, & Castro, 2010).

More often, we fail to recognize that the linguistic demands of DLL's everyday practices are far more complex than often acknowledged (Faulstich Orellana, 2009). As an example, children who are learning English or who have bilingual capacities often serve as language and sociocultural brokers for their non-English-speaking family members across a range of financial, medical, and educational institutions (Jimenez, 2001). Yet, these children's classroom experiences neither recognize nor make use of such important cognitive literacy activities and sociocultural accomplishments, and while a host of other "diverse" cultural practices are welcomed into learning communities, robust notions of linguistic diversity rarely are. There are economic, sociopolitical, and educational consequences to failures of leveraging and extending students' linguistic toolkits in our learning communities, and given the broader economic and sociopolitical goals often articulated in regards to education (e.g., economic competitiveness), we call attention to research that shows the cognitive, sociopolitical, and economic benefits to bilingualism and biliteracy. As sociologists Rumbaut and Massey (2013) have noted, plurilingualism is a tremendous advantage in the globalized economy, and the loss of non-English languages would in fact come at a significant cost to the U.S. and indeed the global economies (p. 13). This recognition of bilingualism, biliteracy, and biculturalism as resources we might leverage is foundational to designing more expansive communities of literacy learning—environments that reflect the polylingual and polycultural character of *all* youths' lives, and the practices in which they participate (Gutiérrez, Bien, & Selland, 2011).

BEST PRACTICES IN ACTION

Teachers and other practitioners are designers: designers of both curricula and practices. More importantly, we think practitioners should be prepared to also be designers of new futures, of possible lives for all youth, particularly DLLs, and youth from historically marginalized communities for whom literacy is key (Gutiérrez, 2008). In this section, we highlight approaches to teaching DLL youth that focus on the importance of meaning making, and on the role of everyday knowledge and practices in developing consequential forms of literacy in generative communities of learning. From this perspective, a premium is placed on understanding and leveraging students' practices, not just in school, but across the settings of everyday life—from youth interest-driven practices, to those organized by family and other adults, to disciplinary practices in more formalized settings.

When we focus on youths' practices, and what youth actually do routinely with literacy in a variety of contexts, we can greatly enhance our understanding of the linguistic repertoires youth develop as they move within and across practices. Recognizing the dynamic linguistic practices of youth is useful in shifting the focus from deficit perspectives about youth and communities' language practices toward the design of learning environments that leverage students' history of involvement with literacy. To this end, we present a set of design principles to help educators craft communities of learning that will leverage everyday practices toward more expansive forms of literacy production, underscored by the point that developing English language skills should not replace students' full linguistic toolkits, but build on them to develop consequential and expansive forms of literacy.

Design Principles

- Recognize the variability and regularity in any group of DLLs as central to understanding students' educational strengths and potential,
- Understand the kind of cognitive activity and sociocultural knowledge that DLLs are leveraging, as they navigate a range of contexts with differing language demands.
- Identify and employ strategic and appropriate forms of assistance that are embedded into meaningful practices.
- Recognize the language demands of the practices in which DLLs participate, in the classroom and beyond.
- Extend support for DLLs who are developing capacities in two languages simultaneously and the resulting demands.
- Draw on the existing toolkits that all children bring to the classroom (e.g., even pre-school children who are developing their home language but who have little-to-no knowledge of English have linguistic repertoires that can be leveraged).

- Design literacy practices that utilize everyday linguistic and socio-cultural practices, as these are key to building academic and disciplinary knowledge.
- Design literacy practices that socialize youth to and through their participation in robust and consequential learning activity.

With these principles in mind, we review a number of considerations that should help teachers organize rich learning environments for DLL youth across grade levels who are also learning to read and write in English, as well as appropriating disciplinary content knowledge.

Rising to the Concrete: Leveraging Everyday Knowledge and Linguistic Practices

Today's youth move across a range of contexts and produce artifacts that reflect the intercultural, hybrid, and multimodal practices of which they are part. These dynamic repertoires, developed across their ecologies of interest and everyday lives, should be cultivated as an important dimension to learning (Alim & Paris, 2017). In terms of supporting the development of robust and consequential forms of learning, we underscore the importance of understanding the *everyday* in developing expansive forms of language and literacy learning both in and out of school. Leveraging the everyday includes home language practices, and involves more than making learning more relevant and engaging; it also means situating literacy learning in the particular sociocultural and linguistic histories of students.

Learning from a sociocultural perspective (Vygotsky, 1987) suggests that learning is made consequential by grounding abstract knowledge into the everyday. Significantly, this view of learning challenges assumptions that there is a "lower, 'Level 1' kind of learning/thinking," which precedes and must be mastered in order to acquire, "higher, 'Level 2' learning/ thinking . . . in the mastery of school" (Laboratory for Comparative Human Cognition, 1989, p. 75). Such theories of teaching and learning, and of DLLs themselves, are erroneous, and necessarily limit possible learning outcomes (Gutiérrez, 2012). Rather, successful learning involves bringing more complex, future-oriented practices into the present experiences and endeavors of learners (Cole, 1992).

These conclusions are supported by insights from the National Literacy Panel's meta-analysis of literacy development studies for DLLs, which found that DLL youth rarely struggle with or lack basic alphabetic skills (August & Shanahan, 2006). Moreover, research tells us that learning a language and learning to be literate in both the first and second language involves both discrete skills and higher-level strategies, as well as acquiring the sociocultural knowledge of how and when to use language and literacy practices (Escamilla et al., 2014). Instruction, then, should focus on higher-level text skills and their sociocultural meanings and uses, blending "top-down" and "bottom-up" instruction to ensure that students' classroom literacy practices are modeled on the sorts of tasks they will ultimately be asked to do in school and life in the future, and those that are present already in their daily practices.

To illustrate how to bring the future into the present, and the role of the everyday in literacy learning, we highlight a classic study by Moll and Diaz (1987) that documented how a combination of institutional, ideological, and pedagogical forms worked to constrain the learning of bilingual Spanish–English speakers. Employing a sociocultural methodology with observer–participant accounts, Moll and Diaz examined the consequences of instruction and its social organization on the reading development of two groups of children who were assessed to be bilingual in spoken English and Spanish. The researchers observed children in two different classrooms, with students in each classroom grouped by high, medium, and low reading ability. Although all the children could speak English, and had learned to read for comprehension (a higher-order skill) in Spanish, instruction for all groups was designed to "remediate" their reading deficiency with lessons organized around phonetics and pronunciation, and an assumption that they could not read and comprehend English. Moll and Diaz found that given these conditions, even children in the highest level reading group made little progress, and had few opportunities to engage in elaborated talk or linguistic development.

In search of an alternative way to support bilingual children and leverage their full linguistic repertoires, Moll and Diaz designed an intervention in which children would read the English texts to themselves, but were allowed to discuss the meaning of the texts in Spanish, English, or a combination of the two with peers and teachers—a practice common in their own speech community. With attention focused on what children could understand from what they had read, and the encouragement of a collaborative community of learners engaging with literacy, decoding, and meaning making, the children's estimated grade level for comprehension significantly increased. Research tells us that "such gains in comprehension and making sense of texts should not be surprising, as mature reading and mathematical thinking require both top-down (Level 2) and bottom-up (Level 1) processes" (Laboratory for Comparative Human Cognition, 1989, p. 75). This is precisely the type of back-and-forth learning we see in Moll and Diaz's intervention. Such work argues what many in this research community believe: a theory of learning and instruction driven by a reductive view of DLLs' literacy abilities is wrong in principle and pernicious in practice (Gutiérrez, 2012, p. 20).

These findings have been supported in subsequent work with DLLs. Researchers have noted (Iddings, Combs, & Moll, 2012) that when instruction and policy restricts the role of home language in learning, particularly content knowledge, learning is constrained. Specifically, reductive English-only literacy programs eliminate students' linguistic repertoires—powerful mediators in students' learning—and create what can be termed an "Arid Zone," where meaningful learning opportunities and resources, including peers, texts, bilingual teachers, and more "dry up," further marginalizing the DLLs and truncating their opportunities to expand learning and develop new linguistic identities (Iddings et al., 2012). It is worth noting that this "Arid Zone" dynamic is possible even when curriculum and programming are purportedly welcoming to bilingualism. Cervantes-Soon (2014), examining a dual language program serving both DLLs and monolingual English speakers learning a new language, found that when language learning was separated from the home practices of DLL youth in favor of solely accommodating the practices of the monolingual English-speaking youth, the literacy development of DLL students deteriorated. In short, building communities of bi/multilingual literacy learning requires appreciation for all students' practices, and should challenge students to adjust equally to all of the everyday literacy practices that exist in a diverse classroom setting.

As a final example, in contrast to "Arid Zones," Pacheco (2012) incorporated the unique learning, thinking, and knowledge DLLs develop in home–community spaces into a curriculum. In this work, she drew on the notion of "everyday resistance" to illustrate a particular set of enacted political actions and practices that Latinx students developed to negotiate the demands of their politically charged contexts. As these students came together to develop coordinated and strategic challenges to particular social and educational policies, they engaged in joint sense making, problem solving, and social analysis. This everyday resistance involved practices related to designing, planning, and carrying out collective actions and activities, which, over time, cultivated complex linguistic and sociocultural resources that served as thinking and analytic tools for learning in school contexts. Thus, individual and collective practices of everyday life and resistance, fully recognized, were indispensable to the success of DLL youth both in school, and beyond.

Designing Instruction to Reflect Students' Everyday Linguistic and Sociocultural Practices

Following Moll and Diaz (1987), we include several additional examples of approaches that illustrate design principles that engage youth in mature literacy activities to leverage and build skills for future literacy practices.

One such example is found in the work of Razfar (2010). In a study of the common, everyday literacy practice of corrective feedback and repair with DLL youth, Razfar found that the design and ideology guiding the deployment of this practice was integral to its success. Traditionally, Razfar notes, corrective feedback is cognitively and individually based; student utterances and attempts at growth are evaluated by the instructor for their form and content, and an individual assessment is given to students based on the accuracy of their response. The impulse of the practice is positive—to provide constructive feedback—but the effect can serve to undermine the DLL student's confidence and ownership of learning, as well as his or her very identity as a user of English, as the correction is likely to be felt as deeply personal, causing the student emotional stress. Thus, this often naturalized use of immediate and direct corrective feedback around basic language use can function negatively, as a socialization practice that shapes limited views of how language is used, in what contexts, and by whom. The cultural dissonance that DLL youth often experience in this practice can push them toward an *identity* as someone who can*not* use the language correctly.

However, as Razfar explores, when instructional designs account for the multilayered challenges of dual language learning, alternative discourse practices become possible. In a yearlong ethnographic study of a second grade class of DLLs, Razfar traced the ways in which a focal teacher constructed her discourse around moments of corrective feedback. He observed that when the teacher's practices were aimed toward the construction of teacher–student relationships based on *confianza,* or sustained mutual trust, corrective feedback became a positive practice. Rather than individual and error-centered, feedback was constructive, communal, and caring in nature, and focused on growth and meaning for the entire community of learners, rather than strictly on the form a single individual displayed. Further, the discourse through which corrective feedback was delivered displayed empathy and care for students, as well as inviting the use of native language to support and make sense of the student's nascent attempts at English usage.

The result was a classroom culture in which both student and teacher understood that the use of corrective feedback was aimed at broadening and supporting all participants' linguistic repertoires of practice. Because the design of the practice of corrective feedback was responsive to their burgeoning language usage, and the anxiety associated with these initial attempts at a new language identity, students were able to see themselves as valuable and important language users in a supportive community, and more easily accessed and engaged with critical thinking tasks. Students were able to build positive peer relationships as they participated in academic tasks and skills, and gained an improved sense of ownership and agency in their language usage. In short, corrective feedback rooted in mutual *confianza,* and the recognition of the challenges DLLs experience supported students and prompted them to take more risks and to pursue more opportunities to critique and expand their own English language and literacy skills.

Hybrid Language Practices: Drawing on Students Existing Toolkits

Similar to Razfar, Martínez (2013) offers evidence of the pedagogical and learning benefits of drawing on the existing toolkits that all children bring to the classroom. This study in an East Los Angeles middle school focused on the role students' language ideologies played in their learning and identities. Martínez found that the practices of this English-only school had consequences for the ways students viewed their own first-language practices. Consequently, they saw little benefit or value in using their home language and everyday linguistic practices, and were socialized in subtractive ways to view English as dominant and qualitatively better, instead of recognizing their daily code-switching and translanguaging practices as intellectually demanding and complex.

Recognizing bilingualism as a resource to be valued and additively framed, the focal teacher in Martinez's study encouraged sense making and self-expression through Spanish and Spanglish (in which English and Spanish were blended). While home languages remained subordinated in the classroom—English literacy and expression remained the object of the course—providing opportunities to view the home language as a meaningful and productive tool in learning allowed students to recognize Spanglish as a means toward "cultural maintenance." This shift in language ideology (how they viewed their own languages) opened up opportunities for students to increase their comprehension. Moreover, it began to cultivate a critical language awareness that fostered more agency and ownership in their learning, challenging deficit interpretations of themselves and their linguistic abilities that had limited their investment in learning and language acquisition.

Explicit Skill Instruction in Sociocultural Practice: Intentional Support Embedded into Meaningful Practices

As we noted earlier, consequential instruction for DLLs involves much more than direct instruction around isolated, segmented aspects of literacy (e.g., phonics, decoding). Moreover, we agree that preparing DLL youth and other nondominant students to deal with such "gate-keeping" tasks as required by standardized and other discrete assessments is a professional and ethical imperative (Delpit, 1986). Yet these sorts of explicit instruction must be embedded in meaningful, contextually significant practices. As articulated by one of our design principles, practitioners need to identify areas for explicit support, and employ strategic and appropriate forms of assistance to support the development of skills in meaningful practices. This is key. Learning discrete skills out of the context of meaningful and rigorous practices only helps to "encapsulate schooling" (Engeström, 2004) in ways that make literacy, and particularly language learning, inert and disconnected.

Let us consider vocabulary instruction, a seemingly narrow unit of instructional focus. Research has shown word development to be hugely important for DLL youth, as limitations in vocabulary create one of the largest barriers toward the higher-level thinking objectives of DLL youth and to subsequent academic success and progress (August & Shanahan, 2006; August, Carlo, Dressler, & Snow, 2005; McKeown & Beck, 2004; Scarcella, 2003). However, we know from this research that to be effective for DLL youth, vocabulary instruction must be rooted in everyday practices and build from students' knowledge of their first-language (e.g., employing cognates), while attending in explicit ways to complex understandings of foundational words (August et al., 2005; Beck, McKeown, & Kucan, 2002; Carlo et al., 2004; Lesaux, Kieffer, Faller, & Kelley, 2010; Vaughn et al., 2009). Thus, carefully designed vocabulary instruction can serve as an illustrative practice, both because of its importance to the development of DLL students' linguistic repertoires and because engaging vocabulary instruction requires thoughtful design of ways to situate learning in meaningful, rigorous, complex, and rich literacy practices.

A stellar example of how explicit instruction can be organized in thoughtful and relevant ways appears in the intervention designed by Lesaux et al. (2010). In this study, Lesaux and her team deployed a multiweek, daily intervention program for classrooms with many—though not exclusively—DLL middle schoolers. The intervention included several units organized around engaging, interest-driven informational text, and a limited number (eight to nine words every 2 weeks) of thoughtfully selected, high-utility academic words. At the conclusion of the program, the researchers found significant positive effects for students in meanings of taught words, morphological awareness, and definitions in text, as well as marginally significant gains in depth of word knowledge and at least one measure of reading comprehension. While DLL students still lagged behind their peers, their gains were promising.

One of the features that made this vocabulary intervention successful is how it situated vocabulary instruction into meaningful social, community literacy practices. First, the program was organized as a routine daily practice in these classrooms, structured such that students were continually exposed to vocabulary words across multiple contexts, with nuanced definitions, and in a range of authentic ways. Second, the instruction engaged students with texts that were meaningful to longer-term objectives, and useful in whole-group and small-group discussions, game play, artifact creation, and writing activities that were part of broader community goals, promoting the use of focal, high-utility words across a range of compelling social and interactional contexts. Finally, because the words were embedded in many different contexts and media, explicit instruction around topics such as morphology, prefixes and suffixes, varied definitions, and decoding particular word parts had utility to student's engagement in a meaningful social activity, and could be succinct, limited, and focused.

Of relevance to practice, teachers initially skeptical of their students' ability to complete the higher-level tasks embedded in the program were surprised to find that within the context of interest-driven social practice, the youth participants excelled at even rigorous tasks. By designing a space in which both word learning and learning how to learn words became valued and meaningful practices, the importance and function of learning and acquiring relevant vocabulary increased. Essentially, vocabulary learning had a function in their everyday activity, and in valued literacy and interactional practices in school. As such, students not only appropriated new vocabulary, but also learned the sociocultural value of developing these new literacy skills. An important implication here is that when skills are embedded within rich, meaningful, and well-designed community literacy practices, youth can engage with and master skills far more quickly, and in more compelling ways, than through isolated, reductive, direct skill instruction.

We highlight this study because it aligns with our design principles as they might be applied to explicit instruction. This rich example of socializing students to and through rich, embedded community literacy practices has been reinforced by subsequent studies (e.g., August, Artzi, & Barr, 2016), making it is easier to see how explicit instruction around discrete, seemingly reductive tasks (e.g. vocabulary, grammar) might be made consequential—and engaging—when organized in ways that challenge youth to develop literacy skills as they engage in mature endpoint activities. As a final note, while we believe this study was an excellent example of designing intentional instruction into meaningful practices, we would note that the Lesaux et al. (2010) study did not make any direct mention nor seem to make any intentional use of students' first languages. We refer back to Moll and Diaz (1987) and Garcia's various studies (2009, 2017) to reiterate the importance of translanguaging, and leveraging children's everyday language practices and home repertoires in dynamic ways, to augment consequential reading skills. For example, leveraging students' understandings of cognates and exploring translated meanings in texts in their home language, and inviting discussion in home languages, are key features of enriched, high-level learning for DLL youth, and powerful tools for developing academic language and vocabulary in both English and their first languages. As in the Moll and Diaz (1987) study, the organization of such practices does not require any expertise in the second language by the practitioner; instead, the community of learning can be designed so that students of varied linguistic backgrounds might share and explore understandings and build new vocabulary across their languages in valued interactions with peers.

REFLECTIONS AND FUTURE DIRECTIONS

All youth have the right to participate in meaningful, collaborative, and consequential learning activity. In line with our sociocultural view of learning and development (Vygotsky, 1978), we want to invite educators to see learning as a necessarily social, communal process that must be *made* to become consequential by active processes of design. Practices are not static and unchanging. They are dynamic, and co-constituted by the people participating in them, and the tools available. From this perspective, we hope that educators will begin to see best practices not as things that are implemented—discrete strategies we deploy or enact—but lived. Best practices must be situated in carefully designed learning ecologies that shape, and are shaped by, the everyday practices and goals of the community. In order to leverage students' full repertoires, those repertoires must be appreciated, and invited in as an integral part of the rigorous literacy practices in a classroom. Only when we as educators appreciate, understand, and embody a high valuation of these practices can we push for complexity, while providing the right kind and amount of support to extend students' learning.

Today's youth, particularly DLL youth and youth from historically marginalized communities, are increasingly disconnected from school and its practices. As our nation's demographics change, so too must our pedagogies, ideologies, and instructional designs shift, to ensure our literacy practices differentiate, accommodate, and extend the translingual linguistic repertoires that characterize DLLs, and increasingly, will characterize the linguistic repertoires of all students. We must strive for learning that leverages socially relevant and culturally sustaining practices in new designs; connects the everyday with school, work, and interest-driven activity; and provides a variety of opportunities to use communicative and written language, and to try out how language is used across social contexts, and from different identity positions.

ENGAGEMENT ACTIVITIES

As we look toward practices that can be applied expediently in classrooms, we reiterate the importance of teachers thinking of and positioning themselves as designers of community possibility. Teachers need rich understandings of the social context and everyday practices of DLLs in general, as well as their own students in particular, to thoughtfully adapt and create a variety of practices and strategies that can enhance and enrich student learning. Here, we identify four examples of professional practices for supporting DLLs, and hope educators who take up these practices will situate them in ways that have resonance for their local contexts and students.

1. **Take a Process Approach to Classroom Engagement.** Often in classrooms, it is easy to focus on the ultimate product, and forget about the small, constituent literacy practices that make up the process of getting there. For DLLs, this is even more critical, for final products in English (like a full essay, or even participation in a class discussion in English) can be anxiety-inducing, and the steps to get there successfully unseen sticking points of confusion or frustration. To avoid this, structure your classroom practices to emphasize the different parts of the process that lead to a final product, even if it seems altogether straightforward and mundane. Implemented in ways that invite translanguaging and build *confianza,* a focus on the process can help educators to tease out, better understand, and make the valued practices we want our communities of learners participating in clear, and allow DLLs to locate where their home practices and linguistic repertoires can aid them as assets.

2. **Cognitive Mapping.** Research tells us that for DLLs, visual artifacts can be extremely valuable tools for learning and English language development. Particularly when engaging around disciplinary terms, concepts, and academic language, invite students to construct dynamic "cognitive maps" that leverage their full linguistic repertoires. Rather than employing static, prefabricated graphic organizers, encourage this as a creative process, in which collaborative groups craft their own arrangement/display, according to their own schemas for understanding, and full linguistic resources, to help them visually map out a term, concept, theme, or the like. Archive these, posting them in the classroom as co-constituted reference guides DLLs can continually refer back to.

3. **Translingual Dialogue Journals.** Invite students to construct a translingual (i.e., using their full linguistic resources in whatever

ways they need to) dialogue journal as an ongoing literacy practice in the classroom. This student artifact can function as a way for the educator, and potentially other students, to regularly engage with each other's writing as an ongoing reference manual and resource, and allow students a defined place in which to record and experiment with new or interesting grammar/sentence structures or vocabulary words as they encounter them. This practice reinforces literacy as a shared, communal activity that happens in dialogue with others, and gives the educator the opportunity to support students' ownership of literacy learning as something that is ongoing and valuable to their meaningful participation in mature, high-interest endpoint practices. Finally, translingual journals provide both safety for a student to experiment with language with an educator's support, and space for educators to ensure students are seeing their own bi/multilingualism in additive, positive ways.

4. **Personal Second-Language Learning.** As Snow, Burns, and Griffin (1998) note, knowledge about language is crucial to helping teachers perform effectively in the classroom, yet most teachers of DLL students know very little about the linguistic or sociocultural challenges of language acquisition. With this in mind, we recommend teachers, particularly those who teach large populations of DLLs, to challenge themselves to learn a second language, particular one that many of your students speak. This endeavor has important pedagogical and sociocultural possibilities, as the experience of learning a second language permits teachers to develop a deeper appreciation of the complexity and the demands of language acquisition, appreciate the importance of using one's own linguistic toolkit as a resource for learning and meaning making, and open potential lines of communication and trust with students and families. While immersive experiences are ideal, a variety of free Smartphone language-learning apps that are now available make taking up this task even more possible.

REFERENCES

Alim, H. S., & Paris, D. (2017). What is culturally sustaining pedagogy and why does it matter? In D. Paris & H. S. Alim (Eds.), *Culturally sustaining pedagogy: Teaching and learning for justice in a changing world* (pp. 1–24). New York: Teachers College Press.

Almanza de Schoenwise, E., & Klingner, J. (2012). Linguistic and cultural issues in developing disciplinary literacy for adolescent English language learners. *Topics in Language Disorders, 32*(1), 51–68.

August, D., Artzi, L., & Barr, C. (2016). Helping ELLs meet standards in English language arts and science: An intervention focused on academic vocabulary. *Reading and Writing Quarterly, 32*(4), 373–396.

August, D., Carlo, M., Dressler, C., & Snow, C. (2005). The critical role of vocabulary development for English language learners. *Learning Disabilities Research and Practice, 20*(1), 50–57.

August, D., & Shanahan, T. (2006). *Developing literacy in second-language learners: Report of the National Literacy Panel on Language Minority Children and Youth.* Mahwah, NJ: Erlbaum.

Batalova, J., & McHugh, M. (2010a). *States and districts with the highest number and share of English language learners.* Washington, DC: Migration Policy Institute.

Batalova, J., & McHugh, M. (2010b). *Top languages spoken by English language learners nationally and by state.* Washington, DC: Migration Policy Institute.

Beck, I., McKeown, M., & Kucan, L. (2002). *Bringing words to life.* New York: Guilford Press.

Capps, R., Fix, M., Murray, J., Ost, J., Passel, J., & Herwantoro, S. (2005). *The new demography of America's schools: Immigration and the No Child Left Behind Act.* Washington, DC: Urban Institute.

Carlo, M., August, D., McLaughlin, B., Snow, C., Dressler, C., Lippman, D., . . . White, C. (2004). Closing the gap: Addressing the vocabulary needs of English language learners in bilingual and mainstream classrooms. *Reading Research Quarterly, 39*(2), 188–215.

Carlo, M., & Bengochea, A. (2011). Best practices in literacy instruction for English language learners. In L. Gambrel & L. Morrow, *Best practices in literacy instruction* (4th ed., pp. 117–137). New York: Guilford Press.

Carnock, J. T. (2017). Southeast is fastest growing region for English learners. Retrieved June, 4 2018, from *www.newamerica.org/education-policy/edcentral/southeast-els.*

Cervantes-Soon, C. G. (2014). A critical look at dual language immersion in the new Latin@ diaspora. *Bilingual Research Journal, 37*(1), 64–82.

Cole, M. (1992). Culture and cognitive development: From cross-cultural comparisons to model systems of cultural mediation. In A. F. Healy, S. M. Kosslyn, & R. M. Shiffrin (Eds.), *From learning theory to cognitive processes: Essays in honor of William K. Estes* (pp. 279–305). Hillsdale, NJ: Erlbaum.

Delpit, L. (1986). Skills and other dilemmas of a progressive black educator. *Harvard Educational Review, 56*(4), 379–386.

Engeström, Y. (2004). Non scolae sed vitae discimus: Toward overcoming the encapsulation of school. *Learning and Instruction, 1,* 243–259.

Escamilla, K., Hopewell, S., Butvilofsky, S., Sparrow, W., Soltero-González, L., Ruiz-Figueroa, O., & Escamilla, M. (2014). *Biliteracy from the start: Literacy squared in action.* Philadelphia: Caslon.

Faulstich Orellana, M. (2009). *Translating childhoods: Immigrant youth, language and culture.* New Brunswick, NJ: Rutgers University Press.

García, O. (2009). Education, multilingualism and translanguaging in the 21st century. In T. Skutnabb-Kangas, R. Phillipson, A. K. Mohanty, & M. Panda (Eds.), *Social justice through multilingual education* (pp. 140–158). Bristol, UK: Multilingual Matters.

García, O. (2011). *Bilingual education in the 21st century: A global perspective.* New York: Wiley.

Garcia, O. (2017). Translanguaging in schools: Subiendo y bajando, bajando y subiendo as afterword. *Journal of Language, Identity, and Education, 16*(4), 256–263.

García, O., & Kleifgen, J. A. (2010). *Educating emergent bilinguals: Policies, programs, and practices for English language learners.* New York: Teachers College Press.

Gottlieb, M., Cranley, M. E., & Cammilleri, A. (2007). *Understanding the WIDA English language proficiency standards: A resource guide.* Madison: Board of Regents of the University of Wisconsin System.

Gutiérrez, K. (2008). Developing a sociocritical literacy in the third space. *Reading Research Quarterly, 43*(2), 148–164.

Gutiérrez, K. (2012). Re-mediating current activity for the future. *Mind, Culture, and Activity: An International Journal, 19,* 17–21.

Gutiérrez, K., Bien, A., & Selland, M. (2011). Polylingual and polycultural learning ecologies: Mediating emergent academic literacies for dual language learners. *Journal of Early Childhood Literacy, 11*(2), 232–261.

Gutiérrez, K., & Rogoff, B. (2003). Cultural ways of learning: Individual traits or repertoires of practice. *Educational Researcher, 32,* 19–25.

Gutiérrez, K., Zepeda, M., & Castro, D. (2010). Advancing early literacy learning for all children: Implications of the NELP report for dual language learners. *Educational Researcher, 39*(4), 334–339.

Iddings, A. C., Combs, M. C., & Moll, L. (2012). In the arid zone: Drying out educational resources for English language learners through policy and practice. *Urban Education, 47*(2), 495–514.

Jimenez, R. T. (2001). "It's a difference that changes us": An alternative view of the language and literacy learning needs of Latina/o students. *The Reading Teacher, 54*(8), 736–742.

Laboratory for Comparative Human Cognition. (1989). Kids and computers: A positive vision of the future. *Harvard Educational Review, 59*(1), 73–86.

Lesaux, N. K., Kieffer, M. J., Faller, S. E., & Kelley, J. G. (2010). The effectiveness and ease of implementation of an academic vocabulary intervention for linguistically diverse students in urban middle schools. *Reading Research Quarterly, 45,* 196–228.

Martínez, R. (2013). Reading the world in Spanglish: Hybrid language practices and ideological contestation in a sixth-grade English language arts classroom. *Linguistics and Education, 24,* 276–288.

McKeown, M. G., & Beck, I. L. (2004). Direct and rich vocabulary instruction. In J. F. Baumann & E. J. Kame'enui (Eds.), *Vocabulary instruction: Research to practice* (pp. 13–27). New York: Guilford Press.

Moll, L. C., & Diaz, E. (1987). Change as the goal of educational research. *Anthropology and Educational Quarterly, 18,* 300–311.

Motha, S. (2014). *Race, empire, and English language teaching: Creating responsible and ethical anti-racist practice.* New York: Teachers College Press.

Nakamoto, J., Lindsey, K. A., & Manis, F. R. (2007). A longitudinal analysis of English language learners word decoding and reading comprehension. *Reading and Writing: An Interdisciplinary Journal, 20,* 691–719.

National Center for Education Statistics. (2017). Local Education Agency (School District) Universe Survey Data. Retrieved June 4, 2018, from *https://nces.ed.gov/ccd/pubagency.asp*.

National Clearinghouse for English Language Acquisition (NCELA). (2011). *The growing number of English learner students, 2009–2010*, Washington, DC: Author. Retrieved June 4, 2018, *https://ncela.ed.gov/growing-number-english-learner-students-2009-2010*.

National Clearinghouse for English Language Acquisition (NCELA). (2018). *SY 2015–2016 Consolidated State Performance Report, Part I and Part II–State by State Reports*. Washington, DC: Author. Retrieved June 4, 2018, from *www2.ed.gov/admins/lead/account/consolidated/index.html#sy15-16*.

National Education Association. (2008). *English language learners face unique challenges: Policy brief*. Washington, DC: Author. Retrieved June, 4, 2018, *http://citeseerx.ist.psu.edu/viewdoc/summary?doi=10.1.1.190.2895*.

Ochs, E. (1993). Constructing social identity: A language socialization perspective. *Research on Language and Social Interaction, 26*(3), 287–306.

Ochs, E., & Schieffelin, B. (2011). The theory of language socialization. In A. Duranti, E. Ochs, & B. Schieffelin (Eds.), *The handbook of language socialization* (pp. 1–21). Malden, MA: Wiley-Blackwell.

Ochs, E., & Schieffelin, B. (2017). Language socialization: An historical overview. In P. A. Duff & N. H. Hornberger (Eds.), *Encyclopedia of language education, 2nd edition: Vol. 8. Language socialization* (pp. 3–16). New York: Springer.

Otheguy, R., García, O., & Reid, W. (2015). Clarifying translanguaging and deconstructing named languages: A perspective from linguistics. *Applied Linguistics Review, 6*(3), 281–307.

Pacheco, M. (2012). Learning in/through everyday resistance: A cultural–historical perspective on community resources and curriculum. *Educational Researcher, 41*(4), 121–132.

Peña, E., & Kester, E. S. (2004). Semantic development in Spanish–English bilinguals. In B. A. Goldstein (Ed.), *Bilingual language development and disorders in Spanish–English speakers* (pp. 105–128). Baltimore: Brookes.

Quijano, A. (2000). Coloniality of power and Eurocentrism in Latin America. *International Sociology, 15*(2), 215–232.

Razfar, A. (2005). Language ideologies in practice: Repair and classroom discourse. *Linguistics and Education, 16*, 404–424.

Razfar, A. (2010). Repair with *confianza*: Rethinking the context of corrective feedback for English learners (ELs). *English Teaching: Practice and Critique, 9*(2), 11–31.

Rogoff, B. (2003). *The cultural nature of human development*. New York: Oxford University Press.

Rumbaut, R., & Massey, D. (2013). Immigration and language diversity in the United States. *Daedalus, 142*(3), 141–154.

Santa Ana, O. (Ed.). (2004). *Tongue-tied: The lives of multilingual children in public education*. New York: Rowman & Littlefield.

Scarcella, R. (2003). *Academic English: A conceptual framework*. Los Angeles: University of California Language Minority Research.

Schmidt, R. (2000). *Language policy and identity politics in the United States*. Philadelphia: Temple University Press.

Snow, C. E., Burns, M. S., & Griffin, P. (1998). *Preventing reading difficulties in young children*. Washington, DC: National Academy Press.

Strauss, V. (2014, August 21). For first time, minority students expected to be majority in U.S. public schools this fall. *Washington Post*. Retrieved from *www.washingtonpost.com/news/answer-sheet/wp/2014/08/21/for-first-time-minority-students-expected-to-be-majority-in-u-s-public-schools-this-fall/?noredirect=on&utm_term=.4b7283346c2e*.

Taylor, P. (2014). *The next America: Boomers, millennials, and the looming generational showdown*. New York; Public Affairs/Perseus Book Group.

U.S. Census Bureau. (2015). Table 1: Detailed languages spoken at home by English proficiency 2009–2013, Oct. 2015. In C. Ryan, *Language use in the United States: 2011* (p. 3). Washington, DC: Author.

Vaughn, S., Martinez, L. R., Linan-Thompson, S., Reutebuch, C. K., Carlson, C. D., & Francis, D. J. (2009). Enhancing social studies vocabulary and comprehension for seventh-grade English language learners: Findings from two experimental studies. *Journal of Research on Educational Effectiveness, 2*, 297–324.

Vygotsky, L. S. (1978). *Mind in society*. Cambridge, MA: Harvard University Press.

Wong-Fillmore, L., & Snow, C. (2005). What teachers need to know about language. In C. T. Adger, C. E. Snow, & D. Christian (Eds.), *What teachers need to know about language* (pp. 7–54). Washington, DC: Center for Applied Linguistics.

Zong, J., & Batalova, J. (2015). *The limited English proficient population in the United States*. Washington, DC: Migration Policy Institute.

CHAPTER 7

Best Practices in Adolescent Literacy Instruction

DOUGLAS FISHER
NANCY FREY

This chapter will:

- Explore the theory, research, and best practices related to content areas and disciplinary literacy.
- Emphasize the value of students collaborating with their peers in learning environments.
- Analyze close reading practices, including annotation, text-based discussions, and writing with evidence as approaches that mobilize both content-area reading approaches as well as disciplinary approaches.

Mauricio is a 10th grader at the school where we teach. We asked him to keep track of all of the things he read for a day. His log included text messages, community signs, a history textbook, Snapchat, an online article for his science class, several Google page results, the novel he was reading for English, and flyers on the walls of the school announcing various events. The vast majority of what Mauricio reads on a daily basis is informational in nature. He mostly reads to find information, some of it by his choice and some of it for school. Luckily, Mauricio has been taught to read for information and easily comprehends the various texts he reads. Importantly, much of the reading Mauricio read involved collaboration with others. For example, his reading of the science article involved an extended collaborative conversation with his peers. And the novel he was reading was discussed as part of his book club. Mauricio's learning is enhanced when he is provided opportunities to interact with his peers.

READING FOR INFORMATION IN SECONDARY SCHOOLS

Reading for information is a specific kind of reading and accounts for the bulk of the reading adults do. While reading for information has some core processes in common with reading for pleasure, there are differences that have instructional implications. Getting lost in a story requires a certain set of skills, whether you are nine or 49, including an understanding of plot-driven literature in which characters interact in specific settings. These narrative structures are useful in that they provide readers with a window on and a mirror to the world (Cullinan, 1989). Some literature allows us to learn about people we might never meet and visit places we may never travel to in our lifetimes—the window metaphor. And some literature allows us to see and affirm ourselves and people like us, as if in a mirror. Of course, literature can be used to help students understand content as well. For example, students can read historical fiction to broaden their understanding of various time periods.

But an understanding of plot-driven narrative texts will not provide the reader with the skills necessary to read for information. Expository, or informational, texts do not rely on plots, settings, dialogue, and conflicts to make their point. These texts differ in that they attempt to explain the social, physical, and biological worlds in which we live. They have different text structures, such as problem–solution or cause–effect, and often contain text features such as figures, charts, diagrams, and headings that contain valuable information.

That's not to say that informational texts are better. Reading both narrative and expository texts is important; they do different things for our brains. It's just that teaching one, and not the other, is more common. As Duke (2000) noted, a scarcity of informational texts are used in the primary grades. Without experience with informational texts, some students struggle in school, failing to gain knowledge through wide reading. And their middle and high school teachers wonder why they can't gain information from the texts they're reading. The solution isn't as easy as assigning more informational texts in the primary grades. Students have to be taught how to read, write, speak, listen, and think in each of the disciplines in which they are expected to perform. In other words, reading like a scientist really is different from reading (or writing for that matter) like a historian or an art critic. The remainder of this chapter focuses on best practices in content-area literacy, a long and distinguished field that has focused on helping teachers and students use literacy across the disciplines. We expand the discussion to encompass a newer construct known as "disciplinary literacy." Before we do that, however, we first note the value of students collaborating with their peers.

COLLABORATION: A KEY TO ADOLESCENT LITERACY

As we noted with Mauricio's learning, student-to-student interaction is important and can improve learning. A lot of evidence demonstrates that collaborative conversations improve the speed of learning. As an example, Hattie (2009) conducted a review of several thousand meta-analyses to create his now famous list of what works best. High on the list, with an effect size of 0.82, is classroom discussion. Also high on the list is cooperative versus independent learning, with an effect size of 0.59, and cooperative versus competitive learning at 0.54. In other words, there is plenty of evidence for us to recommend that significant numbers of instructional minutes be devoted to students working together. As you will see in the "Best Practices in Action" sections that follow, high-quality instructional routines often allow students to work with their peers.

EVIDENCE-BASED BEST PRACTICES

Early reading research efforts focused on specific processes, such as decoding or comprehension. Much of this early research focused on young students learning to read. The seminal text by Hal Herber (1970) changed that. Herber suggested that researchers and teachers should focus on reading in content areas. Many of the ideas in Herber's book, widely accepted as the first comprehensive text on content-area literacy, are still used today. As we discuss further in the section that follows, there are a number of effective approaches for fostering students' reading, writing, speaking, and listening in every content area. Having said that, there are two areas of research that inform our work today.

For several decades, content-area teachers were told, "Every teacher is a teacher of reading." Unfortunately, this isn't accurate when you consider the complexity of the reading process as identified in this book. Reading instruction requires a deep knowledge of language structure and function (Schleppegrell, 2013). Instead of thinking that every teacher is a reading teacher, today we note that learning is based in language (Fisher,

Frey & Hattie, 2016). This is more than a semantic change. It's a conceptual change focused on the things that have to happen in a classroom for students to learn. An understanding that learning is based in language helps teachers structure their instructional time such that students read, write, and speak, not just listen, in the classroom. Providing students time to use language as part of their content-area instruction has the power to significantly improve achievement (Fisher & Frey, 2014).

Another difference since Herber's seminal work centers on disciplinary literacy. Shanahan and Shanahan (2008, 2012) examined literacy learning and concluded that there are three stages of development: basic literacy, intermediate literacy, and disciplinary literacy (see Figure 7.1). Basic literacy represents the foundational and generalizable skills that are needed for all reading tasks—decoding skills, comprehension of print and literacy conventions, recognition of high-frequency words, and usual fluency routines.

As students progress beyond this stage—typically in the upper primary grades—they move into intermediate literacy. This stage involves the development of skills that allow readers to use some generic techniques to understand their literacy tasks. At this stage, students are better able to

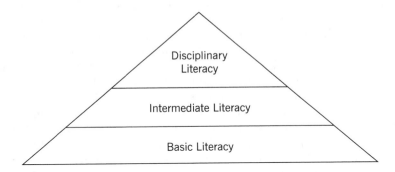

Basic Literacy: Literacy skills such as decoding and knowledge of high-frequency words that underlie virtually all reading tasks.

Intermediate Literacy: Literacy skills common to many tasks, including generic comprehension strategies, common word meanings, and basic fluency.

Disciplinary Literacy: Literacy skills specialized to history, science, mathematics, literature, or other subject matter.

FIGURE 7.1. The increasing specialization of literacy development. From Shanahan and Shanahan (2008, p. 44). Copyright 2008 by the President and Fellows of Harvard College. Reprinted by permission.

employ various cognitive comprehension strategies and can utilize fix-up procedures to address misunderstandings. Additionally, they are able to take notes, activate background knowledge, summarize their thinking, and so on.

Beyond this second stage, disciplinary literacy becomes the focus. The skills involved in this stage are usually not formally taught and are difficult to learn due to the abstract nature of many discipline-specific texts. Moreover, disciplinary literacy is constrained in terms of its applicability to a wide range of reading materials. Specifically, an English teacher who is proficient in teaching literacy skills related to reading classic and contemporary novels may not be so skilled at guiding students to comprehend a technical biology article from a professional journal.

In order for students to gain discipline-specific literacies necessary for content learning, they must be able to transform texts in their minds and on paper. In the next section, we explore instructional practices necessary for this to occur. However, these hinge on two assumptions about text difficulty and reading volume. In the absence of these assumptions, best practices for transforming texts have limited effectiveness.

In discussing best practices, it is useful to identify assumptions on which these practices are predicated. Our first assumption is related to text difficulty. As Allington (2002) emphatically states, "You can't learn much from books you can't read" (p. 16). In fact, there is no evidence that 11-grade learners reading at the fifth-grade level will benefit from independently reading 11th-grade texts without instruction and support. Discarding the textbook altogether is not advised, but a student who is reading well below grade level is going to need supplemental texts that will allow him or her to extract information in a meaningful way. Thankfully, readings on a wide range of topics are widely available using digital search engines. In addition, textbook publishers have responded to the demand for a range of texts and modalities. Most of the instructional materials on the market today offer parallel texts written 2 or more years below grade level, as well as digital versions that are read aloud by a pre-recorded voice, allowing the user to follow along in the text. These text-based supports allow struggling readers to benefit more fully from transformational instruction by lowering the barriers presented by texts that are too difficult to read.

Our second assumption is that students read widely. A steady diet of daily reading does wonders for building background knowledge about the range of topics needed across the curriculum (Fisher, Grant, & Ross, 2010). A study of educational success among students in 27 countries found that coming from a home with 500 books was the strongest predictor of a child's level of educational attainment—stronger than parents' occupation, education, or demographics (Evans, Kelley, Sikora, & Treiman, 2010). And while it may not be feasible to stock their home libraries, our students' use of daily opportunities to read from an array of texts has a positive effect on their content learning. When these two assumptions are in place—texts across a gradient of difficulty and daily opportunities to read—the effects of best practices are magnified.

BEST PRACTICES IN ACTION FOR CONTENT LITERACY

Educators have long known that learning is an active process that requires the student to manipulate information in order to make it his or her own (Bransford, Brown, & Cocking, 1999). Inadequate instructional practices rely on transmission, rather than transformation, of knowledge. In each of the following sections, we begin our discussion about best practices for adolescents by exploring content-area reading. Then we turn our attention to disciplinary reading. As Shanahan and Shanahan (2008) noted, one is not better than the other. Their model implies that disciplinary literacy rests on strong generic literacy skills.

Developing and Activating Background

There are at least two approaches for developing background knowledge: direct and indirect. Direct approaches immerse the student in the learning moment and include field trips, internships, and other methods of experiential learning that provide them with fodder to talk with others about their experiences. Indirect approaches are those that take place in the classroom and do not require relocating students to another environment. These indirect approaches include the aforementioned wide reading, as well as vocabulary instruction.

Vocabulary instruction, which is discussed more thoroughly in another chapter in this book, is essential to content-area learning. Students arrive at the classroom door with incomplete vocabulary knowledge that is specific to the discipline. This can be misleading for students, who may believe that because they can furnish one definition, they know everything they need to know about a term. This is especially true for multiple-meaning words that are influenced by the context. For instance, the words *root, bark,* and *cone* are as essential to a botany unit as *xylem* and *monocot*. However, neglect of these multiple-meaning words, while favoring the obvious scientific vocabulary, can create gaps in student knowledge. In turn, this leads to incomplete background knowledge for future learning.

Graphic Organizers

Graphic organizers are a tool that students can use fairly generically across content areas. Venn diagrams, concept maps, semantic webs, compare-and-contrast charts, cause-and-effect charts, and the like, allow students to create visual representations of what they have read, heard, or seen. Transforming a piece of text into a graphic and visual form requires that students reread and engage in critical thinking about what they read. Graphic organizers have been used with students of all ages and across the disciplines (McCrudden & Rapp, 2017). They have been used with students with disabilities (Gajria, Jitendra, & Sood, 2007), English language learners (Rubinstein-Ávila, 2006), and students identified as gifted and talented (Cassidy, 1989). In sum, graphic organizers are an effective way for students to learn, and remember, content. Unfortunately, sometimes graphic organizers are simple photocopies and function more like worksheets rather than thinking tools. Let's consider a nonexample and a more effective example.

The misuse of a graphic organizer occurs when students are asked to copy information onto the tool, often while the teacher does all of the work and thus all of the thinking. For example, the students in Ms. Hardy's sixth-grade science class were each provided with a photocopy of a Venn diagram. Following her reading of an informational text that compared cuttlefish and squid, the students copied the information that she wrote and projected with a document camera. By the end of the lesson, each student had an exact replica of the teachers' graphic organizer but they had done none of the analysis or thinking to produce it. While the product is impressive, the students in Ms. Hardy's class are not benefiting from the use of graphic organizers as a tool for transforming text. They are no more likely to use a Venn diagram when confronted with a text that compares and contrasts information. And they are not very likely to remember the specific information about cuttlefish and squid.

The students in Ms. Epstein's seventh-grade earth science class have a very different experience with graphic organizers. They were taught various tools at the beginning of the year and are encouraged to select a tool that fits with the information presented. During the unit on volcanoes and earthquakes, for example, students are provided with readings from textbooks, the Internet, and a number of additional informational sources. On one particular day, students are reading the textbook in class. Listening in while a group works illustrates the ways in which graphic organizers can be used to ensure understanding. Jessica used a Venn diagram to collect information from the chapter about the similarities and differences between earthquakes and volcanoes. Marco used a flow chart to document the process, which includes the relationship between the two actions that occur when tectonic plates move. Daisy created two semantic maps to identify the meanings of the terms, examples of each, as well as the processes that created them. Their discussion highlights the effectiveness of student-created graphic organizers.

DAISY: So, the plates kinda rub together for both, right?

MARCO: Yeah, when the plates rub, it's the start of the process. But right here (*points to a part of his graphic organizer*), there's a difference. In this direction, you get a volcano but in this direction you get an earthquake. See?

JESSICA: I get it. It's like what I wrote in common. They both have a start with the tectonic plates of the Earth. And they both occur around the edges of plates, or the breaks in the plates.

DAISY: Yeah, and we got some bad ones. Like the one in San Francisco.

Their conversation continues and the students regularly make reference to the tools they have created. The result of their work was increased understanding of the content as well as reinforcement of the different ways to transform a text and really understand it.

Note Taking

Note taking is another generic content-area tool that students can use across classes and content areas. Most experts in a discipline know how to take notes, even though what they pay attention to and record may be different. Note taking occurs as students listen or when they take a piece of text and distill its essential features, key ideas, or main points to record in their notes. Notes should not be inclusive of all of the information presented, as that would be redundant (the reader could simply reread the text or play the digital recording over again). Instead, notes should highlight content and serve an external storage function.

While taking notes is a strong predictor of test performance (Peverly, Ramaswamy, & Brown, 2007), students often do not know how to take good notes. In a study of the implementation of several content-literacy instructional routines, teachers noted that students had difficulty with identifying main ideas and summarizing, and that their instruction in taking and making notes improved student performance (Fisher, Frey, & Lapp, 2009).

As with other instructional procedures used to improve students' understanding of the content, note taking can go astray. When Mr. Thibodeaux created a fill-in-the-blank page for a reading he assigned students, his students did not learn to think deeply about the text. Instead, they were on a mission to find the right answer to write on the line. They didn't ever really read the text and certainly didn't think about the information in their quest to finish the task.

When Devon took notes from a primary-source document about Mount Vesuvius in his middle school social studies class, he transformed the text and included visuals and words. His teachers taught him how to identify key ideas and summarize through their modeling. For example, several months before Devon's reading about the tragic events in Italy in 79 CE, his English teacher modeled her thinking and note making by using a number of informational articles. While reading about the creation of the QWERTY keyboard, she paused every so often. Devon's English teacher makes comments such as, "This seems really important because the author took the time to write about it and include an illustration. I think that will need to be included in my notes." With practice and instruction, students can be taught to store content-area information in their notes. And this process will serve them well, whether they are in a college class or at a business meeting. We all rely on notes as reminders and triggers for our memory.

Writing to Learn

Writing to learn is yet another way for students to develop their generic literacy skills. When students write, they think. Writing requires students to consider what they already know, what they have read, and what they think. Writing to learn is not process writing, meaning that teachers do not evaluate students' writing for mechanics and grammar. Instead, student responses are used to check for ascertaining that the writer has developed an understanding of the content. As McDermott (2010) noted, "Instead of having students parrot science facts back to the instructor, writing-to-learn activities focus on the production of nontraditional writing assignments—such as poems, brochures, or letters—to develop student understanding" (p. 33).

As with all instructional routines designed to improve student performance, writing to learn can be used in ways that are ineffective. For example, when ninth-grade humanities teacher Ms. Haddock asked her students to "write about a personal experience with travel," the responses varied widely and were really of no use in activating students' background knowledge about immigration in preparation for their study of *The Circuit* (Jiménez, 1997). In this case, the prompt was not created in such a way as to ensure learning from and while writing. There are a number of prompts that can be used effectively in writing to learn. Fisher and Frey (2008) provide the following list of examples paraphrased below:

- *Admit slips.* Upon entering the classroom, students write on an assigned topic such as "What did you notice was important in yesterday's discussion?" or "Explain the difference between jazz and rock."
- *Found poems.* Students reread an assigned text and find key phrases that "speak" to them, then arrange these into a poem structure without adding any of their own words (Dunning & Stafford, 1992).
- *Cinquains.* A five-line poem in which the first line is the topic (a noun), the second line is a description of the topic in two words, the third line is three *-ing* words, the fourth line is a description of the topic in four words, and the final line is a synonym of the topic word from line one.
- *Yesterday's news.* Students summarize the information presented the day before, either from a film, lecture, discussion, or reading.
- *"What if" scenarios.* Students respond to prompts in which information is changed from what they know and they predict outcomes. For example, students may be asked to respond to "What would be different if the Civil War was fought in 1920?"
- *Take a stand.* Students discuss their opinions about a controversial topic such as "Just because we can, should we clone people?"
- *Exit slips.* Used as a closure activity at the end of the period, students write on an assigned prompt such as "The three best things I learned today are. . . . "

BEST PRACTICES IN ACTION
FOR DISCIPLINARY LITERACY

A decade ago, a chapter on adolescent literacy might have ended with the discussion on content-area literacy. We now know a lot more, and disciplinary literacy is gaining traction and attention. Having said that, we think it's important to note that there is a role for both generic, content-area literacy and disciplinary literacy. As Brozo, Moorman, Meyer, and Stewart (2013) noted, there is a "radical center" in which these two ways of thinking about adolescent literacy can both be used. To our thinking, teachers toggle back and forth between generic and disciplinary literacy, much like the experts in their respective fields do.

Remember Mauricio from the opening of this chapter? He was a novice and used a lot of generic approaches. Some would argue that his instruction should focus on disciplinary literacy. So we asked a historian named Matt, not a history teacher, to track his literacy use during the day. Like Mauricio, he engaged in a number of generic literacy tasks, such as taking notes during a lecture, noting new terms that he had not heard before, and checking his Facebook page. But he also used a number of discipline-specific approaches. For example, he received a new issue of a professional journal and noted his use of sourcing and corroborating. He wrote in the margins of a journal article, focusing on what he thought was bias in the way the author presented some facts. He considered the context of the time in history, including the political, cultural, and social forces that influenced thinking. Unlike Mauricio, Matt used both generic and disciplinary approaches to his literacy, and so can students.

Disciplinary Literacy in History

Discipline-specific literacy in social studies and history demands that students are able to read, discuss, and write critically about historical events and documents. Wineburg's (1991) comparative analysis of high school history students and historians exposed a glaring gap in the use of analytic thinking by the two groups. High school students were much more vulnerable to simply accepting the content of the documents at face value, while historians routinely interrogated the text. Stahl and Shanahan (2004) identified three essential literacy practices of historians, namely, that they identify the source of the information, corroborate the contents through other reliable sources, and contextualize the information within the milieu of the time. Monte-Sano and De La Paz (2012) have researched how the construction of document-based questioning prompts influence whether students use or fail to use these practices. They found that prompts written to spur thinking about sourcing ("What was happening in the world that motivated them to give these speeches?"), causation ("Why did they speak out?"), or corroboration ("What are the similarities and differences between these two documents?") resulted in higher-quality writing (p. 279). On the other hand, situated prompts that asked students what they would do ("Write a letter to the secretary-general.") resulted in lower-quality historical reasoning because students wrote from a contemporary perspective, rather than a historical one.

Discipline-Specific Literacy in Science

In contrast, scientific literacy requires that students apply knowledge across texts and science fields in order to understand concepts. For example, understanding the process of osmosis requires knowledge of biology, chemistry, and physics. Faggella-Luby, Samson Graner, Deshler, and Valentino Drew (2012) state that "novice readers often ignore, discount, or compartmentalize information," unlike scientists who "deeply engage with concepts across science genres" and fields (p. 71). The inability to think across science content limits students' ability to create scientific texts, such as reporting on results of lab experiments. Nam, Choi, and Hand (2011) recommend use of a science-writing heuristic to promote such critical thinking. Throughout the lab, the science teacher pauses to promote written student inquiry:

- *Question*: What are my questions I hope to answer through this experiment?
- *Test*: What tests can I conduct?
- *Observe*: What are my observations?
- *Inquiry*: What are my data?
- *Claim and Evidence*: What do I claim? What is my evidence?
- *Collaboration*: How do my claims compare to others?
- *Reflection*: How have my ideas changed from the beginning?

In this model, science writing isn't viewed as a single element of literacy, but rather as the convergence of all elements of literacy. Students read and discuss the work of others, make observations, analyze data, and write about them. In comparative studies of middle school science students, the researchers found that public discussion and negotiation of the investigation resulted in higher levels of application of scientific argumentation in their summary writing (Nam et al., 2011).

In the next section, we discuss four instructional approaches that provide meaningful access to complex texts and content. These text-based supports allow struggling readers to benefit more fully from transformational instruction by lowering the barriers presented by texts that are too difficult to read. Importantly, these supports—close reading, annotation, discussion, and writing with evidence—require the use of all facets of literacy.

MOBILIZING CONTENT-AREA AND DISCIPLINARY APPROACHES TO IMPROVE STUDENTS' THINKING AND LEARNING

There are a number of ways that the two major initiatives focused on improving adolescent literacy can be combined to improve learning for middle and high school students. In this chapter, we focus on close reading as an instructional routine that provides an example of the type of learning that students can do in their classes. We'll follow Kim Elliot, a high school biology teacher, as she leads her students through lessons featuring these practices.

Close Reading

The practice of close analytic reading of complex text is not new, having been applied for nearly a century in college classrooms across the world. High school educators have relied for many years on the works of Adler and Van Doren (*How to Read a Book* [1972]) and Paul and Elder (*The Thinker's Guide to How to Read a Paragraph* [2008]) to guide students through careful inspection of a text. Having said that, not all texts deserve this kind of attention. Paul and Elder (2008, Reading for a Purpose, ¶ 5) advise that the first step is determining the purpose of the reading:

1. *Sheer pleasure*: requires no particular skill level.
2. *To figure out a simple idea*: which may require skimming the text.
3. *To gain specific technical information*: skimming skills required.
4. *To enter, understand, and appreciate a new world view*: requires close reading skills in working through a challenging series of tasks that stretch our minds.
5. *To learn a new subject*: requires close reading skills in internalizing and taking ownership of an organized system of meanings.

When a sufficiently complex text does warrant careful inspection, close reading instruction is in order. In our experience, we have found that short passages, be they wholly self-contained or excerpted from a longer reading, work best. This allows students to zoom in on a particularly challenging text, one rich with disciplinary knowledge, in order to deeply understand its content. High school biology teacher Kim Elliot did just that during a unit on evolution. She selected a passage from *The Panda's Thumb: More Reflections in Natural History* (Gould, 1980). "I chose this reading as part of a larger study of contrivances, or imperfect but functional adaptations, in organisms," she said. "My students will also be reading and discussing other examples, like Darwin's work on the study of floral diversification." She determined the purpose of the reading—to learn a new subject—and identified the main points. "I want them to understand that these adaptations are the product of whatever the organism had available, and how these resulting contrivances are a bit of evolutionary 'make do.' What I mean by that is that although it isn't perfect, it's functional and pretty clever," she said.

Her close reading consists of a minimal amount of frontloading. Students had previously learned about the basic elements of evolution earlier in the week. "They need some prior knowledge to draw upon if they're going to understand this article," Ms. Elliot remarked. A hallmark of a novice learner is that he or she is not good at knowing what information he or she will need for a task, and therefore he or she frequently overlooks existing knowledge he or she possesses when learning something new. "In the past I probably would have spent 20 minutes reteaching them what they had previously learned before we ever got to the article," she said. "But that's not what scientists do. They have to consolidate what is known and what is unknown. I realized that when I do all the frontloading they didn't have to think about what they need. It's like packing for a trip. It's more challenging when you have to decide what goes in the suitcase yourself, as opposed to having someone pack it for you."

Students first begin to transform information in their minds by making connections to what they already know. This requires them to leverage the *right* prior knowledge in order to begin building a schema for new information. "That's tough for them," said the science teacher. "But I need for them to consider and either discard or select relevant information for themselves," she said. "I can't always be the one doing all the thinking for them."

Ms. Elliot usually has students read the passage once to themselves "to get the flow of the information" and "if it's really tough I'll read it aloud to them while they follow along." Students who need more support might listen to an audio recording, or read the text in shorter chunks. Ms. Elliot said, "When I first started I thought I would really have a hard time with my students who read below grade level, but in practice that hasn't been the case because there's so much rereading and discussion that the kids who don't get it the first time begin to understand it better as we proceed."

Ms. Elliot often thinks aloud about a portion of the passage to model scientific thinking. "I added a labeled diagram of a panda's paw to the reading," said Ms. Elliot. "The part I chose to model was how I drew on the anatomy unit we had completed a few months ago to understand the terms in the article and the diagram. I thought aloud about the adductor and abductor muscles in order to show them how I was drawing on knowledge from a previous unit to understand."

Annotation

The practice of annotating a text, that is, marking and writing on the text in a meaningful way, is as old as books themselves. Even centuries ago when a monastery's library might only hold 10 or 20 books, monks made annotations on sacred texts. There are several reasons for annotating text, first and foremost because it promotes cognitive interaction and metacognitive thinking. It can also contribute to discipline-specific understanding of texts. Monte-Sano (2011) described the efficacy of annotations to support the development of historical reasoning in high school. Initially students annotated little or not at all, but with practice and feedback from their teacher on the annotations, students in the study were increasingly adept at using multiple, contrasting pieces of evidence to support claims and interpretations.

Science students must locate and construct valid arguments based on evidence (Driver, Newton, & Osborne, 2000). However, novice science students often simply consume texts whole without noticing the evidence forwarded to support a claim. Annotation practices invite students to slow down, reread, and interact with texts. During Ms. Elliot's close reading of the passage from *The Panda's Thumb* (Gould, 1980), students were required to annotate. "The second time they read through the text, I tell them to annotate," she said. "We've done quite a bit of work as a school on annotation so that students are comfortable doing this."

Her school has developed guidelines for doing so, and encourages students to customize their annotations as they become more skilled. Schoolwide annotation practices, derived from the work of Adler and Van Doren (1972) include:

- Underline the major points using your pen or pencil.
- Circle keywords or phrases that are confusing or unknown to you.
- Write a question mark (?) for areas you are wondering about during the reading. Be sure to write your question!
- Use an exclamation mark (!) for things that surprise you and briefly note what it was that caught your attention.

"Some teachers use highlighters as well, although I don't because I want them to spend more of their attention on making notes to themselves, rather than filling the page with bright colors. I know when I look back at some of my old college textbooks I have no idea why I highlighted something. I wasn't annotating," she said. Student annotations also give her insight into what a student is noticing and not noticing. "When I have a student who is struggling with understanding and interpreting a complex text, I ask her to show me her annotations," Ms. Elliot said. "Sometimes it's practically blank, which tells me they aren't reading for detail. Other times I see the questions they have written and places where they have marked their confusion. It helps me laser-in on what the roadblock might be." In the case of this passage, the main idea was in the second sentence, and easily overlooked by most of her students during the early phase of the close reading lesson: "Our textbooks like to illustrate evolution with examples of optimal design—nearly perfect mimicry of a dead leaf by a butterfly or of a poisonous species by a palatable relative. But ideal design is a lousy argument for evolution" (Gould, 1980, p. 20).

Ms. Elliot observed the annotative behaviors of her students, making notes to herself about who noticed and who did not. Rather than correct this immediately (a temptation to be sure), she used this information to guide discussion of the main idea and key details, reminding students to continue to annotate throughout the discussion phase of the close reading lesson.

Discussion

Meaningful talk about complex text drives close reading lessons. As noted earlier, students engage in repeated readings and annotate in order to transform thoughts and questions onto paper. But without discussion, these practices are far less effective. It also requires a skilled teacher to lead the discussion, not just host an extended question-and-answer session. The use of accountable talk practices (Michaels, O'Connor, Hall, & Resnick, 2010) ensures that students practice the three principles of discussion: accountability to the classroom community, to the knowledge base, and to the practice of reasoning and logic as an intellectual pursuit. In practice, it is common to consider the student side of accountable talk; in truth, it begins with the teacher's consistent use of these same principles. Michaels et al. (2010) recommend that teachers use the following conversational moves to promote accountable talk and avoid regressing to a "chalk and talk" session (italics are direct quote from pp. 27–32):

- *Marking*: "That's an important point." By marking student comments, you alert others to key points that you want to forward.
- *Challenging students*: "What do *you* think?" This is an effective conversational move for turning the conversation back to them. Remember, you already know the content. They're the ones who need to discover it.
- *Keeping the channels open*: "Did everyone hear that?" Large classrooms can make it difficult for students to follow discussions. By asking questions like this from time to time, you mark important points and moderate sound levels.
- *Keeping everyone together*: "Who can repeat . . . ?" This invites students to expand on the comments of others, and reminds them about the importance of listening in discussion.
- *Linking contributions*: "Who wants to add on . . . ?" Many people refer to it as "piggybacking." Adolescents need to acquire the ability to link and synthesize commentary.
- *Verifying and clarifying*: "So, are you saying . . . ?" The teacher is not only a facilitator, but also a guide who elevates the conversation. Restatements such as this can expand academic language and highlight where gaps in knowledge or logic still need to be addressed by the group.

- *Pressing for accuracy*: "Where can we find that?" We use this question frequently, especially with text-based discussion, to guide listeners about how evidence is located. At other times, it can help a speaker discern between hearsay and evidence.
- *Building on prior knowledge*: "How does this connect?" Link the concepts and texts under current discussion to those that have been read and discussed in previous lessons.
- *Pressing for reasoning*: "Why do you think that?" The intent of a question like this is to move the conversation from opinion to argument. This encourages the speaker to provide facts, cite textual evidence, or identify when the circumstance is ambiguous.
- *Expanding reasoning*: "Take your time; say more." The teacher delivers this message to signal the class about the importance of hearing every voice. Some students are quick to answer and can easily dominate. This conversational move validates those who arrive at conclusions as they speak.
- *Recapping*: "What have we discovered?" Extended discussions can end too abruptly and leave participants wondering about larger ideas. This conversational move invites summary and synthesis.

Many secondary students wrongly view the teacher as the primary source; he or she is not. These conversational moves keep the discussion going and challenge students to collectively locate answers within and across texts and experiences. While these conversational moves are generalizable across readings, text-dependent questions are developed with a specific reading in mind. Text-dependent questions cause students to engage in meaningful rereading, and advance their comprehension beyond surface-level comprehension. A three-part cognitive path that works for us is: *What does the text say? How does the text work? What does the text mean?* The first path through a reading invites discussion about the main ideas and details, while the second path asks students to look at the structure. The third path—W*hat does the text mean?*—requires students to infer across the text and make intertextual comparisons. Unfortunately, too often students never progress beyond the first cognitive path and therefore have little experience at deepening their comprehension.

Kim Elliot, a biology teacher, designs text-dependent questions in advance of the close reading in order to guide student thinking. Their initial readings of the text involve the entire passage; as they examine structure and deeper meaning their rereadings sometimes consist of a few sentences or paragraphs:

- *How the text works—General understandings and key details*: How did the panda's thumb evolve? Is this a perfect design or an imperfect one?

- *How the text works–Structure and vocabulary*: How does the author vacillate between posing questions and furnishing information? To what effect? What is an "opposable thumb"? What are the similarities and differences between the panda's paw and the human hand?
- *What the text means–Author's purpose*: How does Gould demonstrate his progression in understanding imperfect design? What is his stance regarding imperfect design?
- *What the text means–Inferencing across the text*: How does the last paragraph of the reading compare and contrast with the first?
- *What the text means–Intertextual connections*: Reexamine the section on evolutionary design in our textbook. Should it be expanded to include examples of imperfect design? Why or why not?

"I don't always use all the questions I prepare, and I don't follow them in a lockstep order," said Ms. Elliot. "It really varies by class period. At times the group comes together very early on in arriving at conclusions or anticipating a point before I have even posed the question. Other times I need to lead them a bit more," she said. "But I'm finding that by having my questions ready, I am much better at listening for learning and inquiry, and not just 'correct answers.' I'm clearer on what I want them to learn from the piece," she offered.

Writing with Evidence

While the quality of notes is a strong predictor of test performance (Peverly et al., 2007), students often do not know how to take good notes. In a study of the implementation of several content-literacy instructional routines, teachers noticed that students had difficulty with identifying main ideas and summarizing, and that their instruction about taking and making notes improved student performance (Fisher, Frey, & Lapp, 2009). At the same time, secondary students find the volume of information they must acquire and process each day challenging.

Another major challenge for secondary students is the increased emphasis on writing to inform, explain, and persuade. Students in middle school may find this especially difficult, given the diminished attention paid in the classroom to writing personal responses. The core standards describe three text types—narrative, informational, and argumentative—that are mixed and matched for a variety of purposes. Rather than writing a one-dimensional piece, students are more often required to combine these in a variety of ways. For example, the passage read by Ms. Elliot's biology class included narrative paragraphs (those in which the author recounted his visit to a zoo as a child), informative paragraphs (those devoted to the anatomy of the panda paw), and argumentative statements (those that linked claims to evidence). However, without good notes to draw upon, students are not adequately prepared to write using evidence. Instead, they rely too heavily on what they have personally experienced, or what they recall from a text read days or weeks ago. In both cases, the result is vague, weakly constructed information.

A third challenge to writing with evidence is that many secondary students write infrequently. A national survey of high school science, social studies, and English teachers found that 47% did not assign a multiparagraph essay even once a month, and 71% did not assign one weekly (Kiuhara, Graham, & Hawken, 2009). We would be appalled if reading assignments were so paltry, and yet the dearth of writing that occurs in high school classrooms is somehow more acceptable to some. It is hard to imagine how students will ever become stronger writers when they engage in actual writing so infrequently.

Ms. Elliot knows that science students need to write regularly. Many of their science writing assignments are text-based. "We call them Science Weeklies at my school," she explained. Students must summarize and synthesize readings drawn from close readings in the classroom and their own outside readings. At the conclusion of the close readings she conducts, she asks her students to use their annotations to create collaborative graphic organizers, another means for transforming the text on paper. Venn diagrams, concept maps, semantic webs, compare-and-contrast charts, cause-and-effect charts, and the like, allow students to create visual representations of what they have read. Transforming a piece of text into a graphic and visual form, as noted earlier, requires that students reread and engage in critical thinking about what they read.

The students in Ms. Elliot's class were taught various organizing tools at the beginning of the year and are encouraged to select the tool that fits with their purpose. After the close reading, students convened in small collaborative groups to expand their annotations using graphic organizing tools. Rather than decide for them, and thus do the critical thinking for them, Ms. Elliot made a variety of graphic organizers available for them to use as models. Students worked together to ensure that key points were recorded. At the end of the week, they will be writing a summary and critique of this reading for their Science Weekly, equipped with evidence to draw from the text.

REFLECTIONS AND NEW DIRECTIONS

The field of adolescent literacy continues to evolve, and a growing body of research is focused on identifying the nature and characteristics of discipline-specific literacies. While much has been written about textbooks in content areas, there is less knowledge in the profession about the ways in which content experts read and understand information in their chosen fields.

A related topic of research is on reading comprehension of digital texts, especially those that are on the Internet. This is an expanding knowledge base in the literacy field, and raises questions about the ways in which we use digital texts, with whom, as well as how we teach and assess it. The interactive nature of Internet spaces is challenging us about how we teach students to find, use, create, and share information.

A common objection we field from content teachers is that these practices take too much time. "How will I cover all my content?" they argue. We contend that they are correct *if they presume to leave everything else as is*. A close reading is hard to squeeze in to a 60-minute period that has always featured 45 minutes of lecture each day. To be sure, the process of teaching students to think, not just consume, is a daunting one. Many students in our classrooms today have relatively little experience at engaging in inquiry; they have become accustomed to being taught exactly what will be on the test and not much more. But our goal is to turn out thinkers, not encyclopedias. That spirit of inquiry, the ability to question and probe texts and with it the thinking of others, is where we are setting the bar for ourselves as a profession. And we can't achieve a higher goal simply through maintaining the status quo.

CONCLUDING REMARKS

Content-area literacy is an important consideration for learners whether they are in preschool or in college. Informational texts differ from narrative texts, and students need to be taught to read—and be encouraged to read—both. As we have noted, there are a number of best practices for helping students learn content, all of which have a basis in language. While we no longer think of all teachers as teachers of reading, teachers can use language—specifically reading, writing, speaking, listening, and viewing—to ensure student understanding. Content-area literacy draws on each of the literacy components addressed in this book, from decoding to vocabulary to comprehension, to enable readers to make sense of the complex and amazing world around them.

And discipline-specific literacy is also an important consideration for adolescent learners. As we have noted, there are a number of best practices for helping students apprentice into the traditions of a given discipline, whether that be art, music, history, science, mathematics, or literary theory. Disciplinary literacy also draws on each of the literacy components addressed in this book from vocabulary to comprehension, to enable readers to make sense of the complex and amazing world around them, but extends students' thinking to include the ways in which experts in that discipline go about their work.

ENGAGEMENT ACTIVITIES

1. Identify the background knowledge necessary to understand this chapter. Do the same thing with an upcoming lesson for your students and identify the generic literacy approaches that will be useful in addressing gaps in knowledge.

2. Identify the differences in the ways different content areas approach reading and writing. How is it that scientists read or write and how is that different from other disciplines?

3. Consider an upcoming lesson. How might you change that lesson to include the evidence-based practices discussed in this chapter? Is there a piece of text that students could read closely?

4. Select a piece of text worthy of instruction. Develop a series of text-dependent questions that require students to return to the text to determine the answers. Review the questions to ensure that they are not limited to recall questions, but rather include a full range of thinking.

RESOURCES

For additional information on instructional approaches, see:

Fisher, D., Frey, N., Hattie, J., & Thayre, M. (2017). *Teaching literacy in the visible learning classroom, 6–12.* Thousand Oaks, CA: Corwin.

Graham, S., & Perin, D. (2007). *Writing next: Effective strategies to improve writing of adolescents in middle and high schools* (Carnegie Corporation Report). Washington, DC: Alliance for Excellent Education.

REFERENCES

Adler, M. J., & Van Doren, C. (1972). *How to read a book.* New York: Touchstone.

Allington, R. L. (2002). You can't learn much from books you can't read. *Educational Leadership, 60*(3), 16–19.

Bransford, J. D., Brown, A. L., & Cocking, R. C. (Eds.). (1999). *How people learn: Brain, mind, experience, and school.* Washington, DC: National Academy Press.

Brozo, W. G., Moorman, G., Meyer, C., & Stewart. T. (2013). Content area reading and disciplinary literacy: A case for the radical center. *Journal of Adolescent and Adult Literacy, 56*(5), 353–357.

Cassidy, J. (1989). Using graphic organizers to develop critical thinking. *The Gifted Child Today, 12,* 34–36.

Cullinan, B. E. (1989). *Literature and the child* (2nd ed.). San Diego, CA: Harcourt Brace Jovanovich.

Driver, R., Newton, P., & Osborne, J. (2000). Establishing the norms of scientific argumentation in classrooms. *Science Education, 84*(3), 287–312.

Duke, N. K. (2000). 3.6 minutes per day: The scarcity of informational texts in first grade. *Reading Research Quarterly, 35,* 202–224.

Evans, M. D. R., Kelley, J., Sikora, J., & Treiman, D. J. (2010). Family scholarly culture and educational success: Books and schooling in 27 nations. *Research in Social Stratification and Mobility, 28*(2), 171–197.

Faggella-Luby, M., Sampson Graner, P., Deshler, D., & Valentino Drew, S. (2012). Building a house on sand: Why disciplinary literacy is not sufficient to replace general strategies for adolescent learners who struggle. *Topics in Language Disorders, 32*(1), 69–84.

Fisher, D., & Frey, N. (2014). Close reading as an intervention for struggling middle school readers. *Journal of Adolescent and Adult Literacy, 57,* 367–376.

Fisher, D., Frey, N., & Hattie, J. (2016). *Visible learning in literacy.* Thousand Oaks, CA: Corwin.

Fisher, D., Frey, N., & Lapp, D. (2009). Meeting AYP in a high need school: A formative experiment. *Journal of Adolescent and Adult Literacy, 52,* 386–396.

Fisher, D., Grant, M., & Ross, D. (2010). Building background knowledge. *The Science Teacher, 77*(1), 23–26.

Gajria, M., Jitendra, A., & Sood, S. (2007). Improving comprehension of expository text in students with LD: A research synthesis. *Journal of Learning Disabilities, 40*(3), 210–225.

Gould, S. J. (1980). *The panda's thumb: More reflections in natural history.* New York: Norton.

Hattie, J. (2009). *Visible learning: A synthesis of over 800 meta-analyses relating to achievement.* New York: Routledge.

Herber, H. L. (1970). *Teaching reading in content areas.* Englewood Cliffs, NJ: Prentice-Hall.

Jiménez, F. (1997). *The circuit: Stories from the life of migrant child.* Albuquerque: University of New Mexico.

Kiuhara, S. A., Graham, S., & Hawken, L. S. (2009). Teaching writing to high school students: A national survey. *Journal of Educational Psychology, 101*(1), 136–160.

McCrudden, M., & Rapp, D. (2017). How visual displays affect cognitive processing. *Educational Psychology Review, 29*(3), 623–639.

McDermott, M. (2010). More than writing-to-learn. *The Science Teacher, 77*(1), 32–36.

Michaels, S., O'Connor, M. C., Hall, M. W., & Resnick, L. B. (2010). *Accountable Talk® Sourcebook: For classroom conversation that works* (Version 3.1). Pittsburgh, PA: University of Pittsburgh Institute for Learning. Retrieved from *iflpartner.pitt.edu/index.php/download/index/ats.*

Monte-Sano, C. (2011). Beyond reading comprehension and summary: Learning to read and write in history by focusing on evidence, perspective, and interpretation. *Curriculum Inquiry, 41*(2), 212–249.

Monte-Sano, C., & De La Paz, S. (2012). Using writing tasks to elicit adolescents' historical reasoning. *Journal of Literacy Research, 44*(3), 273–299.

Nam, J., Choi, A., & Hand, B. (2011). Implementation of the science writing heuristic (SWH) approach in 8th grade science classrooms. *International Journal of Science and Mathematics Education, 9*(5), 1111–1133.

Paul, R., & Elder, L. (2008). *The thinker's guide to how to read a paragraph: The art of close reading.* Tomales, CA: Foundation for Critical Thinking.

Peverly, S., Ramaswamy, V., & Brown, C. (2007). What predicts skill in lecture note taking? *Journal of Educational Psychology, 99*(1), 167–180.

Rubinstein-Ávila, E. (2006). Connecting with Latino learners. *Educational Leadership, 63*(5), 38–43.

Schleppegrell, M. (2013). The role of metalanguage in supporting academic language development. *Language Learning, 63,* 153–170.

Shanahan, T., & Shanahan, C. (2008). Teaching disciplinary literacy to adolescents: Rethinking content-area literacy. *Harvard Educational Review, 78*(1), 40–59.

Shanahan, T., & Shanahan, C. (2012). What is disciplinary literacy and why does it matter? *Topics in Language Disorders, 32*(1), 7–18.

Stahl, S. A., & Shanahan, C. H. (2004). Learning to think like a historian: Disciplinary knowledge through critical analysis of multiple documents. In L. T. Jetton & J. A. Dole (Eds.), *Adolescent research and practice* (pp. 94–115). New York: Guilford Press.

Wineburg, S. S. (1991). On the reading of historical texts: Notes on the breach between school and academy. *American Education Research Journal, 28,* 495–519.

PART III

EVIDENCE-BASED STRATEGIES FOR LITERACY LEARNING AND TEACHING

Best Practices for Developmental Word Study in Phonics, Vocabulary, and Spelling

DONALD R. BEAR

This chapter will:

- Introduce developmental word knowledge.
- Describe fundamentals of word study for all learners.
- Share word study activities by developmental stage.
- Demonstrate how word study is integrated instructionally in daily teaching routines.
- Illustrate how word study is organized to create a community of learners.

EVIDENCE-BASED BEST PRACTICES
IN WORD STUDY INSTRUCTION

This chapter explores the many dimensions of word study and how to teach phonics, vocabulary, and spelling developmentally. It discusses the research base that underlies word study, and then offers a variety of effective practices and routines in the context of key ingredients of an effective word study program. You will see how word study is integrated in reading and writing instruction.

What Is Word Study?

Word study is an approach to teaching students developmentally and explicitly the underlying properties of how words are spelled and what they mean. In this approach, phonics, vocabulary, and spelling are taught through active learning to enable students to explore deeply the relations among words, and understand the principles of how words are spelled (Templeton & Bear, 2018). Why word study? Reading and writing proficiency depend upon the accurate and rapid recognition and understanding of words in context, and the accurate and easy production of words in writing (Bear, Invernizzi, Templeton, & Johnston, 2016).

The developmental approach springs from the discovery that spelling provides a *window* into students' developing word knowledge (Henderson & Beers, 1980; Read, 1971). Students' correct spelling reveals what they know, and their misspellings show us the edges of their learning, what they are using and confusing, and their instructional levels (Invernizzi, Abouzeid, & Gill, 1994). Students' correct and incorrect spellings reflect their understanding of the principles underlying English orthography, their knowledge of how words are spelled, and the knowledge they use when they read and write (Invernizzi & Hayes, 2004, 2011).

Literacy Development and Word Study

Word study begins with assessing students' development. Five stages of spelling development serve as the basis for placing students' instructionally (Henderson, 1981, 1990); see Figure 8.1. Once students' stages are known, choosing what to teach to whom is fairly straightforward.

The five stages can each be divided into early, middle, and late gradations of the stage to make it easier to think about the continuum of development. Developmentally, given the gradual nature of learning, there are overlaps between stages. The three gradations add clarity in the discussion of what invariably are fuzzy boundaries between stages. For example, one teacher may describe a student as being in the *late letter name* stage and another may say that the learner is in the *early within word pattern* stage. These gradations also make it easier to think about groups for differentiated instruction when children at the end of one stage may be grouped with students at the beginning of the next stage. In the next section, each of the stages is discussed in more detail, and is accompanied by a presentation of effective word study practices. Below each heading, an approximate grade and reading lexile span for each stage is presented.

Emergent → Letter Name– → Within Word → Syllables & → Derivational
                Alphabetic   Pattern   Affixes   Relations

FIGURE 8.1. Five stages of spelling in English.

Word Study with Emergent Bilinguals

Emergent bilinguals compare the orthographies and the oral languages they know with spelling and speaking in English. There are 60 million emergent bilinguals in the United States who are learning English, and there are countless students all around the world who are learning English as a foreign language. While nearly 80% of English learners in the United States speak Spanish, in some districts there are as many as eight dozen different languages. There is a wide range of learning experiences and achievement among students: some students know no other written language than English, which is a second oral language; other students start learning English early and are nearly equally proficient in two languages; and still other students speak and read with modest proficiency one language at home and are learning a second language at school.

Students use what they know in one orthography to learn the orthography in others, and instruction builds on this knowledge (San Francisco, Mo, Carlo, August, & Snow, 2013). Students benefit from instruction in which they examine contrasts between their first languages and English (Helman, Bear, Templeton, Invernizzi, & Johnston, 2012; Swan & Smith, 2001). Most programs with English learners provide instruction to clarify confusions in the contrasts between English and home languages. For example, Spanish speakers learning English may sort pictures and words that begin with the /sh/, /h/, and /s/ and /ch/, /c/, and /h/ sounds to clarify the differences between /ch/, a sound both in English and Spanish, and /sh/, a sound that is not a part of Spanish.

For emergent bilinguals, bilingual word study adds depth to their knowledge of written languages. There are many phonological and alphabetic contrasts that are relatively obvious, for example, the spelling substitution of *b* for *p* among Spanish-speaking students in the letter name stage (e.g., spelling *ship* as SIB). Emergent bilinguals who are unfamiliar with long vowel patterns benefit from sorting pictures of unfamiliar long vowel sounds, and then during the within word pattern, students study the patterns to spell long vowel words in English (e.g., patterns like CVCe in *name;* CVVC in *neat;* CVV in *may*) (Bear, Helman, & Woessner, 2009).

Spelling Assessments and Word Study

The goal of spelling assessments is to understand children's progress and then to plan appropriate instruction. Spelling inventories and spelling observation guides are formative assessments that chronicle changes in students' orthographic knowledge. Given the reciprocal relationship between spelling and reading (Ehri, 2014; Perfetti, 1997), spelling analyses can also help teachers to think about assigning students to their guided reading groups.

There are several spelling inventories in common use, and all are easy to administer and score to determine a stage of development or grade level (Bear et al., 2016; Ganske, 2013; Invernizzi, Meier, & Juel, 2003; Morris, 2016; Schlagal, 1992). The reliability and validity of several inventories have been established for different stages and grades, for Spanish, and for academic vocabulary inventories (Ford, Invernizzi, & Huang, 2014; Helman et al., 2012; Sterbinsky, 2007; Townsend, Bear, Templeton, & Burton, 2016). The specific features the inventories measure reflect development and not an entire scope and sequence. Teachers keep both the spelling samples, feature-scoring guides, and writing samples to plan instruction and to share in parent–teacher meetings. In addition to these assessments at the beginning and end of the year, teachers conduct periodic assessments to examine more complete sets of features. These progress-monitoring assessments allow more flexibility in teaching and circumvent the dreadful, repetitive study of features and principles students have already studied and mastered. For example, if students can spell short vowel words with excellent accuracy, there is no need to assign short vowel word study. The inverse is also true; if students cannot spell half the short vowel words correctly, they may be just memorizing words without seeing how the short vowel patterns bring the words together.

To illustrate how spelling is used to assess word knowledge to guide word study, consider Marie's uncorrected, first-draft writing, and her spelling sample from the Elementary Spelling Inventory (Bear et al., 2016). During a tutoring session, Marie wrote a short piece about her hobby, cooking, and her interest in opening a restaurant. She has spelled many words correctly including several short vowel words and high-frequency words. Marie spelled several blends correctly and spelled the voiced *th* digraph in *there* (*THEAR*), and omitted the letter *h* in the voiceless *th* in *think* (TINK) and in the *wh* in *when* (WIN). Marie made similar errors in the spelling assessment that was administered at the beginning and end of tutoring. She made another *b–d* letter reversal and misspelled several short vowels. At times, Marie used her knowledge of the CVCe pattern to spell long vowels, as in PLASE for *place* and BRITE for *bright*. Several consonant digraphs and blends were spelled correctly while others were omitted. From what she is experimenting with in her misspellings, we have a good indication of what Marie knows about English orthography (see Figure 8.2).

As we explore teaching practices in the next section, you will see what stage of spelling development Marie is in, and the types of word study instruction that were a part of her tutoring. For now, know that Marie was a fourth grader at this time, and was a struggling reader and

(a)

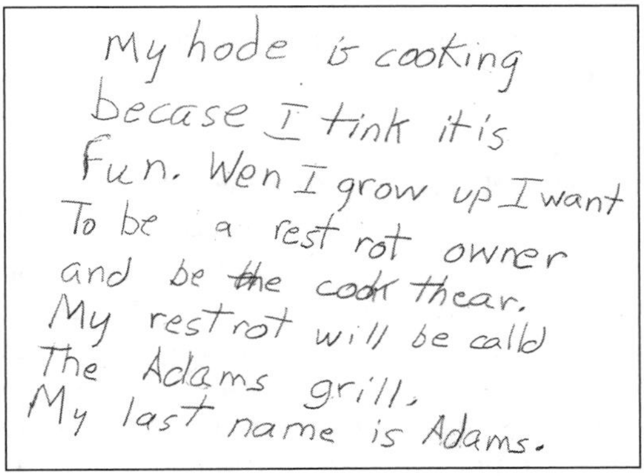

My hode is cooking
becase I tink it's
Fun. Wen I grow up I want
To be a rest rot owner
and be the cook thear.
My restrot will be calld
The Adams grill,
My last name is Adams.

(b)

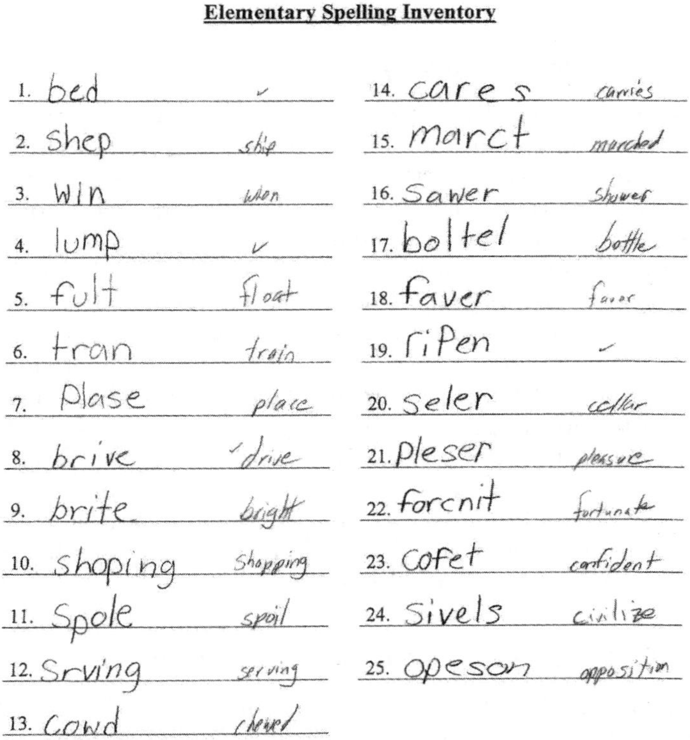

Elementary Spelling Inventory

1. bed	✓	14. cares	carries
2. shep	ship	15. marct	marched
3. win	when	16. sawer	shower
4. lump	✓	17. boltel	bottle
5. fult	float	18. faver	favor
6. tran	train	19. ripen	✓
7. plase	place	20. seler	cellar
8. brive	drive	21. pleser	pleasure
9. brite.	bright	22. forcnit	fortunate
10. shoping	shopping	23. cofet	confident
11. spole	spoil	24. sivels	civilize
12. srving	serving	25. opeson	opposition
13. cowd	cowed		

FIGURE 8.2. (a) An example of Marie's spelling and writing. (b) Marie's performance in the Elementary Spelling Inventory.

writer who had been receiving language instruction with a speech and language specialist.

WORD STUDY COMMUNITIES

To build a community of what some respectfully and good-naturedly call *word nerds,* teachers share their own interest in words, and encourage students to share interesting words and phrases. According to Pearson (2013), there are 10 indicators of a successful word study community. One of the key indicators is student talk about and reflection on word study. We all have seen how important student discussions are to teach comprehension, and the same is true for word study. I discuss briefly how to get students to talk about how talking builds communities of learners.

Student Talk Builds Community

Teachers guide word study lessons through a Socratic approach to teaching in which open-ended questions lead to an explicit examination of underlying spelling principles. We ask each other how words are related: "What do you notice about these words?"; "How do they look alike?"; "What meaning connections can we make?"

Open-ended questions are a tool for reflection and sharing in small groups. For example, we teach students to ask each other to reflect on their word pairs and categories when they play games and check each others' word sorts: "How are those words alike?"; "What do all of those words have in common?"; "What other words fit that pattern?" Through differentiated word study, classmates who are proximal partners developmentally, in a Vygotskian sense, sort and discuss words, and through these shared language experiences their thinking advances. Students examine phonics, spelling, and vocabulary by comparing, contrasting, and categorizing word features through hands-on activities, games, online dictionary searches, and repeated practice sorting.

Ten Indicators of Effective Word Study Instruction

In a study designed by Gehsmann, Millwood, and Bear (2012) to validate a word study observation tool and to examine effective practices and classrooms, the researchers found that 10 indicators described effective teaching: differentiated word study grouping; preparation and organization of materials; teacher talk that facilitates student reflection and clarifies concepts; substantial student-to-student talk; extension and transference to reading and writing; instructional routines for daily and weekly activities; student reflection; notebook use; engagement; teacher knowledge and classroom management. This guide includes specific ways teachers encourage student reflection, and other indicators draw attention to instructional materials and routines. Literacy coaches and teachers review these indicators periodically and they concentrate on a few indicators at a time in their professional development communities. The best practices to follow are found in classrooms where these indicators have been observed, especially student talk and reflection.

BEST PRACTICES IN ACTION ACROSS THE STAGES

Word study can be differentiated by the five stages of spelling. In this section, the characteristics of each stage are introduced, accompanied by word study activities representative of that stage. First, consider how word study is introduced.

Lesson Plan Format for Explicit Word Study Instruction

Word study usually begins with a set of words or pictures that are organized in groups of four or five words or on pictures that illustrate particular concepts. Most word study activities focus on the concepts or orthographic principles for students' developmental levels, but sorts can be about anything you want students to compare and contrast, as in the *concept sort* activity described in the next section. Word study can be introduced in small-group and sometimes in whole-class instruction. A lesson that is explicit but also guides students to discover the categories may take 15 minutes on the first day. On subsequent days, the word study may be quite brief in independent, partner, and small-group activities assigned each day.

There are four basic steps to introduce word study explicitly in teacher-defined, "closed sorts" in which teachers show students how to sort the words or pictures by specific categories. Words are printed on approximately 1" by 2" rectangles on one page, and, usually, prior to meeting, students cut up the page to create a stack of 24 or so words or pictures. Demonstrations are conducted with paper sorts at a table, with broadcasts on screens and smart boards, and with enlarged cards at pocket charts with students manipulating the cards by the established categories.

Teacher Demonstrates

Let students know that this is how you want them to proceed on their own. Read the words aloud with students and discuss the meaning of a few words the students may not know. Ask them to explain what the categories for sorting might be. Guide students to establish the categories, and together sort two or three examples for each category. Pass out the cards and ask students to say the word or picture aloud, and then say the key word of each column to compare. Students then place the word or picture into the correct category and explain their thinking: "Why did you place the word there?" In a beginning-sound picture sort, a student may explain, "I put the *candy* with *cow* because they sound alike at the beginning. They begin with the letter *c*." Be methodical in these comparisons, showing students how to say the words on the cards and compare them to key words, saying the words aloud, and explaining their thought processes with the stem: "I put these cards here because. . . . "

Students Sort and Check

Students sort with partners or individually. Students should sort accurately and correct errors when they read through the words in each category. If there are more than four words students cannot read, that sort may be too difficult and a step back to an easier sort is in order.

Students Reflect

This is a crucial aspect that is easy to pass over. After students have sorted and checked, they explain how words in each column are related. They provide reasons why they sorted the way they did.

Teacher Extends

Repeated practice is essential for students to glean the invariance within each category. Extend activities are introduced to students in small groups. To extend the examination of the categories, an array of activities like the ones described stage-by-stage below are assigned for seatwork, centers, or home. This introductory lesson is used in word study throughout the following stages.

Management schedules and individual contracts are two ways to set out 3-, 4-, or 5-day routines. Here is a 5-day word study schedule to adapt:

- Day 1: Demonstration activity with teacher, and cut and bag the new sort;
- Day 2: Practice sorting, write the sort in the word study notebook, and sort with a partner;
- Day 3: Sort three times, go on a word hunt, add new words found to your notebook, and play the game for the new sort;

- Day 4: Sort twice and explain the sort to a partner, write a reflection in your word study notebook, or do a blind sort with a partner- or student-led group;
- Day 5: Spelling assessment, introduce the game, check your word study notebook, and word-hunt with a partner.

This instructional pacing is adapted to students' learning, and is differentiated in ways presented in the following discussion of word study in the five stages.

Emergent Stage Word Study

Reading Stage: Emergent Reading; Grade Range, PreK–Middle K

There are six elements to consider during this stage. The skills that underlie these elements must come together before conventional literacy proceeds: (1) oral language, its concepts and vocabulary; (2) alphabet awareness; (3) phonological awareness; (4) letter–sound knowledge; (5) concepts about print; and (6) the concept of word in text (Johnston, Invernizzi, Helman, Bear, & Templeton, 2015). The first element, language, its concepts and vocabulary, is foundational and begins early, even in utero (Partanen et al., 2013). We know that children who by age 4 have been identified as having a significant language delay are likely to have reading difficulties later (Anthono et al., 2012; Snowling & Melby-Lervá, 2016). So, a rich language base is crucial to literacy, and literacy experiences must start early. Elements 2–5 are well known and their importance is well documented (Blachman, Schatschneider, Fletcher, Murray, Munger, & Vaughn, 2014).

TEACH CONCEPT OF WORD IN TEXT

The concept of word in text (COW-T), the sixth element, is less well known, and is assessed as the ability to point accurately to the words of a text students have memorized (Flanigan, 2007; Morris, Bloodgood, Lomax, & Perney 2003). Without a COW-T, students do not acquire sight words with any ease or make phonic generalizations beyond letter–sound correspondences (cf. Mesmer & Williams, 2015). Primary teachers have known about COW-T and it is even discussed in *To Kill a Mockingbird* (Lee, 1960, p. 23), when Scout observed that she "could not remember when the lines above Atticus's moving finger separated into words . . . " (Bear, 1991); we would say that indeed, when the lines "separated into words," Scout had acquired a beginning COW-T. Teaching COW-T is accomplished the same way it is assessed, by having students practice pointing to the words of a rhyme or student dictation that they have memorized.

START SOUND PLAY EARLY IN RHYTHMIC ACTIVITIES

A precursor of emerging phonological awareness and COW-T may be further up the language stream with children's awareness of oral, rhythmic structures. Before the segmentation of syllables into beginning and ending sounds, children acquire the prosodic understanding of the syllable within the phrase. In research with 4- to 7-year-olds, children delayed in language development improved in phonological awareness when they engaged in musical and particularly rhythmic activities (Bhide, Power, & Goswami, 2013; Forgeard, Schlaug, Norton, Rosam, Iyengar, & Winner, 2008; Goswami, Gerson, & Astruc, 2010; Moritz, Yampolsky, Papadelis, Thomson, & Wolf, 2013; Nelson, 2016).

INTRODUCE PICTURE SORTS OF BEGINNING CONSONANTS

Once students have a beginning COW-T, they start to sort pictures by beginning consonants. With frequently occurring consonants, students compare and contrast the sounds they hear and feel at the beginning when they name the pictures. We may start with *b, m, r,* and *s* as the first four beginning consonants we present. The sorts are introduced following the lesson plan format described above.

A common activity is for students to "Draw and Label" pictures of words with beginning consonants and then write the names of the pictures with as many letters of the words as they can (HRT for *heart*). "Letter Spin" is a popular matching activity for children to take home to practice letter recognition. Make a spinner divided into the number of letters being used. Students spin the letter and then find that letter chip, and they say the name of the letter. Play continues until all the letters are identified. Additional letters and spinners can be added.

Letter Name–Alphabetic Stage Word Study

Reading Stage: Beginning Reading, Lexile Range:
Up to 400; Grade Range: K–Middle 2

The name of this stage highlights two principles students use when they spell: (1) they use the names of the letters to spell (e.g., TIM for *time*) and (2) they use the alphabetic principle to make one-to-one correspondences between letters and sounds. Early in this stage, their invented spellings show that they are experimenting mostly with beginning consonant sounds, and then ending consonants, along with particularly prominent sounds in words like an *f* in the middle of *elephant*. Once students have learned the letter–sound correspondences of beginning and final consonants, they move on to study short vowels starting with short vowel word families like the *-at* family (*cat, fat, bat, rat*).

To spell short vowels, students match articulatory gestures, how it feels in the mouth when they say the short vowels, to the letter names (Henderson & Beers, 1980; Read, 1971). For example, students in this stage may spell short *i* sounds with the letter name *e* as in *bee* because the letter name *e* feels closest to the way the short *i* is articulated. Beginning readers are word-by-word readers, they read disfluently, and they point to the words as they read. Their rates range from 40 to 80 words per minute.

SHORT VOWEL FAMILIES

Students study the onset (beginning consonant) and rime (the word family) of the basic word families for the short vowels (e.g., *-ad, -an, -at, -ed, -en, -et*). Sometimes instruction is too focused on families and students become inflexible and find it difficult to say that vowels across families are similar, for example, that *bat* and *mad* sound alike in the middle. Guide students to study short vowels across the short vowel families.

Game playing picks up during this stage. Students enjoy Tic-Tac-Toe or the longer version, Black-Out; Go Fish; and easy board games using the words and pictures they are studying.

PERSONAL READERS FOR REPEATED READING AND COLLECTING SIGHT WORDS

The personal reader is a place to store materials that early-and-middle-letter name stage students use in repeated reading (Bear et al., 2016). Repeated reading is a productive way to learn sight words including high-frequency sight words. Favorite and memorable poems, individual dictations, or paragraphs from memorable stories are reproduced in 26-point type and placed in students' personal readers. At this stage, to a degree, the more rereadings the students can get in, the more sight words they will learn. After reading their personal reader entries several times, students may review a sheet of possible sight words they can harvest, or they may underline sight words that they are confident that they "really know" when the words are printed out of context. Early letter name spellers collect a few words from what they reread repeatedly. Gradually, passages can be expanded to one or two paragraphs or stanzas.

Sight word acquisition from the personal reader selections is monitored closely at least until students have a sight word collection of approximately 100 words. The first 50–80 words are critical. While the task is time-intensive, teachers must keep track of how many sight words students have learned. A page with two columns of numbered lines is placed in the personal reader for teachers to write the new sight words learned and for students to review. Teachers scan these pages regularly for record keeping.

THE CONSONANT–VOWEL–CONSONANT PATTERN

During the last third of this stage, students learn about the consonant–vowel–consonant (CVC) pattern, the primary pattern for short vowel patterns in English. If a word follows the CVC pattern, it probably has a short vowel. In parallel with the short vowels, students also examine consonant digraphs and blends. Once students see digraphs and blends as a unit, they understand that words like *spill, black,* and *thump* are CVC-pattern words. Within each short vowel, the vowels differ a bit, but together they are more alike compared to long vowels; for example, consider the differences among these short vowels and then check for the larger differences with the long vowels: *bad, bat, ban, ball* to *bade, bait, bane, bale.* The CVC pattern makes it easier to compare words across short vowels especially as *r*-controlled words come up for study (e.g., *far, her, fir, fur*). One of the last features students learn to spell in this stage is preconsonantal nasals as in *bump* and *stand.* Once students have learned these subtle and low-frequency preconsonantal nasals they are ready to study long vowel patterns.

Short vowels like short *i* and short *e* can be difficult for emergent bilinguals to discriminate (Helman, 2004). There are a number of charts that explicate the short vowel contrasts that may be confusing for students from a variety of languages (Helman et al., 2012). Consonant blends and digraphs can also confuse emergent bilinguals, especially when those sounds and letter pairs do not exist in their other languages. This discussion of patterns becomes a regular part of students' reflections; now, they look for how words sound in the middle, and how short vowels words look alike in terms of the CVC pattern.

Within Word Pattern Stage Word Study

Reading Stage: Transitional Reading, Lexile Range: 400–700; Grade Range: 1–Middle 4

The study of the other patterns in single-syllable words in English becomes the dominant emphasis during this stage. Early in this stage, instruction begins with the study of sound differences among the long and short vowels in picture sorts or word sorts with pictures at the top of each sorting column. After examining sound contrasts, students review the short vowel, CVC pattern, and compare it to the long vowel consonant–vowel–consonant–little *e* (CVCe) pattern. The internal vowel pattern, CVVC, is examined next. This pattern is less frequent than the CVCe pattern, and involves a number of variations. The open-syllable CVV pattern comes next and the letter *y* reaches into complex vowels like /oi/ as in *boy* and *coil*. Some vowels are more difficult than others. The long *u*, as in *mule*, can be hard to discriminate. The complex vowel sounds and patterns have several variations, and are less frequent (e.g., *book/fool, scout/scowl*). This is also a time when students study more complex *r*-influenced vowels (e.g., *-ir, -ier -ire, -oar, -ore, -ure*).

This is a time when emergent bilinguals can learn about the sounds of novel vowels in English through picture sorts. Sorting pictures by sound gives students practice saying the sounds in a consistent fashion. Finally, at the end of this stage, students can spell nearly all single-syllable words correctly. This stages closes with the study of homophones and homographs. Word study with dictionaries becomes more important to understand multiple meanings (*steak/stake; root* (verb)/*root* (noun).

These transitional stage students make dramatic changes in their reading. At the beginning of this stage students read easy nonfiction texts, easy series like some in the *I Can Read* series published by HarperCollins, the *Nate the Great* series (Sharmat, 2006), and extended pattern books like *Down by the Bay* (Raffi, 1999). Students gradually read longer, more complex materials with embedded phrases and more polysyllabic words that include individual books and series like *Horrible Harry* (Kline, 2002), *Junie B. Jones* (Park, 2015), and *Tree House Mysteries* (Osborne, 2001), all well known at this level. What is fascinating is that silent reading rates begin to outstrip oral reading rates around 100 words per minute, and because it is more efficient, students become silent readers if accuracy is sufficient. In listening to oral reading, teachers notice the fluency increasing, but in the beginning and middle of the transitional stage there is a relative lack of expression, particularly of words that are in focus and could be emphasized prosodically to highlight intentions. Through activities like Readers Theater, poetry readings, and chorales students acquire reading expression that helps them to read aloud effectively, and to think deeply to comprehend.

GAMES AND CHARTS

A wide variety of games are played during this stage. Students like to play Homophone Rummy, and the circular Race Track game with long vowel words and patterns. Students also like to work with partners to make charts of related words. For example, in Figure 8.3 we see students making a chart of long *o* and *e* words and short *e* words that students will later

FIGURE 8.3. Students create a word study chart for long and short vowels.

analyze by patterns. These charts are posted and students add words as they find them.

STRUGGLING READERS

Some students do not learn the patterns in this stage; they continue to misspell long and complex vowels; they read too slowly to read grade-level complex texts without support, and they find it difficult to keep up with the reading and writing demands. Their academic scores may flatten at a third- or fourth-grade level. Some struggling readers with strong verbal skills may be able to reach middle school grade-level comprehension, but by high school their lack of orthographic knowledge is likely to hold them back given the increasing demands to read a large amount of complex, domain-specific vocabulary.

Marie, whom we met earlier, was struggling as a reader in fourth grade. Her guided reading levels were in the G and H and 300–500 lexile ranges. While Marie knew how to spell many words correctly like *rest, lump, cook, want,* and *last,* she was learning how to spell words with short vowels (SHEP for *ship,* WIN for *when*), and she was also experimenting with spelling long vowels and diphthongs (PLASE for *place,* BRITE for *bright,* THEAR for *there,* COWED for *chewed,* SAWER for *shower*). To determine a stage, we could say that Marie is in the late letter name or the early part of the within word pattern stage. Instructionally, to strengthen her foundational knowledge and to have a common metalinguistic language, the tutor and Marie began with a fast-paced examination of short vowel patterns, consonant blends and digraphs, and the CVC pattern. After six tutoring sessions Marie began to study the common long vowel patterns. She started with comparing short and long vowel sounds, and then studied the CVCe pattern. The chart presented in Figure 8.3 was developed by Marie and a partner and was posted for a time during her second semester of tutoring in the literacy center.

Syllables and Affixes Stage Word Study

Reading Stage: Intermediate Reading, Lexile Range: 500–1,000; Grade Range: 3–8

In this stage students study two-syllable words and the ways syllables combine. Morphology, the study of meaningful word parts, is the focus during this stage, beginning with the study of inflected morphology like the *–ed*, and *-ing* suffixes. From an abundance of research, it is clear that teaching morphology impacts literacy achievement (Carlisle, 2010; Goodwin, Huggins, Carlo, August, & Calderon, 2013). Students build on their knowledge of the CVC pattern and long vowel patterns to contrast the spelling patterns of short and long vowels and how adding suffixes impacts spelling. This includes the principles of *e*-drop + *-ing* for long vowels, and consonants doubling for short vowels *(save/saving* compared to *sit/sitting)*. Next, students examine closed (CVC) and open (CV) syllables as they learn to add various suffixes to words, for example, *-ing*, *-ly*, and *-ed*. In their study of open and closed syllables, students learn these patterns: VC/CV (*skipping*), V/CV (*reason*), VC/V (*river*), VCC/CV (*pumpkin*), VC/CCV (*pilgrim*), and VV (*riot*).

In these upper stages, students are maturing as readers. Independent reading is silent, and students learn study skills and how to adjust reading rates for different purposes. They become familiar with various genres, and learn how to read in various disciplines.

VOCABULARY NOTEBOOKS

Every student in this stage has a vocabulary notebook, and these notebooks can be arranged in a variety of ways. If the notebook is online, students have an area, like a folder, for different content areas. In their English language arts classes, students develop sections in their notebooks for the vocabulary from novels, for domain-specific words in their disciplinary studies, and an open or miscellaneous area for words that come up daily. Sometimes the vocabulary notebook includes *golden lines* students collect. These are quotes that they find in their reading or listening that strike them as important, telling, eloquently phrased, or intriguing. Guided reading lessons often begin with students sharing a few vocabulary words and golden lines they found when they read; this puts students' talk at center stage, and helps to build a community of learners (Templeton et al., 2015).

ACADEMIC VOCABULARY: GENERAL AND DOMAIN SPECIFIC

In this and the next stage, students delve into academic vocabulary and multisyllabic word study in which they study general and domain specific academic vocabulary (see Chapter 5). General academic vocabulary occurs in all academic texts and across disciplines (Nagy & Townsend, 2012). The study of general vocabulary is enhanced when students study related words. Students' learning is also enhanced when they see multiple examples of the word parts. For example, in studying general vocabulary words like *significant,* several other related words can be presented (*sign, signal, significance*). These other words help to anchor the meaning for students. Another way to broaden exposure and increase context to learn general academic vocabulary is by discussing formulaic phrases or sequences (Schmitt, 2004). For example, in examining the word *though,* it will help to add phrases like *even though,* or to study polysemous words like *degree* in frequently occurring formulaic phrases as in *degree to which* or *fifth degree,* or *30 degrees Fahrenheit,* etc.

Games and word sorts continue to play a role in word study routines at these upper levels. Students continue to enjoy racetrack games and generating charts of related words, for example, words that begin with the same prefix, such as *prefabricated, pretend, preamble,* and *pretest.*

Derivational Relations Stage Word Study

Reading Stage: Advanced Reading, Lexile Range: 740–1,000; Grade Range: 5–12

Our vocabularies grow throughout our lifetimes. Students in this stage concentrate on word roots and their derivations, as well as less common affixes. This stage involves a number of exercises that show students that by looking at word parts they can identify word families, affixes, and roots, and in so doing, make *meaning connections.* With several examples of related words before them, students learn that they do not have to memorize each word, but that vocabulary study is generative (Templeton, 2015). When we teach one word we teach 10, and when we teach a root, learning is exponential. Figure 8.4 illustrates how with plenty of examples the meaning of roots can be inferred, in this case, *liber*. We are always looking for related words to deepen learning.

MAKING THE MEANING CONNECTION

The links between meaning and spelling are important to uncover for vocabulary growth. By making meaning connections in spelling students find how literally thousands of words are related. They learn underlying principles that explain what happens to pronunciation and spelling when syllables, usually suffixes, are added to words: "Words similar in meaning can be similar in spelling despite changes in sound" (Templeton, 1992, p. 194). Specific principles include vowel alteration and reduction when vowels change as syllables are added to base words (*comp**o**se/comp**o**sition*), and prefix assimilation which explains what happens when some prefixes connect to base words (e.g., the *in-*, meaning not, turns into *im-* before a *p* (*impossible, improbable;* similar changes are made for the prefixes *il-* and *ir-*). While there are many principles to explore, this is also a time for students to look carefully at the vocabulary they find while they read both in English language arts and in their other content areas. The next activity can be adapted across disciplines in the intermediate and secondary grades.

SIX-STEP, DEEP, AND GENERATIVE VOCABULARY STUDY

Students study several words deeply each week. This activity is introduced over several sessions by showing students how to choose words and the rest of the process as follows.

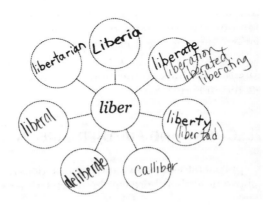

FIGURE 8.4. Root web for *liber*.

1. Find a word worth studying. Choose important and useful words.
2. Record the sentence or the most important parts of a long sentence.
3. Take apart. Break off the prefixes and suffixes and look for the base word or root. Make a list of related words by word parts: prefixes, base or root, and suffixes.
4. Make meaning connections. What meaning do these words or word parts (e.g., *aqua, aqua green, aquarium, Aquarius–water*) share?
5. Use references to find out more about the word parts and add information to your entry for this word.
6. Develop materials and a plan to display and share what you learned with classmates.

ETYMOLOGIES AND REFERENCES

Students in the upper levels of orthographic knowledge need dictionaries and word origin references to dig more deeply into word histories. After a few lessons in which students are shown how to read the abbreviations and some of the historical information, they are shown how to enter selected materials into their vocabulary notebooks (Templeton et al., 2015). Online references include all types of dictionaries in specific disciplines, dictionaries of etymologies, visual displays of related words, translation dictionaries, dictionaries for emergent bilinguals, and other online resources that expand each day. Here are some popular websites students refer to regularly: *dictionary.com, etymonline.com, myetymology. com, onelook.com, visualthesaurus.com, visuwords.com,* and *vocabulary.com.* We aim to have 10 copies of unabridged dictionaries and four copies of etymological reference books by Ayto (1990), Hoad (1986), and Shipley (2001) available in our English language arts classrooms. There are dozens of books that explore idioms, vocabulary in specific disciplines, and interesting phrases. Students use these resources to create word webs in which they explore the meaning connections among words that share the same root as they did in Figure 8.4.

REFLECTIONS AND FURTHER DIRECTIONS

Word study is an approach to teaching, and the practices and principles of word study like those described here can be used with existing materials and resources. There are four essential elements of this approach to word study: (1) the developmental sequence for differentiation; (2) integration of phonics, spelling, and vocabulary; (3) students' reflections and discussions; and 4) practice activities, sorts, and games. The impact of these activities warrants further study through practice-embedded research in which teachers, researchers, and students investigate together (Snow, 2015). Like the comprehension focused Directed Reading–Thinking Activity (DRTA), which is responsive to students' predictions and reflections (Stauffer, 1975), word study takes students' developmental lead and puts them in a position to reflect on the sounds, meaning, and spellings of words (Zutell, 1996).

Word study is available digitally and online. How will digital experiences change instruction? Ideally, sorting words with partners will be just as useful online as it is with paper cards. Algorithms and artificial intelligence to examine eye movements, speech, and writing for students' accuracy, speed, and reflections can be used to adapt learning presentations to be more responsive instructionally as students move along the developmental continuum. Educators and researchers have found value in having students write words (Berninger & Wolf, 2009), and in word study, this is accomplished when students write words in lists by pattern. A digital stylus provides this experience, and with the right software, guidance in forming letters and words can be provided, and may be found to be as useful as writing on paper.

The goal of word study is to improve reading and writing; conceived in this way, spelling instruction is a more purposeful activity that is not just a rote memorization task (Graham & Santangelo, 2014; Massengill, 2006). The spelling activities in word study are dynamic and tailored to students' growth, and they impact students' reading, vocabulary, and conceptual knowledge (Conrad, 2008; Ehri, 2014; Rosenthal & Ehri, 2008; Treiman, 1998). For many teachers and parents, word study is a new way of thinking about spelling instruction and it will be important to share this larger goal, the developmental model, and the research to show how word study impacts literacy.

ENGAGEMENT ACTIVITIES

1. **Explicit Word Study Lesson Plan.** Refer to the four steps in the lesson described above to plan an explicit word study lesson. Form a small group of students in the same stage. Either choose an existing word list or sort, or develop a sort that includes three or four categories of words that follow different patterns. Include a few words that are "oddballs" that do not fit the established categories. Practice the demonstration and plan a few open-ended questions to ask, like "What did you notice about these words?" Plan a few ways like think–pair–share, or charting, for students to interact and discuss how words are related.

After the lesson, reflect on how it went. Was the sort at the students' instructional level? Could they read the words, sort accurately, and talk about the categories? Were their reflections accurate? What extension activities will give students the daily practice they need?

2. **Spelling and Reading Connections.** Based on what you have learned about the stages of spelling and reading, see if you can observe a synchrony in students' development. You may want to use one of the spelling assessments discussed here or simply gather free, uncorrected writing samples and assign a stage of spelling based on the description of the stages. Compare students' reading and spelling achievement. See if you have developmental groups in the sample that would make it possible to provide word study and guided reading instruction together to small groups of students.

   Examine anomalies by examining the relationships among reading accuracy, word recognition, and comprehension, when, for example, you have a good reader who is a poor speller. Sometimes there is a synchrony in word reading and spelling, but given students' strong language and thinking, their comprehension is more advanced than their word knowledge would predict.

3. **Games.** Develop three copies of one game that uses related words or pictures that match students' developmental levels. Refer to games mentioned in this chapter including Go Fish, Tick-Tac-Toe, the Racetrack game, and Concentration. Be sure to plan for students' reflections in which they explain how words are alike before completing a match. Ask students to give you feedback on the game: Was the game easy to follow? Was the game entertaining? What did they learn about words? What games might students want to make?

4. **Academic Vocabulary.** Understanding disciplinary vocabulary is essential to comprehension. To teach vocabulary in one unit of study, identify key vocabulary words that are important to comprehend a section in students' readings. Choose five domain-specific words and three general vocabulary words that are essential to understand the text. Prepare a list of related words for the vocabulary including generative vocabulary (*microbe: micro-, microbiotic, microcosm, micro-organism*), and phrases (*good microbes, environmental microbiology, cold-loving microbes, microbiologists, soil microbes*). Ask students to brainstorm related words and share from your list those they do not mention. *Onelook.com, etymonline.com,* and *visuwords.com* are fine resources for this vocabulary study.

Have students work with you and partners to choose two of the five domain-specific and two of the general vocabulary words, and then have students make a chart of related vocabulary words for each word. Ask them to include phrases and drawings of the concept to accompany the chart. These charts can be posted around the room or shared online.

Consider using or adapting the six-step, deep, and generative vocabulary routine discussed above. In other lessons, show students how to use the upper-level resources discussed in the derivational relations stage.

REFERENCES

Anthoni, H., Sucheston, L. E., Lewis, B. A., Tapia-Páez, I., Fan, X., Zucchelli, M., . . . Pennington, B. F. (2012). The aromatase gene CYP19A1: Several genetic and functional lines of evidence supporting a role in reading, speech and language. *Behavior Genetics, 42*(4), 509–527.

Ayto, J. (1990). *Dictionary of word origins.* New York: Arcade.

Bear, D. R. (1991). "Learning to fasten the seat of my union suit without looking around": The synchrony of literacy development. *Theory into Practice, 30*(3), 149–157.

Bear, D. R., Helman, L., & Woessner, L. (2009). Word study assessment and instruction with English learners in a second grade classroom: Bending with students' growth. In J. Coppola & E. V. Primas (Eds.), *One classroom, many learners: Best literacy practices for today's multilingual classrooms* (pp. 11–40). Newark, DE: International Reading Association.

Bear, D. R., Invernizzi, M., Templeton, S., & Johnston, F. (2016). *Words their way: Word study for phonics, vocabulary, and spelling instruction* (6th ed.). Boston: Pearson.

Bhide, A., Power, A., & Goswami, U. (2013). A rhythmic musical intervention for poor readers: A comparison of efficacy with a letter-based intervention. *Mind, Brain, and Education, 7*(2), 113–123.

Blachman, B. A., Schatschneider, C., Fletcher, J. M., Murray, M. S., Munger, K. A., & Vaughn, M. G. (2014). Intensive reading remediation in grade 2 or 3: Are there effects a decade later? *Journal of Educational Psychology, 106*(1), 46–57.

Carlisle, J. F. (2010). Effects of instruction in morphological awareness on literacy achievement: An integrative review. *Reading Research Quarterly, 45*(4), 464–487.

Conrad, N. J. (2008). From reading to spelling and spelling to reading: Transfer goes both ways. *Journal of Educational Psychology, 100*(4), 869–878.

Ehri, L. C. (2014). Orthographic mapping in the acquisition of sight word reading, spelling memory, and vocabulary learning. *Scientific Studies of Reading, 18*(1), 5–21.

Flanigan, K. (2007). A concept of word in text: A pivotal event in early reading acquisition. *Journal of Literacy Research, 39*(1), 37–70.

Ford, K. L., Invernizzi, M. A., & Huang, F. (2014). Predicting first grade reading achievement for Spanish-speaking kindergartners: Is early literacy screening in English valid? *Literacy Research and Instruction, 53*(4), 269–286.

Forgeard, M., Schlaug, G., Norton, A., Rosam, C., Iyengar, U., & Winner, E. (2008). The relation between music and phonological processing in normal-reading children and children with dyslexia. *Music Perception, 25*(4), 383–390.

Ganske, K. (2013). *Word journeys* (2nd ed.). New York: Guilford Press.

Gehsmann, K. M., Millwood, K., & Bear, D. R. (2012, December). *Validating a classroom observation tool for studying developmental word study instruction.* Paper presented at the 62nd annual conference of the Literacy Research Association, San Diego, CA.

Goodwin, A. P., Huggins, A. C., Carlo, M. S., August, D., & Calderon, M. (2013). Minding morphology: How morphological awareness relates to reading for English language learners. *Reading and Writing, 26*(9), 1387–1415.

Goswami, U., Gerson, D., & Astruc, L. (2010). Amplitude envelope perception, phonology and prosodic sensitivity in children with developmental dyslexia. *Reading and Writing, 23,* 995–1019.

Graham, S., & Santangelo, T. (2014). Does spelling instruction make students better spellers, readers, and writers? A meta-analytic review. *Reading and Writing, 27,* 1703–1743.

Helman, L. A. (2004). Building on the sound system of Spanish: Insights from the alphabetic spellings of English language learners. *Reading Teacher, 57,* 452–460.

Helman, L. A., Bear, D. R., Templeton, S., Invernizzi, M., & Johnston, F. (2012). *Words their way with English learners* (2nd ed.). Boston: Pearson/Allyn & Bacon.

Henderson, E. H. (1981). *Learning to read and spell: The child's knowledge of words.* DeKalb: Northern Illinois Press.

Henderson, E. H. (1990). *Teaching spelling* (2nd ed.). Boston: Houghton Mifflin.

Henderson, E. H., & Beers, J. (Eds.). (1980). *Developmental and cognitive aspects of learning to spell: A reflection of word knowledge.* Newark, DE: International Reading Association.

Hoad, T. F. (1986). *The concise Oxford dictionary of English etymology.* New York: Oxford University Press.

Invernizzi, M., Abouzeid, M., & Gill, J. T. (1994). Using students' invented spelling as a guide for spelling instruction that emphasizes word study. *Elementary School Journal, 95,* 155–167.

Invernizzi, M., & Hayes, L. (2004). Developmental-spelling research: A systematic imperative. *Reading Research Quarterly, 39,* 216–228.

Invernizzi, M., & Hayes, L. (2011). Developmental patterns of reading proficiency and reading difficulties. In A. McGill-Franzen & R. L. Allington (Eds.), *Handbook of reading disability research* (pp. 196–207). New York: Routledge/Taylor & Francis.

Invernizzi, M., Meier, J., & Juel, C. (2003). *PALS 1–3 Phonological Awareness Literacy Screening* (4th ed.). Charlottesville, VA: University Printing Services.

Johnston, F., Invernizzi, M., Bear, D. R., & Templeton, S. (2015). *Words their way for preK–K.* Boston: Pearson.

Kline, S. (2002) *Horrible Harry fifteen megapack* (Books 1–15). New York: Scholastic

Lee, H. (1960). *To kill a mockingbird*. New York: Lippincott.

Massengill, D. (2006). Mission accomplished . . . it's learnable now: Voices of mature challenged spellers using a word study approach. *Journal of Adolescent and Adult Literacy, 49,* 420–431.

Mesmer, H. A. E., & Williams, T. O. (2015). Examining the role of syllable awareness in a model of concept of word: Findings from preschoolers reading. *Reading Research Quarterly, 50*(4), 483–497.

Moritz, C., Yampolsky, S., Papadelis, G., Thomson, J., & Wolf, M. (2013). Links between early rhythm skills, musical training, and phonological awareness. *Reading and Writing, 26*(5), 739–769.

Morris, D. (2016). *Morris Informal Reading Inventory: Preprimer through grade 8.* New York: Guilford Press.

Morris, D., Bloodgood, J. W., Lomax, R. G., & Perney, J. (2003). Developmental steps in learning to read: A longitudinal study in kindergarten and first grade. *Reading Research Quarterly, 38,* 302–328.

Nagy, W., & Townsend, D. (2012). Words as tools: Learning academic vocabulary as language acquisition. *Reading Research Quarterly, 47*(1), 91–108.

Nelson, S. D. (2016). The effects of an integrated rhythmic and literacy intervention on the development of phonological awareness and rhythm skills of preschoolers. *Iowa State University Capstones: Graduate Theses and Dissertations.* Retrieved from *https://lib.dr.iastate.edu/etd/15984.*

Osborne, M. P. (2001). *Magic tree house* (boxed set, books 1–4): *Dinosaurs before dark; The knight at dawn; Mummies in the morning; and Pirates past noon* (S. Murdocca, Illus.). New York: Random House.

Park, B. (2015). *Junie B. Jones complete first grade collection* (Books 18–28 with paper dolls in boxed set). New York: Random House.

Partanen, E., Kujala, T., Näätänen, R., Liitola, A., Sambeth, A., & Huotilainen, M. (2013). Learning-induced neural plasticity of speech processing before birth. *Proceedings of the National Academy of Sciences of the USA, 110*(37), 15145–15150.

Pearson. (2013). *Words Their Way® classroom observation tool: Indicator reference guide.* Upper Saddle River, NJ: Author.

Perfetti, C. A. (1997). The psycholinguistics of spelling and reading. In C. A. Perfetti, L. Rieben, & M. Fayol (Eds.), *Learning to spell: Research, theory, and practice across languages* (pp. 21–38). Mawah, NJ: Erlbaum.

Raffi. (1999). *Down by the bay.* New York: Knopf Books for Young Readers.

Read, C. (1971). Preschool children's knowledge of English phonology. *Harvard Educational Review, 41,* 1–34.

Rosenthal, J., & Ehri, L. C. (2008). The mnemonic value of orthography for vocabulary learning. *Journal of Educational Psychology, 100*(1), 175–191.

San Francisco, A. R., Mo, E., Carlo, M., August, D., & Snow, C. (2013). The influences of language of literacy instruction and vocabulary on the spelling of Spanish–English bilinguals. *Reading and Writing, 19*(6), 627–642.

Schlagal, R. (1992). Patterns of orthographic development into the intermediate grades. In S. Templeton & D. R. Bear (Eds.), *Development of orthographic knowledge and the foundations of literacy: A memorial festschrift for Edmund H. Henderson* (pp. 31–52). Hillsdale, NJ: Erlbaum.

Schmitt, N. (Ed.). (2004). *Formulaic sequences: Acquisition, processing and use.* Philadelphia: Benjamins.

Sharmat, M. W. (2006). *Nate the great.* New York: Yearling Press.

Shipley, J. (2001). *The origins of English words.* Baltimore: Johns Hopkins University Press.

Snow, C. S. (2015). 2014 Wallace Foundation Distinguished Lecture: Rigor and realism: Doing educational science in the real world. *Educational Researcher, 44,* 460–466.

Snowling, M. J., & Melby-Lervå, M. (2016). Oral language deficits in familial dyslexia: A meta-analysis and review *Psychological Bulletin, 142*(5), 498–545.

Stauffer, R. G. (1975). *Directing the reading–thinking process.* New York: HarperCollins.

Sterbinsky, A. (2007). *Words Their Way spelling inventories: Reliability and validity analyses.* Memphis, TN: Center for Research in Educational Policy, University of Memphis.

Swan, M., & Smith, B. (2001). *Learner English: A teacher's guide to interference and other problems* (2nd ed.). Cambridge, UK: Cambridge University Press.

Templeton, S. (1992). Theory, nature, and pedagogy of higher-order orthographic development in older students. In S. Templeton & D. R. Bear (Eds.), *Development of orthographic knowledge and the foundations of literacy: A memorial Festschrift for Edmund H. Henderson* (pp. 253–277). Hillsdale, NJ: Erlbaum.

Templeton, S. (2015). Learning, reading, and writing words closely and deeply: The archaeology of thought. In D. A. Sisk (Ed.), *Accelerating and extending literacy for diverse learners: Using culturally responsive teaching* (pp. 105–120). Lanham, MD: Rowman & Littlefield.

Templeton, S., Bear, D. R., Invernizzi, M. R., Johnston, F., Flanigan, K., Townsend, D. R., . . . Hayes, L. (2015). *Vocabulary their way: Word study with middle and secondary students.* Boston: Pearson.

Templeton, W. S., & Bear, D. R. (2018). Word study research. In D. Lapp & D. Fisher (Eds.), *Handbook of research in the teaching of English* (4th ed., pp. 207–232). New York: Routledge.

Townsend, D., Bear, D., Templeton, S., & Burton, A. (2016). The implications of adolescents' academic word knowledge for achievement and instruction. *Reading Psychology, 37*(8), 1119–1148.

Treiman, R. (1998). Why spelling?: The benefits of incorporating spelling into beginning reading instruction. In J. L. Metsala & L. C. Ehri (Eds.), *Word recognition in beginning literacy* (pp. 289–313). Mahwah, NJ: Erlbaum.

Zutell, J. (1996). The directed spelling thinking activity (DSTA): Providing an effective balance in word study instruction. *The Reading Teacher, 50*(2), 98–108.

CHAPTER 9

Best Practices in Vocabulary Instruction

KATHY GANSKE

This chapter will:

- Highlight what we know about vocabulary teaching and learning.
- Describe the importance of classroom communities for vocabulary development.
- Present evidence-based practices for teaching vocabulary, including academic vocabulary.
- Consider future directions for vocabulary teaching, learning, and research.

Scholarly writings often report that just a hundred words make up about 50% of all writing in English (*https://en.oxforddictionaries.com/explore/what-can-corpus-tell-us-about-language*)). Imagine that! Just a hundred of the nearly 2.5 billion words that worldwide comprise 21st-century English texts, from novels to emails! (Oxford English Corpus; *https://en.oxforddictionaries.com/explore/oxford-english-corpus*). An impressive figure, but bear in mind that the other 50% carry most of the meaning. Consider the 52 words from the first two sentences of the chapter, excluding numbers and citations. Of these, 26 are among the 100 most common words: *that, just, a, make, up, about, of, all, in, that, just, a, of, the, that, from, to, an, but, in, that, the, other, most, of, the.* These high-frequency words help structure the sentences and tie ideas together but add little to our understanding of the content, compared to the rest: *Scholarly, writings, often, report, hundred, words, writing, English, Imagine, hundred, nearly, billion, words, worldwide, comprise, century, English, texts, novels, emails, impressive, figure, bear, mind, carry, meaning.* The importance of vocabulary knowledge for readers' comprehension has long and widely been recognized as critical for students' success in school and beyond (e.g., Davis, 1968; National Reading Panel, 2000; National Governors Association & Council of Chief State School Officers, 2010; National Early Literacy Panel, 2008). Yet, there is also evidence that vocabulary may not be addressed, or at least not effectively addressed, in primary and middle school classrooms (Lawrence, White, & Snow, 2010; Wright & Neuman, 2014). This chapter explores the why and how of developing children's vocabulary knowledge.

EVIDENCE-BASED BEST PRACTICES:
A RESEARCH SYNTHESIS

Larger vocabulary size has been associated with better comprehension and better performance on standardized test measures (Stahl & Fairbanks, 1986). Readers who know more words have an easier time comprehending and, in turn, acquiring new words (e.g., Nagy, 2005; Stanovich, 1986).

Word Learning

According to Perfetti's lexical quality hypothesis (LQH; 2007), readers who know more words are better at learning new words *and* they learn the words better. They acquire understanding of word features, such as the sounds and spellings, morphology, and syntax, as well as the word meanings. The features interconnect with a reader's personal experiences, producing a high-quality abstract word representation that reflects not just its original context but information associated with multiple situations and concepts and the reader's broader knowledge. Consider the word *devour,* which means to "eat up or consume greedily." For me the word evokes associations with several experiences. One relates to a childhood memory of watching our family dog eat its food as a kitten sat nearby and my worry that the snapping jaws might miss their mark. Others connect to a *Jurassic Park* movie in which one dinosaur makes a meal of another, to my eating of a burger after a long and strenuous hike, and even to my immersion in a new book by a favorite poet—Mary Oliver or Billy Collins. My high-quality representation for the word includes robust meaning connections and word features that together facilitate my retrieval and application of the word in different situations (Perfetti, 2007).

 Unfortunately, the kind of cycle of success just described is not one that all children experience. Children from lower SES backgrounds and language minority students often do not have the kind of vocabulary knowledge used in school and needed for success (August, Carlo, Dressler, & Snow, 2005; Graves, August, & Mancilla-Martinez, 2013; Hart & Risley, 1995), and they may have limited exposure to this kind of language outside of school (Schleppegrell, 2004). Without such vocabulary knowledge, it can be difficult or impossible to access academic content (Nagy & Townsend, 2012; Zwiers, 2007), particularly since teachers may assume students know the words and not teach them (Corson, 1997; Snow, Lawrence, & White, 2009). Even words and phrases like *nevertheless, because,* and *for example,* known as *connectives* (Crosson & Lesaux, 2013), can cause comprehension breakdowns.

Various terms have been used to describe academic vocabulary that crosses disciplines, including *general* or *Tier 2* words—*evidence, justify, confer*—and *domain-specific* or *Tier 3* words—*triangle, calculate, habitat* (Beck, McKeown, & Kucan, 2013; Nagy & Townsend, 2012). Tier 1 words are high-frequency words that tend to be known. Consider: Each of the first 60 words on the Coxhead's (2000) Academic Word List (AWL), a well-known list of 570 general academic words, occurs about once in every 4.3 pages of academic text (p. 228). It is not surprising that there is interest in seeing academic vocabulary instruction addressed, even in early grades and preschool (Barnes, Grifenhagen, & Dickinson, 2016; Foorman et al., 2016).

How Many Words Do Children Need to Know?

Compounding some children's problem of limited vocabulary knowledge is the tremendous number of words they are exposed to during their schooling. Estimates as to how many words this is vary due to different methods of counting the words. Generally, counts are based on word families, so a "word" such as *define* also includes *definition, defining, redefined, definable, undefined,* and numerous other forms of the word. Typical counts range from about 88,000 to 180,000 words, if proper nouns, multiple meanings, and idioms are included (Nagy & Anderson, 1984; Anderson & Nagy, 1992). The result is much greater, if calculated via one of the big data sets used by corpus linguists who can search curricular materials across grade levels and publishers (Fitzgerald, Elmore, Kung, & Stenner, 2017). Differences aside, the number is staggering; clearly, the more of these words readers know, the easier it will be for them to comprehend school texts.

How Many Words Do Children Learn?

An even bigger challenge than estimating how many words children will face during their schooling may be estimating the number of words children learn. Drawing on a wealth of research, Graves (2016) estimates that linguistically advantaged children may start first grade with oral vocabularies of about 10,000 words and graduate from high school with reading and oral vocabularies of about 50,000 words. By contrast, the vocabularies of linguistically less-advantaged children may be about half these sizes. This discrepancy is concerning given that differences in vocabulary tend to persist (Biemiller, 2001; Juel, Biancarosa, Coker, & Deffes, 2003) and vocabulary knowledge in first grade can predict reading achievement in middle and high school (Cunningham & Stanovich, 1997). Graves further posits that in order to learn 50,000 words by grade 12 children need to learn some 3,000 to 4,000 words a year from kindergarten to 12th grade. Other research estimate that 1,000 to 3,000 words are actually learned each year across the school years (Biemiller, 1999; Nagy, 2007; Nagy & Anderson, 1984). In either case, children seem to learn far more words than we teach them (Nagy & Herman, 1987; D'Anna, Zechmeister, & Hall, 1991), which suggests that their learning is incidental, occurring in a variety of contexts—book reading, talk and discussion in school, electronic media, conversations out of school with friends and family, and so on.

What Does It Mean to *Know* a Word?

Although we often talk about knowing this or that, when it comes to knowing a word it is a bit more complicated because, as revealed in the previous discussion of Perfetti's LQH theory (2007), word knowledge is multifaceted and does not equate merely to knowing a definition (Johnson & Pearson, 1984; Nagy & Scott, 2000). Anderson and Freebody (1981) highlight two fundamental aspects of word knowledge: *breadth* of knowledge, "the number of words for which a person knows at least some of the significant aspects of meaning" (p. 92), and *depth* of knowledge, or knowing "all the distinctions that would be understood by an ordinary adult under normal circumstances" (p. 93). Over time, we deepen our understanding of the word as we learn additional meanings and nuances. Although it is important to know a lot of words, an instructional focus on breadth can come at the expense of depth of understanding due to the greater number of words receiving attention (Coyne, Loftus, Zipoli, & Kapp, 2009).

Readers may wonder: How many interactions with a word does a student need to "own" it, namely, to be able to use it readily and appropriately. There is no fixed number of experiences, but it will likely take more than one (Graves, 2016). McKeown, Beck, Omanson, and Pople (1985) found that 12 exposures positively impacted reading comprehension, while four did not. With each encounter more information is stored in memory until the beginning vague notion of the word becomes a reliable understanding of it. Depending on student interest in the word and the meaningful nature of the interaction, some words will require more interactions. Exposure to the word in multiple contexts and through differing perspectives is key (Beck et al., 2013; Stahl, 2003).

Another facet of word knowledge is realizing that a word can have more than one meaning, understanding the meanings, and knowing when to use them. Contrary to many conceptualizations of word knowledge, Cronbach's (1942) five dimensions (see Table 9.1) capture both depth and breadth of understanding a word, including knowledge of individual and multiple meanings and appropriate use of the word. Gaining understanding of multiple meanings is especially important in light of the fact that polysemous words, those with multiple meanings, make up 70% of some 9,000 words identified as essential for elementary students to know (Johnson, Moe, & Baumann, 1983).

Others besides Cronbach (1942) have developed means for describing the extent to which a word is known. Dale (1965) described a stage-like progression—never saw the word before, heard of the word, vague idea of the word meaning, could define and use the word—to capture

TABLE 9.1. Cronbach's Five Dimensions of What It Means to Know a Word

Dimension	Demonstrated trait	Example of knowledge use
Generalization	Define the word.	"*Tattoo*: a permanent mark on the skin made by pricking or scarring."
Application	Use the word correctly or define its correct usage.	"The sailor had an anchor *tattoo* on his right arm."
Breadth	Know multiple meanings for a word.	"Two other meanings for *tattoo* are a drum or bugle signal that calls soldiers and sailors back to camp, and to beat or tap rhythmically."
Precision	Know when, and when not, to use a word.	"My brother's nervous tapping on the table was like a *tattoo*, but you probably wouldn't say the siren wailed like a *tattoo*, because it's constant."
Availability	Apply the word in discussions and thinking.	"We could plan to include a tattoo when the band gets to the cemetery on Memorial Day."

Note. From Ganske (2012). Copyright 2012 by The Guilford Press. Reprinted by permission.

the incremental nature of word learning. The scale is one that teachers still often use to assess children's knowledge of vocabulary prior to a unit of study (Blachowicz, 1986; Ganske, 2008) and that students use to self-assess understanding. Bravo and Cervetti (2008) created a similar tool for use with content area vocabulary. Beck, McKeown, and Omanson (1987) offer a classification system comprising five levels that is similar to Dales' (1965) but more nuanced:

- no knowledge of the word
- general sense of the word (such as *abdicate* has something to do with kings and queens or *ridicule* is something bad)
- narrow context-bound knowledge, as for instance, knowing that *devour* means to "eat up greedily" but not knowing we can devour a book just as easily as a sandwich
- knowledge of a word but inability to recall and use it in appropriate situations
- rich, decontextualized knowledge of a meaning, its connection to other words, and its extension to metaphorical uses.

Nation (2001) identifies three critical facets relevant to language minority students' vocabulary learning that include receptive and productive skill:

- form (pronunciation, spelling, word parts)
- meaning (including forms in which the word occurs, understanding the meaning and the concept behind the word, associations with other words)
- use (such as grammatical functions, other words used with the word, and when and where the word is used).

Other scholars have described the characteristics of knowing a word in different ways (e.g., Calfee & Drum, 1986; Johnson & Pearson, 1984; Kame'ennui, Dixon, & Carnine, 1987; Nagy & Scott, 2000, Qian, 2002).

CLASSROOM AS A COMMUNITY
FOR LEARNING VOCABULARY

Because children learn most words incidentally and classrooms are one of the spaces in which this occurs, it is important that the classroom environment supports and encourages vocabulary learning. Brophy (2008) discusses three traits relevant to classroom communities: *social milieu, expectancy,* and *value.* In classrooms that function as communities, students feel part of a social fabric yet have some autonomy and competence. Tasks are at "just right" levels of challenge to enable students to feel they have the power to improve over time. Furthermore, when activities are interesting and students know why they are engaging in them, students are motivated and value the learning. These three qualities are foundational to classroom settings that support and promote children's vocabulary knowledge and language learning.

Language, as the primary means by which we develop and share understandings, is critical in the development of students' thinking (Vygotsky, 1978). The quality of teacher talk has been associated with student learning, including vocabulary learning (e.g., Barnes & Dickinson, 2017; Denton, 2013, 2016; Dickinson & Porche, 2011; Johnston, 2004; Nystrand, Wu, Gamoran, Zeiser, & Long, 2003). Across the grades, teachers' emphases on rich language during discussion has been shown to lead to greater student comprehension (Murphy, Wilkinson, Soter, Hennessey, & Alexander, 2009). Similarly, in early childhood classrooms teachers' use of rich language has related to improvements in language and academic performance, both short and long term (Barnes & Dickinson, 2017). However, when teaching sophisticated vocabulary, Barnes and Dickinson suggest that shorter sentences may be helpful in preventing cognitive overload.

Quantity of talk also matters. Increases in student talk, with attendant decreases in teacher talk, have been associated with greater student learning (Nystrand et al., 2003); unfortunately, in many classrooms, teacher talk dominates and what could be discussion is often a mini-interrogation (Ganske & Jocius, 2013). In a meta-analysis to uncover supports for vocabulary learning, Ford-Connors and Paratore (2015) found a number of benefits for discussion and instructional conversations, including (1) opportunities for students to hear and use target words in real contexts; (2) student interactions that promote word learning and conceptual understanding; (3) word learning through anticipation of participating in discussions, as well as actual participation; (4) deepening of content understanding; and (5) development of word consciousness. Greater student gains were linked to teachers who encouraged the use of rich language and higher-level thinking and who forged connections to students' prior experiences and their content and strategy learning. Abundant, high-quality talk in classrooms by teachers and students supports learning and achievement.

High-quality interactive read-alouds can add to the sense of classroom community and can have a positive impact on young children's vocabulary knowledge (e.g., Beck & McKeown, 2001; Dickinson, 2001; Hargrave & Sénéchal, 2000). During the reading teachers model and engage students in higher-level thinking. They ask questions to prompt discussion about vocabulary and comprehension, define words, and reread the text (Wasik,

Hindman, & Snell, 2016). Props, retellings, and extension activities are also sometimes used. Biemiller and Boote (2006) found that rereading the same story led to a 12% increase in children's understanding of target vocabulary, and by adding direct explanations of meanings during the reading vocabulary increased by 22%. Books should be sophisticated enough to afford teaching five to ten words, but if this is not the case, McGee and Schickendanz (2007) suggest incorporating sophisticated words into comments or the introduction. They suggest that words be defined by (1) a short phrase that illustrates the meaning (*sly* means he's "tricky" and "sneaky"); (2) pointing to illustrations clues; (3) enactment through gestures (*slump*); (4) voice expression (*whined, pleaded*); and (5) reading pace (reading fast to show that the character's words *gushed*). The quality of the interactions during read-alouds matters, as the talk about the text, both during the reading and at other times, has been shown to affect children's growth in receptive vocabulary knowledge more than the number of reading events (Roberts, Jurgens, & Burchinal, 2005). Read-alouds should be a staple of the literacy diet in early-grade classrooms; I would argue further—in *any* classroom.

A classroom climate in which reading is valued also can promote vocabulary development. Teachers of young children who value reading are likely to read aloud more. In the case of older students, how much students read contributes significantly to growth in both their vocabulary and their general knowledge (Cunninngham & Stanovich, 1991). Text complexity is also a factor; texts must be sophisticated enough to expose the reader to new and difficult vocabulary. Despite the promise, the fact is many adolescents do not like to read and do not read enough to affect vocabulary growth (Graves, 2016; Ford-Connors & Paratore, 2015). Clearly, to leverage vocabulary development through incidental learning, teachers of older students need to be able to motivate readers.

Other classroom environmental factors may bear on students' vocabulary learning. For example, a large class size may make it difficult for teachers to scaffold students' learning (Bowne, Yoshikawa, & Snow, 2016). Teachers' expectations of students' language needs may lead them to use less rich and less complex language and vocabulary and teacher turnover may result in less robust language environments (Barnes & Dickinson, 2017).

Word consciousness, or awareness of and interest in words (Anderson & Nagy, 1992; Graves & Watts-Taffe, 2002), may be considered another trait of a classroom community and an important part of a comprehensive program to develop vocabulary knowledge (e.g., Bauman, Kame'enui, & Ash, 2003; Graves, 2016; Scott & Nagy, 2009). In word-conscious classrooms, teachers promote interest in words by drawing attention to interesting language and providing opportunities, activities, and materials for students to play with words and heighten their appreciation of language. Fascinating words like *flibbertijibbet* (a silly, scatter-brained, or talkative person), unusual pronunciations and spellings (e.g., *queue-/kēyū/*); a personal connection (*spoke*—"That's what's on my bicycle!" as one first grader suddenly realized); and word play—puns, idioms, oxymora, metaphors, riddles and jokes, palindromes, etc.—can pique interest in and curiosity about words. Teaching about changes in meaning across time is another way to develop word consciousness. One of my first experiences with this aspect of word consciousness was with the word *school*, which originally meant "leisure," an awareness that stuns many intermediate-grade students.

Scott and Nagy (2009) identify knowledge and beliefs that are a part of word consciousness. These include (1) knowing a word is about more than simply knowing a definition, (2) word learning occurs in small steps and across time, (3) one strategy does not work for all words, and (4) context, definitions, and word parts afford valuable information about word meaning, especially when considered collectively.

I personally have found that after developing word consciousness students tend to ask more questions about unfamiliar words, enjoy sharing favorite words, monitor their reading and talk for interesting uses of language, and feel a sense of empowerment for learning. Their metalinguistic awareness helps them to better understand word meanings in context through the use of morphological, syntactic, and semantic clues and to appreciate language when reading and writing.

In summary, classroom communities that effectively promote vocabulary learning are likely to have the following five characteristics:

- High, but realistic expectations for students' learning
- Valuing of reading and read-aloud interactions
- Rich language discussions and student-generated talk, scaffolded by teachers' thoughtful consideration of students' needs
- Word consciousness and an awareness of why vocabulary matters
- Word-learning activities and tasks that are designed to be motivating and appropriately challenging.

BEST PRACTICES IN ACTION

This section describes three practices for developing vocabulary knowledge: context clues, morphology, and the teaching of academic vocabulary and multiple meanings in primary-grade classrooms.

Teach Context Clues

Since wide reading is thought to be one way children can learn many words (Biemiller & Slonim, 2001; Nagy, Anderson, & Herman 1987), and context is one source of information for understanding unfamiliar words (Scott & Nagy, 2009), it is important to teach learners how to use this resource (Ford-Connors & Paratore, 2015; Fukkink & deGlopper, 1998). Students in more advanced grades and with more advanced reading ability can best leverage context clues (Nagy et al., 1985; Shefelbine, 1990; Swanborn & deGlopper, 1999). Struggling readers often neither read widely nor make effective use of strategies (Baker, Simmons, & Kame'enui, 1995). They tend to have more limited vocabulary and less relevant background knowledge, which makes inferring meanings more difficult (Perfetti, Marron, & Foltz, 1996), so much so that when the conceptual load is great students may be unable to learn any words from context (Nagy et al., 1987). Texts with less-dense contexts can be beneficial, namely texts with one unfamiliar word in 25, rather than one in 10 (Na & Nation, 1985). Also, instruction may need to involve simpler strategies, more explicit instruction, and intense practice (Elleman, Steacy, Olinghouse, & Compton, 2017).

Students who effectively use context look for and consider information from available clues within the surrounding sentences, such as

- Rephrasing of the word's meaning or provision of its actual definition: "She was famished and ready to eat just about anything."
- Examples: "When he reported to his friends that he had told his teacher a dinosaur ate his homework, they all scoffed, booing, laughing, and teasing him."
- Comparison that may include a simile or synonym: "When she gaped at the tree, her mouth opened wider than a balloon." "When my cat gets rambunctious, my mom wishes he was less active."
- Contrasts: "You are really tardy today; from now on I expect you to be on time."

For young children the clues might be in illustrations that accompany the text. Accessibility of a clue may depend on the reader's/listener's background experiences, and in some texts there may not be clear clues. In general, the more times students are exposed to a word the more likely they will be to learn it (Horst, Cobb, & Meara, 1998; Nagy, Anderson, & Herman, 1987).

To teach use of context clues, teachers might develop a routine for two to three times a week in which they present students with a short paragraph or sentence that includes a targeted clue and an unfamiliar word.

In the beginning, teachers solve the word by using a think-aloud strategy to help students grasp the process. Gradually, students take over the problem solving. In time, the paragraphs can include multiple words and clues. The target word should be unfamiliar to students; when necessary to ensure this, a nonsense word can be embedded or substituted for a real word in the paragraph. Each word-solving experiences should be followed by a brief discussion of the process. Use of context clues as a strategy needs to be taught—students should not merely be reminded to use them. Younger children respond well to the idea of being "detectives" in search of clues and then using the clues to solve the word mystery. One teacher I know even adds a cardboard magnifying glass prop to the learning.

Teach Morphology

Being able to identify and understand the meaning units or *morphemes* (prefixes, suffixes, and roots) that comprise multisyllabic words can aid the development of students' vocabulary knowledge (e.g., Baumann et al., 2002; Bowers, Kirby, & Deacon, 2010; Goodwin & Ahn, 2010), including struggling readers and bilingual students (e.g., Goodwin & Ahn, 2013; Harris, Schumaker, & Deshler, 2011; Silverman et al., 2013). This is a strategy that students can really leverage since about 60% of the nearly 90,000 words they encounter can be understood with morphology (Nagy & Anderson, 1984).

Instruction in morphology should begin with morphemic units that are more transparent and of higher frequency. For example, the prefixes in *untie, redo,* and *incorrect* are obvious and are attached to base words, making the reader's task of understanding the new words a fairly easy one. By contrast, consider that the prefix *in-* is also found in *irregular* and *immobile* but a spelling change masks the identity of each word, resulting in a less-apparent meaning connection. The nine prefixes and several suffixes shown in Table 9.2 comprise 76% of all prefixed words and 80% of all suffixed words (White, Sowell, & Yanagihara, 1989). These are well worth students knowing. Yet, when White et al. tested third- and fourth-grade students, they found that just 63% of them knew even the most common prefix, *un-*. A small set of Greek and Latin roots (14 total) also hold much potential for enabling students to understand unfamiliar words: they can be combined with other morphemes to create 100,000 words (Brown, 1947). However, it is important to note that these roots can be quite opaque. Think, for example of *sist*, which means "to stand," "to endure," or "to persist," as in *resistant* (which literally means to "be in a state to persist again"). The meaning connections are even less evident when the spelling for *sist* changes to *stat, sta,* and *stan.* Yet, even with their potential to be complex, roots are an important tool students should

TABLE 9.2. Power-Packed Prefixes and Suffixes

Prefixes	Suffixes
un- (not, opposite of)	-s, -es
re- (back, again)	-ed
in-, im-, il-, ir (not)	-ing
dis- (opposite of)	-ly
en-, em- (put into)	-er, -or (agent)
non- (not)	-ion, -tion, -ation, -ition
in-, im- (in, into)	
over- (too much)	
mis- (badly, wrongly)	
Percentage of all prefixed words: 60%	Percentage of all suffixed words: 80%

learn when they are ready for the challenge. Root study can begin with those that are more transparent, such as *audio, bio, phon, vis,* etc.

Affixes and roots should be explicitly taught. Word webs are excellent for this exercise. The prefix, suffix, or root targeted for instruction is written in the center, with student-generated words that include the affix or root added to the web, as shown in Figure 9.1. Teachers should discuss any nonexamples (such as *unite* for *un-*) that may be suggested, as well as relevant meaning connections. For instance, in the Figure 9.1 example, students might be invited to explain the connection of *tri* to *triangle* (a shape or object that has three angles). This talk often arouses curiosity that leads to talk of other words, such as *trident* and the fact that *dent* means "tooth" (*dental, dentist*), so *trident* literally means "three teeth," a good name for a three-pronged spear. During reading, students should be encouraged to apply their knowledge of the morpheme in one word to the unfamiliar word and draw on clues from the context. (For further discussion and activities related to morphology, see Ganske, 2008, 2014).

Teach Individual Words: Leverage Word Study Time

Academic Vocabulary

As valuable as read-aloud time is for advancing children's knowledge of sophisticated vocabulary, some researchers (Carlisle, Kelcey, & Berebitsky, 2013; Silverman & Crandell, 2010) have suggested the need to explore additional times of the school day. My current work is focused on developing younger children's knowledge of academic vocabulary and

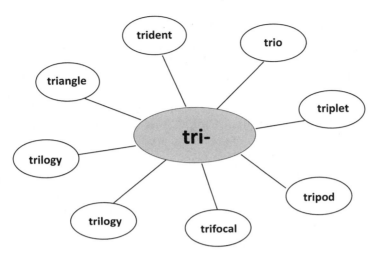

FIGURE 9.1. Word web for the prefix *tri-*. From Ganske (2014). Copyright 2014 by The Guilford Press. Reprinted by permission.

everyday words through connections to word study portions of the day (Ganske, 2016, 2017). The projects show promise for advancing learners' vocabulary knowledge. The academic vocabulary part of the work involves a 10-minute whole-class discussion/teaching lesson to introduce children to a general academic vocabulary word—*confer, evidence, interpret, appropriate,* or the like—that has applicability to the talk of small-group word study instruction and other parts of the day. Children read the word with the teacher, brainstorm thoughts about its meaning, and share their ideas and make connections, as the teacher questions, clarifies, and extends the children's learning. A short transcript segment focused on a first-grade teacher's talk about *explicit* with her class follows (for several complete examples, see Ganske, 2018).

The children's sharing after brainstorming makes clear that they initially think the word has something to do with "accurate," a previously taught word, then with "clear," "organized," "great," and finally with "having lots of details." The teacher pauses the group:

TEACHER: Oooooh! Now we're really there. We're coming to this idea. Details. What if I said to you, Child A, "I know you just had a difficult time with a friend on the playground . . . " (This is all pretend) " . . . could you please be very explicit about what happened?" What do you think I mean by that?

CHILD: Like talk it out; like talk with somebody.

TEACHER: Talk it out. . . . Would you just say, "It happened. We ran. We ran into each other." No. You would probably be very, very explicit. You would say, "First, Child B came running around the playground, and then Child C came running from the other side, and they didn't see each other, and they ran into each other. They both fell to the ground. Child C was upset and Child B hurt herself." So you are very explicit. You are very very clear. There are lots of details. And you're very clear.

CHILD: And you have to be accurate because you don't want to lie to the teacher.

TEACHER: Right. In order to be explicit, you have to be accurate. Anyone want to add on?

CHILD: I think it means to kind of say the truth.

TEACHER: Ahhh. Exactly. What if I said to you, "I'm going to the carnival." Who likes the carnival? "And at the carnival there is one Ferris wheel and two guys that sell cotton candy and there is one, no two, roller coasters and a hot air machine." I'm being very explicit. I'm giving a very clear, truthful, and accurate statement. There is no question about what is at the carnival, is there? What if I said, "I think there's some cool stuff there." Is that being explicit? No, it's just kind of general. If I said, "The boy walked across the street." OK. But what if I said, "The boy zoomed across the street." Better; it's more explicit. You can see that image in your head. So, today during word study I may ask you to be more explicit, explain yourself, be more clear.

Although the lesson ends here, during small-group word study, the teacher integrates *explicit* into the talk of her teaching and will encourage the children to use the word as well, across time. Each week she introduces a new word and each week she uses it, along with words from previous weeks, during word study talk and at other times of the day. In the lesson just described, to teach the word she used examples, synonyms, anotonyms, visualization, multiple contexts, real-world connections, and actively engaged students' interest by having them speculate on the word's meaning. During the sharing she honored every child's ideas through comments such as "What a great start; let's add on to that. She's already on the right track" and to a child who thought the word might mean "nice," she said "He took kind of a different turn. Maybe looking for a different meaning of *explicit*. Good risk taking there." The end result? Very engaged learners who are eager to contribute to the conversation. This same type interaction and explicit instruction around academic vocabulary could happen at any grade level.

Words with Multiple Meanings

Explicit instruction through discussion also can be used to teach polysemous words, words with multiple meanings, such as *ring*: "on a finger, round shape, action, place for performance in a circus, doorbell sound," etc. Polysemous words can be problematic for readers, especially language-minority students (Beck et al., 2013; Ford-Connors & Paratore, 2015). Word study is a prime time to develop young children's awareness of multiple meanings, since words used in the categorization activities that are a common part of word study tend to be Tier 1 words, words the children can read and with which they have some familiarity, but not necessarily with additional meanings. I've often watched young children grow excited when they discover that *bark* is not just the sound a dog makes and *ring* can mean something other than a jewelry item. To expand children's understanding of everyday words during word study small-group interactions, I recommend choosing two of the sort words (everyday words) to discuss. When using the SAIL (survey, analyze, interpret, link) framework (Ganske, 2016), this occurs during the survey part of the lesson. Ask children to share what they think the word means, and then expand their understanding by introducing them to an additional meaning. Explanation and kid-friendly definitions work well, but it is also helpful to show a photo on a tablet or a real object, or to enact the word, especially for language-minority students. Because the words are everyday words, such as *run* and *horn*, there will be opportunities for young learners to think about and use the words outside of school; it is also beneficial to review the words at the start of the next week's lesson.

REFLECTIONS AND FUTURE DIRECTIONS

It is widely accepted that vocabulary knowledge is critical for reading comprehension and that vocabulary knowledge is malleable; yet, as previously pointed out, vocabulary instruction does not always happen, at least not effectively. This needs to change. Learners of all ages deserve access to (1) positive learning environments in which reading and writing are valued and curiosity and interest in word learning are fostered; (2) opportunities to engage in meaningful talk about words; (3) tools for understanding words, such as how to use context clues and morphology; and (4) direct teaching of academic and polysemous words in ways that actively engage them and provide contexts to practice their use.

ENGAGEMENT ACTIVITIES

1. Incorporate cognate study into the study of morphology. Cognates are words that share similar spellings, meanings, and syntax across languages (transportation/*transportación*), such as English and Spanish. Because they are fairly common in picture books (Hernandez & Montelongo, 2018) even young children can be engaged in learning about them. What English words in your favorite picture books have Spanish cognates? Crosscheck your ideas with the list of cognates at the ¡Colorín Colorado! website, *www.colorincolorado.org/sites/default/files/Cognate-List.pdf,* or at *textproject.org.*

2. Compare academic word lists, such as Coxhead's AWL (2000); Hiebert's version of the AWL, which is filtered to include just 343 of the 570 that are among the 4,000 simple word families; Biemiller's Words Worth Teaching (2010); or some of Beck, McKeown, & Kucan's (2008) Tier 2 Word Candidates drawn from specific stories. Which words would be good choices for your students and would afford you and them multiple opportunities to use the words in the classroom?

3. Take note of vocabulary teaching and learning in your classroom. For a week, keep a tally or otherwise record how often you talk about vocabulary with your students. What is the quality of the interaction, and what role do students take? How do you follow up and encourage them? You might even record, for relistening purposes, one of the interactions. What challenges and successes do you notice?

REFERENCES

Anderson, R. C., & Freebody, P. (1981). Vocabulary knowledge. In J. Guthrie (Ed.), *Comprehension and teaching: Research reviews* (pp. 77–117). Newark, DE: International Reading Association.

Anderson, R. C., & Nagy, W. E. (1992, Winter). The vocabulary conundrum. *American Educator, 16,* 14–18, 44–47.

August, D., Carlo, M., Dressler, C., & Snow, C. (2005). The critical role of vocabulary development for English language learners. *Learning Disabilities Research and Practice, 20,* 50–57.

Baker, S. K., Simmons, D. C., & Kame'enui, E. J. (1995). *Vocabulary acquisition: Curriculum and instructional implications for diverse learners* (Tech. Rep. No. 14). Eugene: University of Oregon, National Center to Improve the Tools of Educators.

Barnes, E. M., & Dickinson, D. (2017). The relationship of Head Start teachers' academic language use and children's receptive vocabulary. *Early Education and Development, 28*(7), 794–809.

Barnes, E. M., Grifenhagen, J. F., & Dickinson, D. K. (2016). Academic language in early childhood classrooms. *The Reading Teacher, 70*(1), 39–48.

Baumann, J. F., Edwards, E. C., Font, G., Tereshinski, C. A., Kame'enui, E. J., & Olejnik, S. (2002). Teaching morphemic and contextual analysis to fifth-grade students. *Reading Research Quarterly, 37*(2), 150–178.

Beck, I. L., & McKeown, M. G. (2001). Text talk: Capturing the benefits of read-aloud experiences for young children. *The Reading Teacher, 55,* 10–20.

Beck, I. L., McKeown, M. G., & Kucan, L. (2008). *Creating robust vocabulary: Frequently asked questions and extended examples.* New York: Guilford Press.

Beck. I. L., McKeown, M. G., & Kucan, L. (2013). *Bringing words to life: Robust vocabulary instruction* (2nd ed.). New York: Guilford Press.

Beck, I. L., McKeown, M. G., & Omanson, R. C. (1987). The effects and uses of diverse vocabulary instructional techniques. In M. G. McKeown & M. C. Curtis (Eds.), *The nature of vocabulary acquisition* (pp. 147–163). Hillsdale, NJ: Erlbaum.

Biemiller, A. (1999). *Language and reading success.* Cambridge, MA: Brookline Books.

Biemiller, A. (2001). Teaching vocabulary: Early, direct, and sequential. *American Educator, 25,* 24–28.

Biemiller, A. (2010). *Words worth teaching: Closing the vocabulary gap.* Columbus, OH: McGraw-Hill SRA.

Biemiller, A., & Boote, C. (2006, February 1). An effective method for building meaning vocabulary in primary grades. *Journal of Educational Psychology, 98*(1), 44–62.

Biemiller, A., & Slonim, N. (2001). Estimating root word vocabulary growth in normative and advantaged populations: Evidence for a common sequence of vocabulary acquisition. *Journal of Educational Psychology, 93*(3), 498–520.

Blachowicz, C. I. Z. (1986). Making connections: Alternatives to the vocabulary notebook. *Journal of Reading, 29,* 643–649.

Bowers, P. N., Kirby, J. R., & Deacon, S. H. (2010). The effects of morphological instruction on literacy skills: A systematic review of the literature. *Review of Educational Research, 80*(2), 144–179.

Bowne, J. B., Yoshikawa, H., & Snow, C. E. (2016). Relationships of teachers' language and explicit vocabulary instruction to students' vocabulary growth in kindergarten. *Reading Research Quarterly, 52*(1), 7–29.

Bravo, M. A., & Cervetti, G. N. (2008). Teaching vocabulary through text and experience in content areas. In A. E. Farstrup & S. J. Samuels (Eds.), *What research has to say about vocabulary instruction* (pp. 130–149). Newark, DE: International Reading Association.

Brown, J. I. (1947). Reading and vocabulary: 14 master words. In M. J. Herzberg (Ed.), *Word study* (pp. 1–4). Springfield, MA: G. & C. Merriam.

Calfee, R. C., & Drum, P. A. (1986). Research on teaching reading. In M. D. Wittrock (Ed.), *Handbook of research on teaching* (3rd ed., pp 804–849). New York: Macmillan.

Carlisle, J. F., Kelcey, B., & Berebitsky, D. (2013). Teachers' support of students' vocabulary learning during literacy instruction in high poverty elementary schools. *American Educational Research Journal, 50*(6), 1360–1391.

Corson, D. (1997). The learning and use of academic English words. *Language Learning, 47,* 671–718.

Coxhead, A. (2000). A new academic word list. *TESOL Quarterly, 34,* 213–238.

Coyne, M. D., Loftus, S., Zipoli, R., & Kapp, S. (2009). Direct vocabulary instruction in kindergarten: Teaching for breadth versus depth. *Elementary School Journal, 110*(1), 1–18.

Cronbach, L. J. (1942). An analysis of techniques for diagnostic vocabulary testing. *Journal of Educational Research, 36,* 206–217.

Crosson, A. C., & Lesaux, N. K. (2013). Connectives: Fitting another piece of the vocabulary instruction puzzle. *The Reading Teacher, 67*(3), 193–200.

Cunningham, A. E., & Stanovich, K. E. (1997). Early reading acquisition and its relation to reading experience and ability 10 years later. *Developmental Psychology, 33*(6), 934–945.

Dale, E. (1965). Vocabulary measurement: Techniques and major findings. *Elementary English, 42*(8), 895–901, 948.

D'Anna, C. A., Zechmeister, E. B., & Hall, J. W. (1991). Toward a meaningful definition of vocabulary size. *Journal of Reading Behavior, 23,* 109–122.

Davis, F. B. (1968). Research in comprehension in reading. *Reading Research Quarterly, 3,* 499–545. Retrieved from *www.jstor.org/stable/747153.*

Denton, P. (2013). *The power of our words: Teacher language that helps children learn* (2nd ed.). Turners Falls, MA: Northeast Foundation for Children.

Denton, P. (2016). *The power of our words for middle school: Teacher language that helps students learn.* Turners Falls, MA: Northeast Foundation for Children.

Dickinson, D. K. (2001). Book reading in preschool classrooms: Is recommended practice common? In D. K. Dickinson & P.O. Tabors (Eds.), *Building literacy with language: Young children learning at home and school* (pp. 175–203). Baltimore: Brookes.

Dickinson, D. K., & Porche, M. V. (2011). Relation between language experiences in preschool classrooms and children's kindergarten and fourth grade language and reading abilities. *Child Development, 82,* 870–886.

Elleman, A. M., Steacy, L. M., Olinghouse, N. G., & Compton, D. L. (2017). Examining child and word characteristics in vocabulary learning of struggling readers. *Scientific Studies of Reading, 21*(2), 133–145.

Fitzgerald, W. J., Elmore, J., Kung, M., & Stenner, A. J. (2017). The conceptual complexity of vocabulary in elementary-grades core science program textbooks. *Reading Research Quarterly, 52*(4), 417–442.

Foorman, B., Beyler, N., Borradaile, K., Coyne, M., Denton, C. A., Dimino, J., . . . Wissel, S. (2016). *Foundational skills to support reading for understanding in kindergarten through 3rd grade* (NCEE 2016-4008). Washington, DC: National Center for Education Evaluation and Regional Assistance, Institute of Education Sciences, U.S. Department of Education. Retrieved from *http://whatworks.ed.gov.*

Ford-Connors, E., & Paratore, J. R. (2015). Vocabulary instruction in fifth grade and beyond: Sources of learning and productive contexts for development. *Review of Educational Research, 85*(1), 50–91.

Fukkink, R. G., & deGlopper, K. (1998). Effects of instruction in deriving word meaning from context: A meta-analysis. *Review of Educational Research, 68*(4), 450–469.

Ganske, K. (2008). *Mindful of words: Spelling and vocabulary explorations 4–8.* New York: Guilford Press.

Ganske, K. (2012). If you want students to learn vocabulary—Move beyond copying words. In D. Lapp & B. Moss (Eds.), *Exemplary instruction in the middle grades* (pp. 205–224). New York: Guilford Press.

Ganske, K. (2014). *Word journeys: Assessment-guided phonics, spelling, and vocabulary instruction* (2nd ed.). New York: Guilford Press.

Ganske, K. (2016). SAIL: A framework for promoting next generation word study. *The Reading Teacher, 70*(3), 337–346.

Ganske, K. (2017, December). *Words for academic vocabulary exploration and study–WAVES.* Paper presented at the 66th annual meeting of the Literacy Research Association, Orlando, FL.

Ganske, K. (2018). *Word sorts and more: Sound, pattern, and meaning explorations K–3* (2nd ed.). New York: Guilford Press.

Ganske, K., & Jocius, R. (2013). Small-group word study: Instructional conversations or mini-interrogations? *Language Arts, 91*(1), 23–40.

Goodwin, A. P., & Ahn, S. (2010). A meta-analysis of morphological interventions: Effects on literacy achievement of children with literacy difficulties. *Annals of Dyslexia, 60*(2), 183–208.

Goodwin, A. P., & Ahn, S. (2013). A meta-analysis of morphological interventions in English: Effects on literacy outcomes for school-age children. *Scientific Studies of Reading, 17*(4), 257–285.

Graves, M. F. (2016). *The vocabulary book: Learning and instruction* (2nd ed.). New York: Teachers College Press.

Graves, M. F., August, D., & Mancilla-Martinez, J. (2013). *Teaching vocabulary to English language learners.* New York: Teachers College Press, International Reading Association, Center for Applied Linguistics, and Teachers of English to Speakers of Other Languages.

Graves, M. F., & Watts-Taffe, S. M. (2002). The place of word consciousness in a research-based vocabulary program. In A. E. Farstrup & S. J. Samuels (Eds.), *What research has to say about reading instruction* (3rd ed., pp. 140–165). Newark, DE: International Reading Association.

Hargrave, A. C., & Sénéchal, M. (2000). A book reading intervention with preschool children who have limited vocabularies: The benefits of regular reading and dialogic reading. *Early Childhood Research Quarterly, 15,* 75–90.

Harris, M. L., Schumaker, J. B., & Deshler, D. D. (2011). The effects of strategic morphological analysis instruction on the vocabulary performance of secondary students with and without disabilities. *Learning Disability Quarterly, 34*(1), 17–33.

Hart, B., & Risley, T. R. (1995). *Meaningful differences in the everyday experiences of young American children.* Baltimore: Brookes.

Hernández, A. C., & Montelongo, J. A. (2018). Word study with Spanish–English cognates. In K. Ganske, *Word sorts and more* (pp. 81–92). New York: Guilford Press.

Horst, M., Cobb, T., & Meara, P. (1998). Beyond a Clockwork Orange: Acquiring second language vocabulary through reading. *Reading in a Foreign Language, 11*(2), 207–223.

Johnson, D. D., Moe, A. J., & Baumann, J. F. (1983). *The Ginn word book for teachers: A basic lexicon.* Boston: Ginn.

Johnson, D. D., & Pearson, P. D. (1984). *Teaching reading vocabulary.* New York: Holt, Rinehart and Winston.

Johnston, P. H. (2004). *Choice words: How our language affects children's learning.* Portland, ME: Stenhouse.

Juel, C., Biancarosa, G., Coker, G., & Deffes, R. (2003). Walking with Rosie: A cautionary tale of early reading instruction. *Educational Leadership, 60*(7), 12–18.

Kame'enui, E. J., Dixon, D. W., & Carnine, R. C. (1987). Issues in the design of vocabulary instruction. In M. G. McKeown & M. E. Curtis (Eds.), *The nature of vocabulary acquisition* (pp. 129–145). Hillsdale, NJ: Erlbaum.

Lawrence, J. F., White, C., & Snow, C. E. (2010). The words students need. *Educational Leadership, 68*(2), 23–26.

McGee, L. M., & Schickedanz, J. A. (2007). Repeated interactive read-alouds in preschool and kindergarten. *The Reading Teacher, 60*(8), 742–751.

McKeown, M. G., Beck, I. L., Omanson, R. C., & Pople, M. T. (1985). Some effects of the nature and frequency of vocabulary instruction on the knowledge of use of words. *Reading Research Quarterly, 20*(5), 522–535.

Murphy, P. K., Wilkinson, I. A., Soter, A. O., Hennessey, M. N., & Alexander, J. F. (2009). Examining the effects of classroom discussion on students' comprehension of text: A meta-analysis. *Journal of Educational Psychology, 101,* 740–764.

Na, L., & Nation, I. S. P. (1985). Factors affecting guessing vocabulary in context (less dense contexts. *RELC Journal, 16*(1), 33–42.

Nagy, W. E. (2005). Why instruction needs to be long-term and comprehensive. In E. H. Hiebert & M. L. Kamil (Eds.), *Teaching and learning vocabulary: Bringing research to practice* (pp. 27–44). Chicago: Routledge.

Nagy, W. (2007). Understanding words and word learning. In S. Rosenfield & V. Berlinger (Eds.), *Implementing evidence-based academic interventions in school settings* (pp. 479–500). New York: Oxford University Press.

Nagy, W. E., & Anderson, R. C. (1984). How many words are there in printed school English? *Reading Research Quarterly, 19,* 304–330.

Nagy, W. E., Anderson, R., & Herman, P. (1987). Learning word meanings from context during normal reading. *American Educational Research Journal, 24*(2), 237–270.

Nagy, W. E., & Herman, P. A. (1987). Depth and breadth of vocabulary knowledge: Implications for acquisition and instruction. In M. C. McKeown & M. E. Curtis (Eds.), *The nature of vocabulary acquisition* (pp. 19–35). Hillsdale, NJ: Erlbaum.

Nagy, W. E., & Scott, J. A. (2000). Vocabulary processing. In M. L. Kamil, P. B. Mosenthal, P. D. Pearson, & R. Barr (Eds.), *Handbook of reading research* (Vol. 3, pp. 269–274). Mahwah, NJ: Erlbaum.

Nagy, W. E., & Townsend, D. (2012). Words as tools: Learning academic vocabulary as language acquisition. *Reading Research Quarterly, 47,* 91–108.

Nation, I. S. P. (2001). *Learning vocabulary in another language.* Cambridge, UK: Cambridge University Press.

National Early Literacy Panel. (2008). *Developing early literacy: A scientific synthesis of early literacy development and implications for intervention.* Washington, DC: National Institute for Literacy. Retrieved from *https://lincs.ed.gov/publications/pdf/NELPReport09.pdf.*

National Governors Association Center for Best Practices & Council of Chief State School Officers. (2010). *Common Core State Standards for English language arts and literacy in history/social studies, science, and technical subjects.* Washington, DC: Authors.

National Reading Panel & National Institute of Child Health and Human Development. (2000). *Report of the National Reading Panel: Teaching children to read: An evidence-based assessment of the scientific research literature on reading and its implications for reading instruction: Reports of the subgroups.* Washington, DC: National Institute of Child Health and Human Development, National Institutes of Health.

Nystrand, M., Wu, L. L., Gamoran, A., Zeiser, S., & Long, D. (2003). Questions in time: Investigating the structure and dynamics of unfolding classroom discourse. *Discourse Processes, 35,* 135–198.

Perfetti, C. A. (2007). Reading ability: Lexical quality to comprehension. *Scientific Studies of Reading, 11*(4), 357–383.

Perfetti, C. A., Marron, M. A., & Foltz, P. W. (1996). Sources of comprehension failure: Theoretical perspectives and case studies. In C. Cornoldi & J. Oakhill (Eds.), *Reading comprehension difficulties: Processes and intervention* (pp. 137–165). Mahwah, NJ: Erlbaum.

Qian, D. D. (2002). Investigating the relationship between vocabulary knowledge and academic reading performance: An assessment perspective. *Language Learning 52*(3), 513–536.

Roberts, J., Jurgens, J., & Burchinal, M. (2005). The role of home literacy practices in preschool children's language and emergent literacy skills. *Journal of Speech, Language, and Hearing Research, 48,* 345–359.

Schleppegrell, M. J. (2004). *The language of schooling: A functional linguistics perspective.* Mahwah, NJ: Erlbaum.

Scott, J., & Nagy, W. (2009). Developing word consciousness. In M. Graves (Ed.), *Essential readings on vocabulary instruction* (pp. 106–117). Newark, DE: International Reading Association.

Shefelbine, J. L. (1990). Student factors related to variability in learning word meanings from context. *Journal of Literacy Research, 22*(1), 71–97.

Silverman, R. D., & Crandell, J. D. (2010). Vocabulary practices in prekindergarten and kindergarten classrooms. *Reading Research Quarterly, 45*(3), 318–340.

Silverman, R. D., Proctor, C. P., Harring, J. R., Doyle, B., Mitchell, M. A., & Meyer,

A. G. (2013). Teachers' instruction and students' vocabulary and comprehension: An exploratory study with English monolingual and Spanish–English bilingual students in grades 3–5. *Reading Research Quarterly, 49,* 31–60.

Snow, C., Lawrence, J., & White, C. (2009). Generating knowledge of academic language among urban middle school students. *Journal of Research on Educational Effectiveness, 2,* 325–344.

Stahl, S. A. (2003, Spring). Words are learned incrementally over multiple exposures. *American Educator, 27*(1), 19–18, 44.

Stahl, S. A., & Fairbanks, M. M. (1986). The effects of vocabulary instruction: A model-based meta-analysis. *Review of Educational Research, 56,* 72–110.

Stanovich, K. E. (1986). Matthew effects in reading: Some consequences of individual differences in the acquisition of literacy. *Reading Research Quarterly, 21,* 360–407.

Swanborn, M. S., & deGlopper, K. (1999). Incidental word learning while reading: A meta-analysis. *Review of Educational Research, 69,* 261–285.

Vygotsky, L. S. (1978). *Mind in society.* Cambridge, MA: Harvard University Press.

Wasik, B. A., Hindman, A. H., & Snell, E. K. (2016). Book reading and vocabulary development: A systematic review. *Early Childhood Research Quarterly, 37*(4), 39–57.

White, T. G., Sowell, J., & Yanagihara, A. (1989). Teaching elementary students to use word-part clues. *The Reading Teacher, 42,* 302–308.

Wright, T. S., & Neuman, S. B. (2014). Paucity and disparity in kindergarten oral vocabulary instruction. *Journal of Literacy Research, 46,* 330–357.

Zwiers, J. (2007). Teacher practices and perspectives for developing academic language. *International Journal of Applied Linguistics, 17,* 93–116.

CHAPTER 10

Best Practices in Narrative Text Comprehension Instruction

JANICE F. ALMASI
SUSAN J. HART

This chapter will:

- Discuss issues related to the role of word recognition and the role of knowledge in comprehension instruction.
- Discuss the importance of teaching readers to be strategic versus teaching strategies.
- Assert that the 21st-century informational age requires readers to become transformed into strategic learners.
- Explain the role of context, explicit instruction, agency and metacognition, and transfer in teaching readers to become transformed into strategic learners.

The first section of this chapter reviews what current and seminal research says about comprehension, while the second section describes the fundamental changes that need to occur to recontextualize comprehension as a means of cultivating strategic and reflective learners. The third section describes adjustments that can be made within literacy classrooms to foster an environment that is conducive to a "transformational view" of narrative text comprehension instruction.

EVIDENCE-BASED BEST PRACTICES:
A RESEARCH SYNTHESIS

Two issues have been at the forefront of comprehension research and practice: the role of *word recognition* and the role of *knowledge* in instruction aimed at improving comprehension. Understanding these perspectives helps situate why comprehension instruction needs to transform into a mindset that will prepare learners for the 21st century.

The Role of Word Recognition in Instruction Aimed at Improving Comprehension

Many researchers and practitioners subscribe to the notion that the ability to decode words is central to successful comprehension. The logic underlying this perspective is based on the premise that if one can decode the words in a text, then comprehension should be adequate, if one's listening comprehension is also adequate. This perspective is rooted originally in automaticity theory (Fleisher, Jenkins, & Pany, 1979; LaBerge & Samuels, 1974; Samuels, 2004) and more recently in Hoover and Gough's (1990) "simple view" of reading, which argued that skilled reading consisted simply of decoding and linguistic comprehension.

These theories are most evident in emergent literacy practices and instruction with struggling readers where much of the instruction is focused on word recognition (including phonics and phonemic awareness instruction) and fluency, and little instruction is focused on comprehension. The logic behind this practice is that "students need to learn to read the words first, we will focus on comprehension afterward."

If these theories were accurate, then it would be inconceivable that readers could decode words accurately and struggle with comprehension. Valencia's research (Riddle Buly & Valencia, 2002; Valencia, 2011) indicated that readers who struggle vary greatly. Nearly 20% of all struggling readers in her research could decode words accurately and read fluently; however, their comprehension was weak. Leach, Scarborough, and Rescorla's (2003) research found that nearly half of the fourth graders in their study had late-emerging comprehension difficulties (i.e., comprehension difficulty emerged after third grade). Of those students, one-third had comprehension difficulty, but could decode words accurately.

These studies dispel the notion that accurate decoding alone guarantees comprehension. A significant number of readers who struggle with comprehension do so despite having adequate word recognition skills.

Programs and legislation that aim to teach all children to read by grade three often focus on teaching children to read words accurately and with fluency. The Reading First programs of the 2000s were an example of such legislation. Reading First was intended to provide explicit instruction in phonics, phonemic awareness, fluency, vocabulary, *and* comprehension; however, ensuing instructional practice focused largely on phonics, phonemic awareness, and fluency. Ultimately, when the final report of Reading First's impacts was released, findings indicated that these code-based interventions had no significant impact on comprehension for children in grades 1, 2, or 3 (Gamse, Jacob, Horst, Boulay, & Unlu, 2008).

Almasi, Palmer, Madden, and Hart's (2011) review of research on interventions that foster narrative comprehension for struggling readers found similar results. Those interventions focused solely on decoding and/or fluency were not as successful at enhancing comprehension as interventions that included both decoding and comprehension instruction. Furthermore, interventions that focused exclusively on comprehension were consistently successful at enhancing comprehension. In a more quantitative analysis of research, Edmonds and colleagues (2009) examined studies in which three types of interventions were used to enhance comprehension: (1) fluency/word-study interventions, (2) comprehension interventions (e.g., teaching single strategies, teaching multiple strategies, or using graphic organizers), and (3) multicomponent interventions, which included either word study and comprehension or fluency and comprehension. Their analysis found that comprehension interventions were superior to all other types of intervention for enhancing comprehension, and the most effective interventions were those that taught multiple strategies. In particular, teaching multiple strategies was effective for struggling readers and students with disabilities. Likewise, Snowling and Hulme's (2011) review of research suggested that students who struggle with comprehension do not benefit from interventions focused on decoding. Instead, they benefit more from interventions focused on either oral language, vocabulary, or metacognitive strategies.

These reviews of research confirm the conclusion that while the ability to decode words and read with fluency is necessary for successful reading, and vital *for* comprehension, the ability to decode by itself is not sufficient to ensure successful comprehension. These research findings should put to rest the notion that an instructional emphasis on decoding (i.e., phonics, phonemic awareness) by itself, or even in large part, leads to significant impacts on comprehension—it does not.

Rather than viewing comprehension as "simply" a by-product of decoding and linguistic comprehension, the evidence suggests that comprehension is a more complex process in which readers actively construct mental representations of the text. Kintsch's (1998) construction–integration model of comprehension best represents thinking from this perspective. The construction–integration model of comprehension suggests that readers construct meaning simultaneously by deriving meaning from the textbase and integrating it with relevant information from their prior knowledge and experience. The integration of the textbase and his or her prior knowledge enables the reader to make connections to the text and arrive at his or her own personal interpretation of the text, which Kintsch (1998) refers to as a "situation model" (p. 49). Knowledge of comprehension strategies and the ability to be strategic is part of each reader's prior knowledge that is activated and used when needed to construct a situation model (Graesser, 2007).

The Role of Knowledge in Comprehension

The role of knowledge in comprehension is one with which the field continues to grapple. The issue revolves primarily around the degree to which content knowledge and process knowledge contribute to comprehension. Some have argued (e.g., Hirsch, 2006; McKeown, Beck, & Blake, 2009; Neuman, 2006) that having relevant content knowledge (e.g., domain knowledge, prior knowledge, vocabulary) is critical to comprehension. These scholars contend that readers must have specific knowledge of content and concepts in the text to be able to understand it. Others contend that it is essential that readers possess process knowledge related to what comprehension strategies to use, and procedural and conditional knowledge related to where, when, and how to use those strategies (e.g., Duke & Pearson, 2008–2009; Pressley, 2000; Pressley et al., 1992). The question of interest for practitioners is: "Does a reader have difficulty comprehending because he or she lacks knowledge of the words and concepts in the text, or does he or she lack knowledge of the process of knowing when/how to access that knowledge?"

Beginning with the National Reading Panel (2000), government-issued reports regarding research-based comprehension practice have consistently found that there is strong research evidence to support teaching comprehension strategies to both young readers (e.g., Shanahan et al., 2010) and adolescent readers (Kamil et al., 2008; Scamacca et al., 2007; Torgesen et al., 2007). Unfortunately, recent standards documents (Common Core State Standards [CCSS]; National Governors Association & Council of Chief State School Officers [NGA & CCSSO], 2010) do not mention strategy instruction, choosing instead to focus on the resulting products of comprehension that are most closely aligned with literal interpretations and close readings of the text that emphasize literal recall, making logical inferences, citing textual evidence to support conclusions, and analyzing the structure of texts. The result of such standards-based instruction has meant that, in practice, teachers are often unaware of what to teach children to arrive at the end product: successful comprehension.

Those arguing on behalf of content knowledge suggest that a focus on teaching comprehension strategies has undermined comprehension because the curriculum has neglected content knowledge and the vocabulary that is gained when learning content (Hirsch, 2006). The argument is predicated on the notion that "if you can't understand what the words mean or the concepts in the text, then comprehension is impossible." The instructional implications are that teachers need to build vocabulary and provide core knowledge to enhance comprehension. Unfortunately, many times those who struggle to comprehend do so regardless of whether they have content knowledge. As well, those who argue in favor of the content knowledge position are often long on rhetoric and short on empirical evidence. McKeown and colleagues (2009) is often cited as a study that supports the content knowledge position in that the fifth graders in the content knowledge condition were more successful at oral recall of narrative text than students in the strategies condition. However, all students did equally well on another measure of comprehension, the sentence verification technique. Thus, the results are mixed, and unfortunately there were several issues with the quality of the study. The study was not conducted with struggling readers (or poor comprehenders); did not control for variations in content knowledge; and used intact classrooms, but did not analyze results in a way that would control for the problems of using intact classrooms. Most importantly, the strategy instruction condition did not consist of instruction that most experts in strategy instruction would call "authentic strategy instruction." Thus, the study that is most often cited as evidence in support of the content knowledge position produced mixed results and had several methodological issues that render the findings suspect.

Although there is little substantive evidence to support the content knowledge position, there is, however, evidence that refutes the content knowledge position, and there are decades of research that support strategies instruction. The remainder of this review focuses on that body of research.

Nation's (2005) review of the research suggested that, while poor comprehenders tend to have weak expressive and receptive vocabularies, and that this lack of word-level knowledge contributes to poor comprehension, it is not likely that weak vocabulary entirely accounts for comprehension difficulties. For example, 7- and 8-year-old poor comprehenders continued to struggle to make inferences and understand text in studies where great care was taken to make sure all students had relevant content knowledge and vocabulary (Cain & Oakhill, 1999; Cain, Oakhill, Barnes, & Bryant, 2001). These findings suggest that something beyond vocabulary and content knowledge accounts for successful comprehension. Poor comprehenders in these studies understood relevant vocabulary, had the requisite content knowledge, and could find the location of the pieces of information they needed in the text to make an inference, yet they still could not make accurate inferences. In other words, this study ruled out the possibility that insufficient content knowledge caused these students' comprehension failure. The instructional implication based on this research is that poor comprehenders need to learn *how* to access knowledge and *how* integrate it to make inferences. Simply having content knowledge was insufficient for comprehension. These readers needed the process knowledge of how, when, and where to integrate knowledge across sentences to make inferences. These poor comprehenders needed strategy instruction.

Embedded Nature of Strategy Instruction in Comprehension Instruction

Those who argue in favor of strategy instruction do not deny that content knowledge is important; instead, they argue that strategy instruction is needed for many learners to become independent, self-regulated readers so they can learn relevant content from text. Palincsar and Schultz (2011) suggested that strategy instruction is intended to teach readers a "repertoire of thinking tools that should be used in opportunistic ways, determined by the demands of the text and the goals of the reader" that are taught "in the service of advancing knowledge building" (p. 91).

Strategies are cognitive and metacognitive processes that are deliberately and consciously employed as a means of attaining a goal (Almasi & Fullerton, 2012; Paris, Lipson, & Wixson, 1983; Pressley, Borkowski, & Schneider, 1989). Afflerbach, Pearson, and Paris (2008) distinguished strategies from skills by noting that intentionality, awareness, and goal-directedness are the hallmarks of strategic action.

The key aspect of this definition is that strategic behaviors are actions employed by an agentic individual. Often educators speak of strategies as if they are nouns rather than actions. This may be because much of the early research on strategy instruction focused on identifying what good and poor readers did while reading to enhance their comprehension. These "good and poor reader studies" helped the field understand what good readers were thinking and doing while reading. Instructional practice based on these findings attempted to teach struggling readers to engage in those strategies that good readers did while reading. Typically, these strategies were taught in isolation and they were taught quickly—sometimes over the course of a few lessons or a few weeks.

Reviews of these studies identified several powerful strategies that had significant impacts on comprehension, including comprehension monitoring, constructing mental images, identifying story grammar components, generating questions while reading, making inferences, and summarizing (e.g., Almasi et al., 2011; Gersten, Fuchs, Williams, & Baker, 2001; National Reading Panel, 2000; Pressley, 2000). Inadvertently, these studies may have led to current instructional practice in which strategies are often taught one at a time and in isolation. The other inadvertent outcome that may have emerged is that, due to the isolated nature of the instruction, teachers often prompted students to employ a specific strategy, rather than encouraging students to make their own decisions about whether to use the strategy or not. The results of these studies have shown that students are able to learn how to use a strategy to improve short-term comprehension, but over time these comprehension gains were not sustained. Unfortunately, the field has experienced a return to studies of isolated strategy instruction in recent years. Like earlier studies, more recent studies of summarization (e.g., Furtado & Johnson, 2010) and inferencing (e.g., Hall, 2016; McMaster et al., 2012) have found that teaching these strategies to students who struggle enhances their comprehension, while studies that focused on teaching metacognitive strategies in digital environments have had mixed results (e.g., Lan, Lo, & Hsu, 2014). In general, research has indicated that teaching strategies one at a time is not as effective as teaching them as an integrated set (Reutzel, Smith, & Fawson, 2005).

Although well meaning, teaching isolated strategies may also lead to the unintended practice in which students are not aware of alternative strategies or processes for making sense of text. As well, as Aukerman (2013) noted, such instruction may lead to the notion that there is only one "right" way to use strategies or that there are "better" strategies to use to construct meaning. Aukerman (2013) referred to strategy instruction as "comprehension-as-procedure pedagogy" (p. A4), and suggested that under such circumstances readers develop the notion that there is a "prespecified," or correct, way of using strategies to construct meaning.

Wilkinson and Son (2011) acknowledged the plethora of studies that support strategy instruction; however, they argued that research on strategy instruction has been unable to find particular combinations of strategy use that are effective and that research has been unable to determine whether the strategies that are taught are what causes the increases in comprehension. Both criticisms are valid; however, they reflect unintended consequences from research focused on teaching isolated strategies.

Research has also shown that the ability of such short-term, isolated strategy instruction to yield long-term benefits and transfer to all reading contexts is questionable (Almasi et al., 2011; Pressley, 2000). Many of these studies of isolated strategy instruction do not provide students with the type of explicit instruction that enables them to internalize the strategic processing necessary to transfer what they learned to other contexts. Instruction that fosters transfer includes opportunities for readers to talk not only about the strategies they use, but also about the conditions under which they may or may not use them. That is, readers must think about and consider where, when, and why they might use a particular strategy as they make decisions about whether to use a certain strategy to meet their reading goal.

In short, studies of isolated strategy use focus on teaching students the "strategy" rather than teaching students "to be strategic." Subsequently, teachers have come to focus on strategies as things to be taught, rather than as actions to be fostered. The difference between teaching students a "strategy" versus teaching students to be "strategic" is that strategic actions require intentionality—they require a reader who is *actively processing the text* and *making decisions about it* (Afflerbach et al., 2008; Paris, Wasik, & Turner, 1991; Pressley et al., 1989). Such readers continually monitor the reading experience and consciously make decisions as to where, when, how, and why they should apply strategic behaviors and actions (e.g., activating background knowledge to make connections, visualizing, making predictions, making inferences, identifying text structure, monitoring comprehension, summarizing) as warranted by the conditions surrounding the reading event. Thus, teaching readers to be strategic not only involves teaching them about the strategy, but also teaching them about the conditions under which one might *use* the strategy.

Instruction should, therefore, be focused on assisting readers in *becoming* strategic. That is, instruction should help readers learn how to become metacognitively aware so that they can actively make decisions on their own about how to make sense of the text. It does not mean that they should be taught a prescribed pattern of strategy use, or combinations of strategies, aimed at making sense of text. It means teaching students to become independent decision makers while they are reading. When taught as an integrated set, comprehension strategy instruction should take on a more dialogic characteristic that is focused on helping readers work through comprehension difficulties using a problem-solving approach in which multiple paths (and multiple ways of using combinations of strategies) lead to a successful outcome.

The ability to use a reading strategy to improve comprehension is far more difficult when the goal is to teach students to be strategic. It involves not only teaching students about the strategy, but also teaching them about the subtle nuances related to analyzing the reading task and making decisions about which strategies might best be suited for particular purposes, at particular times, and under particular circumstances. Such instruction takes time. Thus, interventions have been developed to teach readers how to use *sets* of strategies rather than individual strategies.

These interventions focus on teaching students how to recognize where and when they should use strategies, how to select from a variety of strategies, and how to determine whether their choices were moving them toward their goal: comprehension.

Reciprocal Teaching (Palincsar & Brown, 1984), Informed Strategies for Learning (e.g., Paris, Cross, & Lipson, 1984), the Learning Strategies Curriculum (e.g., Schumaker & Deshler, 1992, 2006) and Transactional Strategies Instruction (TSI; Anderson, 1992; Pressley et al., 1992) are examples of interventions that not only teach students how to flexibly use a cohesive set of strategies, but also how to develop metacognitive awareness of the task and self that fosters self-initiated and self-regulated strategy use. Research has shown that each of these interventions has proven successful with readers at various age levels, and some studies have shown that they lead to sustained and significant growth in comprehension over time (Brown, Pressley, Van Meter, & Schuder, 1996; Van Keer, 2004). More recently, Cantrell, Almasi, Rintamaa, and Carter's (2016) study of 2,263 low-achieving adolescents confirmed this finding. Their evaluation found that when adolescents were taught to use an integrated set of reading strategies (the Learning Strategies Curriculum) across 1 year, ninth graders' reading achievement grew significantly. As well, both sixth and ninth graders' motivation for reading was significantly impacted. Likewise, the What Works Clearinghouse's (U.S. Department of Education, 2010) intervention report regarding the efficacy of the set of integrated strategies that comprise Reciprocal Teaching affirmed its significant impact on comprehension.

Because of these research findings, core reading programs (i.e., basal reading programs) have incorporated some of the research related to comprehension strategies instruction (Pilonieta, 2010). However, as Dewitz, Jones, and Leahy (2009) found, the five most widely used commercial core reading programs do not provide the type of explicit instruction, the gradual release of responsibility, or the focus on becoming a strategic user of a set of comprehension strategies that is foundational to comprehension strategies instruction. Furthermore, Dewitz, Leahy, Jones, and Sullivan (2010) found these core programs woefully inadequate in their attempt to provide students with the procedural and conditional knowledge associated with strategy use. What continues to be problematic is that teachers tend to misunderstand what strategic processing involves, focus on isolated strategy use rather than strategic processing, and concentrate on activities rather than strategies. Teachers may engage students in an activity, but they do not provide the requisite instructional elements to teach *strategic processing*. Very often, the teacher him- or herself performs the strategies rather than teaching students how to use the strategy independently. That is, a teacher may set a purpose for reading rather than teaching the students how, when, and why they should set their own purposes while reading. Thus, students are not actively engaged in the decision-making process regarding what strategies to use and when to use them. As a result, they do not learn to become planful, self-regulated readers who possess a repertoire of strategies to assist them as they read. Readers who struggle are at a disadvantage in this scenario.

In summary, the previous review of reading comprehension research provided an overview of two generations of comprehension strategies research that has led to two different perspectives on instruction. The first perspective is what we will call the "isolation view" in which strategies are taught in isolation and their use is often prompted by teachers. This viewpoint has parallels to the industrial-age worldview discussed by Shantz and Rideout (2003) that situates knowledge as a possession of something outside of yourself. It was a mindset that underlined the standardization and training perspective of the 20th century. A common metaphor is that readers acquire a "toolbox" of different strategies (Almasi & Fullerton, 2012). From this perspective the strategies, or "tools," used by the reader are outside of the reader (kept in a metaphorical toolbox) and accessed when needed. A more knowledgeable other, such as a teacher, might let you know which tool to select and when to use it: "Today we're going to learn about the parts of a story. Stories include setting, characters, plot, and a solution. Here is a story map for you to fill out after you read the story. It will help you remember what you have read."

The "transformational view," which is what this chapter seeks to encourage, emphasizes the importance of teaching strategies in a manner that enables students to *become* strategic. This viewpoint highlights the shift in paradigm needed in education to empower students and teachers to have a growth mindset. Dweck (2016) posited that learners who believe their ability is malleable and who become more proficient with hard work exemplify a growth mindset. The reader no longer reaches for a tool from a toolbox that is outside of him or her; the reader actually *is* the tool. The tools are within the reader, and the reader must consider reader factors, textual factors, and contextual factors to determine what strategy works best in each situation. The reader embodies the tools/strategies. That is, the reader becomes the tools/strategies and the tools/strategies become the reader. The reader is transformed by using the strategies. Teachers from this perspective do not tell readers when to use a strategy; instead, they say things like "Today we are going to read a story. What strategies or tools might we use as we are reading to help us understand the story?" This is followed by a discussion among the students as to different types of strategies that they might use to help them as they read. The section that follows provides further explanation of what these best practices look like in action.

BEST PRACTICES IN ACTION

In current practice, educators feel the tension that is created due to the lack of coherence between reading programs and research-based strategies instruction. Core reading programs, like those that Dewitz, Jones, and Leahy (2009) evaluated, establish a precedent as to how comprehension instruction will occur within classrooms. Within the environments perpetuated by such reading programs, strategy instruction is prescriptive in nature, matching the strategy as outside of the learner or fixed mindset of generations past. It removes the social context of learning and expects all students to use the same strategies, in the same way, for the same outcome. Learners are viewed in this perspective as separate from the context of learning. Separating content and learning leads to a different understanding of how people conceptualize the nature of knowledge and learning.

Some would argue that the goal of comprehension is to extract the meaning from the text. This perspective implies that there is only one correct interpretation of a text and the reader must discover it. From this perspective, knowledge is located outside of the learner, and the learner must acquire that knowledge to successfully comprehend text. Again, this is a fixed perspective that was created so all students conformed to an industrial mindset.

This viewpoint of students as products, detached from their own learning processes has dominated our schools. As the No Child Left Behind Act (2001) embraced the "Big Five": (1) phonemic awareness, (2) phonics, (3) fluency, (4) vocabulary, and (5) comprehension (National Reading Panel, 2000), core reading programs followed in line and perpetuated a decontextualized nature of teaching strategies in isolation (Dewitz et al., 2009). In terms of comprehensive literacy instruction, this perspective brought with it a mind-set that emphasized "the simple view" of reading comprehension (Hoover & Gough, 1990). Such a developmental perspective stresses individual skills such as decoding, listening, fluency, and vocabulary/content knowledge as steps to achieve comprehension. Hoffman (2017) stated that such a perspective might work for literacy growth if literacy instruction and literacy learning were not such complex processes.

However, literacy learning is not simple. It is complex, and alternate perspectives suggest that there are multiple ways of knowing, or understanding a text, and the reader's job is to construct meaning in a manner best suited to his or her goals as a reader and the context. From this perspective, knowledge is located within the learner, and the learner must actively construct meaning to successfully comprehend text. Preparing students for the 21st century, an informational age where things will constantly change and their ability to adapt knowledge and become strategic will help them problem-solve, is part of the paradigm shift needed in education to help support students in the skills necessary to be successful in life.

The remainder of this chapter extends the conversation about comprehensive literacy instruction to recognize the social context of literacy learning as it relates to reading comprehension. This chapter attempts to change the conversation by focusing on how to teach readers to be strategic, while recognizing the social nature of comprehension processes and learning. Figure 10.1 depicts a more comprehensive and contextual view of how strategies can be implemented within a literacy environment so that students can become strategic and reflective within a classroom culture that values the growth mindset and fosters educational grit within the learning process. Figure 10.1 illustrates how four elements work together to create a learning environment that fosters independent, self-regulated comprehension: (1) context, (2) explicit instruction, (3) agency and metacognition, and (4) scaffolding. The following ideas, based on Almasi and Fullerton's (2012) critical elements of strategy instruction model, will help classroom teachers and interventionists to identify critical features necessary to help readers become strategic.

Context: Mindset, Grit, and the Learning Process

The instructional context in Figure 10.1 represents the overall instructional environment and everything contained within that environment. Context is critical for solid comprehension strategy instruction because it is through context that students become acculturated into the language of strategies, observe strategic behaviors and actions, and participate in strategic processing firsthand. Sociocultural perspectives on learning (e.g., Vygotsky, 1978) suggest that learning is a "cognitive apprenticeship" (Rogoff, 1990, p. i) that occurs when learners interact socially with others who might guide, support, or stretch their thinking so that they can learn how to use and implement the strategies that will be needed to become a literate member of the culture. In an instructional context focused on transformational comprehension, this means that students learn how to be strategic. There is not one tool they grab and use, instead strategic learners read the entire context and use information within the context to determine what part of their knowledge will support them in the problem-solving process. For example, a reader might need a different strategy, or may need to act in a different manner when reading in an online environment than when reading traditional text (Coiro & Dobler, 2007; Leu et al., 2008), or when reading in a Western society that places greater value on "school literacy" or "written literacy" than in a society

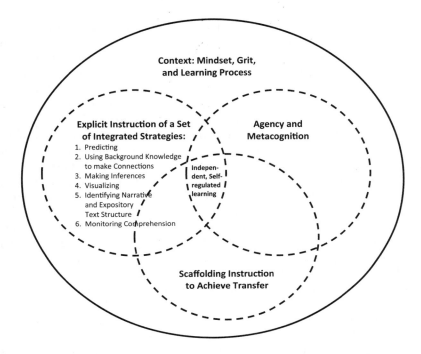

FIGURE 10.1. Key elements in a transformational view of comprehension strategy instruction.

that values "oral literacy," where a higher demand is placed on memory. Johnston (2004) noted that classrooms are sites where "children are *becoming* literate" (p. 22). It is where they are developing social and personal identities about who they are as readers, writers, and thinkers. It is where they explore, try out, and try on various ways of being, acting, and thinking as they negotiate their own identities. In this sense, then, the classroom instructional context is a space in which readers author themselves (Holland, Lachicotte, Skinner, & Cain, 1998), which means there is a great deal of playful experimentation needed, particularly as readers attempt new or different ways of accomplishing tasks and goals. This is not a space where there are "right" or "wrong" ways of "doing" reading or comprehending. It is a space where readers construct and build their own understanding of themselves and of what works for them and under what conditions. Thus, the instructional context must be a safe space that is free of the hazards that lead children to become cautious, fearful, anxious, and passive participants in their own learning. Often such hazards arise when children are assessment-focused or performance-oriented, as

Prawat (1989) described them. Their goal might be to "get done," which might lead them to rush through or skim a text so they finish, rather than engage in strategic behaviors that would assist their comprehension but cause them to take longer. A transformational classroom should provide an experience for students that fosters experiences that allow students to process various types of information and use their knowledge of strategies to solve problems. This approach takes a context where a growth mindset is vital. In such an environment students must learn how to "monitor what's going on, but their own internal monologue is not about judging themselves and others. They are sensitive to positive and negative information and attuned to its implications for learning but harness it into a part of their internal dialogue of, 'What can I learn from this: How can I improve?'" (Dweck, 2016, p. 225).

Creating this "safe" environment means creating a space in which it is "OK" to be uncertain or wrong, and in fact, it is celebrated when students say "I don't get it" or "I'm confused." The teacher's response, in a safe space, would be, "Wonderful! Owen I'm so glad you could recognize when your reading doesn't make sense! That shows you are a good reader because you know when the text doesn't make sense! What didn't make sense to you?" In these classrooms, which prepare students for the social contexts of the 21st century, the teacher creates a safe space where students can openly discuss what they don't understand and test new or different ways of making sense of text. These safe spaces include many opportunities for readers to talk with other readers about the texts, what they understood (or did not understand), and how they went about making sense of the text (e.g., what strategic processes they used, when they used them, where they used them, and why they used them). Teachers in these classrooms are not asking comprehension questions or noting who understood and who did not. Instead, teachers who create safe spaces make note of students' strategic processing and under what circumstances.

In the above scenario, the teacher might ask other students if they had a similar problem: "Did anyone else have difficulty understanding that part? Let's talk about what strategies we can use to help ourselves when the text doesn't make sense." The teacher might then use the teachable moment to begin a very brief explanation of "fix-up strategies" that we might use when the text doesn't make sense, such as rereading, reading ahead to clarify meaning, or discussing the difficult part with another person.

Explicit Instruction

A critical feature of context focuses on the nature of the instruction itself. Explicit instruction is represented in Figure 10.1 as a key element within the context. It is an aspect that is often heralded as being vital to best practice, but in reality does not occur. Explicit instruction involves teacher modeling, explanation, and think-alouds that help children understand what strategic processes are, how to use them, under what conditions they might be used, and why they might be used. In the research literature, this is known as declarative, procedural, and conditional knowledge (Paris et al., 1983). In Figure 10.1 the seven research-based comprehension strategies are represented within explicit instruction as a list, but they should be thought of as a flexible and interconnected set of strategies. Teachers should teach this set of strategies using explanation, modeling, thinking aloud, and long-term guided practice in a variety of settings. Explicit instruction provides a framework for teachers to show how to problem-solve with the seven comprehension strategies as a part of the process of students becoming strategic.

Brown (2008) found that teachers trained to use TSI provided much richer explanations of the processes involved in strategic thinking. The TSI teachers described the reasons for using particular strategies at particular times and the processes underlying their use. They also provided a great deal of modeling and verbalized about the thought processes they used while reading, whereas non-TSI teachers did not. In addition, TSI teachers provided commentary on and elaborated students' thought processes to take advantage of teachable moments.

For example, a teacher might provide an explanation of various fix-up strategies and then think aloud about how to use one of them in the context:

"OK, so Owen said that he didn't understand what the author, Stephen Mooser, meant in the sentence, 'Happy HICCUP Halloween.' That is confusing and it doesn't seem to make sense. When we are reading and the text doesn't make sense we can use our fix-up strategies. So, I might think, 'Wait a second that doesn't make sense. I'd better stop and use a fix-up strategy.' One fix-up strategy we can use is to read ahead slowly and see if the meaning clears up. That just means reading ahead a little farther and being very alert and cautious while I read. So, as I read ahead slowly I'm going to keep trying to think of that HICCUP in the middle of the sentence that didn't make sense and see if the next couple of sentences help clarify the meaning. I'm going to try that."

The teacher would then continue by reading aloud from the text (in this example, the text was Stephen Mooser's *The Ghost with the Halloween Hiccups*):

[*Teacher reading aloud*] "Oh my," said Laura. "You have the hiccups." "All HICCUP day," said Mr. Penny." [*Teacher thinking aloud*] "OK, now I've read ahead a little further to see if the meaning cleared up. I noticed that Laura told Mr. Penny that he had the hiccups. So, I guess that means Mr. Penny has the hiccups. Then there is another odd sentence with HICCUP in the middle of it. I noticed that there are quotation marks around the sentence 'All HICCUP day' and that usually means someone's talking. So, if he has the hiccups and he's talking . . . well, that reminds me of when I have hiccups. Sometimes if I have hiccups and I try to talk, I hiccup in the middle of the sentence I'm trying to say. Maybe that's it! Could it be that the author, Stephen Mooser, is trying to show us how Mr. Penny was talking by inserting an actual HICCUP right in the middle of his sentence? Let me go back and reread that sentence and make a pretend HICCUP in the place where the word hiccup is capitalized, 'All [makes a hiccup sound] day.' Does that make sense now?"

In this think-aloud the teacher fluidly integrated several aspects of strategy instruction. She provided a *think-aloud* of what she might think while she was reading if that same sentence didn't make sense to her. Then she included an *explanation* of what one fix-up strategy, reading ahead, is and how to do it. She then *modeled* the fix-up strategy by reading ahead from the spot where Owen had difficulty. After she read aloud she used several comprehension strategies: she *summarized* what she read, *made a connection to her background knowledge* about what happens to her when she has the hiccups, and then she used the *rereading fix-up strategy* to check (*monitor*) her comprehension.

Ultimately, she is showing the students how to weave together a variety of strategies to make sense of the text—the "read ahead slowly" fix-up strategy gets linked to two of the seven comprehension strategies, "summarization" and "using background knowledge to make connections to bring meaning to the sentence," before she goes back to use the "rereading fix-up strategy" to check her understanding, which is yet another one of the seven comprehension strategies (monitoring comprehension). In this small example, we can see how complicated the reading process actually is. When we read successfully we never use just one strategy. Instead, we integrate the entire set of strategies together in different combinations as in the example above. Explicit discussion of this strategy, coupled with ample experiences that allow for students to do the same in a safe space, are all integral in the social process of becoming strategic. The example continues below to describe how the teacher can reflect on the process with the students.

After the think-aloud, the teacher might turn the conversation back to the students to ask them if they interpreted the sentence in a different way or used different strategies: "Did anyone understand that sentence in a different way? Did anyone use other strategies to help them make sense of that sentence?" By doing this the teacher opens the door to a safe environment where different combinations of strategies can be used and different interpretations of the text are valued. What we see in this example is a teacher who is providing explicit instruction, but she is grounding it in authentic reading experiences and continually turns the context back over to the students.

Another aspect of explicit instruction includes providing lots of guided practice for readers to use and try out ways of recognizing and using strategic behaviors in varied contexts. This guided practice should take place over time and should gradually shift the responsibility for strategic thinking, actions, and behaviors to students so that over time students are able to engage in these processes independently and of their own volition. This is where Dewitz and colleagues (2009) found that core reading programs lagged in their attempts at reproducing research-based best practices in comprehension strategy instruction. These programs simply did not provide sufficient opportunities for students to use what they had learned in multiple contexts and under varying conditions. As well, too much teacher guidance did not enable students to assume responsibility for their own learning.

Explicit instruction should also occur in authentic reading contexts. That is, readers need to practice being strategic using authentic texts of all sorts: picture books, informational texts, comic books, graphic novels, magazines, digital texts, and so on. Transfer will not occur unless readers can think about how they might be strategic in different contexts (e.g., in school, out of school) and under different circumstances (e.g., when they are fatigued, unmotivated, stressed).

Unlike direct instruction, explicit instruction does not break the reading process down into separate parts or subskills. Each time reading occurs it should reflect the entire reading process with authentic texts. That is, strategic reading requires students to read whole texts—not chunks of texts, or a couple of sentences, or sentences with blanks in them, or words (or parts of words) in isolation. For readers to truly understand what it means to be strategic, they must encounter the reading process in its complex entirety. It is like learning to drive a car. Imagine if we taught teenagers how to drive by having steering practice using fake steering wheels in a classroom. After steering practice, imagine the teacher providing braking practice by having students pumping imaginary brakes followed by acceleration practice using imaginary accelerator pedals. Inauthentic sites of practice do not provide learners with the realities they will encounter when they must coordinate all those separate pieces into a coherent whole while also making decisions about where and when to brake and under what conditions you might need to brake more quickly. So it is with reading and learning to be strategic—we must provide authentic learning contexts in which readers learn to negotiate and manage the entire process all at once. This means being an active participant in the process and learning to make decisions. It also means allowing students to experience being strategic in various scenarios that utilize 21st-century experiences.

Pearson and Dole (1987) noted that during explicit instruction there are no "correct" answers. There are multiple sets of strategies, combinations of strategies, and strategic behaviors that can be used to accomplish a given reading task. If we use the driving scenario again, it is like using multiple or different routes to arrive at the same place for a meeting. Everyone can arrive at the same place by using different paths. So it is with strategic processes in reading—different readers can use different strategies, combinations of strategies, and strategic behaviors to accomplish the same goal: comprehension of text.

The final feature of explicit instruction is that the feedback that teachers offer should be suggestive rather than corrective. If there are no "correct" answers, then the feedback we offer students should provide alternate suggestions or different ways of approaching the task. As well, we can provide opportunities for students to share the different strategies they use with each other so they can see how other readers approach and accomplish tasks.

Agency and Motivation

"Agency" refers to the notion that people are active participants in their life events, not simply a product of those events (Bandura, 2008). In reading, this means that the reader plays an active role in, and influences, the way the reading event occurs. That is, the reader is an agent who has an influence on how the reading event will proceed and what strategic behaviors and actions will be used. In many classrooms that teach "strategies," however, it is often the teacher who takes on a great deal of authority in terms of making decisions about what strategies will be taught, to whom, with what texts, and when. At times teachers determine what graphic organizers will be used, with what texts, and when they will be filled out. In a classroom that fosters agency, the teacher enables and empowers students to make such decisions themselves. At the heart of agentic behavior is metacognition. That is, students can influence and make decisions about the reading process when they are able to evaluate their progress to determine whether their reading is successful or unsuccessful and then to make adjustments as needed so that they can reach their goal.

Johnston (2004) suggested ways in which teachers' language can enable agentic behaviors. He noted that teachers foster agency by providing opportunities for students to stop and talk about their thinking. For example, during a read-aloud teachers might stop at points that are particularly thought-provoking or that are prime opportunities for predicting and say, "What are you thinking? Share your thoughts with a partner." These stopping points provide an opportunity for children to verbalize their thought processes. This is not simply "sharing." The goal is for students to verbalize the thought processes that are going through their minds during the reading process. In this way, metacognitive awareness is built.

Instructional opportunities that foster verbalization also occur when students can figure out something while reading. For example, if a young reader recognizes a word such as "laundry" that he or she ordinarily would not recognize, the teacher might say, "You figured that out. How did you do that?" As Johnston (2004) has noted, the teacher's question does not have a "correct" answer. Instead, it is an invitation to tell a narrative about how the student solved a problem. The story is a process-oriented story in which the student shares the strategy or combination of strategies that he or she used to solve the problem "Well, I looked at the picture and saw dirty laundry on the floor. Then I noticed a slot in the wall with a word that began with *L* on it. I figured the word must be *laundry*." By verbalizing these thought processes, students see a variety of ways they can solve similar problems.

Thus, teachers can encourage metacognitive behaviors by asking open-ended questions that encourage students to share their own thought processes. Other examples include, "Why doesn't that make sense to you?"; "What did you do to figure that out?"; and "How did you know that?" Brown's (2008) study showed that TSI teachers tended to ask students to explain their thinking whereas non-TSI teachers did not. Such questions led the students in the TSI classrooms to clarify and justify their thinking and they could draw upon their personal experiences and evidence from the text to do so.

The language that students use to respond to such questions brings awareness to what are typically "covert" or hidden thought processes (Prawat, 1989). The thoughts become an object for others to reflect upon and evaluate. Vygotsky (1978) has noted that such "egocentric" speech is the basis for inner speech. When this type of language is in its external and public form, it becomes available for everyone to ponder. During that thinking, some individuals may think about how that process might be helpful to them, such as "Oh, I never thought about doing it that way. I'll have to try that." Such reflection then opens the doors for the individual to try it on his or her own. When a person attempts such behaviors on his or her own, it shows that he or she is beginning to internalize the process. These attempts, however, also illustrate the need (as mentioned above) for creating a safe space because these initial attempts are just that—initial—and we want students to be willing to take risks to try new ways of thinking and processing text. As students become more metacognitive, they can recognize when text doesn't make sense, which means they recognize the need for strategic action. Such recognition leads to action, which leads to agency. Students determine *whether* they need to be strategic, *when* they need to be strategic, *where* they need to be strategic, and *how* to be strategic. Such agentic behavior is necessary to help students transform themselves from passive to active participants in the reading process.

Scaffolding Instruction to Achieve Transfer

Decades of research have shown that strategy instruction improves reading comprehension; however, the troublesome aspect is helping readers transfer such instruction to different contexts. Providing sufficient guided practice under varying conditions is critical to transfer. One way to provide such guided practice is by incorporating strategies instruction into every aspect of the classroom, in every discipline. This includes creating a safe context and providing opportunities for student verbalization that lead to agency in *every* learning opportunity—during read-alouds, during shared reading, during guided reading, and after independent reading. This form of scaffolding is flexible and might occur during whole-class, small-group, or individualized instruction. TSI is a model of instruction that incorporates these principles into every reading event because the teacher–student and student–student conversations that characterize TSI can occur during the reading of any text, including online reading. The type of teacher scaffolding that occurs during TSI is not preplanned. It requires a trained teacher who can identify opportune, teachable moments as students are reading text in authentic contexts. Brown (2008) has noted that teachers gradually release responsibility to students by engaging in think-alouds in which they explain and model their own thought processes to students. TSI teachers grab teachable moments during authentic reading experiences to demonstrate the type of strategic thinking and behaviors they engage in naturally.

At other times, particularly with readers who struggle, scaffolding that leads to transfer needs to be planned more deliberately. During this type of scaffolding, the teacher might select a strategy, a combination of strategies, or a strategic behavior on which to focus instruction. These preplanned lessons might be conducted during guided reading groups . so that students can practice using the focal strategies with texts at their independent or instructional reading level. This type of instruction should not occur with texts that are at a frustrational level for students.

Almasi and Fullerton's (2012) critical elements of strategy instruction model describes a means of planning instructional lessons so that teacher-scaffolded support is gradually reduced. In this model, two dimensions of scaffolded support are considered: (1) the amount of cognitive effort a reader must expend, and (2) the nature of the instructional tasks and texts used during the lesson. The amount of cognitive effort a reader must expend is greater when the reader must complete the reading tasks independently because all of the burden for reading and enacting strategic behaviors belongs to the reader; however, the amount of cognitive effort diminishes when the reader can complete the reading task with a partner, a small group, or with the whole class. By using various grouping patterns, the teacher can provide guided practice and scaffolding in different ways.

The amount of scaffolded support can also be varied by teaching students how to engage in strategic behaviors using different types of tasks and texts in lessons. If we define "text" broadly so that it includes any sign or symbol that communicates a message, then texts would include movies, cartoons, pictures, wordless picture books, texts that are read aloud, texts read during shared reading, and texts read independently. This broad conceptualization of "text" means that initial strategy lessons can introduce readers to difficult strategies such as comprehension monitoring without requiring them to decode the text. In this manner, struggling readers can learn very high-level cognitive strategies at a young age. By introducing readers to strategic processing in this manner it helps them learn the language of being a strategic reader.

Focal lessons aimed at teaching students new strategies or strategic behaviors (e.g., making predictions, monitoring comprehension, summarizing, visualizing, making connections, making inferences) that they did not know about previously might begin with very concrete lessons using video excerpts from movies, television, or digital programs. In this type of lesson, teachers can provide explicit instruction for students using "texts" where the reader can focus solely on the strategic processing rather than having to bear the additional burden of decoding. For example, Mrs. Macklin noticed that her second graders often made "wild" predictions that were based more on their background knowledge and didn't use the text to help form the prediction. She decided to model how to predict by using a video clip from a TV show in which she could stop the video at a highly predictable, or "cliff hanger" point and think aloud about the thoughts going through her mind as she formed a prediction, "Well, I'm really excited to see the next part because I noticed _____ and that makes me think that _____ is going to happen next." At this point she might open the discussion up for the students to share their thoughts: "Does anyone else have a prediction about what might happen next in the show?" As students share their ideas, Mrs. Macklin will try to encourage them to verbally share the thought processes they are using as they form their predictions and link those ideas to some evidence in the show that they have already seen, "Oh, you think _____ is going to happen? What did you notice in the show so far that makes you think that?" Mrs. Macklin would then continue using the think-aloud with whole-class input during this lesson in which the "text" is a TV show.

After teaching this type of lesson, follow-up guided practice lessons can be planned that vary either the type of text or task (e.g., teaching students how to make predictions with a wordless picture book or during a read-aloud while keeping it as a whole-class or small-group activity so the cognitive effort needed will still be low) and/or the amount of cognitive effort needed (e.g., making predictions from a video with a partner or independently). The goal in this form of scaffolding is to alter the types of texts, tasks, and grouping arrangements during follow-up guided practice sessions so that over time we are releasing the responsibility for strategic processing to students. Eventually students will be using the strategy with text written at their instructional level independently. By planfully mapping out these two dimensions of scaffolding during instruction, responsibility is gradually released to students, which leads to transfer.

In summary, the four key ingredients to support an environment that cultivates strategic and reflective learning are (1) context, (2) explicit instruction, (3) agency and metacognition, and (4) scaffolding. These four components are essential within a setting that values the learning process because they provide a space where students' prior experiences, individual perceptions, and own pace of learning are valued.

It is within such an environment that we begin to recognize it is not just about the strategy you teach: environment matters. Research has shown that teaching strategies in isolation is not effective—we must provide a space for students that cultivates their transformation into independent, agentic learners who recognize that context matters as they decide when and how to use strategies that best meet their needs.

REFLECTIONS AND FUTURE DIRECTIONS

This chapter aimed to change the discourse surrounding comprehension strategy instruction from ideas about how to teach the seven research-based strategies to ideas about how to teach students to be strategic. This focus will help teachers achieve the most elusive aspect of comprehension instruction: transfer. Transfer happens when students become agentic. They see the value of thinking strategically and use it to make their own decisions about how to solve problems as they read.

The benefit of this approach to comprehension instruction is that we know it works. The research reviewed in this chapter is quite conclusive that teaching readers to be strategic results in long-term gains in comprehension. There are several limitations to consider, however. One is that learning to teach in this manner is difficult and can take years to learn how to do well (Brown & Coy-Ogan, 1993; Duffy, 1993a, 1993b; El-Dinary & Schuder, 1993). Research that is more recent has begun to tackle that issue using technology-based methods of teacher training (Graves, Sales, Lawrenz, Robelia, & Richardson, 2010). Another issue is that most assessments of comprehension focus on the *product* of comprehension, which often relies on memory and recall of text and the ability to make inferences. The reliance on literal and inferential questions as the primary ways of assessing comprehension means that instruction tends to approximate the text. Assessments that focus more on the *processes* used to make sense of text would be better aligned with an emphasis on teaching students to be strategic (Almasi & Fullerton, 2012; Carlson, Seipel, & McMaster, 2014; van den Broek & Espin, 2012). Currently, we rely on self-reports of strategy use (which are not always reliable) or think-aloud protocols (which are time- consuming to administer and labor-intensive to code) as the primary ways of assessing strategic processing. Developing new ways to assess strategic processing (and valuing them) would begin to change the instructional emphasis in our schools and classrooms.

CONCLUDING REMARKS

For decades, we have emphasized the importance of teaching students comprehension strategies. However, shifting the emphasis from "the strategy" to "the student" is critical. This shift requires teachers to move from focusing on the strategies that are taught to *focusing on the context in which they are taught*. The focus on context ensures that we create learning opportunities that make it safe for readers to try on new ways of thinking and acting. A safe space accompanied by explicit instruction means that the context is ripe for readers to explore their own identity as readers and construct meaning. When we also include lots of opportunities for students to verbalize and share the thought processes they use while reading, this enables them to become more metacognitively aware while reading. Such metacognitive awareness enables readers to evaluate their reading progress and make decisions about what strategic processes may be needed to successfully attain their goals. When readers are active participants who make their own decisions about the reading process, they possess agency, which is the key to transformation.

This chapter suggests that by recognizing the underlying belief systems that are perpetuated by various programs, change can begin to occur in educational environments. If learners are valued within their own comprehension instruction, positive change will be reflected in the way in which these learners negotiate/identify themselves as learners. By cultivating an environment that values the learner as inextricably linked to his or her own learning process, learners' agency will improve and positively impact their ability to transform themselves into lifelong learners who are strategic and reflective.

ENGAGEMENT ACTIVITIES

1. Develop a list of ideas for creating a safe environment for strategy use.

2. Discuss the importance of teaching students to be strategic readers who determine when and where strategic action should take place as they read.

3. The CCSS related to literal recall, making logical inferences, citing textual evidence to support conclusions, and analyzing the structure of texts are long-term goals. Discuss how comprehension strategy instruction provides the means of attaining those goals.

RESOURCES AND FURTHER LEARNING

Almasi, J. F., & Fullerton, S. K. (2012). *Teaching strategic processes in reading* (2nd ed.). New York: Guilford Press.
Dewitz, P., Leahy, S., Jones, J., & Sullivan, P. M. (2010). *The essential guide to selecting and using core reading programs.* Newark, DE: International Reading Association.
Johnston, P. H. (2004). *Choice words: How our language affects children's learning.* Portland, ME: Stenhouse.

REFERENCES

Afflerbach, P., Pearson, P. D., & Paris, S. G. (2008). Clarifying differences between reading skills and reading strategies. *The Reading Teacher, 61*(5), 364–373.
Almasi, J. F., & Fullerton, S. K. (2012). *Teaching strategic processes in reading* (2nd ed.). New York: Guilford Press.
Almasi, J. F., Palmer, B. M., Madden, A., & Hart, S. (2011). Interventions to

enhance narrative comprehension. In R. Allington & A. McGill-Franzen (Eds.), *Handbook of reading disability research* (pp. 329–344). New York: Routledge.

Anderson, V. (1992). A teacher development project in transactional strategy instruction for teachers of severely reading-disabled adolescents. *Teaching and Teacher Education, 8*(4), 391–403.

Aukerman, M. (2013). Rereading comprehension pedagogies: Toward a dialogic teaching ethic that honors student sensemaking. *Dialogic Pedagogy: An International Online Journal, 1,* A1–A30.

Bandura, A. (2008). Reconstrual of "free will" from the agentic perspective of social cognitive theory. In J. Baer, J. C. Kaufman, & R. F. Baumeister (Eds.), *Are we free?: Psychology and free will* (pp. 86–127). New York: Oxford University Press.

Brown, R. (2008). The road not yet taken: A transactional strategies approach to reading comprehension instruction. *The Reading Teacher, 61*(7), 538–547.

Brown, R., & Coy-Ogan, L. (1993). The evolution of transactional strategies instruction in one teacher's classroom. *Elementary School Journal, 94*(2), 221–233.

Brown, R., Pressley, M., Van Meter, P., & Schuder, T. (1996). A quasi-experimental validation of transactional strategies instruction with low-achieving second-grade readers. *Journal of Educational Psychology, 88*(1), 18–37.

Cain, K., & Oakhill, J. V. (1999). Inference making ability and its relation to comprehension failure in young children. *Reading and Writing Quarterly: An International Journal, 11,* 489–503.

Cain, K., Oakhill, J. V., Barnes, M. A., & Bryant, P. E. (2001). Comprehension skill, inference-making ability, and their relation to knowledge. *Memory and Cognition, 29*(6), 850–859.

Cantrell, S. C., Almasi, J. F., Rintamaa, M., & Carter, J. C. (2016). Supplemental reading strategy instruction for adolescents: A randomized trial and follow-up study. *Journal of Educational Research, 109*(1), 7–26.

Carlson, S. E., Seipel, B., & McMaster, K. (2014). Development of a new comprehension assessment: Identifying comprehension differences among readers. *Learning and Individual Differences, 32,* 40–53.

Coiro, J., & Dobler, E. (2007). Exploring the online comprehension strategies used by sixth-grade skilled readers to search for and locate information on the Internet. *Reading Research Quarterly, 42,* 214–257.

Dewitz, P., Jones, J., & Leahy, S. (2009). Comprehension strategy instruction in core reading programs. *Reading Research Quarterly, 44*(2), 102–126.

Dewitz, P., Leahy, S., Jones, J., & Sullivan, P. M. (2010). *The essential guide to selecting and using core reading programs.* Newark, DE: International Reading Association.

Duffy, G. G. (1993a). Rethinking strategy instruction: Four teachers' development and their low achievers' understandings. *Elementary School Journal, 93*(3), 231–247.

Duffy, G. G. (1993b). Teachers' progress toward becoming expert strategy teachers. *Elementary School Journal, 94*(2), 109–120.

Duke, N. K., & Pearson, P. D. (2008–2009). Effective practices for developing reading comprehension. *Journal of Education, 189*(1–2), 107–122.

Dweck, C. S. (2016). *Mindset: The new psychology of success.* New York: Random House.

Edmonds, M. S., Vaughn, S., Wexler, J., Reutebuch, C., Cable, A., Tackett, K. K., & Schnakenberg, J. W. (2009). A synthesis of reading interventions and effects on reading comprehension outcomes for older struggling readers. *Review of Educational Research, 79*(1), 262–300.

El-Dinary, P. B., & Schuder, T. (1993). Seven teachers' acceptance of transactional strategies instruction during their first year using it. *Elementary School Journal, 94*(2), 207–219.

Fleisher, L. S., Jenkins, J. R., & Pany, D. (1979). Effects on poor readers' comprehension of training in rapid decoding. *Reading Research Quarterly, 15*(1), 30–48.

Furtado, L., & Johnson, L. (2010). Enhancing summarization skills using twin texts: Instruction in narrative and expository text structures. *The Reading Matrix, 10*(2), 271–281.

Gamse, B. C., Jacob, R. T., Horst, M., Boulay, B., & Unlu, F. (2008). *Reading First Impact Study Final Report Executive Summary* (NCEE 2009-4039). Washington, DC: National Center for Education Evaluation and Regional Assistance, Institute of Education Sciences, U.S. Department of Education.

Gersten, R., Fuchs, L. S., Williams, J. P., & Baker, S. (2001). Teaching reading comprehension strategies to students with learning disabilities: A review of research. *Review of Educational Research, 71*(2), 279–320.

Graesser, A. C. (2007). An introduction to strategic reading comprehension. In D. S. McNamara (Ed.), *Reading comprehension strategies: Theories, interventions, and technologies* (pp. 3–26). New York: Erlbaum.

Graves, M., Sales, G. C., Lawrenz, F., Robelia, B., & Richardson, J. (2010). Effects of technology-based teacher training and teacher-led classroom implementation on learning reading comprehension strategies. *Contemporary Educational Technology, 1*(2), 160–174.

Hall, C. S. (2016). Inference instruction for struggling readings: A synthesis of intervention research. *Educational Psychology Review, 28,* 1–22.

Hirsch, E. D. (2006). Building knowledge: The case for bringing content into the language arts block and for a knowledge-rich curriculum core for all children. *American Educator, 30* (1), 8–17.

Hoffman, J. V. (2017). Comprehension is *not* simple: Considering the persisting dangers in the simple view of reading comprehension. In S. E. Israel (Ed.), *Handbook of research on reading comprehension* (2nd ed., pp. 57–69). New York: Routledge.

Holland, D., Lachicotte, W., Skinner, D., & Cain, C. (1998). *Identity and agency in cultural worlds.* Cambridge, MA: Harvard University Press.

Hoover, W. A., & Gough, P. (1990). The simple view of reading. *Reading and Writing: An Interdisciplinary Journal, 2,* 127–160.

Johnston, P. H. (2004). *Choice words: How our language effects children's learning.* Portland, ME: Stenhouse.

Kamil, M. L., Borman, G. D., Dole, J., Kral, C. C., Salinger, T., & Torgesen, J.

(2008). *Improving adolescent literacy: Effective classroom and intervention practices: A practice guide* (NCEE No. 2008-4027). Washington, DC: National Center for Education Evaluation and Regional Assistance, Institute of Education Sciences, U.S. Department of Education. Retrieved from *http://ies. ed.gov/ncee/wwc*.

Kintsch, W. (1998). *Comprehension: A paradigm for cognition*. New York: Cambridge University Press.

LaBerge, D., & Samuels, S. J. (1974). Toward a theory of automatic processing in reading. *Cognitive Psychology, 6*(2), 293–323.

Lan, Y.-C., Lo, Y.-L., & Hsu, Y.-S. (2014). The effects of meta-cognitive instruction on students' reading comprehension in computerized reading contexts: A quantitative meta-analysis. *Educational Technology and Society, 17*(4), 186–202.

Leach, J. M., Scarborough, H. S., & Rescorla, L. (2003). Late-emerging reading disabilities. *Journal of Educational Psychology, 95*(2), 211–224.

Leu, D. J., Jr., Coiro, J., Castek, J., Hartman, D. K., Henry, L. A., & Reinking, D. (2008). Research on instruction and assessment in the new literacies of online reading comprehension. In C. C. Block & S. R. Parris (Eds.), *Comprehension instruction: Research-based best practices* (2nd ed., pp. 321–346). New York: Guilford Press.

McKeown, M. G., Beck, I. L., & Blake, G. K. (2009). Rethinking reading comprehension instruction: A comparison of instruction for strategies and content approaches. *Reading Research Quarterly, 44*(3), 218–253.

McMaster, K. L., van den Broek, P., Espin, C. A., White, M. J., Rapp, D. N., Kendeou, P., & Carlson, S. (2012). Making the right connections: Differential effects of reading intervention for subgroups of comprehenders. *Learning and Individual Differences, 22,* 100–111.

Nation, K. (2005). Children's reading comprehension difficulties. In M. J. Snowling & C. Hulme (Eds.), *The science of reading: A handbook* (pp. 248–266). Malden, MA: Wiley Blackwell.

National Governors Association & Council of Chief State School Officers. (2010). *The Common Core Standards for English language arts and literacy in history/social studies, science, and technical subjects*. Washington, DC: Authors. Retrieved from *www.corestandards.org*.

National Reading Panel. (2000). *Teaching children to read: An evidence-based assessment of the scientific research literature on reading and its implications for reading instruction* (Report of the Subgroups). Washington, DC: U.S. Department of Health and Human Services, Public Health Service, National Institutes of Health, and the National Institute of Child Health and Human Development.

Neuman, S. B. (2006). How we neglect knowledge—and why. *American Educator, 30*(1), 24–27.

No Child Left Behind Act of 2001, Pub. Law 107-110, 115 Stat. 1425.

Palincsar, A. S., & Brown, A. L. (1984). Reciprocal teaching of comprehension-fostering and comprehension-monitoring activities. *Cognition and Instruction, 1,* 117–175.

Palincsar, A. S., & Schultz, K. M. (2011). Reconnecting strategy instruction with its theoretical roots. *Theory into Practice, 50,* 85–92.

Paris, S. G., Cross, D., & Lipson, M. Y. (1984). Informed strategies for learning: A program to improve children's reading awareness and comprehension. *Journal of Educational Psychology, 76,* 1239–1252.

Paris, S. G., Lipson, M. Y., & Wixson, K. K. (1983). Becoming a strategic reader. *Contemporary Educational Psychology, 8,* 293–316.

Paris, S. G., Wasik, B. A., & Turner, J. C. (1991). The development of strategic readers. In R. Barr, M. L. Kamil, P. Mosenthal, & P. D. Pearson (Eds.), *Handbook of reading research* (Vol. 2, pp. 609–640). New York: Longman.

Pearson, P. D., & Dole, J. A. (1987). Explicit comprehension instruction: A review of research and a new conceptualization of instruction. *Elementary School Journal, 88*(2), 151–165.

Pilonieta, P. (2010). Instruction of research-based comprehension strategies in basal reading programs. *Reading Psychology, 31,* 150–175.

Prawat, R. S. (1989). Promoting access to knowledge, strategy, and disposition in students: A research synthesis. *Review of Educational Research, 59*(1), 1–41.

Pressley, M. (2000). What should comprehension instruction be the instruction of? In M. L. Kamil, P. B. Mosenthal, P. D. Pearson, & R. Barr (Eds.), *Handbook of reading research* (Vol. 3, pp. 545–561). Mahwah, NJ: Erlbaum.

Pressley, M., Borkowski, J. G., & Schneider, W. (1989). Good information processing: What it is and how education can promote it. *International Journal of Educational Research, 13,* 857–867.

Pressley, M., El-Dinary, P. B., Gaskins, I., Schuder, T., Bergman, J. L., Almasi, J., & Brown, R. (1992). Beyond direct explanation: Transactional instruction of reading comprehension strategies. *Elementary School Journal, 92*(5), 513–555.

Reutzel, D. R., Smith, J. A., & Fawson, P. C. (2005). An evaluation of two approaches for teaching reading comprehension strategies in the primary years using science information texts. *Early Childhood Research Quarterly, 20,* 276–305.

Riddle Buly, M., & Valencia, S. W. (2002). Below the bar: Profiles of students who fail state reading assessments. *Educational Evaluation and Policy Analysis, 24*(3), 219–239.

Rogoff, B. (1990). *Apprenticeship in thinking: Cognitive development in social context.* New York: Oxford University Press.

Samuels, S. J. (2004). Toward a theory of automatic information processing in reading, revisited. In R. B. Ruddell & N. J. Unrau (Eds.), *Theoretical models and processes of reading* (5th ed., pp. 1127–1148). Newark, DE: International Reading Association.

Schumaker, J. B., & Deshler, D. D. (1992). Validation of learning strategy interventions for students with LD: Results of a programmatic research effort. In B. Y. L. Wong (Ed.), *Intervention research with students with learning disabilities* (pp. 22–46). New York: Springer-Verlag.

Schumaker, J. B., & Deshler, D. D. (2006). Teaching adolescents to be strategic learners. In D. D. Deshler, E. S. Ellis, & B. K. Lenz (Eds.), *Teaching adolescents with disabilities: Strategies and methods* (pp. 121–156). Thousand Oaks, CA: Corwin Press.

Shanahan, T., Callison, K., Carriere, C., Duke, N., Pearson, P. D., Schatschneider, C., & Torgesen, J. (2010). *Improving reading comprehension in kindergarten through 3rd grade: A practice guide* (NCEE 2010-4038). Washington, DC: National Center for Educational Evaluation and Regional Assistance, Institute of Education Sciences, U.S. Department of Education. Retrieved from *http://whatworks.ed.gov/publications/practiceguides.*

Snowling, M. J., & Hulme, C. (2011). Evidence-based interventions for reading and language difficulties: Creating a virtuous circle. *British Journal of Educational Psychology, 81,* 1–23.

Torgesen, J. K., Houston, D. D., Rissman, L. M., Decker, S. M., Roberts, G., Vaughn, S., . . . Lesaux, N. (2007). *Academic literacy instruction for adolescents: A guidance document from the Center on Instruction.* Portsmouth, NH: RMC Research Corporation, Center on Instruction.

U.S. Department of Education, Institute of Education Sciences, What Works Clearinghouse. (2010, September). Reciprocal teaching. Retrieved from *https://ies.ed.gov/ncee/wwc/Docs/InterventionReports/wwc_rec_teach_091410.pdf.*

Valencia, S. W. (2011). Reader profiles and reading disabilities. In A. McGill-Franzen & R. L. Allington (Eds.), *Handbook of reading disability research* (pp. 25–35). New York: Routledge.

van den Broek, P., & Espin, C. A. (2012). Connecting cognitive theory and assessment: Measuring individual differences in reading comprehension. *School Psychology Review, 41*(3), 315–325.

Van Keer, H. (2004). Fostering reading comprehension in fifth grade by explicit instruction in reading strategies and peer tutoring. *British Journal of Educational Psychology, 74,* 37–70.

Vygotsky, L. S. (1978). *Mind in society.* Cambridge, MA: Harvard University Press.

Wilkinson, I. A. G., & Son, H. (2011). A dialogic turn in research on learning and teaching to comprehend. In M. L. Kamil, P. D. Pearson, P. Afflerbach, & E. Moje (Eds.), *Handbook of reading research* (Vol. 4, pp. 358–387). New York: Routledge.

CHAPTER 11

Best Practices in Informational Text Comprehension Instruction

NELL K. DUKE
NICOLE M. MARTIN

This chapter will:

- Describe characteristics of the classroom community that can support students in learning to comprehend informational text.

- Identify evidence-based strategies for scaffolding comprehension and developing strategic comprehenders of informational text.

- Describe a unit that enacts research-supported practices and supports development of many skills related to informational text comprehension.

THE CLASSROOM AS A COMMUNITY OF LEARNING ABOUT INFORMATIONAL TEXT COMPREHENSION

When you picture the circumstances in which poetry or narrative text is written, you probably picture an individual writer, alone with his or her thoughts at a typewriter or computer. Informational text is sometimes written this way as well, but quite often it is written in the context of a community: a cast of journalists produces a print or online news site, a group of product testers provides feedback to the writer of a technical manual, a team of researchers collaborate to produce a medical resource, and so on. Similarly, the reading of informational text is often not a lone act, but one carried out in conversation with others. Readers of a print or online news site talk with friends about what they have read, send or post comments for other readers, perhaps even submit a letter to the editor; officemates work together to follow a technical manual; a family discusses what they have learned about a pressing health problem from the medical resource.

As much as possible, we want to create a community for reading informational text in the classroom as well. Among other things, we want students to:

- *collaborate* around informational reading, whether by partner reading, text discussion, exchanging texts of interest, or cooperatively writing informational texts using a range of sources they have collected.
- *be curious,* such that when they are wondering or debating about something, they look it up for one another or read about and enact an investigation to resolve their dispute. We want them to be interested in how effective readers comprehend informational text and how they can learn to better do so themselves.
- *be purposeful,* thinking about how they can use informational text individually and collectively to meet goals such as deepening their knowledge, addressing a problem, meeting a need, or enjoying an event. We have observed even young children using informational text to communicate in powerful ways and even effect change in the world outside of school.
- *critique,* particularly as they get older, rather than simply accepting any given source at face value. We want them to evaluate the credibility of sources, cross-check information, and bring a critical eye to how others have presented information.
- *savor reading,* greeting new informational texts and topics with a collective sense of excitement and recognizing that skilled informational reading is not about reading fast but about reading and rereading with understanding top of mind.

Teachers play an important role in establishing a classroom community in which students demonstrate the qualities that we have just described. Doing so requires an understanding of evidence-based best practices in informational text comprehension, the topic to which we turn next.

EVIDENCE-BASED BEST PRACTICES: A RESEARCH SYNTHESIS

We believe a long-term and situated view of informational text comprehension instruction in learning communities is important. Rather than expecting students to learn from generic approaches to instruction or from one lesson or unit of study, decades of research suggest that learning communities are more likely to learn how to comprehend informational text well when opportunities to comprehend informational text alongside strategic teaching are included.

Characteristics of Skilled Comprehension

We begin our discussion of evidence-based best practices by highlighting four characteristics of skilled comprehension that have implications for how we teach.

Skilled Comprehension Is Strategic

To comprehend text, readers actively and flexibly use a range of strategic processes, such as previewing, activating background knowledge, and setting reading purposes (Duke & Pearson, 2002; Pressley & Afflerbach, 1995). Students need to learn "to be active in the way that good comprehenders are active" (Block & Pressley, 2007, p. 225). They also need to learn that strategy use is contingent (Almasi & Hart, 2011). Readers select processes that will be useful for the text being read. This means helping students become adept at flexibly applying processes readers have used to comprehend informational text. Examples from prior research are listed in Table 11.1.

Skilled Comprehension Is Genre-Specific

Comprehension is genre-specific to a significant degree (Duke & Roberts, 2010). Genres have different purposes and characteristics, and the processes involved in comprehending one genre are not isomorphic with those involved in comprehending another. This means the ability to comprehend texts in one genre well does not guarantee proficiency at comprehending texts in another genre. Readers read informative/explanatory text differently than, for example, narrative text (e.g., Kucan & Beck, 1996). Informative/explanatory texts often include large amounts of information about topics unknown or less familiar to readers; may be designed to develop understanding of abstract and complex ideas and relationships; and may use specialized vocabulary, text structures, and text features (e.g., Duke & Tower, 2004; Pappas, 2006). To comprehend informative/explanatory texts, readers elaborate on authors' ideas, make more of particular kinds of connections, notice interesting details, and attend to informational text structures—a distinct contrast to processes used for narrative text comprehension (such as predicting what will happen next

TABLE 11.1. Ten Processes Used to Comprehend Informational Text

Name	Description	Sample guiding questions
Setting reading purposes	Readers think about what they want to accomplish with the reading and make decisions about how they will read.	*What is my goal? Do I need to read the whole text or just part of it? Do I need to study it or just search for information?*
Connecting to prior knowledge	Readers think about what they already know and how this knowledge might connect with the text.	*Have I read or learned about this before? What have other authors or people said about this? Am I familiar with the way this text is structured, and what does this mean for my reading?*
Predicting	Readers think about what will come next in the text. They check and revise their previous predictions and generate new ones.	*What will I learn next? Did the author talk about what I expected? Given what I just read, does my prediction still make sense?*
Inferring	Readers draw conclusions about information not stated or shown in the text.	*For this to make sense, what needs to be true? What has the author left out that might be important?*
Interpreting graphics and text features	Readers think about the meanings of the text's graphics and other features, as well as how these connect to the text's words and main ideas.	*What does this show? What is most important about it? What can I learn from it?*
Evaluating content	Readers think about their reactions to the text's words, graphics, ideas, and implications.	*What do I think about this? Do I agree or disagree, and why?*
Monitoring (and fixing up) comprehension	Readers think about their reading and comprehension processes. Whenever they encounter problems while they are reading, they take action until the problems are solved.	*Does this make sense? Am I understanding this well? What can I do to help myself understand this better?*
Questioning	Readers ask questions about the text, authors' ideas, and their own thinking.	*Why is this true? What does that mean?*
Summarizing	Readers think about what they have read or learned. They may focus on recalling the text, paragraphs, and/or sentences.	*What has the author said so far? What did I learn in this paragraph?*

and identifying specific story elements). Even within the broad category of "informational text," readers may read texts differently. For example, in one study (Martin, 2011), the second author found that second- through fifth-grade students used different processes when reading procedural text (such as monitoring processes and monitoring problems) than when reading biography or persuasive text (such as inferencing and summarizing). In summary, teaching comprehension of a genre means using that genre during informational text comprehension instruction.

Skilled Comprehension Is Situated

Comprehension is affected by multiple factors, and neither developing nor teaching comprehension is one-size-fits-all (e.g., Connor et al., 2009; Riddle Buly & Valencia, 2002). Reader factors—including the reader's word identification skills, fluency, prior knowledge, interests, and vocabulary—can affect what is understood and learned from text (e.g., Duke & Carlisle, 2011; Fox & Alexander, 2009). These reader factors intersect with text, task, and contextual factors (RAND Reading Study Group, 2002; Valencia, Wixson, & Pearson, 2014). For example, a student who possesses knowledge that the text's author assumes the reader has will have a different comprehension experience than a student who does not possess that knowledge. The reading context, such as whether it occurs in a quiet space or one full of distractions, or the cultural context in which the reading occurs, is also influential (and differentially influential for different readers). Finally, the reading task—including how much support is involved (see later in this section), how motivated the learner is to engage in that specific task, and the demands of the task itself—all influence comprehension. With informational text, sometimes we have the task of comprehending within and across a set of texts on a common topic. Other times our task is to comprehend a single informational text. Sometimes our task involves reading for general edification, other times there is a specific need to apply what is learned from the text. For students to manage a broad range of tasks, learning communities must offer experiences with that broad range within and across each grade and take into account students' knowledge and skills during informational text comprehension instruction.

Skilled Comprehension Is Developmental

Comprehension begins early and develops over time (Duke & Carlisle, 2011; Paris, 2005). Based on available evidence, a federal panel has determined that comprehension instruction should occur with intensity even in kindergarten through third grade (Shanahan et al., 2010). Students in these grades—including children who cannot yet read independently—have been shown in research to develop knowledge of informational text language and structures, display interest in reading informational text, use mental processes to comprehend texts, and benefit from informational text comprehension instruction (e.g., Duke & Kays, 1998; Mantzicopoulos & Patrick, 2010; Pappas, 1993). However, students' comprehension of informational text increases throughout elementary and high school. For instance, Judith Langer (1986) asked third, sixth, and ninth graders to read and recall story and informational passages. Ninth graders recalled on average 19% more of the informational passage and included more informational text language and structures than third graders. Interventions designed to improve informational text comprehension have been effective from at least as early as first grade (e.g., Kraemer, McCabe, & Sinatra, 2012) through adulthood (e.g., Kauffman, Zhao, & Yang, 2011). This suggests informational text comprehension instruction should be an instructional focus across multiple grades, perhaps at every grade. Importantly, unlike, for example, alphabet knowledge, one can never "master" comprehension. Comprehension of new types and topics of text can be challenging even for a highly proficient reader.

These four characteristics of skilled comprehension—that it is strategic, genre-specific to a significant degree, situated or influenced by multiple factors (including text, reader, task, and contextual factors), and developmental—have informed work on how to develop informational text comprehension ability. In the following sections, we identify some key practices for informational text comprehension development.

Providing an Informational-Text-Rich Learning Community

The evidence base calls for learning communities to offer many opportunities for students to comprehend informational text (discussed later in this section) supported by strategic teaching (discussed in a subsequent section) (e.g., Almasi & Hart, 2011; Block & Pressley, 2007). As students listen to and read authentic text for authentic purposes, comprehension strategy instruction, text structure instruction, text discussion, and scaffolding of the text-to-be-read is used to help them learn to comprehend informational text.

Listening to and Reading Informational Text

Exposure to informational text is foundational to students' development of informational text comprehension. One important mechanism for exposing students to informational text is the read-aloud. We have long known read-alouds can help students to become acquainted with informational text language and structures, to understand how adults and their peers think about informational text, and to develop content-area knowledge (e.g., Kraemer et al., 2012; Wan, 2000). Linda Kraemer and her colleagues (2012) examined the effects of informational text read-alouds on 77 first graders' listening comprehension and book preferences in four classrooms. Teachers continued their normal read-aloud routines. In two of the classrooms, a researcher also read informational text aloud three times a week for a month. Kraemer and her colleagues observed increased growth in students' comprehension of informational text (but not book preferences) when compared to their peers.

Stephanie Strachan (2015) found growth in kindergartners' knowledge of informational text, as well as their social studies knowledge, after just five read-alouds of informational text related to economics concepts. These read-alouds were characterized as interactive, with the reader engaging in the following practices as described by Strachan (2015, p. 212):

> (1) asking questions about key concepts in the texts, such as "What else do we need? What did this book tell us?"; (2) asking questions that encourage connections to the text, such as "Can you think of some goods and services that your family buys?"; (3) rephrasing or extending children's responses, such as, "She said that if it's raining or cold, we have to live in a house or some type of shelter to protect us"; (4) explaining concepts from the text that seem confusing or that students have questions about, such as when a student asked if the photo depicted California and I responded, "Let's see. There is a map"; (5) asking children to repeat key words, such as "everyone say, protect"; (6) using gestures to illustrate concepts and asking children to do the same, such as touching one's fingers together to demonstrate that goods are physical things we purchase; and (7) practicing using text features to find information in the texts.

Students also have an important role to play in interactive read-alouds, responding to teacher questions individually and chorally, asking questions themselves, making comments to the whole group, and discussing the text with a partner.

As students develop, they begin to read informational text themselves. As you might expect, students who engage in more informational text reading are likely to be more skilled at informational text comprehension. For example, Heather Schugar and Mariam Dreher (2017) found that fourth graders performed better on the informational reading portion of the National Assessment of Educational Progress (NAEP) when they reported engaging in more out-of-school reading activities including reading to learn and reading on the Internet. In the following section, we discuss one way we can motivate more informational reading.

Comprehending Authentic Texts for Authentic Purposes

Students' development is accelerated, evidence suggests, when their listening to and reading of informational text includes authentic texts and authentic purposes. By this, we mean asking students to comprehend texts "that occur outside of [only] a learning-to-read-and-write context" and that are read and written "for the purposes for which they are read or written outside of a learning-to-read-and-write context and purpose" (Purcell-Gates, Duke, & Martineau, 2007, p. 14).

We have observed the power of comprehending authentic texts for authentic purposes in our own work (e.g., Duke, Caughlan, Juzwik, & Martin, 2011; Purcell-Gates et al., 2007). Consider, for example, a study that one of us (Nell) conducted with colleagues (Purcell-Gates et al., 2007). In the study, second- and third-grade teachers were encouraged to incorporate authentic reading and writing activities—such as creating brochures for a local nature center or writing procedural texts to teach neighboring classrooms how to conduct physics experiments—into science lessons. When students' growth was measured throughout the 2 years of the study, we found that students' reading and writing grew at a faster rate in classrooms with more authentic reading and writing of science informational and procedural texts.

Studies of integrated science-literacy instruction in learning communities also offer evidence of the value of authentic reading and writing activities. Concept-Oriented Reading Instruction (CORI) (e.g., Guthrie et al., 2004, 2009) and Science IDEAS (e.g., Romance & Vitale, 2012) illustrate their potential for increasing students' informational text comprehension. In CORI, students read informational text, conduct scientific inquiries, and participate in hands-on activities in order to develop expertise in scientific content to share with others. In one study of CORI, during a 12-week unit, teachers taught multiple comprehension processes (activating background knowledge, creating graphic organizers, identifying text structures, questioning, searching for information, and summarizing). John Guthrie and his colleagues (2004) compared CORI students' comprehension and motivation to that of peers who had received "strategy instruction" (SI) and "traditional instruction" (TI). The researchers found that "CORI students were more motivated than SI and TI students and were more strategic readers than SI students" (p. 415). (For a meta-analysis of CORI research, see Guthrie, McRae, & Klauda, 2007. For more information about CORI, see *www.cori.umd.edu*.)

Similarly, in Science IDEAS, teachers teach comprehension processes such as activating prior knowledge and summarizing (e.g., Romance & Vitale, 2012). Students work to solve problems and develop scientific expertise. Students complete hands-on science activities; read informational text; take notes, create concept maps, and write summaries in student journals; collaborate in projects and real-world application activities; and review their learning. An examination of a decade of Science IDEAS research concluded that "increasing time for integrated science instruction in grades K–5 will not only result in stronger preparation of students for secondary science, but also concurrently improve student proficiency in reading comprehension (in general) and content-area reading comprehension (more specifically) across grades 3–8" (p. 513). (For more information, see *www.scienceideas.org.*)

Strategic Teaching to Support Students' Comprehension of Informational Text

We are using the term "strategic teaching" to refer to teachers' purposeful use of best practices to extend students' comprehension when they are listening to and reading informational text. Because learning about comprehension processes, text structures, and discussion moves or strategies for discussing text is the means and not the end goal, coordinating teaching with texts' demands and students' needs in learning communities is essential for students' ability to comprehend informational text on their own. As we discuss in the following sections, comprehension strategy and text structure instruction, text discussion, and scaffolding of the text-to-be-read can improve students' informational text comprehension.

Comprehension Strategy Instruction

Comprehension strategy instruction involves explaining, modeling, practicing, and applying mental processes to comprehend text (e.g., Duffy, 2014). For example, one panel of scholars (Shanahan et al., 2010) recommended that teachers teach students to engage in:

- Activating prior knowledge/predicting
- Questioning
- Visualizing
- Monitoring, clarifying, and fix-up
- Drawing inferences
- Summarizing/retelling

Researchers have frequently observed that students who experience comprehension strategy instruction learn the mental processes being studied and exhibit higher levels of informational text comprehension than their peers (e.g., Duke, Pearson, Strachan, & Billman, 2011; Gersten, Fuchs, Williams, & Baker, 2001). Moreover, a direct comparison of teaching a single process at a time versus multiple processes within a short time has hinted that teaching multiple processes may better support students' informational text comprehension development (Reutzel, Smith, & Fawson, 2005), perhaps because students can see how readers select, use, and coordinate more than one process at a time and practice doing the same themselves.

Text Structure Instruction

Readers use informational text structures—organizational patterns such as *cause and effect, comparison and contrast, description, problem and solution,* and *sequence*—to comprehend informational text (e.g., Meyer & Poon, 2001). Researchers have repeatedly provided evidence that teaching students to identify and use these text structures improves their comprehension of informational text (e.g., Hebert, Bohaty, Nelson, & Brown, 2016; Williams et al., 2005). For example, Joanna Williams and her colleagues (2005) investigated the effects of teaching the compare–contrast text structure to second graders and concluded that "students who received the Text Structure program not only learned what they were taught but were also able to demonstrate transfer of what they had learned to content beyond that used in instruction" (p. 546). For nine lessons, teachers and students reviewed lesson objectives, studied words authors use to signal the compare–contrast text structure, and read aloud and discussed informational text. Then they discussed key vocabulary concepts, analyzed the texts' compare–contrast structure, and recorded their ideas on graphic organizers. Students also responded to three short-answer comprehension questions, wrote summaries, and reviewed what they had learned. Later, with texts they had never seen before, students' comprehension was compared to that of second graders who had participated in business-as-usual instruction or lessons focused on learning science content. Students who had participated in the text structure instruction were more able to remember, find, and use the compare–contrast text structure and signal words than their peers. Indeed, looking across 19 studies of informational text structure instruction, researchers found a substantial mean effect, with higher effects in the elementary grades, when instruction lasted 11–20 hours, and when just one or two text structures were the focus of instruction (Pyle et al., 2017).

Discussion

Text discussions have also been linked to students' comprehension development (e.g., Gambrell & Almasi, 1996; Murphy, Wilkinson, Soter, & Hennessey, 2009). Researchers have tested several discussion approaches with informational text and have noted their positive effects on students' comprehension. Karen Murphy and her colleagues (2009) reviewed research on text discussion and concluded that text discussions have "the potential to increase student comprehension, metacognition, critical thinking, and reasoning, as well as students' ability to state and support arguments" (p. 743). Similarly, greater reported opportunity to engage in discussion about reading is associated with higher informational comprehension scores on the NAEP (Schugar & Dreher, 2017). Table 11.2 describes three evidence-based approaches to discussing informational text. In addition, please note the practice of interactive read-alouds shared earlier in this chapter. Interactive read-alouds also involve discussion and help to foster informational reading ability.

Scaffolding of Text-to-Be-Read

Scaffolding of the text-to-be-read precedes or accompanies students' listening to and reading of informational text and is designed to support their comprehension of that text. Because students' comprehension of future text is also important, we believe scaffolding needs to be used alongside other best practices.

There is evidence that prereading activities and visual aids lead to significant increases in students' comprehension of informational text (e.g., Griffin & Tulbert, 1995). Prereading activities are instructional routines teachers use to prepare students for reading. Visual aids are concrete tools that may be used to structure readers' thinking. For example, Sandra McCormick (1989) studied the effects of previewing social studies texts with 76 fifth graders for 2 weeks. For 10 minutes, students discussed their background knowledge, a summary of the text, and key vocabulary. Students' comprehension was judged to be "superior" to their unaided reading. Additionally, Bonnie Armbruster and her colleagues (1991) examined the effects of framing—using graphic organizers that depict a text's structure and capture its main ideas—while reading social studies textbooks. In 12 fourth- and fifth-grade classes (365 students), teachers (1) completed frames in front of students while discussing texts, (2) asked students to complete and discuss their own frames, or (3) followed lessons in teachers' manuals. Researchers found students who studied or completed the frames outscored their peers. Although the fifth graders appeared to benefit more than the fourth graders, the combined results of four rounds of instruction showed framing was "more effective than the discussion and questioning practices recommended by the teachers' editions" (p. 411).

In summary, the evidence base has shown that comprehension strategy instruction, text structure instruction, text discussion, and scaffolding

TABLE 11.2. Three Approaches to Discussion of Informational Text

Name	Overview	Central tenets
Collaborative Strategic Reading (CSR) (e.g., Klingner et al., 2001)	Students take on roles and work together in small groups to use four comprehension strategies while reading informational texts.	The discussion format includes comprehension strategy instruction and cooperative learning. Teachers preteach CSR in whole-group lessons. They model and think aloud, and students role-play. Students learn to (1) activate their prior knowledge and make predictions (*previewing*), (2) find words and ideas that are unknown or confusing to them and apply "fix-up" strategies (*click and clunk*), (3) summarize (*get the gist*), and (4) construct questions about what they read (*wrap up*).
Questioning the Author (QtA) (e.g., Beck & McKeown, 2006; Beck, et al., 1996)	Teachers lead discussions focused on understanding authors' messages.	Teachers and students co-construct meaning during the first reading of a text. Teachers encourage students to view their text as the product of writers who have knowledge and opinions but are also capable of error and bias. Teachers use questions such as "What is the author trying to say?"; "How does that fit in with what the author already told us?"; and "Did the author explain that clearly? Why or why not?" (Beck et al., 1996, p. 390).
Reciprocal Teaching (RT) (e.g., Palincsar & Brown, 1984; Rosenshine & Meister, 1994)	Students discuss the text together in small groups. They collaborate to apply comprehension strategies in informational text.	Teachers teach four comprehension processes (*predicting, questioning, clarifying,* and *summarizing*) and gradually release responsibility for the discussions to students. Teachers tell students when, how, and why each process may be useful, as well as paraphrase, clarify, and extend students' comments and questions when needed. In small-group discussions, students add to summaries, ask additional questions, seek and offer help with confusing sections, and/or respond to each other's thoughts.

of the text-to-be-read can help students to comprehend informational text. As one part of a learning community's instructional agenda that also includes opportunities to listen to and read authentic texts for authentic purposes, strategic teaching may support students' informational text comprehension and development.

BEST PRACTICES IN ACTION

In this section, we describe a single unit that employs evidence-based best practices described in the previous section.[1] This unit is designed for first graders, but could be taught at any grade level with appropriate embedded practices and expectations. The unit includes writing as well as reading, as research suggests is well advised (Graham & Hebert, 2011). The unit also involves a great deal of science content, which the studies reviewed earlier suggest will enhance informational comprehension development as well as motivation.

The teacher begins by reading aloud a magazine article about a senior center where seniors are engaged in a great deal of physical activity (students in higher grades could potentially read the text themselves). Students are impressed by a photo of a senior doing bicep curls and the description of a senior whose goal is to swim 50 miles a year! During the read-aloud, the teacher asks questions to engage students in specific comprehension processes, such as asking students, "What are we learning about these seniors?" to encourage summarizing, a strategy she reviews from a previous unit. She also asks about key details in the text, such as the specific activities in which the seniors are engaged. After reading, the teacher leads children in a discussion, based on the reading and their prior knowledge, about why it's important for seniors to be active.

Standards Connection: *This opening experience provides an opportunity to engage students in reading text closely in order to support them in comprehending not only explicit information in the text but also information that is implicit. By asking students to draw on the reading in their discussion, the teacher is engaging students in citing textual evidence. Asking students to summarize the text is also an important component of this opening experience.*

Next, the teacher tells students that based on the discussion, she thinks they would be great at persuading other seniors to exercise or exercise more! After a brief conversation about past situations in which students have attempted to persuade or convince someone of something,

---

[1] This unit description is based on a unit developed by one of us (Nell) in conjunction with Scholastic, Inc. as part of the *Information in Action* (2014, 2015) project.

the teacher shares some exciting news . . . there is a senior center just down the road from them! She looks it up on the Internet and reads portions of the site to students. She asks students whether they would like to try to persuade seniors at this center to exercise, if they don't already, and keep exercising if they do. Students turn and talk with one another about this possibility. The teacher pulls the group back together and learns that students are very interested in trying to persuade seniors to exercise.

Over the next several days, the teacher shares with students a range of pamphlets designed to persuade people to act in a certain way, such as to eat healthy, using proper car restraint systems for children, and get regular checkups. These pamphlets serve as models and inspiration for students for the pamphlets they plan to write. Students analyze the pamphlets (at least those that they are able to read themselves) using a graphic organizer for persuasive text (see Figure 11.1). The teacher explicitly teaches students to attend to text structure when reading and about the persuasive text structure they are repeatedly encountering. With prompting from the teacher, they also notice specific strategies the authors use to persuade—not only providing reasons for their opinions, but also using persuasive photographs, presenting graphs and statistics, and appealing to readers' emotions.

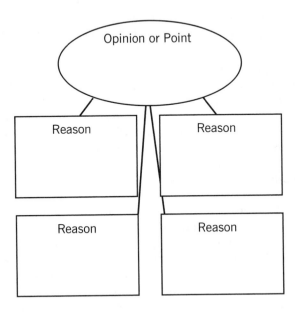

FIGURE 11.1. A graphic organizer for a persuasive text. For older students, evidence and other elements would be added.

Standards Connection: *Studying the pamphlets is a form of metatextual meaning activity that involves thinking about text as text. Many standards documents call for various metatextual skills throughout the grade levels. For example, standards often call for students to identify the structure of texts. For persuasive texts specifically, standards may call for students to analyze and evaluate how an author makes his or her argument, including the claims, reasons, and evidence provided or absent from the text.*

With a sense now of what a persuasive pamphlet contains, students embark on conducting research to inform the writing of their own pamphlets. This includes hands-on experiences, such as graphing their heart rate before and after exercise and interviewing personnel from the senior center, as well as the use of written text to gather information. The teacher ensures that there are many books, magazine articles, and websites available in the classroom that provide information about different types of exercise in which seniors can engage and the effects of exercise. The teacher encourages students to make use of a range of these resources and to integrate information from across them. She briefly preteaches some key vocabulary related to exercise and physiology that students might encounter in their reading. Students meet in student-led small groups in which they use the four strategies of the Collaborative Strategic Reading approach (see Table 11.2) to tackle reading some of the more difficult sources. During this time, the teacher meets with the small groups to compare the information presented in different sources and to assist students in synthesizing information across sources.

Standards Connection: *Standards often expect students to compare texts to one another and to integrate information across many texts, including not only traditional written texts but also visual texts, hands-on experiences, and so on. Learning vocabulary related to a grade-level topic is also commonly expected.*

At this point, students begin detailed planning of the pamphlets they will write, using the same graphic organizer they used for the reading (Figure 11.1). In addition to an opinion/reasons structure, each pamphlet is to include photographs or illustrations and at least one graph, such as a graph some students read on the number of years that different amounts of exercise add to your life. The teacher notes for students that rereading is an important strategy when writing based on informational sources. Students reread the sources and notes they have collected as they work to incorporate the information into their pamphlets. The teacher helps students to think carefully about what that might be most persuasive and appropriate for seniors. Arguing that exercise will help seniors get in shape for football is not very appropriate; arguments that exercise can improve balance and longevity are.

Standards Connections: *The ability to draw on and integrate a range of sources to inform one's writing is expected in many standards documents. So* *too are students expected to construct written arguments influenced by what they have read and incorporating visual devices as appropriate. The goal is for students to develop arguments–or any writing–to be appropriate for the audience, in this case senior citizens who might be considering exercising or exercising more.*

After students have completed their drafts, they read one another's pamphlets and provide feedback. Students are eager to revise and edit to make their pamphlets as persuasive as possible to seniors. Some students turn back to the informative/explanatory texts available on exercise in order to gain yet more information to enhance their pamphlet. The teacher is pleased to see this additional informational text reading, as she is working to balance the amount of informational versus literary reading over the course of the school day. Excitement is palpable as the day arrives for students to deliver their pamphlets to the senior center. The results reflect their hard work in comprehending and composing informational text (see Figure 11.2).

FIGURE 11.2. Excerpts from a first grader's brochure persuading senior citizens to exercise.

REFLECTIONS AND FUTURE DIRECTIONS

Research offers many insights and practices that support a complex, integrated unit such as the one described in this chapter. At the same time, there are areas in need of additional research and development activity. Early in the chapter, we identified four characteristics of skilled comprehension. Unfortunately, these characteristics are not equally distributed among students. An important area for research and development is how best to differentiate informational text instruction so as to develop strong informational comprehension skills among all students. Another key area for continued research and development, implied by the middle sections of the chapter, deals with how to teach students to engage in strategic comprehension, particularly within specific disciplines—for example, how to teach students to read primary-source documents in ways that historians do or how to teach students to read laboratory reports the way biologists do. Such research and development is particularly needed in the elementary years, in which much less research on the topic has been conducted. Related to this, more research and development work is needed on integrated reading, writing, and content-area learning, such as in the unit described in the previous section. Another critical direction for future work lies in how to help teachers to design and implement comprehension-fostering units such as the one described. We know that project-based units like this are educationally promising but also difficult to implement without a high degree of support (e.g., Halvorsen et al., 2012). Yet the research reviewed in this chapter and elsewhere suggests that such units provide a rich context for the development of informational comprehension. We wish readers of this volume success in this difficult but rewarding endeavor.

ENGAGEMENT ACTIVITIES

1. Attempt to read a piece of informational text that is quite difficult for you (e.g., a research article in a field that is unfamiliar to you). Notice how strongly your content knowledge affects your comprehension. Notice the strategies you use to try to help yourself comprehend. How do they compare to those in Table 11.1?

2. Examine a classroom's books and other reading materials as well as the daily schedule. How much opportunity are students provided to interact with informational text? Is informational text incorporated throughout the available reading materials and throughout the school day?

3. Examine a set of curricular resources that include attention to informational text comprehension. To what extent are the best

practices described in this chapter reflected? What additional practices are used? Which practices are missing?

4. Work to design your own unit modeled after the one described in the "Best Practices in Action" section and informed by the findings in the section "Evidence-Based Best Practices: A Research Synthesis."

REFERENCES

Almasi, J. F., & Hart, S. J. (2011). Best practices in teaching comprehension. In L. M. Morrow & L. B. Gambrell (Eds.), *Best practices in literacy instruction* (4th ed., pp. 250–275). New York: Guilford Press.

Armbruster, B. B., Anderson, T. H., & Meyer, J. L. (1991). Improving content-area reading using instructional graphics. *Reading Research Quarterly, 26,* 393–416.

Beck, I. L., & McKeown, M. G. (2006). *Improving comprehension with Questioning the Author: A fresh and expanded view of a powerful approach.* New York: Scholastic.

Beck, I. L., McKeown, M. G., Sandora, C., Kucan, L., & Worthy, J. (1996). Questioning the Author: A yearlong classroom implementation to engage students with text. *Elementary School Journal, 96,* 385–414.

Block, C. C., & Pressley, M. (2007). Best practices in teaching comprehension. In L. B. Gambrell, L. M. Morrow, & M. Pressley (Eds.), *Best practices in literacy instruction* (3rd ed., pp. 220–242). New York: Guilford Press.

Connor, C. M., Piasta, S. B., Fishman, B., Glasney, S., Schatschneider, C., Crowe, E., . . . Morrison, F. J. (2009). Individualizing student instruction precisely: Effects of child × instruction interactions on first graders' literacy development. *Child Development, 80,* 77–100.

Duffy, G. G. (2014). *Explaining reading* (3rd ed.). Portsmouth, NH: Heinemann.

Duke, N. K., & Carlisle, J. F. (2011). The development of comprehension. In M. L. Kamil, P. D. Pearson, E. B. Moje, & P. Afflerbach (Eds.), *Handbook of reading research* (Vol. 4, pp. 199–228). London: Routledge.

Duke, N. K., Caughlan, S., Juzwik, M. M., & Martin, N. M. (2011). *Reading and writing genre with purpose in K–8 classrooms.* Portsmouth, NH: Heinemann.

Duke, N. K., & Kays, J. (1998). "Can I say 'once upon a time'?": Kindergarten children developing knowledge of information book knowledge. *Early Childhood Research Quarterly, 13,* 295–318.

Duke, N. K., & Pearson, P. D. (2002). Effective practices for developing reading comprehension. In A. E. Farstrup & S. J. Samuels (Eds.), *What research has to say about reading instruction* (3rd ed., pp. 205–242). Newark, DE: International Reading Association.

Duke, N. K., Pearson, P. D., Strachan, S. L., & Billman, A. K. (2011). Essential elements of fostering and teaching reading comprehension. In S. J. Samuels & A. E. Farstrup (Eds.), *What research has to say about reading instruction* (4th ed., pp. 51–93). Newark, DE: International Reading Association.

Duke, N. K., & Roberts, K. M. (2010). The genre-specific nature of reading comprehension. In D. Wyse, R. Andrews, & J. Hoffman (Eds.), *The Routledge international handbook of English language and literacy teaching* (pp. 74–86). London: Routledge.

Duke, N. K., & Tower, C. (2004). Nonfiction texts for young readers. In J. V. Hoffman & D. L. Schallert (Eds.), *The texts in elementary classrooms* (pp. 125–144). Mahwah, NJ: Erlbaum.

Fox, E., & Alexander, P. A. (2009). Text comprehension: A retrospective, perspective, and prospective. In E. Israel & G. G. Duffy (Eds.), *Handbook of research on reading comprehension* (pp. 227–239). New York: Routledge.

Gambrell, L. B., & Almasi, J. F. (Eds.). (1996). *Lively discussions!: Fostering engaged reading.* Newark, DE: International Reading Association.

Gersten, R., Fuchs, L. S., Williams, J. P., & Baker, S. (2001). Teaching reading comprehension strategies to students with learning disabilities: A review of research. *Review of Educational Research, 71,* 279–320.

Graham, S., & Hebert, M. (2011). Writing to read: A meta-analysis of the impact of writing and writing instruction on reading. *Harvard Educational Review, 81,* 710–744.

Griffin, C. C., & Tulbert, B. L. (1995). The effect of graphic organizers on the comprehension and recall of expository text: A review of the research and implications for practice. *Reading and Writing Quarterly, 11*(1), 73–89.

Guthrie, J. T., McRae, A., Coddington, C. S., Lutz Klauda, S., Wigfield, A., & Barbosa, P. (2009). Impacts of comprehensive reading instruction on diverse outcomes of low- and high-achieving readers. *Journal of Learning Disabilities, 42,* 195–214.

Guthrie, J. T., McRae, A., & Klauda, S. L. (2007). Contributions of Concept-Oriented Reading Instruction to knowledge about interventions for motivations in reading. *Educational Psychologist, 42,* 237–250.

Guthrie, J. T., Wigfield, A., Barbosa, P., Perencevich, K. C., Taboada, A., Davis, M. H., . . . Tonks, S. (2004). Increasing reading comprehension and engagement through Concept-Oriented Reading Instruction. *Journal of Educational Psychology, 96,* 403–423.

Halvorsen, A., Duke, N. K., Brugar, K. A., Block, M. K., Strachan, S. L., Berka, M. B., & Brown, J. M. (2012). Narrowing the achievement gap in second-grade social studies and content area literacy: The promise of a project-based approach. *Theory and Research in Social Education, 40,* 198–229.

Hebert, M., Bohaty, J. J., Nelson, J. R., & Brown, J. (2016). The effects of text structure instruction on expository reading comprehension: A meta-analysis. *Journal of Educational Psychology, 108,* 609–629.

Kauffman, D. F., Zhao, R., & Yang, Y. (2011). Effects of online note taking formats and self-monitoring prompts on learning from online text: Using technology to enhance self-regulated learning. *Contemporary Educational Psychology, 36,* 313–322.

Klingner, J. K., Vaughn, S., Dimino, J., Schumm, J. S., & Bryant, D. (2001). *From clunk to click: Collaborative Strategic Reading.* Longmont, CO: Sopris West.

Kraemer, L., McCabe, P., & Sinatra, R. (2012). The effects of read-alouds of expository text on first graders' listening comprehension and book choice. *Literacy Research and Instruction, 51,* 165–178.

Kucan, L., & Beck, I. L. (1996). Four fourth graders thinking aloud: An investigation of genre effects. *Journal of Literacy Research, 28,* 259–287.

Langer, J. A. (1986). *Children reading and writing: Structures and strategies.* Norwood, NJ: Ablex.

Mantzicopoulos, P., & Patrick, H. (2010). "The Seesaw is a machine that goes up and down": Young children's narrative responses to science-related informational text. *Early Education and Development, 21,* 412–444.

Martin, N. M. (2011). *Exploring informational text comprehension: Reading biography, persuasive text, and procedural text in the elementary grades.* Unpublished doctoral dissertation, Michigan State University, East Lansing, MI.

McCormick, S. (1989). Effects of previews on more skilled and less skilled readers' comprehension of expository text. *Journal of Reading Behavior, 21,* 219–239.

Meyer, B., & Poon, L. W. (2001). Effects of structure strategy training and signaling on recall of text. *Journal of Educational Psychology, 93*(1), 141–159.

Murphy, P. K., Wilkinson, I. A. G., Soter, A. O., & Hennessey, M. N. (2009). Examining the effects of classroom discussion on students' comprehension of text: A meta-analysis. *Journal of Educational Psychology, 101,* 740–764.

Palincsar, A. S., & Brown, A. L. (1984). Reciprocal Teaching of comprehension-fostering and comprehension-monitoring activities. *Cognition and Instruction, 2,* 117–175.

Pappas, C. C. (1993). Is narrative "primary"?: Some insights from kindergarteners' pretend readings of stories and information books. *Journal of Reading Behavior, 25,* 97–129.

Pappas, C. C. (2006). The information book genre: Its role in integrated science literacy research and practice. *Reading Research Quarterly, 41,* 226–250.

Paris, S. G. (2005). Reinterpreting the development of reading skills. *Reading Research Quarterly, 40,* 184–202.

Pressley, M., & Afflerbach, P. (1995). *Verbal protocols of reading: The nature of constructively responsive reading.* Hillsdale, NJ: Erlbaum.

Purcell-Gates, V., Duke, N., & Martineau, J. A. (2007). Learning to read and write genre-specific text: Roles of authentic experience and explicit teaching. *Reading Research Quarterly, 42,* 8–45.

Pyle, N., Vasquez, A. C., Lignugaris/Kraft, B., Gillam, S. L., Reutzel, D. R., Olszewski, A., . . . Pyle, D. (2017). Effects of expository text structure interventions on comprehension: A meta-analysis. *Reading Research Quarterly, 52,* 469–501.

RAND Reading Study Group. (2002). *Reading for understanding: Toward an R&D program in reading comprehension.* Santa Monica, CA: Rand Education.

Reutzel, D. R., Smith, J. A., & Fawson, P. C. (2005). An evaluation of two approaches for teaching reading comprehension strategies in the primary years using science information texts. *Early Childhood Research Quarterly, 20,* 276–305.

Riddle Buly, M., & Valencia, S. W. (2002). Below the bar: Profiles of students who fail state reading assessments. *Educational Evaluation and Policy Analysis, 24,* 213–239.

Romance, N. R., & Vitale, M. R. (2012). Expanding the role of K–5 science instruction in educational reform: Implications of an interdisciplinary model for integrating science and reading. *School Science and Mathematics, 112,* 506–515.

Rosenshine, B., & Meister, C. (1994). Reciprocal Teaching: A review of the research. *Review of Educational Research, 64,* 479–530.

Schugar, H. R., & Dreher, M. J. (2017). U.S. fourth graders' informational text comprehension: Indicators from NAEP. *International Electronic Journal of Elementary Education, 9*(3), 523–552.

Shanahan, T., Callison, K., Carriere, C., Duke, N. K., Pearson, P. D., Schatschneider, C., & Torgesen, J. (2010). *Improving reading comprehension in kindergarten through 3rd grade: A practice guide* (NCEE 2010-4038). Washington, DC: National Center for Education Evaluation and Regional Assistance, Institute of Education Sciences, U.S. Department of Education. Retrieved from *http://whatworks.ed.gov/publications/practiceguides.*

Strachan, S. L. (2015). Kindergarten students' social studies and content literacy learning from interactive read-alouds. *Journal of Social Studies Research, 39*(4), 207–223.

Valencia, S., Wixson, K., & Pearson, P. (2014). Putting text complexity in context: Refocusing on comprehension of complex text. *Elementary School Journal, 115,* 270–289.

Wan, G. (2000). Reading aloud to children: The past, the present, and the future. *Reading Improvement, 37,* 148–160. Retrieved from *http://projectinnovation. com/Reading_Improvement.html.*

Williams, J. P., Hall, K. M., Lauer, K. D., Stafford, B., DeSisto, L. A., & deCani, J. S. (2005). Expository text comprehension in the primary grade classroom. *Journal of Educational Psychology, 97,* 538–550.

CHAPTER 12

Best Practices in Fluency Instruction

MELANIE KUHN
TIMOTHY RASINSKI
CHASE YOUNG

This chapter will:

- Discuss the role of fluency in the reading process and in reading achievement.
- Present effective approaches to fluency instruction.
- Suggest future directions for research.

Fluency is an integral component in reading development and text comprehension and, over the past two decades or so, it has become central to the literacy curriculum of many primary and elementary schools. In fact, reading fluency is considered by many (e.g., National Governors Association and Council of Chief School Officers, 2010) to be a foundational skill, or a competency that should be acquired early since it lays the foundation for further growth in reading. However, fluent reading is often considered to be nothing more than a label for accurate, automatic word recognition (Fletcher, Lyon, Fuchs, & Barnes, 2007), a (mis)understanding that has been driven, in large part, by a system of assessments or fluency programs that overemphasize students' reading rate (e.g., Kuhn, Schwanenflugel, & Meisinger, 2010; Rasinski, Reutzel, Chard, & Linan-Thompson, 2011).

Further, fluency is seen by many as primarily an oral reading activity. Given that most reading beyond the primary grades is silent, fluency instruction is often considered to be inappropriate beyond third grade (Rasinski et al., 2011). Taken together, the dominance of these perspectives has meant that the perceived importance of fluency in the reading process has lessened of late (Cassidy, Ortlieb, Grote-Garcia, 2016; Rasinski, 2016). Unfortunately, by focusing exclusively, or even primarily, on accurate and automatic word recognition, students can develop a skewed view of what skilled readers do.

From our perspective, the above positions are problematic both in their portrayal of fluency's role in the reading process and in the negative impact they can have on instruction. We instead consider fluency to be a critical component in skilled reading and its instruction. Further, research indicates that disfluency is a factor for a significant percentage of students who experience reading difficulties (e.g., Rasinski & Padak, 1998; Paige, Rasinski, & Magpuri-Lavell, 2012; Valencia & Buly, 2004). However, we also recognize that fluency instruction needs to be placed in the proper perspective. To determine this role, it is essential to remember *two* components of fluent reading are integral to literacy development: automaticity (LaBerge & Samuels, 1974) and prosody (Benjamin & Schwanenflugel, 2010). This understanding recognizes that fluency is not only characterized by both elements, but that they both make distinct contributions to comprehension (Benjamin, Schwanenflugel, & Kuhn, 2009; Hiebert, Samuels, & Rasinski, 2012).

Our goals for this chapter include a discussion of what we consider to be a more appropriate role for fluency instruction in the classroom; the provision of several effective instructional approaches, some of which expand the ways in which fluency can be developed; and how future research may inform both theory and practice.

EVIDENCED-BASED BEST PRACTICES: A RESEARCH SYNTHESIS

To understand why it is essential to include more than speeded word recognition in fluency instruction, it is important to consider how both automaticity and prosody contribute to its development. Here, we discuss the role of both.

Contribution of Automatic Word Recognition to Comprehension

When it comes to word recognition, skilled readers recognize the vast majority of words both accurately and effortlessly. As a result, they do not need to spend a great deal of time identifying the words in a text. This is important because, as with any cognitive task, individuals have a limited amount of attention available while reading (e.g., Adams, 2011; Samuels, 2004), so, whatever attention they spend on one task (word recognition) is attention that is unavailable for another task (comprehension).

Beginning readers find themselves experiencing the reverse (Adams, 2011). Since they are just developing their decoding skills, they need to focus a great deal of their attention on word recognition, leaving them little attention for comprehension. One of our roles as educators is to help students move from purposeful decoding to word identification that is effortless or automatic. There is a general consensus that this can best occur through practice, practice that consists not only of work on word recognition, but also on the supported reading of a wide variety of connected text (e.g., Kuhn et al., 2010; Rasinski, 2011). As a learner repeatedly encounters words, these words become more thoroughly embedded in the learner's memory and he or she requires less attention to decode them accurately. Eventually, the words become part of a reader's sight-word vocabulary, generally over the course of three to eight repetitions (e.g., Torgesen, 2005).

Contribution of Prosody to Reading Fluency

While automaticity has a central role in the development of fluent reading, it is critical to stress that fluency consists of more than simply reading words quickly and accurately; it also involves prosodic reading, or those melodic elements of language that, when taken together, constitute expressive reading (e.g., Kuhn et al., 2010). These include intonation, stress, tempo, and appropriate phrasing. When learners apply these elements correctly, oral reading should take on the qualities of fluent speech. Further, readers who incorporate prosody provide evidence of an otherwise invisible process, that of comprehension. This is because prosody contributes to shades of meaning and a richer understanding of what is written.

Recent research also indicates that prosody contributes to comprehension above and beyond that made by automatic word recognition (Benjamin et al., 2009; Benjamin & Schwanenflugel, 2010). While we know that prosody is closely tied to comprehension, the exact nature of the relationship is a matter of additional research (e.g., Does understanding the text allow for prosody?; Does prosody lead to better understanding?; or Is the relationship reciprocal?; Kuhn et al., 2010). No matter what the relationship, however, the use of expression contributes to learners' engagement with text, helping to bring text to life and adding nuance to their reading.

The Classroom as a Community of Learning: Fluency

According to Gunning (2012), rather than focusing on the individual student, effective literacy programs focus on building a sense of community. "As the importance of learning from others through scaffolding, discussion, cooperative learning, and consideration of multiple perspectives has become apparent, it is clear that the focus must be on group learning and building a community of learners" (p. 487). Most fluency instruction validates this perspective in multiple ways. To begin with, all of the approaches we recommend incorporate some form of scaffolding, and many include either cooperative learning, multiple perspectives recognized through discussion, or both.

What we feel is especially important about these approaches, however, is the fact that they allow all students to benefit from the reading of the same texts. While it is the case that your learners may need more or less scaffolding with any given material, they will all learn by reading and discussing the same selection, even if it is challenging for them. Fluency strategies designed for large groups or the entire class help make such texts accessible to everyone. By implementing an approach that assists your students in this way, you are ensuring that all of your students are all being introduced to, and have the opportunity to internalize, challenging vocabulary and conceptual knowledge that can serve to counter the achievement differences that exist in your classroom.

BEST PRACTICES IN ACTION

Fluency Instruction and the Literacy Curriculum

Given that fluency is an important contributor to comprehension, it is critical that effective instructional approaches are used for its development. Such approaches need to go beyond simply asking students to read text rapidly; they must present learners with a richer and more nuanced understanding of skilled, fluent, and meaning-filled reading (Kuhn et al., 2010; Rasinski, 2011). Importantly, several principles underlie effective fluency instruction (Kuhn & Levy, 2015; Rasinski, 2005), qualities that can be integrated across a range of literacy curricula, depending on the needs of your learners.

In this section, we present several approaches that can be implemented as part of your regular classroom instruction; these are designed either for flexible groups (Fluency-Oriented Oral Reading; Kuhn, 2004–2005), as synthesized fluency routines (Fluency Development Lesson and Read Two Impress), or as shared reading approaches for large groups of students (Fluency-Oriented Reading Instruction; Kuhn & Schwanenflugel,

2008). Depending upon your needs, these approaches can serve as regular components of your lesson plans for younger readers who are making the transition to fluency, or they can be integrated into your literacy curriculum as needed for older readers who have not achieved fluency to date. Importantly, they all have a focus on comprehension and prosody, as well as accuracy; as such, we feel they better represent the type of instruction that leads to the development of skilled reading than does instruction that focuses only on rate and accuracy.

Principles of Fluency Instruction

Timothy Rasinski (2005), one of this chapter's authors, outlined four basic principles that underlie effective fluency instruction. While you do not need to implement all four principles simultaneously, you will find one or more of them are present in any effective approach. To begin with, students should have the opportunity to listen to you, or another skilled reader, model fluent reading for them. Such modeling, even if consists of only a few minutes of oral reading a day, provides students with a better sense of what their own reading should sound like, something that is especially important for students whose reading is choppy or staccato.

Next, it is critical that you provide students with support while they themselves are reading aloud. This should involve their listening to a fluent rendering of the text while they practice reading it themselves. Support of this type can come in the form of echo or choral reading with a group, paired reading with a partner, or reading while listening to a prerecorded rendering of the text. This second principle clearly incorporates the first, that of modeling. Third, you should help focus students' attention on reading in meaningful phrases. As with modeling, a focus on phrasing helps students develop a deeper understanding of the importance of prosody while simultaneously helping them move beyond reading that is word by word or that uses phrasing in ways that fail to replicate oral language.

Finally, and most importantly, it is essential that your students have ample opportunities to read. As with most skills, students become better at reading through practice (Allington, 2009; Samuels, 2006), although the nature and purpose of practice—and how much support is required—will vary depending on the needs of the individual learner and the difficulty of the text. Practice can take two different forms (Kuhn et al., 2010; Rasinski et al., 2011). In wide reading, students read a given passage or text once; this is often followed by discussion or follow-up activities to ensure comprehension. Deep or repeated reading, on the other hand, involves students reading a text several times until they are able to read and understand it well before moving on to a new passage.

The four principles outlined above can be used independently, or they can be combined to create synergistic instructional routines. However, there is one aspect of most fluency instruction, that of repetition, that needs to be reconsidered in light of some recent findings (Kuhn et al., 2010; Mostow & Beck, 2005). First, it is important to stress that repetition does, indeed, help students develop their automaticity—as well as their prosody; this, in turn, helps ensure that learners become fluent readers. What needs to be reconsidered is not the repetition, per se, but instead how that repetition occurs. That is, repetition can occur through a traditional repeated reading format in which a given text is read several times.

Alternatively, repetition can result from reading the same words across multiple contexts, that is, by reading a range of texts a single time as opposed to repeatedly. While this may seem counterintuitive, given the number of shared words and syntactic constructions in many texts, especially those designed for young readers (Adams, 1990), it is possible for repetition to occur across a range of reading materials. In this scenario, students are likely to see the same words and grammatical patterns in multiple contexts, for example, words like *the, ran,* and *cat,* and sentence structures such as noun phrase + verb phrase + prepositional phrase (e.g., *The dog ran quickly after the cat*). Further, there is evidence indicating that readers may learn words faster when the words are encountered in a variety of contexts rather than when they are seen repeatedly in the same context (Mostow & Beck, 2005). As a result of this expanded understanding, we present several approaches to fluency instruction that are based on the above principles as well as both the wide and repeated reading of text.

Fluency-Oriented Oral Reading/Wide Fluency-Oriented Oral Reading

As was discussed above, for many years, repetition was considered a key element in fluency development. However, Kuhn and Stahl (2003) noticed that students using a repeated readings approach and students who read equivalent amounts of text with support made similar gains in fluency. In order to explore this finding further, they compared two types of small-group fluency instruction with striving second-grade readers: one used repeated readings, while the other used the wide reading of a number of texts (2004–2005). Additionally, they included a group that listened to, but did not read, the texts used by the fluency groups and a control group.

Both approaches are designed for small groups of students (up to six per group) and involve reading for 15–20 minutes per session three times a week. Since the goal is to scaffold, or support, your students, they should read material slightly beyond their instructional level; for example, students reading at the primer level can read texts ranging from a late first-grade to an early third-grade reading level. The first procedure is a modified repeated readings technique, Fluency-Oriented Oral Reading (FOOR). In this version, you should echo- or choral-read a single trade book three times over the course of a week. For the second approach, Wide

Fluency-Oriented Oral Reading (Wide FOOR), you should echo- or choral-read a different text for each of the three sessions. While discussion of the material should occur naturally as part of the lessons, comprehension and vocabulary instruction do not need to be intentionally planned; instead the emphasis should be on enjoyment of the text and the natural conversations and discussions that occur as part of the interaction with the text (e.g., Dong, Anderson, Kim, & Li, 2008).

In the initial study, both the FOOR and the Wide FOOR groups outperformed their peers (who either listened to the stories or did no extra reading) in terms of word recognition in isolation, prosody, and correct words per minute. Additionally, the students in the Wide FOOR group made greater growth on comprehension than their peers in the repeated reading, listening-only, or control groups. This finding may be due to the differences in the approaches; since one text was read repeatedly in the FOOR approach, the students may have focused on improving word recognition and prosody. The use of multiple texts in the Wide FOOR procedure, on the other hand, may have led readers to focus on comprehension. Similar results were found when students using repeated readings were simply asked to read the passage multiple times or were directed to focus on its meaning as well (e.g., O'Shea, Sindelar, & O'Shea, 1985). This indicates the importance of ensuring your learners are thinking about the information the text is trying to convey, even if you do so by simply reminding them to think about what the material is telling them prior to their reading. You can further assist learners in their understanding of the material being read by incorporating vocabulary and comprehension discussions into both of these approaches (e.g., see Stahl, 2008). However, the goal is to improve their fluency, not spend the bulk of your time discussing the text, so remember to keep a balance; your students should be spending the bulk of their time with their eyes on the actual text.

FLUENCY DEVELOPMENT LESSON

The Fluency Development Lesson (FDL) (Rasinski, Padak, Linek, & Sturtevant, 1994) also integrates several of the principles of effective fluency instruction mentioned earlier into a coherent classroom routine. In the FDL, students work daily with a brief text. First, you read a relatively short passage (a 50- to 200-word poem or selection taken from a longer prose piece) to your students two or three times. They follow along silently while listening to your oral reading. After the modeling component, you should discuss the meaning of the text as well as the quality of your oral reading with your students. Next, students read the selection chorally as a group; this allows each student to provide oral support for their classmates. Students then divide into partners and engage in paired repeated reading; at this point, each student reads the selection two or three times while their partner follows along silently and provides support and encouragement. After completing this practice, students are offered the chance to perform the daily text for their classmates either as individuals or in small groups. Finally, you and your students choose words from the text for word study and analysis. As an option, students may also take the assigned passage home for further practice with family members.

An early implementation of the FDL in a self-contained second-grade classroom found significant gains in overall fluency and a trend for improved overall achievement in reading (Rasinski et al., 1994). More recently, Zimmerman, Rasinski, and Melewski (2013) reported substantial gains in word recognition, reading fluency, and comprehension among first- through fourth-grade struggling readers who were receiving FDL instruction as part of a 5-week summer reading clinic. Similarly, DiSalle and Rasinski (2017) report that a 3-month intervention program using the FDL with struggling fourth-grade readers resulted in average gains of over a year in reading comprehension and double the expected gains in reading fluency as measured by reading rate.

READ TWO IMPRESS

Read Two Impress (R2I) is another synergistic approach to developing students' reading fluency (Young, Mohr, & Rasinski, 2015; Young, Rasinski, & Mohr, 2016). It combines the neurological impress method (NIM; Heckelman, 1966) and repeated readings (Samuels, 1979), and serves as an intense intervention for students who struggle to read fluently. Careful and consistent administration of R2I can increase reading rate, prosody, and overall reading ability. In this process, a teacher and student read sections of the same text aloud, but the teacher reads slightly ahead of the student. The student then rereads that section aloud without support.

The first step involves obtaining texts that are approximately 1 year above the students' independent reading level—it is important that you have two copies of the material so that you are each reading from your own text. Because R2I includes ample support, it enables students to successfully read more challenging text. Once a selection is made, you should sit next to the student and begin reading together. When the student is comfortable with this, you can begin reading slightly ahead, typically only a single syllable ahead. By reading in this manner, the student can hear the word just as he or she reads it aloud. It is important that the teacher or tutor make adjustments throughout the reading, so be prepared to speed up or slow down depending on the needs of the reader. While reading aloud, be sure to read with appropriate expression as well. In the early research on NIM, Heckelman (1969) reported that NIM reading "etched" the teacher's prosody into the mind of the student. Although the process is more complicated than this, this procedure allows students to develop into more automatic and expressive readers.

One major difference between this procedure and the original NIM procedure is that, in R2I, the reading is chunked into manageable parts. Picture books can be chunked page by page, and novels by paragraph. After reading the section of text in the NIM style, the students should reread it aloud. This gives the student an immediate opportunity to practice, and provides an immediate opportunity for the teacher to give the student feedback. In most cases, you will hear the student read each section accurately, at a decent pace, and with appropriate expression. However, if a student struggles, you can either read smaller sections or acquire a less challenging book.

The R2I process can continue for the remainder of the tutoring session. Younger students can typically participate for about 15 minutes, while older readers can continue for up to 30 minutes. Significant results have been observed after 4 weeks of daily R2I tutoring (Young et al., 2015). However, if the intervention is working, then you can continue with the process until the student is reading on grade level. It is also important to reevaluate the student's skill with the texts he or she is reading and be sure to increase the text level as frequently as possible, perhaps even once per week. The goal of R2I is to rapidly increase a student's reading fluency, and thereby increase a student's reading proficiency. Thus, the student should be kept on the very outer limits of his or her zone of proximal development (Vygotsky, 1978). Of course, there is no one intervention that works for every student, so if a student has not made significant progress in 3 to 4 weeks, consider using a different intervention.

However, when the method was first developed, two third-grade students made 2.5 years of reading growth on the Developmental Reading Assessment after 10 weeks (Mohr, Dixon, & Young, 2012). This remarkable growth prompted other studies that report large effects on the components of reading fluency and moderate effects on students' overall reading achievement (Young et al., 2015; Young, Durham, & Rosenbaum-Martinez, 2018). And while R2I is time-intensive, previous research on the method found that trained volunteers from various backgrounds were able to successfully administer the intervention with fidelity (Young et al.,

2015). Therefore, you can recruit parents, community members, college students, or anyone willing to dedicate their time to your disfluent readers as long as they are willing to implement the intervention faithfully.

FLUENCY-ORIENTED READING INSTRUCTION/WIDE FLUENCY-ORIENTED READING INSTRUCTION

Fluency-Oriented Reading Instruction (FORI) and Wide Fluency-Oriented Reading Instruction (Wide FORI) are designed for the shared reading component of your literacy curriculum. However, both can be easily modified for small-group instruction or used for tutoring one or two struggling readers. FORI (Stahl & Heubach, 2005) involves a weekly lesson plan that consists of rereading a single challenging selection. On Day 1, the week's selection should be introduced using your typical prereading activities, such as highlighting vocabulary, building background knowledge, or previewing the text. You should then read the week's selection aloud while your students follow along in their own copies. After reading the selection, you should discuss the material with your learners to reinforce the understanding that comprehension is the primary goal of reading.

Day 2 involves echo-reading the selection as a class; this approach can be made even more effective by integrating comprehension questions at natural stopping points throughout the selection (Kuhn, Schwanenflugel, Stahl, Meisinger, & Groff, 2013). Day 3's lesson is the shortest of the week, consisting of a simple choral reading of the material with your students. If time permits, however, you can integrate a second choral reading of the material into your instruction. On Day 4, students should partner-read alternative pages of the text since they should be fairly comfortable with it by this point in the week. Again, if time allows, you may have them reread the selection a second time, with the partners reading the opposite pages of those they read initially. Finally, on Day 5, you should implement your usual postreading extension activities; for example, you might ask your students to summarize the selection, to complete graphic organizers of the material, or to write in response to their reading.

The FORI program provides your students with modeling, support or assistance, a focus on appropriate phrasing, and, perhaps most importantly, ample opportunities to read substantial amounts of connected text. While it is the case that some teachers find the format to be a bit tedious, the vast majority of the students actually enjoyed the consistency of a predictable routine. The one aspect of this approach that is absolutely critical, however, is that the material being used is substantial in terms of both length and content. That means the texts need to be long enough for your students to read for an extended period of time (between 20 and 40 minutes per day) and that they are sufficiently challenging for your learners (e.g., grade-level texts if the majority of your students are reading below grade level and texts that are above grade level if the majority of your students are reading at grade level). When these conditions are in place, FORI has been shown to help students make significant growth in their reading ability.

In many classrooms, there is a particular story or expository piece that is a required part of your weekly literacy curriculum. As a result, you may feel a corresponding sense of accountability attached to these selections. In practice, this can mean that you dedicate a greater proportion of your class time to their instruction. The FORI procedure allows you to develop meaningful lessons around such selections. At the same time, the approach provides room for integrating additional reading materials—and instructional approaches—into your literacy curriculum as well. In fact, FORI should not be viewed as the only component of your literacy instruction; instead, it is important that you include multiple types of literacy learning, such as small-group and individual reading instruction, opportunities to write, and a focus on word study, as part of a balanced curriculum. Although the procedure is quite straightforward, it has been shown to be successful with students who are using complex material; as such, it can go hand-in-hand with the Common Core State Standards (National Governors Association and Council of Chief School Officers, 2010) and other standards that are required by many school districts.

While FORI is effective when concentrating on a single text, Wide FORI incorporates the reading of three texts over the course of a week and has been shown to be at least as effective as FORI at improving students' reading ability (Kuhn & Levy, 2015). Further, since it ensures that your learners encounter a large number of words in multiple contexts and provides your readers with more intact selections, it has the potential to expose your students to a broader range of concepts than does FORI.

The primary text for the Wide FORI lessons is usually the required selection for your literacy curricula, but you can use any shared reading text. Since the approach uses three texts per week, you will only spend 3 days on this selection, rather than the 5 days used in the FORI. Day 1 parallels that of FORI; that is, the text is introduced using your usual pre-reading activities, continues with your reading the selection aloud to your class as they follow along, and concludes by discussing the material with your learners. Day 2 consists of echo-reading the selection, followed by a choral- or partner-reading of the text if time allows. Day 3 involves your implementation of any extension activities that you feel are appropriate for the material and could involve a final reading if you feel it would be beneficial.

The remaining lessons, on Days 4 and 5, incorporate the reading of a second and third selection. You should echo-read these texts with your students and follow up by discussing them with your class. Further, if time allows, you can have your students undertake a second reading of the material; whether you decide to have your learners echo-, choral-, or partner-read at this point should depend on your students' comfort with the material, the text difficulty, and the amount of time available. Again, it is essential that the texts are challenging and long enough to spend 20–40 minutes actually engaged in reading. When using Wide FORI as described here, students have made gains not only in terms of their word recognition and fluency, but on their comprehension as well.

While we consider both approaches to be valuable means of accessing the shared reading component of your literacy curriculum, we would recommend Wide FORI if at all possible. Since learners benefit in multiple ways from exposure to a greater number of texts (i.e., word recognition, fluency, vocabulary, and comprehension), we believe this is the preferable approach (e.g., Hirsch, 2003; Paris, 2005; Stanovich, 1986). While we recognize it will be difficult to get multiple class sets of the typically literacy materials usually used for reading lessons, creative use of alternative materials such as classroom magazines, social studies or science texts, or articles available on the Internet from reliable sources, such as NASA or the Smithsonian, and written for young learners can all be used in their stead. In fact, by broadening our concept of what makes for a good text for literacy learning, we might be able to engage some of the reluctant readers who are less fond of fiction than their peers.

REFLECTIONS AND FUTURE DIRECTIONS

While we have greatly expanded our knowledge of reading fluency over the past two decades (e.g. Kuhn & Levy, 2015; Rasinski, 2010), there are still a number of questions that need to be answered. For example, recent research indicates that fluency can be improved through both a generalized increase in scaffolded reading and the repeated exposure to connected text. If this is the case, continuing research in this area may allow us to create additional instructional approaches while simultaneously developing a better understanding of how fluency contributes to learners' overall reading development.

Next, the appropriate difficulty level for text used in fluency instruction deserves further consideration. Research by ourselves and others (e.g., Stahl & Heubach, 2005; Hollingsworth, 1978) has found that greater progress was made when students were given more challenging materials for repeated or scaffolded wide readings. It is intriguing to consider that elements of fluency instruction may provide some key insights into how students can successfully negotiate the more complex texts they will be encountering as they proceed through their educational career.

The nature of the texts provided for fluency instruction is also an issue that requires further study (Hiebert, 2006; Rasinski et al., 2011). Some scholars (and many commercial fluency programs) argue that the texts for fluency instruction should contain academic content and be specifically designed to include words that students need to learn to recognize automatically. Other scholars suggest the use of texts that have a strong voice in order to provide opportunities to work on prosody, and are meant to be performed (e.g. poetry, Reader's Theater scripts, songs). Such material provides students with a natural context for repeated readings (i.e., rehearsal).

Fluency is most often thought of as an oral reading phenomenon most appropriate for the primary grades. Yet, most reading done by adults and students beyond the initial stages of reading is silent. Studies have found strong correlations between oral reading fluency and silent reading comprehension (Daane, Campbell, Grigg, Goodman, & Oranje, 2005). And, more recently, promising attempts have been made to develop instructional methods for developing silent reading fluency (Rasinski, Samuels, Hiebert, Petscher, & Feller, 2011; Reutzel, Jones, Fawson, & Smith, 2008). Still, future research needs to explore further the nature of silent reading fluency and how it may best be taught in classroom and clinical settings.

Additionally, a growing body of research suggests that fluency concerns may impact students' reading proficiency beyond the primary grades (Paige, Rasinski, & Magpuri-Lavell, 2012; Paige, Rasinski, Magpuri-Lavell, & Smith, 2014; Rasinski et al., 2017; Rasinski, Rikli, & Johnston, 2009). Research needs to explore how fluency continues to be an important competency beyond the primary grades and why significant numbers of students emerge from the primary grades without sufficient proficiency in fluency, how it may be more effectively taught to primary-grade students, and how students beyond the primary grades who still struggle in fluency may receive appropriate instruction in this key area.

Finally, while the role of the teacher in fluency instruction is clearly important, it has not been thoroughly investigated. While wide and repeated readings may seem to be primarily activities students engage in independently, we feel that the teacher must play a significant role in fluency instruction by choosing appropriate texts, modeling fluent reading, encouraging and providing feedback and support for students, and setting the stage for performance (e.g., Rasinski, 2005). Clearly the appropriate role of the teacher during fluency instruction needs further examination and clarification.

CONCLUDING REMARKS

In recent years, there has been a renewed focus on approaches that assist learners with their fluency development. However, we strongly believe that certain forms of assessment, along with their corresponding practices, have skewed conceptualizations of reading fluency. This, in turn, has negatively affected the way in which fluency is taught. We believe the approaches and principles presented here provide an alternative that will help you begin to integrate effective fluency instruction into your classroom. By doing so, your students will not only develop automatic word recognition and integrate expression into their oral reading, they will be better able to read challenging text with understanding, thereby helping them achieving the ultimate goal of reading instruction.

Although several issues related to reading fluency still need to be resolved, we feel strongly that appropriate fluency instruction offers a key to success in reading for many developing and struggling readers. We hope you agree and are willing to give fluency instruction a try!

ENGAGEMENT ACTIVITIES

1. How would you respond to a school administrator or parent who notes that since reading speed (an indicator of reading fluency) is associated with reading proficiency, you should emphasize students improving their reading rate through timed reading activities?

2. Identify three texts on a particular subject that you would like to use in your classroom as part of a Wide-FORI curriculum over the course of a week. How might you choose to present them to your students? Since there are multiple texts, they could be implemented in terms of reading difficulty, from easiest to most challenging. However, given that the primary selection for the week has the greatest amount of scaffolding, you might choose to have them read the most difficult text first, followed by the easiest, and then the text that falls in the middle. Or you might switch the last two readings, using the easiest text last and allowing the students to take primary responsibility for this selection. How would each of these scenarios differ in terms of the support you provide? How do you think each text will aid or support the reading of the next?

3. When first administering the R2I intervention, it can be a bit confusing and somewhat difficult, especially when continuously

adjusting to the students' reading rate. Therefore, we recommend that you try it out with a peer or another adult. First, choose a challenging text and read through the first few pages to ensure you can read the text with accuracy, expression, and at an appropriate pace. You could even use this chapter as an example text. Recruit another adult to help you practice. Follow the steps we described in R2I and administer the intervention. After conducting a brief session, ask yourself, what was challenging about the reading? What do I need to do to become more proficient? Also, think about what went well. You may want to reflect for a while and then try the intervention again. After you feel confident, try R2I with a child. With ample practice, the process becomes quite natural.

RESOURCES FOR FURTHER LEARNING

Kuhn, M. R., & Levy, L. (2015). *Developing fluent readers: Teaching fluency as a foundational skill* New York: Guilford Press.

Rasinski, T. V. (2010). *The fluent reader* (2nd ed.). New York: Scholastic.

Young, C., & Rasinski, T. (2016). *Tiered fluency instruction*. Minneapolis, MN: Capstone.

REFERENCES

Adams, M. J. (1990). *Beginning to read: Thinking and learning about print.* Cambridge, MA: MIT Press.

Adams, M. J. (2011). The relationship between alphabetic basics, word recognition, and reading. In S. J. Samuels & A. E. Farstrup (Eds.), *What research has to say about reading instruction, 4th edition* (pp. 4–24). Newark, DE: International Reading Association.

Allington, R. L. (2009). If they don't read much . . . 30 years later. In E. H. Hiebert (Ed.), *Reading more, reading better.* New York: Guilford Press.

Benjamin, R., & Schwanenflugel, P. J. (2010). Text complexity and oral reading prosody in young readers. *Reading Research Quarterly, 45*(4), 388–404.

Benjamin, R., Schwanenflugel, P. J., & Kuhn, M. R. (2009, May). *The predictive value of prosody: Differences between simple and difficult texts in the reading of 2nd graders.* Presentation at the College of Education Research Conference, University of Georgia, Athens, GA.

Cassidy, J., Ortlieb, E., & Grote-Garcia, S. (2016). What's hot: Texas and the nation. *Texas Journal of Literacy Education, 4*(1), 2–8.

Daane, M. C., Campbell, J. R., Grigg, W. S., Goodman, M. J., & Oranje, A. (2005). *Fourth-grade students reading aloud: NAEP 2002 Special Study of Oral Reading.*

Washington, DC: U.S. Department of Education, Institute of Education Sciences.

DiSalle, K., & Rasinski, T. (2017). Impact of short-term fluency instruction on students' reading achievement: A classroom-based, teacher initiated research study. *Journal of Teacher Action Research, 3,* 1–14. Retrieved from *www.practicalteacherresearch.com/uploads/5/6/2/4/56249715/impact_of_short-term_intense_fluency_instruction_.pdf.*

Dong, T., Anderson, R. C., Kim, I., & Li, Y. (2008). Collaborative reasoning in China and Korea. *Reading Research Quarterly, 43*(4), 400–424.

Fletcher, J. M., Lyon, G. R., Fuchs, L. S., & Barnes, M. A. (2007). *Learning disabilities: From identification to intervention.* New York: Guilford Press.

Gunning, T. G. (2012). *Creating literacy instruction for all students in grades 4–8.* Boston: Pearson.

Heckelman, R. G. (1966). Using the neurological impress remedial reading method. *Academic Therapy, 1,* 235–239.

Heckelman, R. G. (1969). A neurological-impress method of remedial-reading instruction. *Academic Therapy, 4,* 277–282.

Hiebert, E. H. (2006). Becoming fluent: What difference do texts make? In S. J. Samuels & A. E. Farstrup (Eds.), *What research has to say about reading fluency* (pp. 204–226). Newark, DE: International Reading Association.

Hiebert, E. H., Samuels, S. J., & Rasinski, T. (2012). Comprehension-based silent reading rates: What do we know? What do we need to know? *Literacy Research and Instruction, 51*(2), 110–124.

Hirsch, E. D. (2003, Spring). Reading comprehension requires knowledge—of words and the world. *American Educator,* pp. 10–13, 16–22, 28–30.

Hollingsworth, P. M. (1978). An experimental approach to the impress method of teaching reading. *The Reading Teacher, 31,* 624–626.

Kuhn, M. R. (2004/2005). Helping students become accurate, expressive readers: Fluency instruction for small groups. *The Reading Teacher, 58,* 338–344.

Kuhn, M. R., & Levy, L. (2015). *Developing fluent readers: Teaching fluency as a foundational skill* New York: Guilford Press.

Kuhn, M. R., & Schwanenflugel, P. J. (Eds.). (2008). *Fluency in the classroom.* New York: Guilford Press.

Kuhn, M. R., Schwanenflugel, P. J., & Meisinger, E. B. (2010). Review of research: Aligning theory and assessment of reading fluency: Automaticity, prosody, and definitions of fluency. *Reading Research Quarterly, 45,* 230–251.

Kuhn, M. R., Schwanenflugel, P. J., Stahl, K. A. D., Meisinger, E. B., & Groff, C. (2013). Fluency-oriented reading instruction. In T. Rasinski & N. Padak (Eds.), *From fluency to comprehension: Teaching practices that work* (pp. 166–175). New York: Guilford Press.

Kuhn, M. R., & Stahl, S. (2003). Fluency: A review of developmental and remedial practices. *Journal of Educational Psychology, 95,* 3–21.

LaBerge, D., & Samuels, S. J. (1974). Toward a theory of automatic information processing in reading. *Cognitive Psychology, 6,* 293–323.

Mohr, K. A. J., Dixon, K., & Young, C. J. (2012). Effective and efficient: Maximizing literacy assessment and instruction. In E. T. Ortlieb & E. H. Cheek, Jr.

(Eds.), *Literacy research, practice, and evaluation: Vol. 1. Using informative assessments for effective literacy practices.* Bingley, UK: Emerald Group.

Mostow, J., & Beck, J. (2005, June). *Micro-analysis of fluency gains in a reading tutor that listens.* Paper presented at the Society for the Scientific Study of Reading, Toronto, Ontario, Canada.

National Governors Association and Council of Chief School Officers. (2010). *Common Core State Standards.* Retrieved from *www.corestandards.org.*

O'Shea, L. J., Sindelar, P. T., & O'Shea, D. (1985). The effects of repeated readings and attentional cues on reading fluency and comprehension. *Journal of Reading Behavior, 17,* 129–142.

Paige, D. D., Rasinski, T. V., & Magpuri-Lavell, T. (2012). Is fluent, expressive reading important for high school readers? *Journal of Adolescent and Adult Literacy, 56*(1), 67–76.

Paige, D. D., Rasinski, T. V., Magpuri-Lavell, T., & Smith, G. (2014). Interpreting the relationships among prosody, automaticity, accuracy and silent reading comprehension in secondary students. *Journal of Literacy Research, 46* (2), 123–156.

Paris, S. G. (2005). Reinterpreting the development of reading skills. *Reading Research Quarterly, 40*(2), 184–202.

Rasinski, T. V. (2005). The role of the teacher in effective fluency instruction. *New England Reading Association Journal, 41,* 9–12.

Rasinski, T. V. (2010). *The fluent reader* (2nd ed.). New York: Scholastic.

Rasinski, T. V. (2011). The art and science of teaching reading fluency. In D. Lapp, N. Frey, & D. Fisher (Eds.), *Handbook of research on teaching the English language arts* (3rd ed., pp. 238–246). New York: Routledge.

Rasinski, T. V. (2016). Is what's hot in reading what should be important for reading instruction? *Literacy Research and Instruction, 55*(2), 134–137.

Rasinski, T. V., Chang, S.-C., Edmondson E., Nageldinger J., Nigh J., Remark L., . . . Rupley, W. H. (2017). Reading fluency and college readiness. *Journal of Adolescent and Adult Literacy, 60*(4), 453–460.

Rasinski, T. V., & Padak, N. D. (1998). How elementary students referred for compensatory reading instruction perform on school-based measures of word recognition, fluency, and comprehension. *Reading Psychology: An International Quarterly, 19,* 185–216.

Rasinski, T. V., Padak, N. D., Linek, W. L., & Sturtevant, E. (1994). Effects of fluency development on urban second-grade readers. *Journal of Educational Research, 87,* 158–165.

Rasinski, T. V., Reutzel, C. R., Chard, D., & Linan-Thompson, S. (2011). Reading fluency. In M. L. Kamil, P. D. Pearson, B. Moje, & P. Afflerbach (Eds.), *Handbook of reading research* (Vol. 4, pp. 286–319). New York: Routledge.

Rasinski, T., Rikli, A., & Johnston, S. (2009). Reading fluency: More than automaticity? More than a concern for the primary grades? *Literacy Research and Instruction, 48,* 350–361.

Rasinski, T., Samuels, S. J., Hiebert, E., Petscher, Y., & Feller, K. (2011). The relationship between a silent reading fluency instructional protocol on students' reading comprehension and achievement in an urban school setting. *Reading Psychology, 32*(1), 75–97.

Reutzel, D. R., Jones, C. D., Fawson, P. C., & Smith, J. A. (2008). Scaffolded silent reading (ScSR): An alternative to guided oral repeated reading that works! *The Reading Teacher, 62,* 194–207.

Samuels, S. J. (1979). The method of repeated readings. *The Reading Teacher, 32,* 403–408.

Samuels, S. J. (2004). Toward a theory of automatic information processing in reading, revisited. In R. B. Ruddell & N. J. Unrau (Eds.), *Theoretical models and processes* (pp. 1127–1148). Newark, DE: International Reading Association.

Samuels, S. J. (2006). Toward a model of reading fluency. In S. J. Samuels & A. E. Farstrup (Eds.), *What research has to say about fluency instruction* (pp. 24–46). Newark, DE: International Reading Association.

Stahl, K. A. D. (2008). Creating opportunities for comprehension instruction within fluency-oriented reading. In M. R. Kuhn & P. J. Schwanenflugel (Eds.), *Fluency in the classroom* (pp. 55–74). New York: Guilford Press.

Stahl, S. A., & Heubach, K. (2005). Fluency-oriented reading instruction. *Journal of Literacy Research, 37,* 25–60.

Stanovich, K. E. (1986). Matthew effects in reading: Some consequences of individual differences in the acquisition of literacy. *Reading Research Quarterly, 21*(4), 360–407.

Torgesen, J. (2005, September). *Teaching every child to read: What every teacher needs to know.* Paper presented at the Georgia Reading First Pre-Service Conference, Atlanta, GA.

Valencia, S. W., & Buly, M. R. (2004). Behind test scores: What struggling readers really need. *The Reading Teacher, 57,* 520–531.

Vygotsky, L. V. (1978). *Mind in society.* Cambridge, MA: Harvard University Press.

Young, C., Durham, P., & Rosenbaum-Martinez, C. (2018). A stacked approach to reading intervention: Increasing second and third graders' independent reading levels with an intervention program. *Journal of Research in Childhood Education, 32*(2), 181–189.

Young, C., Mohr, K. A. J., & Rasinski, T. (2015). Reading together: A successful reading fluency intervention. *Literacy Research and Instruction, 54*(1), 67–81.

Young, C., Rasinski, T., & Mohr, K. A. J. (2016). Read Two Impress: An intervention for disfluent readers. *Reading Teacher, 69*(6), 633–636.

Zimmerman, B., Rasinski, T., & Melewski, M. (2013). When kids can't read, what a focus on fluency can do. In E. Ortlieb & E. Cheek (Eds.), *Advanced literacy practices: From the clinic to the classroom* (pp. 137–160). Bingley, UK: Emerald Group.

CHAPTER 13

Best Practices in Teaching Writing

TROY HICKS

This chapter will:

- Discuss the role of the writing classroom as a community of learning.
- Synthesize theory and research that supports K–8 writing instruction.
- Present evidence-based practices for teachers of writing.
- Suggest future directions for writing instruction.

A PORTRAIT OF BEST PRACTICES IN TEACHING WRITING

In a contemporary third-grade classroom, we see that writers are intent at their craft, alone and in pairs, sitting at desks, stretched out across the floor, or standing together. Much like the scene that Ray and Laminack describe in their book, *The Writing Workshop: Working through the Hard Parts (and They're All Hard Parts)*, it is "a little noisy in the room, but it doesn't seem like a misdirected, off-task kind of noise. Just the hum of noise you get when people are working alongside one another" (2001, p. 1). Also, just like Ray and Laminack's description, some students are writing in their notebooks, some browse through books to use passages as mentor texts, and others are engaged in quiet discussion during peer review.

However, because it is now 2018, at the time of this writing, a slightly different picture emerges in other parts of the classroom. Christopher Working's third graders are still using notebooks, reading mentor texts, and talking with their peers. The productive hum is still present in Mr.

Working's classroom as students work with their "writing buddies," sometimes sitting side by side, yet they are also peering over one another's Chromebook screens and sometimes providing feedback to one another via Google Docs. Since the early 2000s, millions of laptops and tablets have been introduced into K–12 classrooms, including Mr. Working's, and even five years ago it was estimated that "in 2013, 71 percent of the U.S. population age 3 and over used the Internet" (National Center for Education Statistics, n.d.). Though not specific to reports on children and youth, recent statistics from the Pew Internet Research Center (2018) show that 98% of adults ages 18–29 use the internet, so it is reasonable to assume that the number of children using the internet on a daily basis has grown significantly in the past five years, too.

For Mr. Working's students, this use of the Internet includes a variety of writing tasks using collaborative tools such as Google Docs and communities such as Bookopolis, where students can "buzz a book" and share their reviews. They also offer audio comments on a piece of writing using a web-based application called VoiceThread, and they even employ Twitter, where students summarize key classroom learning each day. In the 21st-century classroom, students are engaged as digital writers, sharing their work within the four walls of their classroom, as well as with other students from around the country.

For Mr. Working's students, the mini-lessons, individual work time, and sharing make the writing process a highly social set of activities in which students understand that "their writing is designed for someone else to read," both inside and outside of their classroom (Working, personal communication, 2017). Students move seamlessly from composing with paper and pencil to their work on keyboards and screens. Writers are able to quickly navigate online spaces for drafting, sharing, and ultimately publishing their writing, including on their own classroom wiki page and blog.

In addition to mini-lessons and whole-group discussion about writing, Mr. Working also confers with his students. Building on the time-honored practice described by teachers who enact the workshop approach (e.g. Calkins, 1994; Calkins, Hartman, & White, 2005), Mr. Working spends a good deal of his time during class conferring with individual writers. Yet, something is a bit different. Mr. Working describes the scene:

> "The interesting thing with technology-based writing is that my conferring doesn't necessarily mean that I am sitting right next to them. Or, it might mean that I am sitting right next to them, but we've both pulled up their writing on my screen and their screen. It changes the kind of ways you might confer. It also allows me to confer outside of the writing workshop so I can get to more kids, or I can have one

purpose during the workshop and one purpose outside of the workshop. But I always have that conferring part. I want to make sure that I give as much feedback to kids as possible."

Mr. Working's classroom—along with three others that we will explore in this chapter—provides a glimpse into best practices for teaching in the contemporary, cloud-based, (digital) writing workshop. Built on the same principles that were originally outlined by Graves (1983, 1994), Calkins (1994; Calkins et al., 2005), Atwell (1998, 2002), Ray (1999, 2006, 2010), Fletcher (1992, 2001; Fletcher & Portalupi, 2011), and a number of their intellectual and pedagogical progeny, the main tenets of Writing Workshop pedagogy still hold true: student choice and inquiry, strategic instruction, conferring practices, and opportunities to share one's writing with a broader audience. Accompanying these principles, teachers are encouraged to create communities of writers who would contribute their own ideas to and ongoing classroom conversation about what it means to be a writer, as well as what it means to create good writing in a variety of contexts. Their classroom practices, as I will argue, have also been explored and validated through empirical research methods.

However, teachers still struggle to figure out timely, efficient ways to help guide students through the writing process, to shepherd them as they provide feedback to one another's work, and to build a classroom community. Moreover, they struggle—for reasons including access to technology as well as with their own pedagogical skills and comfort levels—to incorporate digital writing practices. In fact, given the poor performance of students documented through such measures as the National Assessment of Educational Progress (NAEP) (2017), we could, reasonably, wonder if and how the principles of Writing Workshop instruction are present in the vast majority of classrooms. As one proxy for the quality of student writing across the country, the NAEP, otherwise known as "The Nation's Report Card," indicated that only 24% of students were proficient as writers. Any scan of education-related headlines can confirm that additional state, national, and international testing confirms these dismal results.

Put another way, I paraphrase the quote often attributed to science fiction author William Gibson (assigned to Gibson in O'Toole, 2012). He said that "the future has arrived— it's just not evenly distributed yet." Indeed, while we know that best practices in writing instruction are already here, we also know that they are just not equally present across all classrooms. What, then, accounts for the gap between best practices in writing instruction, with both print and digital tools, and what appears to be occurring in the vast majority of classrooms? Though it is beyond the scope of this chapter to fully document (or attend to) the systemic inequalities that plague our schools—and the inherent consequences that such inequalities lead to regarding literacy achievement (e.g., Kozol, 1992, 2005)—in order to better understand the answer to this question, we must first understand the role of the classroom community and how it affects students' motivations for writing.

THE CLASSROOM AS A COMMUNITY OF LEARNING

In reports of practice over the past four decades, hundreds of teacher researchers and university researchers have documented the ways in which educators can build a supportive, sustained community of writers. Professional organizations such as the National Writing Project (*www. nwp.org*) have adopted, as the core to their purpose, the ideas that teachers should be writers and should model effective writing processes, protocols for providing feedback, and attempts at revision. The National Council of Teachers of English, in its "Professional Knowledge for the Teaching of Writing," argues that teachers must know how "to create a sense of community and personal safety in the classroom, so that students are willing to write and collaborate freely and at length" (National Council of Teachers of English, 2016). In short, research demonstrates that teachers should be writers themselves and, in turn, should foster the classroom community as a space where writers collaborate and grow.

Like Chris Working's classroom, other teachers around the country are taking a similar approach, blending best practices in the teaching of writing with digital writing technologies. They, too, invite their students to create writing that will circulate beyond the walls of their own school, and to use tools in productive, responsible, and, yes, creative ways. Communities of writers are no longer confined to the same physical space at one specific time. As we consider the ways in which teachers can incorporate evidenced-based best practices for teaching writing into their classrooms, we will visit, briefly, with three other teachers who are, like Mr. Working, skillfully integrating technology into their writing workshop classrooms: Kristin Ziemke, Franki Sibberson, and Katharine Hale.

Kristin Ziemke, Third Grade

Students in Kristin Ziemke's third-grade classroom, like generations of writers before them and like many other Writing Workshop classrooms, sit in various locations while they discuss drafts, provide feedback, make revisions, and prepare to publish their work. Built on the foundational work of early advocates of the Writing Workshop model noted above, Ms. Ziemke's approach takes a decidedly digital turn. As described by

Muhtaris and Ziemke in their book, *Amplify: Digital Teaching and Learning in the K–6 Classroom,*

> We keep these leaders and established best practices, which are research based, teacher tested, and kid approved, at the core of all we do. When introducing technological tools, we apply the same practices and strategies we use in reading and writing workshop. We model what we want students to do with the technology and guide them to try it out with us. We then provide ample time for students to practice on their own, experiment, and share as a class, thus building new knowledge collaboratively. (2015, p. 5)

In a personal interview, Ms. Ziemke described how audience and authenticity are central to the work that she does with her students. In addition to hosting writing circles where students share their work in progress, partnering students as editors, and inviting them to share their work with someone outside the classroom, Ms Ziemke describes the ways that her students produce various forms of written compositions such as blog posts, summaries, and even what she describes as "micro writing," such as tweets or social network updates.

Building on her belief that writing well requires students to create a volume of work, have choice in that work, and receive effective responses to that work, Ms. Ziemke frames a core question: "Are we doing real work with kids, or are we just doing work that is for school?" (Ziemke, personal communication, 2017). She encourages writing invitations that help students discover how writing will become "something that they might really use" to persuade, to entertain, or to inform. Like Mr. Working, she expects her students to provide one another with substantive feedback, and then share their work with an audience beyond their classroom.

Franki Sibberson, Fifth Grade

In her classroom, with slightly older students, Franki Sibberson's fifth graders engage in many of the same practices as Ms. Ziemke's students. They, too, have a daily structure for Writing Workshop, including an initial gathering with a mini-lesson, shared writing, and modeling; independent work time with conferring; and a final gathering in which students may share some of what they have written. Similarly, they use paper and pencil as well as devices, including the eight Chromebooks that she has available in the classroom, devices she may be able to obtain from other places in the school, and their own (since the school has a "bring your own device" policy).

For Ms. Sibberson—author of numerous professional books (e.g., Bass & Sibberson, 2015; Sibberson, 2012; Sibberson & Szymusiak, 2016) and, as of the time of this writing, the president-elect of the National Council of Teachers of English—her efforts to stay focused on best practices for writing instruction were, at one time, being sidelined for more intentional focus on learning technology tools. For instance, she discussed the ways in which she would spend days, perhaps as long as a week, helping students learn the technical aspects of using a blog. However, in the past few years, she has spent less time focused on the technology itself, and has noted that her students are figuring out technology more on their own, or with help from their classmates. In turn, she argues that "my mini-lesson work and my work with kids has to be about the actual composition."

Her focus, to put it another way, is on the craft of digital writing, which I have described as a combination of alphabetic text features that help us with thinking like authors do, "yet we also need to begin thinking like artists, web designers, recording engineers, photographers, and filmmakers. In other words, intentional choices about craft can lead to creative work in a variety of writing media" (Hicks, 2013, pp. 18–19).

In this sense, Ms. Sibberson, like Mr. Working and Ms. Ziemke, demonstrates what William Kist (2012) has called a "new literacies workshop" and what I have called a "digital writing workshop" (Hicks, 2009): she offers her students structured, yet flexible, working spaces and routines that blend whole-group, small-group, and individual instruction where students engage, in Kist's words, in "daily work in multiple forms of representation" (2012, p. 17) including text, talk, and multimodal compositions. Still, the principles of workshop instruction remain the same. Ms. Sibberson (personal communication, 2017) notes:

> "Principles stay the same. I think what's happened is there's more possibilities for kids. There's more choice. So, where it used to be everything they did was paper and pencil, and they could decide between lined and unlined paper, when I talk about "choice" now they have lots of choices of devices to use, they have lots of choices of how to publish, they have lots of choices of how to craft, and how to plan. And they have lots of choice on how to decide to share their thinking and who they want to share that with, and how they want to share that, and if they want to share it when it is finished, or whether they want to share it while it is in the midst. And, so I think that whole choice piece has exploded."

As we have seen so far with Mr. Working, Ms. Ziemke, and Ms. Sibberson, the principles around best practice in writing do indeed stay the same across the elementary grades. Let's explore how a teacher of middle school students explores these new possibilities for students.

Katharine Hale, Eighth Grade

Now an instructional coach working with other middle school teachers and teaching her own class of eighth graders, Katherine Hale began her career teaching fifth-grade English language arts. Like Mr. Working, Ms. Ziemke, and Ms. Sibberson, she too has been fortunate enough to work with students in a technology-rich environment where they are able to choose between multiple devices. For instance, she has students using iPads and Chromebooks, as well as their own devices. For Ms. Hale (personal communication, 2017), the key question is this: How do we teach writing in a meaningful way while also asking students to explore the affordances and constraints of various digital writing tools?

> "For example, I know blogs have been around forever. But there's something so flexible about blogs, even though it seems like such an old tool, that it allows for so much more choice than any other tool. . . . Blogging is like a very open canvas. And when you want to try to personalize writing for students and give them choice and give them voice, you need as big and blank of a canvas, I realized, that you can."

Ms. Hale continued with a number of examples from her students' blogging, including examples of students who learned to share their passions and hobbies with the class. In one case, she described how a student's blogging, over an entire year, helped her come to understand more about her own identity development as a transgendered youth.

Ms. Hale, in particular, is especially thoughtful about the ways in which she asks students to use a variety of different digital tools. She notes that, many times, she will introduce a writing prompt or ask students to begin a task, but not require them to use any one tool in particular. Instead, much like the choice they have in terms of topics and genres, students will also have decisions to make about the most appropriate tool for the task at hand. For some, this may mean using Google Docs or a blog, for some it may mean using a mind-mapping program, and for still others it may mean putting the devices away and relying on pencil and paper. By providing her students with the option to compose both analog and digital texts, especially in the early stages of the writing process, Ms. Hale reinforces the best practices that support student agency.

In each of these examples, we can see that what it takes to create a community of writers who are engaged with one another and the many tools available for composition. These teachers, as exemplars of contemporary Writing Workshop instruction, demonstrate that even with many new technologies, the principles and practices that enable students to

produce high-quality writing remain consistent. It is with this understanding that we now more fully explore the evidence-based best practices for
the teaching of writing.

EVIDENCE-BASED BEST PRACTICES
FOR THE TEACHING OF WRITING

Since the introduction of No Child Left Behind Act at the turn of the
twenty-first century and the continued efforts of the Every Student Suc-
ceeds Act, we have lived in an educational paradigm that places more
value on causal, statistically reliable evidence, most notably through
scores on standardized assessments and, more recently, ongoing com-
puter-adaptive assessments. In that vein, writing researchers, especially
over the past two decades, have continued to do significant work conducting studies that meet the criteria of the U.S. Department of Education's Institute of Education Sciences' (IES) rigorous demands from the
What Works Clearninghouse (WWC; 2014). In order to meet the criteria of "strong evidence" that a particular teaching strategy or classroom
practice has a direct, cause-and-effect relationship on students' writing
performance, the study must be designed in an experimental fashion,
much as we would expect from a scientific trial exploring the effects of
a particular drug treatment (as compared to a placebo). To ensure that a
particular teaching strategy is, indeed, effective, researchers design their
studies so there are control and experimental groups, and so the variables are controlled.

Before moving forward, though it is crucial to note that there are
numerous critiques of IES and WWC, as well as this quantitative, empirical approach to studying educational phenomenon; it is beyond the scope
of this chapter to explore these critiques in detail. There are many other
teachers and researchers who have examined best practices in the teaching of writing (e.g., Applebee & Langer, 2013; Hillocks, 1986; Smagorinsky, 2005; Troia & Olinghouse, 2013; Zemelman, Daniels, & Hyde, 2012),
as well as other scholars who have examined the conflicts among research
traditions (e.g., Lagemann, 2002). Suffice it to say, without the voices of
teachers such as Ms. Hale, Ms. Sibberson, Mr. Working, and Ms. Ziemke,
a chapter such as this would, indeed, feel highly decontextualized. Moreover, their insights into the uses of digital writing technologies provide us
with specific, useful models for implementing best practices in our contemporary classrooms. Beyond that, I leave further conversations about
the value of quantitative, qualitative, and mixed methods research for a
different day.

Still, as a matter of establishing "best practices"—and based on these standards defining effective research, in June 2012—IES released an Educator's Practice Guide related to elementary writing instruction through the WWC (Graham et al., 2012), followed by a second guide in November 2016 that focused on secondary writing instruction (Graham et al., 2016). The committees that produced each guide were chaired by prominent writing researcher Dr. Steve Graham of Arizona State University. Previously, Graham had been involved in coauthoring the meta-analysis that led to a 2007 report for the Carnegie Corporation of New York, *Writing Next* (Graham & Perin, 2007), and numerous articles, chapters, and books documenting evidence-based best practices in writing (e.g., Graham, MacArthur, & Fitzgerald, 2013). A leading researcher in this area, Graham's work focuses on meta-analysis (the study of other studies) and effect sizes (the extent to which an educational intervention makes a minimal, moderate, or significant difference in learning).

In addition to the countless number of qualitative studies and action research projects that have been taken up by teachers in the classroom, Graham's quantitative analyses through these reports bring an extra level of statistically valid, empirical gravitas to the argument about evidence-based best practices for writing instruction. Graham's analysis of the statistically significant effects of various teaching strategies corroborates what many experts in our field, as well as countless teacher researchers, have developed through practice: our student writers must be taught the writing process in a strategic, transparent manner; they must be introduced to a variety of audiences, purposes, and genres for writing; and we must support student writers through the social construction of meaning making.

Though this chapter is summarizing a great deal of work from different research traditions, I will state my point simply. Just like the vast majority of climate scientists who agree that the Earth is warming, so, too, the vast majority of writing researchers concur with Graham's body of work and his conclusions. Students need consistent time and space for writing, as well as explicit instruction in writing strategies. They also need timely, specific feedback on their writing from teachers and from peers. In short, evidence-based best practices suggest that writing instruction must be:

- *Strategic and transparent.* In addition to identifying the recursive, interwoven aspects of the writing process such as brainstorming, drafting, revising, and editing, students must be taught explicit strategies for approaching each of these stages.
- *Open to a variety of audiences, purposes, and genres.* Beyond typical school-based writing experiences (such as thesis-driven essays and summaries of other texts), students must be taught about the form

and function of different types of writing, as well as the needs and expectations of diverse readers.

- *Socially engaging throughout the writing process.* Along with responses offered by peers and the teacher in the immediate classrooms, students must have opportunities to share their work, both in process and in final form, with audiences beyond the classroom. Technology, obviously, holds potential to enrich these opportunities.

These practices demand specific expectations of both the teacher and students, including a shared set of social norms and mutual respect. Without a doubt, these norms and expectations can be difficult to establish. However, the risk of foregoing such relationship-building activities is that a writing community will not form and, in turn, writing instruction itself will devolve to a series of disconnected lessons and prompts. Teachers will not engage in substantive, sustained work with their students through mini-lessons and conferring, nor will students provide the kinds of feedback and support to one another that is necessary to grow and maintain the community. While the demographic factors affecting any one classroom can be generally positive, neutral, or negative, we are consistently reminded of the fact that it is the teacher who sets the tone in a classroom. Thus, a writing teacher must set that mood in a positive, productive manner, inviting his or her students to explore writing in meaningful ways. Embracing and employing these evidence-based best practices of transparency, variety, and engagement is one way to create such a classroom community. Let's explore how.

Best Practice 1: Make the Writing Process Transparent

Chief among the conclusions that Graham and his colleagues discovered through their meta-analyses—and that has been echoed throughout the work of other teacher researchers and scholars mentioned above—is that students need clear, specific advice from teachers as they explore the writing strategies of other successful writers. As described in the *Writing Next* report, "Strategy instruction involves explicitly and systematically teaching steps necessary for planning, revising, and/or editing text" (Graham & Perin, 2007, p. 15). In the Writing Workshop model, explicit strategy instruction often occurs in two phases: mini-lessons and conferring.

First, during an initial mini-lesson, the teacher will identify a particular strategy such as including appropriate details to illustrate an example.

Second, during writing conferences, teachers will teach

a strategy for planning, for example, teachers should check to see if students are using the strategy and if their planning skills are improving.

If students are no longer using the strategy, but their planning skills have improved, it may mean they no longer need the strategy. Alternatively, if students continue to struggle with planning components of the writing process, the teacher may need to reteach the strategy to the whole class or provide more opportunities for collaborative practice for a small group of struggling students. (Graham et al., 2012)

A related process is making thinking visible through anchor charts, think-alouds, and recordings. Anchor charts can be used to document writing strategies, text features, and samples from mentor texts. Ms. Ziemke describes how she adapts anchor charts to create heuristics for exploring digital texts, too. For instance, last year, some of her students were curious about the ways in which photos and captions—as well as emojis and hashtags—could be used when composing a post on Instagram. To that end, Ms. Ziemke had students explore other Instagram posts as mentor texts, documenting some of the ways that the photographer would frame an image as well as how he or she would write about the subject. Then, as writers in a multimodal space, they created anchor charts to help think about the many decisions they would make when creating their own photographs, captions, and blog posts.

Another way in which strategies for making the writing process transparent have been affected by technology is through the use of "flipped lessons." Defined broadly as "a pedagogical approach in which direct instruction moves from the group learning space to the individual learning space," opening up the classroom for more collaborative, interactive learning activities, flipped lessons are often created in the form of a video to be shared with students (Flipped Learning Network, 2014). In my interview with Katharine Hale, for instance, she described a number of videos that she created for her students on her "power strategies" for writers, specific techniques that she knew her fifth graders would return to time and time again, such as creating an effective lead or adding dialogue to a story.

No matter what way a teacher chooses to make the writing process transparent, significant evidence—both qualitative and quantitative—has accumulated over the past 20 years documenting the importance of this practice. If we do not guide students by providing specific strategies for approaching different parts of the writing process, they will be unable to use those strategies in their own compositions.

Best Practice 2: Write for a Variety of Audiences and Purposes, and in Many Genres

School-based writing can, unfortunately, fall into a trap of redundant prompts that produce formulaic writing. Warning of this trend decades ago in his book *The Testing Trap: How State Writing Assessments Control Learning,* Hillocks argued forcibly that "in the past 30 years, researchers and theorists have come to know that teaching writing entails teaching thinking. Further, they would argue that people learn through writing" (2002, p. 6). Whitney puts it even more bluntly:

> So much of what happens in school has always seemed . . . well, fake. Competing visions of the possibilities and purposes in the space we call school bring with them competing versions of what it would mean to do authentic work in language arts classrooms—that is, work that is in some way meaningful beyond the context of school. (2011, p. 51)

The ways in which writing instruction leads to such "fake" writing are numerous: decontextualized grammar exercises, prompts that are artificial and do not relate to students' lived lives, assessment practices that value formulaic products over an authentic process, and a lack of consistency in teaching and evaluation practices from classroom-to-classroom and grade-to-grade. In contrast, as Graham et al. summarize in a 2012 report for elementary writers, "Students also should learn that writing is used for a variety of purposes, such as conveying information, making an argument, providing a means for self-reflection, sharing an experience, enhancing understanding of reading, or providing entertainment" (p. 12).

In addition to traditional academic genres, such as the thesis-driven essay, teachers can provide an introduction to additional genres and print and digital mentor texts, incorporating a variety of text features, including multimodality. For instance, there are a variety of multimedia pieces available on the *New York Times Multimedia* website and, for younger audiences, sites like *Wonderopolis*. Students could review these sites and, in turn, create their own multimedia pieces, as students have done by modeling their own inquiry projects on models from *Wonderopolis* (Coiro, Castek, & Quinn, 2016). It is in this spirit that Mr. Working discusses with his students the idea that work they put out on the web should be appropriate for an audience of the 3Ps: your parent, our principal, or the president. He reminds students, for instance, that "if the president reads your tweets, and this is the only perception he has of our school, how is he going to view our school?" The same could be said for blog posts, images, videos, or other pieces of digital writing.

As teachers consider a variety of audiences and genres for their students to explore, Fleischer and Andrews-Vaughn's (2009) "unfamiliar genre" project is one way to get students to understand the conventions of genres that they may not have experienced yet as readers or writers. Additionally, Gardner's book *Designing Writing Assignments* (2008) is an excellent resource, especially chapter 4, "Defining New Tasks for Standard Writing Activities," which includes lists of ideas for alternative audiences, time frames, research sources, genres, and positions for writers to take (moreover, the entire book is available as a free PDF download from Writing Across the Curriculum Clearinghouse at Colorado State University).

By engaging students in a variety of writing activities—and encouraging them to explore the nuances that different audiences, purposes, and genres will provide—teachers will help their students become more confident and capable in a variety of writing contexts.

Best Practice 3: Support Writers' Growth through Social Engagement

The third and final point that echoes throughout each of the reports centers on the use of writing as a communicative act. Building on the first two practices—transparency and variety—the third practice demonstrates how important it is that we view writing in a social context. As Karen Bromley stated in her version of this chapter from the fifth edition of this book:

> Writing is a complex interaction of cognitive and physical factors. It is a way to explore thinking and create new knowledge. Writing involves the hand, eye, and both sides of the brain as one makes connections and constructs meaning. It requires knowing the conventions of grammar, spelling, punctuation, and form. It involves small-muscle development and eye–hand coordination to form letters, words, and paragraphs with a pen, pencil, or on a keyboard. It requires having a vocabulary that permits effective self-expression and communication. Writing can be a personal process done solely for oneself or a social process done for and with others. (Bromley, 2014, pp. 289–290)

Or, to draw directly from the fourth recommendation in the report about effective elementary writing instruction, and connect to the themes of this entire volume: "Teachers should establish a supportive environment in their classroom to foster a community of writers who are motivated to write well" (Graham et al., 2012, p. 34). In short, relationships matter in writing classrooms.

PUTTING BEST PRACTICES INTO ACTION

Returning to the four teachers that we met earlier in the chapter will provide us with opportunities to see how they build on established principles and practices of writing instruction in today's contemporary classroom.

When we consider best practices in the teaching of writing today, we cannot do so without a robust discussion of digital literacy and technology. Again, in the fifth edition of this collection Bromley (2014) noted many ways in which technology could enhance student writing and provide opportunities for publication by producing "key pal" exchanges, creating digital stories, using presentation and publication software, and creating wikis. However, in the manner that they are described, these tasks are positioned almost as "add-ons," something to be completed once the real work of writing is done.

If it is not yet clear, my argument in this chapter is that we must approach the union of writing and technology from a slightly different angle. They are, as the four teachers highlighted in this chapter demonstrate, intricately interwoven and unable to be separated. I say this for both practical and theoretical reasons. From the practical standpoint, one–to–one and bring your own device programs are becoming the norm in K–12 schools, even in schools that are less affluent. Technologies such as Google Docs allow for instant collaboration and cloud-based sharing, providing opportunities for teacher response without a great deal of technological hassle. Students are, through their own means or through their formal education, publishing more and more on social media including blog posts, tweets, YouTube videos, podcasts, and other multimedia productions.

What it means to teach writing, then, through a "best practice" lens has changed, even over the past 5 to 10 years. Though I would not want to see my own children—or any child—progress through life having never picked up a pencil or having written in a notebook, we cannot rely on old models of writing instruction, alone, to propel our writers in the 21st century. Instead, we need to adopt a hybrid approach, one that honors what we know about the successful teaching of writing while at the same time integrating technology in critical, creative, and expressive ways.

REFLECTIONS AND FUTURE DIRECTIONS

As noted throughout this chapter, best practices in writing have been known and made evident for decades. In short, we must explicitly model the writing process; explore various audience, purposes, and genres; and invite students to engage in peer, small-group, and whole-class activities related to writing (transparency, variety, engagement). In this sense, the teaching of writing has remained relatively unchanged from the late 1970s or early 1980s until now. We know what the evidence-based best practices are, empirically and experientially, and we know that it is still a struggle to implement them in all classrooms.

In other ways, however, the teaching of writing is drastically different than it has ever been before. As the teachers I've introduced in this chapter demonstrate, in addition to teaching our students how to compose words, sentences, and paragraphs, we are now inviting them to select fonts and colors, identify appropriate images, and where to include hyperlinks. They must also consider other forms of digital writing including video-based compositions and website development. Maps. timelines. emojis. hashtags—all are now a part of the toolset that writers need to be successful in the classroom and beyond.

Considering the evidence explored in this chapter—both empirical evidence from statistical meta-analyses and explorations in the lived lives of teachers—Table 13.1 on p. 305 reiterates the claims about the types of writing (and digital writing) activities that help teachers demonstrate the writing process in a transparent manner, introduce students to a variety of audiences and purposes for writing, and support their growth through social engagement. We must layer in these emerging best practices in teaching digital writing with what we already know to be useful and true for all writing. At the core, transparency, variety, and engagement in our teaching will support the writers in our classrooms. Our challenge now is to reconsider the many ways in which digital writing tools can be layered into these best practices, both in the current moment and as we prepare them for their future academic, professional, and civic lives.

ENGAGEMENT ACTIVITIES

Writing technologies that once included (stone) tablets and static images representing ideas (like hieroglyphics) have come full circle as we now compose on iPads, Surfaces, and Galaxies, and ith still images and video, drawing tools and emojis. However, we cannot underestimate the skill that it takes to engage in the complex task of forming sounds into words, words into sentences, and sentences into coherent paragraphs that connect one idea to the next. Both aspects of writing instruction are important; both must be attended to with urgency and diligence.

Much has been written about best practices related to writing instruction over the past 30 years, and we still have a great deal to learn. Recognizing the complexity of each and every classroom—and the teachers and students who occupy those classrooms—I offer the following activities as potential opportunities to engage students in substantive writing. They are, of necessity, mere snapshots, described in surface-level detail. Still, my hope is that they inspire you to (re)consider the ways in which you are teaching writing now, and the ways that small tweaks to your practice could have significant effects on your students.

1. **Exploring Different Leads.** Beginning with a mini-lesson on effective leads, the teacher has provided her students with three mentor texts from picture books that they have already read. One begins with a quote, one uses onomatopoeia, and the third begins with a surprising detail about one of the characters in the story. Since students have been working on their own narratives for about a week, she invites them to go back into their writers' notebooks, to reread their own stories, and to develop three different leads for their work, considering how readers might react to each one. Then, they can share these leads with two partners and get feedback.

   To extend the opportunity into digital writing, she invites students who are interested to explore another mentor text, an article from the website *Wonderopolis,* and to think about how they could structure their own opening sentences in conjunction with a photograph. Once they have their three leads written, students are welcome to post these leads in their classroom writing community on their blog, or to email the leads to their parents, for peer or outside feedback.

2. **Developing Sentence Variety with Sentence Combining.** Knowing that his students were struggling to write compound and complex sentences, the teacher plans a mini-lesson on sentence combining, focusing specifically on conjunctions. He describes how writers can take sentence segments apart and then put them back together like a puzzle by, quite literally, using laminated cards with the words from a few short sentences upon them and moving them around. He then asks for student volunteers to do the same and, finally, has them find three short sentences in their own writing that they can transcribe onto notecards and then rearrange in different formations on their desks. Then, they take a new version of their compound/complex sentence and write it in their notebook for use in their final draft.

   Exploring a similar approach with a digital writing tool, the teacher also offers students the opportunity to use Padlet. Similar to a corkboard or a wall with sticky notes, Padlet allows students to type individual words, short phrases, or entire sentences on "pads," and then move the pads around on screen. Pads can be copied, and the students can develop multiple combinations showing different kinds of sentence variety. Taking a screenshot of the

Padlet wall, the student can save the final version of the sentence and put it in his or her Google Doc so he or she can type it in there.

3. **Publishing and Celebrating Work.** From opportunities to read aloud during individual conferences to sharing in a small-group or during a whole-class author celebration, the teacher provides

TABLE 13.1. Implications of Evidence-Based Best Practices for Contemporary Writing Classrooms

Evidence-Based Best Practice	Implications for Contemporary Writing Classrooms
Strategic, transparent instruction	• Continue to emphasize specific writing strategies (such as planning, organizing, drafting, revising, and editing) through mini-lessons and conferring, with adequate classroom time for writers to practice their craft. • Make thinking about the writing process visible through the use of anchor charts, think-alouds, and video recordings of classroom instruction, as well as screencast recordings. • Model the composing process using a variety of writing technologies, including digital writing tools such as word processors, blogs, wikis, and other online communities for sharing and responding to writing.
Variety of audiences, purposes, and genres	• In addition to traditional academic genres, such as the thesis-driven essay, provide opportunities to write for a variety of purpose—as well as in numerous genres—for external audiences. • Explore print and digital mentor texts, incorporating a variety of text features (e.g., headings, captions, footnotes) including multimodal features (e.g., hyperlinks, images, video, interactive elements). • Invite outside audiences such as students of the same age, students of different ages, and interested adults to review and respond to student writing.
Social engagement	• Create blocks of time, physical spaces, and routines for Writing Workshop, inviting students to participate in both face-to-face conversation and response using digital tools. • Integrate opportunities for engagement with formative assessment, helping students identify criteria by which they can provide specific feedback to their peers and reflect through self-assessment. • Celebrate and publish student work in a variety of formats, both in print and online (e.g., class books, blogs, podcasts, author's chair)

her students with many opportunities for celebrating their work with classmates, peers, parents, and other interested audiences. Every Friday, writers know that they can sign up for "open mic" time at the end of the language arts block. At the end of each trimester, the teacher works with a selected group of students on the editing team, and they prepare a book of the class's favorite pieces from the previous 12 weeks.

With digital writing, the opportunities for publication and acclaim multiply. A student video production team records their performances (with appropriate student and parent permission). These short clips are uploaded to the class blog, where they are automatically compiled into a weekly e-newsletter. Additionally, the web-editing team prepares social media posts, set to publish automatically throughout the next week, highlighting individual writers.

In each of these three examples—exploring leads, combining sentences, and publishing student work—the work *could* be done without technology (and, arguably, *has* been done successfully without technology by thousands of teachers over decades). Yet, with technology, the processes of writing can become more transparent, varied, and engaging for teachers and students. What once remained within the four walls of the classroom or displayed on the refrigerator at home has now become a part of a sustained, immersive conversation among writers. Moving writers with new opportunities, new audiences, and new technologies, teachers in contemporary classrooms are building on a foundation of best practices while embracing the opportunities that digital writing tools can afford these emerging authors.

REFERENCES

Applebee, A. N., & Langer, J. A. (2013). *Writing instruction that works: Proven methods for middle and high school classrooms.* New York: Teachers College Press.

Atwell, N. (1998). *In the middle: New understandings about writing, reading, and learning* (2nd ed.). Portsmouth, NH: Boynton/Cook.

Atwell, N. (2002). *Lessons that change writers.* Portsmouth, NH: Firsthand/Heinemann.

Bass, W. L., & Sibberson, F. (2015). *Digital reading: What's essential in grades 3–8.* Urbana, IL: National Council of Teachers of English.

Bromley, K. (2014). Best practices in teaching writing. In L. B. Gambrell & L. M. Morrow (Eds.), *Best practices in literacy instruction* (5th ed., pp. 288–314). New York: Guilford Press.

Calkins, L. (1994). *The art of teaching writing* (2nd ed.). Portsmouth, NH: Heinemann.

Calkins, L., Hartman, A., & White, Z. R. (2005). *One to one: The art of conferring with young writers.* Portsmouth, NH: Heinemann.

Coiro, J., Castek, J., & Quinn, D. J. (2016). Personal inquiry and online research. *The Reading Teacher, 69*(5), 483–492.

Fleischer, C., & Andrew-Vaughan, S. (2009). *Writing outside your comfort zone: Helping students navigate unfamiliar genres.* Portsmouth, NH: Heinemann.

Fletcher, R. J. (1992). *What a writer needs.* Portsmouth, NH: Heinemann.

Fletcher, R. (2011). *Mentor author, mentor texts: Short texts, craft notes, and practical classroom uses.* Portsmouth, NH: Heinemann.

Fletcher, R., & Portalupi, J. (2001). *Writing Workshop: The essential guide.* Portsmouth, NH: Heinemann.

Flipped Learning Network. (2014, March 12). Definition of flipped learning. Retrieved September 22, 2017, from *https://flippedlearning.org/definition-of-flipped-learning.*

Gardner, T. (2008). *Designing writing assignments.* Urbana, IL: National Council of Teachers of English. Retrieved from *https://wac.colostate.edu/books/gardner.*

Graham, S., Bollinger, A., Booth Olson, C., D'Aoust, C., MacArthur, C., McCutchen, D., & Olinghouse, N. G. (2012, June). *Teaching elementary school students to be effective writers: A practice guide* (NCEE 2012-4058). Washington, DC: National Center for Education Evaluation and Regional Assistance, Institute of Education Sciences, U.S. Department of Education. Retrieved from *http://ies.ed.gov/ncee/ wwc/PracticeGuide/17.*

Graham, S., Fitzgerald, J., Friedrich, L., Greene, K., Kim, J. S., & Booth Olson, C. (2016, November). *Teaching secondary students to write effectively* (NCEE 2017-4002). Washington, DC: National Center for Education Evaluation and Regional Assistance, Institute of Education Sciences, U.S. Department of Education. Retrieved from *https://ies.ed.gov/ncee/wwc/PracticeGuide/22.*

Graham, S., MacArthur, C. A., & Fitzgerald, J. (Eds.). (2013). *Best practices in writing instruction, second edition.* New York: Guilford Press.

Graham, S., & Perin, D. (2007). *Writing next: Effective strategies to improve writing of adolescents in middle and high schools.* New York: Carnegie Corporation of New York. Retrieved from *www.carnegie.org/publications/writing-next-effective-strategies-to-improve-writing-of-adolescents-in-middle-and-high-schools.*

Graves, D. H. (1983). *Writing: Teachers and children at work.* Exeter, NH: Heinemann Educational Books.

Graves, D. H. (1994). Conditions for effective writing. In *A fresh look at writing* (pp. 103–114). Portsmouth, NH: Heinemann.

Hicks, T. (2009). *The digital writing workshop.* Portsmouth, NH: Heinemann.

Hicks, T. (2013). *Crafting digital writing: Composing texts across media and genres.* Portsmouth, NH: Heinemann.

Hillocks, G. (1986). *Research on written composition: New directions for teaching.* Urbana, IL: National Conference on Research in English.

Hillocks, G. (2002). *The testing trap: How state writing assessments control learning.* New York: Teachers College Press.

Kist, W. (2012). Middle schools and new literacies: Looking back and moving forward. *Voices from the Middle, 19*(4), 17–21.

Kozol, J. (1992). *Savage inequalities: Children in America's schools.* New York: Harper-Perennial.

Kozol, J. (2005). *The shame of the nation: The restoration of apartheid schooling in America*. New York: Crown.

Lagemann, E. C. (2002). *An elusive science: The troubling history of education research*. Chicago: University of Chicago Press.

Muhtaris, K., & Ziemke, K. (2015). *Amplify: Digital teaching and learning in the K–6 classroom*. Portsmouth, NH: Heinemann Educational Books.

National Assessment of Educational Progress. (2017, December 18). Scheduled NAEP writing assessments, past results, trends, methods. Retrieved December 30, 2013, from *http://nces.ed.gov/nationsreportcard/writing*.

National Center for Education Statistics. (n.d.). NCES fast facts: Computer and Internet use. Retrieved October 1, 2017, from *https://nces.ed.gov/FastFacts/display.asp?id=46*.

National Council of Teachers of English. (2016, February 28). Professional knowledge for the teaching of writing. Retrieved May 21, 2018, from *www2.ncte.org/statement/teaching-writing*.

O'Toole, G. (2012, January 24). The future has arrived—It's just not evenly distributed yet. Retrieved September 22, 2017, from *https://quoteinvestigator.com/2012/01/24/future-has-arrived*.

Pew Research Center. (2018). *Internet/broadband fact sheet*. Retrieved from *www.pewinternet.org/fact-sheet/internet-broadband*.

Ray, K. W. (1999). *Wondrous words: Writers and writing in the elementary classroom*. Urbana, IL: National Council of Teachers of English.

Ray, K. W. (2006). *Study driven: A framework for planning units of study in the writing workshop*. Portsmouth, NH: Heinemann.

Ray, K. W. (2010). *In pictures and in words: Teaching the qualities of good writing through illustration study*. Portsmouth, NH: Heinemann.

Ray, K. W., & Laminack, L. L. (2001). *The Writing Workshop: Working through the hard parts*. Urbana, IL: National Council of Teachers of English.

Rouse, M. (n.d.). What is Google Docs? Definition from WhatIs.com. Retrieved October 1, 2017, from *http://whatis.techtarget.com/definition/Google-Docs*.

Sibberson, F. (2012). *The joy of planning: Designing minilesson cycles in grades 3–6*. Portland, ME: Choice Literacy.

Sibberson, F., & Szymusiak, K. (2016). *Still learning to read: Teaching students in grades 3–6*. Portland, ME: Stenhouse.

Smagorinsky, P. (2005). *Research on composition: Multiple perspectives on two decades of change*. New York: Teachers College Press.

Troia, G. A., & Olinghouse, N. G. (2013). The Common Core State Standards and evidence-based educational practices: The case of writing. *School Psychology Review, 42*(3), 343–357.

What Works Clearinghouse. (2014, March). Procedures and standards handbook, version 3.0. Institute of Education Sciences. Retrieved from *https://ies.ed.gov/ncee/wwc/handbooks*.

Whitney, A. E. (2011). In search of the authentic English classroom: Facing the schoolishness of school. *English Education, 44*(1), 51–62.

Zemelman, S., Daniels, H., & Hyde, A. (2012). *Best practice: Bringing standards to life in America's classrooms* (4th ed.). Portsmouth, NH: Heinemann.

CHAPTER 14

Best Practices in Reading Assessment

PETER AFFLERBACH
BYEONG-YOUNG CHO
MARIA ELLIKER CRASSAS
JONG-YUN KIM

This chapter will:

- Describe the current state of literacy assessment.
- Examine characteristics of effective literacy assessment.
- Suggest means for implementing and sustaining best practices in literacy assessment with the advent of standards initiatives.
- Provide examples of best practices with literacy assessment.

This chapter focuses on classroom-based reading assessments that have positive influence on the teaching and learning of reading. We consider best practices in reading assessment in relation to the contexts in which teaching and learning happen, and where assessment is proposed, mandated, developed, conducted, interpreted, and used. In many states and school districts, there is a hyperfocus on high-stakes summative testing. This may result in lack of attention to classroom-based reading assessment. The most pressing challenges to best practice in classroom assessment of reading include the following:

- assessing both reading processes and reading products
- assessing reading skills and strategies and the assessment of how students use what they understood from reading

- assessing reading from multiple sources including the Internet/ hypertext
- assessing the cognitive, affective, and conative factors that influence students' reading development
- using both formative assessment and summative assessment in a productive and complementary manner
- assuring that reading assessment contributes to students' developing ability to self-assess
- providing professional development opportunities that help teachers develop expertise in reading assessment.

When we are able to work with assessment to serve all of the above purposes, we have faith that assessment supports the classroom community and that the needs of teachers and students are met. Moreover, these best practices in reading assessment promote dynamic interactions between teachers and students and between students themselves. Best practices in reading assessment are grounded in the knowledge and insight provided by research. This chapter offers an account of effective reading assessments that reflects our most current, evidence-based understandings of reading and of assessment.

EVIDENCE-BASED BEST PRACTICES
IN READING ASSESSMENT

In theory, the means to meet reading assessment challenges is readily available, and it emanates from our knowledge about reading (National Assessment Governing Board, 2012; Snow, 2002; Stanovich, 1986) and effective reading assessment (Darling-Hammond, 2010; Morsy, Kieffer, & Snow, 2010). All assessment must have a connection to the phenomena it would measure. Fortunately, we have substantial evidence-based conceptualizations of reading and its development. The strategies and skills that must develop for students to grow into accomplished readers are well researched (Pressley & Afflerbach, 1995), in traditional print and in more recent Internet/hypertext settings (Cho, 2013; Rouet, 2006). In addition, research demonstrates that accomplished student readers use prior knowledge (Kintsch, 1998), inferential reasoning (Graesser, Mills, & Zwaan, 1997), and evaluative mindsets (Wiley et al., 2009) as they read. Research also provides details about how motivation and engagement (Guthrie, Wigfield, & You, 2012), self-efficacy (Schunk & Bursuck, 2016), metacognition (Veenman, 2016), and epistemic beliefs (Braten, Britt, Stromso, & Rouet, 2011) influence students' reading and reading development. Ongoing research and the refinement of theoretical models of reading greatly enhance our understanding of what student readers need to succeed, and they should inform the instruction and assessment that we use to foster student readers' growth.

Concurrent with the evolution of our understanding of reading development is our knowledge about effective reading assessment. Many forms of reading assessment, informed by research in educational measurement, have the potential to positively influence instruction and learning. The careful examination of what we will assess in reading places us in a position to create assessment materials and procedures that are sensitive to the nature of students' development (Pellegrino, Chudowsky, & Glaser, 2001). Our ability to give full accounting of the construct of reading, combined with our knowledge about assessment and psychometrics, contribute to our confidence in the assessments we design and use. In turn, this ability and this knowledge give us confidence in the inferences about student accomplishment that we make from assessment results. Designing assessments in accordance with our collected wisdom about the reading construct, and combining this with our best understanding of effective assessment, allows for accurate and useful inferences from reading assessment information.

Consider an example of how this process should work. We know from research that successful, developing readers must decode printed text, often relying on phonics early in their reading careers. Part of decoding involves learning to identify pairs of consonants, in isolation and as they appear in words, and knowing the unique sounds that these consonant blends make. Allowing for dialect variations, we know that the *ch-* consonant blend makes predictable sounds and we can use assessments that allow us to measure students' ability to recognize *ch-* in print, to determine its sound counterparts, and to correctly pronounce, or "say," the *ch-* blend.

We can listen to our students as they pronounce the *ch-* blend in words and in isolation. We can listen to their story reading when the text contains words with the *ch-* blend. We can examine their invented spelling to see how it approximates the *ch-* sound. We can use a published phonics assessment. Because we are careful with our understanding of the *ch-* blend and how we assess students' ability to produce the sounds, we can make accurate inferences about their developing ability to do so. From students' performance on these assessments we infer their phonics skills and decoding strategies. With confidence in our conceptualization of phonics and in the materials and procedures we use to assess phonics, we are afforded confidence in the inferences we draw from assessment results. We can use the results of our assessment in a formative manner, to immediately shape our understanding of the developing reader and subsequent instruction. We can also use the results in a summative manner, as they provide evidence that the student has (or has not) met a key learning goal. Finally, we note that this process works for any and all student reading outcomes—ranging from learning sound–symbol correspondences to synthesizing and critiquing information from multiple texts.

While research and theory provide us with a broad understanding of reading, reading assessments tend to be narrowly focused. We must strive to develop assessments that describe the complexity of student reading growth. Davis (1998) reminds us that assessment is always a sample and approximation of the thing we want to describe. Moreover, Davis notes that many of our assessments are "thin." Reading assessment yields results that describe but a portion of reading, and this should temper the inferences we make about students' growth and learning. For example, performance assessments are developed to help us understand students' increasingly complex strategy use and higher-order thinking in relation to standards initiatives. Yet, these assessments are often silent about students' motivations, or self-efficacy, factors that clearly influence students' reading, strategy use, higher-order thinking, and reading achievement.

While our theoretical and practical knowledge of reading and reading assessment is rich, the realization of useful reading assessment is often impoverished. Many states, school districts, and schools use assessment programs formed by tradition and habit, rather than informed by current understanding of reading and assessment. For example, while there have been considerable advances in our understanding of reading and reading assessment, students' adequate yearly progress is measured by tests that look much like those used 50 years ago. The use of single test scores to judge students' reading achievement and teachers' accountability often skews schools' reading assessment agenda and funding. While major professional organizations advise against using a single text score to make consequential decisions about students (American Educational Research Association/American Psychological Association/National Council on Measurement in Education, 1999), much school capital is invested in testing. Purchasing, training, practicing, administering, scoring, and teaching related to high-stakes tests each reduce the already limited school resources that might be more wisely used.

BEST PRACTICES IN READING ASSESSMENT IN ACTION

Effective reading assessment is based on the detailed understanding of reading and of assessment. Reading assessment should produce information that is useful to different audiences for their different purposes, especially teachers and students. Classrooms are the obvious venue for realizing the promise of effective reading assessment. However, in spite of the considerable growth in our understanding of how to develop and use classroom-based reading assessments (Calfee & Hiebert, 1996), implementation is generally slow.

Effective reading assessment is that which informs important educational decisions. A first concern for classroom teachers is collecting and using reading assessment information to shape instruction and learning. Consider the students who populate our classrooms. In a classroom of 25 or 30 students, we expect that each will vary in terms of his or her reading strategies and skills, prior knowledge for texts, motivation, and self-esteem as readers. They will vary in the attributions they make for their reading success or failure and they will vary in terms of their agency, or the degree to which they feel they are in control of the reading they do. These individual differences contribute to varied performances and achievement in reading. We need assessments that describe student readers' characteristics in diverse classrooms, characteristics that can influence their reading achievement. Understanding these student characteristics is a key to effective instruction, and careful classroom-based assessment informs teachers and serves as a basis for this instruction. Assessment done during reading lessons and on a daily basis, over marking periods, and across the school year, *is* high-stakes assessment, for without it there is not progress toward reaching daily, weekly, and annual reading goals.

Reading assessment is most useful when it provides teachers with detailed and up-to-date information about their students' reading development. The zone of proximal development (Vygotsky, 1978) is the space in which students learn new things in relation to their existing knowledge and competencies, and in relation to teachers' instruction and support. Thus, teacher accountability is closely tied to the ability to identify students' zones of proximal development, and then teach in these zones. Here, the centrality of classroom-based assessment is evident. We need formative classroom-based assessments that help us identify teachable moments for each student, that give us the detail we need to effectively teach to students' needs, and that describe the important outcomes of effective reading instruction. A robust classroom assessment program continually provides detailed information about students' current competencies and next steps: It informs our ongoing work in the zone of proximal development.

EXAMINING BEST PRACTICES IN READING ASSESSMENT

In this section, we describe reading assessment materials and processes that represent best practices in classroom-based reading assessment. We provide an overview of particular forms and foci of assessment, explain why they are necessary in a comprehensive assessment program, and describe the means to implementing them. These assessments include reading inventories and miscue analysis, performance assessments, teacher questioning, observations and surveys of student growth, and checklists.

Reading Assessments That Focus on Reading Processes and Products

All assessment involves making inferences about students' growth and achievement. We reason about the extent of students' reading development using our assessment of the processes and products of their reading. Process assessments focus on students' strategies, skills, and task performances as they are being used. In contrast, product assessments focus on what students produce as a result of reading. Much attention is given to product assessments, especially tests, often at the expense of process assessment. This creates an untenable situation. Consider that one result of the ambitious efforts to create world-class reading standards is that students must read increasingly challenging texts, and perform increasingly complex tasks. Many standards initiatives are linked to performance assessments that tell us if a student has met a particular standard. However, teachers and students need detailed assessments that describe the nature of student achievement on the path to meeting these standards. We have elaborate assessments related to the end goal, or product. However, we often are lacking comprehensive and integrated assessment coverage of the processes that student readers must learn and use on their way to meeting the goal. Attainment of complex standards is less certain when teachers and students do not have valid assessment information that describes their daily progress toward the teaching and learning goals.

Reading processes are those strategies and skills that readers use when they decode words, determine vocabulary meaning, read fluently, and comprehend (Afflerbach, Pearson, & Paris, 2008). Process-oriented reading assessment focuses on the strategies and skills that students use to construct meaning from text. Such assessment allows teachers to assess in the midst of students' reading. For example, as we listen to the student applying phonics knowledge to sound out the *ch-* consonant blend, we are in the midst of the student using decoding processes. When we observe a student rereading a sentence to clarify its meaning, we are in the midst of a metacognitive process. When a student critiques a lack of evidence to support the author's claim, we are witnessing evaluative, higher-order thinking processes. Our process assessment helps us determine the strategies and skills that work or do not work as the student constructs meaning. Moreover, assessment of reading processes takes place as students actually read, providing insights into how reading strategies and skills work together.

In contrast, product-oriented reading assessment gives an after-the-fact account of student reading achievement. We have to work backward to imagine what processes contributed to the product. Typical reading product assessments are quizzes, tests, and after-reading questions related to students' comprehension of text. Of course, the information provided by product assessments can help us determine students' achievement in relation to important reading goals, such as content-area learning and meeting standards. Moreover, when we examine test scores, we can make inferences about students' achievement in relation to lesson and unit goals and curriculum standards, but, unfortunately, we are limited to making backward inferences about what worked (or didn't work) as the student read, and as we earlier taught. If we are interested in making inferences about how our instruction contributed (or didn't contribute) to the students' achievement, a similar series of backward inferences is necessary. This is an important fact about product assessments: They are relatively limited in their ability to provide detail on what students can and can't do as they read. An apt analogy is one in which we try to determine why a soccer team won or lost a game by examining the final score. Certainly, the final score is important, but it tells us nothing about the means by which it was achieved. There may be very little for us to go on if we are interested in gaining useful information from the assessment about how to do better—as teachers, and as student readers.

In contrast, classroom-based assessment of reading processes can provide us with detailed information on how students process text and construct meaning in real time. Here, our inferences are based on our assessment of the processes themselves. A prime example of assessment that focuses on readers' processes is miscue analyses (Clay, 1993; Goodman & Goodman, 1977), in which the teacher focuses on a student's oral reading behaviors. Assessment here is "online" or in real time, and we get information about students' reading processes as they actually read. Accordingly, miscue analysis can illustrate how students decode print, engage prior knowledge, read fluently, construct meaning, and monitor the meaning-making process. It can inform the teacher about student strengths or weaknesses in sound–symbol correspondences, or in literal and inferential comprehension. The inferences we make about students' strengths and needs come from the actual account of reading processes. With oral reading data, we may observe that a student is not consistently monitoring comprehension, as the student continues to read even when he or she is making meaning-changing miscues. We are able to pinpoint the problem, and we may be able to provide instruction to address a detailed, precise need based on our process-oriented reading assessment information.

Assessing Reading Skills and Strategies and How Students Use What They Understood from Reading

Students must comprehend the texts they read and they must also be able to use the information they gain from reading to perform reading-related tasks. In the early grades, a considerable portion of assessment dwells on students' development of the mechanics of reading. This is followed by reading assessment that focuses on the reader's comprehension of text. We can assess students' ability to determine or construct main ideas and we can ask students to locate or identify details in texts. When we ask students to summarize a text, we are continuing a focus on constructing meaning. Each of these assessments focuses on comprehension as the final goal of reading. We must remember that reading to answer comprehension questions, while common school practice, is rarely encountered in the reading done outside of school. Thus, reading assessment should also focus on how students use the meaning they construct from text in reading-related tasks. When students read guidelines for conducting hands-on experiments to help guide their science inquiry, or they read Native American narratives on the influence of colonization so that they can create a dramatic presentation, their reading involves these two significant goals: to comprehend text and to use what is comprehended in a related task or performance. Of course, such reading is the norm outside of the classroom. So it should be in classrooms, too.

Performance assessment features in the high-stakes assessments associated with the standards initiatives and related assessment consortia (Smarter Balanced Assessment Consortium, 2012; Partnership for Assessment of Readiness for College and Careers, 2013) and focuses on the things we expect students to do with the knowledge they gain from reading (Baxter & Glaser, 1998). For example, fifth-grade students read instructions and guidelines for conducting a hands-on science experiment. Of course, we focus on their comprehension, but we are also very interested in their application of what they have learned (or comprehended) in the conducting of the science experiment. This includes the correct sequencing of steps in scientific inquiry, identification of laboratory tools, and following experiment safety procedures. The performance assessment accommodates our need to measure and describe the link between comprehension of text and how students use what they comprehend. Performance assessment has the added attraction of using rubrics that help students conceptualize suitable levels of performance at a specific task: rubrics provide students with a blueprint of what they must do to achieve a superior score, and the performance assessment illustrates for students what is needed. The rubric also provides the means for students to check their progress toward reaching a particular performance level, and to practice self-assessment. Performance assessments and their related rubrics can help students continue to learn how to do assessment for themselves.

Assessing Reading and Higher-Order Thinking

Many reading comprehension assessments focusing on student understanding of a text use multiple-choice items. After students read a given text, they choose the best answer from among alternatives, with questions focusing on identifying the main idea, remembering details, and inferring vocabulary and sentence meaning. These tests often fail to tap into students' higher-order thinking skills and strategies in reading, which include analysis and synthesis, application, and evaluation. This is unfortunate, as students must be able to read complex texts closely by analyzing the language and structure contributing to the meanings in text, integrating the ideas and thoughts from the text, and interrogating the usefulness of the text based on the readers' goals.

The need to create assessments capable of describing students' higher-order strategies and skills in reading is clear. Bloom's (1956) taxonomy (Anderson & Krathwohl, 2001) proposes that establishing a literal understanding of text involves basic comprehension, while related cognitive processes of applying, analyzing, synthesizing, and evaluating represent higher-order thinking in reading. We offer two examples of reading assessment that can provide information about students' higher-level thinking: students' generating critical questions about their reading, and students composing integrative essays when learning from multiple source texts.

In order to create critical questions, a student must identify or construct main ideas in text, determine the author's intention, and use the meaning constructed to formulate questions. Consider students who are asked to generate a critical question about a text that focuses on global warming, climate change, and the means of addressing both. Before engaging in this task, students must first identify the main idea: carbon dioxide levels and average temperatures continue to rise globally. They also must understand the author's intention: to convince readers to take action to combat global warming. Having met these reader goals, students can then ask informed critical questions, such as how persuasive the author was or what sources the author used to make his or her argument. Based on the students' critical questions, teachers can assess the extent to which a student has understood the text, and how this understanding is used by the student to create a meaningful question. Second, writing an integrative essay based on the reading of multiple texts helps us understand a student's comprehension of each text and his or her ability to combine information from across texts into a coherent whole (Wolfe & Goldman, 2005). In this task, a well-developed assessment rubric serves two roles: it is a scaffolded guide for students' higher-order thinking, and it provides scoring guidelines for a classroom teacher to assess students' work. We note that our second example involves writing in a major role, and that writing ability may be confounded with reading ability. Such is literacy use outside of the classroom. Determining the relative contribution of reading and writing to student's performance is challenging.

Assessing Reading from Multiple Sources Including the Internet/Hypertext

Students are expected to think, read, write, and communicate responsively while exploring and comprehending diverse sources of information in digital media (Alvermann, 2002; Leu, Kinzer, Coiro, Castek, & Henry, 2013). Because the Internet is the locus of increasingly larger numbers of public, social, and interactive media, reading the Internet includes core competencies of navigating, evaluating, and using multiple texts and sources that students locate on the Internet (Goldman & Scardamalia, 2013). As recent curricular reforms emphasize, Internet reading competence not only plays a foundational role in information gathering, knowledge building, and academic learning in diverse school subjects, but such competence allows students to become civic participants in public discourse that relates to sometimes contentious social issues (National Council for the Social Studies, 2013).

Describing what students know and can do with Internet-related literacies is a priority for assessment, both nationally and internationally (e.g., National Assessment of Educational Progress [NAEP], Programme for International Student Assessment [PISA], Progress in International Reading Literacy Survey [PIRLS], two Common Core assessment consortia). Following is a description of the assessment of student performance in an online inquiry task, using both formative and summative approaches. In the related unit, students learn the strategies and attitudes required for productive online inquiry learning. In this example, the goals of student learning are informed by a seventh-grade standard:

> Conduct short research projects to answer a question, drawing on several sources and generating additional related, focused questions for further research and investigation (CCSS.ELA-LITERACY.W.7.7).

To reach this standard, students must be adept at online inquiry, and understand what makes online text environments unique, when compared with print-based situations. The Internet affords readers' text choices, access to authentic materials, and exploration of multiple sources. However, the Internet can present student readers with fragmented information, untrustworthy sources, and a maze-like information space. With this contextual understanding, we can deconstruct the above standard to anticipate what student readers must do to attain it. Students must:

- Conduct short research for a given question (e.g., by planning the information search, by generating keywords and search terms).
- Identify and use several source texts (e.g., identifying sources that represent different perspectives, arguments, and facts; evaluating the source's reliability; judging the usefulness of the sources for their reading goals).
- Generate focused questions for further investigation (e.g., evaluating different arguments, narrowing down the key aspect of the issues and problems, identifying the gap between what is known and what needs to be known).

We can frame these requisite abilities with the following description: Students will be able to formulate a relevant written question that provokes subsequent thinking on the given topic. The question should reflect what students learn from online sources, the working knowledge that they construct from reading, and the inquisitiveness that motivates a follow-up inquiry. Students may fail at the initial task of question generation if they are not efficient in generating topic-related search terms, conducting focused online searches, and comprehending and assessing reliable sources of information. Also, if students do not possess sufficient prior knowledge or are incapable of integrating the knowledge to their reading, generating questions will be a challenging task. However, if students are active in monitoring and managing their information location and source evaluation, they will be able to gather relevant knowledge to deepen their thoughts on the topic, and this can complement their relatively sparse prior knowledge.

As described in the standard, the assessment task should have a predetermined inquiry question to invoke the students' online searching. For example, when the students learn about the controversial practice of mountaintop removal (MTR) coal mining, an initial inquiry question can be broad (e.g., What is the environmental impact of MTR?) because later the students can use the initial question to develop the focus for a self-initiated inquiry. The outcome of the specification is the targeted outcome for assessment. A key question is: How can I draw the evidence to support my judgment of student performance?

One example could be creating a checklist to assess the process of student reading in the online inquiry task. The teacher uses the checklist while observing students' online reading, keeping track of student performance, and gathering evidence. Figure 14.1 presents a version for teacher use, modified from one in Cho and Afflerbach (2015).

Another assessment relates to "Generating focused questions for further investigation," where the outcome of student performance is an inquiry question formulated from his or her online inquiry. The rubric is built around multiple criteria for generating a high-quality inquiry question. Table 14.1 provides a sample analytical rubric suited for the task of question generation as the outcome of online inquiry performance, as developed in a previous study on adolescents' critical questioning in an online inquiry task (Cho, Woodward, Li, & Barlow, 2017).

Just as reading the Internet represents a challenging frontier for student readers, developing assessments that describe this reading demands insight and creativity by teachers. The sample rubric and checklist provided here offer one possible approach to assessing a particular aspect of student development related to reading on the Internet.

Assessing Cognitive, Affective, and Conative Reading Outcomes and Reader Characteristics

Current high-stakes assessments, early reading screening instruments, and the majority of classroom reading assessments focus on the strategies and skills that contribute to reading comprehension, an important cognitive achievement. Assessment measures the cognitive development of student readers, but there is little or no attention paid to other factors that support and enhance (or stifle) reading development. Experienced classroom teachers and parents know that reading strategies and skills are essential to students' reading success, but do not guarantee this success. A host of factors influences reading development and reading achievement, including motivation and engagement, self-efficacy (Bandura, 2006), epistemic beliefs, and agency (Afflerbach, Cho, Kim, Crassas, & Doyle, 2013).

Successful readers are engaged readers (Guthrie & Wigfield, 1997; Schiefele, Schaffner, Moller, & Wigfield, 2012). These students are motivated to read, they identify themselves as readers, they persevere in the face of reading challenges, and they consider reading to be an important part of their daily lives. When we think of our teaching successes, do we think of students who earned high test scores? Or do we think of students who went from reluctant readers to enthusiastic readers? Do we think of students who evolved from easily discouraged readers to readers whose motivation helped them persevere through reading challenges? Do we remember students who avoided reading at all costs transforming themselves into students who learned to love reading? Certainly, we can count such students and our positive influence on them among our most

Target skills and mindsets: These are what you want to assess!	Student performance: Keep these questions in mind and at hand during the observation of student reading!	Teacher observation: Check the appropriate box!		
		No evidence	Performed but disconnected	Relevant and consistent
Exploring and selecting reliable web sources	Does the student activate prior knowledge?			
	Does the student refine the research topic into a relevant search term?			
	Does the student seek to find sources to answer the given question?			
	Does the student reject the sources irrelevant to the question?			
Interconnecting and learning from multiple sources	Does the student relate the current source to the previously identified sources?			
	Does the student notice whether the sources support, conflict with, or never relate to each other?			
	Does the student attempt to build a global understanding of the sources read?			
	Does the student notice the need for further searches of facts, claims, or evidence?			
Challenging and evaluating web sources	Does the student perceive who created the source and when and where it was created?			
	Does the student bring the criteria to assess the accuracy and credibility of the sources?			
	Does the student assess whether the reading of the source meaningfully contributes to the reading goals?			
	Does the student assess whether the reading of the source adds new knowledge as compared to the previous ones?			
Monitoring and managing the process of online reading	Does the student select hyperlinks in relevant and coherent manners?			
	Does the student find sources that clearly relate to the inquiry question?			
	Does the student choose a reasonable number of useful sources given the scope of the inquiry focus?			
	Does the student mind whether he or she makes progress toward the goal?			

FIGURE 14.1. Assessment checklist for online inquiry processes.

TABLE 14.1. Scoring Rubric for Students' Question Generation Response

Criterion quality	Relevance	Validity	Significance
Complete	The response is completely relevant to the topic, uses information gained during the research, and presents multiple relevant sources that were used to support the response.	The response integrates question and justification logically into a coherent argumentative perspective, develops claims supported by more than one idea or single fact, and uses information easily identified as credible.	The response reflects important and critical issues related to the topic, promotes critical thinking, and provokes discussion including a wide variety of facts and perspectives, which would result in heightened understanding.
Adequate	The response is adequately relevant to the topic, includes information gained during the research, and presents sources.	The response relates question and justification to a similar argumentative perspective, includes claims using more than a single fact, and uses information mostly identified as reliable.	The response reflects somewhat important or critical issues in relation to the topic, might promote critical thinking, and might provoke discussion including some different facts and perspectives, which would result in increased understanding.
Partial	The response is partially relevant to the topic, alludes to information gained during the research, and may use a source.	The response includes question and justification that fit loosely together and so may not maintain an argumentative perspective, has claims that are not supported well by facts, and may misuse some unreliable and/or biased information.	The response reflects issues in relation to the topic that might not be important and critical, might not promote critical thinking, and is likely to provoke brief discussion at best, which might result in shallow understanding.
Lacking	The response is irrelevant to the topic, is vaguely or not at all related to information or sources found in the search, and thus fails to address any aspect of the topic.	The response includes a question and justification but they do not fit together or are superficial, presents few or no claims supported by facts, and offers no or little evidence that reliable information was used.	The response fails to reflect important or critical issues in relation to the topic, would not promote critical thinking, and would not provoke discussion that would increase understanding.

worthy teaching accomplishments. The lesson here is that successful student readers are not just good strategy-and-skill readers; they are efficacious, motivated, and they believe in their ability to read. Accomplished teachers know the great impact of those factors on student reading and reading development. Thus, our assessments must inform us about how these powerful factors are operating in each student.

If we are serious about accountability, we need assessments that demonstrate that high-quality teaching and effective reading programs influence student readers' growth. This growth can include positive motivation, perseverance in the face of difficulty, appropriate attributions made for reading success and failure, and self-esteem as a reader (Afflerbach, 2016). We need assessments that are capable of measuring and describing student growth that is complementary to reading strategy and skill development. We are fortunate to have such measures. For example, we can conduct surveys and inventories of students' reading motivation (Gambrell, Palmer, Codling, & Mazzoni, 1996), attitudes toward reading (McKenna & Kear, 1990), and reading self-concept (Chapman & Tunmer, 1995). Together, these and related assessments can help us understand and describe growth that is related to the already assessed cognitive development. They move us toward a fuller measure of the accomplishments of students and their teachers.

Using Formative Reading Assessment and Summative Reading Assessment

We are a society enamored with numbers. Schools, school districts, classrooms, states, teachers, and students are evaluated and ranked in relation to annual series of tests, or summative reading assessments. These assessments report important summary information about students' reading strategies and skills. They summarize reading achievement as a grade-level equivalent, a raw score, and a percentile rank. Summative assessment is important as it helps us understand if students reach grade-level benchmarks, unit and lesson goals, and standards in classrooms, districts, and states. However, summative assessment is, by nature, after the fact of teaching and learning. We do not have as rich an opportunity with summative assessment, compared with formative assessment, to inform instruction and to address students' individual needs as they are developing (Mansell, James, & the Assessment Reform Group, 2009).

In spite of this limitation, summative assessment is used to make highly consequential decisions. Accountability, sanction, reward, school success, and school failure are often determined through a process that uses a single summative assessment score. The pressure to focus on such summative assessment takes resources from our formative assessment efforts, the very type of assessment that helps teachers and schools demonstrate accountability on a daily basis. Formative assessment, in contrast, is conducted with the goal of informing our instruction and improving student learning. At the heart of effective reading instruction is the classroom teacher's detailed knowledge of each student. This knowledge is constructed through ongoing formative assessments, conducted across the school day and the school year, like the process-oriented reading assessment discussed earlier in this chapter.

For example, teacher questioning may be tailored so that it provides formative assessment information. The teacher adept at asking questions during instruction understands how well students are "getting" the lesson. The teacher's questions can focus on strategies and skills; cognitive, affective, and conative influences on reading achievement; and content-area learning that are a result of reading. Then, the teacher uses information provided by students' responses to questions to build a detailed sense of how students are progressing toward lesson goals and where to place an ongoing instructional focus. Consider a fifth-grade teacher's questions to her students as they read a chapter in a science textbook:

"What is an ecosystem?"
"On what balances does an ecosystem depend?"
"Can you explain your reasoning?"
"Where do you get the information contained in your explanation?"

Questions like these evoke responses that demonstrate degrees of student understanding. From students' responses, the teacher constructs his or her own understanding of their achievement.

The degree of detail that is provided by formative assessment may help a classroom teacher determine a teachable moment, identify the need for reteaching an important concept or skill related to ecosystems, or move forward to new instruction with confidence that students possess the requisite knowledge to succeed. In an effective assessment program, formative assessment describes students' ongoing reading growth as it occurs, and summative assessment provides summary statements about students' literacy achievement. States and school districts should attend to the linkages between summative assessments and the formative assessments used in the classroom. Successful teachers frequently use formative assessments in their classrooms because they know the importance of understanding students' reading development on a daily basis. Understanding whether students achieve the final goal of a reading assignment is different from understanding whether the students is progressing smoothly toward the final goal.

Using Assessment to Help Students Learn to Do Assessment Themselves

Many students move through school with reading assessment done to them or for them. Students read, take a quiz or test, and hand it in. Their work is evaluated and graded, and then returned to the student. The student earns a score, but gains no understanding of how assessment works. A result is that many students think of assessment as a "black box" (Black & William, 1998). A serious consequence of this approach to reading assessment is that students do not learn to do reading assessment for themselves. Even as we ask questions in class, without our explanation of why we ask these questions or how we arrive at our evaluations of student responses, students will not understand how the evaluation of their reading is made. Across school years there may be lost opportunities for students to learn to conduct reading assessment on their own, and students remain outsiders to the culture of reading assessment.

Our classroom-based assessment should provide students with the means to eventually assume responsibility for assessing their own reading. Accomplished readers regularly assess their ongoing comprehension of text and their progress toward reading-related goals, as they are metacognitive. This ability is not innate: it is learned from models of doing assessment that the students eventually internalize. In fact, a hallmark of the successful reader is the ability to monitor his or her reading and then conduct ongoing assessment of his or her reading progress (Pressley & Afflerbach, 1995; Veenman, 2016; Whitebread et al., 2009).

To foster student independence with assessment, we should provide opportunities in which they learn the value of self-assessment and the means to do accurate and useful assessment for themselves. A good start is modeling simple and straightforward assessment routines, and helping students learn to initiate and successfully complete these routines independently. For example, consider the checklist used by a second-grade teacher. As students read, she regularly asks the students to refer to the checklist and engage in the assessment thinking that it requires. She models using the checklist and expects that her students will learn to use it themselves as they read independently. The checklist includes the following:

_____ I check to see if what I read makes sense.
_____ I remind myself why I am reading.
_____ I focus on the goal of my reading while I read.
_____ I check to see if I can summarize sentences and paragraphs.
_____ If reading gets hard, I ask myself if there are any problems.
_____ I try to identify the problem.

_____ I try to fix the problem.

_____ When the problem is fixed, I get back to my reading making sure I understand what I've read so far.

The teacher also models the use of the checklist by asking related questions of herself when she reads to the students, and thinks aloud about why she asks the questions and her answers to the questions. This predictable presentation of self-assessment routines can help set developing readers on a healthy path to self-assessment.

Checklists can be adjusted to the content and complexity of instructional goals. For example, if we are interested in fostering students' ability to self-assess their critical reading, we may devise a checklist with the following items:

_____ I check the text to see if the author provides evidence to support claims.

_____ I compare the information in the text with what I already know about the topic.

We do not give up our responsibility to conduct classroom-based reading assessments when we promote student self-assessment. Rather, we look for opportunities to use our assessments to help students learn to do assessment themselves. If in all of our teaching related to reading students do not begin to learn how to do self-assessment, they will not become truly independent readers.

Providing Professional Development Opportunities for Teachers to Develop Expertise in Reading Assessment

Successful classroom-based reading assessment demands teacher expertise, and professional development is the means for helping teachers develop that expertise. Specifically, teachers must be supported in developing effective formative assessments. The complex text and task combinations that comprise standards initiatives demand focused, expert assessment as teachers help their students progress toward attainment of standards. Teachers as assessment experts examine what aspect of reading to assess, choose the text and task to best capture it, make inferences about the students' reading from the assessment information, and transform the understanding of students' reading into informative feedback for students to use for self-assessment of their strengths and weaknesses.

Teacher and school accountability are commonly associated with the results of high-stakes testing. We believe that accountability can be demonstrated in other places as well. Unfortunately, in the contest for scarce school resources, tests often win and formative assessment often loses. The costs involved in developing, buying, administering, and scoring tests are considerable. The school funds spent on high-stakes tests are taken from limited school budgets. This means that money spent on tests cannot be spent on initiatives that would actually help teachers become better at classroom-based assessment.

Lack of professional development opportunities prevents many teachers from becoming practicing experts in classroom-based reading assessments (Black & William, 1998). Teachers can develop expertise with classroom assessment when they are supported by their administrators and school districts (Johnston, 1987). Specifically, professional development can help teachers learn and use effective reading assessment materials and procedures that best inform the daily teaching and learning in the classroom (Stiggins, 1999). As we noted earlier, the array of factors that we must assess is large, ranging from reading strategies and skills (the traditional focus of assessment), to motivation, self-efficacy, and metacognition. Just as there are zones of proximal development for students' strategy and skill development, there are zones of proximal development for students' motivation, self-efficacy, and metacognition.

Regular and detailed assessments provide information that helps teachers recognize and utilize the teachable moment. These daily successes sum to the accomplished teaching and learning that is reflected in accountability tests. But accountability is not achieved through testing—it is achieved through the hard work that surrounds successful classroom assessment and instruction. Professional development also helps teachers construct reliable product assessments, such as quizzes, tests, and report cards. Professional development helps teachers become educated consumers and users of the variety of reading assessments that are available.

SUMMARY

Effective reading assessment is necessary for reading program success, and balance is necessary for effective reading assessment. Current reading assessment practice is marked by imbalances that influence teaching and learning. As teachers, we are challenged to provide effective instruction for each and every student. Effective instruction is dependent on assessment that helps teachers and students move toward and attain daily and annual reading goals. This chapter describes what is needed if reading assessment is to reflect our best, most recent understandings of reading and how to measure reading development. We are not wanting for description and detail of how classroom-based reading assessment helps our teaching and how our teaching helps student readers develop. There must be a concerted effort to bring classroom-based reading assessment into the spotlight and to deliver on its promise.

High-quality classroom assessment of reading is as much a product of teacher expertise and effort as it is of political power, popular will, and continuing education (Afflerbach, 2017). Many people believe that tests are at best a key to school excellence, and at worst a nuisance. But a populace that equates testing with best practice in assessment needs further education. As well, full accounting of the costs of current reading assessment programs, especially high-stakes tests, may help the general public understand how much school resources are given to reading assessment that yields information that is of relatively little use for teachers. Teachers must earn and maintain the trust that is currently given, by some, to high-stakes standardized tests. If in our schools and classrooms we are able to demonstrate the superior nature of particular reading assessment information, we may gain converts to classroom assessment.

High-quality reading assessments today are more integral to the daily lives of teachers, students, and classrooms. When we focus on process assessment, we can accurately determine what aspect of a summarization strategy students do and don't understand. When we assess and determine how a student's motivation grows as the result of gaining control of the act of reading, we are describing a compelling success story. And when we share our reading assessment knowledge with our students, we are preparing them to conduct assessment of their own reading, fostering independence.

REFLECTIONS AND FUTURE DIRECTIONS FOR READING ASSESSMENT

When classroom teachers can conduct assessment in a reliable and valid manner, public trust will be gained. Earlier, we sketched the importance of professional development to teachers' growing ability to conduct classroom reading assessments and effectively use their results. However, there is little research that describes how teachers develop as assessment experts, or that demonstrates what type of classroom assessment training most benefits teachers and their students.

A related area for future research and action is the public perception of assessment. We are a society that has valued scientific inquiry, along with research results and agendas for action that are informed by such inquiry and results. Why, then, do our most consequential reading assessments and their uses appear relatively uninformed by our most recent understandings? Similarly, why do states and school districts spend the bulk of their assessment budgets on test purchasing, administering, scoring, and reporting? This problem is exacerbated by the federal mandate of testing all students in grades 3 through 8 in reading, yet the problem existed prior to the passage of the No Child Left Behind Act of 2001. Working to change citizens' understanding of testing should accompany efforts to better our classroom assessments.

A final area for future research relates to the effects of reading assessment on student reading achievement. Despite the importance of reading assessment in determining student achievement and related consequences, reading assessment itself is not a common focus of research (Afflerbach, Cho, Kim, & Clark, 2010). Reading assessment is used as the measure of student achievement in many research designs. There are few studies that describe how assessment can contribute to student learning and achievement, although work in this area is promising (Black & William, 2012; Crooks, 1988). Research should help us determine the relationship of reading assessment with students' reading achievement. Classroom-based reading assessments, especially those that focus on formative assessment, the assessment of processes and the application of knowledge gained from reading, should positively impact teaching and learning.

CONCLUDING COMMENTS

We conclude this chapter with concern, and with optimism. Our concern is fueled by the fact that high-stakes tests continue to monopolize the vocabulary of school success. Test scores are what we talk about when we talk of reading achievement. In addition, the resources that high-stakes tests demand continue to prevent the allocation of needed resources to formative assessment. This is an untenable situation, given the centrality of formative assessment to student success at increasingly demanding curriculum. We note that it is simple to infer the need for massive formative assessment in support of students striving to meet high standards. In contrast, the mechanisms and funding that are necessary to foment such change are complex, and not well explicated.

In contrast, our optimism is fueled by the fact that eminently useful reading assessment materials and procedures exist and are continually being developed, indicating that part of the hard work is already done. We have the means to develop reading assessment that is central to the identification and accomplishment of teachable moments and reading assessment that reflects student achievement in relation to our most recent understanding of reading. This must be complemented by teachers' professional development, public commitment to examine our new conceptualizations of reading and reading assessment, and endorsement of those assessments that best describe and support students' reading achievement.

ENGAGEMENT ACTIVITIES

The following activities are designed to encourage readers of this chapter to investigate balance and imbalance in reading assessment:

1. Conduct task analyses of a local or state standard related to the students you teach. Task analyses give us detailed knowledge of the things we ask students to do. This puts us in a position to assess our assessments. Are they sensitive to all the growth that students may exhibit? Do they favor one type of achievement while ignoring others? Task analyses not only help us determine the suitability of the assessment, they prompt our attention to aspects of reading strategies and tasks that may be the focus of instruction. Knowing the assessment in this case helps us think about teaching, assessment, and balance in assessment. As you conduct your task analysis, determine all the factors that must be operating for student success.

2. Develop an account of all the relevant factors that influence students' growth in reading, focusing on cognition, affect, and conation. Next, compare this account with the reading assessments that you use in the course of a school year. What is the "coverage" of these assessments? Is each and every factor that influences students' reading growth given assessment attention? What factors are overrepresented? What factors are underrepresented?

3. Consider how you can use formative assessment to identify students' zones of proximal development as students work toward attainment of a specific, complex reading and learning goal. What formative assessment information, focused on student cognition and affect, will inform your daily reading instruction in relation to that standard? How will you use the formative assessment information as students move toward attainment of the goal?

4. Based on your account of the reading assessments mandated in your school, and the coverage of these assessments, create a presentation for teachers and school administrators that advocates for optimal assessment. In the presentation, describe what you believe to be the areas that receive adequate reading assessment coverage, and those that are not sufficiently assessed. Suggest specific reading assessment materials and procedures that can contribute to better balance in reading assessment.

REFERENCES

Afflerbach, P. (2017). *Understanding and using reading assessment, K–12* (3rd ed.). Alexandria, VA: Association for Supervision and Curriculum Development.

Afflerbach, P. (2016). *Handbook of individual differences in reading: Reader, text, and context.* New York: Routledge.

Afflerbach, P., Cho, B.-Y., Kim, J.-Y., & Clark, S. (2010). Classroom assessment of literacy. In D. Wyse, R. Andrews, & J. Hoffman (Eds.), *The international handbook of English, language and literacy teaching* (pp. 401–412). London: Routledge.

Afflerbach, P., Cho, B.-Y., Kim, J.-Y., Crassas, M. E., & Doyle, B. (2013). Reading: What else matters besides strategies and skills? *The Reading Teacher, 66,* 440–448.

Afflerbach, P., Pearson, P. D., & Paris, S. (2008). Clarifying differences between reading skills and reading strategies. *The Reading Teacher, 61*(5), 364–373.

Alvermann, D. E. (Ed.). (2002). *Adolescents and literacies in a digital world.* New York: Peter Lang.

American Educational Research Association/American Psychological Association/National Council on Measurement in Education. (1999). *The standards for educational and psychological testing.* Washington, DC: Author.

Anderson, L., & Krathwohl, D. (2001). *A taxonomy for learning, teaching and assessing: A revision of Bloom's taxonomy of educational objectives.* New York: Addison, Wesley Longman.

Bandura, A. (2006). Guide for constructing self-efficacy scales. In F. Pajares & T. Urdan (Eds.), *Self-efficacy beliefs of adolescents* (pp. 307–337). Charlotte, NC: IAP.

Baxter, G., & Glaser, R. (1998). Investigating the cognitive complexity of science assessments. *Educational Measurement: Issues and Practice, 17*(3), 37–45.

Black, P., & William, D. (1998). Assessment and classroom learning. *Educational Assessment: Principles, Policy and Practice, 5,* 7–74.

Black, P., & William, D. (2012). Assessment for learning in the classroom. In J. Gardner (Ed.), *Assessment and learning* (2nd ed., pp. 11–32). London: SAGE.

Bloom, B. S. (Ed.). (1956). *Taxonomy of educational objectives: The classification of educational goals. Handbook 1: Cognitive domain.* New York: Longman.

Braten, I., Britt, M. A., Stromso, H. I., & Rouet, J.-F. (2011). The role of epistemic beliefs in the comprehension of multiple expository texts: Toward an integrated model. *Educational Psychologist, 46*(1), 48–70.

Calfee, R., & Hiebert, E. (1996). Classroom assessment of reading. In R. Barr, M. Kamil, P. Mosenthal, & D. Pearson (Eds.), *Handbook of reading research* (2nd ed., pp. 281–309). Mahwah, NJ: Erlbaum.

Chapman, J. W., & Tunmer, W. E. (1995). Development of young children's reading self-concepts: An examination of emerging subcomponents and their relationship with reading achievement. *Journal of Educational Psychology, 87,* 154–167.

Cho, B.-Y. (2013). Adolescents' constructively responsive reading strategy use in a critical Internet reading task. *Reading Research Quarterly, 48*(4), 329–332.

Cho, B.-Y., & Afflerbach, P. (2015). Reading on the Internet: Realizing and constructing potential texts. *Journal of Adolescent and Adult Literacy, 58*(6), 504–517.

Cho, B.-Y., Woodward, L., Li, D., & Barlow, E. (2017). Examining adolescents' strategic processing during online reading with a question-generating task. *American Educational Research Journal, 54*(4) 691–724.

Clay, M. (1993). *Reading Recovery: A guidebook for teachers in training.* Portsmouth, NH: Heinemann.

Crooks, T. (1988). The impact of classroom evaluation on students. *Review of Educational Research, 58,* 438–481.

Darling-Hammond, L. (2010). *Performance counts: Assessment systems that support high-quality learning.* Washington, DC: Council of Chief State School Officers.

Davis, A. (1998). *The limits of educational assessment.* Oxford, UK: Blackwell.

Gambrell, L., Palmer, B., Codling, R., & Mazzoni, S. (1996). Assessing motivation to read. *The Reading Teacher, 49,* 518–533.

Goldman, S. R., & Scardamalia, M. (2013). Managing, understanding, applying, and creating knowledge in the information age: Next-generation challenges and opportunities. *Cognition and Instruction, 31,* 255–269.

Goodman, K., & Goodman, Y. (1977). Learning about psycholinguistic processes by analyzing oral reading. *Harvard Educational Review, 47,* 317–333.

Graesser, A. C., Mills, K. K., & Zwaan, R. A. (1997). Discourse comprehension. *Annual Review of Psychology, 48,* 163–189.

Guthrie, J. T., & Wigfield, A. (1997). *Reading engagement: Motivating readers through integrated instruction.* Newark, DE: International Reading Association.

Guthrie, J. T., Wigfield, A., & You, W. (2012). Instructional contexts for engagement and achievement in reading. In S. L. Christenson, A. L. Reschly, & C. Wylie (Eds.), *Handbook of research on student engagement* (pp. 601–634). New York: Springer.

Johnston, P. (1987). Teachers as evaluation experts. *The Reading Teacher, 40,* 744–748.

Kintsch, W. (1988). The role of knowledge in discourse comprehension: A construction–integration model. *Psychological Review, 95*(2), 163–182. .

Leu, D. J., Kinzer, C. K., Coiro, J., Castek, J., & Henry, L. A. (2013). New literacies: A dual-level theory of the changing nature of literacy, instruction, and assessment. In D. E. Alvermann, N. J. Unrau, & R. B. Ruddell (Eds.), *Theoretical models and processes of reading* (pp. 1150–1181). Newark. NJ: International Reading Association.

Mansell, W., James, M., & the Assessment Reform Group. (2009). *Fit for purpose: A commentary by the Teaching and Learning Research Programme.* London: Economic and Social Research Council, Teaching and Learning Research Programme.

McKenna, M. C., & Kear, D. J. (1990). Measuring attitude towards reading: A new tool for teachers. *The Reading Teacher, 43,* 626–639.

Morsy, L., Kieffer, M., & Snow, C. (2010). *Measure for measure: A critical consumer's guide to reading comprehension assessments for adolescents.* New York: Carnegie Corporation.

National Assessment Governing Board. (2012). *Reading framework for the 2013 National Assessment of Educational Progress.* Washington, DC: American Institutes for Research.

National Council for the Social Studies. (2013). The college, career, and civic life (C3) framework for social studies state standards: Guidance for enhancing the rigor of K–12 civics, economics, geography, and history. Retrieved September 17, 2017, from *www.socialstudies.org/sites/default/files/c3/C3-Framework-for-Social-Studies.pdf.*

Partnership for Assessment of Readiness for College and Careers. (2013). *PARCC task prototypes and new sample items for ELA/literacy.* Retrieved September 17, 2013, from *https://parcc.pearson.com/practice-tests/english.*

Pellegrino, J., Chudowsky, N., & Glaser, R. (2001). *Knowing what students know: The science and design of educational assessment.* Washington, DC: National Academy Press.

Pressley, M., & Afflerbach, P. (1995). *Verbal reports of reading: The nature of constructively responsive reading.* Hillsdale, NJ: Erlbaum.

Rouet, J.-F. (2006). *The skills of document use: From text comprehension to web-based learning.* Mahwah, NJ: Erlbaum.

Schiefele, U., Schaffner, E., Moller, J., & Wigfield, A. (2012). Dimensions of reading motivation and their relation to reading behavior and competence. *Reading Research Quarterly, 47,* 427–463.

Schunk, D., & Bursuck, W. (2016). Self-efficacy, agency, and volition. In P. Afflerbach (Ed.), *Handbook of individual differences in reading: Reader, text, and context* (pp. 54–66). New York: Routledge.

Smarter Balanced Assessment Consortium. (2012). Sample items and performance tasks. Retrieved September 17, 2013, from *www.smarterbalanced.org/sample-items-and-performance-tasks.*

Snow, C. (2002). *Reading for understanding: Toward an R&D program in reading comprehension.* Washington, DC: RAND Corporation.

Stanovich, K. (1986). Matthew effects in reading: Some consequences of individual differences in the acquisition of literacy. *Reading Research Quarterly, 21,* 360–407.

Veenman, M. (2016). Metacognition. In P. Afflerbach (Ed.), *Handbook of individual differences in reading: Reader, text, and context* (pp. 26–40). New York: Routledge.

Vygotsky, L. (1978). *Mind in society: The development of higher psychological processes.* Cambridge, MA: Harvard University Press.

Whitebread, D., Coltman, P., Pasternak, D., Sangster, C., Grau, V., & Demetriou, D. (2009). The development of two observational tools for assessing metacognition and self-regulated learning in young children. *Metacognition and Learning, 4,* 63–85.

Wiley, J., Goldman, S. R., Graesser, A. C., Sanchez, C. A., Ash, I. A., & Hemmerich, J. A. (2009). Source evaluation, comprehension, and learning in Internet science inquiry tasks. *American Educational Research Journal, 46*(4), 1060–1106.

Wolfe, M. B. W., & Goldman, S. R. (2005). Relations between adolescents' text processing and reasoning. *Cognition and Instruction, 23,* 467–502.

PART IV

PERSPECTIVES ON
SPECIAL ISSUES

CHAPTER 15

Best Practices in Teaching the New Literacies of Online Research and Comprehension

LISA ZAWILINSKI
ELENA FORZANI
NICOLE TIMBRELL
DONALD J. LEU

This chapter will:

- Define a dual-level theory of New Literacies. It will then show how one lowercase theory, the New Literacies of online research and instruction, is useful to guide instruction, especially when developing a community of learners.

- Explain how we should interpret best practices in reading with both a lens to the future and a lens to the past, integrating instruction in the New Literacies of online research and comprehension with traditional reading comprehension.

- Provide 10 research-based principles that inform instruction in New Literacies and provide two specific ideas to implement each principle in the classroom.

EVIDENCE-BASED BEST PRACTICES IN NEW LITERACIES: FORGING NEW COMMUNITIES OF LEARNING ONLINE

The Internet is a disruptive technology (Christensen, 1997), altering traditional elements of society from sport, to business, to politics. The

337

disruptive impact of the Internet also alters the nature of literacy as new technologies and new social practices generate additional, new literacies (Leu, Kinzer, Coiro, Castek, & Henry, 2013). New online communication tools also make possible new communities of learners by extending collaborative learning projects into classrooms in other parts of the world, helping to develop richer understandings of culture, language, and contexts (Larson & Dwyer, 2015). Clearly, literacy has become a deictic, or dynamic, construct.

How we adapt to a dynamic definition of literacy in the classroom will define our students' success in both school and life. Given the continuous changes taking place, one might even suggest that learning how to learn new literacies is more important than learning a fixed set of skills from one specific type of literacy. Every specific literacy that you know today will change repeatedly and substantially during your lifetime.

Some believe there is little to teach; our students are already "digital natives," skilled in online new literacies (Prensky, 2001). Interestingly, this is not the case. It is true that today's students have grown up in an online world and are developing proficiency with gaming, social networking, video, and texting (Alvermann, Hutchins, & DeBlasio, 2012). However, this does not necessarily mean they are skilled in the effective use of online information, perhaps the most important aspect of the Internet. Indeed, recent research is showing how limited students are regarding locating and critically evaluating information online. Many students find it difficult to judge the accuracy, reliability, and bias of information that they encounter during online research (Forzani, 2015; Graham & Metaxas, 2003; Sanchez, Wiley, & Goldman, 2006).

NEW LITERACIES: THEORY AND RESEARCH

As we try to understand these new literacies, we encounter a conundrum: How can we develop adequate understanding when the very object that we seek to study continuously changes? Our field has never before faced an issue such as this, since literacy has generally been static, permitting us, over time, to carefully study and understand it. One way out of this conundrum may be to think about literacy on two different levels, using a dual-level theory of New Literacies (Leu et al., 2013).

A dual-level theory of New Literacies conceptualizes literacy at lowercase (new literacies) and uppercase (New Literacies) levels. Lowercase theories of new literacies explore specific aspects of the changes taking place (e.g., Lewis & Fabos, 2005; Street, 2003). Lowercase theories of new literacy are better able to keep up with the rapidly changing nature of literacy since they are closer to the specific types of changes that rapidly take place. Multiple lowercase theories also permit our field to maximize the lenses we use and the technologies and contexts we study. Every scholar who studies new literacy issues is generating important insights for everyone else, even if we do not share a particular lens, technology, or context. How, though, do we come to understand these insights, taking place in many different fields from many different perspectives? For this, we require a second level of theory, an upper-case theory of New Literacies.

New Literacies, as the broader concept, benefits from work taking place in the multiple, lowercase dimensions of new literacies by identifying the common findings that appear. Leu et al. (2013) suggest that this broader New Literacies theory currently includes these common findings:

1. The Internet is this generation's defining technology for literacy and learning within our global community.
2. The Internet and related technologies require additional new literacies to fully access their potential.
3. New literacies are deictic.
4. New literacies are multiple, multimodal, and multifaceted.
5. Critical literacies are central to new literacies.
6. New forms of strategic knowledge are required with new literacies.
7. New social practices are a central element of new literacies.
8. Teachers become more important, though their role changes, within new literacy classrooms. (p. 1158)

This chapter will use the findings from this broader New Literacies theory to provide the context for understanding one lowercase form, the new literacies of online research and comprehension (Leu et al., 2015).

The New Literacies of Online Research and Comprehension

Online research and comprehension is a self-directed text construction and comprehension process that frames online reading comprehension as problem-based inquiry with online information. It includes the reading skills, strategies, dispositions, and social practices that take place as we use the Internet to conduct research, solve problems, and answer questions. At least five processing practices occur during online research and comprehension, each requiring additional new skills and strategies when they take place online: (1) reading to identify important questions, (2) reading to locate information, (3) reading to evaluate information critically, (4) reading to synthesize information, and (5) reading and writing to communicate information.

How does the nature of reading and writing change online? What, if any, new literacies do we require? We are just discovering some of the answers to these questions (Afflerbach & Cho, 2008). First, it appears that online reading comprehension typically takes place within a problem-solving task. In short, online reading comprehension is online research. Second, online reading also becomes tightly integrated with writing as we communicate with others to learn more about the questions we explore and as we communicate our own interpretations. A third difference is that readers do not solely construct meaning as they read online, they also construct the texts as they make decisions about what to read and where to go to get the needed information. A fourth difference is that new technologies such as browsers, search engines, wikis, blogs, e-mail, and many others are required. Additional skills and strategies are needed to use each of these technologies effectively. Keyword entry in a search engine, for example, becomes an important new literacy skill during online reading because it is required in search engines, an important new technology for locating information. Finally, and perhaps most importantly, online reading may require even greater amounts of higher-level thinking than offline reading. In a context in which anyone may publish anything, higher-level thinking skills such as critical evaluation of source material become especially important online.

There are several reasons why the new literacies of online research and comprehension are important to classroom reading programs. First, they focus directly on information use and learning, so these skills are central to learning at all levels. Second, the ability to read and use online information effectively to solve problems defines success in both life and work. Third, these new literacies are not always included in literacy programs (International Reading Association, 2009). Finally, our students often appear to lack these skills (Forzani, 2015).

Standards

New Literacies and the new literacies of online research and comprehension are being recognized in recent policy initiatives. A number of nations have integrated these skills into curriculum and educational standards, seeking to prepare youth for work and life in an online age of information.

Australia

Australia has recently developed the Australian Curriculum (Australia Curriculum, Assessment and Reporting Authority [ACARA], n.d.). This initiative tightly integrates literacy and the Internet within the English curriculum and suggests that online research and communication are essential elements in this area:

Information and Communication Technology [ICT] capability is an important component of the English curriculum. Students use ICT when . . . they conduct research online, and collaborate and communicate with others electronically. (ACARA, n.d., General Capabilities, Information and Communication Technology Competence section, para. 2)

Canada: Manitoba

The province of Manitoba has developed an educational framework called Literacy with ICT Across the Curriculum (Minister of Manitoba Education, Citizenship, and Youth, 2006). This initiative recognizes that reading has changed and that online reading is a problem-solving task, requiring new skills to locate, evaluate, synthesize, and communicate in online contexts. It describes these new online literacies as

identifying appropriate inquiry questions; navigating multiple information networks to locate relevant information; applying critical thinking skills to evaluate information sources and content; synthesizing information and ideas from multiple sources and networks; representing information and ideas creatively in visual, aural, and textual formats; crediting and referencing sources of information and intellectual property; and communicating new understandings to others, both face to face and over distance. (Minister of Manitoba Education, Citizenship, and Youth, 2006, p. 18)

The United States

In the United States, somewhat common standards have now appeared across many states designed to prepare students for college and careers in the 21st century. One of the key design principles of these new standards appears to be the integration of online research and comprehension skills within the classroom. These include locating, evaluating, synthesizing, and communicating with online information:

To be ready for college, workforce training, and life in a technological society, students need the ability to gather, comprehend, evaluate, synthesize, and report on information and ideas, to conduct original research in order to answer questions or solve problems, and to analyze and create a high volume and extensive range of print and nonprint texts in media forms old and new. The need to conduct research and to produce and consume media is embedded into every aspect of today's curriculum. (National Governors Association & Council of Chief State School Officers [NGA & CCSSO], 2010, p. 4)

Three changes are especially noticeable in the many new standards documents appearing in nations around the world:

1. There is a greater focus on reading informational texts.
2. Higher-level thinking is emphasized.
3. Digital literacies are integrated throughout the English language arts standards.

Each of these reflects the shift in reading from page to screen that we have described as important to the new literacies of online research and comprehension. While there is more that can be done (Drew, 2012), a number of standards include these new literacies of online research and comprehension.

READING STANDARDS WITH DUAL LENSES: A LENS TO THE FUTURE AND A LENS TO THE PAST

Interestingly, the word "Internet" is never used in the reading standards now appearing in the United States (Leu et al., 2011). Because of this oversight, many will ignore instruction in online reading, thinking that U.S. standards only reference traditional, offline reading comprehension.

Why? The answer is related to prior knowledge. One of the most consistent patterns in reading research is the finding that the prior knowledge we bring to a text profoundly shapes our interpretation of it. Given that most of our prior knowledge about reading is derived from an understanding of reading in offline contexts, the U.S. standards are likely to be interpreted in relation to offline reading comprehension, not online reading comprehension. Another way of looking at this issue is to suggest that many educators will read standards only with a lens to our past, and not a lens to our future, failing to include instruction in important online reading skills. Figure 15.1 illustrates the problem in relation to a common reading standard, often referred to as *close reading*. The standard states, "Read closely to determine what the text says explicitly and to make logical inferences from it; cite specific textual evidence when writing or speaking to support conclusions drawn from the text" (NGA & CCSSO, 2010).

With our extensive prior knowledge derived from offline reading, we naturally interpret this standard, using a lens to our past, and teach inferential reasoning with narrative text offline. On the other hand, if we read this standard by using a lens to the future, we would think of the inferential reasoning required to read in different contexts online, perhaps the reading of search engine results. When we read search engine results to select the best site for our needs we are required to make many inferences about what we would find at each link. Many students do not read search engine results; they simply click and look their way down each list of search results, reviewing each web page, often skipping right past

Reading with a lens to the past

- We would use narrative text.
- We would teach inferential reasoning about setting, events, problems, solutions, characters, etc.
- Typical discussion questions might include:
  o Tell us what you think will happen next?
  o What evidence in your text suggests this answer?

Reading with a lens to the future

> **Ancient Egypt**
> www.ancientegypt.co.uk/ ▾
> The British Museum gives information on **Egyptian** life, gods and goddesses, mummification, rulers, pyramids, temples, time, trade, and writing, as well as games ...
>
> **Ancient Egypt — History.com Articles, Video, Pictures and Facts**
> www.history.com/topics/ancient-egypt ▾
> The **ancient Egyptian** civilization endured for more than 5000 years, and at its peak was one of the richest and most powerful in the world.
>
> **6th Grade Social Studies - Ch. 4 & 13 Ancient Egypt**
> www.anoka.k12.mn.us › ... › AMSA Teacher Web pages Perm... ▾
> Chapter 4 & 13 Learning Activities. Learning Targets. I can: • understand the importance of the Nile River. • understand that **Egyptian** governments changed over ...

- We would use informational text such as search engine results.
- We would teach how to infer information from search result listings.
- Typical discussion questions might include:
  o Which of these sites is a commercial site?
  o What evidence in the text suggests this?
  o Which of these sites comes from England? Which comes from Minnesota?
  o What evidence in the text suggests this?

FIGURE 15.1. Reading standards with a lens to the past and a lens to the future.

a useful resource. Instruction in how to make inferences and use textual evidence to support those inferences would be very useful to students. Educators who read with both a lens to the past and a lens to the future would interpret a close reading standard by teaching both types of close reading.

These two lenses operate within most other standards in reading, too. Consider, for example, a common standard related to point of view, *Assess how point of view or purpose shapes the content and style of a text.* Someone reading this standard with a lens to the past would interpret it by teaching point of view within narratives, engaging students in discussions about the point of view held by different characters. Someone reading this standard with a lens to the future would interpret it by teaching point of view in relation to the evaluation of a website's reliability, where point of view is one of several important elements to consider when evaluating the reliability of information that is found online. Since the word "Internet" or "online" never appears in the reading standards of the United States, and since we are only beginning to develop our knowledge of online reading, we run the risk of interpreting nearly all of the standards in reading with a lens to our past, implementing them only within traditional print contexts. Such an outcome will limit instruction, denying important learning opportunities to our students.

BEST PRACTICES IN ACTION:
PRINCIPLES AND PRACTICES IN NEW LITERACIES

How can we begin to think about instruction in New Literacies, consistent with newly appearing standards? We provide 10 principles and two instructional ideas that you can use to implement each principle.

Begin Teaching and Learning New Literacies as Early as Possible

Schools should begin to integrate online experiences and new literacies instruction as soon as children begin their literacy education program (Forzani & Leu, 2012). A useful first step is to use online resources to support foundational offline reading skills in PreK, kindergarten, and first grade. These sites teach early offline reading skills while also providing important early experiences with navigating an online interface. In addition, even the youngest students can now easily create digital texts, blending foundational with digital skills to safely share information with others. In short, new technologies allow you to combine both an instructional lens to our past and a lens to our future.

PBS KIDS Island

PBS KIDS Island (*http://pbskids.org/island*) offers a number of free games across literacy areas and development. From letter identification at *Likety Letter Bingo* to *Super Whys Reading Challenge* that focuses on comprehension of simple sentences, students will enjoy a number of literacy challenges. Moreover, skills like signing in and using the back arrow on a browser are beginning New Literacies skills practiced while navigating the site. PBS KIDS Island requires a free account. We recommend that teachers create a single user account and password for their class or create individual accounts for each student using e-mail addresses from a student-safe e-mail tool like ePals (*ePals.com*).

Book Creator for Digital Information Sharing

Many new literacies can be practiced alongside traditional beginning writing and reading skills while creating digital texts. Even our youngest students can successfully create e-books given the numerous features available to them (Zawilinski, 2016). Creating digital books with young students provides a scaffold to later, online communication experiences.

Book Creator (*https://app.bookcreator.com/books*) is an e-book creation technology that is only available for the Chrome browser (available on most laptop and desktop computers and iOS and android mobile devices). The Chrome browser version allows teachers and students to create 40 e-books for free. Students can share their knowledge via drawing, typing, audio, and images. Imagine creating a digital book for your class where each student creates his or her own page. This helps students learn about each other, identify commonalities, and build community. Similarly, as students explore and learn new features, they can share these features with one another. Finally, completed books can be shared traditionally, face to face within the classroom community, or digitally, e-mailed beyond the classroom.

Use New Literacies to Help the Last Student Become First

Make it a policy to always teach a new technology to your weakest reader(s) first. This enables struggling readers and writers to become literate in this new literacy before other, higher-performing students in reading. They can then teach this new literacy to others who are not literate with the new form. This is a powerful principle that positions weaker readers as experts. It should always be used. Unfortunately, the opposite often happens. Struggling readers frequently are denied access to online experiences because their offline literacy skills are thought to be insufficient to permit success. Avoid this problem by helping your weakest students become literate in a new technology first.

Teach Blogging and Wiki Skills to Struggling Readers First

When you begin to use wikis and blogs in your classroom, make certain that you use these opportunities, too, to help the last become first with New Literacies. Imagine a first or fifth grader who has been struggling with literacy learning suddenly becoming the class expert on how to create a new blog comment or post. A few minutes of coaching on the necessary steps puts this student in the expert seat. The rest of the class then relies on this student for instruction and coaching. This student's role in the classroom shifts as he or she shares responsibility for teaching important reading and writing skills.

Reframe Social Media Hashtagging as a Literacy Skill

The popularity of using hashtags on social media sites can be reframed in the classroom as a new literacy skill. Hashtags enable readers to use a keyword or topic in order to facilitate a search, and on social media they are also used to attract followers. By considering the appropriate hash tags students are forced to identify relevant key ideas, themes, or issues, and make connections to other prior reading experiences. By inviting struggling readers to create a set of hashtags suitable for the text or topic, the teacher can position them as the expert "taggers" for the class. As each reading text is encountered and discussed in the classroom, this student is in charge of issuing the relevant hashtag and explaining the reason for their categorization.

Integrate New Literacies Instruction into Traditional Literacies Instruction

Rather than teaching new literacies skills separately, integrate them into your regular classroom instruction. Teachers can do this by using the Technological Pedagogical Content Knowledge (TPACK) framework and simultaneously drawing on these three different types of knowledge (Mishra & Koehler, 2006). Digital literacies skills can be used to support traditional literacy skill development to differentiate instruction and to learn how to collaborate with others within a community of learners.

Digital literacies skills are also integrated with traditional literacies skills throughout the Common Core Standards (NGA & CCSSO, 2010). By integrating new literacies skills with traditional literacies skills throughout the curriculum, students learn how to use technology in the service of disciplinary skills such as interpreting literature, engaging in science experiments, learning about historical events, and solving math problems. They also learn how to use technology in the context of other tasks, making the technology skills "sticky" and helping students learn how to use the same technology skills across multiple different contexts.

Employ Internet Reciprocal Teaching

Online reading requires a mix of both traditional and new literacies skills. When teaching students online research and comprehension skills, help them build on the traditional, offline research and comprehension skills they already possess. Internet reciprocal teaching (IRT; Leu et al., 2008) can be used to model the integrated use of both kinds of skills when reading online and to help students develop their own inquiry practices. IRT has demonstrated efficacy in the classroom for developing online research and comprehension skills (Leu et al., 2008). Even students with little online reading experience will feel more confident as they use some skills with which they are already familiar. Those students who are already familiar with traditional reciprocal teaching will have the added advantage of being comfortable with the teaching strategy in a traditional literacy context as well.

Use Explanatory Screencasts to Share Learning

When a student has developed a sound understanding of a new topic, or mastered a new skill, he or she is typically called on to explain his or her learning in writing for an audience of one: his or her teacher. Explanatory screencasts are an effective formative or summative learning task that enable students to share their understanding of a topic with a community of learners. A screencast is a recording taken of a computer screen that is often accompanied by voiceover narration, screen annotations, and title slides, and is created using either built-in software in the device or through free online tools such as Screencast-O-Matic (*www.screencast-o-matic.com*). For example, if students have learned about weather systems in school, they might annotate a weather map on a laptop or tablet while explaining aloud the meaning of each symbol on the synoptic chart in order to help other students learn the same information. Once the screencast is captured and edited, the final product can be published on YouTube or educational sites such as Educreations (*http://educreations.com*) or Explain Everything (*https://explaineverything.com*), which creates an authentic audience for the students and positions them as contributors to the digital world rather than remaining simply as consumers.

Teach Online Search Skills Because These Are Important to Success in the New Literacies of Online Research and Comprehension

The ability to read and locate online information is important. If one cannot locate information online, it becomes very hard to solve a problem with online information and to learn in online spaces. Several reading skills and strategies are required: generating effective keyword search strategies; reading to infer which link may be most useful among a set of search engine results; and efficiently scanning for relevant information within websites. Each is important to integrate into classroom reading programs.

Use Google Search Education or KidzSearch

Search engines regularly add new search capabilities that are not always known to users. To keep up to date with those that are added to Google, visit "Google Search Education" at *www.google.com/intl/en-us/insidesearch/searcheducation/index.html*. Here you will find lesson plans, activities to improve your own search skills, daily search challenges for your students, and training webinars for both you and your students. There is a similar teaching tool for the KidzSearch search engine at *www.kidzsearch.com/ boolify*. KidzSearch is a kid-safe search engine that returns results with images.

Play "One Click"

To develop better close reading skills during the reading of search results, play "One Click." Conduct a search for any topic that you are studying in class. If you lack an interactive whiteboard or a projector, print out enough copies of the first page of search results for each student. Distribute these. Then see if students can locate the best link on the search results page for each question that you ask such as, "Which link will take you to a site developed by an Egyptologist?" or "Which site on this page is a commercial site and will probably try to sell you something?" Each question should require students to make an inference from the limited information appearing in the search results list. If you have an interactive whiteboard or a projector, do the same but ask students to come to the projected screen and point to the answer they think is correct, explaining their reasoning and teaching others, showing them the evidence that they used.

Use Online Reading Experiences to Develop Critical Thinking Skills and a Generation of "Healthy Skeptics"

A central objective of any instructional program in New Literacies is to develop students who read as "healthy skeptics." We seek to raise a generation of students who always question the information they read for reliability and accuracy, always read to infer bias or point of view, and always check the sources they encounter while reading. The Internet demands these skills. Although these skills have always been necessary with offline texts (Bråten, Strømsø, & Britt, 2009), the proliferation of unedited information and the merging of commercial marketing with educational content (Fabos, 2008) presents additional challenges that are quite different from traditional print and media sources, requiring new strategies during online reading. Your leadership in this area will ensure that students in your district graduate with the critical evaluation skills required in an online age.

Use Source Plus

Schools increasingly require students to list the sources of any online information used in a report. Take this one step further and require students to add a sentence for each source, indicating how they determined it was reputable and reliable. Before students do this on their own, model how you think through determining the reliability of a site. After modeling your own thinking, students can discuss together whether they think a website is reliable enough to use as a source to answer the question. Students likely will have their own research questions that they can bring to this task for practice as well.

Employ Discovery Questions

To teach source evaluation skills, have small groups conduct research to answer a three-part problem such as this:

1. How high is Mt. Fuji in feet?
2. Find a different answer to this same question.
3. Which answer do you trust and why do you trust it?

As you observe students begin work on the third part of the problem, you likely will see a student begin to use the strategy that you have targeted: locating and evaluating the source of the information. When you see someone use this strategy, perhaps by clicking on a link to "About Us," interrupt the other groups and have this student teach the strategy to the class, explaining how he or she evaluates a source for expertise and reliability. There are many inconsistent facts online that can also be used, just like this, to teach source evaluation, including: "How long is the Mississippi River?" or "What is the population of San Francisco?"

Integrate Online Communication into Lessons

It is easy to integrate the Internet into classrooms through the use of online communication tools such as e-mail, wikis, and blogs, as well as the child-safe social networks for schools that are now beginning to appear. Each creates a wonderfully natural way in which to develop a classroom community of effective online information use (Zawilinski, 2012). Importantly, they may also be used to keep parents informed about what is taking place in classrooms.

As we begin to integrate these online communication tools into our classrooms, we should not ignore concerns about child safety. When we begin, we may wish to restrict communication only to our students and to a community of people whom we can trust, such as parents and other teachers and students. There are many versions of wikis, blogs, and e-mail that can provide these protections. Typically, they do this in three ways. First, most permit you to restrict access. You can often list the addresses of people you wish to be able to view, add, or edit information. Second, many tools, especially child-safe e-mail tools, permit you to approve any message before it is sent. Finally, most prohibit e-mail from outside coming in as well as e-mails going to addresses outside the e-mail system that you use.

Investigate Other Teachers' Use of Blogs, Wikis, and E-Mail

To gather ideas about how online communication tools can be used effectively in classrooms, simply search online to see how other teachers do this (Zawilinski, 2009). Using Twitter hashtags such as #educhat, #engchat, or #edtechchat is one way of connecting with teachers and sharing blog and wiki resources. Another is to search online with keywords such as first-grade classroom blog, fourth-grade classroom blog, classroom wiki, or classroom e-mail. Send links of good classroom models to other teachers in your school to review and consider.

Find Child-Safe E-Mail at ePals and Gaggle

Both ePals (*www.epals.com*) and Gaggle (*www.gaggle.net*) provide child-safe e-mail for free and paid services, respectively. Many teachers begin student e-mail use by choosing settings that limit the exchange of e-mail to students in the classroom. Later, teachers adjust settings to permit e-mail to students in other classrooms in the school. Finally, they open settings to other students around the world who have been admitted into the system. At each step you can monitor all correspondence if you wish.

Identify Ways to Include New Literacies Instruction When There Is Resistance to It

Schools sometimes limit the amount of technology instruction students receive for fear that it will take time away from more traditional instruction. Likewise, technology coordinators may place restrictions on classroom access to Internet tools for one reason or another. As a literacy educator, it is important to find ways to incorporate new literacies instruction into your curriculum so students can gain these valuable skills. You should determinedly work to make child-safe access to online tools and resources easier for students in your classroom.

Use the Word "Pilot"

When tools are blocked in your district, a useful strategy for incorporating new literacies instruction is to meet with your principal and suggest that a "pilot" be implemented in your classroom for the online technology that you wish to use. Prepare for this meeting carefully. Describe what the technology does, how it will increase opportunities for students, and how you will ensure child safety. Also suggest that a note be sent to parents to inform them about what will be taking place, why it is important, and to request their permission. Thus, anxieties are reduced and, after a successful pilot, your school may be more receptive to additional innovations.

Many new tools may be "piloted." Edmodo (*www.edmodo.com*) is an educational tool for online collaboration that uses an interface similar to that of social networks. Should it be blocked by your district, ask to conduct a pilot of this tool in one classroom to evaluate its potential for other classrooms. G Suite for Education (*https://edu.google.com/k-12-solutions/g-suite/?modal_active=none*), an online set of tools, is another good option for conducting a pilot. While more and more schools are seeing the usefulness of Google tools for their students, many still block this tool. Google offers free online tools, including Google Docs for word processing, spreadsheets, forms, presentations, and drawing pages. Word-processing and other files may be used by anyone with permission from the creator. Thus, multiple students and teachers can collaboratively work on a single document at once. Using this tool as part of a pilot is a low-risk way to begin implementing technology into the classroom.

Teach New Literacies Skills within Disciplinary Areas

If you cannot give up instructional time during your literacy block to teach new literacies skills, integrate these skills into your science and social studies curriculum. Students can gain valuable online research skills, for example, while learning about important historical issues and events. Or, students can conduct a collaborative research project on a topic that is already part of the science curriculum. As students engage in research projects with one another, they learn how to locate, evaluate, synthesize, and communicate information online in a collaborative context. At the same time, students learn how to be part of a scientific community of learners, an important goal in many science curriculums.

Use Performance-Based Assessments for Evaluating Students' Ability with New Literacies

Effective instruction is informed by effective assessment. While no assessment is perfect (Darling-Hammond, 2010), some have argued that performance-based assessments do this better than many other forms of assessments (Wiggins, 1998). Performance-based assessments provide more diagnostic information than do many other types of assessments, for they are administered while students perform an authentic task. Some initial models for assessing the new literacies of online research and comprehension have appeared. For example, the PISA Digital Reading Assessment (Organization for Economic Co-operation and Development [OECD], 2011) evaluated 15-year-olds from a number of different countries. In addition, the Progress in International Reading Literacy Study (PIRLS) provides another new assessment of reading in response to this changing dynamic, ePIRLS (Mullis, Martin, & Sainsbury, 2013). ePIRLS (*https://timssandpirls.bc.edu*) is an innovative, performance-based assessment of students' ability to read and learn online with school-based assignments in science and social studies. The ePIRLS assessments are delivered on a computer and include lessons in social studies and science, web pages, information graphics, animations, multiple tabs, pop-up windows, and an avatar that guides students through the online reading, research, and learning tasks. As students make decisions, their online reading ability is evaluated.

Another approach is the Online Research and Comprehension Assessment, or ORCA (Leu, Kulikowich, Sedransk, & Coiro, 2009). Each online research task in science is directed through chat messages from an avatar student within a social network. Students locate four different websites and summarize the central information from each using their notepad. They also evaluate the source reliability of a website and write a short report of their research in either a wiki or an e-mail message. The assessments have demonstrated high levels of both reliability and validity (Leu, Coiro, Kulikowich, & Cui, 2012). To gain greater understanding of what performance-based assessments of online research and comprehension will look like in the future, you may view a video of one student completing one of the assessments: *http://neag.uconn.edu/orca-video-ira*.

Use Informal Observation Strategies

While we wait for better formal assessments, you can use informal observations of students conducting online research to gain important diagnostic information about an individual student's ability. Give students a short online research project and carefully observe how they locate, evaluate, synthesize, and communicate information online during their research. Careful observation is a teacher's best instructional friend. Another way to gather informal, performance-based assessment data is through think-alouds. As students learn about online research, invite one student to think aloud using the projected screen so the entire class can see online research and comprehension strategies in action. This will provide students with new strategies and provide you with important insights about needed skill development.

Leverage Screen-Sharing Software

Consider the use of screen sharing, or monitoring, software on your computer in one-to-one computing classrooms. This software places a thumbnail image of each student's device screen on the teacher's computer, which may be used to observe students to evaluate their strengths and needs. Importantly, it may also be used to display a student's screen when the student is teaching the class an important new skill that he or she has discovered. There are many different screen-sharing software programs including Apple Remote Desktop (*www.apple.com/remotedesktop*) or Apple Classroom (for iPads) (*https://itunes.apple.com/us/app/classroom/ id1085319084?mt=8*), Reflector (for tablet devices) (*www.airsquirrels.com/ reflector*), LanSchool (*www.lenovosoftware.com/lanschool*), Netop Vision (*www.netop.com/edu.htm*) and others.

Use Collaborative Online Learning Experiences with Classroom Partners in Other Parts of the World

Some teachers are beginning to explore the future of classroom instruction and develop new classroom learning communities. They connect with other classrooms around the world to engage in collaborative classroom learning projects. These classrooms use educational forums, collaborative writing tools, video conferences, wikis, and simple web page development tools to learn, exchange information, and work on collaborative research projects. With these projects, students increase their New Literacies skills while they develop a richer understanding of content and a greater understanding of the differences that define our planet. Most importantly, these experiences provide students with preparation for the world they will soon enter, especially in the workplace.

Connect and Communicate with Other Classrooms

Use professional learning networks on ePals, Twitter, Google+, or other educational communities to connect with several teachers at your grade level, possibly in different countries, and set up a weekly message exchange project. Invite each participating classroom to send the other classrooms a weekly message, describing what took place in their classroom on one day. Thus, each classroom will receive a number of messages from around the world each week. Share copies of the messages with students on a projected screen, or via the class website, to help students develop new friends and a richer understanding of the world around them. In younger grades, ask your class to dictate a response each week, while you transcribe it, or have them film or audio-record their message. In older grades, assign the message project to a different group each week. Have another group serve as editors to read, suggest revisions, and edit the work. Then send it out to the other participating classes. With these message projects, you will begin to develop new communities of learners around the world.

Find an International Classroom and Work on a Common Project

Once regular communication and a rapport is established with an international classroom, work with the other teacher to set up a common project. One such project is a virtual field trip. Use tools such as Google Expeditions (*https://support.google.com/edu/expeditions/answer/6335093?hl=en*) or Skype in the Classroom (*https://education.microsoft.com/skype-in-the-classroom/overview*) to locate a suitable "destination" for both classes to "visit." If a simultaneous virtual field trip cannot be arranged, have classes conduct their visits asynchronously. The following day set up a video conference using Skype (*www.skype.com/en*) or Google Hangouts (*https://hangouts.google.com*), or a collaborative writing space such as a wiki or Google Doc (*www.google.com/docs/about*), for students to reflect on what they observed and experienced, taking note on the differing perspectives offered by students. As an alternate common project, invite the partnering classroom to use Google Earth (*www.google.com/earth*) and Streetview (*www.google.com/streetview*) to visit some of the nearest attractions to your school and share their observations about the geography, architecture, and points of historical interest from the perspective of a virtual "tourist." Have your class reciprocate the visit and share similar findings.

Recognize That a New Literacies Journey Is One of Continuous Learning

As new technologies appear on the Internet, New Literacies and new opportunities for instruction continuously appear (International Reading Association, 2009). They remind us that our New Literacies' future is really a journey, not a destination. The regular appearance of New Literacies requires additional roles for teachers and students. For teachers, it means bringing both a lens to the future and a lens to the past to learning standards, integrating online literacy experiences into the classroom in a regular and thoughtful fashion. This will require knowing which online reading and writing skills are important to support. It will also mean developing learning experiences for these skills. In addition, it means learning from other colleagues, an important source of information in a world where it is hard for any one person to keep up with all of the changes that are taking place. It also means being on the lookout for new skills and strategies that students in your class manifest, so you can then distribute these skills to your other students and to fellow teachers. For students, it means having regular, consistent, and safe access to online technologies in the classroom and at home. When this is not possible at home, it becomes even more important for it to be available at school.

Build an Online Support System

Keep a running list of the best new online tools and resources that you encounter. Regularly distribute these through your school's social network, e-mail, wiki, blog, or Twitter feed, and encourage others to do the same. Consider sharing resources with teachers outside of your school community by using online professional learning networks linked through wikis or Twitter hashtags. This will quickly build a community around the effective integration of online new literacies into classrooms.

Build and Maintain an Expert List

Create and maintain an "Expert List" in your classroom or on your class blog or wiki. As you observe students who demonstrate new and useful online reading and writing strategies, add the name of the student and the skill he or she displayed to the Expert List, where everyone can see it. Frequently refer to this list during instruction, making it a resource just as a word wall may be for spelling. When students ask the teacher for help, he or she can refer them first to the Expert List to see if any classmates know how to do the skill the student needs help with. In this way, the community of learners has many teachers (the students themselves), not just the classroom teacher.

REFLECTIONS AND FUTURE DIRECTIONS

In a world in which change takes place to literacy every single day, it is impossible to accurately predict precisely what literacy instruction will be in the future. We believe, however, that the new literacies of online research and comprehension will always be central for learning, though these new literacies will continuously evolve. We also believe that the future will include online technologies for literacy that do not exist now, requiring even newer skills and strategies to be developed by our students.

These changes will require each of us to always have one lens turned to the future so that we might continuously learn about even newer online tools that we can use in our classrooms, preparing our students for all that they so richly deserve.

ENGAGEMENT ACTIVITIES

1. Scaffold online communication with younger students by creating an "About Us" class e-book. Using apps or browser-ready tools like Book Creator (*https://bookcreator.com*), young students build basic, new literacies skills, while simultaneously solidifying the classroom community as they note similar interests and experiences.

2. Integrate New Literacies within traditional literature circles. The Visualizer can use a web whiteboard (see *https://awwapp.com*) to sketch his or her favorite part. The group can also create and share digital post-its before or during the meeting using Padlet (*https://padlet.com*). Create new roles like the "Author Investigator" who can search online for relevant author information to share with the group.

3. Develop a lens to the future for the CCSS in reading. Review the Common Core State Standards for your grade level. How can you implement each one in a way that uses a lens to the future to develop online reading research and comprehension skills? What activities mentioned in this chapter can you begin to implement now?

REFERENCES

Afflerbach, P., & Cho, B.-Y. (2008). Determining and describing reading strategies: Internet and traditional forms of reading. In H. S. Waters & W. Schneider (Eds.), *Metacognition, strategy use, and instruction* (pp. 201–255). New York: Guilford Press.

Alvermann, D., Hutchins, R. J., & DeBlasio, R. (2012). Adolescents' engagement with Web 2.0 and social media: Research, theory, and practice. *Research in the Schools, 19*(1), 33–44.

Australian Curriculum, Assessment and Reporting Authority. (n.d.). The Australian curriculum, v3.0. Retrieved from *www.australiancurriculum.edu. au/Home*.

Bråten, I., Strømsø, H. I., & Britt, M. A. (2009). Trust matters: Examining the role of source evaluation in students' construction of meaning within and across multiple texts. *Reading Research Quarterly, 44*(1), 6–28.

Christensen, C. M. (1997). *The innovator's dilemma: When new technologies cause great firms to fail.* Boston: Harvard Business School Press.

Darling-Hammond, L. (2010). Performance-based assessment and educational equity. *Harvard Educational Review, 64*(1), 5–31.

Drew, S. (2012). Open up the ceiling on the Common Core State Standards. *Journal of Adolescent and Adult Literacy, 56,* 321–330.

Fabos, B. (2008). The price of information: Critical literacy, education, and today's Internet. In J. Coiro, M. Knobel, C. Lankshear, & D. Leu (Eds.), *Handbook of research on new literacies* (pp. 839–870). Mahwah, NJ: Erlbaum.

Forzani, E. (2015, April). *Investigating the effects of gender and socioeconomic status on students' ability to critically evaluate online information in science.* Paper presented at the annual meeting of the American Educational Research Association, Chicago, IL.

Forzani, E., & Leu, D. J. (2012). New literacies for new learners. *Educational Forum, 76*(4), 421–424.

Graham, L., & Metaxas, P. T. (2003). Of course it's true: I saw it on the Internet! *Communications of the ACM, 46*(5), 71–75.

International Reading Association. (2009). *IRA position statement on new literacies and 21st century technologies.* Newark, DE: Author. Retrieved from *www.literacyworldwide.org/docs/default-source/where-we-stand/new-literacies-21st-century-position-statement.pdf?sfvrsn=ec4ea18e_6.*

Larson, L., & Dwyer, B. (2015). Digging deeper with reader response: Using digital tools to support comprehension of literary texts in online learning environments. In T. Rasinski, K. E. Pytash & R. E. Ferdig (Eds.), *Using technology to enhance reading: Innovative approaches to literacy instruction* (pp. 121–130). Bloomington, IN: Solution Tree.

Leu, D. J., Coiro, J., Castek, J., Hartman, D., Henry, L. A., & Reinking, D. (2008). Research on instruction and assessment in the new literacies of online reading comprehension. In C. C. Block & S. R. Parris (Eds.), *Comprehension instruction: Research-based best practices* (pp. 111–153). New York: Guilford Press.

Leu, D. J., Coiro, J., Kulikowich, J., & Cui, W. (2012, December). *Using the psychometric characteristics of multiple- choice, open Internet, and closed (simulated) Internet formats to refine the development of online research and comprehension assessments in science: Year three of the ORCA project.* Paper presented at the annual meeting of the Literacy Research Association, San Diego, CA.

Leu, D. J., Forzani, E., Rhoads, C., Maykel, C., Kennedy, C., & Timbrell, N. (2015). The new literacies of online research and comprehension: Rethinking the reading achievement gap. *Reading Research Quarterly, 50*(1), 37–59.

Leu, D. J., Kinzer, C. K., Coiro, J., Castek, J., & Henry, L. A. (2013). New literacies: A dual level theory of the changing nature of literacy, instruction, and assessment. In N. Unrau & D. Alvermann (Eds.), *Theoretical models and processes of reading* (6th ed., pp. 1150–1181). Newark, DE: International Reading Association.

Leu, D. J., Kulikowich, J., Sedransk, N., & Coiro, J. (2009). *Assessing online reading comprehension: The ORCA project.* Research grant funded by the U.S. Department of Education, Institute of Education Sciences.

Leu, D. J., McVerry, J. G., O'Byrne, W. I., Kiili, C., Zawilinski, L., Everett-Cacopardo, H., . . . Forzani, E. (2011). The new literacies of online reading comprehension: Expanding the literacy and learning curriculum. *Journal of Adolescent and Adult Literacy, 55*(1), 5–14.

Lewis, C., & Fabos, B. (2005). Instant messaging, literacies, and social identities. *Reading Research Quarterly, 40,* 470–501.

Minister of Manitoba Education, Citizenship, and Youth. (2006). A continuum model for literacy with ICT across the curriculum: A resource for developing computer literacy. Retrieved from *www.edu.gov.mb.ca/k12/tech/lict/teachers/show_me/continuum.html.*

Mishra, P., & Koehler, M. J. (2006). Technological pedagogical content knowledge: A new framework for teacher knowledge. *Teachers College Record, 108*(6), 1017–1054.

Mullis, I. V. S., Martin, M. O., & Sainsbury, M. (2013). PIRLS 2016 reading framework. In I. V. S. Mullis & M. O. Martin (Eds.), *PIRLS 2016 Assessment Framework* (p. 11–29). Chestnut Hill, MA: TIMSS & PIRLS International Study Center, Boston College. Retrieved from *timssandpirls.bc.edu/pirls2016/framework.html.*

National Governors Association for Best Practices & Council of Chief State School Officers. (2010). *Common Core State Standards for English language arts and literacy in history/social studies, science, and technical subjects.* Washington, DC: Author. Retrieved from *www.corestandards.org.*

Organization for Economic Co-operation and Development. (2011). PISA 2009 results: Students on line: Digital technologies and performance (Vol. 6). Retrieved from *www.oecd.org/education/school/programmeforinternationalstudentassessmentpisa/pisa2009resultsstudentsonlinedigitaltechnologiesandperformancevolumevi.htm.*

Prensky, M. (2001). Digital natives, digital immigrants. *On the Horizon, 9*(5), 1–6.

Sanchez, C. A., Wiley, J., & Goldman, S. R. (2006). Teaching students to evaluate source reliability during Internet research tasks. In S. A. Barab, K. E. Hay, & D. T. Hickey (Eds.), *Proceedings of the Seventh International Conference on the Learning Sciences* (pp. 662–666). Bloomington, IN: International Society of the Learning Sciences.

Street, B. (2003). What's new in new literacy studies? *Current Issues in Comparative Education, 5*(2), 1–14.

Wiggins, G. (1998). *Educative assessment: Designing assessments to inform and improve student performance.* San Francisco: Jossey-Bass.

Zawilinski, L. (2009). HOT blogging: A framework for blogging to promote higher order thinking. *The Reading Teacher, 62,* 650–661.

Zawilinski, L. (2012). *An exploration of a collaborative blogging approach to literacy and learning: A mixed method study.* Unpublished doctoral dissertation, University of Connecticut, Storrs, CT.

Zawilinski, L. (2016). Primary grade students create science eBooks on iPads: Authentic audiences, purposes and technologies for writing. *New England Reading Association Journal, 51*(2), 81–90.

CHAPTER 16

Organizing Effective Literacy Instruction

Differentiating Instruction to Meet Student Needs

D. RAY REUTZEL
SARAH K. CLARK

This chapter will:

- Provide an overview of the global and national context in which organizing for classroom literacy instruction is embedded.

- Present the evidence-based elements of effective literacy instruction addressing state standards and *response to intervention* (RTI) models.

- Discuss the use of assessment data to inform changes to state standards and instructional expectations and RTI literacy instruction.

- Describe the use of an array of effective literacy instructional practices to use with state standards and RTI.

- Offer alternative grouping approaches as a part of effective literacy instruction to use state standards and RTI.

- Illustrate the scheduling of a literacy instructional block to support effective literacy instruction in an age of greater accountability, state standards, and RTI.

EVIDENCE-BASED BEST PRACTICES:
DIFFERENTIATING LITERACY INSTRUCTION IN A
COMMON CORE AND RESPONSE TO INTERVENTION ERA

Many, if not most, citizens living in our ever-shrinking, globally connected world would agree that the ability to read is a critical factor in living a healthy, happy, and economically productive life. On the other hand, the inability to read often denies individuals and groups access to many significant educational, social, health care, and economic opportunities. Years ago these facts were widely heralded in a report titled *Becoming a Nation of Readers* (Anderson, Hiebert, Scott, & Wilkinson, 1985). Unfortunately, more recent U.S. evidence seems to point to a nation of *nonreaders*. We are as a people literate but often uninformed. We tend to spend much of our time engaged in almost any other conceivable activity except sustained, deep reading. As a nation we spend less time reading than watching TV or surfing on the Internet. A 2018 national survey revealed that U.S. adults spend 2.8 hours per day watching TV, as compared to .25–.33 hours per day in reading books (Bureau of Labor Statistics, 2018). In fact, a National Endowment for the Arts survey in 2016 found that 14% fewer Americans had read any work of literature in the year past, as compared to American adults in 1982. And book reading has generally declined since U.S. adults' reading of literature was first measured in 1982. Jenkins (2008) found in a survey that 58% of U.S. adults don't read a book again after high school graduation, and 42% of college graduates never read a book again after college graduation. Eighty percent of U.S. families didn't buy or read a book in the previous year, and 70% had not been in a bookstore in the preceding 5 years. These statistics paint a picture of a U.S. population that is able to read, but isn't inclined to do so. This situation does not bode well for a democratic republic such as ours that is highly dependent upon a well-informed populace.

As troubling as these facts are, it is only compounded when national statistics are presented showing a substantial and continuing achievement gap between the rich and the poor, and between Asian and Caucasian students and students of other ethnic and linguistic minorities. And as if that isn't troubling enough, there are international data showing U.S. students' achievement in the bottom half of 30 comparable and competitive nations in math and in the middle in reading science achievement (Organisation for Economic Cooperation and Development, 2016). This tale of a nation with increasing numbers of nonreaders encumbered by two achievement gaps, one national and one international, has led in the past decade to two important educational reforms that are shaping the literacy instruction of today and tomorrow, as well as influencing the classroom environment that supports literacy instruction. The first of these two educational reforms is the increasing use of *response to intervention* (RTI) models adopted to close the national achievement gap by delivering timely interventions to students who are falling behind their national peers. The second reform is the adoption and implementation of the Common Core State Standards or adjustments and adaptions of these Common Core State Standards in individual state standards intended to close the international achievement gap between the United States and other developed nations and return the United States to a more advantaged status in the global economy.

Gap 1: The U.S. Achievement Gap

The first achievement gap, which is largely a national concern, has centered on a persistent reading achievement gap. Since 1992, black, Hispanic, and Native American students have continued to lag significantly behind their white and Asian peers in reading achievement. By the mid-1990s, political opinions had coalesced around the need for sweeping reforms in literacy instruction and assessment. The politically charged "perfect storm" around literacy was initiated with the National Assessment Educational Progress national report card on reading confirming that the achievement gap between white and Asian students and those in other economic, ethnic, linguistic, and cultural groups had widened to an all-time high (Williams, Reese, Campbell, Mazzeo, & Phillips, 1995).

The U.S. Congress and the U.S. Department of Education reacted to this devastating news by forming several blue ribbon panels charged with examining research on proven teaching practices and then sharing their findings with the public. The National Reading Panel (National Institute of Child Health and Human Development, 2000) examined the teaching of reading in elementary and secondary schools; the National Literacy Panel for Language Minority Children and Youth (August & Shanahan, 2006) explored literacy development and instruction for second-language learners; and the National Early Literacy Panel (2008) looked at beginning literacy learning for preschoolers and kindergartners. Reports from these three panels have been most influential in reforming public policy and instructional practice in reading. Though these research findings were not only quickly adopted by commercial reading program publishers, they were codified into law as a part of the federal government's No Child Left Behind Act (e.g., Reading First, Early Reading First), which included far-reaching policy and legislative changes to federally funded Title I and Head Start programs.

Though there has been modest progress in closing the national reading achievement gap, results of these initiatives have been disappointing. Although the achievement gap narrowed to its lowest measured level since

1992, it is clear that children in specific ethnic groups, often those living in poverty, continue to fail to read at grade level at more than twice the rate of those living out of poverty, and in Asian and White ethnic groups. Too many students in the most rapidly growing segment of U.S. society, namely black, Hispanic, and Native American children, continue to perform at levels below their peers nationally in basic reading proficiency.

The RTI model is a relatively recent addition to the special education law entitled, Individuals with Disabilities Education Act (IDEA). RTI is a recommended process for schools to follow when working with children who are struggling to learn to read or who are failing to read on grade level (Gersten et al., 2008). The underlying premise of RTI is that the instruction students receive, or have received previously, is not sufficient to meet the needs of the learner. DuFour, DuFour, Eaker, Many, and Mattos (2016) when describing the core purpose of professional learning communities (PLCs), assert that multitiered intervention systems, like those required as part of implementing an RTI model of support are needed to ensure that every student exits the year having acquired the essential literacy skills, knowledge, and behaviors required for success at the next grade level. Teachers learn in PLCs how to provide struggling students the additional time and support they will need to master the requirements of a grade-level curriculum because many students enter the classroom each year lacking the essential literacy foundational skills that they should have mastered in prior years.

There are three levels or tiers of instruction that make up the RTI model. First, there is Tier 1 instruction that consists of the standards and objectives taught at each grade level. Tier 1 instruction is intended for the whole class or heterogeneous small groups with differentiated levels. This instruction is usually from a research-based core literacy program taught with the goal of fidelity to the program. In instances where student progress is not being met in Tier 1 instruction, there is a pressing need to address the instructional effectiveness and the curriculum materials in use. For those students who lag behind their peers or who lack competence in one or more key literacy skills, Tier 2 is needed. Tier 2 reading instruction provides targeted, small-group literacy instruction that meets the specific needs of each individual struggling reader. It relies on reading assessment data to help determine those needs and to design meaningful instruction. Schools sometimes have a district-adopted program for teachers to use in Tier 2 instruction. If the student does not respond to Tier 2 intervention, then a more intensive form of instruction should be implemented. The third and final tier is Tier 3 instruction, sometimes referred to as the "double dose" intervention. Students can be serviced individually, although most Tier 3 instruction continues in small groups and are taught by the teacher, reading specialist, or special educator. In recent years, teachers are seeing more and more students who require Tier 3 instruction, but who do not qualify for special education assistance. This shift requires the classroom teacher to take on more responsibility for differentiating the literacy instruction to meet the needs of students who fall far behind his or her peers in reading ability.

A variety of reading assessments play an important role in assisting the teacher in providing the correct form of instruction to each of the students in the class. Types of reading assessments include screening, diagnostic, progress-monitoring, and outcome assessments. Some of these are used before, some during, and some after the reading process. Teacher observations also provide the necessary information needed to make instructional decisions, as do regular consultations with reading specialists and/or reading coaches who utilize assessment data to inform instructional decisions. The RTI model operates in a functional way to close the national achievement gap between those who typically perform well without supplementary reading instructional attention and those who typically lag behind (Reutzel & Cooter, 2016).

Gap 2: The International Reading Achievement Gap

The second achievement gap, an international concern, has resulted from academic achievement comparisons of U.S. graduating high school seniors with graduates from 34 other highly developed nations and economies. These comparisons have revealed that U.S. students lag approximately 2 years behind the academic performance levels of similarly aged graduating students in other developed nations. An increasingly influential group of corporate, governmental, and public policy advocacy groups see these two literacy-related achievement gaps as threats to the U.S. economy and even our national security (Brill, 2011; Darling-Hammond, 2010; Friedman & Mandelbaum, 2011; Neuman & Celano, 2012; Perry, 2011; Weber, 2010).

The Progress in International Reading Literacy Study (PIRLS) released in 2011, is an international comparative study of fourth-grade student literacy-related achievement (Wagner, 2008). In 2011, 57 educational systems participated in the PIRLS comparison and five nations scored higher than the United States, and others scored significantly higher. As Geoffrey Canada states in the book *Waiting for Superman*, "the steady progress of the American education system has ground to a halt. As countries in the rest of the word have continued to advance, U.S. reading and math scores have frozen in place" (Weber, 2010, p. 17).

There is increasing concern about how U.S. students compare with students from the other 34 developed nations in the world on competitive rankings in literacy, science, and mathematics (Wagner, 2008). According to the Programme for International Student Achievement (See PISA,

2015) (Organisation for Economic Co-operation and Development, 2016), the United States ranks 24th in literacy, 25th in science, and 41st in mathematics among 74 developed comparable nations. These rankings continue to highlight a considerable gap in the nation's student academic outcomes when compared to students in other developed nations. This fact in turn raises concerns about U.S. students' abilities to compete in an increasingly competitive world economy in the future.

Although increased attention given to teaching children the essential or critical components of the literacy process in the past decade has resulted in moderate national effects (Mathes et al., 2005; Rathvon, 2004; National Early Literacy Panel, 2008; National Assessment of Educational Progress, 2015), the detrimental national and international achievement gaps continue to persist. In an effort to "raise the bar" of literacy achievement expectations to assure readiness of U.S. students for career and college upon high school graduation, the National Governors' Association (NGA) and the Council of Chief State School Officers (CCSSO) joined together in the adoption, implementation, and assessment of the *English Language Arts (K–12) Common Core State Standards* (ELA K–12 CCSS) (NGA & CCSSO, 2010).

As of this writing, 42 states, the District of Columbia, four U.S. territories, and the Department of Defense Education Activity have adopted the Common Core State Standards (CCSS) in the English language arts (K–12) in some form. This state-by-state adoption of learning standards represents the first time in U.S. history that there has been a near border-to-border coordination of learning goals. The vast majority of teachers and students nationally use the CCSS for English language arts (K–12) or something closely related to them.

Not only do the CCSS represent the most extensive basis in history for national agreement on learning standards concerning what students should know and be able to do in literacy, these new standards are markedly higher than past standards in terms of what they expect teachers to accomplish with their students (Carmichael, Martino, Porter-Magee, & Wilson, 2010; McLaughlin & Overturf, 2013; Morrow, Shanahan, & Wixson, 2013). In the past, educational standards have usually been written using a developmental model from youngest to oldest learners. The designers of the CCSS seem to have followed the recommendations of the late Stephen Covey (2004)'s *Seven Habits of Highly Effective People*: they began with the end in mind. In other words, they reverse-engineered the CCSS by starting with what is expected of college- and career-ready high school seniors, and then reverse-engineered the CCSS for younger learners from there. As Shanahan (2013, p. 208) wrote,

> Past standards have represented what educators thought they could accomplish, while the CCSS are a description of what students would

need to learn if they are to leave school able to participate in U.S. society and to compete globally by working or continuing their education.

The CCSS are without a doubt more demanding of both teachers and students. They represent a forward-looking, 21st-century representation of what the high school graduating student needs. As expected in the initial stages of implementation and assessment, school administrators and teachers saw fewer students meeting these higher literacy standards.

In addition to higher standards and expectations, the CCSS highlight connections across subject areas (Stage, Asturias, Cheuk, Daro, & Hampton, 2013) and elevate the expectations of teachers to teach all children to read and write well enough to succeed in college and career. Thus, using the evidence-based standards of effective literacy instruction from the first decade of the new millennium (National Reading Panel, 2000; National Early Literacy Panel, 2008), teachers now have an objective clearly in view—helping students achieve the new and more demanding performances outlined in the CCSS (NGA & CCSSO, 2010). The intention of this instruction is to lift all students to international standards of proficiency in reading and writing, which will close the international achievement gap by offering evidence-based and standards-based high-quality Tier 1 literacy instruction across the grades as is typically explicated in an RTI model of instructional delivery (Vaughn, Fuchs, & Fuchs, 2008).

If there is one clear message that classroom teachers should take away from this brief recitation of issues related to literacy instruction and assessment, it is the significance that the United States now places on the ability of its citizens to read and read well. Consequently, it has been in the past and indeed is today a continuing national priority for our citizens to once again become a nation of readers. Teachers occupy a unique and important position to positively affect the literacy achievement of the next generation by organizing for and delivering effective literacy instruction that meets the needs of *all* students preparing them for successful careers and college and becoming lifelong readers.

The next section of this chapter is devoted to best practices of literacy instruction in action. We begin with a description of Tier 1 literacy instruction that incorporates elements of evidence-based reading and writing instruction into three allocated time blocks. Following this description, we discuss how teachers can organize their classrooms to support Tier 2, small-group, targeted literacy instruction, which is derived from administration of progress-monitoring assessments that reveal students' skill, strategy, or conceptual instructional needs. We provide illustrations of how to manage the complexities of the classroom environment where whole-class, small-group, and individual instruction is the new normal or the expected practice in literacy instruction.

BEST PRACTICES IN ACTION

A Classroom Vignette

Mrs. Lopez takes a deep breath as she shuts the classroom door. The next morning a new school year begins and 26 second graders will walk through the doorway ready for another year of learning and growth. Mrs. Lopez has worked tirelessly to get the classroom ready to meet the diverse needs of each of her students and is excited for the days ahead. Her colorful and brightly lit classroom welcomes students and encourages deep thinking and creativity.

Mrs. Lopez's classroom is well organized and designed to meet the needs of each individual student and to accommodate multiple types of learning settings that will include small-group instruction, whole-class instruction, and individual learning centers. The classroom is rich with print including the daily schedule, the objectives for the day, a message center, word walls, collections of environmental print, labeled objects, poetry, songs, handwritten notes, newspaper articles, and a wide variety of literature and informational texts placed strategically throughout the classroom. A large colorful rug with space for each child to sit comfortably provides a perfect spot for read-alouds, discussions, singing, and conversations as a class and this arrangement lends itself easily to whole-class and/or Tier 1 instruction. A horseshoe table is set up nearby for Mrs. Lopez to move into small-group, teacher-directed, and differentiated literacy instruction. These smaller groups allow for targeted Tier 2 and Tier 3 instruction. Instructional materials such as vocabulary cards, small whiteboards and markers/erasers, text sets, and word sort cards are all readily available at the table.

Stationed throughout the room are multiple literacy centers designed to provide students with an opportunity to practice the skills and instruction provided during whole-class and small-group instruction. These centers are based on student needs and emphasize topics such as phonological awareness, phonics, fluency, vocabulary, comprehension, writing, and the integration of reading and writing with science and social studies content. These intentional and carefully crafted learning centers provide opportunities for students to practice what has been modeled and taught and to apply new learning in an unrushed and individualized setting.

Mrs. Lopez has organized a writing center stocked with multiple forms of paper, writing tools, computers with Internet access, individual computer tablets with word processors and access to *Dictionary.com* and *Thesaurus.com,* dry-erase boards, and a printer standing by for students to print and publish their writing.

An independent reading area has also been established complete with beanbag chairs and pillows intended to provide a relaxing space for students to relax and do some independent reading in a quiet nook in the classroom. Along with a classroom library filled with literature and informational texts on a wide variety of topics, there are also computer tablets available for students to read digital texts and to use Applications such as *Epic!–Books for Kids* to enrich learning and reading opportunities for students.

Additional individualized centers include opportunities for students to read about and conduct science experiments, to explore historical documents, and to engage in disciplinary literacy throughout the school day. The last learning center provides opportunities for students to practice paired or budding reading fluency and houses digital recorders, headphones, browsing boxes for reading practice, and materials for evaluating self and others' reading fluency. These fluency activities include practice to improve rate, accuracy, and expression.

Given the opportunity, Mrs. Lopez would tell us all about the planning, thought, and preparation that has gone into designing an effective and efficient classroom. She knows how critically important the classroom environment is to the academic success of her students. She has designed her classroom environment to include the following: (1) intentional implementation of a variety of grouping strategies, (2) access to wide variety of high-quality texts including both print and digital, and (3) inclusion in a classroom management plan that encourages both self-regulation and a feeling of community and connection. These complex organizational components, like so much of effective literacy instruction, are the products of teacher knowledge, skill, and ingenuity.

As you can tell from this vignette, Mrs. Lopez attends to the individual differences students bring with them to school, and she is well aware that not all students respond to instruction in the same way or with similar enthusiasm. Mrs. Lopez also understands that every child needs to be taught, to varying degrees, all of the components of evidence-based literacy Tier 1 instruction that addresses the grade-level CCSS (Neuman & Gambrell, 2013) or individualized state standards. This is not meant to imply that a one-size-fits-all instructional approach using state core literacy standards will be effective with all children, but that this only frames a base set of learning expectations. After teachers provide high-quality, Tier 1 instruction, they collect and analyze progress monitoring data and design Tier 2, and, if needed, Tier 3, targeted literacy instruction delivered in small groups to fill gaps and strengthen the acquisition of necessary literacy skills and to meet the higher standards and expectations set for students today.

The Daily Literacy Block: Organizing an Effective Instructional Routine

Students develop a sense of security when the events of the school day revolve around a sequence of familiar activities. Although variety is the spice of life, students find comfort in familiar instructional routines and schedules in a well-organized classroom (Holdaway, 1984). There are any number of ways to organize the activities and instruction of the school day. It is important, however, that children experience a variety of interactive settings as a whole class, in small groups, and individually each day. Groups should be flexible, meet the needs of the students, incorporate assessment data to inform instructional decisions, and involve the "best practices" of literacy instruction. It is also important that children receive daily planned, intentional, and explicit instruction in the critical components, strategies, and skills of learning to read and write successfully.

One such approach used to organize the school day is the *daily literacy instruction block* based in part on the recommendations of Shanahan (2004) and also based on the work of Mathes et al. (2005) relating to the value of small-group reading instruction. This organizational framework, the daily literacy instruction block (see Figure 16.1), is a functional and flexible instructional scaffolding model used by teachers in classrooms to provide interactive, shared, whole-class, and small-group differentiated reading and writing experiences for children similar to such other organizational plans as the four-block plan by Patricia Cunningham (Cunningham, Hall, & Defee, 1998). Additionally, the daily literacy instruction block incorporates terminology used in instructional learning standards to ensure alignment. A variety of assessments including screening, diagnostic, progress-monitoring, and outcome assessment play key roles in assisting the teacher make instructional decisions that meet the developmental needs of students.

The daily literacy instruction block is divided into four clearly defined instructional times and activity blocks: *(1) foundational skills instruction, (2) comprehension strategy instruction, (3) writing and spelling instruction,* and *(4) targeted small-group instruction.* The daily literacy instruction block incorporates into its structure the critical components of reading and writing instruction recommended in this chapter and in several national reading research reports, including decoding and word recognition instruction, fluency development, writing, vocabulary and comprehension strategy instruction, and guided oral reading (August & Shanahan, 2006; Snow, Burns, & Griffin, 1998; National Reading Panel, 2000; National Early Literacy Panel, 2008). The daily literacy instruction block is designed for 180 minutes of allocated daily instructional time in grades K–6 and incorporates both Tier 1 and Tier 2 instruction. This is an uninterrupted block

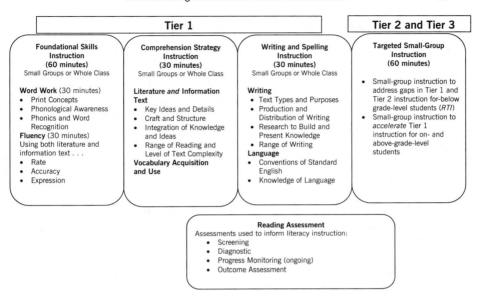

Tier 1			Tier 2 and Tier 3
Foundational Skills Instruction (60 minutes) Small Groups or Whole Class	**Comprehension Strategy Instruction (30 minutes)** Small Groups or Whole Class	**Writing and Spelling Instruction (30 minutes)** Small Groups or Whole Class	**Targeted Small-Group Instruction (60 minutes)**
Word Work (30 minutes) • Print Concepts • Phonological Awareness • Phonics and Word Recognition **Fluency** (30 minutes) Using both literature and information text . . . • Rate • Accuracy • Expression	**Literature *and* Information Text** • Key Ideas and Details • Craft and Structure • Integration of Knowledge and Ideas • Range of Reading and Level of Text Complexity **Vocabulary Acquisition and Use**	**Writing** • Text Types and Purposes • Production and Distribution of Writing • Research to Build and Present Knowledge • Range of Writing **Language** • Conventions of Standard English • Knowledge of Language	• Small-group instruction to address gaps in Tier 1 and Tier 2 instruction for-below grade-level students (*RTI*) • Small-group instruction to *accelerate* Tier 1 instruction for on- and above-grade-level students

Reading Assessment
Assessments used to inform literacy instruction:
- Screening
- Diagnostic
- Progress Monitoring (ongoing)
- Outcome Assessment

FIGURE 16.1. Daily literacy instruction block.

of time to ensure instructional density and proper pacing with focused attention on the tasks. The structure of the time allocations found in the daily literacy instruction block is outlined in Figure 16.1.

Tier 1 Literacy Instruction: Meeting the Demands of Instructional Standards

Tier 1 literacy instruction is grade-level-appropriate instruction for *all* students. This means that achieving the state core literacy standards are expected of all students at each subsequent grade level. Students must meet new expectations in reading foundations, literature, informational text, writing, listening and speaking, and language in each grade level and be able to read and write increasingly complex texts. In order to meet these new standards, teachers will need to allocate instructional time and focus to the "just right set" of evidence-based instructional priorities. Many core reading programs adopted by school districts align with their state standards, but teacher knowledge and instructional approach remain highly important in Tier 1 literacy instruction. In what follows, we outline the priorities for time allocation and instructional focus in Tier 1 reading instruction that is intended to meet the new and higher expectations of state standards.

Reading Foundational Skills Instruction (60 Minutes)

The *foundational skills* instructional block is functionally divided into two key components including *word work* (30 minutes) and *fluency* (30 minutes). The purpose of the *word work* component of the foundational skills instruction is to develop children's (1) phonological and phonemic awareness, (2) concepts about print, (3) letter recognition and production, (4) decoding and word recognition, and (5) spelling concepts, skills, and strategies.

WORD WORK (30 MINUTES)

Effective instructional practices used during this time allocation include shared reading of enlarged texts (including charts, posters, use of lessons and text on the smart board, overhead transparencies, and big books), the co-construction of interactive written sentences and brief stories, making and breaking words using manipulative letters, and choral response techniques using such tools as gel, white dry erase, or magna-doodle boards. We cannot overemphasize the importance of providing the whole class with direct, explicit instruction on each of these word-related skills, strategies, and concepts. Children need clear explanations such as "think-alouds" coupled with expert modeling of reading and writing behaviors, and guided application of these concepts, skills, and strategies during this time allocation as well. We also strongly recommend that daily lessons focus on both decoding and spelling—reading and writing processes that help children better understand the reciprocal nature of all reading and writing processes. While explicit instruction and modeling are necessary, games and word play can also be used as an instructional approach during word work to increase student engagement in these foundational literacy skills.

FLUENCY (30 MINUTES)

The *fluency* component of the foundational skills instruction begins with explicit explanation, description, and modeling of reading fluency as defined in the research and professional literature: (1) accuracy, (2) rate, and (3) expression, so that children learn how to read fluently using a broad range of texts (Reutzel & Juth, 2014). Children need to see and hear models of what fluent reading sounds like and what it does not sound like. After explaining, defining, describing, modeling, demonstrating, and discussing fluent reading, teachers use various formats for choral reading, such as echoic (echo chamber), unison (all together), antiphonal (one side against another), line-a-child, and so on. For those who are unfamiliar with these choral-reading variations, we recommend reading Opitz and Rasinski's (2008) *Good-Bye Round Robin,* or Rasinski's (2003) *The Fluent Reader.* Once children sense their emerging fluency, they want to demonstrate it to others. Children love to perform their practiced oral reading for an audience of either parents or other students in the school building. When preparing an oral reading performance, teachers might use one of three well-known oral reading instructional approaches: (1) Readers' Theater, (2) radio reading, and (3) recitation (Opitz & Rasinski, 2008). Remember that fluency achieved in just one type of task or text type is insufficient, and that children require instruction and practice with a variety of reading fluency tasks and a variety of text types (literature and informational texts) and levels of challenge (Reutzel, 2012). This will teach students that fluency can vary depending on the genre (fictional vs. nonfictional reading), topic of the text (familiar or unfamiliar ideas and vocabulary), and that reading at a comfortable, not necessarily a fast, pace to achieve comprehension is a trait of a good reader.

Oral reading fluency can also be supported through silent reading when specific supportive conditions are present. Reutzel, Jones, Fawson, and Smith (2008) describe a process known as scaffolded silent reading (ScSR) where students are guided through book selection lessons to select a book they can and do read. Students set goals, conference with the teacher, and complete response projects to share what they learned with others from reading a book silently. ScSR has been shown to result in fluency gains equal to those found with repeated oral reading with feedback as recommended by the National Reading Panel (Reutzel, Fawson, & Smith, 2008).

Comprehension Instruction (30 Minutes)

The purpose of the *comprehension* instructional block is to develop children's (1) vocabulary and (2) comprehension. Effective instructional practices used within this time segment include explicit instruction of vocabulary concepts, using a variety of methods and requiring a variety of responses (Beck, McKeown, & Kucan, 2013; McKenna, 2002; Stahl & Nagy, 2006), and wordplay (Johnson, 2001).

VOCABULARY INSTRUCTION

To support the growth of one's vocabulary, it is important to remember that there are four different types of vocabularies (listening, speaking, reading, and writing) and teachers should work to strengthen each of these during instructional time. Students learn vocabulary at different levels beginning at the unknown, moving to acquainted, and finally a word becomes established within a student's vocabulary (National Reading Panel, 2000). Graves (1987) articulated six tasks that should be incorporated during vocabulary instruction: (1) learning to read new words, (2) learning new meanings for old words, (3) learning new words that represent known concepts, (4) learning new words that represent new concepts, (5) clarifying and enriching meaning of known words, and (6) moving words from receptive to expressive vocabulary.

While teachers can use the vocabulary recommended in the core reading program to assist in the comprehension of the current story, that doesn't have to be the only vocabulary instruction that takes place. Additional new words can be introduced to the students, added to the word walls, highlighted during read-alouds, and encouraged in student writing. Bowne, Yoshikawa, and Snow (2017) found that content-focused vocabulary instruction was very effective in developing and sustaining vocabulary growth in young learners. This is especially true when children are engaged in whole-class, conceptually rich discussions on a wide range of interesting topics. Furthermore, Snell, Hindman, and Wasik (2015) advised teachers to use child-friendly definitions, ask questions and have conversations about unfamiliar words, reread books, engage children in retelling activities that use newly learned vocabulary words, and integrate new words with other activities throughout the school day. Thus, teachers who provide opportunities for students to read, write, question, and converse about new and unfamiliar words are providing meaningful vocabulary instruction.

COMPREHENSION INSTRUCTION

Effective comprehension strategy instruction includes both dialogic collaboration and conversation around a variety of texts and the teaching of a variety of comprehension strategies including (1) questioning, (2) discussing text structure, (3) using graphic organizers, (4) explaining inferences, (5) predicting, (6) monitoring, (7) summarizing, and (9) background knowledge activation or building (Dole & Liang, 2006; Pyle et al,, 2017; Wilkinson & Son, 2011). Providing the whole class with direct explicit instruction on each of these comprehension skills, strategies, and concepts continues to be considered a "best practice" of literacy instruction. With comprehension, using both literature and informational texts is essential to align with core state literacy standards as well as providing opportunities for students to interact with each other and with the teacher around the contents and structure of the texts they are reading—often referred to as "close readings" (Cummins, 2013; Reutzel, Clark, Jones, & Gillam, 2016; Shanahan, 2012a, 2012b). To strengthen comprehension, children need clear explanations, "think-alouds" coupled with expert modeling of comprehension thought processes and behaviors, as well as teacher-guided application of these concepts, skills, and strategies in the reading of many texts at different levels and in many genres. It is also strongly recommend that teachers consider teaching multiple comprehension strategies such as *reciprocal teaching* (Palincsar, 2003), *concept-oriented reading instruction* (Guthrie, 2003; Swan, Coddington, & Guthrie, 2010), and *transactional strategies* (Brown, Pressley, Van Meter, & Shuder, 1996; Reutzel, Smith, & Fawson, 2005) to be used collectively and strategically while interacting with a variety of texts over long periods of time (National Reading Panel, 2000; Reutzel et al., 2005).

Additionally, children need to be taught how different texts are organized through close readings of a text (Shanahan et al., 2010; Shanahan, Fisher, & Frey, 2012). Understanding text structure aids comprehension. The use of retelling, as well as guide sheets or graphic organizers, helps students organize information and understand text more clearly. For example, literature texts typically include the following features: (1) setting, (2) characters, (3) conflict or problem, (4) goal or plot (rising action, climax, falling action), and (5) resolution. The use of story maps supports the comprehension of literature texts because they require students to engage in the text and assist in self-monitoring (Davis & McPherson, 1989; Reutzel & Cooter, 2018). Informational texts are structured differently than literature texts and follow one of five informational text structures: (1) descriptive, (2) sequence, (3) problem–solution or question–answer, (4) compare and contrast, and (5) cause–effect (Jones, Clark, & Reutzel, 2016). Helping students learn to navigate informational texts and learn how to use information text features such as the table of contents, the glossary, the index, the graphics (including maps, pictures, and graphs) as well as the inserts and bubble call-outs, can support and deepen student comprehension of these types of texts (Roberts et al., 2013).

Writing and Spelling Instruction (30 Minutes)

The purpose of the *writing and spelling* instructional block is to develop children's (1) composition skills, (2) spelling, (3) mechanics, (4) grammatical understandings, and (5) literary and writing genre concepts, skills, and strategies.

WRITING INSTRUCTION

Graham, Gillespie, and McKeown (2013) stressed the key elements of effective writing instruction should include opportunities for students to write frequently across the curriculum, to write for many different purposes, to have access to good models for the types of writing, to use word processing as the primary writing medium, to have support gathering and organizing ideas, and to receive intentional and direct teaching of writing skills and strategies immersed with regular feedback and assessment.

During writing instruction, a variety of emphases should be incorporated including fluency development, exploring writing types and the purposes of writing, producing and distributing writing, researching and presenting knowledge in writing, and experiencing a range of writing experiences that allows for both extended and shorter periods of time writing independently and with scaffolding and support (Graham, McKeown, Kiuhara, & Harris, 2012; Troia, 2014; Troia & Olinghouse, 2013). Students need to develop the ability to fluently produce letters, words, and sentences in order to allow for thoughts to be efficiently represented (Coker, 2006; Graham et al., 2012.) Time should be given in the earliest stages of writing development for helping children acquire handwriting or keyboarding skills that allow them to transcribe thoughts efficiently into words, phrases, and sentence.

Once transcription is fluent, effective instructional practices used within this writing time allocation include modeled writing by the teacher; a writer's workshop with drafting, conferencing, revising, editing, publishing, and disseminating; and explicit whole-class instruction on each of these writing skills, strategies, and concepts. Simply setting up a Writer's Workshop in the classroom, however, is not sufficient. Most students do not have enough experience with generating ideas for writing, understanding how to select writing topics, utilizing advance planning for writing, understanding how to produce and organize text, understanding writing mechanics, and using the steps of revision or editing (Harris, Graham, Mason, & Friedlander, 2008). Therefore, children need clear explanations, "think-alouds" coupled with expert modeling of writing behaviors, and guided application of these writing concepts, skills, and strategies during this time allocation as well. It is also a "best practice" to learn about writing through reading and studying the styles of the authors of children's literature. Many students can model those authors that use description imagery, sensory details, figurative language, good plot structure, or characterization.

Harris and Graham (2016) reiterated that skilled writing is complex and requires much self-regulation and multiple opportunities for practice before a student can become an effective writer. Incorporating writing strategy instruction such as the self-regulated strategy development (SRSD) instructional approach developed by Harris and Graham (Harris et al., 2008) allows teachers to create a personalized writing instruction experience for each student. The SRSD model is organized in progressive stages including (1) developing background knowledge, (2) discussing it, (3) modeling it—collaborative modeling, (4) memorizing it, (5) supporting it, and (6) independent performance. These stages are not followed in a lock-step manner but rather are designed to be adjusted according to the needs and abilities of each individual student. Incorporating writing instructional strategies such as the SRSD allows the teacher not only to teach a variety of writing types, address each phase of the writing process, and the opportunity to teach or reinforce writing strategies and skills, but it allows the teacher to emphasize and explain the steps of the writing process (Graham & Harris, 1992). We also strongly recommend that daily lessons provide a time allocation for sharing children's writing in an "author's chair" or using some other method of disseminating and sharing children's writing products. Writing instruction is often done at the pace of the writer with different children at different stages of the writing process. Some may be publishing while other's may be at the editing stage. Differentiated instruction is especially important in this area with the teacher constantly aware of the pacing and stages of each child (Graham & Harris, 2016; Harris, Graham, & Adkins, 2015).

SPELLING INSTRUCTION

Enlisting a variety of spelling instructional strategies is also recommended so as to provide a variety of learning activities and to maintain student interest. Graham and Santangelo (2014) noted strong support for teaching spelling as it improved spelling performance when compared with no spelling instruction. An emphasis on helping students to recognize spelling patterns can alleviate confusion about spelling (Helman, Bear, Invernizzi, Templeton, & Johnston, 2013). Using spelling instructional strategies such as the *spelling in parts* (SIP) strategy designed by Powell and Aram (2008) assists students in learning new spelling patterns and provides strategies for students to use when they encounter larger words and need to break them down into smaller, more manageable chunks. While many Tier I programs offer spelling lists that focus on a phonics skill each week, teachers should remain purposeful in their practice options for the selected spelling words, rather than relying on the traditional approach of copying words five times each on Monday, sentences on Tuesday, definitions on Wednesday, and so forth. Planning meaningful spelling instruction teaches students about the English language, offers varied ways to practice words with similar word affixes (prefixes, suffices, or word roots), and adds to the student's growing vocabulary.

Tier 2 Literacy Instruction: Closing the Achievement Gap

Tier 2 literacy instruction, in an RTI model of instructional delivery, is intended to close gaps in students' skills, knowledge, or strategies as revealed in regular progress monitoring of instructional effectiveness. If a student is found to be lagging behind his or her peers in literacy growth, then further diagnostic assessment is employed to determine the area(s) of weakness so that the teacher can deliver targeted, small-group instruction to quickly close this gap and return students to Tier 1 instruction. In Tier I instruction, varied grouping is often employed by the classroom teacher to include whole-class, small-group, partners, and individual work time. With Tier 2 literacy instruction, small-group instruction has been found to be most effective, rather than whole-class instruction. In what follows, we discuss how to organize the classroom to support small-group, targeted reading instruction to support the delivery of Tier 2 literacy instruction.

Targeted Small-Group Instruction (60 Minutes)

Targeted small-group instruction time is a designated time for the classroom teacher to provide Tier 2 instruction to struggling readers who need more time and help and are below grade level in their reading skills. This time can also be used to accelerate and enrich literacy instruction for students who are performing on or above grade level. Managing the Tier 2 small group instruction time is a complex effort for most teachers. A teacher must be thoughtful of the behaviors and active learning of all class members while assessing, teaching, and working with the Tier 2 program or specific lesson for each group that meets. We recommend that the teacher, rather than a parent helper, or teaching assistant, work with Tier 2 intervention students because of the teacher knowledge and literacy training that a teacher can offer a student who is struggling. It's important that students clearly understand the expectations for this time so as to use their time wisely in completing literacy tasks, and also to minimize off-task behaviors that can occur when the teacher is working with small groups (Morrow, Reutzel, & Casey, 2006; Morrow, 2010). We show in Figure 16.2 options for managing the Tier 2 small-group literacy instruction environment. Options provide effective classroom management suggestions and range from simple to increasingly complex management options.

The first option is the most *simple* of the four options. During the simple option, the majority of the students work independently or with a partner completing <u>daily</u> assigned literacy tasks that are completed at student desks. These tasks can be listed menu-style where students select the tasks they would like to complete each day, or tasks can be specifically assigned by the teacher. The teacher is stationed in the small-group differentiated reading area of the classroom prepared to offer differentiated reading instruction. The teacher works with small groups of students who are pulled from the whole class and then students rotate back when the

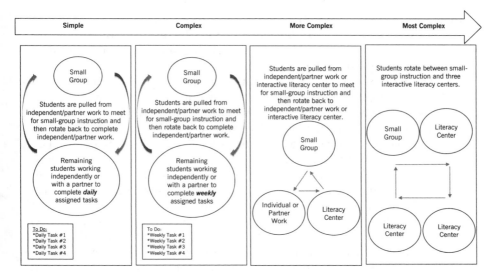

FIGURE 16.2. Four options for managing Tier 2 small-group instruction.

next group is called. The classroom has a quiet working noise level to help each student focus on the varied tasks.

The second or the *complex* option looks very similar to the first option except that the majority of the students are working independently or with a partner completing weekly assigned literacy tasks that are completed at student desks. The students working on literacy tasks independently or with a partner have a week to complete the assigned tasks so work on each task may spill over from one day to the next. These tasks may be listed menu-style where students select the tasks they would like to complete over the course of the week or tasks can be specifically assigned by the teacher. The teacher is stationed in the small-group differentiated reading area of the classroom prepared to offer differentiated reading instruction.

The third option is the *more complex* option. This option is similar to the first two options except that a literacy center has been introduced to the rotation. Students are either working independently or with a partner on their self-selected menu or teacher assigned literacy tasks, or they are working in a small group with the teacher, or they are working in another small group at the literacy center. Students may be assigned a specific time to go to the literacy center or students may be invited to go to the literacy center after their assigned tasks are completed. This is sometimes called the workshop model. It is important that the teacher create a way to keep students accountable for the work in each center to ensure that it is not just keeping the students quiet while the intervention groups are meeting, but that the instructional time being spent is valued and connected to the learning plan that week.

The fourth and *most complex* option occurs when the teacher works with small, targeted instruction reading groups and the remaining students are rotating through three or more literacy centers. The teacher is stationed in the small-group differentiated reading area of the classroom prepared to offer small-group targeted reading instruction. The children are called to their small reading group (homogeneous group) from an assigned "center rotation" group (mixed-abilities group). Literacy centers are teacher-selected, -designed, and -provisioned. Literacy centers focus on activities and tasks that reinforce and support Tier 1 and Tier 2 instruction. These activities are centered on word work, fluency, vocabulary, comprehension instruction, and writing and spelling. The fourth and most complex option requires that the literacy center activities and tasks are clearly understood, independent of teacher supervision, and able to be completed within the time allowed. It is also important that tasks completed at literacy centers have a component of accountability and performance. We caution teachers against the creation of too many learning centers. In the early part of the year, fewer centers are easier for both teachers and students to handle. As the year progresses, adding a few new centers, especially optional centers, can add variety to this time block. As time progresses and children acquire more experience with the rotation between learning centers, we have found it better to assign children specific tasks to be completed during this time period rather than a time-controlled rotation through various literacy centers. Many teachers model in detail the literacy centers at the beginning of the week, check for understanding, and then use the remaining time that day and the rest of the week to focus solely on Tier 2 instruction. It is important to note that this option of Tier 2 instruction requires upfront planning and material preparation from the teacher so that students have access to the centers and can remain independent, allowing the teacher to focus on the small-group focused tasks. Establishing clear procedures for this work time, teaching those expectations, and practicing them with the students initially and again whenever needed will maintain the consistent positive working tone that is needed for *all* students to succeed.

REFLECTIONS AND FUTURE DIRECTIONS

Teachers accommodate individual student needs in literacy instruction increasingly by providing high-quality Tier 1 literacy instruction to help all children meet the expectations of core state literacy standards using literacy progress-monitoring, screening, diagnostic, and outcomes assessment within an RTI framework to help those who struggle to catch up and keep up with their peers. Throughout the history of classroom literacy instruction, several variations on ability grouping and whole-class instruction and seatwork have persisted despite a large body of relevant research pointing to many negative outcomes for students and teachers related to these grouping strategies (Rupley & Blair, 1987). More recent research has consistently demonstrated the advantages of providing students with small-group, differentiated literacy instruction targeting specific identified needs and teaching to meet those needs (Mathes et al., 2005; Tyner, 2009).

CONCLUDING COMMENTS

More research is needed to determine the effects of implementing the state standards on students' reading achievement over time. We also need research to determine the effects that newly created standardized assessments will ultimately have on literacy instruction. For example, we don't know if this educational reform will yield outcomes similar to previous reforms on the behaviors of teachers, leading them to reduce literacy instruction to the pursuit of higher test scores. Further, we do not know how the lack of professional development support around implementing the core state literacy standards will affect literacy teachers' instruction and the curricula used or developed in schools (Reutzel, 2013). The years ahead are filled with hope and promise of improved outcomes for U.S. students as core state standards and RTI take hold in classrooms, but whether or not this promise will be realized as hoped has yet to be determined.

ENGAGEMENT ACTIVITIES

1. Discuss why the pursuit of established, grade-level Common Core State Standards within an RTI model or framework can lead to successfully differentiating literacy instruction to meet the needs of *all* learners.

2. Observe several targeted, small-group literacy instructional sessions in at least one classroom and take field notes. Then, interview four or five children in various groups about their perceptions of the differentiated instruction they receive in Tier 2 small-group settings. Does the instruction look different for each

group, or is the level of text the only change observed with the same routine in each group meeting? Do you think that changing the text level is sufficient differentiation to be effective for all children?

3. When given a reading or writing task to perform individually *or* in a cooperative learning group, what is the result on students' performance? Is quality higher or lower? Do individuals or groups use learning time more efficiently? Is the performance or product given by individuals or cooperative learning groups higher or lower? How do children of varying abilities and skill levels feel about the group processes and products?

4. Discuss whether it is important for teachers to know what children are learning from time spent in learning centers? If it is important, how can teachers require accountability from children for learning activities found in typical independent learning centers—like a buddy or paired-reading fluency center, for example?

5. Although teachers often want to provide targeted, differentiated small-group literacy instruction in their classrooms, they do not know how to manage the activity of all of the children while teaching a small group. What options are described in this chapter that can be used to accomplish this aim?

REFERENCES

Anderson, R., Hiebert, E., Scott, J., & Wilkinson, I. (1985). *Becoming a nation of readers*. Washington, DC: National Institute of Education.

August, D., & Shanahan, T. (2006). *Developing literacy in second-language learners: A report of the national literacy panel on language-minority children and youth*. Mahwah, NJ: Erlbaum.

Beck, I. L., McKeown, M. G., & Kucan, L. (2013). *Bringing words to life, 2nd edition*. New York: Guilford Press.

Bowne, J. B., Yoshikawa, H., & Snow, C. E. (2017). Relationships of teachers' language and explicit vocabulary instruction to students' vocabulary growth in kindergarten. *Reading Research Quarterly, 52*(1), 7–29.

Brill, S. (2011). *Class warfare: Inside the fight to fix America's schools*. New York: Simon & Schuster.

Brown, R., Pressley, M., Van Meter, P., & Schuder, T. (1996). A quasi-experimental validation of transactional strategies instruction with previously low-achieving second-grade readers. *Journal of Educational Psychology, 88*, 18–37.

Bureau of Labor Statistics. (2018). *American time use survey–2017 results*. Washington, DC: United States Department of Labor.

Carmichael, S. B., Martino, G., Porter-Magee, K., & Wilson, W. S. (2010). *The state of state standards—and the Common Core—in 2010.* Washington, DC: Thomas B. Fordham Institute.

Coker, D. L. (2006). Impact of first-grade factors on the growth and outcomes of urban school children's primary-grade writing. *Journal of Educational Psychology, 98,* 471–488.

Covey, S. (2004). *The 7 habits of highly effective people.* New York: Simon & Schuster.

Cummins, S. (2013). *Close reading of informational texts: Assessment-driven instruction in grades 3–8.* New York: Guilford Press.

Cunningham, P. M., Hall, D. P., & Defee, M. (1998). Nonability-grouped, multilevel instruction: Eight years later. *The Reading Teacher, 51*(8), 652–664.

Darling-Hammond, L. (2010). *The flat world and education: How America's commitment to equity will determine our future.* New York: Teachers College Press.

Davis, Z. T., & McPherson, M. D. (1989). Story map instruction: A road map for reading comprehension. *The Reading Teacher, 43*(3), 232–240.

Dole, J. A., & Liang, L. A. (2006). Help with teaching reading comprehension: Comprehension instructional frameworks. *The Reading Teacher, 59*(8), 742–753.

Fisher, D., Frey, N., & Lapp, D. (2012). *Text complexity: Raising rigor in reading.* Newark, DE: International Reading Association.

Friedman, T. L., & Mandelbaum, M. (2011). *That used to be us: How American fell behind in the world it invented and how we can come back.* New York: Farrar, Straus & Giroux.

Gersten, R., Compton, D., Connor, C.M., Dimino, J., Santoro, L., Linan-Thompson, S., & Tilly, W. D. (2008). *Assisting students struggling with reading: Response to intervention and multi-tier intervention for reading in the primary grades. A practice guide* (NCEE 2009-4045). Washington, DC: National Center for Education Evaluation and Regional Assistance, Institute of Education Sciences, U.S. Department of Education. Retrieved from *https://ies.ed.gov/ncee/wwc/ Docs/PracticeGuide/rti_reading_pg_021809.pdf.*

Graham, S., Bollinger, A., Olson, C. B., D'Aoust, C., MacArthur, C., McCutchen, D., & Olinghouse, N. (2012). *Teaching elementary school students to be effective writers: IES practice guide* (NCEE 2012-4058). Washington, DC: Institute of Education Sciences, U.S. Department of Education.

Graham, S., Gillespie, A., & McKeown, D. (2013). Writing: Importance, development, and instruction. *Reading and Writing, 26*(1), 1–15.

Graham, S., & Harris, K. R. (1992). Self-regulated strategy development: Programmatic research in writing. In B. Y. L. Wong (Ed.), *Contemporary intervention research in learning disabilities* (pp. 47–64). New York: Springer.

Graham, S., & Harris K. R. (2016). Evidence-based practice and writing instruction. In C. MacArthur, S. Graham, & J. Fitzgerald (Eds.), *Handbook of writing research* (2nd ed., pp. 211–226). New York: Guilford Press.

Graham, S., McKeown, D., Kiuhara, S., & Harris, K. R. (2012). A meta-analysis of writing instruction for students in the elementary grades. *Journal of Educational Psychology, 104*(4), 879–896.

Graham, S., & Santangelo, T. (2014). Does spelling instruction make students better spellers, readers, and writers?: A meta-analytic review. *Reading and Writing, 27*(9), 1703–1743.

Graves, M. F. (1987). The roles of instruction in fostering vocabulary development.

In M. G. McKeown & M. E. Curtis (Eds.), *The nature of vocabulary acquisition* (pp. 165–184). Hillsdale, NJ: Erlbaum.

Guthrie, J. T. (2003). Concept-oriented reading instruction. In C. E. Snow & A. P. Sweet (Eds.), *Rethinking reading comprehension* (pp. 115–140). New York: Guilford Press.

Harris, K. R., & Graham, S. (2016). Self-regulated strategy development in writing: Policy implications of an evidence-based practice. *Policy Insights from the Behavioral and Brain Sciences, 3*(1), 77–84.

Harris, K. R., Graham, S., & Adkins, M. (2015). Practice-based professional development and self-regulated strategy development for Tier 2, at-risk writers in second grade. *Contemporary Educational Psychology, 40*, 5–16.

Harris, K. R., Graham, S., Mason, L. H., & Friedlander, B. (2008). *Powerful writing strategies for all students*. Baltimore: Brookes.

Helman, L., Bear, D. R., Invernizzi, M., Templeton, S., & Johnston, F. (2013). *Words their way: Within word pattern sorts for Spanish-speaking English learners*. Boston: Pearson.

Holdaway, D. (1984). *Stability and change in literacy learning*. Portsmouth, NH: Heinemann.

Jenkins, J. (2008). *Dan Poynter's ParaPublishing.com: Jerrold Jenkins Survey*. Retrieved August 23, 2013, from *http://parapublishing.com/sites/para/resources/statistics.cfm*.

Johnson, D. D. (2001). *Vocabulary in the elementary and middle school*. Boston: Allyn & Bacon.

Jones, C. D., Clark, S. K., & Reutzel, D. R. (2016). Teaching text structure: Examining the affordances of children's informational texts. *Elementary School Journal, 117*(1), 143–169.

Mathes, P. G., Denton, C. A., Fletcher, J. M., Anthongy, J. L., Francis, D. J., & Schatschneider, C. (2005). The effects of theoretically different instruction and student characteristics on the skills of struggling readers. *Reading Research Quarterly, 40*(2), 148–183.

McKenna, M. C. (2002). *Help for struggling readers: Strategies for grades 3–8*. New York: Guilford Press.

McLaughlin, M., & Overturf, B. J. (2013). The Common Core: Insights into the K–5 standards. *The Reading Teacher, 66*(2), 153–164.

Morrow, L. M. (2010). Preparing centers and a literacy-rich environment for small-group instruction in early reading. In M. C. McKenna, S. Walpole, & K. Conradi (Eds.), *Promoting early reading: Research, resources and best practices* (pp. 124–141). New York: Guilford Press.

Morrow, L. M., Reutzel, D. R., & Casey, H. (2006). Organizing and managing language arts teaching: Classroom environments, grouping practices, exemplary instruction. In C. Weinstein & C. Evertson (Eds.), *Handbook of classroom management: Research, practice, and contemporary issues* (pp. 559–581). Hillsdale, NJ: Erlbaum.

Morrow, L. M., Shanahan, T., & Wixson, K. K. (Eds.). (2013). *Teaching with the Common Core Standards for English language arts, PreK–2*. New York: Guilford Press.

National Assessment of Educational Progress, Department of Education, Institute of Education Sciences, National Center for Education Statistics. (2015). The nation's report card, 2015: Mathematics and reading assessments. Retrieved July 24, 2017, from *www.nationsreportcard.gov/reading_math_2015*.

National Early Literacy Panel. (2008). *Developing early literacy: Report of the National Early Literacy Panel*. Jessup, MD: National Institute for Literacy.

National Endowment for the Arts. (2016). The survey of public participation in the arts (SPPA), 2013–2015. Retrieved July 24, 2017, from *www.arts.gov/artistic-fields/research-analysis/arts-data-profiles/arts-data-profile-10*.

National Governors Association & Council of Chief State School Officers. (2010). *Common Core State Standards for English language arts and literacy in history/ social studies, science, and technical subjects*. Retrieved September 25, 2013, from *www.corestandards.org*.

National Institute of Child Health and Human Development, National Institutes of Health. (2000). *Report of the National Reading Panel: Teaching children to read: An evidence-based assessment of the scientific research literature on reading and its implications for reading instruction: Reports of the subgroups*. Washington, DC: Author.

Neuman, S. B., & Celano, D. (2012). *Giving our children a fighting chance: Poverty, literacy, and the development of information capital*. New York: Teachers College Press.

Opitz, M. F., & Rasinski, T. V. (2008). *Good-bye round robin: 25 effective oral reading strategies, updated edition*. Portsmouth, NH: Heinemann.

Organisation for Economic Co-operation and Development. (2016). *PISA 2015: Results in focus*. Paris: Author.

Perry, S. (2011). *Push has come to shove: Getting our kids the education they deserve– Even if it means picking a fight*. New York: Crown.

Powell, D. A., & Aram, R. (2008). Spelling in parts: A strategy for spelling and decoding polysyllabic words. *The Reading Teacher, 61*(7), 567–570.

Pyle, N., Vasquez, A. C., Lignugaris-Kraft, B., Gillam, S. L., Reutzel, D. R., Olszewski, A., . . . Pyle, D. (2017). Effects of expository text structure interventions on comprehension: A meta-analysis. *Reading Research Quarterly, 52*(1), 1–33.

Rasinski, T. V. (2003). *The fluent reader: Oral reading strategies for building word recognition, fluency, and comprehension*. New York: Scholastic.

Rathvon, N. (2004). *Early reading assessment: A practitioner's handbook*. New York: Guilford Press.

Reutzel, D. R. (2012). Hey teacher, when you say fluency, what do you mean?: Developing fluency and meta-fluency in elementary classrooms. In T. V. Rasinski, C. Blachowicz, & K. Lems (Eds.), *Fluency instruction: Research-based best practices* (2nd ed., pp. 114–140). New York: Guilford Press.

Reutzel, D. R. (2013). Implementation of the Common Core Standards and the practitioner: Pitfalls and possibilities. In S. B. Neuman, L. B. Gambrell, & C. Massey (Eds.), *Quality reading instruction in the age of Common Core Standards* (pp. 59–74). Newark, DE: International Reading Association.

Reutzel, D. R., Clark, S. K., Jones, C. D., & Gillam, S. L. (2016). *Young meaning makers: Teaching comprehension, K–2*. New York: Teachers College Press.

Reutzel, D. R., & Cooter, R. B. (2018). *Teaching children to read: The teacher makes the difference, 8th edition*. Boston: Pearson.

Reutzel, D. R., Fawson, P. C., & Smith, J. A. (2008). Reconsidering silent sustained reading: An exploratory study of scaffolded silent reading (ScSR). *Journal of Educational Research, 102*(1), 37–50.

Reutzel, D. R., Jones, C. D., Fawson, P. C., & Smith, J. A. (2008). Scaffolded silent reading (ScSR): An alternative to guided oral repeated reading that works! *The Reading Teacher, 62*(3), 194–207.

Reutzel, D. R., & Juth, S. (2014). Supporting the development of silent reading fluency: An evidence-based framework for the intermediate grades (3–6). *International Electronic Journal of Elementary Education, 7*(1), 27–46.

Reutzel, D. R., Smith, J. A., & Fawson, P. C. (2005). An evaluation of two approaches for teaching reading comprehension strategies in the primary years using science information texts. *Early Childhood Research Quarterly, 20*(3), 276–305.

Roberts, K. L., Norman, R. R., Duke, N. K., Morsink, P., Martin, N. M., & Knight, J. A. (2013). Diagrams, timelines, and tables—Oh, my!: Fostering graphical literacy. *The Reading Teacher, 67*(1), 12–24.

Rupley, W. H., & Blair, T. R. (1987). Assignment and supervision of reading seatwork: Looking in on 12 primary teachers. *The Reading Teacher, 40*(4), 391–393.

Shanahan, T. (2004, November). *How do you raise reading achievement?* Paper presented at the Utah Council of the International Reading Association Meeting, Salt Lake City, UT.

Shanahan, T. (2012a). What is close reading? Shanahan on Literacy Blog. Retrieved August 30, 2013, from *http://shanahanonliteracy.com/blog/what-is-close-reading#sthash.n9G9p9tv.dpbs.*

Shanahan, T. (2012b). Planning for close reading. Shanahan on Literacy Blog. Retrieved August 30, 2013, from *http://shanahanonliteracy.com/blog/close-reading-with-struggling-adolescents#sthash.2JnyPXQt.dpbs.*

Shanahan, T. (2013). Common Core State Standards: Educating young children for global excellence. In D. R. Reutzel (Ed.), *Handbook of research-based practice in early education* (pp. 207–221). New York: Guilford Press.

Shanahan, T., Callison, K., Carriere, C., Duke, N. K., Pearson, P. D., Schatschneider, C., & Torgesen, J. (2010). *Improving reading comprehension in kindergarten through 3rd grade: A practice guide* (NCEE 2010-4038). Washington, DC: National Center for Education Evaluation and Regional Assistance, Institute of Education Sciences, U.S. Department of Education. Retrieved September 25, 2013, from *https://ies.ed.gov/ncee/wwc.*

Shanahan, T., Fisher, D., & Frey, N. (2012). The challenge of challenging text. *Educational Leadership, 69*(6), 58–62.

Snell, E. K., Hindman, A. H., & Wasik, B. A. (2015). How can book reading close the word gap?: Five key practices from research. *The Reading Teacher, 68*(7), 560–571.

Snow, C. E., Burns, M. S., & Griffin, P. (1998). *Preventing reading failure in young children.* Washington, DC: National Academy Press.

Stage, E. K., Asturias, H., Cheuk, T., Daro, P. A., & Hampton, S. B. (2013). Opportunities and challenges in next generation standards. *Science, 340*(6130), 276–277.

Stahl, S. A., & Nagy, W. E. (2006). *Teaching word meanings.* Mahwah, NJ: Erlbaum.

Swan, E. A., Coddington, C. S., & Guthrie, J. T. (2010). Motivating silent reading in classrooms. In E. H. Hiebert & D. R. Reutzel (Eds.), *Revisiting silent reading: New directions for teachers and researchers* (pp. 95–111). Newark, DE: International Reading Association.

Troia, G. A. (2014). *Evidence-based practices for writing instruction* (Document No. IC-5). University of Florida, Collaboration for Effective Educator Development, Accountability, and Reform Center. Retrieved from *http://ceedar.education.ufl.edu/tools/innovation-configuration.*

Troia, G. A., & Olinghouse, N. G. (2013). The Common Core State Standards and evidence-based educational practices: The case of writing. *School Psychology Review, 42*(3), 343–357.

Tyner, B. (2009). *Small-group reading instruction: A differentiated teaching model for beginning and struggling readers* (2nd ed.). Newark, DE: International Reading Association.

Vaughn, S., Fuchs, D., & Fuchs, L. S. (Eds.). (2008). *Response to intervention: A framework for reading educators*. Newark, DE: International Reading Association.

Wagner, T. (2008). *The global achievement gap: Why even our best schools don't teach the new survival skills our children need–and what we can do about it*. New York: Basic Books.

Weber, K. (Ed.). (2010). *Waiting for Superman: How we can save America's failing public schools*. New York: Public Affairs.

Wilkinson. I. A. G., & Son, E. H. (2011). A dialogic turn in research on learning and teaching to comprehend. In M. L. Kamil, P. D. Pearson, E. Moje, & P. Afflerbach (Eds.), *Handbook of reading research* (Vol. 6, 359–387). New York: Routledge.

Williams, P. L., Reese, C. M., Campbell, J. R., Mazzeo, J., & Phillips, G. W. (1995). *NAEP 1994 reading: A first look*. Washington, DC: Educational Testing Service for the National Center for Educational Statistics, Office of Educational Research and Improvement, U.S. Department of Education.

CHAPTER 17

Best Practices in the Physiological, Emotional, and Behavioral Foundations of Literacy Achievement

DIANE H. TRACEY

This chapter will:

- Examine the construct of a "classroom as a community of learners" through the lens of the student as a "whole" person.

- Provide a theoretical and research synthesis regarding the physiological, emotional, and behavioral foundations of literacy achievement.

- Discuss best practices to support students' physiological, emotional, and behavioral foundations of literacy learning.

- Offer engagement activities to facilitate students' physiological, emotional, and behavioral growth.

THE CLASSROOM AS A COMMUNITY OF LEARNERS

One way to conceptualize any student's school experience is as a member of a classroom community of learners. The construct of a classroom as a community of learners suggests a broad orientation to one's educational journey. In this conceptualization, the student is not traveling alone; rather, he or she is a member of a group and, as such, both contributes to and is affected by that group. Furthermore, a classroom community construct suggests a multidimensional understanding of the transactions between students, teachers, parents, and administrators. These transactions are not limited in scope to the realm of the cognitive; they are social, emotional, cultural, and linguistic. The construct of the classroom as a community of learners is therefore consistent with the understanding of the student as a "whole" person—a physical, emotional, social, cognitive, and, if one's belief system allows, spiritual being. Stated alternatively, the classroom as a community of learners construct refutes the idea that any student is simply cognitive in nature, and is highly consistent with the thesis of the present chapter regarding students' physiological, emotional, and behavioral foundations as critical to their literacy achievement.

EVIDENCE-BASED BEST PRACTICES: A RESEARCH SYNTHESIS

Theory

One theorist who brought attention to the role of the physiological, emotional, and behavioral foundations of learning is Abraham Maslow (1943, 1954). In 1943, Maslow put forth a theory of psychological motivation known as Maslow's hierarchy of needs. In this work, Maslow proposed that humans have five hierarchical levels of needs: physiological needs, safety needs, love and belonging needs, self-esteem needs, and self-actualization. Maslow hypothesized that a person's needs are sequential in nature, such that lower-level needs have to be satisfied before one can be motivated to focus on upper-level needs. Maslow's hierarchy of needs is depicted in Figure 17.1.

Maslow's position that students' foundational physiological, emotional, and social needs must be met to optimally facilitate academic achievement (associated with upper-level esteem and self-actualization needs) is gaining quantitative research support (Taormina & Gao, 2013; Noltemeyer, Bush, Patton, & Bergen, 2012). For example, Taormina and Gao (2013) conducted a statistical investigation of the theory in which they created measures to assess the satisfaction of each of Maslow's five levels of need. Taormina and Gao (p. 155) reported: "strong support for the validity and reliability of all 5 [of Maslow's] need measures. Significant, positive correlations among the scales were also found; that is, the more each lower-level need was satisfied, the more the next higher level need was satisfied."

The triune brain model (Chopra & Tanzi, 2012) provides a second theoretical frame supporting the foundational importance of physiological needs in human functioning. This model attempts to capture the

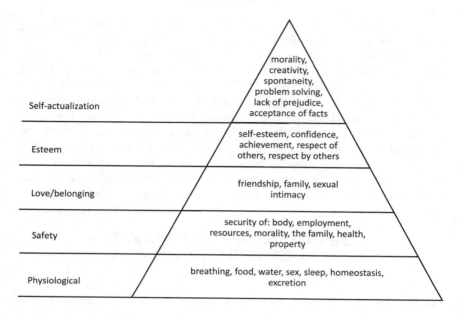

FIGURE 17.1. Maslow's hierarchy of needs. From Factoryjoe, Wikimedia, under the Creative Commons Attribution-Share Alike 3.0 Unported license.

biological evolution of the human brain over hundreds of millions of years. The model is consistent with Maslow's theory because it places physiological needs as the earliest in brain evolution, followed by the development of emotions and then cognition. Chopra and Tanzi (2012) wrote:

> In the triune (three-part) model of the brain, the oldest part is the reptilian brain, or brain stem, designed for survival [e.g., physiological functioning]. It houses vital control centers for breathing, swallowing, and heartbeat, among other things. It also prompts hunger, sex, and the fight-or-flight response. The limbic system was the next to evolve. It houses the emotional brain and short-term memory. Emotions based on fear and desire evolved to serve the instinctive drives of the reptilian brain. The most recent development is the neo-cortex, the region for intellect, decision-making, and higher reasoning. As our reptilian and limbic brains drive us to do what we need for survival, the neo-cortex represents the intelligence to achieve our ends while also placing restraints on our emotions and instinctive impulses. (p. 112)

Figure 17.2 shows an illustration of the biological evolution of the brain reflecting the foundational position of the physiological needs followed sequentially by the emotional and then cognitive systems.

Maslow's theory (1943, 1954) regarding a hierarchy of human needs, Taormina and Gao's (2013) quantitative research supporting Maslow's theory, and biological evidence from the triune brain model (Chopra & Tanzi, 2012) provide a compelling argument for the foundational importance of physiological and emotional factors in supporting cognitive (literacy) growth. The remainder of this chapter highlights research and educational implications related to this theoretical position.

Research Regarding the Physiological Foundations of Literacy Achievement

Three factors dramatically affect physiological well-being: nutrition, sleep, and exercise. Below, research summarizing the relationships between each of these factors and academic achievement is briefly summarized. A fuller discussion of this body of research is published elsewhere (Tracey & Morrow, 2017).

Nutrition

To help conceptualize the importance and scope of worldwide child hunger and nutrition, the World Food Programme (2016) reported that approximately 3.1 million children die per year from malnutrition, and that approximately 45% of all worldwide child deaths in 2011 were related to hunger. Approximately 40% of all preschool-age children in developing countries are judged to be iron-deficient (World Hunger Education

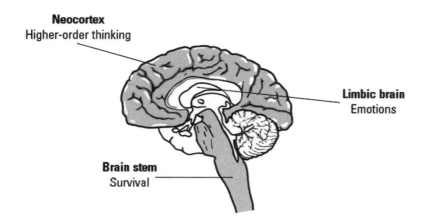

FIGURE 17.2. The triune brain. From Erlauer (2003). Republished with permission from the Association for Supervision and Curriculum Development. Permission conveyed through Copyright Clearance Center, Inc.

Service, 2016), and 71% of iron-deficient children score below average in academic performance (Halterman, Kaczorowski, Aligne, Auinger, & Szilagyi, 2001). Poverty is the primary cause of worldwide child hunger and starvation (World Hunger Education Service, 2016).

Malnutrition and hunger are not limited to children who live in developing countries. In a recent *New York Times* article, Carroll (2016) reported that hunger affects approximately 15 million children living in the United States, or about one in seven households. Bomer and Maloch (2013) articulated that in 2011, 20.6% of U.S. families with children experienced food insecurity (unreliable access to affordable, nutritious food). This included 36.8% of single-women headed households and 24.9% of single-men headed households. In addition, approximately 25% of all black households and 26% of all Latino households were food-insecure (Bomer & Maloch, 2013). Consistent with worldwide hunger statistics, American children living in poverty are overwhelmingly more at-risk for malnutrition than their middle-class peers (Carroll, 2016). For example, in a study of approximately 1,000 preschool-age children, Bucholz, Desai, and Rosenthal (2011) found a positive relationship between Head Start participation (indicating low socioeconomic status) and inadequate intake of protein, calcium, thiamin, riboflavin, niacin, and selenium.

What, then, are the academic consequences related to hunger, malnutrition, and food scarcity? In a recent review of cognitive implications of childhood nutrition, Kahn, Raine, Donovan, and Hillman (2014) wrote that "emerging evidence suggests that cognitive and brain health may be profoundly affected by weight status and nutritional intake" (p. 63). They stated that "nutrition may directly or indirectly influence cognitive performance via several pathways including provision of key substrates for optimal brain health, modulation of gut bacteria, and alterations in systematic energy balance" (p. 51). In summarizing a meta-analysis of 160 studies examining the relationships between nutrition and brain function, Wolpert and Wheeler (2008) emphasized the importance of omega-3 fatty acids for healthy, flexible, neural synapse function, and noted that too much "junk food" (food high in sugar, salt, and/ or fat that has little nutritional value) can increase the chance of cell damage through the creation of free radicals, and damage the plasticity of synaptic relays. Kahn, Raine, Donovan, and Hillman (2014) confirmed maternal nutritional deficiencies related to children's cognitive deficits for folate, vitamin B_{12}, iron, zinc, and protein, and suspected the role of vitamin D deficiency in cognitive dysfunction.

For older children, Erikson (2006) cited evidence of increased risks of attention-deficit/hyperactivity disorder and dyslexia in individuals with omega-3 dietary deficiencies. Since omega-3 fatty acids (which are not naturally produced in the body but are found in abundance in salmon, walnuts, and kiwi) strengthen synaptic plasticity, and synaptic plasticity is closely linked to learning, Wolpert and Wheeler (2008) wrote that it is not surprising that deficiencies in omega-3s are associated with lower reading and writing achievement. Erikson (2006) also found that a lack of protein was associated with poor student performance. Zhang, Herbert, and Muldoon (2005) found that the consumption of polyunsaturated fats and increased cholesterol levels were both associated with decreased academic performance. On this point, Dr. Gomez-Pinella, professor of neurosurgery at the University of California, Los Angeles, succinctly wrote, "Junk food and fast food negatively affect the brain synapses" (as quoted in Wolpert & Wheeler, 2008, p. 1). Mosconi et al. (2014) summarized, "We are what we eat: the nutritional content of what we eat determines the composition of our cell membranes, bone marrow, blood, hormones, and is therefore the foundation on which our body and brain are built" (p. 1).

Examined from a public, economic perspective, research conducted in Copenhagen found that "nutrition interventions generate returns among the highest of 17 potential development investments" (Khandelwal, Siegel, & Narayan, 2013, p. 131). Best practices for educators associated with the foundational, importance of students' nutrition will be discussed later in this chapter.

Sleep

A second, foundational, physiological need is adequate sleep. An abundance of research indicates that the amount and types of sleep that one experience are significantly related to learning (Euston & Steenland, 2014; Gillen-O'Neal, Huynh, & Fuligui, 2013; Yang et al., 2014). The theoretical mechanism underlying these research findings is *sleep-dependent memory consolidation* (Scullin, 2013). Sleep-dependent memory consolidation theory posits that specific brain functions take place during sleep that actually consolidate memories and learning. The biological process behind this theory is the growing of dendric spines. Dendric spines are docking stations in the brain that allow neurons to connect. The connection of neurons is then the biological equivalent of learning. Yang and colleagues (2014) demonstrated that dendric spines grow during sleep and do not grow in the absence of sleep.

Park (2014) also wrote about the neuroanatomical consequences of sleep deprivation. She argued that "brain cells that don't get their needed break every night are like overworked employees on consecutive double shifts—eventually they collapse. . . . Once those brain cells are gone, they're gone for good" (para.5).

Given the chemical and neuroanatomical changes that take place during sleep (and in the absence of adequate sleep), it is intuitive and well documented that, at all ages and stages of development, sleep and learning are highly related. For example, in one study of 15-month-old babies, it was found that napping was necessary for them to learn a new grammatical language pattern (Hupbach, Gomez, Bootzin, & Nader, 2009). Similarly, as reported by Ravid, Afek, Suraiya, Shahar, and Pillar (2009, p. 577), Touchette et al (2007) studied approximately 1,500 children, ages two-and-a-half to six, and found "significant associations between shortened sleep duration, hyperactivity, impulsivity, and lower scores on neuro-co-developmental tests."

In somewhat older children, Ravid et al. (2009) revealed that the correlation between kindergarten students' sleep and grades at the end of first grade was highly significant ($r = .64$, $p < .01$). These results have been corroborated with studies of middle-school students (Drake et al., 2003). At the high school level, Gillen-O'Neel, Huynh, and Fuligni (2013) concluded, "Our findings complement sleep research that has demonstrated that students who, on average, sleep for more hours tend to have more positive academic outcomes such as higher grades and better school behaviors" (p. 139).

Despite the documented relationship between sleep and academic performance, Park (2014) wrote that 25% of teens report falling asleep in class at least once a week. Recently, the National Centers for Disease Control and Prevention have labeled the extent of sleep deprivation in the United States to be a public health epidemic (Park, 2014). Best practices for educators associated with the foundational importance of students' sleep will be discussed later in this chapter.

Exercise

In addition to reporting on the physiological factors of nutrition and sleep, an extensive body of literature underscores the powerful effects of exercise on students' cognitive abilities The benefits associated with regular exercise for students include improved academic achievement at school as measured by grades and by standardized test scores (Burrows, Correa-Burrows, Orellana, Lizana, & Ivanovic, 2014; Chaddock-Heyman, Hillman, Cohen, & Kramer, 2014; Hillman, 2014; Wojcicki & McAuley, 2014); and improvements in cognitive control (including attention) and memory (Chaddock-Heyman et al., 2014; Hillman, 2014; Wojcicki & McAuley, 2014). In addition, examinations of brain structure, as measured by magnetic resonance imaging (MRI), and brain function, as measured by electroencephalography (EEG), both show evidence of positive changes associated with exercise (Chaddock-Heyman et al. 2014). Burrows et al. (2014) wrote, "A potential link between exercise and academic performance can be explained by both physiological and psychological factors such as increased blood and oxygen flow to the brain, reduction of stress, improvement of mood, and increased synaptic plasticity" (p. 1600).

Given the scientific evidence regarding the positive correlations between physical exercise, cognitive functioning, and academic achievement, the current state of exercise among American youth is deeply disturbing. Hillman (2014) reported a dramatic reduction of physical activity in modern society, and Wojcicki and McAuley (2014) wrote, "The health related literature suggests that physical activity levels among children and adolescents have witnessed significant declines over the last several decades" (p. 7). Wojcicki and McAuley noted, according to the Centers for Disease Control and Prevention (CDC), that children and adolescents should participate in 60 minutes of daily, moderate-to-vigorous aerobic activity, although it is not necessary for the 60 minutes to be continuous. At the same time, the CDC (2012) found that more than 70% of American youths do not meet that benchmark. Furthermore, Wojcicki and McAuley (2014) reported that only 30% of American youth receive daily physical education classes, while almost 50% do not participate in any form of vigorous physical activity during the week. Best practices for educators associated with the foundational importance of students' exercise will be discussed later in this chapter.

Research Regarding the Emotional Foundations of Literacy Achievement

In 2014, cognitive and affective neuroscientist Mary Helen Immordino-Yang, from the University of Southern California, won the prestigious Early Career Award from the American Education Research Association for her work investigating the relationships between emotions and learning. Together, the work of Immordino-Yang (2015), Maslow (1943, 1954), Taormina and Gao (2013), and Chopra and Tanzi (2012) provide a compelling argument for the human emotional system being situated between lower-level physiological needs and higher-level cognitive needs. As a result of this placement, the emotional system can be viewed as undergirding, and playing a central role in, higher levels of cognitive functioning, such as literacy learning. Research in the areas of the relationship between stress and academic achievement (Anthony, DiPerna, & Amato, 2014; Berg, Rostila, Saarela, & Hjern, 2014; Gautam & Pradhan, 2017; Potter, 2010), attachment theory (Ainsworth, 1969; Bowlby, 1969, 1980), teacher–student relationships (Bernstein-Yamashiro & Noam, 2013; Krstic, 2015), and affective neuroscience (Immordino-Yang, 2011, 2015; Immordino-Yang & Faeth, 2009) support this theoretical position.

Stressors are the thoughts, feelings, and life events that cause individuals to feel tension and pressure (Gautam & Pradhan, 2017). According to

Gautam and Pradhan, stressed children can show symptoms of anxiety, shyness, aggressiveness, social phobia, disengagement, depression, loss of energy, elevated blood pressure, difficulty concentrating, impatience, and nervousness. Consistent with theories that posit a close relationship between emotion and cognition, increased student stress is inversely associated with academic achievement; that is, as students' stress levels increase, their academic performance decreases (Anthony et al, 2014; Berg et al., 2014; Gautam & Pradhan, 2017; Potter, 2010). Stress levels are particularly high for students from low-income, urban backgrounds (Harpin, Rossi, Kim, & Swanson, 2016), children from homes in which parents have divorced (Anthony et al., 2014; Potter, 2010), and children from homes in which parents have died (Berg et al., 2014) or have chronic illnesses (Chen & Fish, 2013).

Another source of students' emotional equilibrium, or disequilibrium, is related to the concept of *attachment* (Bowlby, 1969). Attachment refers to an individual's ability to form relationships with others. Ainsworth (1969) conducted research on Bowlby's attachment theory (1969) and found that, as a result of mother–infant interactions, infants develop one of three types of attachment patterns early in life: (1) secure, (2) anxious–ambivalent, or (3) anxious–avoidant attachment patterns. Subsequently, a broad research base has documented that infant attachment style becomes a key pervasive personality characteristic (Ahmad & Sahak, 2009). Of critical importance to educators, consistent research shows that a child's attachment pattern is related to his or her academic learning, with securely attached children having higher overall academic achievement including math ability, reading ability, and reading comprehension than insecurely attached children (Kristic, 2015; Mackay, Reynolds, & Kearney, 2010). Krstic (2015) explained that attachment patterns are related to early cognitive development because securely attached children feel freer to explore their environments than do their insecurely attached peers; securely attached children then learn from these explorations. Recent research documenting a central, positive relationship between attachment style and student achievement has also been reported by Mackay, Reynolds, and Kearney (2010); Maltais, Duchesne, Ratelle, and Fend (2015); Marzban, Ejei, and Bahrami (2014); White (2013); and Wolfgang (2013).

In addition to the emotional variables of stress and attachment style, school-based learning is affected by the quality of teacher–student relationships (Bernstein-Yamashiro & Noam, 2013; Krstic, 2015; Maltais et al., 2015; Marzban et al., 2014; Mackay et al., 2010; Wolfgang, 2013). Research projects show that high-quality teacher–student relationships are characterized by a student's sense that the teacher understands and cares about him or her as a person, the student's perception that he or she is supported and respected by the teacher, an overall positive feeling between the teacher and student, and a student's sense that he or she is physically and emotionally safe with the teacher (Bernstein-Yamashiro & Noam, 2013). Bond and Dykstra (1967) were two of the earliest researchers to demonstrate the importance of the classroom teacher in literacy instruction. These researchers found that the quality of the classroom teacher was more closely related to students' literacy achievement than were specific teaching methods or materials. Since then, high-quality teacher–student relationships have been found to positively correlate with: higher student test scores (Lee & Loeb, 2000; Yonezawa, McClure, & Jones, 2012), improved student engagement and motivation (Yonezawa et al., 2012), and reduced high-school dropout rates (Bernstein-Yamashiro & Noam, 2013). Bernstein-Yamashiro and Noam (2013) found that "a lack of connection to caring adults at school is cited as a major variable of student alienation, failure, and disaffection from school, and finally dropout" (p. 17). Given that 25% of all students do not graduate from high school, and that that figure doubles for low-income students from minority backgrounds, Bernstein-Yamashiro and Noam underscored the importance of teacher–student relationships for high-risk students.

Neuroscientific investigations also verify the foundational contributions of emotions in learning (Immordino-Yang, 2011, 2015). In evidence, the current American Educational Research Association's (AERA) website now states, "Extensive research makes clear that the brain networks supporting emotion, learning, and memory are intricately and fundamentally intertwined" (AERA website, 2016)). Immordino-Yang (2015) echoed this finding: "It is literally neurobiologically impossible to build memories, engage complex thoughts, or make meaningful decisions without emotion." More specifically, while literacy educators have, for several decades, understood the academic benefits of helping students make connections between what they are reading and what they already know (Bouchamma & Poulin, 2014), the work of Immordino-Yang and colleagues shows that it is the emotional connections between what students are reading and themselves that are essential for "truly useful, transferable, intrinsically motivated learning" (Immordino-Yang, 2015). Immordino-Yang and Faeth (2009) wrote:

> The message from social and affective neuroscience is clear: no longer can we think of learning as separate from or disrupted by emotion, and no longer can we focus solely at the level of the individual student in analyzing effective strategies for classroom instruction. Students and teachers socially interact and learn from one another in ways that cannot be done justice by examining only the "cold" cognitive aspects of academic skills. Like other forms of learning and interacting, building

academic knowledge involves integrating emotion and cognition in social context. Academic skills are hot!" (p. 67)

Research Regarding the Behavioral Foundations of Literacy Achievement

As demonstrated thus far, students' literacy achievement is undergirded by their physiological and emotional well-being. In addition, students' literacy achievement is closely related to their classroom behavior and to the overall climate in their classroom (Baker, 2006; Hamre & Pianta, 2005). According to Kaplan Toren, and Seginer (2015), the classroom climate consists of three primary components: (1) teacher–student relationships, (2) peer relationships, and (3) educational atmosphere. The classroom educational atmosphere includes constructs such as classroom management, classroom organization, grouping practices, instructional differentiation, and instructional scaffolding (Kaplan Toren & Seginer, 2015). Students learn best when they can focus on the task at hand, and when the classroom climate is organized, focused, supportive, and warm (Pianta, LaParo, & Hamre, 2008). In contrast, when students have trouble staying on task, and when the classroom is chaotic, disorganized, and marked by tension and aggression, lower student achievement is evidenced (Pianta et al., 2008).

In a meta-analysis of 54 controlled intervention studies focused on classroom management and academic achievement, Korpershoek, Harms, de Boer, van Kuijk, and Doolaard (2016) determined that effective classroom management is a "precondition for learning" (p. 670). Effective classroom management is associated with "improved time-on-task, improved instruction practices, and increased opportunity to learn" (p. 670). In their analysis, they divided their examination into interventions that focused on (1) changing teachers' behaviors (e.g., making rules and keeping order), (2) improving teacher–student relationships, (3) improving students' behaviors (e.g., self-regulation), and (4) improving students' relationships with each other through enhanced empathy training. The interventions that had the greatest effectiveness were those that focused on enhancing students' relationships with each other. Another finding from the meta-analysis was that preventative classroom management techniques, such as building positive teacher–student relationships and including students in classroom rule making, were more highly associated with student achievement than were reactive classroom management techniques such as punishment. They concluded, "The results of the meta-analysis confirm the finding of generally positive effects of classroom management interventions on student outcomes in primary education" (p. 668). Best practices for educators associated with the foundational importance of students' classroom behaviors will be discussed later in this chapter.

BEST PRACTICES IN ACTION

Best Practices Regarding the Physiological, Emotional, and Behavioral Foundations of Literacy Achievement

This chapter is built upon the afore-described theory and research showing that students' cognitive activities, such as literacy achievement, are highly related to their well-being in the areas of physiological, emotional, and behavioral functioning. Furthermore, the chapter presents physiological, emotional, and behavioral aspects of functioning as foundational to literacy achievement. From this view, students' physiological, emotional, and behavioral needs must be assessed and addressed *prior to,* or at least at the same time as, literacy abilities. To solely address students' literacy needs, in the absence of also considering their physiological, emotional, and behavioral needs, is presented as erroneous practice. Below, best practices for assessing and supporting students' physiological, emotional, and behavioral wellbeing are presented.

Best Practices to Promote Physiological Well-Being in Students

Best practices for promoting physiological well-being among students begin with being aware of, and informed about, the degree to which students' nutritional, sleep, and exercise needs are being met in daily life. Regardless of students' age, the first month of school is the ideal time to bring attention to the physiological foundations of learning, and to how well students' needs are being met in this area. Teachers can begin by providing students with age-appropriate information about the links between nutrition, sleep, exercise, and learning, and then assess how well they seem to be doing in these areas. One way to gather this information is to have students complete a nutrition, sleep, and exercise log for 1 week. Parents can help younger children complete these logs, which may help the family unit develop a heightened awareness of the relationship between their child's physiological needs and academic success. After teacher review, the logged activities can be discussed in class. Sample questions for discussion are "What kinds of foods are students eating for breakfast, lunch, dinner, and snacks?" and "What are the nutritional values of these items, and how might they affect brain function?" Class discussions can also be generated for sleep and exercise. The daily recommended guidelines for nutrition, sleep, and exercise for students at particular levels of development should be discussed, and comparisons and contrasts between actual and ideal levels of practice should be highlighted.

Following an initial assessment and discussion of physiological well-being, teachers need to help students keep their attention on these foundational aspects of learning throughout the school year. Charts that track students' nutrition, sleep, and exercise activities can be created and posted in the classroom. Students who meet recommended guidelines for nutrition, sleep, and exercise can be rewarded for continuing to do so, while students who do not yet meet these guidelines can be rewarded for improvement. One-to-one individual discussions between students and teachers can be provided for students who do not make improvements, and parent involvement can be sought.

In addition to assessing and tracking students' activities in the areas of nutrition, sleep, and exercise, educators need to model and support healthy living in the classroom. Teachers can post their own nutrition, sleep, and exercise activities, and strive to focus on improvement if their own practices don't meet adult guidelines. Teachers can also set rules for the kinds of snacks that students are allowed to have in the classroom, and encourage all students to have water bottles containing fresh water at their desks at all times. Teachers can keep healthy snacks in school to share with students who are in need. With regard to exercise, the website GoNoodle (*www.gonoodle.com*) provides movement and mindfulness videos appropriate for in-classroom use. Teachers can intersperse these videos throughout the school day to help students increase exercise minutes that they can then add to their logs and charts. With regard to sleep, teachers can provide a quiet place for students to rest if they come to school overly tired. Of course, chronic problems with nutrition, sleep, and exercise, and, even more troubling, signs of physical abuse, must be brought to the attention of school resource personnel.

Best Practices to Promote Emotional Well-Being in Students

Literacy educators who concur with the idea that emotional well-being undergirds academic and literacy success will want to address, as much as possible, their students' emotional well-being at home and in school. Issues within students' homes like divorce, illness, death of a family member, job loss, moving, financial stress, incarceration, deportation, domestic violence, addiction, and/or birth of a sibling can all cause disequilibrium and stress for students of all ages. Students' emotional well-being will also be related to their relationships with peers and teachers at school, and to their abilities to adequately meet academic demands.

To explore the emotional dimensions of students' lives, educators need to open the lines of communication between students and themselves. Again, this is consistent with research showing that open, trusting, and secure relationships between teachers and students are associated with students' higher academic achievement (Krstic, 2015). Young children can be helped to use dramatic play items or to draw pictures to process thoughts and feelings that may be troubling to them. Older students can be helped to put their thoughts and feelings into a written form. Students can also place personal pieces of writing to the teacher in a classroom mailbox. The use of high-quality children's (or adolescents') literature in the classroom can further support students' communication about difficult topics, as can interactive dialogue journals between teachers and students. All students can be helped to put their thoughts and feelings into spoken words. Casual experiences, such as shared, small-group lunches between teachers and students, and after-school activities can provide opportunities for student–teacher relationship building and emotional communication. Teachers should not, of course, be expected to solely handle students' extreme emotional problems, and should reach out to a guidance counselor, peer, or supervisor if significant emotional challenges are present in any student's life. That said, given the central role of emotions to learning in general, it appears that assessing and appropriately responding to students' emotional needs are important components of facilitating their literacy achievement, as significant emotional distress at home and/or at school will typically adversely affect literacy achievement (Anthony et al., 2014; Berg et al., 2014; Gautam & Pradhan, 2017; Potter, 2010).

When initiating conversation with a student, it is advisable to first ask permission to speak with him or her. For example, the teacher can say, "Roger, I noticed that you seemed upset today. Is it OK if we talk about this?" If the student says that he or she doesn't want to talk about it, the teacher can reply, "I understand. I just want you to know that I care about how you are doing and feeling. If you change your mind, please know that I am here for you. Also, if you want to write to me about what's on your mind, you can leave a note for me in the classroom mailbox." If the student is willing to speak with the teacher, the teacher can then say something like, "Can you help me to better understand why you kept your head down on your desk today?" After the student explains what is bothering him or her, the teacher can ask the student if he or she has any ideas about what will help the situation. The teacher can also offer a suggestion. This is best done if preceded by the question, "Is it OK with you if I offer an idea of something that might help?" Often, it is therapeutic to simply let a student know that the teacher cares, is available to listen, and that the teacher understands his or her feelings.

In addition to opening the lines of communication with students, some educators find it beneficial to emphasize the concept of *resilience* in their classrooms (Parker-Pope, 2017). Resilience is the ability to persevere in the face of life's obstacles. Proponents of resilience training suggest that resilience consists of learnable behaviors. These behaviors include:

1. Practicing optimism.
2. Reframing problems as challenges.
3. Viewing stress as a way to improve performance.
4. Forgiving oneself for setbacks.
5. Remembering past successes.
6. Deliberately going outside of one's comfort zone to strengthen resilience.
7. Recognizing that stress will never be completely eliminated from one's life.

Instead, students can focus on their responses to stress with the knowledge that they can, with practice, get better at responding to it (Parker-Poe, 2017). The concept of *grit,* also popular right now in the educational literature, is very similar to that of resilience (Rimfeld, Kovas, Dale, & Plomin, 2016).

Yet another route to address students' emotional well-being in the classroom is through mindfulness meditation. In mindfulness meditation, students learn how to increase a sense of relaxation and peace within themselves by using a variety of breathing and thinking practices. Internet websites such as GoNoodle and Headspace (*www.headspace.com*) can be useful resources for teachers wanting to address their students' emotional needs in this way. Mindfulness meditation has been shown to improve both behavioral and academic outcomes (Harpin, Rossi, Kim, & Swanson, 2016). For example, in one 10-week study, urban fourth graders showed improvements in pro-social behaviors, emotional regulation, and academic performance (Harpin et al., 2016). Teachers and researchers can use the Child and Adolescent Mindfulness Measure (Greco, Baer, & Smith, 2011) to assess the impact of mindfulness meditation on their students.

Educators may also want to explore the use of yoga in the curriculum. The word "yoga" means "to yoke," and in yoga practice the mind, body, and spirit (as represented by the breath) are linked. Recent studies on the use of yoga in schools suggest that it can improve emotional equilibrium, attention, and self-esteem (Hagins & Rundle, 2016). Simultaneously, yoga can decrease anxiety, problematic behavior, and negative thought patterns (Hagins & Rundle, 2016). The goal of many school yoga programs is to improve school achievement through students' increased self-regulation and executive function. While the emotional benefits of yoga practice to students are well documented, research on academic outcomes is more mixed, with some studies showing clear academic gains associated with its use, and other studies showing no difference when contrasted with other interventions (Kauts & Sharma, 2009).

The lens of affective neuroscience provides state-of-the-art, quantifiable research findings that validate the central role of emotions in literacy learning (Immordino-Yang, 2015). Although the use of affective neuroscientific tools such as functional magnetic resonance imagining (fMRI) is not likely for most school-based literacy educators right now, for literacy researchers, this avenue of work is a meaningful and open investigative opportunity.

Best Practices to Promote Behavioral Well-Being in Students

Administrators, teachers, and professional development providers who are interested in classroom climate as an influence on students' literacy achievement can inform themselves more fully about the Classroom Assessment Scoring System (CLASS) (Pianta et al., 2008). This instrument quantitatively assesses traditional instructional variables such as behavior management, instructional formats, and concept development, but also addresses less traditional variables such as teacher sensitivity and regard for students' perspectives. Six versions of the CLASS have been developed to date: infant, toddler, Pre-K, K–3, upper elementary, and secondary. The instrument has been validated in over 2,000 classrooms and is widely used by Head Start, the Gate's Foundation, and researchers interested in measuring teacher–student interactions and classroom climate. Pianta et al. (2008) reported that classrooms in which teachers and students "enjoy warm and supportive relationships with each other," display positive affect and communication, and in which "the teacher and students consistently demonstrate respect for one another" (p. 23) are repeatedly, and statistically, associated with higher student academic outcomes than are classrooms that score lower on these measures. They reported similar associations for the variables of teacher sensitivity ("the teacher's awareness of, and responsivity to, students' academic and emotional needs"; p. 22) and the teacher's regard for student perspectives ("the degree to which teachers place an emphasis on students' interests, motivations, and points of view"; p. 22). Additional resources for improving classroom management are the book *One, Two, Three Magic for Teachers: Effective Classroom Discipline Pre-K through Grade 8* (Phelan & Schonour, 2004) and the website for ClassDojo (*www.classdojo.com*).

REFLECTIONS AND FUTURE DIRECTIONS

Theories and research in the areas of physiological, emotional, and behavioral foundations of academic achievement show that the factors responsible for students' literacy achievement are not solely cognitive in nature. To the contrary, these bodies of work indicate that students' school success is strongly influenced by, and related to, their physiological, emotional, and behavioral dimensions of well-being. As a result, it is imperative that physiological, emotional, and behavioral factors be considered when assessing and designing programs of instruction for literacy growth. The model presented in Figure 17.3, put forth here as the literacy achievement hierarchy, suggests a hierarchy of factors to be assessed and included in instructional design.

Although, at first glance, the proposed model appears very similar to Maslow's hierarchy of needs, the literacy achievement hierarchy includes the central role of students' behavior and literacy skills as contributing factors to life success, whereas Maslow's hierarchy of needs does not. Thus, the literacy achievement hierarchy centrally positions the role of students' literacy abilities in their path toward self-actualization. Furthermore, the model indicates that students' physiological, emotional, and behavioral factors be evaluated and addressed when considering their literacy achievement. Due to the primacy of these factors in the hierarchy, it is highly recommended that these factors be considered foundational, and addressed *prior to* cognitive factors when assessing and designing instructional plans for students' literacy growth. Moving forward, it is also recommended that research be conducted on the statistical degree to which physiological, emotional, and behavioral characteristics contribute to students' literacy success. As stated at the outset of this chapter, it is presumed erroneous that only cognitive factors and cognitive interventions are responsible for students' literacy attainment.

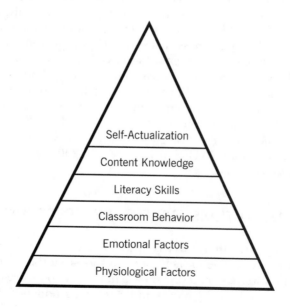

FIGURE 17.3. The literacy achievement hierarchy.

CONCLUSION

Students' literacy learning at school takes place within communities of learners. While academic engagement, motivation, and achievement remain top priorities in these classrooms, the purpose of the present chapter is to highlight the underlying roles of students' physiological, emotional, and behavioral well-being within these communities. If literacy educators focus solely on literacy instruction, great opportunities to support their students' literacy growth will be missed. As such, this chapter highlights the physiological, emotional, and behavioral dimensions of students' lives, and describes ways in which these dimensions can be assessed and addressed in the classroom. Fully attending to the underlying physiological, emotional, and behavioral needs of our communities of learners is a key part of optimizing their literacy achievement.

ENGAGEMENT ACTIVITIES

1. **Nutritional, Sleep, and Exercise Logs.** Readers of this text can bring greater attention to the critical importance of students' physiological well-being in literacy achievement through the use of nutrition, sleep, and exercise logs with their students. Each day, students can track the items that they eat, their hours of sleep, and the amount of exercise that they obtain. Students can share their logs and discussions can ensue. Prizes can be awarded for students' successes and improvements in these areas. The more that teachers emphasize the importance of physical foundations in their classroom, the greater their students' literacy success will be.

2. **Teacher–Student Dialogue Journals.** One of the most effective ways to support students' emotional well-being is by strengthening teacher–student relationships. Dialogue journal entries facilitate this goal. In dialogue journaling, students are encouraged to write to their teachers once a week about anything that is on their minds. Teachers then read the journal entries and write back. Journal entries should not be graded or marked for grammatical accuracy or spelling. Rather, they should be viewed as a vehicle for better understanding students' lives and needs.

3. **Peace Corners.** Students' physiological, emotional, and behavioral needs can be supported with the inclusion of peace corners in classrooms. Peace corners are places where students can go when they need to build peace, quiet, and equilibrium within

themselves. Access to soothing music, meditation, reading, and writing materials can be provided. Peace corners address students' physiological, emotional, and behavioral needs in a compassionate and supportive manner.

REFERENCES

Ahmad, A., & Sahak, R. (2009). Teacher–student attachment and teachers' attitudes toward work. *Journal of Educators and Education, 24,* 55–72.

Ainsworth, M. D. S. (1969). Object relations, dependency, and attachment: A theoretical review of the infant–mother relationship. *Child Development, 40,* 969–1025.

American Educational Research Association. (2016). Retrieved July 1, 2016, from *www.aera.net/Portals/38/docs/Annual_Meeting/2016%20Annual%20Meeting/2016%20Knowledge%20Forum/Immordino.pdf.*

Anthony, C., DiPerna, J., & Amoto, P. (2014). Divorce, approaches to learning, and children's academic achievement: A longitudinal analysis of mediated and moderated effects. *Journal of School Psychology, 52*(3), 249–261.

Baker, J. A. (2006). Contributions of the teacher–child relationships to positive school adjustment during elementary school. *Journal of School Psychology, 44,* 211–229.

Berg, L., Rostila, M., Saarela, J., & Hjern, A. (2014). Parental death during childhood and subsequent school performance. *Pediatrics, 133*(4), 682–689.

Bernstein-Yamashiro, B., & Noam, G. G. (2013). Teacher–student relationships: A growing field of study. *New Directions for Youth Development, 137,* 15–26.

Bomer, R., & Maloch, B. (2013). Lunch, teeth, body, and mind: Children's learning and well-being. *Language Arts, 90*(4), 273–280.

Bond, G. L., & Dykstra, R. (1967). The cooperative research program in first-grade reading instruction. *Reading Research Quarterly, 2*(4), 5–142.

Bouchamma, Y., & Poulin, V. (2014). Impact of reading strategy use on girls' and boys' achievement. *Reading Psychology, 35,* 312–331.

Bowlby, J. (1969). *Attachment and loss: Vol. 1. Attachment.* New York: Basic Books.

Bowlby, J. (1980). *Attachment and loss: Vol. 3. Loss, sadness, and depression.* New York: Basic Books.

Bucholz, E. M., Desai, M. M., & Rosenthal, M. S. (2011). Dietary intake in Head Start versus non-Head Start preschool-aged children: Results from the 1999–2004 National Health and Nutrition Examination Survey. *Journal of the American Dietetic Association, 111*(7), 1021–1030.

Burrows, R., Correa-Burrows, P., Orellana, A. A., Lizana, P., & Ivanovic, D. (2014). Scheduled physical activity is associated with better academic performance in Chilean school-age children. *Journal of Physical Activity and Health, 11,* 1600–1606.

Carroll, A. E. (2016, May 23). Sorry, there's nothing magical about breakfast. *New York Times,* p. A3.

Chaddock-Heyman, L., Hillman, C. H., Cohen, N. J., & Kramer, A. F. (2014). The importance of physical activity and aerobic fitness for cognitive control and memory in children. *Monographs of the Society for Research in Child Development, 79*(4), 25–50.

Chen, Y., & Fish, M. (2013). Parental involvement of mothers with chronic illness and children's academic achievement. *Journal of Family Issues, 34*(5), 583–606.

Chopra, D., & Tanzi, R. E. (2012). *Super brain*. New York: Three Rivers Press.

Drake, C., Nickrl, C., Burduvali, E., Roth, T., Jefferson, C., & Badia, P. (2003). The Pediatric Daytime Sleepiness Scale (PDSS): Sleep habits and school outcomes in middle school children. *Sleep, 26*(4), 455–458.

Erlauer, L. (2003). *The brain-compatible classroom: Using what we know about learning to improve teaching*. Alexandria, VA: Association for Supervision and Curriculum Development.

Erikson, J. (2006, November/December). Brain food: The real dish on nutrition and brain function. *WisKids Journal*.

Euston, D. R., & Steenland, H. W. (2014, June 6). Memories: Getting wired during sleep. *Science, 344*(6188), 1087–1088.

Gautam, P., & Pradhan, M. (2017). Stress as related with conduct and achievement in adolescent students. *Indian Journal of Health and Wellbeing, 8*(5), 382–387.

Gillen-O'Neal, C., Huynh, V. W., & Fuligui, A. (2013). To study or to sleep?: The academic costs of extra studying at the expense of sleep. *Child Development, 84*(1), 133–142.

Greco, L., Baer, R. A., & Smith, G. T. (2011). Assessing mindfulness in children and adolescents: Development and validation of the Child and Adolescent Mindfulness Measure (CAMM). *Psychological Assessment, 23*(3), 606–614.

Hagins, M., & Rundle, A. (2016). Yoga improves academic performance in urban high school students compared to physical education: A randomized controlled trial. *Mind, Brain, and Education, 10*(2), 105–116.

Halterman, J. S., Kaczorowski, J. M., Aligne, C. A., Auinger, P., & Szilagyi, P. G. (2001). Iron deficiency and cognitive achievement among school-aged children and adolescents in the United States. *Pediatrics, 107*, 1381–1386.

Hamre, B. K., & Pianta, R. C. (2005). Can instructional and emotional support in the first-grade classroom make a difference for children at risk of school failure? *Child Development, 76*, 949–967.

Harpin, S., Rossi, A., Kim, A., & Swanson, L. (2016). Behavioral impacts of a mindfulness pilot intervention for elementary school students. *Education, 137*(2), 149–156.

Hillman, C. H. (2014). An introduction to the relation of physical activity to cognitive and brain health, and scholastic achievement. *Monographs of the Society for Research in Child Development, 79*(4), 1–6.

Hupbach, A., Gomez, R. L., Bootzin, R. R., & Nader, L. (2009). Nap-dependent learning in infants. *Developmental Science, 12*(6), 1007–1012.

Immordino-Yang, M. H. (2011). Implications of affective and social neuroscience for educational theory. *Educational Philosophy and Theory, 43*(1), 98–103.

Immordino-Yang, M. H. (2015, May 4). Why emotions are integral to learning: An excerpt from Mary Helen Immordino-Yang's new book. Retrieved July 12, 2016, from *www.noodle.com/articles/why-emotions-are-integral-to-learning-mary-helen-immordino-yang*.

Immordino-Yang, M. H., & Faeth, M. (2009). The role of emotion and skilled intuition in learning. In D. Sousa (Ed.), *Mind, brain, and education* (pp. 66–81). Bloomington, IN: Solution Tree Press.

Kahn, N. A., Raine, L. B., Donovan, S. M., & Hillman, C. H. (2014). The cognitive implications of obesity and nutrition in childhood. *Monographs of the Society for Research in Child Development, 79*(4), 51–71.

Kaplan Toren, N., & Seginer, R. (2015). Classroom climate, parental educational involvement, and student functioning in early adolescence: A longitudinal study. *Social Psychology of Education, 18*(4), 811–827.

Kauts, A., & Sharma, N. (2009). Effect of yoga on academic performance in relation to stress. *International Journal of Yoga, 2*(1), 39–43.

Khandelwal, S., Siegel, K. R., & Venkat Narayan, K. M. (2013). Nutrition research in India: Underweight, stunted, or wasted? *Global Heart, 8*(2), 131–137.

Korpershoek, H., Harms, T., de Boer, H., Van Kuijk, M., & Doolaard, S. (2016). A meta-analysis of the effects of classroom management strategies and classroom management programs on students' academic, behavioral, emotional, and motivational outcomes. *Review of Educational Research, 86*(3), 643–680.

Krstic, K. (2015). Attachment in the student–teacher relationship as a factor of school achievement. *Teaching Innovations, 28*(3), 167–188.

Lee, V., & Loeb, S. (2000). School size in Chicago elementary schools: Effects on teachers' attitudes and students' achievement. *American Educational Research Journal, 37*(1), 3–31.

Mackay, T., Reynolds, S., & Kearney, M. (2010). From attachment to attainment: The impact of nurture groups on academic achievement. *Education and Child Psychology, 27*(3), 100–110.

Maltais, C., Duchesne, S., Ratelle, C. F., & Feng, B. (2015). Attachment to the mother and achievement goal orientations at the beginning of middle school: The mediating role of academic competence and anxiety. *Learning and Individual Differences, 39,* 39–48.

Marzban, A., Ejei, J., & Bahrami, F. (2014). Causal model of attachment impact on academic achievement with regard to the mediator of curiosity. *Journal of School Psychology, 18*(3), 118–128.

Maslow, A. H. (1943). A theory of human motivation. *Psychological Review, 50,* 370–396.

Maslow, A. H. (1954). *Motivation and personality.* New York: Harper & Collins.

Mosconi, L., Murray, J., Davies, M., Williams, S., Pirraglia, E., Spector, N., . . . de Leon, M. (2014). Nutrient intake and brain biomarkers of Alzheimers' disease in at-risk, cognitively normal individuals: A cross-sectional neuro-imaging pilot study. *BMR Open.* Retrieved from *http://library.kean. edu:2078/10.1136/bmjopen-2014-004850.*

Noltemeyer, A., Bush, K. J., & Bergen, D. (2012). The relationship among deficiency needs and growth needs: An empirical investigation of Maslow's theory. *Children and Youth Services Review, 34,* 1862–1867.

Park, A., Sifferlin, A., & Oaklander, M. (2014, September 11). The power of sleep. *Time, 184*(11), 52–58.

Parker-Pope, T. (2017, August 1). How to build resilience in midlife. *New York Times,* pp. D1–D6.

Phelan, T. W., & Schonour, S. J. (2004). *1, 2, 3 magic for teachers: Effective classroom discipline pre-K through grade 8*. Naperville, IL: Sourcebooks.

Pianta, R. C., La Paro, K. M., & Hamre, B. K. (2008*). Classroom Assessment Scoring System (CLASS): K–3*. Baltimore: Brookes.

Potter, D. (2010). Prosocial wellbeing and the relationship between divorce and children's academic achievement. *Journal of Marriage and the Family, 72*(4), 933–946.

Ravid, S., Afek, I., Suraiya, S., Shahar, E., & Pillar, G. (2009). Sleep disturbances are associated with reduced school achievements in first-grade pupils. *Developmental Neuropsychology, 34*(5), 574–587.

Rimfeld, K., Kovas, Y., Dale, P., & Plomin, R. (2016). True grit and genetics: Predicting academic achievement from personality. *Journal of Personality and Social Psychology, 111*(5), 780–789.

Scullin, M. K. (2013). Sleep, memory, and aging: The link between slow-wave sleep and episodic memory changes from younger to older adults. *Psychology and Aging, 28*(1), 105–114.

Taormina, R. J., & Gao, J. H. (2013). Maslow and the motivation hierarchy: Measuring satisfaction of needs. *American Journal of Psychology, 126*(2), 155–177.

Touchette, E., Petit, D., Seguin, J. R., Boivin, M., Tremblay, R. E., & Montplasir, J. Y. (2007). Associations between sleep duration patterns and behavioral/cognitive functioning at school entry. *Sleep, 30*, 1213–1219.

Tracey, D. H., & Morrow, L. M., (2017). *Lenses on reading: An introduction to theories and models*. New York: Guilford Press.

White, K. M. (2013). Associations between teacher–child relationships and children's writing in kindergarten and first grade. *Early Childhood Research Quarterly, 28*(1), 166–176.

Wojcicki, T. R., & McAuley, E. (2014). Physical activity: Measurement and behavioral patterns in children and youth. *Monographs for the Society for Research in Child Development, 79*(4), 7–24.

Wolfgang, J. D. (2013). *The longitudinal effect of traumatic stress and attachment difficulties on academic achievement of young children*. Unpublished doctoral dissertation, University of Florida, Gainesville, FL.

Wolpert, S., & Wheeler, M. (July 9, 2008) Food as brain medicine. *UCLA Magazine Online*. Retrieved from *http://magazine.ucla.edu/exclusives/food_brain_medicine*.

World Food Programme. (2016). *Hunger statistics*. Retrieved from *www.wfp.org/hunger/stats*.

World Hunger Education Service. (2016). *Hunger notes*. Retrieved from *www.worldhunger.org*.

Yonezawa, S., McClure, L., & Jones, M. (2012). *Personalization in schools: The students at the center series*. Boston: Jobs for the Future.

Zhang, J., Herbert, J., & Muldoon, M. (2005). Dietary fat intake is associated with psychosocial and cognitive functioning of school-aged children in the United States. *Journal of Nutrition, 135*, 1967–1973.

CHAPTER 18

Building Strong Home, School, and Community Partnerships through Culturally Relevant Teaching

JEANNE R. PARATORE
PATRICIA A. EDWARDS
LISA M. O'BRIEN

This chapter will:

- Present evidence to support the importance of parent involvement in children's school success.
- Explain the importance of teachers developing and acting on a mindset that aligns with evidence that parents and teachers together can "grow" into productive partnerships.
- Discuss the importance of teachers enacting outreach strategies to engage parents as partners.
- Describe the families that populate our schools as a basis for understanding and planning appropriate forms of parent involvement.
- Explore culturally relevant teaching and its relationship to building effective and sustaining home, school, and community partnerships.
- Connect culturally relevant teaching to home–school partnerships.
- Share examples of home–school partnerships that are aligned with both culturally relevant teaching and principles of effective parent involvement.
- Conclude with guiding principles and reflections on future directions.

In this chapter, we argue that building productive and sustained home, school, and community partnerships is grounded in three fundamental ideas. First, children are better positioned for school success when their parents and their teachers form productive and sustained partnerships; and such partnerships are more likely to develop when teachers implement deliberate and thoughtful outreach efforts. Second, culturally relevant teaching—an approach to instruction that embraces cultural and linguistic differences as strengths and valid and valuable learning opportunities—is fundamental to equitable and just teaching for all of our students; further, enacting the principles of culturally relevant teaching requires that teachers acquire deep knowledge of their students, their families, and their experiences. Third, parent–teacher partnerships that are designed to support the exchange of information about school, home, and community experiences are likely to deepen teachers' understandings about their students and, as such, provide the foundation for culturally relevant teaching.

To build these arguments, first, we review evidence related to the importance of home–school partnerships; second, we explore the consequential role teachers play in developing and sustaining meaningful partnerships, including the importance of developing a growth mindset in relation to themselves and also in their work and conversations with both their students and their students' families; third, we describe the demographics of families teachers can expect to meet and partner with in today's schools and classrooms; fourth, we define culturally relevant teaching and its importance to achieving equitable and just teaching for all our students; fifth, we connect culturally relevant teaching to home–school partnership building; and sixth, we provide a few examples of home–school partnerships that are grounded in culturally relevant teaching (CRT). We conclude with summative guiding principles and reflections about future directions.

EVIDENCE-BASED BEST PRACTICES

A Research Synthesis: The Importance of Parent Involvement in Children's Schooling

The importance of parent involvement in children's academic success has been well documented and widely accepted. Based on a comprehensive research synthesis, Henderson and Mapp (2002) reported that academic effects are demonstrated across broad and varied measures: students of involved parents have higher rates of school attendance, better social skills and behavior, higher grades and test scores, lower rates of retention, and higher rates of high school graduation and postsecondary study.

These findings are further strengthened by additional, large-scale studies that postdate Henderson's and Mapp's review. For example, Houtenville and Conway (2008) sought to determine both the educational and economic effects of parent involvement. They analyzed a large data set (10,382 eighth-grade students) from the National Education Longitudinal Study (NELS). They found parental effort to have significantly positive effects on student achievement, "along the order of four to six years of parental education or more than $1000 in per-pupil spending" (p. 450).

We also know, however, that some studies have yielded findings of unproductive parental involvement programs (e.g., Mattingly, Prislan, McKenzie, Rodriguez, & Kayzar, 2002; St. Pierre, Ricciuti, & Rimdzius, 2005), and these reports raise questions about precisely what makes some programs succeed, while others fail. Some studies help answer these questions by examining how various types of parent involvement differentially influence student outcomes. In a meta-analysis of 51 studies (total sample 13,000 students), Jeynes (2012) examined the effects of several forms of parent involvement on the academic achievement of preschool through 12th-grade students. He found that regardless of program type, parent involvement programs were significantly related to students' academic achievement (0.3 SD), with slightly greater effects for older students (0.33 SD) than younger students (0.31 SD). Further, he found that parent involvement programs emphasizing parent–child shared reading (i.e., any program that encouraged parents and their children to read together) and parent–school partnerships (i.e., any efforts that support parent and teacher collaboration as equal partners in enhancing children's academic and/or behavior outcomes) had the largest effects (0.51 SD, 0.35 SD, respectively) as compared to programs emphasizing checking homework and communication between parents and teachers (0.27 SD, 0.28 SD, respectively). English-as-a-second-language instruction (i.e., efforts to improve parents' English so as to empower their school involvement) or Head Start programs emphasizing parent involvement did not yield a significant effect on students' academic achievement.

In their work, Fan, Williams, and Wolters (2012) focused on school motivation, a key contributor to academic achievement (e.g., Guthrie & Wigfield, 2000), and studied how various aspects of parent involvement influenced school motivation among students of differing ethnic backgrounds (12,721 tenth-graders including Asian American, Hispanic, Caucasian, and African American students). Fan et al. found that although parent involvement in the form of holding high aspirations enhanced all students' school motivation, differences in effects of other practices were observed across ethnic groups regardless of socioeconomic status. For example, parent–school communication regarding benign or positive issues (e.g., course selection, help with homework), as opposed to negative issues (e.g., poor behavior or low academic performance), was positively related to Hispanic students' intrinsic motivation for English language arts (ELA), but had no effect on Asian American, Caucasian, or African American students' intrinsic motivation for ELA. Similarly uneven effects were observed when the form of involvement was participation in school functions: it contributed to enhanced intrinsic motivation and self-efficacy for ELA for Caucasian students; for African American students, parent participation in school functions was positively related to students' self-efficacy but negatively related to intrinsic motivation; and for Asian American or Hispanic students' motivation, parent involvement in school functions had no association with ELA.

Altschul (2011), too, found that the form of parent involvement mattered. In this study, at-home parent involvement for Mexican American students ($N = 1,609$) was associated with enhanced academic achievement (i.e., standardized measures of reading, math, science, and history), while parent involvement in school functions had no effects.

Additional evidence of differences according to families' ethnic backgrounds is found in an earlier study by Jeynes (2003). He conducted a meta-analysis of 20 studies (total sample of 12,000 students) of effects of parent involvement on academic achievement of students of different ethnic backgrounds (African American, Latino, Asian) in grades K–12. In examined studies, parent involvement was represented in various ways, including parent communication with children about school, checking children's homework, holding high expectations for academic success, encouraging outside reading, and attending school functions. Parent involvement had significant positive effects for all racial groups, although these effects were not equal. African American and Latino groups benefited more than Asian American groups. In addition, parent involvement had positive effects on all academic measures (e.g., grade point average [GPA], achievement tests), but effects were greater on achievement tests than on GPA.

Also seeking to understand factors that related to parent involvement effects, Dearing, Kreider, Simpkins, and Weiss (2006) examined the role of parent education. In a longitudinal study of low-income children ($N = 281$) whose parents were involved in an intervention program with services for children (high-quality preschool) and parents (education and job training) during the children's kindergarten year, Dearing et al. found that effects varied by maternal education. That is, there was a relationship between the intervention, higher levels of parent involvement, and higher levels of literacy performance among children whose parents were less educated, but no relationship when parents were relatively more educated. Further, when parent involvement in children's schooling increased between kindergarten and fifth grade, children of both high- and low-education families achieved higher literacy performances, suggesting that benefits accrue when involvement is not only sustained, but also heightened. Moreover, despite an achievement gap across children of high- and low-education mothers when parent involvement was low, this gap disappeared when parent involvement levels were high.

In our view, the combined evidence supports a clear claim that parent involvement in their children's learning has noteworthy academic benefits for nearly all children. Moreover, when children have mothers with less education, parent involvement exerts an even more powerful influence on children's literacy performance, even eliminating the achievement gap that typically separates the performance of children of low- and high-education mothers. Further, the evidence that relationships vary depending on the form of parent involvement and by education levels and the race/ethnicity of the family suggests that parents in diverse communities may enact their involvement in differing, yet meaningful, ways.

The Teacher's Role in Parent Involvement: Developing and Acting on a Growth Mindset

Few teachers reading the evidence about the importance of parent involvement will be surprised—their own observations and experiences confirm the outcomes of formal investigations. However, some teachers—especially those who practice in low-income communities—believe that, for the most part, the parents of the children with whom they work are disengaged and uninterested in their children's learning (e.g., Edwards, 2016; Greene, 2013; López-Robertson, Long, & Turner-Nash, 2010.). Studies indicate that some teachers believe so strongly in parents' lack of interest and motivation related to their children's schooling that they even fail to reach out to them, assuming their efforts will meet with resistance (e.g., Edwards, 2009). In the words of Carol Dweck (2016), some teachers have a "fixed mindset" (p. 8) that creates an expectation of failure and limits both the scope and the effectiveness of actions intended to engage parents in collaborative activities.

Some may be surprised, then, by findings that the extent to which parents become involved in their children's schooling is not explained by families' education, economic status, language, or culture; rather, actions teachers take are instrumental in levels of parent involvement. Based on evidence collected from a sample of over 1,200 parents of elementary school children, Epstein (1986) concluded:

> Parents' education did not explain experiences with parent involvement unless teacher practices were taken into account. In the classrooms of teachers who were leaders in the use of parent involvement,

parents at all educational levels said they were frequently involved in learning activities at home. (p. 291)

This study, though persuasive in both its size and definitive finding, is now over 30 years old, so one might reasonably ask if this finding is likely to hold up in today's schools and classrooms. To answer this question, we turn next to a number of more recent studies. In the first, Sheldon (2003) collected data from 113 public schools in one urban, low-income school system. He found that high-quality parent involvement programs correlated strongly with teachers' and administrators' outreach practices, noting, in particular, positive effects of schools' deep and broad efforts "to involve hard-to-reach families and the community in the school and in students' learning" (p. 160). In a later study, using school attendance as the target variable, Sheldon (2007) measured changes in students' attendance, explaining that higher rates of attendance correlate with higher performance on standardized achievement tests and lower rates correlate with increased risk of school dropout. He compared attendance rates in schools in the state of Ohio with and without schoolwide school, family, and community partnerships. In schools with schoolwide partnership programs, rates of student attendance increased, while in schools without schoolwide partnership programs, rates of student attendance decreased. Moreover, as he found in the earlier study, the "driving mechanism" (p. 267) causing this effect was school outreach to families.

In another large-scale investigation (N = 19,375 kindergartners), Cooper (2010) sought to determine specific moderators (e.g., income status, parental education, teacher education) of the relationship between family poverty and school-based parent involvement. School-based parent involvement was defined as parents who "attended a PTA meeting, attended an open house, attended a parent advisory group or policy council, attended a school or class event, attended a regularly scheduled parent–teacher conference, volunteered at school, participated in fundraising, or contacted teacher or school since the start of kindergarten" (p. 483). Cooper found that among poor parents with little education, school-based involvement was low; however, among poor parents with high levels of education (i.e., a college degree or higher), parents had "slightly higher school-based involvement than their non-poor counterparts" (p. 487). Further, the negative association between poverty and school-based parent involvement was moderated by teachers' level of education—that is, the negative association weakened when teachers held graduate-level degrees. Yet, additional analyses indicated that when teachers initiated school-based parent involvement, high-income parents benefited more than low-income parents, as the gap in levels of involvement between the two groups became wider. Cooper speculated that the types of parental involvement that teachers typically advocate may favor the abilities, experiences, and predispositions about schooling of high-income parents, and as such, prominent outreach efforts may be a better "match" for high-income parents.

Park and Holloway (2013) also examined effects of school-outreach efforts on parent involvement. Analyzing data from 3,248 parents of high school students (African American, Caucasian, and Latino), like the studies by Epstein (1986), Sheldon (2003, 2007), and Cooper (2010), they found that school-outreach efforts were strongly associated with school-based involvement, particularly if efforts were perceived by parents as informative (e.g., how to help child with homework, why a child is placed in particular groups or classes, parents' expected role at school). Additional analyses also indicated that among high-poverty parents, self-efficacy—the belief that they have the capacity to perform the help in beneficial ways—was a powerful predictor of school involvement. Finally, Park and Holloway (2013) found that ethnicity was not a factor in *whether* parents engaged in their child's education, but that there were differences in *how* parents of differing ethnic backgrounds were involved (when accounting for mother's educational attainment and family income). For example, African American and Latino parents were less likely to participate in school-based involvement (e.g., attend general school meetings, parent–teacher organization meetings, class events, volunteer in class) than Caucasian parents. This finding lends yet more support to the claim that the particular forms of parent involvement advocated by teachers are consequential in engaging all parents.

Walker, Ice, Hoover-Dempsey, and Sandler (2011), too, found evidence that both the forms of parent involvement and the ways teachers support parent involvement matter. They investigated school-based and home-based involvement practices among low-income, immigrant Latino parents of first- through sixth-grade children ($N = 147$). Results indicated that home-based involvement was predicted by partnership-focused role construction (i.e., the belief that schools and parents share responsibility for students' educational outcomes) and by specific invitations from the parents' children. School-based involvement was predicted by specific invitations from teachers (as opposed to "a welcoming environment"), but was also mediated by parents' perception of time and energy for their involvement.

When taken together, these findings provide solid evidence that parents of diverse ethnic and economic backgrounds participate in their child's schooling in ways that enhance their children's achievement; however, the particular ways in which parents become engaged may differ from familiar and predominant forms of parent involvement, making teachers' efforts to engage parents puzzling and complex. In particular, initiatives are generally successful when (1) teachers (rather than children) initiate specific invitations for parent involvement; (2) parents and teachers co-construct roles and responsibilities; (3) the forms of involvement are a "good fit" for parents' schedules and family commitments; and (4) teacher actions support parents' ability (and in turn, self-efficacy) relative to the focal tasks and activities.

However, even in the face of compelling evidence, it is important to recognize and acknowledge that, at times, the ability of individuals to act on findings may be limited by the aforementioned "fixed mindset." As Dweck (2016) explained, for those who hold a fixed mindset, "risk and effort are two things that might reveal your inadequacies or show that you were not up to the task. In fact, it's startling to see the degree to which people with the fixed mindset do not believe in putting in effort or getting help" (p. 9). Dweck's words about fixed and growth mindsets and parents and teachers are largely intended to address how these individuals speak to children about their strengths and needs. But, here, we interpret and apply her ideas to how teachers speak to parents about their children's abilities and behaviors and also the abilities and behaviors of parents themselves. Dweck, like many others (e.g., Denton, 2008; Johnston, 2004, 2012), emphasizes that our words matter—they convey to children attitudes about identity and ability—attitudes that then influence the dispositions they develop and the actions and strategies they learn to implement. We argue here that the words we, as teachers, say and the ways we say them matter, also, to parents—and have the potential to shape the identities they build as learning partners and the actions and strategies they become empowered to take.

In sum, as we think about how to make a difference through leadership and professional development, we must consider not only what is known about effective home–school partnerships, but also what is known about developing dispositions that enable acting on the evidence. Shifting from a fixed to a growth mindset is not a simple action—it does not happen without a combination of guidance and time. But making teachers aware of it and then working toward it—in relation to their views of themselves, their students, and their students' families—may be a necessary first step to developing productive home–school partnerships.

In the next section, we turn our attention to developing an understanding of the families we must be prepared to serve as the demographics in U.S. schools continue to change.

The Families in Our Schools

As classroom teachers, we see at firsthand the changing demographics of our classrooms—our students represent increasingly varied ethnicities and races, countries of origin, first languages, and religions. According to the Annie B. Casey Foundation (2017), "In 13 states and the District of

Columbia, children of color are the majority of the child population, and demographers predict that children of color will be the majority of all children in America by 2020" (p. 17).

Also changing, but perhaps less visible in the faces and voices of our children, is the economic security of the children who populate our classrooms. The Southern Education Foundation reported that in 2015 low-income students for the first time represented "a majority of the school-children attending the nation's public schools" (2015, p. 2). According to a report from the Annie B. Casey Foundation (2017), the number of children living in poverty in 2015 was one in five. For children of color, the rate is far worse, with 36% of African American children, 34% of Native American children, and 31% of Latino children living in poverty as compared to 12% of their non-Hispanic Caucasian peers. Data released in 2016 (Semega, Fontenot, & Kollar, 2017) indicated poverty affects families in every U.S. region, with a rate of 13% for those living within metropolitan statistical areas (16.8% among those in principal cities) and 16.7% among those living outside metropolitan areas. The overall numbers are staggering: "The federally defined label of low-income applies to more children today than it did a decade ago, before the onset of the Great Recession. In total, 31 million kids—43% of the nation's children—now live in families that are low-income" (Annie E. Casey Foundation, 2017).

The effects of living in poverty on children's learning are well documented and far-reaching. Briefly stated, from inception and throughout their childhood, children living in poverty are likely to experience poor nutrition and poor health care, and these factors contribute to diminished engagement, concentration, and memory. These behaviors, in turn, are likely to diminish children's opportunities to learn, resulting in a substantial achievement gap among poor children when compared to their middle- and high-income peers; higher rates of school dropout—equal to four and one-half times that of higher-income peers; and greater risk of behavioral and emotion problems (see, e.g., Biddle, 2013).

Although such data can lead to discouragement and even despair, they should not. There is evidence that excellent schools can make a difference (e.g., Reeves, 2005; Taylor & Pearson, 2002; Teddlie & Stringfield, 1993), especially when teachers add productive parent involvement efforts to the instructional strategies they undertake as part of teaching reform (e.g., Allen, 2007; Chrispeels & Rivero, 2001; McIntyre, 2010). In an especially powerful statement, under the subheading "Seeing Clearly," Jensen (2013) cautioned: "Remember, students in poverty are not broken or damaged. In fact, human brains adapt to experiences by making changes—and your students can change. You can help them to do so by understanding . . . and addressing . . . differences with purposeful teaching" (pp. 29–30).

Although Jensen, perhaps, intended this statement to apply to changes in our students' brains, we suggest that as teachers, we, too, must reflect on and consider how we must change our perceptions and our practices so that we are able to "see clearly" and more fully understand and know our students and their families. We believe we can do this by attending to the principles of CRT, and we turn to those next.

Defining Culturally Relevant Teaching

For at least the last 40 years, anthropologists, sociolinguists, and teacher educators (e.g., Au & Jordan, 1981; Mohatt & Erickson, 1981; Jordan, 1985) have used terms such as *culturally appropriate, culturally congruent, culturally responsive, culturally compatible,* and *culturally sustaining* to describe pedagogies that are intended to respond to the diversity of students who populate our classrooms and expand every student's opportunities. Over 20 years ago, Gloria Ladson-Billings used the term culturally relevant teaching (CRT) to describe "a pedagogy that empowers students intellectually, socially, emotionally, and politically by using cultural referents to impart knowledge, skills, and attitudes" (1994, pp. 17–18). She explained that CRT is grounded in three essential tenets: "students must experience academic success; they must develop or maintain cultural competence; and students must develop a critical consciousness through which they challenge the status quo of the social order" (1995a, p. 160). Ladson-Billings argued that although CRT closely resembled critical pedagogy, it differed in its commitment to "collective, not merely individual, empowerment" (p. 160).

Despite its decades-long history, it is fair to say that CRT is not yet fully understood, nor is it broadly implemented. In part, this may be because CRT is grounded in a belief that the differences among ethnic and cultural groups are normative to the human condition and valuable to both personal and societal development (Gay 2010)—a belief that is a clear departure from the oft-held view that cultural and linguistic differences contribute to children's learning difficulty and may be at the root of underachievement. As described by Gay (2013), embracing the view that cultural and linguistic differences forecast an array of valuable opportunities to be embraced rather than problems to be solved requires the development of a complex and multifaceted view of the relationship between culture and learning, as well as deep knowledge of the backgrounds and experiences of the children in our classrooms:

> Culturally responsive teaching is the behavioral expressions of knowledge, beliefs and values that recognize the importance of racial and cultural diversity in learning. It is contingent on . . . seeing cultural

differences as assets; creating caring learning communities where culturally different individuals and heritages are valued; using cultural knowledge of ethnically diverse cultures, families, and communities to guide curriculum development, classroom climates, instructional strategies, and relationships with students; challenging racial and cultural stereotypes, prejudices, racism, and other forms of intolerance, injustice, and oppression; being change agents for social justice and academic equity; mediating power imbalances in classroom based on race, culture, ethnicity, and class; and accepting cultural responsiveness as endemic to educational effectiveness in all areas of learning for students from all ethnic groups. (p. 50)

For the purposes of this chapter, we have taken as a given that readers have a disposition toward CRT—that is, we assume that readers value and recognize the importance of racial and cultural diversity in learning. But we think it's fair to expect that even teachers predisposed to CRT may not be clear or confident about ways to develop deep knowledge and understanding of children, their families, and their communities—of the sort that enables CRT. That is, how does a typical teacher go about acquiring all of this knowledge about his or her students' background and experiences and then making sense of it in ways that advance teaching and learning? One can expect that some of this information can be gathered as teachers interact with students day in and day out. But the depth and breadth of the information that is shared may be diminished by a number of factors, including limited instructional time; the extent to which children are able or willing to fully describe and share their experiences and knowledge; perhaps limited even by the types of questions teachers think to ask. So, although these routine conversations are valuable and essential, they likely are not enough. In the next section, we examine the teaching practices and routines enacted by teachers who engage in culturally relevant pedagogies.

Culturally Relevant Teaching as the Foundation for Connecting Teachers, Families, and Communities

Drawing from the work of many (e.g., Ladson-Billing, 1994, 1995a, 1995b; Gay 2010, 2013; Paris, 2012), teachers who enact CRT practices engage in the following instructional actions and routines:

1. They believe that every child has the capacity to succeed; they maintain and meet high expectations by joining a cognitively challenging curriculum with explicit instruction, expert scaffolding, and many opportunities for their students to practice and apply

new understandings in meaningful and purposeful contexts in and out of school.

2. They create classroom environments in which everyone's culture is valued. They recognize children's cultural differences as opportunities to learn about each other and about the world in which we live.

3. They use their knowledge of their students' cultural backgrounds and experiences to guide curricular and instructional decision making. They search for and integrate familiar materials (e.g., multimodal texts and experiences common in classrooms and also in students' homes and communities) as important curricular and instructional resources.

4. They familiarize themselves with their students' cultural contexts and experiences and they help their students view their experiences outside of school as valid and valued ways of knowing and learning.

5. They recognize and build on the social nature of learning by situating instructional experiences within collaborative contexts in which students can share their own ideas, question and challenge the ideas of others, and co-construct meaning and understanding.

6. They view learning as an iterative, inquiry-based process in which knowledge is not static or mastered but rather re-created and recycled through many collaborative opportunities to investigate, explain, question, and refine or revise understandings about important ideas.

As is readily apparent, to act on these principles, teachers must acquire far more than the superficial knowledge of their students' ethnicities, races, and languages—they must establish methods or routines for *really* getting to know their students, their families, and their communities. Their search for understanding must be intentional and deliberate, uncovering families' experiences, interests, achievements, problems, and challenges, while also sharing children's classroom and school experiences. This collaborative knowledge sharing, in turn, is expected to allow teachers, family, and community members to meaningfully and productively build on their collective "funds of knowledge" (Moll & Greenberg, 1991) so that students learning in and out of school is both coherent and purposeful. In the next section, we provide examples of initiatives that can lead to collaborative knowledge building and strong home, community, and school relationships; and how those relationships, in turn, contribute to a classroom learning context in which teachers deliberately and intentionally connect new knowledge to children's school, home, and community experiences.

BEST PRACTICES IN ACTION:
COLLABORATIVE KNOWLEDGE BUILDING

Perhaps the most well known and thoroughly studied example of an approach to parent–teacher relationship-building is the work of Moll and his colleagues (e.g., Moll & Greenberg, 1990; González, Moll, & Amanti, 2005; Moll & Cammarota, 2010) on identifying *funds of knowledge* present in households of the children we teach. As described by González et al. (2005),

> The concept of *funds of knowledge* . . . is based on a simple premise: People are competent, they have knowledge, and their life experiences have given them that knowledge. Our claim is that first-hand research experiences with families allow one to document this competence and knowledge. It is this engagement that opened up many possibilities for positive pedagogical actions. (p. *x*)

The Fund of Knowledge project is grounded in "respectful talk between people who are mutually engaged in a constructive conversation" (González et al., p. 8). Participating teachers learn to visit homes not for the purpose of teaching parents what to do, but instead, to deepen their understanding of what parents know and do as part of their daily family, community, and work experiences. To do so they observe, question, and discuss, with a focus on gaining a deeper understanding of their children's lives outside of school. In addition, teachers meet as an after-school study group to discuss their observations and the knowledge they have gained and to articulate the ways they can act on the information. That is, they reflect on what they have learned and determine how they can use the information to connect children's learning experiences in school, at home, and in the classroom. Participating teachers described their experiences as transformative. One teacher explained:

> Participating in the project helped me to reformulate my concept of culture from being very static to more practice-oriented. This broadened conceptualization turned out to be the key which helped me develop strategies to include the knowledge my students were bringing to school in my classroom practice. (pp. 99–100)

A second example of an approach designed to support parent–teacher relationship building, the Parent Story approach, is drawn from the work of Edwards, Pleasants, and Franklin (1999):

> Parent stories can provide teachers with the opportunity to gain a deeper understanding of the "human side" of families and children

(i.e., why children behave as they do, children's ways of learning and communicating, some of the problems parents have encountered, and how these problems may have impacted their children's views about school and the schooling process. (p. xviii)

Edwards et al. explained that through parent stories, teachers have the opportunity to see and understand the ways home and school cultures may differ and the challenges that these differences create for students; they can learn about individual and social pressures facing families; and they can also learn about parents' aspirations and expectations for their children. Armed with this knowledge, teachers can come to recognize their own strengths and responsibilities in helping parents meet certain challenges, and they can also learn to seek help for issues outside of their expertise.

To collect family stories, Edwards et al. suggest seven major steps. First, teachers seek at least one colleague who is also interested in collecting family stories, so that they can share their experiences—positive and negative—along the way and have a partner with whom to problem-solve. Second, teachers systematically review records of each of the children in their classrooms, and, to start, choose one student about whom they have concerns or questions. Third, teachers prepare questions related to 11 categories: (1) parent–child family routines; (2) child's literacy history; (3) teachable moments (e.g., explicit or implicit home learning opportunities); (4) home life (e.g., discipline, parent–child relationship, problems); (5) educational experiences (outside of home, e.g., library visits, summer activities); (6) parents' beliefs about their child; (7) child's time with others; (8) parent–child sibling relationships; (9) parents' hobbies, activities, and interests in books; (10) parent–teacher relationship; and (11) parents' school history and ideas about school. (See Edwards et al., 1999, pp. 36-40, for a suggested list of interview questions.) Fourth, teachers identify a time and place to have the conversation with the parent(s), and as they talk, they either audio-record or take written notes to assist them later as they reflect on and consider ways to act on the information they have gathered. Fifth, teachers review and reflect on the information shared by parents. Edwards et al. (1999) provide specific steps to follow, including composing a list of the positive and negative aspects of the "story," recording facts that "stick out" in your mind, and generating new questions. Sixth, the teacher uses his or her notes to develop some instructional ideas that help the child in the classroom and support learning at home. Seventh, the teacher implements his or her ideas in the classroom and meets with parents to explain how they might help the child at home.

The Funds of Knowledge and Parent Story approaches are especially comprehensive and potentially very instructive. However, building parent–teacher relationships need not be quite as formal a process as each of these requires. Allen (2007), for example, emphasized ways by which teachers might take advantage of existing daily and weekly routines to create spaces for conversations with parents. In communities in which parents walk their children to school, a teacher positioned at an appropriate location can initiate "handoff chats" (p. 71), sharing information about the child's progress, providing parents an opportunity to ask a question about a homework assignment, and so forth. Other examples include *getting-to-know-you* conferences with each parent early in the school year, characterized as a "listening conference" (p. 72) during which parents share their knowledge and insights about their children; and weekly communication about classroom work that includes an envelope containing a sample of the child's work, a comment from the teacher about the child's learning progress, and a space for parents to write their own response to the child's work and progress.

Gillanders, McKinney, and Ritchie (2012) describe a collaborative inquiry approach they used to understand low-income minority parents' goals for the education of their young children and to align their instruction with the input they received. In particular, the researchers found that teachers used the information to design more effective home visits; to provide parents clear and straightforward information about their children's performances; to design homework tasks that parents could understand and support; and to explore opportunities for parents and teachers to develop social networks so that they could keep the conversations going.

In a project initially intended to stem the long-recognized challenge of summer reading loss, Compton-Lilly, Caloia, Quast, and McCann (2016) used home visits and interviews to understand how their students and family members engaged in book reading. They described the "lessons learned" as follows:

> Clearly, parents were highly motivated and interested in supporting their children with literacy. We learned important lessons not only about their interests and passion toward literacy but also about their resourcefulness. Parents were agential and creative not only in the ways they located books for their children but also in the networks they accessed to help their children and in their willingness to support their children, even when they were not confident in their own abilities. (p. 62)

As we reflect on these ideas and consider the ways that we, as teachers, can effectively build a classroom culture that leads to productive partnerships with our children's families, we are reminded once again of the comments of Lapp (2010) as a clear and helpful reminder of the stance we should take: "As suggested by the African proverb 'he who does not know one thing knows another,' all participants have something to share and therefore all voices should be heard in establishing and maintaining a partnership" (p. 154).

SUMMATIVE GUIDING PRINCIPLES

As we explained at the outset, we grounded this chapter in three fundamental ideas. First, CRT—an approach to instruction that embraces cultural and linguistic differences as strengths and valid and valuable learning opportunities—is fundamental to equitable and just teaching of all of our students; further, enacting the principles of CRT requires teachers to acquire deep knowledge of their students, their families, and their experiences. Second, children are better positioned for school success when parents and teachers form productive and sustained partnerships, and such partnerships are more likely to develop when teachers implement deliberate and thoughtful outreach efforts. Third, parent–teacher partnerships that are designed to support the exchange of information about school, home, and community experiences are likely to deepen teachers' understandings about their students and, as such, provide the foundation for CRT.

We noted that at times administrators and teachers respond to these key ideas with comprehensive (and often time-consuming) efforts. But one need not start out by attempting a full-scale initiative. To start, we can set the stage for productive parent–teacher partnerships by adhering to a few basic guiding principles:

1. Productive home–school partnerships are grounded in strong parent–teacher relationships that grow out of interactions that are focused on the *exchange* of information between parents and teachers, such that teachers gain a deeper understanding of the family's routines and interests, their children's particular interests and predispositions, and so forth; and parents gain a deeper understanding about the school, the classroom, and actions they might take to support their children's learning. Such interactions are grounded in a growth mindset, a belief and disposition that all parents and teachers—independent of differences in language, culture, education, or social class—can together grow into productive and collaborative partners in support of children's learning. Such interactions are also frequent and ongoing, enabling both parents and teachers to co-construct understandings of school, home, and community connections and to develop strategies and practices to integrate their understandings within activities in and out of school.

2. High levels of parent involvement are associated with effective out-reach efforts. These include attention to the particular needs of the families in the community and are typically characterized by flexible scheduling of events and distribution of notices and materials in the parents' first languages. In addition, teachers and administrators identify and enlist the support of friends, relatives, and community leaders who are influential with a particular family or with the various subcultures within a community.

3. When parent involvement activities are intended to support specific elements of children's literacy development, teachers and administrators identify the specific knowledge and skills parents need to effectively support the target learning, and they plan and offer workshops and training sessions that support parents' efficacious implementation of the focal activity.

REFLECTIONS AND FUTURE DIRECTIONS

As we think about where we are and where we need to be, we note that the bulk of the evidence that underlies the basic premises within this chapter is not new. Although we continue to test and validate additional ways to act on what we know about developing productive home–school partnerships, the fundamental ideas have been well established for decades. Nonetheless, in-service teachers are often observed relying on age-old parent involvement practices—for example, back-to-school nights; field trip chaperones; homework helpers—with seemingly little awareness that we have a strong knowledge base confirming that such practices are a poor "fit" for the families of the children who now populate their classrooms; or that we know quite a bit about the types of practices that are likely to be a good "fit." It is unlikely that this is indicative of teachers' reluctance to embrace or outright resistance to change; rather, it is more likely that it is a reflection of the lack of emphasis on developing understandings about parent involvement and productive home–school partnerships as part of preservice teacher education programs. Year after year, surveys indicate that first-year teachers identify their lack of knowledge about how to work with families as one of their greatest challenges (Chen, 2017; Flannery, 2010). As we look to the future, we see two essential needs. One is to help in-service teachers to become familiar with and to act on what we know about effective home–school partnerships. This will require substantial professional development in combination with effective school leadership. The second is to improve the preservice teacher education curriculum, such that novice teachers enter the classroom prepared to develop the types of parent–teacher relationships that will help build deep knowledge and understanding of children's experiences outside of school and help teachers integrate their knowledge as they build their curriculum.

ENGAGEMENT ACTIVITIES

1. In this chapter, we argue that getting to know students' families and communities is essential for building and sustaining productive home–school partnerships. Review the instructional actions and strategies taken by teachers who enact culturally relevant pedagogies. Choose one or two practices that are not part of your current teaching repertoire. How might you modify your teaching routines to incorporate the target teaching action(s)?

2. Select one of the "exemplary" home–school partnership programs described in this chapter and complete an analysis of the ways its practices align with the principles of CRT and the principles of productive home–school partnerships. Is this a program you might implement in your own school or classroom? Why or why not?

3. Many teachers and administrators are committed to both CRT and developing and sustaining home–school partnerships, but they find that their efforts fall short. Gather a group of two or three colleagues and together consider the commonly implemented parent involvement strategies used in your own classrooms or your school. Based on the ideas presented in this chapter, how might these strategies or practices be changed or modified to align with evidence of effective home–school partnerships?

REFERENCES

Allen, J. (2007). *Creating welcoming schools: A practical guide to home–school partnerships with diverse families*. New York: Teachers College Press.

Altschul, I. (2011). Parental involvement and the academic achievement of Mexican American youths: What kinds of involvement in youths' education matter most? *Social Work Research, 35*(3), 159–170.

Annie B. Casey Foundation. (2017). More kids living in low-income families today than before the recession. Retrieved October 13, 2017, from *www.aecf.org/blog/more-kids-living-in-low-income-families-today-than-before-recession*.

Au, K., & Jordan, C. (1981). Teaching reading to Hawaiian children: Finding a culturally appropriate solution. In H. Trueba, G. Guthrie, & K. Au (Eds.),

Culture and the bilingual classroom: Studies in classroom ethnography (pp. 69–86). Rowley, MA: Newbury House.

Biddle, B. (Ed.). (2013). *Social class, poverty, and education*. New York: Routledge.

Chen, G. (2017, June 22). 10 major challenge facing public schools. *Public School Review*. Retrieved October 14, 2017, from *www.publicschoolreview.com/blog/10-major-challenges-facing-public-schools*.

Chrispeels, J. H., & Rivero, E. (2001). Engaging Latino families for student success: How parent education can reshape parents' sense of place in the education of their children. *Peabody Journal of Education, 76*(2), 119–169.

Compton-Lilly, C., Caloi, R., Quast, E., & McCann, K. (2016). A closer look at summer reading programs: Listening to students and parents. *The Reading Teacher, 70*(1), 59–67.

Cooper, C. E. (2010). Family poverty, school-based parental involvement, and policy-focused protective factors in kindergarten. *Early Childhood Research Quarterly, 25*(4), 480–492.

Dearing, E., Kreider, H., Simpkins, S., & Weiss, H. B. (2006). Family involvement in school and low-income children's literacy: Longitudinal associations between and within families. *Journal of Educational Psychology, 98*(4), 653–664.

Denton, P. (2008). The power of words. *Educational Leadership, 66*(1), 28–31.

Dweck, C. (2016). *Mindset: The new psychology of success. How we can learn to fulfill our potential*. New York: Random House.

Edwards, P. A. (2009). *Tapping the potential of parents: A strategic guide to boosting student achievement through family involvement*. New York: Scholastic.

Edwards, P. A. (2016). *New ways to engage parents: Strategies and tools for teachers and leaders, K–12*. New York: Teachers College Press.

Edwards, P. A., Pleasants, H. M., & Franklin, S. H. (1999). *A path to follow: Learning to listen to parents*. Portsmouth, NH: Heinemann.

Epstein, J. (1986). Parents' reactions to teacher practices of parent involvement. *Elementary School Journal, 86*, 277–294.

Fan, W., Williams, C. M., & Wolters, C. A. (2012). Parental involvement in predicting school motivation: Similar and differential effects across ethnic groups. *Journal of Educational Research, 105*(1), 21–35.

Flannery, M. E. (2010, September 13). Top eight challenges teachers face this school year. *NEA Today*. Retrieved October 14, 2017, from *http://neatoday. org/2010/09/13/top-eight-challenges-teachers-face-this-school-year-2*.

Gay, G. (2010). *Culturally responsive teaching* (2nd ed.). New York: Teachers College Press.

Gay, G. (2013). Teaching to and through cultural diversity. *Ontario Institute for Studies in Education of the University of Toronto: Curriculum Inquiry, 43*(1), 48–70.

Gillanders, C., McKinney, M., & Ritchie, S. (2012). What kind of school would you like for your children?: Exploring minority mothers' beliefs to promote home–school partnerships. *Early Childhood Education Journal, 40*, 285–294.

González, N., Moll, L. C., & Amanti, C. (2005). *Funds of knowledge: Theorizing practices in households, communities, and classrooms*. Mahwah, NJ: Erlbaum.

Greene, S. (2013). *Race, community, and urban schools: Partnering with African American families*. New York: Teachers College Press.

Guthrie, J. T., & Wigfield, A. (2000). Engagement and motivation in reading. In M. L. Kamil, P. B. Mosenthal, P. D. Pearson, & R. Barr (Eds.), *Handbook of reading research* (pp. 403–424). Mahweh, NJ: Erlbaum.

Henderson, A. T., & Mapp, K. (2002). *A new wave of evidence: The impact of school, family, and community connections on student achievement.* Austin, TX: National Center for Family and Community Connections with Schools.

Houtenville, A. J., & Conway, K. S. (2008). Parental effort, school resources, and student achievement. *Journal of Human Resources, 43*(2), 437–453.

Jensen, E. (2013). How poverty affects classroom engagement. *Educational Leadership, 70*(8), 24–30.

Jeynes, W. (2003). A meta-analysis: The effects of parental involvement on minority children's academic involvement. *Education and Urban Society, 35*(1), 202–218.

Jeynes, W. (2012). A meta-analysis of the efficacy of different types of parental involvement programs for urban students. *Urban Education, 47*(4), 706–742.

Johnston, P. H. (2004). *Choice words: How our language affects children's learning.* Portland, ME: Stenhouse.

Johnston, P. H. (2012). *Opening minds: Using language to change lives.* Portland, ME: Stenhouse.

Jordan, C. (1985). Translating culture: From ethnographic information to educational program. *Anthropology and Education Quarterly, 16,* 105–123.

Ladson-Billings, G. (1994). *The dreamkeepers: Successful teaching for African-American students.* San Francisco: Jossey-Bass.

Ladson-Billings, G. (1995a). "But that's just good teaching!": The case for culturally relevant pedagogy. *Theory into Practice, 34*(3), 159–165.

Ladson-Billings, G. (1995b). Toward a theory of culturally relevant pedagogy. *American Educational Research Journal, 32,* 465–491.

Lapp, D. (2010). Stories, facts, and possibilities: Bridging the home and school worlds for nonmainstream students. In D. Fisher & K. Dunsmore (Eds.), *Bringing literacy home* (pp. 136–158). Newark, DE: International Reading Association.

López-Robertson, J., Long, S., & Turner-Nash, K. (2010). First steps in construction counter narratives of young children and their families. *Language Arts, 88,* 99–103.

Mattingly, D. J., Prislan, R. A., McKenzie, T. L., Rodriguez, J. L., & Kayzar, B. (2002). Evaluating evaluations: The case of parent involvement programs. *Review of Educational Research, 72*(4), 549–576.

McIntyre, E. (2010). Issues in funds of knowledge teaching and research: Key concepts from a study of Appalachian families and schooling. In M. L. Dantas & P. C. Manyak (Eds.), *Home–school connections in a multicultural society: Learning from and with culturally and linguistically diverse families* (pp. 201–217). New York: Routledge.

Mohatt, G., & Erickson, F. (1981). Cultural differences in teaching styles in an Odawa school: A sociolinguistic approach. In H. Trueba, G. Guthrie, & K. Au (Eds.), *Culture and the bilingual classroom: Studies in classroom ethnography* (pp. 105–119). Rowley, MA: Newbury House.

Moll, L. C., & Cammarota, J. (2010). Cultivating new funds of knowledge through research and practice. In K. Dunsmore & D. Fisher (Eds.), *Bringing literacy home* (pp. 289–305). Newark, DE: International Reading Association.

Moll, L. C., & Greenberg, J. (1990). Creating zones of possibilities: Combining social contexts for instruction. In L. C. Moll (Ed.), *Vygotsky and education: Instructional implications and applications of sociohistorical psychology* (pp. 319–348). Cambridge, UK: Cambridge University Press.

Paris, D. (2012). Culturally sustaining pedagogy: A needed change in stance, terminology, and practice. *Educational Researcher, 41*(3), 93–97.

Park, S., & Holloway, S. D. (2013). No parent left behind: Predicting parental involvement in adolescents' education within a sociodemographically diverse population. *Journal of Educational Research, 106*(2), 105–119.

Reeves, D. B. (2005). High performance in high-poverty schools: 90/90/90 and beyond. In J. Flood & P. L. Anders (Eds.), *Literacy development of students in urban schools: Research and policy* (pp. 362–388). Newark, DE: International Reading Association.

Semega, J. L., Fontenot, K. R., & Kollar, M. A. (2017). *Income and poverty in the United States: 2016.* Washington, DC: U.S. Census Bureau Current Population Reports, U.S. Government Printing Office. Retrieved May 15, 2018 from *www.census.gov/content/dam/Census/library/publications/2017/demo/P60-259. pdf.*

Sheldon, S. B. (2003). Linking school–family–community partnerships in urban elementary schools to student achievement on state tests. *Urban Review, 35*(2), 145–164.

Sheldon, S. B. (2007). Improving student attendance with school, family, and community partnerships. *Journal of Educational Research, 100*(5), 267–275.

Southern Education Foundation. (2015). A new majority research bulletin: Low income students now a majority in the nation's public schools. Retrieved October 13, 2017, from *www.southerneducation.org/Our-Strategies/Research-and-Publications/New-Majority-Diverse-Majority-Report-Series/A-New-Majority-2015-Update-Low-Income-Students-Now.*

St. Pierre, R. G., Ricciuti, A. E., & Rimdzius, T. A. (2005). Effects of a family literacy program on low-literate children and their parents: Findings from an evaluation of the Even Start Family Literacy Program. *Developmental Psychology, 41*(6), 953–970.

Taylor, B. M., & Pearson, P. D. (2002). *Teaching reading: Effective schools, accomplished teachers.* Mahwah, NJ: Erlbaum.

Teddlie, C., & Stringfield, S. (1993). *Schools make a difference: Lessons learned from a 10-year study of school effects.* New York: Teachers College Press.

Walker, J. M. T., Ice, C., Hoover-Dempsey, K. V., & Sandler, H. M. (2011). Latino parents' motivations for involvement in their children's schooling: An exploratory study. *Elementary School Journal, 111*(3), 409–429.

CHAPTER 19

Best Practices in Professional Learning for Improving Literacy Instruction in Schools

SHARON WALPOLE
JOHN Z. STRONG
CARY B. RICHES

This chapter will:

- Argue that professional learning attends to context and combines training, coaching, curriculum, and collaboration.
- Consider recent research on coaching, on professional learning communities, and on integrating technology into professional learning.
- Discuss building a growth mindset for teachers' professional learning.
- Highlight our recent professional learning efforts in elementary and middle school.

THE CLASSROOM AS CONTEXT: MAKING PROFESSIONAL LEARNING COUNT

As we write this chapter, we have ended another year of whirlwind professional learning (PL) efforts—large-scale institutes, classroom-based observation and feedback, classroom-based modeling, grade-level team coaching, schoolwide observation and feedback, online module design, online consultation, and curriculum design work. These efforts were not intended as stand-alone knowledge-building efforts. They were intended to bring ideas to the place that really matters: the classroom. And we face another year with the certainty that some of these efforts will yield changes in teaching and many will not. We suspect that the difference in impact will be coherence. PL must be entirely coherent with the rest of the influences on teaching and learning to have real impact.

Figure 19.1, our representation of Desimone's (2009) call for researchers in the area of PL to embrace complexity, unpacks the many ways that a lack of coherence can scuttle the potential of PL to impact classroom practice. Note that while she used the term "professional development," we will use "professional learning" in this chapter to push back on the idea that teachers can be developed. Outside the circle are some of the forces that influence teaching and learning. The context in which teachers act is complicated by their own characteristics and those of their students, the work of their leadership team, the curriculum they are asked to enact, and the policy context. Inside the circle is the logic model that leads from PL to student achievement. PL designers may or may not attend well to the features of PL. If they do, the PL might influence teacher knowledge and skill and potentially their attitudes and beliefs. If that happens, teachers might change their instruction. If, and only if, teachers change instruction, that change might be associated with changes in achievement. There are a lot of *ifs* in the design of effective PL. To make a difference, we must attend carefully to each of them.

Rather than lament these complex requirements, we join the many

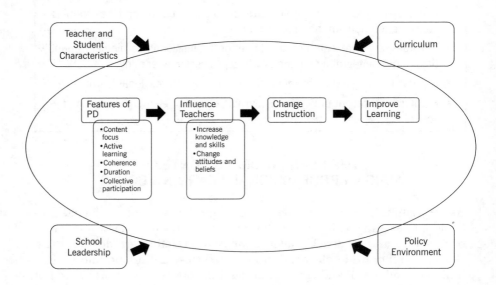

FIGURE 19.1. A representation of Desimone's (2009) call for PD research.

others who have decided to advocate. Even a brief look at PL rallying documents reveals consistency in messaging. We are informed by the Standards for Professional Learning that guide the design of effective PL, including learning communities, leadership, resources, data, learning designs, implementation, and outcomes (Learning Forward, 2011). Consistent with the calls in the oft-cited *How People Learn: Brain, Mind, Experience, and School* (National Research Council, 2000), we seek PL designs that are learner-centered, knowledge-centered, assessment-centered, and community-centered. Recent PL research reveals that these overall goals can be realized in different ways. In settings where teachers are experiencing PL that is watered down or disconnected from practice, their leaders are choosing to ignore the existing research on effective PL or to ignore the complexities of their schools' contexts, or both. We agree with Kennedy (2016) that teachers deserve PL that is designed to motivate them, is intellectually engaging, and provides meaningful support for their everyday work.

We come to this chapter representing three different perspectives on PL design. Sharon Walpole, along with her late research partner, Michael McKenna, has long championed the use of literacy coaches to take large-scale state and federal initiatives and contextualize them for teachers. Sharon is now the director of her university's PL center and will be working with professionals in all content areas to design PL systems. Cary Riches is a district director of curriculum and instruction. She must view PL as a mechanism for communicating and supporting district-level curriculum and strategic planning decisions in a diverse set of schools and classrooms, and she must view it as the only lever she can control as she promises her district's stakeholders better student achievement over time. John Strong is an advanced doctoral student. He must view PL as a necessary and complex mediator in his efforts to design and test instructional interventions. We write this chapter together because we work together and because we have committed our time to the scholarly study and enactment of PL. We have also committed to one another and to teachers that they deserve the best possible PL experiences. We design PL not to "fix" bad teachers; we design PL because teachers deserve the best. Only when they participate in the best PL can we expect new ideas to make their way from theory into practice in real time and in real classrooms.

EVIDENCE-BASED BEST PRACTICES: A RESEARCH SYNTHESIS

Despite the efforts of nearly every school district in the nation and hundreds of university-based researchers, designing and testing the effects of PL remains a difficult task. Gold-standard research requires random assignment and control conditions. Few districts can allow such designs, especially as the stakes are high for teachers and children. Even if teachers were assigned randomly, they might vary in their motivation to participate in the PL (Kennedy, 2016). Not surprisingly, then, in a 2007 review, the What Works Clearinghouse examined 1,300 studies; only nine met this gold standard, and they vary widely in their focus. Taken together, they suggest that at least 14 hours of PL must be included and that initial trainings must be accompanied by follow-up efforts (Yoon, Duncan, Lee, Scarloss, & Shapley, 2007). That is not much to go on.

The news from the research world is not all bad and not all vague. Since the publication of the last edition of this text, we have learned much about the design of PL. Here is the short version. While researchers once viewed types of PL as standing alone, PL research is now exploring the ways that different types of PL interact. Figure 19.2 represents our current understanding of some of the major PL levers that might be used in concert to support teachers and influence their practice. Certainly, teachers continue to report that one-shot trainings are ineffective, as well they should. However, they see utility in a range of other PL experiences that allow deeper processing of ideas (Mundy, Howe, & Kupczynski, 2015). It is our job to craft those experiences so that they work together.

To say that research is providing more and more guidance for PL is not to say that all results are positive. As we view some high-visibility PL failures, we think that they may be explained partially by their lack of attention to the need for coherent systems of collaboration, training, curriculum, and coaching. For example, 2 years of online modules and workshops led to only small improvements in practice (Folsom, Smith,

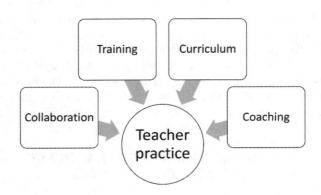

FIGURE 19.2. Influences on teacher practice.

Burk, & Oakley, 2017). Coaching did not add value to a professional development course to enhance early childhood teachers' knowledge, but it did improve teachers' classroom implementation (Neuman & Cunningham, 2009). Large-scale coaching did not add value to training institutes, and neither were associated with gains in knowledge or practice (Garet et al., 2008). Further, large-scale initiatives that combined institutes, follow-up trainings, and coaching built knowledge, but did not influence achievement (Garet, Heppen, Walters, Smith, & Yang, 2016).

While these studies were surely disappointing, we think it is useful to view them as evidence that truly high-quality PL must consider that collaboration, training, curriculum, and coaching are each necessary but none sufficient in PL design. That may be because PL initiatives must face what Kennedy (2016) referred to as "the problem of enactment." Even when teachers learn new practices, they may continue to enact old contradictory practices. New practices are more than new ideas; actually enacting them requires abandonment of previous practices and acknowledging that those practices were ineffective. To increase the chances for enactment, we will first describe recent efforts to improve collaboration, to provide expert coaching, and to take advantage of technology. In addition, we will discuss building a growth mindset within these contexts as part of teachers' PL. Then we will provide two examples of how we have attempted to bring these contexts together.

Professional Learning Communities

Teachers may collaborate in many ways, but their collaboration has been institutionalized and branded in professional learning communities (PLCs). PLCs are ongoing meetings of teachers with like roles and goals. They are commonly used by grade-level teams in elementary school and by content-area teams or interdisciplinary teams in middle and high school. They provide a flexible model for supporting collaboration. Perhaps because of their social nature, such collaborations can influence both instruction and self-efficacy (Cantrell & Hughes, 2008; Dobbs, Ippolito, & Charner-Laird, 2017). PLCs have matured from a stand-alone focus on vision, standards, and examining student data and artifacts (e.g., Dufour, Dufour, Eaker, & Many, 2010). They are now used as a component of multicomponent PL designs. For example, a 2-year initiative to institutionalize disciplinary literacy employed a traditional institute followed by planning sessions and PLCs. This combination of training, attention to curriculum, and collaboration helped teachers move from the technical challenge of enacting disciplinary literacy strategies to an examination of their own beliefs about teaching and learning (Dobbs et al., 2017).

What PLC designs have in common is their collaborative (rather than didactic) approach to knowledge building and reflection, their reliance on and development of teacher leadership, and their ongoing, scheduled nature. The actual protocols that PLCs use may differ. We view a PLC design recently recommended for teachers seeking to evaluate new instructional practices for elementary school literacy as a useful model for many goals. The authors (Kosanovich & Foorman, 2016) of the recommendations identify five steps. In Figure 19.3 we present their steps as a cycle to show that PLCs are an ongoing process that could be applied to a series of topics and strategies over time. For example, a PLC cycle could begin with participants identifying a topic to study before reading about and discussing new strategies in research. After collaborating with peers to role-play the new strategies, teachers reflect on how the strategies compare with their current practices and then plan to implement them. This direct talk about exactly how the new is different from the old is essential. In fact, if teachers do not collaborate to name and unpack these differences, the new ideas may never move from the PLC to the classroom. Instead, teachers will justify their past practice as a type of implementation of the new ideas. If they indeed try something new, teachers can then share their experiences implementing the new strategies in their classroom and problem-solve with their colleagues.

PLCs are certainly not prescriptive, and they could easily operate as

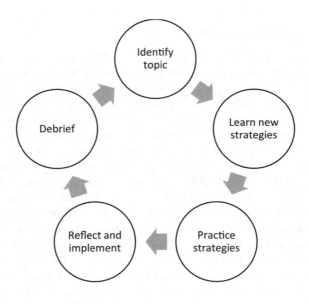

FIGURE 19.3. PLC cycle.

a component of a multipronged PL effort. They could provide structured, ongoing follow-up to trainings, or they could be used to evaluate or create curriculum. Regardless of the topic identified, the call to learn new strategies invites incorporation of research articles or book studies. Kennedy (2016) identified time to read and discuss research as a characteristic of effective PL. PLCs can provide the time and context for such work. A coach could participate as a member of a PLC or act as a resource to help the members identify new strategies associated with their topic. Even better, a coach could provide individualized support as teachers practice, reflect, and implement.

Coaching

Teacher coaching has emerged beyond its status as a promising practice in the PL literature. Coaching, first designed and studied by Joyce and Showers (1982), has stood the test of time. It has been used across all levels of schooling and in all content areas. Research on coaching, too, has moved beyond case studies and into the mainstream of PL research. It has done so while retaining variety in implementation specifics, which we see as positive.

Coaching, broadly speaking, is planned interaction among instructional experts and teachers that is individualized, intensive, sustained, context-specific, and focused. Rather than quibble about the roles and goals of coaches, or about the efficacy of one coaching model over another, we are encouraged that researchers have begun to view coaching in combination with other PL levers. McKenna and Walpole (2008) compared and contrasted coaching models on their intrusiveness and argued that no one model would be appropriate for all settings or goals. Now we know more about why that is true. The PL landscape requires that we consider both the ultimate goal of coaching and the individuals who participate as coaches and coached.

Researchers have explored the interaction of coaching and teachers' experiences and beliefs. Teachers must continually enhance their sense of efficacy, the conviction that their individual and collective efforts can influence their students. Cantrell and Hughes (2008) chronicled a PL model including coaching for teachers of adolescents that unpacks some of these complex interactions. Initial training explained and modeled instructional practices. Teachers collaborated in reading, role playing, planning, and reflection. Monthly coaching supported teachers through planning and modeling. This complex PL design influenced instruction differentially, and efficacy was one of the mechanisms they measured. While teachers with higher initial efficacy were more likely to implement the new instruction quickly, those with higher collective efficacy were more likely to implement later in the year. It may be that a team approach to PL that includes collaborative practice opportunities and extensive coaching leverages individual teacher self-efficacy and builds collective teacher efficacy. Teachers may need both access to instructional experts and time to teach, collaborate, and learn with peers to nurture the belief that they can make a difference together.

We are also much further along in our understanding of the effects of coaching on instruction and achievement. Kraft, Blazer, and Hogan (2016) looked across studies employing causal designs in which the effects of coaching were compared to a control condition. Sometimes, when reviews of evidence are restricted in this way, they yield disappointing results. Put another way, promising practices in less rigorous studies can be ineffective when tested with more rigorous controls. This was not the case for coaching. Coaching in these 44 studies was causally related to large improvements in instruction and small gains in achievement. The largest effects on instruction were realized in preschool and elementary school; effects on achievement were smallest in middle school and very similar in preschool, elementary school, and high school.

While more and more evidence supports the effectiveness of coaching, one of the nagging issues in planning and implementing coaching programs is the logistical nuts and bolts. For coaching to be individualized, teachers need to have their own individual needs addressed. And there are usually a lot of teachers to coach. They often are teaching at the same time, and a coach can only be in one place at one time. Designers of coaching projects may argue that the number of sessions is a crucial design component. However, researchers cannot identify a threshold for face time for coaching to be effective. Perhaps it is the quality and focus, not the quantity, of coaching efforts that may be most important (Kraft, Blazer, & Hogan, 2016).

Finding coaches with an effective combination of knowledge, skills, and experiences remains a challenge to large-scale implementation of the practice. Coaches will be more effective if teachers view them as experienced, familiar with the challenges faced daily in classrooms, and able to draw on a variety of experiences. Coaches are more effective when they treat teachers as colleagues working together to test a model of instruction rather than as problematic professionals who need to improve their knowledge and skills (Kennedy, 2016). The number of professionals who have the ideal combination of content knowledge, personal skills, and classroom experiences will likely always be limited.

Technology-Enhanced Professional Learning

Virtual coaching remains a promising practice with potential for scale-up. At its face, virtual coaching has the potential to address many of the logistical problems with planning and implementing coaching initiatives. Coaches can watch teachers outside of the confines of the school day, watch teachers who teach at the same time, and focus their time on only the instruction that is the object of coaching. They can also engage teachers in targeted, online video discussions, without the need for costly extensions of the school day, extensive use of substitute teachers, or rescheduling of essential student-teacher planning time. With the support of coaching, teachers can work with more teachers, potentially improving the quality of teaching (by reducing the total number of coaches needed per teacher, hire, and support). There are well-thought-out examples of technology use as a part of PL initiatives in the literature.

Technology-enabled scale-up for Targeted Reading Intervention (TRI), a kindergarten and first-grade reading intervention. Teachers first participated in a summer institute, followed by weekly grade-level meetings for children from and monthly follow-up meetings. At the same time, they used a videoconferencing system so that a coach could watch implementation and provide real-time feedback on a weekly to biweekly basis. Teachers reported that the virtual coaching was effective for them, and that the intervention produced positive achievement results (Amendum, Vernon-Feagans, & Ginsberg, 2011; Vernon-Feagans, Kainz, Hedrick, Ginsberg, & Amendum, 2013). This same support system was validated to improve the achievement of English learners using TRI (Amendum, Bratsch-Hines, & Vernon-Feagans, 2018).

My Teaching Partner-Language and Literacy Curriculum (MTP-LL) is a technology-enhanced PL platform with an even broader set of goals. It includes a video library that teachers use to learn new practices, and a cyclical series of web-based coaching opportunities. Teachers upload videos of their instruction, coaches watch the videos and provide feedback, and then the two discuss the instruction on the phone. The coaching component added value to the video library for preschool teachers (Pianta, Mashburn, Downer, Hamre, & Justice, 2008). Combined with workshops, My Teaching Partner—Secondary (MTP-S) has also produced improved achievement in middle school and high school (Allen, Pianta, Gregory, Mikami, & Lun, 2011; Allen, Hafen, Gregory, Mikami, & Pianta, 2015). As technology for collecting, storing, and sharing video examples of real instruction becomes increasingly affordable and easy to use, PL systems that employ technology will likely be more and more common.

Professional Learning for a Growth Mindset

Professional learning might also be used for teachers to learn about practices for promoting a growth mindset, or the idea that intelligence is not fixed and can be developed (Dweck, 2006). Promoting a growth mindset in students has important implications for their literacy achievement. Recent research has found that students' overall and reading-specific growth mindsets were related to their reading comprehension and word-reading outcomes (Petscher, Al Otaiba, Wanzek, Rivas, & Jones, 2017). Despite many teachers' familiarity with the concept of growth mindset, most want more professional development in how to enact growth mindset practices in the classroom (Blad, 2016). Collaborating with other teachers about how to incorporate growth mindset practices should be a part of ongoing professional learning.

Discussions about promoting growth mindsets in students should also support the development of teachers' own growth mindsets, both in their beliefs about their students' abilities and their own teaching abilities (Dweck, 2015; Massey, 2016). To support the ongoing development of growth mindset, teachers might engage in professional learning activities that involve observing other teachers to learn about new practices, giving and receiving constructive feedback, and working collaboratively to solve problems (Massey, 2016).

The Project for Education Research That Scales (2015) present a five-session professional learning cycle for teaching growth mindset that could be implemented in PLCs (Massey, 2016). The five sessions include learning about growth mindset, planning for teaching growth mindset, promoting growth mindset through praise, celebrating and reflecting on mistakes, and planning for implementation of growth mindset. During the sessions, teaching teams engage in various activities, including self-assessment, readings, videos, peer observations and feedback, and group discussions. We support this approach for teaching growth mindset, as it encompasses training, curriculum, coaching, and collaboration into a coherent PL initiative.

BEST PRACTICES IN ACTION

We have been enacting PL in large and small settings, learning as we go. Below we provide two brief descriptions of our efforts, one in elementary school and one in middle school. What they have in common is that they employed a combination of PL strategies to move ideas from research into classroom communities.

Elementary PL Example

Our most recent large-scale effort to design effective PL actually began with failure. After many years of failed efforts to support teachers to modify their curricula to increase rigor, text quality, and time spent in meaningful reading and writing, Sharon Walpole and Michael McKenna designed Bookworms as evidence that research could be the source of pedagogy and great children's authors could be the source of texts. They built an entire curriculum so that their PL efforts could be coherent with a set of affordable tools that teachers could have in their classrooms. Bookworms uses a very small set of instructional routines to enact evidence-based, standards-aligned practices in Tier 1 instruction. It also provides a rich and balanced knowledge-building text context for their multiple-entry Tier 2 skills curriculum (Walpole & McKenna, 2017). Bookworms is an Open Educational Resource with lesson plans available online at *http://openupresources.org*. The classroom materials are only full-length trade books that can be purchased in classroom sets much more inexpensively than commercial curricula. For an independent description and review of Bookworms, see *www.edreports.org/ela/bookworms/index.html*.

Once Bookworms was identified as an enactment of research consistent with standards, Sharon and Michael set out to design comprehensive PL. Figure 19.4 provides a preview of their strategies. First, they considered access. Teachers have scant time for PL, and it is distributed unevenly across schools and districts. Access was expanded with a series of free online PLC modules (currently housed at *comprehensivereadingsolutions.com*). Coaches or teachers could look at the offerings, create a PLC syllabus collaboratively, and set up a protocol for viewing the modules independently and then coming together to collaborate. Over 5 years, more than 133,000 different users have accessed the PL modules; 757 of them completed a survey after completion. Over 90% reported that the modules met their needs, they learned new ideas from the modules, and they intended to implement those ideas in their classrooms.

Next, they designed a series of large training institutes, with presenters selected for their content knowledge and their presentation style. Some institutes were targeted for teachers and others for leaders. Teacher institutes included research-based rationales and then both video models and role-playing activities for instructional routines. Leadership institutes included tools for scheduling instruction and PL, for supporting nonevaluative coaching efforts, and for linking evaluative observation and feedback to the instructional targets. Both types of institutes included student achievement data as it became available and case study descriptions of implementation efforts. Both types allowed collaboration and problem solving with professionals from other schools with similar goals. The institutes invited access to the modules, and usage data from the PL modules indicates that access to the online supports always spiked after face-to-face institutes.

These PL efforts yielded more and more requests for direct onsite coaching and modeling—many more than the authors could handle. They

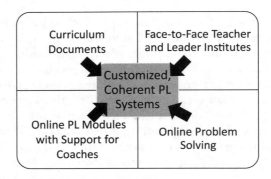

FIGURE 19.4. A coherent set of PL opportunities.

used technology to address this scale-up challenge. With John Strong's help, they collected and posted brief video samples of different parts of whole-class Bookworms lessons at different grade levels. They posted these on the PL site. Then Sharon modeled each of the different types of small-group lessons that are employed in Bookworms. Since each is 15 minutes in length, these videos could be posted in full on a YouTube channel (Walpole, 2017). That channel is new, and it already has over 11,000 views. John also made a viewing guide to direct teachers' attention while watching the videos, highlighting the most common implementation questions that they had addressed in schools.

Sharon and Michael also provided weekly online problem-solving sessions. Using video conferencing, they set up free, open, virtual office hours. These sessions, attended by individuals who had specific questions and by others who simply enjoyed the weekly collaborations, served to connect Bookworms teachers and administrators to one another. None of these PL opportunities were required of Bookworms users; instead, they chose what they wanted to do to enhance their understandings. This combination of written curriculum materials, face-to-face institutes designed separately for teachers and for leaders, online PL modules to enhance collaboration, video modeling, and virtual office hours for problem solving has been an attempt at coherent PL design. Perhaps because of this coherence, Bookworms has evidence of feasibility for teachers and promise for students in the upper elementary grades (Walpole, McKenna, Amendum, Pasquarella, & Strong, 2017).

Middle School PL Example

Our second experience also began with a well-meaning failure. John Strong and Cary Riches designed a year-long PL that incorporated face-to-face training with monthly follow-up activities, including walk-through observations and feedback, instructional coaching for teachers individually and in PLC meetings, and leadership coaching for school administrators. The instructional targets were evidence-based instructional strategies described in *Cracking the Common Core* (Lewis, Walpole, & McKenna, 2014).

First, John presented 9 hours of face-to-face training in a summer institute designed to increase teachers' knowledge of specific instructional routines. He designed the institute in 3-hour segments that focused on building background knowledge before reading, using routines to increase student time and engagement in connected reading, and incorporating text-based discussion and writing after reading. Teachers brought one existing curriculum unit to the workshop. John explained and modeled specific strategies and supported teachers in planning to implement them when using their existing texts. During each session, John gave teachers time to learn new strategies, reflect on how to use them, and collaborate with their colleagues.

Next, John and Cary trained school administrators to use the *Adolescent Literacy Walk-Through for Principals* (ALWP), an observation tool designed to gather data about the frequency of teachers' instructional practices in literacy (Rissman, Miller, & Torgesen, 2009). They did this to ensure that building administrators would be equipped to recognize teachers' efforts. They defined each instructional practice included in the ALWP, described how it aligned with the strategies teachers learned in the initial training, and conducted practice observations with follow-up discussion. Teachers also reviewed the ALWP in a PLC meeting so that the tool their administrators would use would not be threatening or secret.

Over the course of 6 months, John, Cary, and an administrator in each school conducted brief walk-throughs to collect data about teachers' implementation of instructional practices using the ALWP. The walk-throughs were scheduled in advance, and teachers expected them. They hoped to see teachers at their best. Afterward, John provided the walk-through data to teachers during their PLC meetings. They discussed it and problem-solved, and he modeled instructional routines at teacher request.

Throughout the school year, Cary met with each administrator monthly to align his or her evaluative feedback with the strategies teachers learned about in PL activities. Cary also met with the English language arts (ELA) department chair in each school to discuss the challenges that teachers faced enacting the literacy strategies within their existing curriculum units and lesson plans. She provided these teacher leaders with support and feedback on facilitating effective weekly PLC meetings that included reading and discussing research on adolescent literacy.

At the end of the school year, John shared the results of all 94 walk-throughs with ELA teachers and administrators in each school. The results were disappointing. The most frequently observed instructional practices were use of graphic organizers, engaging students in guided practice, and providing opportunities for student collaboration. There was very little teacher modeling or discussion of text.

Even more problematic than the walk-through data, John and Cary observed very little actual reading in these ELA classrooms. If students did read, the texts appeared to be below the grade-level goals for text complexity. At the end of the school year, Cary investigated this issue. Her review of her district's curriculum materials revealed that teachers were in fact using texts that were too easy. She realized that further support of teachers' enactment of the targeted instructional strategies would also require abandonment of previous practices and materials, including most of the texts and curriculum units that these teachers had taught for many years.

It became clear that John and Cary failed to promote a growth mindset among teachers during the year-long PL. As a result, many of the teachers resisted enacting new practices and abandoning those that they had learned through previous PL opportunities. In hindsight, expecting teachers to change their teaching practices after one summer institute, monthly walk-throughs, and coaching was an unrealistic goal. Providing an opportunity for teachers to observe other teachers who had enacted these new practices might have promoted a growth mindset within teachers about their own teaching abilities.

Cary invited all middle school ELA teachers to collaborate in curriculum development after the school year ended. Contrary to the predictions of some of her colleagues, nearly all of the teachers chose to work together on this summer project. Guided by the theory of bounded autonomy (Hill, 1997), Cary set boundaries for text selection and evidence-based instructional strategies that were used to design new curriculum units at all grades. Teachers first read and chose new trade books that reflected grade-level text complexity standards and featured characters from diverse backgrounds and settings. Next, they worked together to design new curriculum units and lesson plans that incorporated the new texts and integrated the instructional strategies they had learned about during the previous school year's PL. Cary introduced how to promote a growth mindset for students and what a growth mindset looks and sounds like for teachers. Many teachers were concerned that the new materials and strategies would require them to completely change their practices and require students to engage in more rigorous work than they had done in the past. However, grade-level teams were given autonomy to match the lesson and unit objectives with the texts and strategies they decided to enact. They worked together to abandon most of the texts and practices that had been in place for many years.

Initial survey results from this year-long PL effort indicated that the teachers were satisfied with the initial training and ongoing support they received. For example, teachers shared that the summer institute was a good introduction to the strategies, and they appreciated the level of support they received through feedback, modeling, and opportunities to practice newly learned strategies. However, the data John and Cary collected and shared revealed very little implementation of the new ideas. Instead of accepting this result, Cary decided to add attention to curriculum design to a PL system that already employed training, collaboration, and coaching. While we don't know yet whether this addition will produce more time in real reading and writing for students, we do know that teachers said that they were motivated to teach the curriculum that they created and were appreciative of ongoing district support.

REFLECTIONS AND FUTURE DIRECTIONS

Like teaching itself, PL design and implementation is not for the faint of heart. Like teaching itself, PL design and implementation requires a constant attention to evidence, a deep sense of empathy and respect for others, a commitment to continuous learning, a desire to enhance self- and collective efficacy, and a willingness to admit to and learn from mistakes. Our vision of the requirements of high-quality PL has widened as research has revealed deeper understandings. PL is not one practice or another. It is an ecosystem whose health requires attention to broad categories of teacher experience with and access to curriculum, training, coaching, and collaboration. It must acknowledge and adapt to the changing characteristics of teachers and students, shape and respond to policy initiatives, and engage educational leaders. Our teachers deserve our best efforts.

ENGAGEMENT ACTIVITIES

1. For teachers: Choose a practice guide (*https://ies.ed.gov/ncee/wwc/ PracticeGuides*) to read and discuss in your PLC. Identify a topic to study, read about evidence-based recommendations, collaborate with other teachers to practice a new strategy, reflect on how it compares with old practices, and make a plan to implement.

2. For administrators: Design an initial training session for instructional leaders in your school to model and explain best practices for literacy instruction. Schedule follow-up activities that include classroom-based observation and feedback, grade-level team meetings, and curriculum development.

3. For coaches: Choose a web-based PL module from our open-access site (*comprehensivereadingsolutions.com*). Make a schedule with colleagues to specify a date by which each person will have viewed the module and completed its associated tasks. Schedule a follow-up meeting for teachers to discuss the module and share what they have learned.

REFERENCES

Allen, J. P., Hafen, C. A., Gregory, A. C., Mikami, A. Y., & Pianta, R. (2015). Enhancing secondary school instruction and student achievement: Replication and extension of the My Teaching Partner–Secondary intervention. *Journal of Research on Educational Effectiveness, 8*(4), 475–489.

Allen, J. P., Pianta, R. C., Gregory, A., Mikami, A. Y., & Lun, J. (2011). An interaction-based approach to enhancing secondary school instruction and student achievement. *Science, 333*, 1034–1037.

Amendum, S. J., Bratsch-Hines, M., & Vernon-Feagans, L. (2018). Investigating the efficacy of a web-based early reading and professional development intervention for young English learners. *Reading Research Quarterly, 53*(2), 155–174.

Amendum, S. J., Vernon-Feagans, L., & Ginsberg, M. C. (2011). The effectiveness of a technologically facilitated classroom-based early reading intervention. *Elementary School Journal, 112*(1), 107–131.

Blad, E. (2016). Teachers seize on "growth mindset," but classroom practice lags. *Education Week, 36*(5), 1–11.

Cantrell, S. C., & Hughes, H. K. (2008). Teacher efficacy and content literacy implementation: An exploration of the effects of extended professional development with coaching. *Journal of Literacy Research, 40*(1), 95–127.

Desimone, L. M. (2009). Improving impact studies of teachers' professional development: Toward better conceptualizations and measures. *Educational Researcher, 38*, 181–199.

Dobbs, C. L., Ippolito, J., & Charner-Laird, M. (2017). Scaling up professional learning: Technical expectations and adaptive challenges. *Professional Development in Education, 43*(5), 729–748.

DuFour, R., DuFour, R., Eaker, R., & Many, T. (2010). *Learning by doing: A handbook for professional learning communities at work* (2nd ed.). Bloomington, IN: Solution Tree.

Dweck, C. S. (2006). *Mindset: The new psychology of success.* New York: Random House.

Dweck, C. S. (2015). Growth. *British Journal of Educational Psychology, 85*(2), 242–245.

Folsom, J. S., Smith, K. G., Burk, K., & Oakley, N. (2017). *Educator outcomes associated with implementation of Mississippi's K–3 early literacy professional development initiative.* Washington, DC: U.S. Department of Education, Institute of

Education Sciences, National Center for Education Evaluation and Regional Assistance, Regional Educational Laboratory Southeast. Retrieved from *http://ies.ed.gov/ncee/edlabs.*

Garet, M. S., Cronen, S., Eaton, M., Kurki, A., Ludwig, M., Jones, W., . . . Sztejnberg, L. (2008). *The impact of two professional development interventions on early reading instruction and achievement.* Washington, DC: National Center for Educational Evaluation and Regional Assistance, Institute of Education Sciences. Retrieved from *http://ies.ed.gov/ncee/pdf/20084030.pdf.*

Garet, M. S., Heppen, J., Walters, K., Smith, T., & Yang, R. (2016). *Does content-focused teacher professional development work?* Washington, DC: National Center for Educational Evaluation and Regional Assistance, Institute of Education Sciences. Retrieved from *https://ies.ed.gov/ncee/pubs/20174010/pdf/20174010.pdf.*

Joyce, B., & Showers, B. (1982). The coaching of teaching. *Educational Leadership, 40*(1), 4–8, 10.

Kennedy, M. M. (2016). How does professional development improve teaching? *Review of Educational Research, 86*(4), 945–980.

Kosanovich, M., & Foorman, B. (2016). *Professional learning communities facilitator's guide for the What Works Clearinghouse practice guide: Foundational skills to support reading for understanding in kindergarten through 3rd grade.* Washington, DC: U.S. Department of Education, Institute of Education Sciences, National Center for Education Evaluation and Regional Assistance, Regional Educational Laboratory Southeast. Retrieved from *http://ies.ed.gov/ncee/edlabs.*

Kraft, M.A., Blazar, D., & Hogan, D. (2016). *The effect of teaching coaching on instruction and achievement: A meta-analysis of the causal evidence.* Working paper, Brown University, Providence, RI.

Learning Forward. (2011). Standards for professional learning. Retrieved from *https://learningforward.org/docs/august-2011/referenceguide324.pdf.*

Lewis, W. E., Walpole, S., & McKenna, M. C. (2014). *Cracking the Common Core: Choosing and using texts in grades 6–12.* New York: Guilford Press.

Massey, S. L. (2016). Leadership in reading. *Illinois Reading Council Journal, 45*(1), 50–55.

McKenna, M. C., & Walpole, S. (2008). *The literacy coaching challenge: Models and methods for grades K–8.* New York: Guilford Press.

Mundy, M., Howe, M. E., & Kupczynski, L. (2015). Teachers' perceived values on the effect of literacy strategy professional development. *Teacher Development, 19*(1), 116–131.

National Research Council. (2000). *How people learn: Brain, mind, experience, and school: Expanded edition.* Washington, DC: National Academies Press.

Neuman, S. B., & Cunningham, L. (2009). The impact of professional development and coaching on early language and literacy instructional practices. *American Educational Research Journal, 46*(2), 532–566.

Petscher, Y., Al Otaiba, S., Wanzek, J., Rivas, B., & Jones, F. (2017). The relation between global and specific mindset with reading outcomes for elementary school students. *Scientific Studies of Reading, 21*(5), 376–391.

Pianta, R. C., Mashburn, A. J., Downer, J. T., Hamre, B. K., & Justice, L. (2008).

Effects of web-mediated professional development resources on teacher–child interactions in pre-kindergarten classrooms. *Early Childhood Research Quarterly, 23*(4), 431–451.

Project for Education Research That Scales. (2015). *Mindset kit–5-sesssion professional learning series: Growth mindset for educator teams.* Retrieved from *www.mindsetkit.org/growth-mindset-educator-teams/growth-mindset-professional-development-materials/5-session-professional-learning-cycle.*

Rissman, L. M., Miller, D. H., & Torgesen, J. K. (2009). *Adolescent literacy walkthrough for principals: A guide for instructional leaders.* Portsmouth, NH: RMC Research Corporation, Center on Instruction.

Vernon-Feagans, L. L., Kainz, K., Ginsberg, M., Hedrick, A., & Amendum, S. (2013). Live webcam coaching to help early elementary classroom teachers provide effective literacy instruction for struggling readers: The Targeted Reading Intervention. *Journal of Educational Psychology, 105*(4), 1175–1187.

Walpole, S. (2017). *Bookworms lessons.* Retrieved from *www.youtube.com/c/bookwormslessons.*

Walpole, S., & McKenna, M. C. (2017). *How to plan differentiated reading instruction: Resources for grades K–3* (2nd ed.). New York: Guilford Press.

Walpole, S., McKenna, M. C., Amendum, S., Pasquarella, A., & Strong, J. Z. (2017). The promise of a literacy reform effort in the upper elementary grades. *The Elementary School Journal, 118*(2), 257–280.

Yoon, K. S., Duncan, T., Lee, S. W.-Y., Scarloss, B., & Shapley, K. (2007). *Reviewing the evidence on how teacher professional development affects student achievement.* Washington, DC: U.S. Department of Education, Institute of Education Sciences, National Center for Education Evaluation and Regional Assistance, Regional Educational Laboratory Southwest. Retrieved from *http://ies.ed.gov/ncee/edlabs.*

Index